Gleanings from Newport Court Files

1659 - 1783

Jane Fletcher Fiske

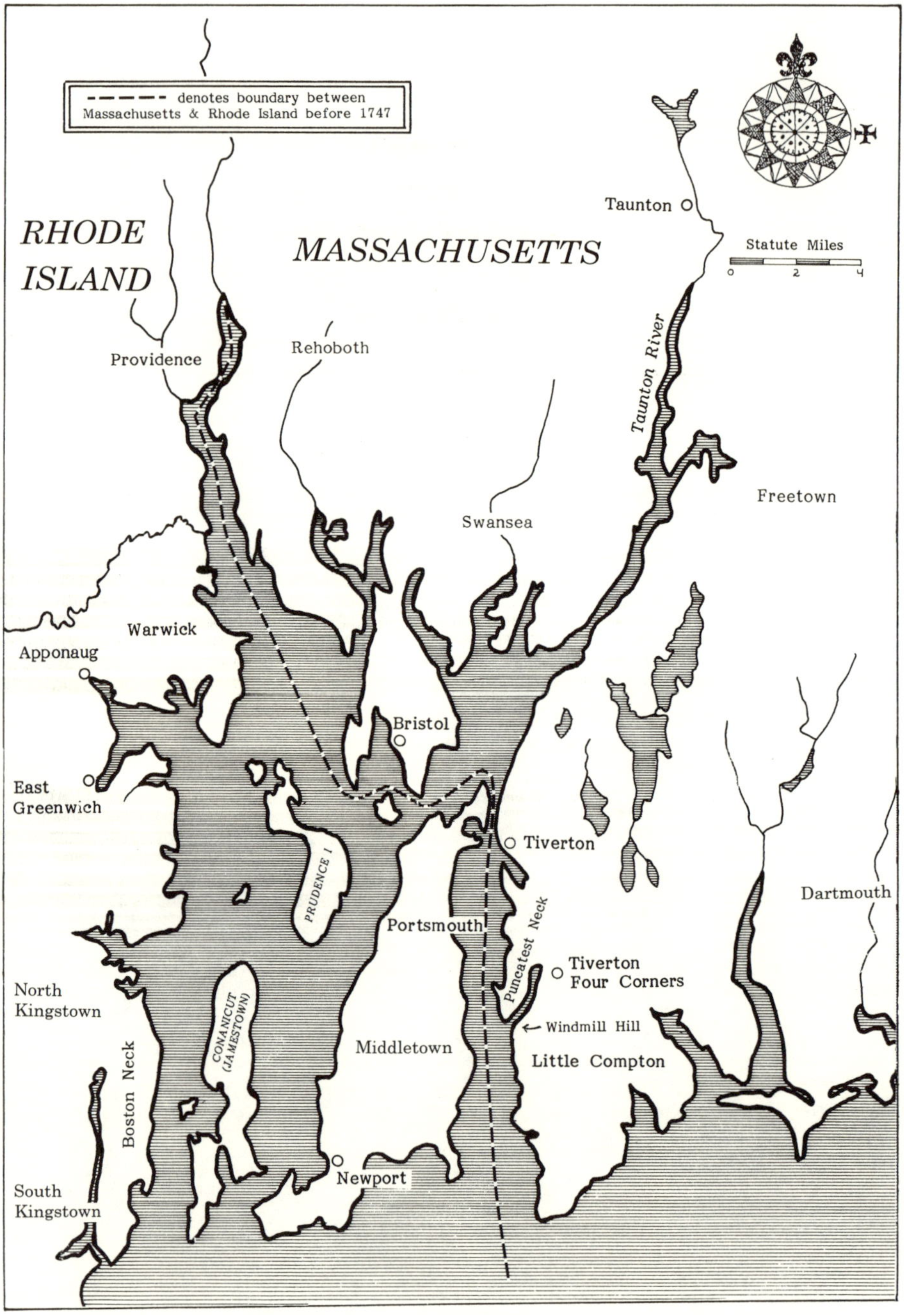

THE NARRAGANSETT BAY AREA

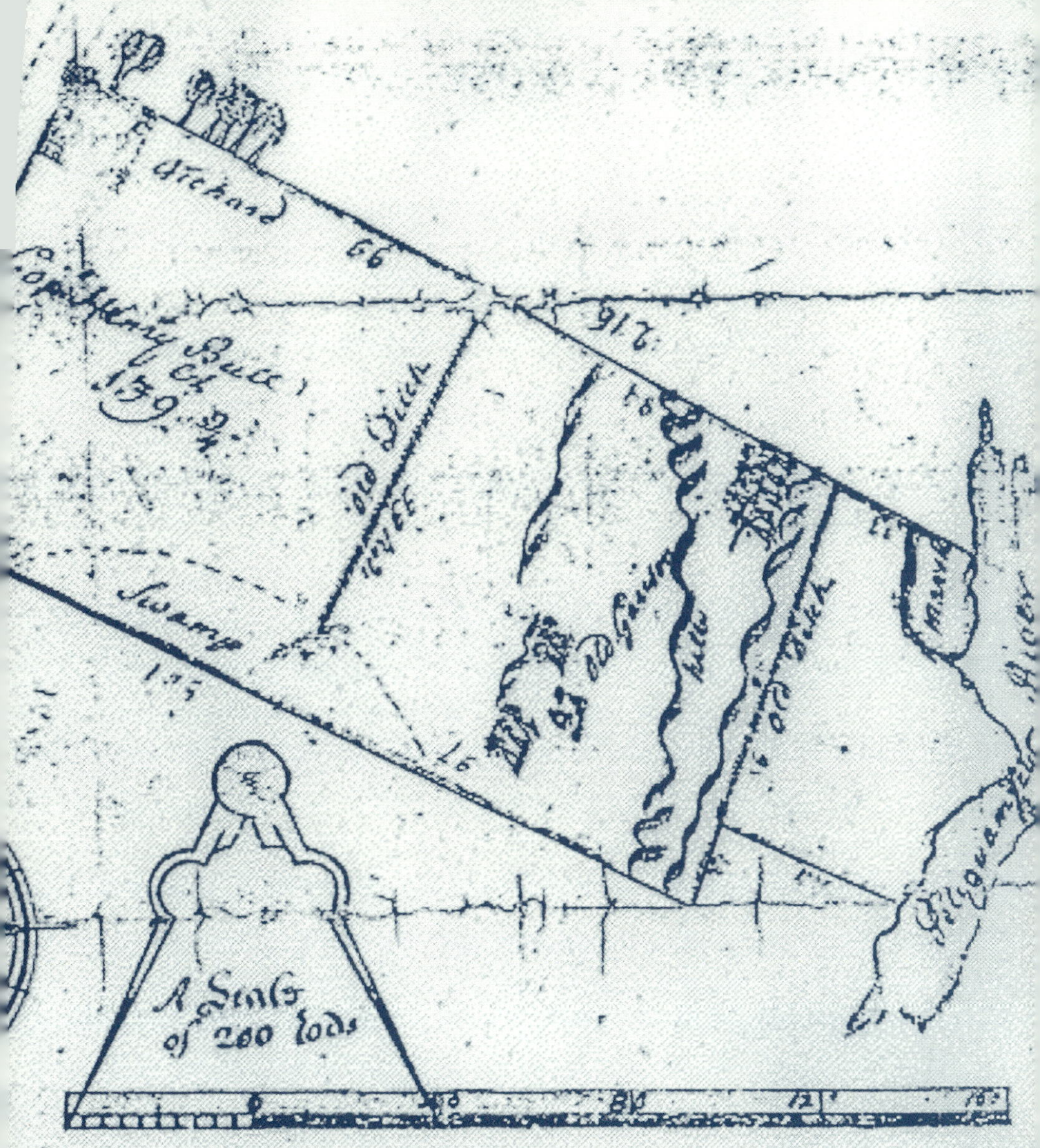

This is a Draft of Capt Henry Bull Lo
in south Kingstown as the fences now
Surveyed & Indrafted by me
Jan: 8: 1729

Gleanings from Newport Court Files

1659 - 1783

Jane Fletcher Fiske

Boxford, Massachusetts
1998

ISBN 0-9615790-1-3

Jane Fletcher Fiske
44 Stonecleave Road, Boxford, MA 01921

TABLE OF CONTENTS

Illustrations

All illustrations are from photocopies.
Please note that numbers refer to items, not to pages.

Endpapers: map (1729/30) showing Bull family land in Kingstown, including site of Jireh Bull's garrison house destroyed in King Philip's War

Frontispiece: Map of Rhode Island and adjacent areas

INTRODUCTION

The records which form the basis for this book have had a long and not uneventful journey from the eighteenth century to the present. Their story begins with the court clerks who laboriously wrote them, undoubtedly with quill pens, on pieces of paper that varied from tiny scraps to ledger pages. Folded into packets, they spent two centuries or more in the dusty vaults of the Newport Court House before they were gathered up by someone in the state government of Rhode Island and carried to the basement of the Veteran's Auditorium in Providence, there joining records from the other county courts. After some years there in scattered confusion, they were deposited in the Providence College Archives (where I used them), and after a few years they were again moved to an attic of the Superior Court Building in Providence. Finally, about a decade ago, the journey ended in a refurbished warehouse in Pawtucket where proper care is finally being given to them.

Over the years, a few scholars of Rhode Island history or genealogy consulted them. There is evidence that John Osborne Austin, compiler of *The Genealogical Dictionary of Rhode Island* (1887), was familiar with their contents on many families up to about 1750. Readers of the long defunct *Narragansett Historical Register* will note in these pages a handful of items which were also published there, such as the list of Newport wills that could not be proved because they had only two witnesses at a time when the law required three. For years, less initiated researchers could access the records only through a card index file kept in the office of the Newport County Court Clerk, and in the late 1970s even this resource was relegated to a spot in the basement where visitors were not permitted to go. The cards referred to the court record books and, even when those books were still available at the court house, they provided only the basic facts of each case and almost none of the colorful detail to be found in the files themselves. Eventually the books, too, were gathered up and taken to Providence.

My own experience with the court records began in 1980, and my work with them has been an adventure. Although I had used the record books in Newport in the 1970s, I first made contact with the files in 1980, when they were stored at Providence College. At the time, I was seeking information on the Cook family of Portsmouth for a genealogy I was compiling and subsequently published.[1] I had in hand several references to the Newport County record books, from the card index mentioned above. It was appar-

1. Jane Fletcher Fiske, *Thomas Cooke of Rhode Island*, 2 vols. (Boxford, Mass., 1987).

ent from my first look at a roomful of cardboard cartons, however, that there was no way I—or anybody else—was going to find anything I might be specifically looking for. The challenge was too great to pass up, however, and with the blessing of the archivist, I lifted out a box whose label indicated its contents as early eighteenth century files, and dug into it, opening file packets that had not been unfolded in many years.

Some time that first morning, I discovered in a file a copy of the will of my own ancestor, Governor Henry Bull of Newport, who died in 1693. Austin in his comprehensive and often definitive *Genealogical Dictionary of Rhode Island* had stated that there were references to a will made by Henry Bull, but no copy had ever been found. Having both stumbled upon something of great importance to myself, and proved Austin wrong after all these years, the lure was irresistible. Thoroughly addicted, for several years I spent at least a day a week in the Archives at Providence College, poring through box after box of small folded packets of court papers, abstracting on pads of yellow lined paper anything that looked interesting from a genealogical, historical, or simply a human interest point of view, making photocopies of documents too lengthy or too important to trust to my abstracting skills. The archival staff there could not have been more cooperative and helpful.

At home I copied my abstracts into the computer. Because the files themselves were so disorganized, any day's notes might fall into quite a number of different years and court terms. Occasionally there was a docket to help, but most often I used the dates given in the files themselves (usually the writ) as the basis for putting them in chronological order. The earliest records I found, in a couple of metal boxes labeled "Miscellaneous," contained some documents which had been removed from their files. These and other copies of early wills and deeds have been arranged by their own dates rather than those of the cases in which they were entered as evidence.

After several years of abstracting, with no clear notion of what I wanted to do with the material other than enjoy it, the need for an index became apparent — I was copying from files I'd already looked at and copied earlier. However, because I was still adding new records, there was no way to meaningfully paginate the collection of abstracts. The problem was solved when a friend suggested numbering by item numbers, or cases, rather than pages. Even these numbers changed as some new material was added, but fortunately my word-processing software included an automatic counter.

At some point the volume of abstracts reached the point where I began to think about publishing. Information found in the files had provided me with material for several articles published in various genealogical journals, and I had been able to supply other searchers with bits and pieces that extended their own knowledge of certain families. Friends and acquaintances were urging me to "do something with" the abstracts.

Decisions about how to present the material were made and changed several times. Finally the arrangement settled into its present form, which I hope will prove to be both easy to use as reference and enjoyable in which to browse.

Understanding and Using the Court Records

The court records of any place provide a treasure-trove of information about the history of that location and the people who lived there. Gaining access to such information, however, requires some understanding of the three different types of court records: Docket Books, Record Books, and Files, and the differences between them.

Dockets were made up by the court clerks, listing cases in the order in which they were to be heard. The docket number was usually written on the back of the file papers included in each case. *Record Books* were also kept by the court clerk, who entered into them the basic and essential data about each case. These books were kept chronologically by court term, and it is to this source that most available indexes to court records refer. Many researchers consult only the Record Books, not realizing that more information may be available.

While one may certainly learn much about each case from the information in the Record Book, it is the actual *file papers*, stored in packets, that bring the protagonists to life and provide the colorful backgrounds of each story. These file papers contain depositions – the statements of people giving testimony – sometimes in the hand of the deponent with his signature, but more often written by a justice of the peace who set the words down the way he heard them. Such phonetic spelling preserves the phraseology and colloquialisms of the time and occasionally must be read aloud to be comprehensible. The files contain the various bills and accountings which were the reasons behind many cases, listing what items or services were being bought, sold, and traded, and by whom. Most important for the genealogical researcher, the files frequently contain copies of wills and deeds on which the cases of the plaintiff and defendant were built. Researchers concerned with Newport history and genealogy – or with that of any other place which may have lost many of its other records – will appreciate the value of such discoveries.

During the Revolutionary War, from December 1776 to December 1779, Newport and the fifteen-mile-long Island of Aquidneck on which it, Middletown, and Portsmouth are situated were occupied by the British.

The town clerk, Walter Chaloner, was, understandably, sympathetic to the enemy, and he left with them, taking along the town records, including the books of vital records, deeds, and town council and probate matters. The ship carrying them ran aground at Hell Gate in New York Harbor and the records were submerged for a few days before they were rescued. They were then left in a warehouse for some time before being returned to Newport at the instigation of George Washington and Nathaniel Greene. It was to be two centuries before preservation efforts were undertaken, and by that time many records had been entirely lost and many more fragmented or faded beyond legibility. Those that remain are at the Newport Historical Society, bound into books that were restored years ago using the "Emery process" whereby pages were encased in layers of thin silk. Despite the restoration, many records are out of their original order, and there are few pages on which the script is both complete and clear. Certainly, the researcher of Newport's past is susceptible to great frustrations.

Court records are the only type of record in Rhode Island that traditionally have been kept in the court houses rather than the town or city halls. As noted earlier, some years ago all Rhode Island court records, both books and files, were gathered up and placed in the Records Center under the Veterans' Auditorium in Providence. Researchers who saw them there report that they were scattered, even on the floor. Sometime in the 1970s the entire collection of was moved to the Archives of Providence College, housed in the basement of the Phillips Library. Students hired at the time the collection was moved to the College attempted to organize the files into cardboard boxes, taping paper slips on the outside of each one indicating what years and court terms were stored therein. About 1988, the records were moved again, to a room in the Providence Court House that involved climbing a ladder and was effectively off-limits to the public. Finally, in the fall of 1989, a new repository in a former mill building at One Hill Street, Pawtucket, was prepared and the removal of the records from the Providence Court House began. By 1995 two grants from the National Endowment for the Humanities helped make it possible to arrange the court records from the entire state at the Pawtucket repository, and to store them under proper conditions. Much work remains to be done, however, and further funds are needed.

The records that until recently were kept at the Newport Court House begin with so-called "Court Book A," recording the business of the General Court of Trials from 1671 to 1721[2] and thus covering the entire colony. After the division of the courts by county in 1721, Newport County had its

2. I have made a literal transcription of the first half of Court Book A, covering 1671 to 1704, and that work will be published as a separate volume.

own Inferior Court of Common Pleas and Superior Court, and record books for these courts are labelled, B, C, D, etc., and covered by the Newport County Index Books held with the records presently at Pawtucket.

The court files, containing the various papers that provided evidence in the cases, fill dozens of large cardboard cartons for Newport alone. Very few files for cases before 1715 have been located, except for some scattered documents which are included in this book.

Providence County records, probably well organized to begin with, fared well; Newport's did not. Over the years that I was actively working with them, the Newport files were not in any chronological or practical order, although papers from certain courts and court terms were grouped together. My notes were originally by Box Number, but these ceased to be useful because the papers were rearranged after they were removed from Providence College. Thus, I am unable to follow one of the cardinal rules in publishing genealogical research — to reference each item in a manner that enables the reader to easily locate the original records. The following explanation, however, may help.

Using These Abstracts

The abstracts are presented as nearly as possible in chronological order. That system breaks down with cases which were appealed to the Superior Court, however, in that sometimes I picked them up in the files of the Inferior Court of Common Pleas where they were first heard, and sometimes in copies made for an appeal to the Superior Court. The verdicts, or judgements of the court, were usually not filed with the other papers, and they ended up as bundles of tiny slips, without any notation to indicate date, name, or docket number of the case; it is thus impossible to know which verdict applied to which case. (One of these slips is shown following No. 817.) The executions — documents attesting that the judgement had been carried out — were frequently also filed separately and are not now with the other papers of any given case.

Until the original records are more accessible, the researcher who wishes to verify and delve further will find the Record Books useful. The Judicial Archives at Pawtucket holds indexes to plaintiffs and defendants in the Record Books for all courts. The dates given in the abstracts published here should make it possible to find the record of each case in the books without too much difficulty. The record should contain the basic facts about each case, including the verdict. The files themselves have been put in some order, but much funding is still needed to obtain the archival help necessary to preserve and properly organize the invaluable little packets of pinned and folded papers that constitute those files.

Any attempt to read these court abstracts without taking the time to understand a few basic points about the language in which the records themselves are written is likely to result in unnecessary frustration. It was my instinct from the beginning of the project that the best way to abstract the records was to preserve their flavor by retaining wherever possible the phraseology and the spelling of the originals, rather than translate them into modern English. At times I have lapsed back and forth between original spelling and its modern equivalent, calling into question my own ability to spell.

Among the few changes in abstracted text are the following: Figures, including dates, which were frequently spelled out fully, even in depositions, have been translated into numbers in the abstracts to conserve space. The words "said" or "aforesaid" appear with monotonous regularity in the original records (as in, "the said Mary Jones inherited the said property from her aforesaid grandfather Joseph Smith"), and these words have sometimes been omitted, or abbreviated to "sd."

One of the characteristics of these records is the use of only a Christian, or given name, in referring to individuals, after the full name is stated once. Thus Benjamin Brenton would be referred to as Benjamin, which is just the opposite of today's normal usage which refers to both men and women alike by surname only.

Many of the terms and phrases used in these records are no longer in familiar use. A common example might be, for an employer to "find diet and lodging" for his servant, which meant that he was to provide food and housing for him. The legal language may seem a bit extravagant at times, as in cases of trover, where it might be claimed that the plaintiff had "casually misplaced" anything from a cow to a canoe, which the defendant had found and "converted to his own use," witholding it from the its rightful owner. A glossary on pages 519-520 provides definitions for some of the more common legal terms used throughout the abstracts.

As with spellings, the order in which words were placed sometimes seems outrageous to a modern reader. If a word, a phrase, or a sentence appears not to make sense, reading it aloud may help. Words which seem to be mixed up suddenly take on meaning when they are spoken with the right inflection. A reader familiar with modern legal language is probably better equipped to understand such phrases as "to the plaintiffs belonging" the first time through, but anyone can quickly get the hang of it.

Modifications in punctuation have been made sparingly, and consist mainly of the addition of commas when deemed necessary to preserve the reader's sanity. Spellings have been left alone as much as possible, to allow the accented voices of the original speakers to come through. Spellings that are strange to us reveal how our ancestors spoke with each other – for example, "shop" is often spelled "shoop," and a name like "Niles" sometimes appears as "Noiles." Colorful language aside, readers are cautioned to remember that testimony given for court cases, whether in court or by deposition, is frequently biased and should be taken with a grain of salt.

Names have been put in bold type at least once within each abstract to make finding them easier.

Finally, please note that the book is organized by item number, rather than by page. Page numbers are intentionally omitted from the abstracts in order to minimize confusion. The glossary, index, and lists at the end are paginated, however.

Two of the transcribed wills, those of Giles Slocum and Thomas Ward, were not found among the Newport court records. They were an extraordinary discovery in the Bristol County, Massachusetts, Registry of Deeds. Both men were of Newport, but neither will has survived there, so I have included them here.

This book contains 1182 abstracts, but there are many more cases that were intentionally omitted, or were missed. Some years are not represented at all because I found no records for them, but further files may have been discovered and included in the collection in the time since I stopped working with it. Most of the simple debt cases which named only plaintiff and defendant were passed over, unless there happened to be mentioned a location, occupation, or some other feature that made it unusual enough to be of possible genealogical interest – sometimes just knowing that an individual was in a particular place at a particular time, or how he signed his name, can be useful. I tried to abstract every trespass case I found, since these often included both genealogical and geographical information. Many of the cases interested me because of the visions they evoked: Amy Buffum's troublesome cow, the tragic attempt by Africans to take over a ship that was bringing them to slavery in North America, Hope Moon climbing out from under William Taylor's bed and coolly lighting a candle, or the predicament of the little Harwood girls at Mistress Watson's dancing school. There is certainly much, much more for the diligent researcher to find in the records now housed in Pawtucket.

Because I am in seventh heaven while working with old records, this experience with the court files has been great fun. Much new information has been brought to light, and my own knowledge of many Rhode Island families has been given new dimension by what I have found there. Most satisfying of all, however, is my sense of having opened a window on the vitality of eighteenth-century Newport.

Acknowledgments

My heartfelt thanks go to the staff of the Providence College Archives: Jane Jackson, the present Archivist; Joseph Urban, who was in charge of the Court Records at the time I discovered them and for several years thereafter; and J. Stephen Grimes, who succeeded Mr. Urban in that position and is still with the records at their new location in Pawtucket. All three have tolerated my fascination with the records and made it as convenient as possible for me to work with them.

I am grateful to my friend, the late Ruth Wilder Sherman, F.A.S.G., for reading the abstracts and urging me to publish them, and to Jerome E. Anderson of the New England Historic Genealogical Society, and Maureen A. Taylor, now of the Rhode Island Historical Society, for their interest and helpful suggestions.

Dr. Elaine Crane of Fordham University has offered me hope that the collection may be of interest to historians as well as genealogists. After my life became too busy for me to continue working with the records, the inquiries of many other people have kept me from abandoning the idea of publication.

Most of all, I thank my husband, John W. Fiske, for his enthusiastic encouragement and help.

Jane Fletcher Fiske
Boxford, Massachusetts
19 June 1998

SEVENTEENTH CENTURY MATERIAL
FOUND IN FILES

Most of the early wills and some of the deeds appear in these pages under the dates when they were written, rather than the dates of the cases for which they were entered into evidence. This editorial decision was made for two reasons:

(1) Such documents were frequently found separated from the cases to which they apply, pulled out by unknown hands in earlier research efforts. Cross-referencing has been used whenever possible, but at the time these abstracts were made the earliest court files were still extremely scattered, and many supporting documents were separated from their original case files.

(2) Because so many of the original Newport wills and deeds were lost in 1779, the presentation here provides a chronological substitute for at least a few of those lost records.

1. 1659, November 19: Deed, **Benedict Arnold** to **Pardon Tillinghast:** . . . I Benadict [*sic*] Arnold of Newport on Rhoad Island in New=England Senr . . . in Consideration of a full and valuable consideration in hand rec^{d} . . . do sell and make over unto Pardon Tillinghast late of Providence and now Inhabitant of Newport aforesd cooper all that my Right Title and Interest in one Certain p[ar]cell of Land whereon is now being and standing the now Dwelling house of the sd Pardon Tillinghast in Newport . . . containeth about the Tenth pte of an acre of Ground . . . bounded as followeth . . . on the East pte which is two Rodds wide att sixteen foot & ½ to the rodd by the high way or street that runneth from Mr Brentons & along towards Benadict Arnolds dwelling house and on the north part by a high way as it is generally Laid by the Town to be two rodd broad & runeth from the forementioned highway or street down to the Sea or harbour of the Town of Newp^{t} and on the South partle by the Land of Benadict Arnold . . . all which premised parcel as before Bounded is now in the possession of the aforenamed Pardon Tillinghast to have hold use possess and Enjoy for himself his heirs Exc^{rs} Adminis^{trs} and assigns as his and their own True rightfull and Lawfull Possession . . . allways provided that in Case the said Pardon Tillinghast do Leave the said Land to Dwell Elsewhere or his Lawfull heires that then he and they shall in ye first place make Tender of the Pr[e]mises with the houseing & fenceing and other Improvements thereon unto the aforenamed Arnold my heirs (& soeforth) before he do Sell or lett it to any other p[er]son or p[er]sons whatsoever . . . sd Arnold allowing for the Land as the sd Pardon payd for it to say Twenty Pounds Sterling and for the building as they . . . or as two other Indeferant p[er]sons chosen shall agree it shall be worth at the time In case that I the sd Arnold my heirs shall desire the same and furthermore I the fornamed Arnold doe Engage for my self my heirs & assigns &c that I and they from time to time shall maintain half the fence on the Line between the said Pardon Tillinghasts Land & that which is aforesd in my p[re]sent possession even at all times when I or they do Inclose the sd Land home to the said Pardons Land and Line aforesd so as that my sd Land be by the Line of fence Secured on that Side and other ways I and they my heirs and so forth are not at any Time to be charged with any parts of the said Line of fence and in wittness of this my lawfull act & deed I hereunto putt my hand and seal . . . dated Nov 19th 1659 Even Now upon this 5th day of June 1660 I haveing a Coppy hereof under the hand of the above named Pardon Tillinghast

Signed sealed & delivered Benadict Arnold
in the p[re]sents of
Samll Edsall [and] the mark of **Wm Vaughan**
Copia Vera Tracta & Rotulis per Richd Ward Towne Clerke ex folio 74

2. 1671, June 13: **The will of William Smyton**:

The Last Will & Testament of William Smyton living in Portsmouth who at ye present being very weak but in perfect memory and having Desire to set his house in order upon yt Consideration I do ordain & appoint my well beloved wife **Sarah Smyton** to be my whole and sole Executrix —

Therefore I do give full power to my sd Wife Sarah to enjoy & possess all my proper and Real Estate during her Natural Life in ye world whether moveable or Immoveables as houses Lands Chattles or Cattle and also Debts due unto me from any person whatsoever. Also my Will is that my wife is to pay all Just and Legal Debts that is due from me to others. Also my Will and desire is after the said Death of my said Wife the Estate then remaining undisposed of to my Children as my wife shall see cause. Also my Will and desire is that my trusty and well beloved friends **William Baulston** in Portsmouth and **Francis Brinley** in Newport to be an assistant to my sd Executrix in matters that may be dubious to her as necessity may require. This I do declare to be my last will & Testament as wittness my hand & seal ye 13 of June 1671

Wittness
Symon Cooper Wm Smyton (Seal)
William Correy

I do attest this to be the last Will and Testament of Wm Smyton
Wm Baulston Asst.

A true Copy of the Original transcribed & compared ye 6 July 1671 as attest John Sanford Town Clerk of Portsmouth
Ye above Written is a true Copy entred & Recorded ye 21 of the 2d Month 1712 pr me John Anthony Town Clerke.

Copia vera Examd pr Richd Ward Recorder

3. 1677, December 24: **The will of Benedict Arnold:**

By the Permission of God Almighty

I Benedict Arnold of Newport in the Colony of Rhode Island and Providence Plantations &c Senior Aged Sixty and two years finding my Self Subject to Weaknesses and Infirmities The usual attendants on aged Persons and

Considering my Days are not like to be many that I have to abide in this Temporall life And now at the writing hereof being (tho somewhat weak of Body Yet) in Perfect Memory & reasonable Understanding And Resolving it necessary for preventing the many Inconveniences that may arise for want of setting my House in Order and Setting my Temporall Estate while I am alive do therefore make this my last Will and Testament in Manner and Form following.

Imprimis And in the first Place I having full assurance of the Infinite Mercy of my Almighty Creator unto my Soul and do cheerfully and willingly recommend the Same into his Blessed Hands from whom I receiv'd it and by whose Grace am made willing to wait his Pleasure for my Change from this Transitory Life unto a Life in and with himself Eternally And my Body unto the Earth from whence by the Almighty Power and Decree of the Same God it was taken Willing & appointing [*page* 2] That after my Decease my Body may be decently Interred by my Executors hereafter in this writing Named and the Charge of the Said Interment to be Defrayed out of my Personal Estate my Body I Desire and appoint to be buried *at the NorthEast Corner* of a Parcel of Ground containing three Rod Square* being part of and lying in my Land in or near the Line or Path from my dwelling House leading to my Stonebuilt Windmill in the Town of Newport abovementioned* The Middle or Center of which Said three Rod Square of Ground is and shall be the Tomb already Erected over the Grave of my GrandChild **Damaris Goulding** there buried on the fourteenth Day of August 1677* And I Desire that my dear and loving Wife **Damaris Arnold** after her decease may be buried near unto me on the South Side of the Place afores^{d} ordered for my own Interment And I do order my Executors to erect decent Tombs over my Grave and her Grave in Such Convenient Time as it may be effectually accomplished And further I Do hereby Solemnly Prohibit the Selling or otherwise Disposing of the said three Rod Square of Ground or any Part Thereof [*page* 3] but that it be wholy reserved to ye Use of my Kindred Relations for so many of them as shall please to Bury their Dead in the said Ground and therefore do Order and appoint that they shall have from Time to Time on all such Occassions to and from the said Burying Place Free Egress and Regress without any Molestation from any that Shall succeed me in the Land about it.

Item, In the next Place I will and Ordain that all my Just Debts Shall be Paid all which at the Writing hereof do not amount to thirty pounds Sterling in New England Money either by Bill or Book due to any or to all Men whatsoever And after clearing all such Debts as Shall appear Just I do Give and Bequeath unto my Dear loving & Beloved Wife Damaris Arnold Aforenamed and to her Proper use and Behoof during her Naturall Life and after her decease to the Proper use and behoof of our beloved Daughter **Godsgift Arnold** and to her Heirs and Assigns to have and to Hold Possess and Enjoy as her and their Own true Right and Lawfull Inheritance for ever That is to say [*page* 4] The Lands & Tenaments thereafter mentioned namely the House and two Acres of Land be it more or less that I Bought of **William Haviland** being and lying in the Precints of the Town of Newport abovesaid bounded on the South and on the East Parts by Land now or late in the Possession of **Thomas Clifton** or his Assigns on the West by a Highway belonging to the Said Town and on the North by Land that I have bequeathed to my Son **Josiah Arnold** and I Order the said Line of fence to be made and for ever maintained by the Occupants of the Premisses which I bought of William Haviland aforesaid as also all the Land which I bought of **William Vahhan** being and lying in the Precincts of the said Town of Newport and by me Named Spring Harbour Lands containing Ninety Acres more or less in two Parcells the greator of which two Parcells is bounded on the North by Land now or late in the Possession of **Henry Bull** On the East by Land in the Possession of the Assigns of **Wm Brenton** Esqr deceased On the South by Land in the Possession of **John Coggeshall Senior** and on the West by a Highway belonging to the Said Town the lesser of the Said Parcells of Land is bounded on the North by Land of Henry Bull aforesaid On [*page 5*] the East by the Highway aforesaid On the South Partly by a Broad way and partly by Land in Possession of the Assigns of **George Gardner** deceased and on the West by a Creek or Cove of Salt Water All which the Premisses together with a Certain Parcell of Land in the Close called Stillhouse Close being and lying in the Precincts of the aforesaid Town containing by Estemation two Acrs and a Quarter more or less in two distinct Parcells each bounded as followeth Namely the bigger Parcell on the North and West in Part by **Roger Gouldings** Land and on said North and East more largely by a Highway belonging to the said Town on the South by my Son **Benedict Arnolds** Land and on the West by a Highway Parallell with the Town Highway leading towards his the sd Benedict Arnolds Land The lesser parcell of the Premisses is bounded on the North by a parcell of Roger Gouldings Land aforenamed On the East by the Highway last mentioned as aforesaid on ye South by Benedict Arnolds Land aforesaid and on the West by the Sea or Harbour of the Town aforementioned And it is Ordered that the Said Benedict Arnold his Heirs and Assigns are to make and for ever maintain a Good Sufficient Fence in the Line between his Said Land and both the Said [*page 6*] Parcells of the Premisses and the least or last Described parcell thereof is to make and for ever Maintain by the Occupants thereof a Good and Sufficient Fence In the Line between it and Roger Gouldings Land thereto adjoyning as aforesaid all which the Premisses parcells of Land lying and being in five Distinct parts each bounded as aforesaid I Do give and bequeath to the only Proper use and behoof of my said Wife **Damaris Arnold** for her Support and in Order also toward the Maintainance of my Daughter **GodsGift Arnold** During the Naturall life of her Mother my Said Wife Damaris Arnold and in the Mean Time to be carefully reserved and kept to the only use and behoof of my Said Daughter GodsGift Arnold after her Said Mothers decease for her my said Daughter GodsGift Arnold To have and to hold use and Enjoy to herself and to her Heirs and Assigns as her and their and every or either their undoubted Right and Lawfull Inheritance forever. [*page 7*]

Item, I Do also Give and Bequeath unto the Proper use and behoof of my said Wife **Damaris Arnold** During her Naturall Life and after her decease to the Use and behoof of my dearly beloved and youngest Daughter **Freelove Arnold** all and Singuler the Lands and Buildings Severally hereafter mentioned in particuler that is to say my Dwelling House and the Lands buildings and Tenements hereafter named Namely one Tract of Land being and lying in the Precincts of the foresaid Town of Newport containing by Estemation Sixteen Acres distinguished into two Parcells by a Highway belonging to the said Town and bounded severally as followeth that is to say the lesser parcell whereon is Erected my Warehouse and Wharf and bounded as followeth On the East by the Highway aforesaid on the South by a Parcell of Land I have bequeathed unto my Son **Oliver Arnold** On the West by the Sea or Harbour of Newport on the North by Land Now or late in the Possession of **Pardon Tillinghast** or his Assigns the other and Greater parcell of the Tracts of Land abovesaid upon which Standeth my Dwelling or Mannor House and other Buildings thereto adjoyning or belonging as also my Stone built Windmill and in the said [*page 8*] Parcell is being and lying the three Rod Square of ground abovesaid that I have set a part for a Burying Place the whole parcell being bounded as followeth on the West by the Highway aforesaid On part of the North and part of the West by a Quillit of Land containing fifty foot Square that I Sold and Now or late in the Possession of **Jeremiah Brown**. and on the Rest of the North by a Highway belonging also as the aforesaid Highway to the said Town on the East by Land Now or late in the Possession of **Walter Clark**, or his Assigns save only as the Town may Order a Highway between and on the South by Land I have bequeathed to my Son **Josiah Arnold** he the said Josiah Arnold his Heirs or Assigns being to make and for ever Maintain a good & Sufficient Fence in the Line between the Premisses and his Said Land Moreover I give and bequeath unto my said Wife Damaris Arnold as above^{d} during her Naturall Life and after her Decease to the Use of our Said Daughter **Freelove Arnold** a certain Tract of Land being and lying in the Precincts of the said Town and by me Called Limmington Farm containing by Estemation one hundred and [*page 9*] Thirty Acres more or less and bounded as followeth that is to Say on the North by the Sea or Harbour of the Said Town for the Greatest part and by Land in Possession of **John Stanton** on the Rest of John Stantons Land aforesaid on the South by the Common and on the West by the Common down to the Sea or Harbour aforesaid the Northermost Part being divided at present by a stone Wall from the Southermost part of the Premisses which as yet is not fenced from the Common on which it is bounded as aforesaid all which the Premissed Tracts and parcells of Land as Distinguished by the Respective Bounds of Each the said Tracts and parcells beforementioned together wth all the Buildings Improvements Fences & Conveniencies upon any and every part of the Premisses Erected or thereupon being or to any part thereof propertly belonging or in any wise thereunto appertaining I Do give and bequeath as abovesaid unto the Proper Use and behoof of my said Wife Damaris Arnold for her Support and in Order toward the Maintanance of my Daughter **Freelove Arnold** aforenamed [*page 10*] During the Naturall Life of her Mother my said Wife Damaris Arnold and all the Premisses I will and order to be Carefully reserved and kept to the use of my Said Daughter Freelove Arnold after her said Mother Damaris Arnolds Decease for her my Said Daughter Freelove Arnold the Premisses and every part and parcell of the same abovementioned to have & to hold possess use and Enjoy to her self my said Daughter Freelove Arnold to her own proper use and behoof and to the proper use and behoof of her Heirs and assigns as her and their and every or either of her or their true Right full and lawfull Inheritance forever.

Item. For the More Comfortable Subsistance of my said Wife and towards ye Maintenance of my two Daughters aforenamed I hereby Will and Order that all my Cattle either Horsekind Neat Cattle Sheep & Swine that are mine in the Precincts of the Town of Newport aforesaid shall all be delivered to and left in the Possession and to ye Use of [*page 11*] My said Wife Damaris Arnold to the End and Purpose before expressed During her Naturall Life and after her decease what of the said Cattle and their Increase shall remain I order to the peculier use and behoof of my said Daughters **GodsGift Arnold** and **Freelove Arnold** to be speedily and equally divided between them their Heirs or Assigns for Stocking their Respective Lands hereby given as aforesaid.

Item, And to the End the Business & work may be carried on the more conveniently I order and appoint that all my Servants of what sort soever and all my Household Stuff and Utensialls shall be and Remain to the Use of my said Wife Damaris Arnold during her Naturall life and after her decease what remains to be divided among my Children to wit to Each my Daughters aforesaid one third part thereof and the other third also to be equally divided between them except my said Wife do otherwise dispose of that part to Some other of our Children before her Death.

Item, Unto my Eldest and well beloved Son **Benedict Arnold** I give and bequeath half of my Neck of Land being the Southermost part of the Island [*page 12*] Called Quananagut lying in Narraganset Bay near Rhode Island in the Colony aforesaid the Said Neck of Land being by me Named Beaver Neck and doth Contain one Thousand Acres Surrounded by the Sea exceptyng where it is joyned to the rest of Quananagut by a Narrow Beech or Sponge of Land called Parting Beech which said Beach where it Joyneth to the Said Neck is to be fenced off therefrom by my said Son Benedict Arnold and a Gate therein to be hanged or Barrs to be put down and upon Occasion of going or Coming into or Out of the Said Neck by any & every of my Sons their Heirs and Assigns to whom I have bequeathed Lands at ye Souther End of the Island to wit my Son **Josiah Arnold** and my Son **Oliver Arnold** Ordering and hereby Providing that there shall be a Mutual

Priviledge & Liberty to my Said Sons Benedict Josiah and Oliver their Heirs and Assigns for ever (being their Lands will lye Joyning or near unto Each other) to pass and repass through one anothers Lands on their Necessary Occasions either of Carting driving Cattle or ye like as also for fishing and fowling about the Shore & Creeks and for Sheltering Boats or Canoes in any the Ponds Coves Creeks or Nookes of ye Sea as [*page 13*] Occasion shall require from Time to Time and also free Passage to and from the Boats over Each others Lands they not otherwise Damnifying one another by leaving open Gates or Barrs or ye like, and Whereas I Give & Bequeath one half of the said Beaver Neck unto my Said Son Benedict Arnold I intend he shall have ye Northermost end thereof & that the Neck shall be equally divided in two as near as may be Overthwart the bredth of it from the East Shore to the West Shore and the Fence that Shall be made & maintained in the Said Line three parts of four beginning at the West End of Said Line shall be made and for ever maintained by my Son Josiah Arnold & by his Heirs and Assigns and the other fourth part of that Line of Fence shall be made and for ever maintained by my Said Son Benedict Arnold and his Heirs and Assigns from Time to Time the Premisses to him Bequeathed is five hundred acres bounded on the South by the aforementioned line On the East by an Arm of the Sea called Macril Cove on the North Partly by the Beach end aforementoned and the rest of ye Pond Eell Pond and the Outlet thereof into the Sea down to the Place called Fox hill and [*page 14*] On the West by the Sea as also to my sd Son Benedict Arnold I Give and Bequeath one third part of my Interest in Dutch Island lying near adjacent to that part of Quanonagut all which the Premisses I will and Order to the Only Use and Behoof of my Said Son Benedict Arnold and his Heirs and Assigns for ever.

Item, Unto my Beloved Son **Josiah Arnold** aforenamed I Give and Bequeath a certain parcell of Land being and lying in the Precincts of ye Town of Newport abovementioned the said Land containing by Estemation four Acres more or less being Eight Rod in bredth from North to South and Eighty Rod in Length from East to West Bounded on the North by Land I have Bequeathed to his Mother **Damaris Arnold** &c on the East by the Land of **Walter Clark** on the South in part by Land Now or later in the Possession of **Thomas Clifton** or his Assigns and partly by the Land abovesaid I bought of **William Haviland** and Bequeathed to the Said Damaris Arnold &c and partly by a Highway belonging to the said Town and on the West by a Highway belonging also to the said Town as also unto my Said Son Josiah Arnold [*page 15*] I Give and Bequeath a Certain Parcell of Land lying in the Said Town containing near a quarter of an Acre being in Length North and South Nine Rod more or less and in bredth East & West Sixty and two foot bounded at Each End by the Street ways belonging to the Said Town and on each Side by Land in the Possession of **Thomas Ward** as also unto my Said Son Josiah Arnold I Give and Bequeath a Certain Parcell of Land being and lying on the South End of Quananagut Island abovementoned in the Neck of Land called Bever Neck the Premisses containing five hundred Acres and bounded as followeth on the North by Land above given and bequeathed to my Son Benedict Arnold and on the East South and West by the Sea and therewith free Egress & Regress to & through the Said Benedict Arnolds Land & to and through the Land I have given to my Son Oliver Arnold Expressed to be mutually used and allowed by the Said Benedict Arnold Josiah Arnold and Oliver Arnold according to my true Intent & meaning in that Matter [*page 16*] And together with the aforesaid Lands I Give and Bequeath unto my Said Son Josiah Arnold one third part of my Interest in the Island called Dutch Island aforementoned all which the Premisses together with the Priviledges advantages & Commodities thereupon or upon any part or parts of the Same Being or thereunto belonging or appertaining are to be & remain to the Only Proper Use of my Said Son Josiah Arnold and his Heirs and Assigns for ever.

Item, Unto my Youngest and well Beloved Son **Oliver Arnold** aforenamed I give and bequeath the Lands Tenements and Hereditaments hereafter mentioned that is to Say a Certain parcell of Land being & lying in the Precincts of the foresaid Town of Newport containing one fourth part of an acre more or less being Six Rod in bredth from North to South and bounded on the North by the Land given and bequeathed to my Wife Damaris Arnold &c as abovesaid On the East by the Street or Highway aforementioned belonging to the sd Town on the South by Land I sold to **Simon Parrott** and on the West by the Sea or Harbour of the Same Town, he the Said Oliver Arnold [*page 17*] His Heirs and Assigns being to make and for ever Maintain a good and sufficient Fence in the Line between the Said Land hereby granted to my Said Son Oliver Arnold And the Land aforementoned lying on the North Side thereof, which I have given unto his Mother my Wife Damaris Arnold as abovesaid the South Line of the Land hereby given to my Said Son Oliver Arnold being to be made & for ever maintained by Simon Parrot his Heirs and Assigns as by the Deed he had of me doth appear as also I give and bequeath unto my Said Son Oliver Arnold a Certain Tract of Land being and lying upon the Island Quananagut abovementioned containing by Estemation three hundred acres more or less and called Cajesset Land bounded as followeth on the North partly by a Highway two Rod wide lying between the Premisses and the Land Now or late in the Possession of **Caleb Carr** Senior or his Assigns and partly by Land Now or late in the Possession of the Assigns of **William Weeden** dec^d^ on the West and on the South by a Tract of Land called ye Township [*page 18*] As on the Platt or Draught of the Said Island it Doth appear and on the Easterly parts the Premisses is bounded by the Sea in the Severall Turnings &c of the Said Land on that part thereof and also together with the foresaid Tract I Give and Bequeath another certain Tract of Land being and lying on the Said Island Quanonagut in a Trianguler form containing Sixty four Acres by the Surveyors Platt of that Island and is bounded as followeth, that is to Say on the North Line by the So called Township Land aforementioned on the Easterly part by the Broad Highway that goeth upon a Slant North Easterly to the Said Township Land so called and on the South and West partly by the End of the beach aforenamed and partly by Eeel Pond aforesaid & by the influx thereof unto my sd Son Oliver Arnold all the Land that Now is my Right to & in that said Tract called the Township the sd Tract containing by the Surveyors Account two hundred and Sixty acres my Said Interest therein being more than one third part of the said [*page 19*] Tract as belonging unto my other Tracts and Shares and to all and every of them in the Said Island as by me purchased and lawfully procured So that my Said Right in the said Tract called the Township is and ought to be eighty three Acres and upwards the Bounds whereof will be as the Committee shall appoint when they divide the Said Tract to the Respective Owners thereof Untill when it is however contained within the Tract aforesaid called the Township Land further I Order that Whereas there is Supposed to be Some Land belonging to **Francis Brinley** that may be forty acres which may fall in or about some part of the Premisses to witt forty acres belonging to a two hundredth part and a three hundreth part of the Said Island &c I say for making up the Said Forty Acres to Said Brinley I Order that he shall have forty acres of the North part of the Trianguler Tract of Land aforementioned as once he proposed or else Some Land at Northern End of Said Island near or next to his Land there which he earnestly desired And to gratify him I have procured to that End to Accomodate him with in way of Exchange for that aforementioned lying [*page 20*] Near the Premisses And I Order that to make the Premisses given to Said Oliver Arnold Five hundred Acres he Shall have it out of my Land that I bought of **John Tripp George Bliss Edward Thurston William Cadman** and **Bartholomew West** as by Deeds in writing it may appear under their hands & Seals and being & lying in the Main Body of said Island Northward from a Tract there granted to **William Brenton Esqr** Deceased by and among the first Purchasers of Said Islands The Names of the Persons of whom I bought the foresaid Lands being written in the Places on the Platt of Said Island shewing where they are to lie And together with the foresaid Lands I Give and Bequeath unto my Said Son Oliver Arnold one third part of my Interest in the Island called Dutch Island aforementioned And also equall Priviledges as is aforepremised & Ordered to either his Brothers Benedict Arnold or Josiah Arnold for free and mutuall Egress & Regress to & through Each others Land on all Occasions as are afore more Particularly expressed [*page 21*] All which the Lands and Priviledges whatever are to be & remain to the Proper use & behoof of my said Son Oliver Arnold & his Heirs and Assigns for ever (with the Fencing and Buildings thereupon.)

Item, I also together with the Lands on Quanonagut aforesaid given and bequeathed to my said Sons **Benedict Arnold Josiah Arnold** and **Oliver Arnold** do by these Presents give and bequeath all my Cattle that are or may hereafter be fọund within any ye Said Lands lying Southward from the

Said **Caleb Carrs** Land whither Horsekind Neet Cattle Sheep and any other Sorts the Said Cattle to be equally Shared amonst them to each of my sd Sons one third part to Stock their Respective Lands by these & Presents given and bequeathed as afores[d].

Item, Whereas I have formerly given unto my well beloved Son **Caleb Arnold** a Considerable Sum as by my Book Accompts may appear to Value of two hundred Pounds Sterling in Currant pay yet in my Tender Respects to my said Son Caleb Arnold I do moreover give and bequeath a certain parcell of Land lying & being in y[e] Precincts of the Town of Newport abovesaid containing a Quarter of an Acre more or less and [*page 22*] Bounded as followeth that is to say on y[e] North by Land Now or late in Possession of the Assigns of W[m] Brenton Esq[r] Dec[d] on the East by the Street way belonging to the Said Town on the South by Land Now or late in the Possession of **Robert Carr** Senior and on the West by the Harbour belonging to the Said Town & together with the Premisses I Give and Bequeath unto my Said Son Caleb Arnold Eight Score Acres of Land being and lying in the Island Quanonagut above mentioned and bounded as followeth that is to say on the North and South by Land in my own Possession or in the Possession of my Assigns at the Writing hereof on the East by the Sea and on the West by the Broad Highway the Premised Land being & lying on the East Side and Northern part of Quanonagut near to the Land of **Francis Brinley** abovementioned all which the Premisses together with all y[e] Commodities thereon or thereunto property belonging and appertaining are to be and remain to the only proper use and behoof of the Said Caleb Arnold for and during his Naturall [*page 23*] Life or untill his Eldest Son then living shall come to the Age of one and twenty Years which said Son of his shall at that Age enter upon & Enjoy the Premisses to him & his Heirs for ever.

Item, Unto my Beloved Daughter **Damaris Bliss** y[e] Wife of **John Bliss** of Newport I Give and bequeath a certain Parcell of Land being and lying in the Precincts of Said Town containing seven & twenty acres more or less and bounded as followeth namely on the North partly by Land I sold to **James Card** lately and partly by Land in y[e] Possession of **Joseph Card** On the East partly by Joseph Cards Land aforesaid and more largely by Land in Possession of **William Weeden** on the South by Land Now or late in the Possession of the Assigns of Lieutenant **Joseph Torry** deceased and on the West by the Great Common of the Said Town the Premisses to be and remain to the only proper Use and behoof of my Said Daughter Damaris Bliss and her Heirs and Assigns for ever.

Item, Unto my beloved Daughter **Penelope Goulding** the Wife of **Roger Goulding** I Give and Bequeath a certain parcel of Land being and lying [*page 24*] In the Precincts of the Town aforesaid the said Land by me Named [? Sc]irtfield and is that w[ch] I purchased of **William Dyer** Senior Now late deceased & containing by measure two and twenty Acres and a half and bounded as followeth that is to say on the North by Land in the Possession of **Peleg Sandford** or his Assigns on the East by the Great Common aforesaid as also on the South by the Same Common and on the West partly by Land Now or late in the Possession of the Assigns of **John Clark** Physician deceased and partly by Land in the Possession of the Assigns of William Dyer aforesaid deceased the Premisses to be and remain to the only use and behoof of my Said Daughter Penelope Goulding & her Heirs for ever.

Item, I Give & Bequeath unto my two Youngest Daughters to witt **Gods Gift Arnold** and **Freelove Arnold** beforenamed to each of them fifty Pounds Sterling New England Silver money to be delivered to each of my Said Daughters at the Age of twenty Years or on y[e] day of their Respective Marriages hereby advising them to [*page 25*] Be advised by their Mother in that Point of Mariage wherein either of them being refractory then the Money ev'n both the Said Fifty Pounds to be delivered to the use of the Obedient Party in that Point & the Same in Case of the Death of either of them in the mean time the whole to the Survivor is to be deliver'd to her use & to No other.

Item, What Silver Spoons Cups Bowles Beakers and Porrengers are Now mine I leave them to the Use of my Said Wife during her Naturall Life or untill in her life Time she shall please to give any of it to either our Sons Daughters or Grand Children and the rest to be reserved and kept to the use of Such of them as my said Wife shall dispose it to be theirs after her decease.

Item, Concerning my Interest in the Purchase of Pettaquamscut in the Narraganset Countrey my Said Interest being one part of Seven of that Purchase both of Lands Mineralls and all other the Comodities Priviledges and Conveniencies on the Said Part of the Said Purchase being or thereunto in any ways belonging or appertaining I do by these presents give and bequeath my sd Seventh Part unto my Said Sons **Benedict Arnold Josiah Arnold** and **Oliver Arnold** together with [*page 26*] My Cattle of all sorts that shall be found upon or about the Premisses to be Equally divided amonst them to the Proper use and behoof of my Said Sons and to every of them their Heirs and Assigns Respectively for ever only excepting and willing with the advice and Consent of the rest of the Partners that Some Tract or Tracts five Miles to the Northward and Westward of the Rock called (by y[e] Indian Natives) Pettaquamscut Rock may be sett a part and proposed to the use of this Colony upon very easy Terms for Accomodating one or two Townships to be ordered and erected by the Gen[rll] Assembly of this Colony in which Said Townships I desire & Order may be accomodated more especially my foresaid three Sons & also my Son **Caleb Arnold** aforenamed as also **Maj[r] John Cranston Cap[t] Peleg Sanford Cap[t] Roger Goulding M[r] James Barker Ensign John Bliss** and **John Coggeshall Sen[r]** with other deserving Persons that may be proposed by the rest of the Partners And I further Will & Order that in Case the Setling of a Town or two be [*page 27*] Not effected Yet however that my sd Sons together with Major Cranston Cap[t] Peleg Sandford Captain Roger Goulding M[r] James Barker Ensign John Bliss and John Coggeshall, Sen[r] aforesaid Shall out of my Own Interest in the Said Tracts five Miles Distant from the Said Rock called Pettaquamscut

Rock Each, and every of them respectively have two hundred and fifty Acres of Land in And of my Said Share to every and either their own Proper use and behoof and to the Use & behoof of their Heirs and Assigns respectively for ever and what shall remain of my Said Part of Said Tract or Tracts distance from and Not lying within the said Distance of five Miles of the said Rock, I Desire my Executors hereafter named to take care thereof and cause it to be disposed toward Erecting and Maintaining a Free School in Newport aforesaid and toword the Relief of Poor People of the Said Town and to be ordered and Disposed of to the said Ends premissed by the Councill of the said Town and their Successors from Time to Time for ever

[*page 28*] Item, For the Better Execution of this my last Will and Testament I Do hereby Nominate appoint Constitute and Ordain to be my Executors these Persons hereafter named to witt My Said Beloved Wife **Damaris Arnold** my Executrix and my Said Sons **Benedict Arnold Josiah Arnold & James Barker Senr** my Executors to assist in the Execution of this my last Will and Testament and what they four my Said Executors or any three or two of them or Survivors of them (my Said Wife Damaris Arnold to be always one while she liveth) shall do or cause to be done in or about the Premisses and in Order to putting this my Will in Actuall Execution according to the Contents and true Intent & meaning of these presents shall be held for firm and good to all Intents and Purposes what ever in the Law as if I my self had actually done the same in my Own Person whilst I was Living In Witness hereof I have set my hand and Seal to every Page of this my Will and Testament and finally to the whole Contents whereof in [*page 29*] This last place This the four and twentieth Day of December in the Nine and twentieth year of the Reign of our Sovereign Lord Charles the Second King of England Scotland France and Ireland &c Annoque Dom: 1677.

Benedict Arnold Senr [Seal]

Sign'd & sealed in the presence of us --
Edmund Calverly
William Heffernon
Beriah Brown

[Codicil]

I Benedict Arnold above named Senior having by the Good Grace and Favour of God had my Days lengthened unto this Time In which Time I having considered more maturely of Some Circumstances in my abovesd Will And being and Remaining through his Grace in Reasonable Understanding and Perfect Memory do find it necessary for the Regulation Explanation and Confirmation of my Said last Will and Testament I add as followeth as to the Place above appointed for my Interment being at the North East Corner of the three rod Square apponted for a Burying Place abovesaid I Do Order and appoint that I and my Wife may be buried in that three Rod Square as near as conveniently may be at the East End of the Tombs [*page 30*] There Erected on my Grand Child **Damaris Gouldings** Grave abovesaid my self on the North and my Said Wife on the South side of me and that my Kindred Relations may as they die be buried at Convenient Distance Round about my Said Grave.

Now whereas in the first Article of this my Will that concerneth ye Disposition of my Lands in Quanonacut it is said that my Eldest Son **Benedict Arnold Junr** shall have for his part in the Middle (of the Neck of Land) called Bever Neck having hereby Ordered that as he is the first in Nomination to whom I have disposed of Land in the said Neck so he shall be the first in Scituation and at the South End of the said Neck which said Part of the Said Neck containeth by estemation five hundred Acres be they more or less and is to be divided in all Equality from the remaining Part of the Said Neck by one Streight Line of Fence beginning at the Eastern Side thereof so to run over to the Western Shore on a streight Line from Sea to Sea and the Said Line of Fence to be made and for ever maintained by the said Benedict Arnold Junr and his Heirs Occupants [*page 31*] of the Said Land And whereas tis Said in the second Article concerning the Premisses that my Son **Josiah Arnold** aforesaid shoud have his Said (Third Part) and Share of the Said Neck at the South End thereof He shall have his on the North Side of and adjoyning unto Benedict Arnold Junr afores^d^ Share upon the South and from thence to Extend Northward unto the Pond called Eel Pond which Said Pond is the Northern Bounds of his the Said Josiah Arnolds Share and he the Said Josiah Arnold is to secure himself on the North and Eastern Parts by Fence or otherwise And from and to the Northward of the Said Pond called Eel Pond home to the Highway of Two Rod wide that lyeth between **Caleb Carrs** Land and the Premisses within which Tract is contained my Farm called Cajesset Farm my Dwelling house and other Houses thereon already erected all which my said Housing and Lands shall be the Proper share and Inheritance of my Son Oliver Arnold And if it shall appear that there is not enough in the Said Tract to make his Share five hundred acres Equall with the Rest he shall have so much Land as to [*page 32*] Make it up according as in an Article to this Effect is more Plainly described to the Northward of the Premisses always to be understood that the Priviledges and Commodities that are Ordered that they the Said Benedict Arnold Junr Josiah Arnold and Oliver Arnold are to have in upon or through each others respective Lands shall be duly observed by Each of them respectively according to the Rules set down in a former Article concerning that Matter with this further Additional Proviso that they the sd three Brothers or either of them shall not alienate by Sale or otherways the Propriety of any Part of their foresaid Lands from their Heirs by these presents given and granted unto them as in a foregoing Article relating to the Premisses is more plainly expressed.

Whereas there are words interlined two in the first page & 42^d^ Line Two in the Third Page 14th Line Five in the Seventh Page the 9th and 10th Lines Eight in the Eighth Page 13 & 24 Lines Eleven in the Ninth Page 23^d^ 26th & 30th Lines and four in the Tenth [*page 33*] Page and fourth Line, As also Words Raised in the Eighth Page in the 13th 14th & 15th Lines In ye ninth Page and 26th Line, and in the tenth Page and 4th Line This may Certify that the Interlining and Rasing was by my Order done before the Signing and sealing hereof being the Tenth Day of June One Thousand Six hundred Seventy and Eight 1678

Benedict Arnold Senr [Seal]

Signd and Sealed in the Presence of us aforenamed
Edmund Calverly Wm Heffernon Beriah Brown
July 1st 1678 Edmund Calverly Wm Heffernon & Beriah Brown appeared before the Councill and attested the aforewritten Will in all the Parts thereof to be the last Will and Testament of the Said Benedict Arnold and that he was in Perfect Memory at the Ensealing and declaring thereof: As attest Thomas Ward Town Cler.
The aforewritten being almost thierty three Pages is a True Copy of the Originall Will Exam: pr Josias Lyndon Cler.
The above written will is Entred on Record in ye Counciells book No 2 & in ye 134 page pr Wes' Clarke Town Clerk

4. 1681, April 20: The will of **Robert Carr Senr**:

The Last Will & Testament of Robert Carr Senr: of Newpt on Rhode Island - being now in my perfect Health & memory & being bound a Voyage to New=York & New=Jersey and being aged & not knowing how the Lord may Deale with me in my Intended Voyage and knowing certainly that I must once Dye, Though as uncertain when, Yet being Desirous to set my house in order. Doe make and appoint this to be my Last Will & Testament.

Imprs: I Commit my Soul into the armes of Jesus Christ my Redeemer and my body to the Dust to be Decently Buried.

And to my Worldly Estate I Dispose of as followeth:

1st: I Give and Bequeath to my Loving Wife all my Houshold Stuff and Moveables, Except my Sheep at Conanicut; and Twenty pounds in Money to be paid her Yearly During her Naturall Life by my Sonns hereafter Named.

2ndly I Give to my Eldest Child **Caleb Carr** all my Land at Conanicut, alias James=Town he paying my Wife ten pounds a Year in Money during her Naturall Life and pay **John Hix** his Children by my Daughter twenty pounds.

3rdly I Give my Son **Robert Carr** & to the Heirs of his body Lawfully begotten my Dwelling Houses & Wharfe from the Corner post that Leads into the Well Yard upon a Streight Line to the Sea only the Priviledge of the Highway between the Houses and the Well Yard to be Common up to **James Browns** House, and the wharfe to be ffree for my sons and daughters for any Goods they shall bring on or of the sd Wharfe: & to have all the Land upon the Streight Line from that post adjoyning to the House & pasture except what is Given to my Son in Law James Brown and the priviledg of the Well, and a way to it, and pay to his Mother seven pounds in money Yearly during her Naturall Life.

4thly I Give to my Son **Esek** all my Land from the Corner post of the Well Yard next the Street so to the Land I sold to **Nicholas Davis** now in possession of

Francis Brinley & **Caleb Carr** Together with the privilidge of the Highway Between the House & ye Land & a Highway Down to the Wharfes & the Privilidge of the Wharfe onely The Well to be Common, & free for my Mantion Dwelling House [*page* 2] & a Highway to it for him & the Heirs of his Body Lawfully begotten To Enjoy the Same & pay to his Mother Yearly three pounds in Money.

5^{thly} I Give & Bequeath to my Daughter **Margarett** all my sheep at Conanicut alias James=Town, & the Horse flesh to be sold and the value of them to be returned to her; Except one Yearling Colt come of a Young Mare wch I gave to my Son Caleb.

6^{thly} I Give & Bequeath to my Son in Law **James Brown** & to his Children he hath by my Daughter **Elizabeth** all that Land he hath built upon & fenced in: with two rodds in Length more Even with his Land as it is fenced in, The uppermost piece behind his house next Mr **Brentons** with the Privilidges of the Highway from the Broad Street to his House and Land.

Lastly I Do Nominate & appoint my beloved Wife Executrix and my Two Sonns Caleb and Robert Carr, Executors to this my Last Will & Testament, and as Overseers: I Desire my brother Caleb Carr, & Walter Clarke to be Overseers, to see my Will to all Intents and purposes performed.

Signed Sealed and Published [*signed*] Robert Carr [seal]
before us Aprill ye 20th:1681
Henry Dyre
John Williams
Proved 4 October 1681, Weston Clarke Town Clerke

4A. The will of Thomas Ward of Newport, dated 9 June 1683, proved 2 June 1690: [*This record was found in the Bristol County Registry of Deeds in Taunton, Massachusetts, in 1985, badly faded and torn, among a pile of original deeds. It probably relates to a Bristol County Court Case ca. 1739. This compiler has a photocopy, some of which cannot be deciphered; the original was turned over to the Bristol County Registrar of Deeds. An extract of the will containing the bequest of Ward's Pettaquamscutt property was also found among the earliest Newport files.*]

[*torn*] all men by these Presents that I **Thomas Ward** of Newport on Rhoad Island In ye Collony of Rhode Island & Providence Plantations in New England &c, being through the Goodness and Mercy of the Lord at Present of sound memory, yet haveing Weakness attending my frail Body, Do make this my Last Will, and Testament Bequeathing my Soul to Jehovah my Maker, and my Body to be Decently Interred In Certain hope, that It Shall be Raised when God shall Judge the World by [Jesus] Christ whom He hath appointed and then for Ever be with the Lord Do for Settling My Temporall Estate make this My Last Will and Testament In Manner following makeing Void all other former Wills [-------] my Exec^{rs} In Convenient Time, to pay all that I Justly owe to any Person or Persons.

Item - I give and bequeath unto my son **Thomas** and to the Heirs of his Body Lawfully Begotten, unto the Third Generation and from thence to Descend to his heirs In Fee Simple, for Ever That Is to Say Two Parcells of Land Lying and Being Scituate In the Precincts of Newport aforesaid and Bounded as followeth, one of them Lying near Green End and Bounded on the north by [ye?] highway & on ye East by [----] Peckhams land on ye South by **John Greens** Land, on the West by land in ye possession of **John Peckham Junr** on which said Peice of Land is scituated a Dwelling house, The other said Peice of Land Being Bounded Eastwardly and Partly Southerly, by ye land of **Lawrance Turner** on ye north Partly by ye Common and Partly on **James Weedens** Land and Partly on **Francis Brinleys** land on ye West Partly on **Francis Brinleys** Land and partly by **Edward Thurstons** Land on ye South Partly by the [*torn*] Newtons [*torn*] said Forge [?] and also one hundred acres lott of [*torn*] being scituate in ye town of Little Compton [*torn*] Collony of New Plymouth in New England and bounded on ye south by **Daniel Greenhills** Land [and] West[erly] by the Bay or Salt Walter near Rhoad Island on the North by Land Commonly called **William** [*illegible*] Land and on the East by the undivided lands and with the one moiety or half Part In [*torn*] of all and singular my Lands Lying and Being In [*torn*] Eastward and Westward side of Taunton River In the Colony of New Plymouth aforesaid and Commonly Called the Freemens lands, and also the one Moiety or Half part In Deal of all and singular my Lands Lying and Being Scituate at Pocasset and Parts adjacent In ye said Collony of New Plymouth and also ye [----] one half Part in Deal of all and Singular my Lands [*torn*] Scituate and [*torn*] called Puncatest Neck and Parts adjacent [-------------]ly south aforesaid and also the Two Westernmost of the Islands commonly called Elizabeth Islands, which are undivided Between **Major Peleg Sanford Philip Smith** and my Self, and also all the Moiety or half part In Deale of all and Singular my Lands Lying and Being Scituate at a Place Commonly Called by the Name of Pettaquamscutt or Pettaquamscutt Purchase in the Colony of Rhoad Island & aforesaid.

Item - I give and Bequeath unto my Daughter **Margaret** and to the heirs of her Body Lawfully Begotten unto the third generation and from thence to Descend to her [heirs] in fee Simple for Ever that Is to say Two parcells of Land Lying and Being Scituate In Newport aforesaid (together with other Lands mentioned In this Section) on one of which said peices of Land Is Scituated my Late Dwelling house and Warehouse, and Is Bounded on ye Eastward Southwestward, and Northwestward by the Streets of the said Town, on ye Northeastward by [---] Arnolds Land The Other of the said Parcells of Land is Bounded on the West by the High Way on ye North by **[Joseph?] Clarks** Land, on ye East by **James Barkers Junrs** Land, on ye South by **Thomas Peckhams** Land and also the One Eighth Part of the Two Estermost of the Islands Commonly Called Elizabeth Islands aforesaid, and also the one moiety or half Part In Deal of all and Singular my Lands Lying and Being In the Township of Dartmouth In New Plymouth Collony aforesaid; and also the one Moiety or half Part in Deal of all and Singular my Lands Lying and Being In the said Town of Little Compton In the said Collony of New Plymouth Together with all and Singular ye privileges thereunto Belonging or In any Wise appertaining to the said Lands Except^g only [--]of this Paragraph or Section in one half of one hundred Acres of Land Lying In Little Compton Before Bequeathed to my Son.

Item - I Give and Bequeath to my Daughter **Mary** and to the Heirs of Her Body Lawfully Begotten unto ye Third Generation and from There to Descend to her heirs in fee Simple for Ever, That Is to Say Two parcells of Lands Lying and Being Scituate In Newport aforesaid (Together with other land Mentioned In this Section, one of which Said Parcells of Land Is Bounded on ye South East and Northwest by the Streets of said Town of Newport on ye Southwest Chiefly by the Land of **Josias Arnold**, on the NorthEast by Land In ye possession of **John Williams** on which said Parcell of Land Is Scituated a Dwelling house, the other of the Said Parcells of Land is Bounded on ye West by ye Common highway leading to Wannamatipanam Hill on ye north by **Thomas Coddingtons** Land, on ye East and Southeast on ye Common and **Samuel Cranstons** Land, [---] one moiety or half Part In Deal of all and Singular my Lands Lying and Being Scituated on ye Eastward and Westward Sides of Tanton River In ye Collony of New Plymouth aforesaid, and Commonly Called ye Freemens Lands, and also the One Moiety or half Part In Deal of all & Singular my Lands Lying and Being Scituate at [?Ponagan]sett and parts adjacent In ye Collony of New Plymouth [----] and also ye one moiety or half part in Deal of all & Singular my Lands Lying and being Scituate at a place Called Puncatest [-------] and ye one moiety or half part of all and Singular my Lands Lying and being In the said Township of Little Compton in ye said Collony of New Plymouth, and also the one moiety or half Part In Deal of all and Singular my lands Lying and Being Scituate at a Place Commonly called and Known by ye Name of Pettaquamscutt or Pettaquamscutt Purchase In the Collony of Rhoad Island &c aforesaid, and also all and Singular my Share of Land Lying and being Scituate In ye Province of New Jersey or New Cesarea Near New York In [----] Together with all and Singular ye Priviledges thereunto Belonging or In any Wise appertaining to the said Lands except only out of this Parragraph or Section one half of One hundred acres of Land Lying in Little Compton before Bequeathed to my Son.

And Further my will is If my Wife shall Bear unto me one other Son in my Life [----------------------] my [----------] according to [-----] of Life, [------------] my children aforenamed shall [-------------------] heirs of their Body as aforesaid, then my said Son, as Shall Be So Born, Shall Inherit (after him or her) and His Heirs according as Is Exprest In ye Bequest to them by Reason of whose Decease they shall Inherit

And Farther my Will Is If my Wife shall Bear unto me a Son as beforementioned and It shall please the Lord to Continue ye Life of my Children above mentioned, then my Son So Born shall [------] fifty pounds out of [---------]

and if my Wife shall Bear unto me a Daughter in my Life Term or after my Decease according to [----] of Life, then my Daughter So Born Shall inherit Two hundred pounds out of my Moveable Estate.

Item - I give and Bequeath unto my Beloved Wife **Amy** [----] fifty Pounds [--] one Bedd and Beddsted with y^{e} [furniture?] thereunto Belonging which she shall choose

Item - I give and Bequeath Ten Pounds for ye use of ye Poor of the Church of God Being Baptized Be[---] and observers of the Seventh Day Sabbath [*page* 4] In the said Town of Newport With which said Congregation I have Fellowship.

Item - I give and Bequeath Five Pounds for ye use of the Poor of the s^{d} Town of Newport . . .

Further my Will is that if my Father and Mother shall be alive or either of them, and shall come into these parts, or not, and shall have need thereof, I give and bequeath unto them or to the survivor of them, ye Sum of ten pounds a year During his or her Life [---] out of the Rents of all my Lands aforementioned [----]ding ye Several Bequests Before In these Presents made thereof and [---] part thereof to pay Proportionably according to the yearly Vallue thereof

Item - I give and Bequeath to **Mary Billing** ye Sum of Two Pounds Ten Shillings

Item - I give and Bequeath to **Samuel Bailey** Twenty Shillings

Item - I give and Bequeath to each of my Executors ye sum of Five Pounds

Item - Further my Will Is [that] all the Remainder of my Estate Be Equally Divided Between my Son **Thomas** and my Two Daughters **Margaret** and **Mary** (and their heirs. If it So Come to Pass that Either [----] Decease Before Partition is made whether it be moveable or Immoveable and to be So Divided that Each of them shall Have ye Stocks of Cattle [----] Lands Bequeathed to Each of them [----] the Precincts or Lines thereof

Lastely of This my Will and Testament I Constitute and appoint Loving friends **Phillip Smith** of Newport on Rhoad Island aforesaid [and] **Joseph Church** of Little Compton in ye Collony of New Plymouth aforesaid [*torn*] Executors hereby Giving and Granting Power [---] unto my Executors or ye Surviver of them to Lease and to farm Lett ye Lands herein Bequeathed unto Either [---] said Children and for their use, until they or Either of them to whom said Lands are Bequeathed shall come to the Age of Fourteen Years In Witness whereof I have hereunto sett my hand & seal this ninth Day of June in ye yeare one thousand six hundred eighty and three [1683]

[*signed*] **Thomas Ward**

Declared to be
[----] and Testament
by the said Thomas Ward
In presence of **Henry Tew**
Anna Williams
Mary Billing

I the above named Thomas Ward Do also nominate and appoint my wife Ammy to be an Executrix to this my Will above written with Equall Power Given to my abovenamed Executors and Further my Will is that Notwithstanding my Daughter Margaret is But of the half Blood [---] my Son Thomas and Daughter Mary [*rest of paragraph indecipherable*]

Henry Tew and Mary Billing personally Appeared before the Council and upon solemn engagement did affirm that they saw Thomas Ward L[ate of] Newport Deceased Sign Seal and own y[e] Within written [*torn*] will and Testament and that they signed the said Will as Witnesses

Taken Before y[e] Council this 2nd Day of June 1690

The foregoing is a True Coppy Taken from y[e] Town Council Book of Newport No. [--] pages 122 123 & 124 Newport Dec[r] 31st 1739

Pr W[m] Coddington Jun[r] [Sub?] Council Clerk

5. 1684, September 22: Deed, **Pardon Tillinghast** and wife **Ledeah** to son **John Tillinghast:**

. . . Pardon Tillinghast of Providence in his Majestys Collony of Rhode Island & Providence Plantations in New England in Americah & Ledah his wife sendeth greeting in our Lord God everlasting, know yee that the said Pardon Tillinghast & Ledeah his wife for & in consideration of full satisfaction to them made before the signing & insealing hereof by John Tillinghast of Newport on Rhode Island aforesaid cooper: have sould given granted alieoned enfeoffed & confirmed & by these presents . . . unto the said John Tillinghast aforesaid cooper his heirs executors administrators & assignes for ever, a cerain peice or parcell of land lying & being in the town of Newport aforesaid & is butted easterly uppon the highway leading down to **Simon Parrets** & southerly uppon the lands which was formerly Mr. **Benedik Arnolls** deceased & Now in the possession of one **Edw[d] Pelham** & Northerly by the highway leading down to the seaside; in bredth in front & reer thirty two foot & a halfe more or less, together with all the buildings there uppon houses & out houses & ware houses, pertiqulerly the hous wherein **George Hallson** Now liveth & the warehous & brewhous & uttensells thereunto belonging or any wais appertaining together with the warehouses & land below the same to seaward soe farr as unto us of right belongeth or in any wais appertaineth & all the . . . right title interest use propriety, possession, claime, & demand what soever of them . . . together with the warehouses & land below the same to seaward soe farr as unto us of right belongeth or in any wais appertaineth . . . for ever to the onely proper use & benefit of the said John Tillinghast his heirs executor administrators & assignes for ever, the said Pardon Tillinghast reserving unto him selfe free of charge for his owne pertiquler goods dureing the time of nine years from the day of the date heerof wharfage & warehous room as he shall have ocation & the said Pardon Tillinghast & Ledeah his wife for them selves theire heirs, executors & administrators doe covenant promiss & graunt to & with the said Jn[o] Tillinghast his heirs executors administrators and assignes by these presents in maner & forme as followeth, that is to say that the said Pardon Tillinghast & Ledeah his wife at the time of the grant & confirmation of the premisses unto the said John Tillinghast his heires &

assignes for ever were the true & lawfullowners of the said premises & that they have in them selves lawfully peaceably & quietly have holde possess & inioy the said granted premises with all the priviledges & appurtenances thereof & thereto belonging or of right to [----] apertaining free & clear & clear & clearly aqquited and what soever had made done or suffered to be done by the said Pardon Tillinghas & Ledeah his wife or their heirs executors administrators or any other person or persons what soever whereby the said Jn° Tillinghast his heires, executors administrators shall or may be at any time heerafter lawfully evicted out of the possession thereof by these present warranting him & them in the quiet & peacable possesion thereof, & shall & will perform & doe or caus to be performed & done any such further act & thing what soever whether by way of acnoledgment of this present deed or in any other kinds that shall or may be for the more full completing confirming & sure makeing according to the true intent heerof & according to the laws of this Collony; In Witnesse whereof the said Pardon Tillinghast & ledeah his wife have heerunto set theire hands & seals this twenty second of November in the year of our Lord one thousand six hundred eighty four.
Eraces made in the nineth & tenth line, & soe signed sealed & delivered
in presence of **Jeremiah Browne** **Esek Carr**
Acknowledged by Pardon Tillinghast 22 of 9^{ber} 1684 before Caleb Carr Assistant. Recorded in "101 page of y^e Book of Land Evidences No. 3 belonging to the town of Newport" **Weston Clarke** Town Clerke

6. 1686, April 13: Deed from **Nathanael Coddington** of Newport, merchant, and **Susannah** his wife, for £400 silver money, to **Noell Mew** of Newport, mariner, for 300 acres of land called Rockey ffarme, bounded southerly by the sea, easterly by the cove and marshes of **John Coggeshall**, northerly partly by land of John Coggeshall and partly the Common . . . in a straight line till the Cove and thence westerly bound by the Common called Cherry Neck and soe runs to the sea . . . excepting a small piece on the Northwest corner . . . with houses, gardens, orchards, woods, ponds, creeks, coves, fences . . .. Acknowledged the same day before Walter Clarke. Witnesses William Allen, Thos Rodman. Taken from Newport Land Evidence Book [1]:298-299.

7. 1690, December 4: **The will of John Tillinghast** [*separated from case; appears to be the original, with seal*]:

John Tillinghast of Newport on Rhoad Island in New England being at present through the mercy of God of good and sound memory yett Considring the Mortallity of All mankind doe thare fore for ye futer settling my Temperall estate make & Ordaine this my Last will and Testament In manner following making null all wills by mee mee [*sic*] made formerly & this onely to be taken as my Last will & testament.

Imp^{rs} my will is that All ye Just debts I owe to Any Person or Persons Be duly and truly payd by my Executrix heare After named with In Convenant time After my deceas –

Item I give and Bequeath to my Deare and Loving wife **Esabell Tillinghast** All my Estate during her naturall Life consisting of houses Lands goods & Chattiell Monies wares or Marchandise Nothing omitted Nor Reserved that I shall Dye possessed of but what I have heare in After Bequeathed –

Item After ye decease of my Loving wife Esbell Tillinghast my will is And I doe give and bequeath to my Eldest Sone **Pardon Tillinghast** all that part of my Land houses ware houses & wharfe beginning at ye Chimney back of my new hous whare in I Lived [to] a line drawn awharte my said Land at ye back of said Chimney [----] to ye sea ye hole breath of my Land with all the Leberties privileges And Appurtances that shall thare unto be Long or In any wise Appertaine to him his Heires and Assignes for Ever.

Item my will is that After ye Deceas of my Loving Wife Esbell Tillinghast & I doe give and bequeath to my Second Sonn **Charles Tillinghast** all the Remainder of my Land & houseing from ye back of my new hous Chimney to ye brooad Streatt runing North & south, with the hous that **Mr Holsell** Now Lives in if it be standing And All other Appurtenances Laberties & priviledges thare unto belonging or in Any wise Appertaining to him his heires And Assignes for Ever –

Item my will is that if Either of my Sonns decease before they Come Come [*sic*] to possess what I have bequeathed by this my will that the surviver posses & Injoy that part of ye Deceased

Item I give & bequeath to my Daughto^{r} **Hannah Tillinghast** tenn pounds in Silver mony to be payd her by my Executrix at Eighteen yeares of Age or Day of Marridg –

Item I give and bequeath to my Daughto^{r} **Mary Tillinghast** tenn pounds in Silver Mony to be payd her by my Executrix at Eighteen years of Age or Day of Marridge –

And if Either of my Daughtors should Dye before shee com to that Age or Day of Marridge then my will is that what I have bequeathed to her shall desend to ye Survivor: & if my two Sons Should Dye then my will is that what I have bequeathed [to them] shall be to my two [daughters] Equally Devided as is before given to m[y] Sons.

Lastly of this my Last will And testament I make ordaine and Appoint my Deare And Loving wife Esbell Tillinghast my [---] And sole Executrix of All my Estate of Houses Lands goods and Chattiell as before mentioned Not Doubting of hir Love & Care of my Deare Chilldren in whose Care in bringing them [up I] Doubt Not According to that small Estate I shall Leave with her: Desiring my ffather to be Assistant to her my wife in w^{t} possible hee Cann. In Wittness to this my Last will And testament I have heare unto sett my hand And Seall this forth day of Desemb^{r} 1690.

Signed sealled & owned
in y^{e} p^{r}esence of
John Carr
Nathanael Sheffield
Wes^{t} Clarke

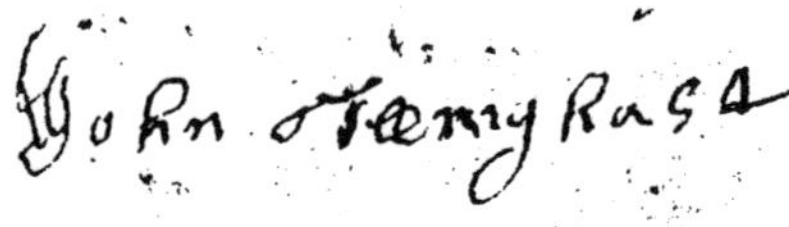

Weston Clarke & Nathaniell Sheffild Appered before y^{e} Counciell y^{e} 7th day of March 1690/91 and did upon their Ingagement owne that they saw John Tillinghast above mentioned Signe Seall & owne this Above written will to be his Last will & testament taken before ye Counciell ye day Above Said Pr Wes^{t} Clarke Clerk Coun^{l} . . . Entred on Record in ye Counciells book n° 2 & in ye 134 page p^{r} Wes^{t} Clarke Town Clerk

8. 1686, October 6: Artickles of Agreement made and Concluded by and between **Richard Wharton** of Boston, Esqr . . . and **Thomas Mumford** of Rochester in ye Kings Province in behalfe of himselfe and Company . . . **Richard Wharton** doth for his part Covenant Grant and agree to and with the said Thomas Mumford and Company that he and they shall have & Peaceably Enjoy the Liberty and freedom of the halfe part of the brook or Stream Runing Against or by the Land of the said Richard Wharton on Boston Neck which brook or Streame is now known or Called by the name of Mattatuxett to sett up a Mill make a mill dam and Joyne it to the Land of the said Wharton with the free use of his ground adjacent to Digg stones and Earth as is Usually Needfull for the Makeing and Upholding of a mill dam or turning the said Streame as he or they See Cause and for the Stoping and pounding the Watter upon the Land of the said Wharton as need shall Require with free Egress and Regress to and from the same for and Dureing the full and Whole time and teirme that the maine fabrick and Principall Worke of the mill Erected by the said Thomas Mumford and Company shall without Generall Reparation be there Continued not hereby Prohibitting the said Mumford & Company from Repaireing the Water Wheel or Cogg Wheel Trunells or any other thing about the said Mill that Requires freequent Amendment Incident to all mills: Allwayes Reserving to the said Wharton his heires and Assignes the Common benefit of the said brook or Streame no way Prejudiciall to the said Mill.

. . .**Thomas Mumford** doth by these presents in behalfe of himselfe and Company Covenant and Agree with: and doth oblidge himselfe to the said Richard Wharton his heires and assignes to pay or Cause to be paid to him or them fourthwith the full Sum of Ten pounds in Curr^{tt} money or the Vallew thereof in such other good payment as Maj^{r} **Richard Smith Capt John Fones** and other of his Majesties Justices of the peace in the Kings Province shall Judge Meet and Equivolent, and that it shall and may be Lawfull for the said Richard Wharton or assignes; at the time of the Ruination and Uselessness of the maine Worke and fabrick of the said Mill . . . to have and Injoy his Right and Liberty hereby Given to the said Mumford and Company and that the said Richard Wharton his heires or assignes shall at his or theire Pleasure Turne the said Streame or Wattercourse againe. Signed by the two parties; witnesses: John Saffin, John Fones, Lodowick Updike. Recorded 7 October 1686 by John Fones, Recorder. Copied from page 62 of the book of Ancient Records belonging to the Narragansett Country . . . 19 July 1722 by Francis Willett, Town Clerk. [*From Northop vs. Mumford, No. 185, in 1723*]

9. 1689/90, January 27: **The will of Caleb Carr**:

I Caleb Carr inhabitant of James Town on Quionnicutt Island in the Collony of Rhoad Island and Providence Plantations in New England Knowing that all men are Mortal, have therefore thought fitt to sett my house in Order by this my Last Will and Testament; and therefore I do bequeath my Soul to God that gave it and my body to the Earth to be Decently Buried.

And in the Next place, I give and bequeath unto my beloved wife, **Philip Carr** all my Estate Real and personal together with all my housing and Lands to be for her use, for the bringing up of my Children untill they come of Age, and that they may be brought up in some Suitable Learning, and my said wife shall possess my housing and Land untill my Son be of Age of Twenty one years But after my Son **Caleb Carr** come to Age, she shall only Enjoy one halfe of the said house with free Egress and Regress so long as she remains a widow, and no Longer, as also my wife shall pay such Legacies as I shall appoint; In the next place, I give unto my Eldest son **Caleb Carr** one halfe of my ffarme, together with my dwelling house and houseing on Quionnicutt Island aforesd, viz. on the North Side of said farme bounded on the North highway to be divided betwixt him and his brother **Wm Carr**, to say, the farme to be divided of an Equall breadth from the Sea to the head Thereof upon a straight line, and my sd son Caleb shall enter upon the said housing and halfe the farme when he comes of Age Only his mother shall Enjoy halfe the house wherein I now dwell during her widow hood as aforesd and the said house and halfe [*torn*] shall be to him, his heirs and successours for Ever, Only he may not sell it to any but his brother **Wm Carr**, and so to remain upon the same Tenure, and my sd son Caleb Carr or his Successours shall pay or cause to be paid unto my beloved wife Philip Carr aforesd six pounds pr Ann^m^ Equivalent to mony dureing her widowhood. In the next place I give and bequeath to my son Wm Carr the other halfe of my sd farme being the south part thereof, adjoyning to the farme that Cousen **Nicholas Carr** possesseth, the sd halfe farme to be Equally divided in breadth betwixt his brother Caleb & him, upon a Straight line from the sea to the head thereof as aforesd wch my said son W^m^ shall possess & enjoy when he comes to the Age of Twenty one Years, to be to him & his heirs successively for Ever, and not to sell it unless it be to his brother Caleb, & that upon the same Tenure, and I appoint my sd son Wm Carr or his Successours when he or they possess, to pay or cause to be paid four pounds pr Ann^m^ Equivalent to mony to my afords^d^ wife Philip Carr dureing her widow hood, Also I give to [*page* 2] my son **Robert Carr** all my Land at Newport on Rhoad Island, lying by the sea side, bounded Northerly by my brother **Robert Carr**'s Land, & Southerly by the house & Land belonging to my Unckle Mr **Caleb Carr**, & Mr **Francis Brinly**, the sd Land to be possesst by him when he comes to the Age of Twenty one Years & to be to him, his heirs and Assignes for Ever. In ye next place I give to my son **Job Carr** all my right of Land in ye Township of James Town on Quionnicutt Island, as also my right of Land on Dutch Island to be to him, his heirs & assignes for Ever; it is also my Will, that if Either my son Robert or my son Job dye before they come to Age, the survivour of them two shall inherit ye Land Appertaining to ye deceased. In ye next place, I give unto my Daughter **Mary Carr** one feather bed & furniture, & five pounds in Stock Equivalent to mony to be paid unto her, when shee is Eighteen years old or at her day of Marriage, wch will be first; In ye next place, I give unto my daughter **Philip Green** [*sic*] one feather bed and furniture, & five pounds in Stock Equivalent in mony to be paid unto her when she is Eighteen years old or at her day of Marriage wch will come first; And finally, I do Constitute my beloved wife Philip Carr aforesd sole Executrix of this my Last Will & Testament, to pay & receive all Just debts & such Legacies as I have appointed her, & I give all such part of my Estate as is not otherwise given away by this Will unto her, & I do desire my honoured father, Maj^r^ **Jno Green** & **Ebenezar Slocum** & my brother in Law **Peter Green** to be overseers of this my Last Will & Testam^t^ & in Witness of this my Last & real Will & Testam^t^ I have hereunto sett my hand & seal this 27th of Jan^ry^ & in the first year of their Maj^ty^ Reign, W^m^ of Great Brittain ffrance & Ireland King &c.

[*signed*] Caleb Carr

The will was witnessed by Caleb Carr Junr, Enoch Place [mark E], and James Green. Mr Caleb Carr and Mr James Green attested it 28 February 1689/90 and it was proved "before ye Gener^l^ Councill there being no Councill in James Town on Quionnicutt" at Newport 3 March 1689/90, Henry Bull, Govr.

10. 1693, January 20 [*separated from case; with records of the Court of Trials 1718-1721*]: Deed from **Ephraim Pearce** of the town of Rehoboth in county of Bristol and **Hannah** his wife to **Thomas Man** of the same place, all their housing and barn with the farm whereon the sd housing doth stand which sd Ephraim and Hannah have som time lived on with ye orchard or orchards nursree or nursrees well or wells sellers . . . with all fence . . . meadow land . . . and halfe a purchase right of ye undivided commons within the township of Providence within the seven mile line. Dated 20 January 1692; acknowledged 16 February 1692/3.

11. 1693, December 11: **The will of Henry Bull** [*original official copy lost when Newport records were damaged in 1779; copy made 14 April 1750 for the case Pitkin vs Easton*]:

Know all Persons to whom these Presents shall come That I **Henry Bull** of Newport on RhodIsland in the Colony of Rhode Island and Providence Plantations in New England being aged and Weak of Body but of Sound Memory and Understanding for ye Settling of my Outward Estate Do make this my Last Will and Testament in manner & form following Utterly Renouncing, and by these presents making Null and Void all other Wills by me formerly made and this shall be taken for my only & Last Will and Testament and No other.

Imprimus. I Give and Bequeath unto my Beloved Wife **Ann Bull** the full and just Sum of One hundred pounds Current Silver Money of New England. The twenty pounds she borrowed of me to pay **George Hath^{o}** for Land she bought of him Shall be part of said Hundred pounds & six Milch Cows and fifty Ewe Sheep which she shall Chuse and also one Horse or Mare which she Shall Chuse among them and two Feather Beds and one Down Bedd with Bedsteads and Furniture to them belonging one of which s^{d} Bedsteds is to be that whereon the Maids Usually Lodge and one fourth part of all my Pewter and Brass and one Years Provision for a family of four Persons as Shall be adjudged by my Overseers hereafter named One Trunk and one Chest which she shall Chuse also all my Negro Servants during her Life and after her Decease they Shall be equally divided between my Grandson **Jireth Bull** & his Sister **Mary Coggeshall** also I Give my Now Dwelling house and Land thereunto belonging, and adjoyning, Containing by Estimation Sixteen Acres to be & remain to the use and behoof of my said Wife Ann Together with ye Use of the Benches Tables Stools & Chairs in sd House for and Dureing Her Natural Life she paying Yearly and every Year in Consideration thereof six pounds Current Money of New England to the

Relict of my Grandson **Henry** deced towards the bringing up of his Children and for and in Consideration of all & Singular the aforementoned Gifts & Bequests unto my said Wife Ann Bull she is to Relinquish & Quitt her Claim of Dowership accept of Them or any of them unto all & every part of my Estate.

Item: I Give and Bequeath unto my Grandson **Jireth Bull** and to the Heirs of his Body Lawfully Begotten unto the third Generation and from thence to be Fee Simple all my Farm Lying and being in the Precinct of the said Town of Newport Bounded on y[e] East by Land in the Possession of **Stephen Mumford** and **Robert Ares** on the South by his own Land on the West by the Sea on the North by Land in y[e] Possession of **Roger Goulding,** together with all & Singular the Priviledges thereto belonging Containing by Estimation One hundred & Eighty Acres and for & in Consideration of which sd Gift my sd Grandson Jireth Bull or his Heirs Shall pay or cause to be paid unto his Sister Mary Coggeshall or to her Heirs One hundred Pounds Current Silver Money of New England within four Years after my decease the which sd Sum of One hundred Pounds if it Shall Not be well & truly paid unto the sd Mary Coggeshall her Heirs according to the true Intent and Meaning hereof I give full Power & Lawfull Authority hereby unto his sd Sister Mary Coggeshall and her Heirs and her and their Lawfull Attorneys to enter into and take into her & their Possession all and Singular the sd Land hereby bequeathed unto my sd Grandson Jireth Bull and Every Part thereof Quietly and Peaceable to Possess the same untill the Profits Issueing out of the sd Lands shall well & truly pay the said Sum of One hundred Pounds.

Item. I Give and Bequeath unto my Great Grandson **Henry Bull** Son to Grandson Henry Bull deced to him and his Heirs my Now dwelling house in Newport after the Decease of my sd Wife Ann Together with all my Lands thereto belonging and adjoyning with all y[e] Priviledges thereto appertaining Containing by Estimation Sixteen Acres bounded Westerly by y[e] Street Northerly by the Orchard that was my Son Jireth Eastward by **John Williams** Land Southward by Land called **Griffens** Land with all and Singular the Houseing thereon and for and in Consideration of which sd Gift my sd Great Grandson Henry Bull or his Heirs shall pay or Cause to be paid within three Years after his Possession of sd House & Land unto his Brother **Ephraim Bull** & Sister **Ann Bull** to each of them or their Heirs Fifty Pounds in Current Money of New England & if my sd Great Grandson Henry Bull Decease before he comes to age then my Will is the sd House and Land shall be equally divided between his Brother Ephraim Bull & Sister Ann Bull.

Item. I Give and Bequeath unto my two Grandsons **Ephraim Bull** and **Ezekiel Bull** and to their Heirs for ever my House and Land in Newport afores[d] commonly called my son Jireth Bulls Deced House and Orchard — about one Acre as it is Now fenced in and to be Divided into Equall Parts this Bequest is to them made up to make up their portions according to the Full intent of their Fathers Will.

Item. I Give and bequeath unto my Grand Daughter **Mary Coggeshall** one Feather Bedd Bedstead & Furniture thereunto belonging which she shall Chuse after my Wife have taken her Choise of One & Fifty Pounds Currant Money of New England which shall be and remain in the Overseers hands till she see Cause to Demand it out.

Item. I Give and Bequeath unto my Grand Daughter **Elizabeth Allen** & hir Heirs for ever my House & Land in Newport Now in Possession of **John Payne** bounded on the South East, South West, & North East by the Highways of the sd Town & Common Lands together with all & Singular the Priviledges and Appurtenances thereto belonging forty sheep & four Young Cattle.

Item. I Give and Bequeath unto my Grand Children **Henry Richman** & **Ann Richman** & their Heirs for ever all that Farm & Tract of Land at Little Compton Now in Possession of their Father Edward Richmond being Butted & Bounded & Contents Expressed in the Deed of Sale to me made and Record[e]d in Bristoll Records Together with all and Singular the Howseing and Appurtenances thereto belonging.

Item. I Give unto my sd Grandson **Henry Richman** thirty pounds Currant Money of New England to be paid unto him when he comes to Age. Item. I Give unto my sd Grand Daughter Ann Richmand thirty Pounds Currant Money of New England to be paid when she Comes to Age or Day of Marraige.

Item. I Give all my Wearing Apparrell unto my three Grand Children **Jireth Bull, Ephraim Bull,** and **Ezekiel Bull.**

Item. I Give unto the Poor two hundred & fifty Pounds of Sheeps wool to be delivered unto Such Persons as my Wife & Trustees Shall See Cause.

Item. I Give & Bequeath unto my Trustees hereafter named Ten pounds and all the Remainder of my Estate of what kind Soever it be off after my funeral Charges, Debts, and Legacies aboves[d] being paid Shall be Equally divided amongst my four Grand Children **Jireth Bull, Mary Coggehall, Ephraim Bull, Ezekiel Bull** and the Children of my Grandson **Henry** Deced as the fifth part the Profit of which said fifth part what it Shall be to be annually paid towards their bringing up.

Lastly. Of this my Last Will and Testament I make Nominate & appoint my Beloved Wife **Ann** my Exec[tx] and my Trusty and Loving friends **John Easton Senior Gov[r] Daniel Gould Senior** of the Town of Newport aforesaid **Thomas Cornell** of the Town of Portsmouth **Benjamin Newbury** of Newport aforesaid Together with her my Executrix and feoffes in Trust to see to the true Performance of this my Last Will and Testament who Shall have Power to Improve according to their Discretion Such part of sd Estate for the use and Profit of the Children & Shall Remain in their Hands without Suffering any Damage if any Detriment shall accrue to said part of Estate through their Endeavour to Improve it and I also Order Will and Declare that if any Person or Persons unto whom I have by this my Last Will Given and Bequeathed any Land or Legacy Shall by any way or Means attempt to make Void or Disannull any Part of this my Last Will and Testament That then and from thenceforth the said Person or Persons so attempting Shall forfeit & Loose all Rights Interest or Title unto the sd Land or Legacy hereby to him or her or them Bequeathed and the Land or Legacy so forfeited and Lost I do hereby Give unto them whom the said Person or Persons shall Attempt to Deprive of his or her Right by this Will Bequeathed Signed by me this 11th of December 1693.

the mark of Henry *H B* Bull

Signed, Sealed, and Delivered by y[e] above named Henry Bull to be his last Will and Testament in the Presence of us William Brinley
Noah Loyd
John Holmes
John Coggeshall
William Brinley, Noah Loyd, John Holmes & John Coggeshall Personally appeared before the Councill and did upon their Engagement Declare that they saw Henry Bull Sign, Seal, & Deliver the above written to be his Last Will & Testament taken before y[e] Council as Attest February 5th 1693.

Weston Clarke Clerk of y[e] Councill

Newport SS: The above and five foregoing Pages are a True Copy taken from the Town Council Book of Newport N° 2. Pages 177 and 178. Newport April 14th 1750. Test W[m] Coddington Jun[r] Council Clerk
A True Copy as on file in the Case Ozias Pitkin & Wife vs George Kinyon tryed at Novemb[r] Court 1753 — Teste J Lyndon Cler.

12. 1693/4, March 8: **The will of Caleb Carr** [*see item 513, 1730*]:

In the name of god Amen the Eight day of March in y[e] year of our Lord God one Thousand six Hundred ninety three or four 1693/4 I Caleb Carr of Newport on Rhoad Island in their Majestys Colony of Rhoad Island Kings province and Providence Plantations in New England in America Seignor being att this time aged this being the year of my age and being now of perfect mind and memory thanks being given unto God, therefore Calling unto mind the mortality of my body, and Knowing that it is appointed for all men once to dye doe make and ordaine this my Last will and Testament in manner and forme folowing that is to say first and Principally I give myself Into the hands of God who give it me & for my Body I Commend it to the Earth to be Buried in Christian & Decent manner and as Touching such worldly Estate wherewith it hath pleased God to bless me in this Life I give Devise Bequeath & dispose I manner & forme following Imprimis that all just debts which I do owe unto any person or persons be paid in Convionant time after my deceas by my Exect[rs] hereafter named.

Item. Unto my Deare wife **Sarah Carr** I give & bequeath fourty pounds in money to be paid her within a years time after my deceas & three gold rings that Now shee hath one of which my will is that shee shall give to my Daughter **Sarah Carr**, and another to my Daughter **Elizabeth Carr** & the other to whome shee pleaseth allso I give & Bequeath to my sd wife Sarah

Carr a silver posneet & the cover belonging to it & two silver spoons one milch cow, fourty sheep and a horse or mare whether of which shee shall make choise of mine also my grate looking glass and the new great Bible further I doe give and bequeath unto my said wife Sarah Carr the fift part of the Beads and Beding pewter & brass & the fift part of all the other household stuff, that I doe Not Now dispose of by this my will Nor shall Not dispose of before the time of my decease further I give & bequeath unto my sd wife Sarah Carr my neagro woman **Hannah** further my will is that my sd wife Sarah Carr shall have after my decese the house where in my son **John Carr** Now liveth on the backside of my dwelling house to live in dureing the time of her widowhood togeather with preveledge in the yard convenient to lay her wood in and use of the well for her own use for herself & family, and the use of the lower garden to the eastward of the yeard as it is Now fenced in with pales and warfage free for her own occations without charge to her.

Item I doe give and bequeath unto my son **Nicholas Carr** and to his Heirs Exect^{rs} Admin^{rs} and assignes for ever my farme lying & being on the Island Conanicutt containeing by estimation seven score acres which I formerly leased unto him for about twenty years as by the said lease may appeare with the dwelling house which Now he dwelleth in thereon and all other out houses buildings and fences thereon and previledges there unto belonging as also that right in the share of Duch Island which belongs to the said farme, further I give and bequeath to my sd son Nicholas Carr his heirs exect^{rs} admin^{rs} and assignes for ever fourty acres of land lying on the west side of the highway over against my brother **Robert Carr** his land on the said Conanicutt Island as also tenn acres of land on the said island which I purchased of **John Peckham** Junr and also twelve acres of land at the head of the fourty acres aforesd with twelve acres I purchased or bought of **Benedict Arnold** further I give and bequeath to my said son Nicholas Carr his heirs exect^{rs} admin^{rs} and assignes for ever one fourth part of my share of land at Golds Island as also twenty five foot in length of land from the west side of my ware house Now standing upon my wharfe here in Newport the said lands to be twenty foot [*page 3*] in Breadth that If he see Cause he may Build upon it or other wayes Improve it further I give and Bequeath unto my said son Nicholas Carr His heirs and Assignes my great Bible my seal ringe, and my Little Cabinet; further my will is that my sd son Nicholas Carr his Heirs or assignes shall Pay or Cause to be Paid unto my now wife Sarah Carr yearly dureing the time of her widowhood twenty shillings a year in wood or provitions Equivalent to money and that my sd son Nicholas Carr shall Have priveledge of my wharfe here in Newport for his own occations –

Item I give and Bequeath unto my son **Caleb Carr** and to his Heirs Exect^{rs} Adminis^{rs} and Assignes for ever the Land at Conanicutt which I bought of **Jirah Bull Thomas Waterman** and **Richard Dunn** with the house and the Houseing now upon it which he now Liveth in withe the Right in Duch

Island Belonging unto the said Land, and also one quarter or one fourth Part of my Land at Golds Island and the gold Ring I do now ware Commonly called hand and hand & hart Between and my Desk with Drawers for writeings further my will is that my sd son Caleb shall pay unto my now wife Sarah Carr yearly Dureing the time of her widowhood twenty Shillings a year in wood or Provitions equivelent to mony Delivered to her here upon the wharfe I do Also give and Bequeath unto my son Caleb Carr his heirs Exec^rs^ Adminis^trs^ and Assignes for ever all my write title and Intrest in the fourty eight acres of Land which was Purchased of the sd Arnold.

Item I give and Bequeath unto my son **John Carr** and to his Heirs Exect^rs^ Administ^rs^ and assignes for ever my Dwelling house that I now Live in above the High way here in Newport with all the out houseing & Lands and Gardians there unto belonging all which Lands I bought of Mr **Benedict Arnold** in his life time all which I do give unto my sd son John Carr as above mentioned only [*page 4*] Reserveing the out house wherein he now Liveth and the gardian next ye said House for my wife **Sarah Carr** to Enjoy and Improve dureing the time of her Widowhood and priveledge in the yard to Lay her wood in to the well for water and to the Celler of the great House to make a Little Rome therein for her own use With priveledge to go there to also I give and Bequeath unto my said son John Carr his Heirs Exect^rs^ Administ^rs^ and Assignes for ever my whole part of Rose Island and the whole of my ware house standing upon my wharf Here in Newport and also my woolen apparrell the grate and Irons the Iron back for the Chimney the grate Tongs and five Shovel one Iron Spit and the grate Table in the hall or Parlour of my Dwelling house and formes Belonging to it —

Item I give and Bequeath unto my son **Edward Carr** and to his Heirs Exect^rs^ Administ^rs^ and Assigne's for ever fifty acres and a half acre of Land at Conanicutt which I Bought of **Jeremiah Willis** and sixty five acres of Land on said Conanicut Island which I bought of **John Green & Henry Bassitt** as Also the writes to Duch Island belonging to ye sd Land with all the Priveledges belonging to those Lands and also one fourth Part of my half of Golds Island and my Indian boy named **Tom** my pare of Little Stillards my wareing Lining and What so ever formely I have given unto him and the Chest that stands in the hall which I had of **Moses Peacheag** the Jew.

Item I give and bequeath unto my son **Francis Carr** and to his Heirs Exect^rs^ Administ^rs^ and Assigne's for ever one half of my Right to the house and Land in Newport that I bought of Mr **Antony Haywood** and also my one half share of Land at Coweset that I bought of Major **John Green**, and also a twenty shilling peice of gold a silver spoon & one fift Part of my Household stuff beds beding and furniture That I may leave behind me at my Desease —

Item I give and Bequeath unto my son **James Carr** and to his Heirs Exect^rs^ Administ^rs^ and Assigne's for ever one half of my Right unto the house and Land in Newport which I Bought of Mr **Antony Haywood** and also all my Rights in [*page 5*] Squamacutt Lands and a peice of gold and a silver spoon and one fift part of my house Hold stuff bed beding & furniture that I may Leave Behind me at my Decase.

Item I give and Bequeath unto my Daughter **Marcy Paine** and her Husband **Thom^{as} Paine** or the Longest liver of them all the land which I purchased of the town of Newport Adjoyning to the house my said son Thom^{as} Paine Hath now Lett unto M^{r} **Wm Brindley** here in Newport Which said house was Purchased of my son Caleb Carr also I give unto them or the Longest liver of them one fourth part of my share of Golds Island and what so ever I have formerly given Her further I give and Bequeath to my said Daughter Mercy Paine my silver Beere bowle to be Kept by her In Rememberance of me as long as she Liveth & at her decease to be Disposed of to whome shee Pleaseth –

Item I give and Bequeath unto my Daughter **Sarah Carr** and to her Heirs Exect^{rs} Administ^{rs} and Assigne's for ever the House and Land there unto belonging which I Bought of **Henery Palmer** here in Newport and also a twenty Shilling peice of gold a silver spoon one fift Part of my House hold Stuff bed beding and furniture That I may Leave behind me at my decease and within two years after my decease five pounds in money to be paid her by my Exec^{trs}

Item I Give and Bequeath unto my Daughter **Elizabeth Carr** and to her Heirs Exect^{rs} Administ^{rs} and Assigne's for ever the house and Land which I Bought of **Ruth Peirce** in ye which **Tho^{mas} Ham** now Liveth here in Newport and also my neagro boy **Jo** and my silver beacor twenty sheet one peice of gold a silver spoon one fift part of my House hold Stuff Bed Beding and furniture that I may Leave behind me at my decase and within two years after my Decase ten pounds in money to be paid her by my Exec^{trs}

[*page 6*] Item I Give and Bequeath to my Grandson **Job Carr** the son of my son **Sam^{ll} Carr** the house wherein **John Davis** now Liveth at the signe of the Ship here in Newport and the long House above it and all the Land bought of Mr **Arnold** Westward of the highway and Northward of a high way which belongs to the said houseing all which I Give and bequeath to my said granson Job Carr his heirs Exect^{rs} Administ^{rs} or Assignes for ever onley Reserving a Cart way to the Ware house and wharfe and my will is that what I have Here Given to my granson Job Carr whall be Kept in The hand of my Exec^{trs} untill he Comes of age and Then Delivered unto him and in the mean Time the Incomes there of to be paid by them towards The bringing of him up.

Item my will is that if any of my sons, **Nicholas Caleb John and Edward Carr** or my granson **Job Carr** son of my son **Sam^{ll} Carr** should dye without Heirs then what I Have Given to Either of them shall be eaqually Divided Amongst the Rest that shall survive of them they my said Sons Nicholas Caleb John and Edwd Carr and Sam^{ll} the father of my granson Job Carr Haveing all had one mother, and if any of my four Children Which I have had by my now wife Sarah Carr should Dye without Heirs then what I have given to either of Them shall be Equally Divided amonst the Rest of

These four for they Likewise had all one mother further My Will is that if my wife **Sarah Carr** the mother of These four Last Children **Frances James Sarah and Eliz**^{beth} which I Had By her see Cause to take all or [*page 7*] Any of them for the bringing of them up then she shall have the Estate which I have given to Them Committed to her management for ye bringing of them up untill they Come of age and then by her Delivered unto them the boys their Parts when they come to be twenty one years of age and the girls their parts at Eighteen years of age or day of marraige but if she Accepts Not thereof then they shall be Taken Care of and brought up to learning at the Discretion of my Exec^{trs} According to this my will and further my will is that if my wife Sarah Carr accept not of nor be satisfied with what I Have given her By this my will in Liue of her Dowery and give Dischare's under her Hand and seal that my Estate shall not be troubled or disturbed by her self or any other person by from or under here in the Hand of those I have bequeathed it unto but on the Contrary shall Cause Disturbance's unto them in the Possession thereof about her Dowery then my Will is that my Execu^{trs} shall Take all my Estate real and personally into Their Hands & whatsoever shee shall Recover shal Be abated out of what Estate I gave unto my four Children which I Had by her and in Liue Thereof only twenty pounds apeice shall be paid To Each of them by my Exec^{trs} Hereafter named and for all other Lands that are mine and not Disposed of by me in this my Will I give and Bequeath to my grand Children to be Eaqually Divided between [*page 8*] Them and of this my Last will and testament I make and ordaine my well Beloved sons Nicholas Carr & Caleb Carr my full and whole Exec^{rs} and if one of them dye then my will is that the other of them that shall survive shall Be full and Whole Exec^{tr} thereunto and do Hereby utterly disallow revoke null and make void all and every other former testaments wills Leagacies Bequeaths and Exec^{trs} by me in any ways before this time willed and Bequeathed Rectifying and Conformeing this and None other to be my Last will and testament in Wittness whereof I have here unto set my hand & seal the day and year above written Signed Sealed and Delivered by ye sd Caleb Carr to be His Last will & testament in the presents of us

Robert Gardner
Nicholas Easton
Ephraim Turner

The will was attested before Benedict Arnold, Assistant, on 8 March 1693/4 by the testator, and was proved 6 January 1695 when Robert Gardner and Ephraim Turner appeared in council and declared that they saw the Late Honoured Governer Caleb Carr Deceased sign seal & own it. On the back of the copy is written "Inclosed is the Last Will and Testament of Caleb Carr of Newport Father to Nicholas Carr and Granfather to Thomas Carr and LikeWise the Last Will and Testament of Nicholas Carr [*see No. 27, below*] abovesd he being Sonn to the abovesd Caleb Carr and Father to the abovesd Thomas Carr."

13. Probably circa 1696? **"A List of the Wills upon the Records of Newport Since the year of 1676 attested only by two Witnesses":**

Phillip Edes 1679 July 7th Witnesses John Woodman William Hichcox
John Coddington 1679 Decr 29th W Francis Brindley William [*torn*]
William Fenner 1680 Aug. 30th W Robert Jnr John Williams
Katherine Salsmon 1680 Aug 12th W Obadeiah Holmes [*torn*]
William Harris Dec. 11th [*sic: no year*] W Thomas Harris Nathanell [*torn*]
Robert Lewis 1682 Ap 12th W Edward Da[*torn*] Weston Clarke
Obediah Holms 1682 April 9th W Edward Marston Weston Clarke
Marmadock Rowndall 1677 10th Nov. W Edward Shipp[--] Elizabeth [---]
John Peckham Jan. 6 - 1681 W John Clark Henry Tew
Jeremiah Brown 1688 April 11th W Samuel Carr Ephraim Tanner [*sic; probably Turner*]
John Thurston Octor 20th 1690 W Mical Daniel Benjamin Toue
Peter Easton Junr [*no date*] W Daniel Gold Thomas Rodman
John Johnson April 1 - 1691 Warter Clarke Thomas Rodman
Clement Weaver 1680 Novr 4th William Hitchcox Thomas Wall
Samuel Wilson September 4th 1690 Thomas Fry Ephraim Turner
William Foster Sep. 29th 1690 Henry Lilly Ephraim Turner
Thomas Emmons Nov. 6th 1695 John Cox John Smith

14. 1698: Deposition of **Thomas Renols** "aged 47 years or there about" before Joseph Clark justice of peace at Westerly, 22 September 1698: "of his certaine knowledge he being there present; that about thirtie two years since or there about Mr **Roger Plaistead,** Mr **Tho: Stanton** & Mr **Robert Cars** man came over on the east side of Paucatuck river, & by virtue of an order they brought from the Kings Comitioners then at Yorke, the abovesaide Plaistead came to **Old goodman Larkins** sellar & demanded possession & the saide Larkin readily gave the saide Plaistead quiet possession & so did my father, the same upon the saide Plaisteads demand, my father & the saide Larkin did also agree wth & engage to paye the saide Plaistead rent so long as they should live there. I doe farther testify that John Babcock did the same . . .." **John Renols** aged 40 years or thereabout "being personaly present at the same time gave oath to the above written, upon his knowledg to be the very truth."

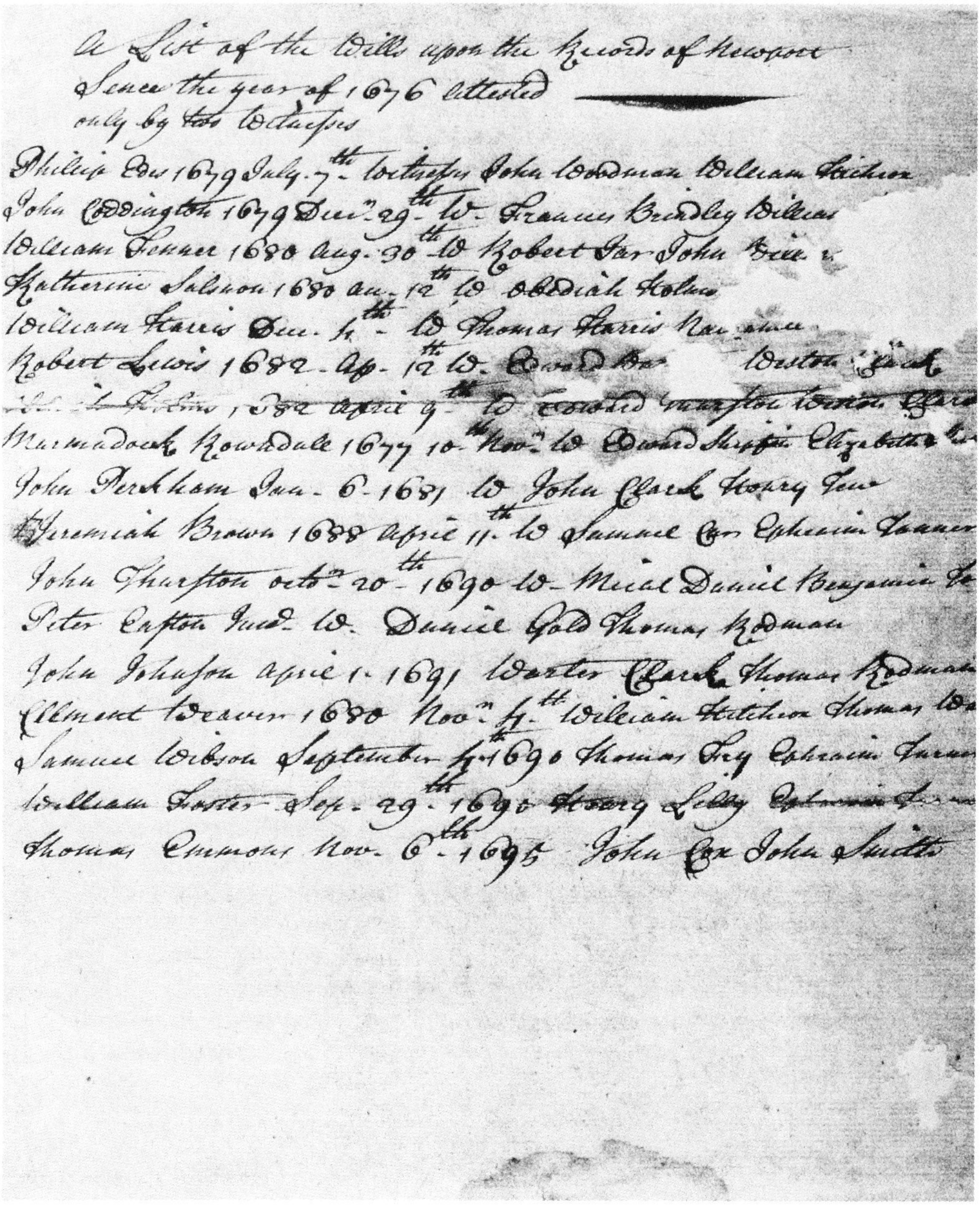

A List of the Wills upon the Records of Newport
Since the year of 1676 attested
only by two Witnesses

Philip Cox 1679 July 7th Witnesses John Woodman William Hitchin
John Coddington 1679 Decr 29th W Frances Brindley William
William Fonner 1680 Aug 30th W Robert Carr John Dice &
Katherine Salsnon 1680 Au 12th W Obediah Holmes
William Harris Dec 4th W Thomas Harris Nav[illegible]
Robert Lewis 1682 Ap 12th W Edward [illegible] Weston [illegible]
~~[illegible] Holmes 1682 April 9th W Edward Thurston Weston Clarke~~
Marmaduck Rowdale 1677 10th Novr W Edward Thurston Elizabeth [illegible]
John Peckham Jan 6 1681 W John Clark Henry Tew
Jeremiah Brown 1688 April 11th W Samuel Cox Ephraim Turner
John Thurston octor 20th 1690 W Mical Daniel Benjamin [illegible]
Peter Easton Indd W Daniel Gold Thomas Rodman
John Johnson April 1 1691 Walter Clark Thomas Rodman
Clement Weaver 1680 Novr 4th William Hitchin Thomas W[illegible]
Samuel Wilson September 4th 1690 Thomas Fry Ephraim Turner
William Foster Sep 29th 1690 Henry Lilly ~~Ephraim Turner~~
Thomas Emmons Nov 6th 1695 John Cox John Smith

List of Newport wills 1676-1695 that had only two witnesses when the law required three [No. 13]

Documents Dated 1700 to 1710

15. 1700, April 4 at Tiverton [*then in Bristol County, Mass.*]: Agreement between **Thomas Townsend** and **Mary** his wife, executrix of the will of **Job Almy,** and **Isaac Martindale** of Newport, now owner of the part and allotment within mentioned late belonging to **Robert Hassard,** that "half the Distance from a Black Oak Tree below the Hill and a little to the Southward of a Marsh or meadow commonly known by the name of Bulgar's Meadow and from thence upon a strait Line to the northermost part of **Daniel Willkes** lott or Land Half the said distance begining from the aforesaid Black Oak Tree to another Black Oak Tree and then upon a strait Line westerly to an apple Tree . . . from thence strait with the River or Pond, the northermost to belong to the aforesd Thomas and Mary Townsend and their heirs . . . the southermost part to belong unto the aforesaid Isaac Martindale. . . ." Witnessed by **Joseph Wanton** and **Samuel Tomkins.**

16. 1702, December 7 - entry from the records of the Newport Town Council: **Gedion Crawfford** as creditor requested administration on estate of **William Smith** deceased "and whereas there is a house standing upon land of Mr. **Robert Carr** that is by agreement to be taken off in some time and was not inventoried. . .is all sum of £28." Inventory taken 27 February 1701/2, sworn to by Mrs. **Mary Smith,** widow. [*See also no. 67.*]

17. 1703, July 8: **The will of Robert Carr** ("Last will of Robert Carr 2nd"):
In the name of God Amen the eighth day of July 1703 I Robart Carr of Newport in the Collony of Rhode Island & Providence Plantations &c, Merchant being weak in body but of Perfect mind and memory Thanks be given to God therefore Calling to mind ye mortality of my body & knowing y^{t} it is appointed for all men once to dye do make & ordain this my last will & testament y^{t} is to Say Principly & first of all I give & Recommend my Soul into ye hands of God that gave it & my body I Recomend to the Earth to be buried in Decent Christian Burial, at ye Discretion of my Executrix hereafter named Nothing Doubting butt at the General Reserection I shall Receive ye Same again by the Mighty Power of God and as touching Such worldly Estate wherewith it hath pleased God to bless me in this Life I Give Bequeath and Dispose of ye same in manner & form (Viz)

Imp^{s} I Give & bequeath to my beloved wife **Elisebeth Carr** all ye benefit of my Reale and personal Estate for ye bringing up of my Children **Robart & Abigail Carr** till they Come of age

Item I Give & bequeath to my beloved wife Elizabeth Carr w^{t} is left of my moveable Estate when my afores^{d} Children are of age to Dispose of as She Shall see meet Except Two feather beds & Furniture & Two Silver Tankerds which I give to my Two Children as hereafter Mentioned

Item I Give and bequeath to my Son **Robart Carr** his heirs and assigns forever my Manssion house and land in Newport aforesaid on the North Side of the high way y^{t} Leads up to **James Brown** his house wth my Shop and all my Land and Wharfe & Ware house that is below ye way of the high Street for him his heirs and assigns freely to posses & enjoy forever Except a Small p^{r}cell or peice of Land Next to the Sea Joyning to ye South side of my wharfe Containing 24 foot in length & 20 foot in bredth which I give & bequeath as hereafter followeth

Item I Give & Bequeath unto my Son **Robart Carr** one half of the four acres & three quarters of Land being a Lott Laid out in ye Comons unto me by the Preprieters of this Island as by Town Records may appear Reference thereunto being had butted and bounded South East of **John Maxon** his land southwest on **Francis Brinley** his land northwest on the Maine Rhoad and all my land upon Block Island according to the deed upon Record to be by him his heirs & assignes freely Possessed & Enjoyed Forever

Item I Give and bequeath unto my son **Robart Carr** one feather bed & furniture with one Silver Tankerd and my Seal Ring to be Delivered to him when he shall Come to age wth all my lands and houses aforesaid for him his heirs and assignes to posses and freely Injoy forever

Item I Give and bequeath unto my Daughter **Abigail Carr** and to her heirs and assigns forever all my lands on the south side of the way that Leads up to **James Browns** & on the North Side of the way that Leads to the Church from s^{d} Browns Gardin Easterly Except What is Given to **George Hix** and a peice of Land I Gave to set a Church of Enland [*sic*] on at the East end of sd Land bounded as followeth on the South Side on Lands of **Francis Brinley** on the East on Land Late in possession of **Peleg Sanford** Deceased ye uper part of the North Side upon **Mr Burtons** Land formerly **Mr Brintons** Land on the West and bounded on the Main Street that Leads unto the Neck and on the North on the high way y^{t} Leads up to **James Browns** & one Small Peice of land on the South Side of my Land next to the sea adjoyning to my Wharfe in Newport aforesaid Containing Twenty four foot in length And Twenty foot in bredth & also one half of the lott of four Acres & three quarters of Land in the Comon Laid out to me by the proprieters aforesaid and butted and bounded South East on **John Maxons** Land south West on **Francis Brinleys** Land north west on the Main Rhode as aforesaid & one feather bed and furniture & one Silver Tankerd for her her heirs and assigns freely to posses and Injoy forever

Item my Will is that all my Debts togeather with my funerall Charges be Justly honerably and Speedily paid

Lastly I Constitute ordaine and appoint my well beloved wife **Elizabeth Carr** my full & Whole Executrix of this my Last will & Testament Contained in two sides of Paper & also nominate appoint Request & Desire my Brother in Law **Robart Lawton** overseer & assistant to my Said Executrix to See this my Last will & Testament Performed And I doe hereby Uterly Disallow Revoake Disanull all & every other & former Testaments Wills Legacies Requests & Executors by me in any ways before named Willed & bequeathed Ratiefying & Confirming this and no other to be my last will and testament

In Witness where of I have herunto Sett my hand & Seal the day and year above on the other side Written

[*signed*] Robert Carr (seal)

Signed Sealed published & Declared by ye s^{d} Robert Carr to be his Last will and Testament in presence of us the subscribers

Alexander Gorden

Robart Gardner

Thomas Fox

18. 1703/4, February 9: **The will of Daniel Updicke**:

In the Name of God Amen I Daniel Updicke of the Parish of St. Dunstans Stepney in the County of Middx marriner being in health of Body and of sound mind and memory doe make & publish and declare this my last Will and Testament in manner following First I Bequeath my Soul unto Almighty God and my Body to the Earth (in case I dye on Shore) to be decently buryed at the discretion of my Executrix hereafter named and as touching and concerning such Temporall Estate as God hath blessed me with I do give Devise and Bequeath the same in manner and form following (that is to say) as touching and concerning that part of my Estate which lyeth in New England in America I doe give and dispose thereof in this manner First I give and Bequeath unto my Sister **Sarah Whitehead** all my stock of Cattle and money which shall be in my Brother **Lodowick Updickes** hands at my decease Item I give and Bequeath unto my Nephew **Richard Whitehead** and to his heires for ever (from and immediately after my decease) all that my parcell of Land lyeing on Boston Neck in New England aforesaid by what name quality or Title the same is known or distinguished. Item I give and Bequeath unto my Nephew **Daniel Updicke** and to his heires for ever (from and immediately after my decease) all that my moiety or halfe part of a certain parcel of Land (the other moiety or halfe part thereof now belonging to my Brother **James Updicke**) lying and being in the Province of New Rochester in New England aforesaid Item as touching and concerning the rest of my Estate being either in old England at Sea or at or in any other part or place beyond the Seas (and not herein before disposed of) I doe give Devise and Bequeath the same as followeth ffirst I give unto my Brother **Lodowick** and to my Brother **James** and to my Sister **Elizabeth Whiteman** to each of them a Ring of a Guinea price to be given to them within Six Moneths next after my decease. Item I give and Bequeath unto the poor of the parish of St. John Baptist and Margate in the Isle of Thannet the Sume of Twenty pounds of lawfull money of

England to be paid within the space of twelve Moneths next after my decease. Item I give and Bequeath unto **Sarah Whitehead** my Neice the Sume of Two hundred Pounds of Lawfull money of England to be paid unto her within twelve months next after my decease. Item I give and Bequeath unto [*page* 2] **Stephen Smith** son of **Matthew Smith** the younger my part of a Ketch called the *Loving Brothers*. Item I give and Bequeath unto **Elizabeth** the Daughter of **Moses Moyse** my part of a Ship called the *Generous Adventure*. Item I give unto my Nephew **Richard Whitehead** the sume of ffifty pounds of lawfull money of England and alsoe all my wearing apparrell. Item all the rest residue and remainder of my Estate Reall and personall of what nature kind or quality soever whether Messuages Lands Tenements Hereditaments Shipping ready money Plate Jewells Rings Goods household stuffe thing and things whatsoever and wheresoever (my Debts ffuneral charges and Legacys thereout first paid and discharged) I give Devise and Bequeath the same unto my well beloved **Wife Martha** and to her heires Exec^{rs} Adm^{rs} and Assignes for ever and I doe hereby nominate and appoint her the said Martha my Wife full and sole Executrix of this my last Will and Testament But in case my said Wife Martha shall happen to have a Child by me Then I doe hereby revoke and make void all Gifts and Legacys above in this my last Will given to any person and persons whatsoever and I doe give Devise & Bequeath all my Estate Reall and personall vizt all my Messuages Lands Tenements Hereditaments Shipping ready money plate Jewells Rings Goods household stuffe thing and things whatsoever and wheresoever unto the said Martha my Wife and to such Child whether Son or Daughter one moyety or halfe part thereof unto my said Wife Martha and the other Moyety or halfe part unto such Child which shall happen to be born of her by me begotten whether son or Daughter share and share alike and I doe hereby revoke disannull and make void all former & other Wills and Testaments by me at any time heretofore made and doe make and declare these presents only for my true and last Will and Testament contained in this one Sheet of written paper In Wittness whereof I the said Daniel Updicke the Testator have to this my last Will and Testament sett my hand and seale this ninth day of ffebruary anno Dom 1703/4 and in the Second year of the Reign of our Sovereign Lady Queen Anne over England &c Item I give to my loving ffriends **Elizabeth Sawyer** of Deale and her son **John Sawyer** to each of them one Guinea of Gold [signed] Daniel Updicke
Witnesses: Elizabeth Sawyer, John Sawyer, and John Taylor, Not. Pub. at Deale. Probated at London 27 March 1704. [P.C.C.] Aston 60

19. 1704, October 29: **The will of Thomas Starr** of Newport, housewright, dated 29 October 1704, signed by mark, and proved 1 January 1704/5. Copy made 17 April 1717 by **William Coddington**, Town Clerk of Newport, from Newport Town Council Book 3, page 147. The testator called himself very sick and weak, and named his loveing wife **Ruth**

executrix. If she remarried, the estate was to be divided equally among the children: **Thomas, Jehosaphat, Sarah, Elizabeth,** and **Hannah,** except for his wife's third, which was to be at her own disposal. Witnesses were **John Stevens, Richard Clarke,** and **Sam[l] Warkman.**

20. 1704, November 4: **The will of Ralph Chapman,** proved in 1711 [*separated from case, which was evidently in 1763, when it was copied*]:

I Ralph Chapman of Newport on Rhode Island being at . . . of the Date hereof of sound memory and disposing mind and knowing that it is appointed once for all men to die I therefore do make this my last will and testament as followeth, re[vok]ing all other will or wills by me at anytime made and if it shall please God to call me from this my natural life . . . this place I order my body to be decently interred by my executrix hereafter named and for y[e] disposal of my worldly goods I give and bequeath as follows.

Imprimis: Whereas I have already done much for my son **Ralph Chapman** yet I give and bequeath unto him my said son twenty shillings to be paid him by my exec[x] herein appointed within one year after my decease and y[t] to be in full of his portion with what already given him.

Item. I give and bequeath unto my son **John Chapman** a cartain peice of land in Newp[t] for a house lot lying and being to y[e] southward side of my dwelling house to be in Length & Breadth on Each Line fifty three feet, and his Lot to begin on y[e] Westward of my Land against the great Street and will be southerly on y[e] Street as goes to **Jireh Bulls,** all which Land as above mentioned I give and Bequeath unto him my said son John Chapman and his heirs & assigns forever.

Item. Unto my son **Isaac Chapman** and his heirs & assigns forever I give and Bequeath a Lot of Land in Newport of fifty three foot to be adjoyning unto y[e] Lot I gave my son John Chapman, being bounded southerly on y[e] Lane goes to **Jireh Bulls,** and will lie on y[e] Eastward of y[e] Lot as abovementioned given my son John Chapman.

Item. Unto my son in law **Jeremiah Gould** I order to be Laid out unto him or his order to y[e] Eastward of y[e] Land I have given my son Isaac a lot of Land, as I have sold unto him and as y[e] deed mentons sixty foot front on y[e] highway leads to Jreh Bull afores[d] and in Breadth fifty three feet.

Item. Unto my four Daughters hereafter mentioned (viz[t]) **Abigail Chapman, Mary Chapman, Lydia Chapman,** and **Catherine Chapman,** and to Each and to Each and either of them, and each or either of their heirs forever I give & Bequeath to Each of them a Lot of Land of fifty three foot in Length or Breadth on Each Line, and bounded southerly on said Street leads to Jreh Bulls, my said Daughter Abigail to have Next Lot Buting on Jeremiah Goulds Lot and so each Lot following after as Mentioned as aboves[d] by Name and Lastly of this my Last Will and Testament I do nominate appoint and Constitute my Well beloved Wife **Mary Chapman** to be my sole Ex[tx] to see my Will Performed and all Lands houses Goods or Chattles of any sort I have I give and Bequeath unto my said Well beloved Wife to her & her heirs and assigns forever to be by her given & Disposed of for such use as she thinks Most Needfull & Convenient for acquiting all my Lawfull Debts and giving What she thinks Convenient to my son **Walter Chapman**, whom I have not already given or Bequeathed any part of my Estate or also to be given to ye Rest of my Children In Testimony hereof I Ralph Chapman have set my hand & seal Newport on Rhode Island November ye fourth 1704.

Signed sealed & declared by Ralph Chapman [*signed*] Ralph Chapman
to be his Last Will & Testament before us and ye words (houses) and (I have) was interlined before signing & sealing
James Cole Wm Anthony Benj^{a} Belcher

1711, September 3: **Capt. James Cole** and **Mr. Benjamin Belcher** appeared [in council] and declared upon oath that they did see Mr. Ralph Chapman sign seal & declare this within written will to be his last will & testament and that they did see Wm Anthony sign as witness to ye sd will with them. Taken in Council as attest pr **Richd Ward** Coun^{l} Clerk

The above and foregoing two pages are a true copy from ye Town Coun^{l} Book of Newport No. 4 Pages 551 & 552 . . . Newp^{t} January 17th 1763 . . . **Wm Coddington** Council Clerk

21. 1704, December 8. **The will of Thomas Mallett** [*copy made for case Wilcox vs Akin, 1723; see No. 179*]. [*This will was among those lost in 1779. This abstract was made from notes taken in 1981. The copy of the will was seen again in 1990, but was then in pieces, with some parts missing.*]

Thomas Mallet of Newport, innkeeper, dated 8 December 1704, sick and weak. Indian man **Abraham** to beloved wife Mary Mallet for 20 years and then to be free . . . to son-in-law Jeremiah Wilcox a case of pistolls with sadle holsters and furniture, two firelock guns which he now hath in possession, one silver hilted sword, and one other sword, and six dozen of plate buttons for a coat. To daughter-in-law Mary Wilcox who now lives in my house, one silver Quart Tankard, one Negro boy named **Andrew.** To Trinity Church in Newport, 40 shillings . . . 20 shillings to the minister who preaches my funeral sermon. Remainder to wife. Signed with a large T; witnessed by **Jonath^{n} Abbot, Thomas Weeden,** and **Thomas Fox.** Proved 5 February 1704[/5].

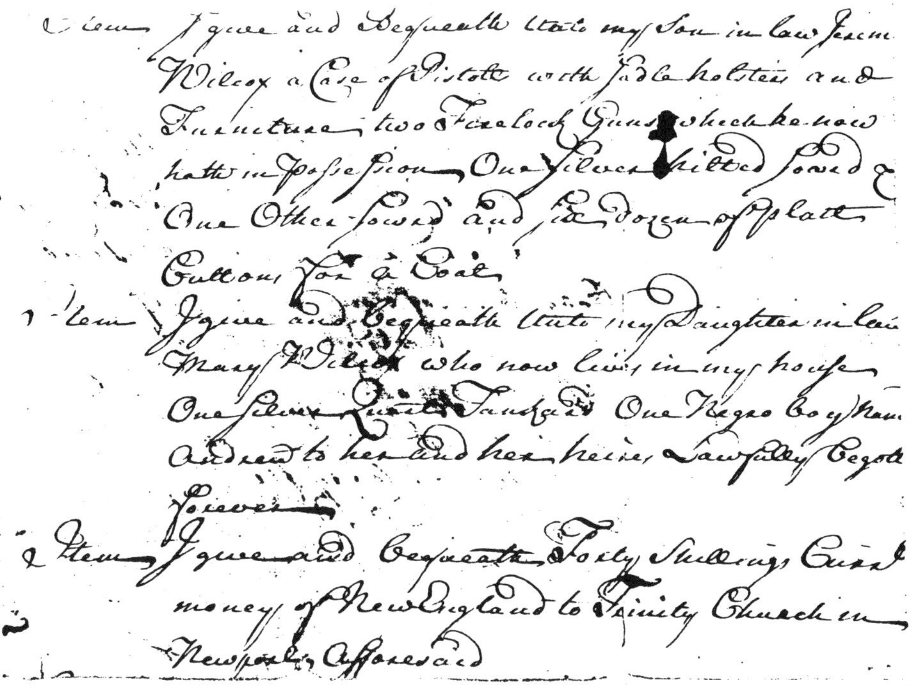

Item I give and Bequeath unto my Son in law Jerem
Wilcox a Case of Pistols with Sadle holsters and
Furniture two Firelock Guns which he now
hath in Possession One Silver hilted Sword &
One Other Sword and six dozen of plate
Buttons for a Coat
Item I give and Bequeath unto my Daughter in law
Mary Wilcox who now lives in my house
One Silver Quart Tankard One Negro boy Nam
Andrew to her and her heires Lawfully Begott
forever
Item I give and bequeath Forty Shillings Curant
money of New England to Trinity Church in
Newport Afforesaid

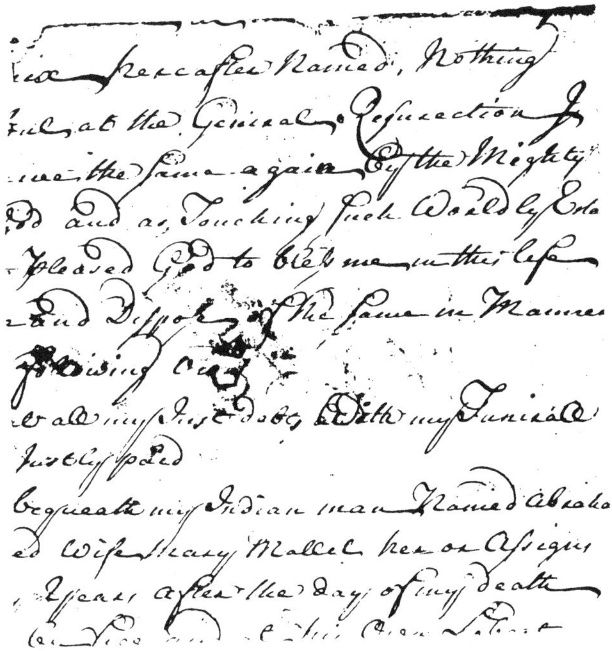

...er hereafter Named, Nothing
...ful at the General Resurrection I
...ive the same again By the Mighty
...od and as Touching such Worldly Esta
...pleased God to bless me in this life
...and Dispose of the same in Manner
following
...o all my Just debts with my Funeral
Justly paid
bequeath my Indian man Named Abraha
...ed Wife Mary Mallet her or Assigns
... years after the day of my death
[illegible]

Above and right:
Surviving fragments of the will of Thomas Mallett dated 1704 [item no. 21]

22. 1705/6, March 16: Warrant [*separated from case*] from **Jeffery Champlin** and **John Eldred**, Assistants, to **Aron Jaquess** Town Sergant of Kingstown: "whereas theire was by Inquissition made on the behalfe of our Sovereigne Lady the Queen this day on a forcable entry made on some lands in Kingstown some time past by **James Wilson** of said town deceased, on the complaint of the guardians to **Henry Bull**, the Jury going out found the force . . . in her Majesties name [we] require you to take what aid needful and remove the force by laying open the ffence made on said lands and deliver possession to the guardians of Henry Bull." The warrant is endorsed "A true Coppy of the originall warrant by me . . . **Aaron Jacways** Town Sergant."

23. 1706, August 1. Indenture of lease [*separated from case*] between Major **John Coggeshall** and his son **Joseph Coggeshall**, both of Newport, and **Edward Thurston** of Newport, cooper, of land whereon Joseph's shop now stands, bounded southerly on land of **Samuell Cranston**, Esq., northerly on land of Major **William Wanton** "by mee purchased of Mr. **Walter Clarke Esqr**," westerly on the sea, and easterly on the highway, Thurston to have also a way 12 feet wide from the street to the wharf. Witnesses were **Benjamin Coggeshall** and **Thos. Peck Jr.**

24. 1708, 22 June: Will of **John Coggeshall** [*copied in March 1724 for case John Coggeshall vs. Freegift Coggeshall et al.; see below, No. 189*].

I John Coggeshall of Newp^{t} in y^{e} Collony of Rhoad=Island And Providence Plantations &c; Senr, being Aged & Weak of Body, but of Sound Sense & memory through the goodness of God to me; and & I had a former will Some years Since but Severall Changes hath fell out Since that, wch Causeth me to make this my Last will & Testam[en]t Hereby revoaking all former wills made by writing word of mouth or other wise whatsoever; & this to Stand as My Last will & Testament. — —

Imp^{rs} I Bequeath my Soul to ye Lord y^{t} gave me Life and being, & my Body to ye Earth to be desently buryed by my Executrix & Executor hereaft^{r} named, on ye East side by my wife **Patience Coggeshall** (soe called) and my will is to be buried without Souldery in armes, & Consearning my Reall & parsonall Estate wch God hath been pleased to be stow upon me I doe order & dispose of in maner as followeth —

Item I Give & Bequeath unto **Freegift Coggeshall** (soe called) Eldest son of ye afore said Patience deceas^{d} a part of my farme I now dwell in, bounded as followeth to begin at The Mouth of y^{e} River wch parts Jahleel Brenton Esquires Land (Lately purchased of **Richard Mew**) & mine, & Soe Northerly [*torn*]edly as y^{e} River runes Vntill it Comes to y^{e} corner of y^{e} Stone wall which Lyes Westerly from my old Dwelling=house & from thence Northerly Upon y^{e} Stone=Wall Soe farr, as turning Eastward, it

Shall Come a Rod northerly ffrom astone=wall (& a row of trees by it) being on y^e^ north side of the house y^e^ sd Ffreegift dwells in & Soe to Continue A rod from sd wall to y^e^ end thereof, & from thence Still on a Straight Line untill it comes to a fence sett up by said ffreegift of post & rayles, and Soe from thence Southerly Untill it Comes to a Stone wall & Soe Easterly upon sd wall Untill it Come to ye Sea, and soe rounding upon ye Sea vntill it Comes to ye aforesd River, All wch sd part of my farme soe Bounded, ye afores^d^ Ffreegift Shall possess & Enjoy presently after my decease wth all Buildings fences Priviledges & apurtenances whatsoever thereunto in any wise appertaining, & to his Heires male Lawfully begotten of his body for ever, y^e^ sd Freegift paying Such Legacys as I Shall hereafter order Him to pay,

Item. I give will unto **James Coggeshall** (soe Called) Second son to y^e^ aforesd Patience, two pounds in Courant Silver Money of New=England to be paid by y^e^ aforesd Freegift presently After my decease, if demanded by said James, he the said James (but Especially his wife) have notoriously [*page* 2] Abused my selfe, my wife & Broth^rs^ Intim[ating? we] were noe better than theeves & murderers as may more particuler appear in a wicked false slanderous Letter (Jezebell Like) she sent to my wife, writen wth her owne hand, her husband maintaining her in it, all which we know & God knowes is false, & we are innocent, soe farr in a probabilyty ye breach mought have been made up, but sinse to provoke me further, she hath By a pretense borrowed a book to Look Something in it, Shee kept it two or three dayes but when it came home We found six choyse manascripts cut out which we very much prised, as a book of physick, dayry, distillations, Dying all Sorts of Coulors, Cookery which being demanded by my Selfe, She put me off, with slite answers, neither denying nor owneing, her husband knowing all those things, But noe Course he takes to Satisfie his parents but Seemes to take her part in all her wicked false Chargis, doing their utmost indevour to Sett my neibours Children & Grand=Children against us, all raised and fomented by her wicked Jealous Spirit, Crying out of Wrongs, but will name noe perticulors & to provoak further, neither of them hath Came to See their father Near upon three years though Somtimes Sick near unto death all which & severall other provocations Which is not Convenient here to be inserted, gives me Just Cause to dissinherit hime Soe farr as I have don,

Item. I give & bequeath unto **Benjamin Coggeshall** (soe Called) Third son of y^e^ aforesd Patience, another part of my ffarme I now dwell in, bounded as followeth first I give unto y^e^ sd Benjamin, all that field Called Vaghans ffield, bounded on y^e^ East upon **John Mumford**s Land, Northerly upon **Jirah Bull**s Land, South upon Stones Layd to wards makeing a Stone=wall untill it meets with y^e^ aforesd John Mounfords Land, westerly upon Land now in y^e^ possession of y^e^ aforesd James. Likewise I give to the aforesd Benjamin all y^t^ Land (as it is now ffenced) which Leads to sd Vahans field to y^e^ place where We used to Catch Sheep, on y^e^ South of y^e^ sd James His house, further I give unto ye aforesd Benjamin, Another part of my farme bounded as followeth to Begin at ye rock which Lyes East from y^e burying place where my father & Mother was buryed, & from thence on a Straight Line westerly untill it Comes a Rod northerly from a Little gate wch opens into a Highway wch Leads into y^e neck & **Jahleel Brentons** Esq^{rs} farme &c: and soe rounding upon y^e high=way untill it Comes to my gate [*torn*] y^e towne of Newport, & soe Southerly upon y^e Stone=wall untill It metes wth y^e Rock aforesd, all wch two parcells of Land y^e sd Benjamin Coggeshall (soe Called) Shall possess & Enioy presently after my decease wth all y^e buildings fences priviledges & appurtenances whatsoever thereunto in any wise appertaining & to his heires male Lawfully begotten of his body for Ever; further my will Is that ye sd Benjamin Shall have free Liberty to mow four Load of marsh in ye Marsh which joyns to ye sd freegifts Marsh, to Say, two Load of marsh & two Load of Creeke grass, wth free ingress, Egress, & Regress to Cary it where he thinks Convenient, for Ever, he paying what Legacyes I shall hereafter order him to pay.

Item. I give & bequeath unto **Joseph Coggeshall** (soe Called) Eldest son of my wife **Mary Coggeshall** (soe Called) y^e moyty or halfe of a piece of Land Lying in y^e towne of Newport which I purchased of **Walter Clark**, bounded on y^e north upon Maj^r **William Wantons** Land, Southerly upon Land of mine, west on the Sea, or harbour & on y^e East upon y^e high=way being About twenty Six foot bredth next y^e high=way, together with y^e buildings whatsoever thereunto apertaining, to him His h[e]ires & assignes for Ever; further my will is y^t y^e aforesd ffreegift shall pay unto y^e aforesd Joseph thirty pounds In Courant Silver money of New=England, y^e halfe of It wch is fiveteen pound, to be paid twelve moneths After my decease, & y^e other fifteen pounds y^e next year after, Leaving it to y^e discretion of his aforesd Mother w^t She & his Bro^r **Abraham** Shall pay as a further Legacy to him,

Item. I give & bequeath unto **Abraham Coggeshall** (soe Called) Second son of my Wife Mary Coggeshall (soe Called) all ye remaining Part of my farme I now dwell in, bounded as followeth on ye East upon Land of **John Munforde** & y^e Sea, Southerly, Easterly upon Land given to y^e aforesd Freegift, Northerly & Northwesterly upon Land given to y^e aforesd Benjamin, Northwesterly & Southwesterly upon Land of Jahleel Brenton Esqr & Capt **John Stantons** Land, further I give unto y^e aforesd Abraham All that Marsh=meddow Called y^e Marsh=Meddow fenced in wth Stone=wall, & Joyning to y^e aforesd ffregifts Marshes, Excepting y^e fore Load of Marsh given to y^e aforesd Benjamin, all wch sd parcels of Land soe bounded y^e sd Abraham Coggeshall (soe Called) shall possess & Enioy presently after my decease, ffor himselfe, & his heires male Lawfully begotten of his Body for Ever, Provided & my will is y^t his Mother Mary Coggeshall (soe Called) shall have ye use & benefit of ye new dwelling house I built Last, untill her decease, & after her Decease shall Returne to ye sd Abraham, & hairs male Lawfully begotten of his body for Ever, wth all y^e Buildings, ffences, Priviledges & apurtenances w^{t}soever thereunto apertaining further my will is his sd mother shall have y^e^ use of Convenient Places to Lay her wood upon, & to keep her horse, a Cow & some poultry, & to Cart her fire=wood as Long as She Liveth, She Paying for y^e^ wood brought to a wharfe in Newp^t^.

Item. I give & bequeath unto **Samuel Coggeshall** (soe Called) y^e^ other Moyty or halfe of y^e^ peece of Land I purchased of Water [*sic*] Clark bounded on y^e^ East upon y^e^ high=way, on y^e^ South upon **Samuel Cranstons** Esqr Land, & on y^e^ west upon y^e^ Sea or harbour & on y^e^ north upon Land given to y^e^ aforesd Joseph his Bro^tr^ being About twenty six foot in bredth next y^e^ high=way, wth all y^e^ priviledges & apurtenances w^t^soever thereunto apertaining, & to his heires & assignes for Ever, to possess presently after my decease, further my will is y^t^ y^e^ aforesd Benjamin Shall pay unto y^e^ aforesd Samuel, fourty pounds in Courant Silv^r^ money of New=England, to say twenty pound a year after my decease, & y^e^ other twenty pound y^e^ next year after, but if y^e^ sd Samuell (being abroad not knowing where he is) [*in the left margin is written* "Samuel sent a Letter in the year 1712, October"] Should be deceased, y^e^ ffourty pound wch y^e^ sd Samuell was to Receive of sd Benjamin He Shall pay unto ye aforesd Joseph or **Elisha Coggeshall** (soe Called) In Equall proportion, Leaveing it to his aforesd mother What she & her aforesd son Abraham shall pay unto ye aforesd Samuell as a further Legacy.

Item. I give & bequeath unto **Elisha Coggeshall** (soe Called) a forth Son of ye aforesd Mary Coggeshall (soe Called) a peece of Land wch I purchased of Mr **Nathanill Coddington**, being sixty foot one way & fifty foot ye other way, as may appear in a deed of Sale under sd Coddingtons Hand & Seal, wth all ye buildings, priviledges & apurtenances w^t^soever thereunto apertaining, to possess & Enioy presently after my decease & to his hires & assigns for Ever; further my will is, that ye Aforesd ffreegift Shall pay unto ye sd Elisha, ffourty pound in Courant Silver money of Newengland, to Say twenty pound three years after my decease, & ye other twenty pound, twelve months next after, Leaving it to his afores^d^ mothers discretion w^t^ She & his afores^d^ Brot^r^ Abraham shall & will give unto ye afores^d^ Elisha as a further Legacy.

Item I give & bequeath unto **Rebeckah** Wife to **John Reynolds**, to **Patience** Wife to **Samuell Rathbone**, to **Content** Wife to **Samuell Norton** Each twenty pounds to be paid by y^e^ afores^d^ Freegift; to Say tenn pounds Each two years after my decease & y^e^ other ten pounds to be paid ten pounds Each, to be paid a year or twelve months after, as an adition to y^t^ I have given them before, the twenty pounds apeece in Courant Silver Money of New=England.

Item I give & bequeath Unto y^e^ three daughters of **Mary Bull** deceased, Wife of **Ephraim Bull,** five pounds apeece, to be paid them at y^e^ age of twenty one years, or day of Marriage, to be paid by y^e^ afores^d^ Benjamin In Courant Silver Mony of New=England —

Item I give & bequeath unto **Patience Lowell**, Wife of **Joseph Lowell** of

Boston five pounds in Courant Silver money of New=England, to be paid to her by y^{e} aforesd Benjamin presently After my decease.

Item I give unto y^{e} afores^{d} **Benjamin**, my Seal=Gould ring and to y^{e} Afores^{d} **Joseph** my Buff Belt wth y^{e} furniture belonging to it, & to y^{e} afores^{d} Abraham my plate=buttons, & y^{e} Littele Sillver dram=Cup, & to y^{e} aforesd^{d} Elisha my Silv^{r} Shooe=buckells & Shurt buttons, ffurther my will is that y^{e} Afores^{d} **Joseph, Abraham, Samuell & Elisha** Shall have all my wearing aparrell both Woollen & Linen, to be Equally divided betwixt them, After my decease.

Item. I give Unto y^{e} afores^{d} **Abraham** all my tacklings be Longing to husbandry, as Cart plows yoakes Chaines, wth all other Tooles &c. Alsoe four sound working Oxen four Cowes fifty good Sound Ewe Sheep all to be delivered to said Abraham presently after my decease, Provided, & my will is, y^{t} ye afores^{d} **Benjamin**, Shall have ye use of sd Cart & Oxen at Convenient times to Cart his owne fire-wood, fenceing Stuff, & other nessessary things for his owne use, doeing ye Oxen noe wrong, wch If he doe to make y^{t} good againe, & if breaks Either Cart or tackling to mend them againe, as they were before.

ffurther my mind & will is y^{t} presently after my decease all my personal Estate Now in my possession (Except w^{t} is disposed of in this my will) as Sheep, neate=Cattle horse kind, swine &c With all my Silver Money, & plate, Likewise all my household utensels, of what nature or kind w^{t}soever, as bedding, Puter, potts & kettles &c I give unto y^{e} aforesd **Mary Coggeshall** (soe Called) whome I make my Executrix, & joyne wth her, her aforesd Son Abraham Executor of this my Last will and testament to the Intent y^{t} all my just depts may be paid, legacys raised & duely paid, ffurther my will is y^{t} what of ye Estate afore given to ye Aforesd Mary Coggeshall (soe Called) Shall remain in her Custody upon her decease Shall be Equally divided betwixt ye Aforesd Benjamin (if he be Marryed & hath a Child) & her aforesd four Sons viz: **Joseph, Abraham, Samuell, & Elisha**, With four daughters, to say, **Mary**, Wife to **Josiah Coggeshall**, **Rebeckah** Wife to **John Reinolds**, **Patience** Wife to **Samuell Rathbone**, & to **Content** Wife to **Samuell Norton**.

ffurther my will is, y^{t} w^{t} I have given unto ye aforesd **Mary Coggeshall** (soe Called) shall be in Liew of all thirds or dowrys w^{t}soever, which may in any wise be demanded by sd Mary, & ffurther my mind and will is y^{t} if ye aforesd **Benjamin** should decease wth out ishue male then his sd porshon of Land given to him as aforesd shall be & accrue to the aforesd **Samuell Coggeshall** (soe Called) & to his heires male Lawfully begotten of his body for ever, paying & doing in all Respects as ye Aforesd Benjamin was to doe but Considering y^{t} ye sd Samuel Have beene abroad in world Severall yeares not knowing if dead or Living, wch when knowing of his decease, or not hearing of him In a Considerable Season, then if sd Benjamin Should decease without Ishue male as aforesd his sd portion of Land shall be & accrue unto **Elisha Coggeshall** (soe Called) & to his heires male Lawfully

Begotten of his body for Ever, paying & doeing in all Respects as ye sd Benjamin was to doe, and if sd Elisha decease w^{th}out Ishue male as aforesd then sd Land shall be & acrew unto **Joseph Coggeshall** (soe Called) & to his heires male Lawfully Begotten of his body for Ever, paying & doeing in all Respects as the sd Benjamin was to doe, a ffurther my will is y^t if ye sd Abraham should decease wth out ishue male Lawfully begotten of his body, then his aforesd portion of Land shall be & acrue to ye aforesd Joseph Coggeshall (soe Called), & to his heires male Lawfully begotten of his body for Ever, paying & doing in all Respects as ye aforesd Abraham was to doe, a ffurther my Mind and will is that if ye aforesd Samuell be deceased (or dye w^{th}out Ishue) then his portion of Land of y^e moity of Land I purchased of **Walter Clark** shall be and accrue unto Joseph Coggeshall (soe Called) & to his heires & assignes ffor ever & ffurther whereas y^e aforesd Benjamin & aforesd Abrahams portions of Land, hath very Little good Planting Land in it for Endien=Corne & the aforesd **Freegifts** Portion of Land is most of it Rich planting Land I doe order and my will is y^t y^e aforesd Benjamin & Abraham shall have two akers a peece of good Land such as he takes in to Plant him selfe paying a reasonable rate for it such as may be Judged by rationel men.

As for fencing, my will is y^t ye aforesd ffreegift shall make & Maintain for Ever, A sufficiente fence in all those Lines where His sd portion of Land doth butt & bound upon ye aforesd Abraham his portion of Land, & ye aforesd Abraham shall make & maintaine a Sufficient fence for Ever, halfe y^t Line (or Lines) of fence where his portion of Land doth butt & bound upon ye aforesd Benjamin his portion of Land, and ye aforesd Benjamin shall make and maintaine a Sufficient fence for Ever, y^t other halfe Line of fence betwixt him & ye aforesd Abraham, allsoe my will is that ye aforesd James & his Wife there heires, Shall maintaine for Ever (or Soe Long as it is in there possession) a Suficiente fence round ye five akers of Land now in their possession, ffurther my will is y^t ye heires of ye aforesd persons Consernd in fencing ye one against ye other shall trully performe in all respects w^t ye afore persons was to doe Concerning fencing ffurther my will is y^t ye sd ffreegift his heires shall have free ingress egress & regress to pass with horse or foot Carting and driveing of Cattle &. Through ye aforesd Abrahams & Benjamin their portion of Land to ye town of Newport & Common dowing as Little damage as may be allsoe ye sd Mary & sd Abraham (or ffreegifts heires) & ye sd Mary & Abrahams heires Shall have ye sd Liberty as is given to sd freegift doeing as Little damage as may be, ffurther my Will is y^t ye aforesd freegift shall have ye use, or benefit of halfe my great barne (to say ye Easterly end, for Ever, or soe Long as he keeps it in good repaire & soe Long as he keeps up ye southerly Little-dores in sufficient repaire, in ye meane time ye aforesd ffreegift shall have free Ingress & regress to Carry in out of sd Barne w^t he shall see Cause to put there with-out molestation and to thrash at Convenient seasons.

ffurther my will is y^t whereas there was Layd out to me a peece of Land out of ye Common in ye South Rockey neck from ye towne of Newp^t Containing about seventy akers Rocks, & all bounded East, Southerly, & westerly, upon **Jahleel Brenton** Esq^{rs} Land, northwesterly upon Capt. **Edward Pelhams** Land, & northerly upon Land now in possession of Mr. **Stephen Mounford**, all wch sd peece of Land soe bounded, I give & bequeath unto Benjamin & Abraham Coggeshall (soe Called) & to their heires, & assignes for Ever, wth all ye fences previledges and apurtenances whatsoever thereunto apertaining, further my will is y^t ye five akers of Land and housen upon it now in ye possession of aforesd James, My will is y^t w^n y^t deed I made to him & his Wife is finished according to ye contents thereof then ye sd Benjamin shall possess & Enioy ye aforesd housen & five akres of Land, for himeselfe, & his heires male Lawfully begotten of his body for Ever,

ffurther my will is y^t whereas ye aforesd **Freegift Coggeshall** (soe Called) had delivered unto him by me when I Leased to hime y^t part of my farme he now dwelleth in, being ye ffirst of march) to hundred good Ewe Sheep & Rams, before Laming time or Shearing time, Six good Cowes, ffive Calves, & four good oxen, all prized by us ye sd John & ffreegift Coggeshall (soe Called) as a hundred & thirteene pounds as money wch sd Stock he was to have the benefitt of so Long as he rented y^t part of my ffarme, now my will is, y^t presently after my decease all ye aforesd stock of Cattel & Sheep, (or ye worth of them) shall be Equally divided betwxt ye aforesd Freegift, Benjamin, & Abraham Coggeshall (soe Called) desiring my overseers (hereafter named) to be helpfull in ye deviding, if they Canot Agree them selves.

ffurther my will is y^t ye buriing place where my ffather & Mother &c Is buried in Shall be a perpetull Buriing place for any of my posterity y^t hath a mind to be Entered therein, & y^t Shall be three rods in Length ffrom North to South, & tow Rod & a halfe wide from East to west, & w^t it wants of ye measure as it is now fenced, shall be made upon ye South End, ye west Side, & my will is y^t ye sd Freegift, Benjamin, & Abraham Coggeshall, (soe Called) shall sett up A Sufficient fence with boards, and soe them & their heires to maintain it for Ever,

I give my Indian woman **Jane** to ye aforesd Mary Coggeshall (soe Called), & any Servant man or boy y^t are prentices I give unto Abraham Coggeshall (soe Called)

Lastly my desire is, y^t my beloved ffrinds **Samuell Cranston** Esqr & Mr **Benjamin Newbery** will take paines to be Overseers in helping & advising my Executrix & Executor for their best advantage, And for gratuity, my will Is y^t my Executrix & Executor Shall provide & give to Each of them A gold=ring of about Twenty Shillings price apiece; And in Witness y^t this Is my Last will & Testament I have hereunto sett my hand & seale this two & Twentieth of June One thousand Seven hundred & Eight.

Signed In y^e p^{r}sence of us — John Coggeshall (seal)
Westin Clark
Edward Thurston

Benj[a] Cranston
William Coddington
Proved 8 November 1708, and recorded by Edw[d] Thurston, Clerk of Council, 24 November 1708 in Newport Town Council Book 4:29 - Copy attested [?1724] by John Hammet, Town Clerk.

25. 1707, November 7: **The will of Peter Brock** [*from case, Phillips vs. Langworthy, 1745*]
November S[t] Iago the 7th day 1707
I Peter Brock of Rhode Island and Providence Plantations in Newport Merchant and Owner of the Good Sloop the Dolphin being Very Weak in Body but of perfect And Sound Memory making this my last Will and Testament Revoaking and Disanulling all Former Wills by me made in Manner and Form Following –
First And Formost I Committ my Soul into the Hands of Almighty God that gave it me and my Body to the Earth to be Decently Entered to the Discreation of my Executors **Thomas Lyndall** & **William James** and as for my Worldly Estate that God hath Endowed me with I Give and Bequeath In Manner and form Following all my Estate both real & personal to **Peter Brock** and **William Brock** and **Sarah Brock** my Three Children all Excepting my Mantioned house and as for all the Rest of my Estate Moneys Jewels Plate bills bonds book debts lands houses Mortgages Shiping profits of shiping & all debts That shall be Made to Peter Brock Sen[r] and also Six hundred pounds in cash in Silver & Gold Which was in my house when I came out I Give to my three Children to be Equally Devided between them three Excepting my house above Mentioned I bequeath the said house to my Dear Wife **Sarah Brock** During her Widowhood and afterwards to become my Eldest Son Peter Brock and if any of my said Children above Mentioned Should Decease before any heirs or Issue then its Inheritance shall be Inheritance Amongst the Survivors also I give & Bequeath to **Thomas Lyndall** ten Pounds & **William James** ten Pounds also I Impower & Authorize my said Executors and I Desire that my Children be Well Educated and Brought up.

[*signed*] Peter Brock

Witnesses: James Tenney, Aquella Gibson, Louronce Gle, Mano Ldices Gle, Gulielmus Worsi
Att a Town Councell of Newport July the 5th 1708: In Councell appeared Thomas Lyndall and William James with the Will & Inventory of Cap[t] Peter Brock late of Newport Deced and Did Exhebit the same before the said Councell they being the Executors to said Will therein Nominated & Appointed which said Will was . . ..

26. 1708 , May 21: **The will of Thomas Peckham:**
In the Name of God Amen, the twentafirst Day of May in the Year of our Lord one thousand seven hundred and eight I Thomas Peckham of Newport on Rhode-Island and Providence Plantations in New-England America Weaver being weak in Body but in perfect Mind and Memory thanks be given unto God, therefore calling to Mind the Mortality of my Body and knowing that it is appointed for men once to die do make and ordain this my last Will & Testament that is to say principly and first of all I give and recommend my Soul into the Hands of God that gave it, and through the Merrit Death and Passion of my Saviour Jesus Christ to have full and free Pardon and forgiveness of all my Sins and to inherit everlasting Life, and my Body I commit to the Earth to be decently buried at the Discretion of my Wife and Children nothing doubting but at the genral Resurection I shall receive the same again by the mighty Power of God, and as touching such worldly Estate wherewith it hath pleased God to bless me in this Life, I give demise and dispose of the same in the following manner [*page* 2] and Forme, that is to say first I will that all my (Just) Debts and Duties as I owe Right or Conscience to any manner of Persons or Persons whatsoever shall be well and truly contented and paid in convenient Time after my decease by my Executor hereafter named.
Item I give and bequeath unto my Son **Thomas Peckham** one shilling in sylver money he having alrady received his Portion.
Item I give and bequeath unto my Daughter **Sarah Underwood** five Pounds in sylver Money to be paid her in one Year after my Decease. Item I give and bequeath unto my Son **Daniel Peckham** one of my Guns and thirty Pounds in sylver money to be paid unto him at the Age of one and twenty Year. Item I give and bequeath unto my Son **James Peckham** my Square Barrel Gun and my now dweling House with a Piece of Land adjoining to sd House as it is now staked out which sd Land being part of the Land which I bought of **Philip Smith** and **William Slade** of Newport aforesd the sd House and Land with the Improvement thereon and all the Priviledges thereto belonging to be and remain unto my Son James Peckham his Heirs Executors Administrators and Assignes for ever [*page 3*] Item I give and bequeath unto my Son **Philip Peckham** all the Remainder of my Lands and Housing with all the Improvements Priviledges & Appertinances whatsoever belonging to sd Land, and Housing with the Stock and Utensils thereto belonging all now in his Possession to him his Heirs Executors Administrators and Assigns for ever. Item I give and bequeath unto my loving Wife all my Cash. Item I give & bequeath unto my two Sons Daniel and James Peckham all my Carpenters Tools to be equally divided betwixt them two. Item I give and bequeath unto my loving Wife **Hannah Peckham** three Pounds in sylver money yearly and every year and the use of my Mare and one Cow with all my household Goods and the Use of my House and Land that I have given unto my son James Peckham during her Widowhood or her natural Life in the Lieu of her

Thirds and for the bringing up of my Son James Peckham: and after the Decease of my Wife my Mare and Cow and all my household Goods with my Carpenters Tools to be equally divided betwixt my two Sons Daniel and James Peckham. Also my Will is that if either of my two Sons Daniel or James [*page* 3] should die before they come to enjoy their Legacies given them that then their Legacy so dying shall be and remain to that Survivor Daniel or James and their Heirs Executors Administrators for ever. Also the Intent and Meaning of my Will is that my Son Philip Peckham shall pay my Son Thomas and my Daughter Sarah Underwood their Legacies and also that three Pounds yearly and every year that is given to my loving Wife Hannah Peckham during her natural Life as abovesd. Also my Will is that my loving Wife shall pay the Legacies by me given unto my two Sons Daniel and James Peckham lastly I do ordain constitute and appoint my loving Son Philip Peckham to be my Lawfull & sole Executor of this my last Will and Testament: and I do hereby utterly disalow revoke and disanul all and every other form and Testament, Will, & Legacies, Bequests and Executors by me in any ways before this Time named willed and bequeathed, ratifying and confirming this and no other to be my last Will and Testament In Witness whereof I have hereunto sett my Hand and Seal the Day and Year above written.

[signed] *Thomas Peckham*

Witnesses: Jeremiah Weeden, William Weeden, Junr, and William Weeden.

In a Codicil dated 16 November 1708, with the same witnesses, Thomas Peckham referred to his will and did "confirm and ratify my said Last Will and Testament and do give and bequeath unto my Son **Daniel Peckham** my Lot of Land that I bought of Maj^{r} **John Bliss** unto him . . . that is to say in the Lieu of the one half of his Legacy given him as is above expressed in my Will." All three witnesses appeared before the Town Council 7 February 1708[/9] to attest their signatures. The will was recorded in Town Council Book 4:50-53, from which it was copied 13 February 1721/2 by Wm. Coddington, Town Clerk.

27. 1709. Will of Nicholas Carr [*from case Thomas Carr vs. Benedict Arnold, 1730; see also Item 12*]:

In the name of God Amen the Tenth Day of Jany in the year of our Lord god 1708/9 I Nicholas Carr of James Town in the Colony of Rhoad Island and Providence Plantations in New England yeoman being weak of Body but of perfect mind and memory thanks be given unto god for the same Therefore calling to mind the mortality of my body and Knowing that it is appointed for all men once to Dye Do make and ordine this my Last will and and testament and for my body I Commend it to the earth, to be Buried in Christian and Decent maner, by my Exec^{tr} here after named, but as for such worldly Estate where With it hath pleased god to bless me with in this Life I give and bequeath and bestowe in maner and forme following Imprimiss that all my Just Debts Which I do owe to any Person or persons which shall be paid In Convenient time after my Decase by my Executor Here after named.

Item I give to my Loveing son **Nicholas Carr** that house and farme with the out houses on said farme that I shall not Dispose of in this my will to be His Heirs Exec^{trs} Admin^{rs} for ever with the Right in duch Island that belongs to said farme and one acre of Land out of **Tom fishes** feild Joynng to the maine high way for a watering Place for his Creatures he my said son Shall fence it out and maintaine the fence for ever if he makes use of sd Land and further my will is that if my son Nicholas Carr should dye without Issew Lawfully begotten of [*page* 2] His body, then my will is that my son **Thomas Carr** shall have the fore said farme to he His heirs Exec^{trs} Admin^{rs} and assignes for Ever, and If my son Thom^{as} Carr should come to Enjoy the afore said farme, my will is that what I have given him now by this my will in Lands shall fall to my son **Benj^{mn}** [Carr *crossed out*] his heirs Exec^{trs} Admin^{rs} and Assgnes for ever to Injoy.

Item I give to my Loveing son **Tho^{ms} Carr** a sertaine Parcell of Land Cont^{ing} Seventy acres be it more or Less Called Thom: fishes feild on the west side of the maine High way on said Island all said Land I give to my son Tho^{ms} Carr to be his heirs Exec^{trs} Admin^{rs} and Assignes for ever and a Right In duch Island that belongs to said Lands, and further I give to my son Tho^{ms} Carr for ever one Pare of oxen fifty Sheep three Cows and one Guine of gold and one silver spoon and one silver Beere Cup marked on the Bottom **T: T:** and all to be Delivered to him when he Comes to the age of twenty & one years old, by my Exec^{trs} hereafter Named, and further my will is that if my son Tho^{ms} Carr should dye without Issew or before he Comes of age to Reseave his portion of Land my Will is that my son Benj^{mn} Carr shall have it To be His heirs Exec^{rs} Admin^{rs} and assignes for ever.

Item I give to my Loveing son **Benjamin Carr** his Heirs Exec^{rs} Administrators and assignes for ever my Little [*page* 3] House that **John Bull** and **Tom percheg** Lives in with a Certaine peice of Land butted Against the Croos Highway south & west on the uper Gardian below my House I Live in and to Run ten Rods North and then a Direct Line to the sea per a line With the Cross high way and three Eights of golds Island to be his Heirs and Assignes for ever and fourty Pounds of Current money one silver Spoon one silver Beere Cup wraughted and one A Rabian peice of Gold all to be Delivered to him when he arives at Twenty and one years of age by my Exec^{tr} Here after Named.

Item I give to my Loveing Daughter **Margret Batty** twenty five Pounds Current money and one Silver porrenger one Silver spoon all to be paid her at my Decase by my Exec^{tr} here after named and the great warming pan bought of **Mr Allins** and all other things that I have given her Before to be hers for ever –

Item I give to my Daughter **Jane Carr** fifty pounds Current money and a feather bed and furniture Worth ten pounds one Silver Cup holds a gill one silver spoon one Warmingpan all to be paid her at my Decase with a Chest of Drawers stands in the grate Chamber –

Item I give to my Daughter **Mercy Carr** fifty Pounds Current money and a feather bed worth ten pounds with furniture one silver spoon all to be paid her at my Decase by my Executor here after Named –

Item I give to my Daughter **Rebeca Carr** fifty pounds Current money of new England and a feather bead worth ten [*page 4*] Pounds with the furniture to it one silver spoon all to be paid her at my Decase by my Exec^{tr} here after named – Item I give to my Daughter **Ann Carr** fifty pounds Current money and one feather Bead with furniture worth ten pounds and one silver spoon all to be paid her at my Decase by my Exec^{tr} here after Named – Item further my will is that my two sons shall be brought up to Learning without Charge to Them by my Exec^{tr} hereafter named and Put out to traides that they shall Like – Item and of this my Last will and testament I make and ordaine my well Beloved son Nicholas Carr my full and whole Exec^{tr} unto this my will and to see it puntially fullfiled to the Real Intent and meaning; and I do hereby utterly Disallow revoke & make null all and every other former Testament wills Leagicies and bequeathed & Exec^{td} by me in any ways before this time willed and bequeathed Rectified & Confirming this & no other to be my Last will and testament written on two sides of one sheet of paper further I do appoint and order my well Beloved Brothers **Cap^{tn} Thom^{as} Paine** and **Edward Carr** both of James Town to be over seears to see this my will performed In wittness whereof I have here unto sett my hand the day and year above written – [Nicholas Carr]

Witnesses: Caleb Carr, John Bull, and Edwd Carr.

Copy taken of the Record of James Town Book of Land Evidence No. 1: pa 123:124:125 Exam^{d} pr T Hull T Clerk

Endorsed on back: ". . . the Last Will and Testament of Caleb Carr of Newport [*see Item No. 12, above*] Father to Nicholas Carr and Granfather to Thomas Carr And Likewise the Last Will and Testament of Nicholas Carr abovesd he being sonn to the abovesaid Caleb Carr and Father to the abovesd Thomas Carr."

28. Will of Charles Dyre, 1709:

In the Name of God, Amen; the Ninth day of May in the year of Our Lord 1709. I Charles Dyre of the Town of Newport on Rhode Island, in the Colony of Rhode Island and Providence Plantations in New England (Yeoman) being sick and weak of Body but in sound and perfect mind and memory thanks be to God for it; But not knowing how soon it may please God to take me out of this Life Do make and appoint this my last Will and Testament, in manner and form following. Principally and first of all I commend my soul to God that gave it me hoping that by the Merits of Christ it may be saved; and my body I Commit to the Earth from whence it came to be buried in Decemt Christian Burial at the discretion of my Executors hereafter mentioned, and as for what worldly Goods and Estate God hath been pleased me withal I Give and bequeath as in Manner following.

Imprimis. My Will and Desire is that my funeral Charges and Just Debts be Duly and truly paid by my Executrix hereafter named.

Item. I Give unto my son **Jams Dyre** and his Heirs lawfully begotten of his Body in Wedlock, all that my Land and Tenements lying and being in the Town of Little Compton in the County of Bristol in the Province of the Massachusetts Bay in New England, the which he now liveth on, part of which Land I had with my Wife **Martha Dyre**, Together with all the Out Houses and all other Liberties and priviledges thereunto belonging or appertaining to them and their Heirs forever.

Item. I Give unto my son **Samuel Dyre** all this my Land and homestead that I now live on, with the Old end of the Dwelling House that standeth on the said lands. Together with the Barns, Stables, Out Houses and all other [*page* 2] Liberties and priviledges thereunto belonging or appertaining. I Give unto him and to his Heirs Lawfully begotten of his Body in Wedlock unto the third Generation, and them and their Heirs forever, He or they paying such Legacies as I have hereafter mentioned and Ordered to be paid by him or them.

Item. I Give to my said son **Samuel Dyre** all that my Lots of land of Commonage lying in the town of Newport on Rhode Island and facing the Lane or highway near the House Called **Thomas Cases** with all the liberties and priviledges and appurtenances thereunto belonging to him and to his Heirs forever and to be at his or their own Disposal.

Item. I Give unto my son **William Dyre,** One hundred pounds in Current Money Silver of New England to be paid unto him or to his Heirs within Two Years after my decease by my son Samuel Dyre, Out of my Estate that I have given unto him.

Item. I Give unto my son **Charles Dyre,** One hundred pounds in Current Silver Money of New England to be paid unto him or to his Heirs within three years time after my decease and to be paid by my son Samuel Dyre or by his Heirs out of my Estate given him.

Item. I Give unto my Daughter **Elisabeth** the now wife of **Thristram Hull** and to her Heirs the sum of Thirty pounds in Current Silver Money of New England to be paid to her or to her heirs in three years time after my decease and to be paid by my son Samuel Dyre or by his Heirs out of my Estate that I have Given him.

[*page 3 is missing from the photocopy made of the 1768 copy; it is abstracted here from another copy made in 1786*:] The piece of ground now called the Burying Ground shall be continued for the same use unto all my after generations that shall see cause to make use of it . . . to be fenced in by my son Samuel.

Item. I give unto my beloved wife Martha the new end of the house, and then to my son Samuel and his heirs unto the third generation. . . To my wife all the household stuff, etc. . . . six of the best cows and 20 ewe sheep. My son Samuel shall take to keep for my wife two cows, six sheep . . .

The residue of the estate to be divided equally between my four sons **James,**

William, Samuel, and **Charles**. Son Samuel to have necessities for farming. Whosover of the children shall be in any ways troublesome or quarrelsome shall be cut off . . . .

Loving brothers **George Brownell** and **Thomas Cornell** and **Benjamin Thayre** to be overseers, to have £3 apiece for their trouble. Wife Martha to be executrix.

Witnesses: **George Hazzard, Jeffery** [*mark, a simple script J*] **Champlin, Nathl Dyre**.

Newport Rhode Island May 9th 1709 – Personally appeared before Me the Subscriber Charles Dyre, and declared this to be his last [*sic*] and Testament by me Jeffery [his mark J] Champlin Assist

Witnesses Jeffery Champlin and Nathaniel Dyre sworn in Council; said they saw George Hazzard sign also as a witness; will recorded by Nath[anie]l Coddington, Co. Clerk [*no date*].

Copied 15 November 1768 from Newport Town Council Book 4, pages 87, 88, 89, 90, and 91, by Wm. Coddington, Council Clerk. Another copy made, "City of Newport, November the 20th 1786, The within and Aforegoing Contained on Six sides then two Sheets of paper . . . a true copy by me taken and compared . . . Peleg Barker Junr, City Clerk."

Documents and Cases Dated 1710 to 1715

29. 1710, September 20: **Will of Robert Carr.**

In the name of god Amen I Robert Carr of Newport on Rhode Island being Ill of body but through Devine favour of Sound and perfect mind & memory as in my life past Calling to mind the Transitoryness of this life, and knowing that it is Appointed for all men Once to dye doe make and appoint this my last Will & Testament in Manner and form Following

Imprimis first and principally I bequeath my soul into the hands of God that gave it hopeing that through the Merrits death and passion of Jesus Christ my Redeamer to have full and free Remission of all my Sins and to Inherit Everlasting life and my body to the earth from whence it was Taken to be Decently buryed at the Descreation of my Executrix hereafter named And as to the Worldly Estate wch God hath pleased to bestow upon me I Give Will & bequeath as Followeth

Item My will is that all my Just debts & Funeral Charges be first paid and Discharged

Item and all the Rest and Residue of my Estate, Personal and Real Estate Whatsoever and Whersoever I Give will and bequeath unto my Dear and Loveing Mother **Elizabeth Carr** her heires and assignes to have and to hold forever whom I also hereby appoint to be my whole and sole Executrix to this my will allowing this & noe Othere to be my last Will & Testament In Witness whereof I have hereunto set my hand & affixed my seal this Twentyeth day of September in the Ninth year of the Reigne of our Sovereign Lady Ann Queen of Great Brittain &c & in the year of our Lord One Thousand Seven hundred & Ten

Signed Sealed published and Robert Carr (Seal)
Declared by the s^{d} Robert Carr
to be his last Will & Testament
in p^{r}sence of James Honyman, John Langford, Nich^{ls} Lange

Proved 2 October 1710; recorded Newport Town Council 4:40-41 by John Hammett, Clerk. Copied 30 July 1724 by Wm Coddington, Council Clerk

30. 1710[/11]. **The will of Anthony Almy,** dated 18 May 1710 [*two copies found, 24 October 1722 and 2 April 1725; the official copy, Newport Town Council Book 4:152-155, was lost in 1779. An inventory survives.*]

In the name of God Amen I Anthony Almy of the Town of Portsmouth in the Collony of Rhod Island & Providence Plantations &c being of perfect mind & memory thanks be given unto God, and now being bound on a voyage to sea, and calling to mind the mortality of my body not knowing how it may please God to deal with me doe make and ordain this my last will & testament as touching such worldly estate as it hath pleased God to bless me withall in this life I give devise and dispose of the same in manner & form following.

Item. I will & bequeath unto my Honoured Mother **Mary Townsend** all my moveable estate in what kindsoever and all such debts that is due unto me from my brother **Job Almy** upon accompt to be at her own disposeing as she shall think fiting for her better support and maintainance and also all y[e] profits & benifitts of all my lands and dwelings dureing her natural life.

Item. I will and bequeath unto my loveing sister **Susanah Almy** her heires and assigns forever the one half part of a six score acre lott lyeing on the eastward side of Punketest outlett and is the second lott in number and is in Pocaset Purchase.

Item. I will & bequeath unto my four loveing cousins namely **John Hix, Robert Hix, Mary Hix** and **Elizabeth Hix** their heires & assigns forever three fifth parts of a fifty acre lott of land lying in a tract of land commonly called Puncetest Outlett to be equally devided among them and is the tenth lott in number.

Item. I will and bequeath unto my cousen **Samuel Snell** son of **Samuel & Mary Snell** all my rights and interest to and in the twenty fourth lott of land in the first devision in Pocaset Purchase in the County of New Bristoll to him his heires and assignes forever.

Item. I will and bequeath unto my cousin **Christopher Townsend** his heires and assignes forever one half part of a six score acre lott of land lying on the Eastward side of Punketest Outlett being the twenty third lott in number and is in Punketest purchase.

Item. I will and bequeath unto my cousin **Solomon Townsend** and his heires and assignes forever the one half part of a six score acre lott of land being the twentieth lott in number and is in the same devision with the twenty third lott before named.

Item. I will and bequeath to my three cousens namely **Deborah Hix, Anne Townsend** and **Hannah Townsend** all my undevided lands in the Collony of Rhod Island and also all my undevided land in the County of Bristoll in the province of the Massachusetts bay to them their heires and assignes forever to be equally devided amongst them.

[*page* 2] And I doe hereby make constitute and appoint my loveing sister **Deborah Hix** my sole executrix of this my last will and testament, and I doe hereby disallow revoke and disanul all and every former testament will legasie bequest or executors heretofore made or suffered to be made by me in any wise allowing and comfirming this and noe other to be my last will and testament in witness hereof I have hereunto sett my hand & fixed my seal in Newport this eighteenth day of May in the year one thousand seven hundred and ten 1710.

[*signed*] Anthony Almy

Witnesses were **Joseph Goldsmith, Peter Treby Jun[r]**, and **James Carey**.

Treeby and Casey appeared before the Council 7 May 1711 and made Oath that they saw the above said Testator M[r] **Anthony Almy** sign seal publish pronounce and Declare the abovesaid Testament to be his last Will & Testament and that they signed as Witnesses Thereunto and also that **Joseph Goldsmith** signed as a Witness with them and that the said Testator was then in his perfect mind and Memory. Attested pr **John Hammet,** C^{l} Court of Probate

This will was sealed up under cover and was this day delivered to me by M^{s} Deberah Hix which I opened and read to her Newport
April 15th 1711 Sam^{ll} Cranston Govr

Memo - Philadelphia Jan^{ry} 8th 1710 : I **Anthony Almy** being now bound a Voyage to sea and haveing a Quarter part of a Sloop Called the *United Friendship* with all her Utensials as she now is floating in Deleware River and not knowing how it may please God to deal with me: If that I dye before I Returne to Rhode Island I give & Desire that **Deborah Hix** take the above premises into her Coustady as her Own proper Estate to act & Dispose of as she shall think fiting as Witness my hand the Day & Year above Written. [*signed*] Anthony Almy

Capt. Joseph Hinchman of Newport . . . made Oath that Mr **Anthony Almy** late Master of the Sloop *United Friendship* did in his presance write w^{t} is Declared on the Other Side of this leaf and in his Sight did Sign the Same with his Own hand, this leaf then being in the Deponents pocket book and was Cut out the day of the date hereof before me In Testimony whereof I have hereunto set my hand this 16 day of April 1711

[*signed*] **Sam^{ll} Cranston** Govr

This leaf with the writing on the other side is by the Councel approved and allowed of to be part of the Will of Anthony Almy deceased and to be anexed to the othere parts of sd will . . . pr John Hammet C^{l} Coun^{cl}

The forgoeing five pages are True Coppy of Anthony Almy Will as is recorded in the Coun^{cl} book No 4 page 152-153-154 & 155 belonging to Newport April 2 1725 . . . Wm Coddington Town Clerke.

31. 1710, September: **John Knight** now resident in Providence . . . eldest son and heir of **John Knight** late of Norwich in ye Collony of Connecticut deces^{d}: grandson and heir of **Richard Knight** of Newport . . . deces^{d} vs. **Peter Wells, Job Babcock, William Tanner, Isaac Shelden, Joseph Car[pen]ter, Peter Crandall, Samuel Hopkins & Gersham Cotterrell** yeomen all of Kingstowne . . . in a plea of partition, damage £800 as per summons dated 15 July 1710. In their plea, by attorney N. Blagrove, the defendants stated that they held no land in common undivided with the plaintiff . . . what land they hold is in fee simple, having received their title from **Henery Hall,** surviving joint tenant of [*torn*] Knight. **David Knight** and **West Clarke** upon their engagement say that Richard Knight of Newport dec^{d} about 31 years agoe.

32. 1711, March 27. **Caleb Carr** son and heir of **Caleb Carr Senr** of Jamestown who was son and heir of **Robert Carr** deceased, vs. **Joseph**

Fry tenant in possession to **Robert Carr Junr**, deceased, in action of trespass to recover 3½ acres in Newport. In a second case, Caleb Carr vs. **Sarah Jackson** tenant in possession for **Elizabeth Carr** in an action of trespass. It was noted that the plaintiff had deceased, which was cause for the action to abate.

33. 1711. **The will of Abial Macomber** [*copy found in case Barker vs Macomber, 1722, No. 172*]:

In the Name of God Amen I **Abiel Macomber** of Newport on Rhoad Island and Providence Plantations in America Marriner am now bound a Voyage to Sea in the Good Sloop Speedwell and not knowing how it may Please God to deal with me in my Voyage and knowing all Men are Mortal & it is appointed for Man once to Dye and now being in health & perfect memory do make this my Last will and Testament Revoking all other Will or Wills heretofore by me made to be Null and Void Ratifieing and alowing this and no other to be of force and Virtue and as for such Goods and outward Estate as it hath Pleased God to Bless me with all I give & Bequeath as followeth

Item I give and bequeath unto my dearly well beloved wife **Susanna Macomber** of Rhoad Island afores[d] all and singular my Goods Chattles Lands Tennements Debts and Sums of Money due owing or Belonging to me any manner of Ways whatsoever or wheresoever and all just sums or sums of Money goods Wares Accompts or what so ever Else shall or may be due or belonging to me hereafter or any ways appertaining to me and I Constitute and appoint Susanna Macomber aforesaid to be Sole Executrix of this my last Will and Testament in Wittness hereof I have hereunto Set my hand and affixed my Seal this Twenty fourth day of September in the Tenth Year of her Majesties Reign Ann Queen of Great Brittain &c Anno Domini 1711

Signed Sealed Published
and Pronounced in Presence
of us the subscribers [*signed*] Abiel Macomber
Ann Brewer
Philip Walker
Jeremiah Childs

Brewer and Childs were sworn 7 January 1722 by William Coddington, clerk of council, and said "it was soe long since that they cannot Remember how it was done . . .."

34. 1711/12, 18 January. **The will of William Collins of Newport** [*copy found in case Collins vs. Tippets, 1725*]:

The testator declared himself very sick and weak, and after the usual preamble about his soul and body, left

. . . to wife **Sarah Collins** one end of my Mansion House during her Natural

Life together with all Household goods Stuff or Furniture w^{t} nature kind or sort whatsoever to be Possessed Enjoyed and Disposed of to her Discretion as also the House on the west End of my Tann Yard to Sell or Dispose of as she sees cause.

Item . . . unto my beloved son William Collins all my Mansion House in said Newport Excepting one End thereof given to his Mother during her Natural Life . . . also a Farm at Naraganset in the Jurisdiction of the Town of Warwick containing about 413 acres as also a Tann Yard in said Newport Excepting what is hereafter Excepted together with my Negro Man Named **Jack** . . . to be possessed . . . when he shall arrive to the Age of 21 years.

Item . . . unto my two Eldest Daughters Namely **Ann** and **Sarah** the House in my Tann Yard the which Dunham and Allin lives in and a piece of land thereunto adjoining the full Depth of the House in length to extend itself Quite a Cross the said Tann Yard to be equally divided between them . . . and to be possessed and Enjoyed by them when they shall arrive to the Age of 18 years . . . Also unto each £50 in current money of New England [at age 18]. Item . . . unto youngest Daughter named **Elizabeth** my House and Land at Green Inn in the Township of Newport containing about 10 acres [at 18].

Lastly I do hereby Nominate Constitute and appoint my trusty and well beloved Brother in Law **Daniel Whitman** and beloved wife Executor and Executrix . . .."

[*signed*] Wm Collins.

Witnessed by **William Martin, James Allen, and John Hammett**. A Memorandum was added, giving to son William Collins £200 at age 21, he to pay to "my said wife £10 Annually during her Natural Life; date and witnesses were the same as for the will. It was proved 4 February 1712 by witnesses John Hammett and James Allen, and recorded 6 February 1712 by Richard Ward, Clerk of Council.

35. 1712: The Will of **John Holmes**:

The Last will and Testament of John Holmes of Newport after my funerall Charges and Just Debts be Paid I Give unto my Son John Holmes and his heirs all that my house and Land Lying in Point Juda in Petesquamscut Purchase in Kings Town Containing three Hundred acres more or less Bounded south by Land of **Thomas** and **John Potter** Westerly by land of **Jahleel Brenton**, and Point Juda Pond Northerly by Land of **Thomas Mumford** East by the sea.

Also I Give unto my son John Holmes and his heirs one acre and three quarters of Land in Newport it being on the Eastern part of my Land by **Mr Bliss** Mill which was Called Common Land.

Also I Give unto my Son **John Holmes** the one half of all my wareing Cloaths wollin and Linnen.

Also I Give unto my Son John Holmes my Silver bowle marked **J H**, and Twelve Pounds in silver moneye my four shares in the Town Wharfe & all my working Gear.

Also my will is that my Son John Holmes Pay unto my wife **Mary Holmes** Ten Pounds pr Year Dureing her Naturall Life.
I Give unto my Son **William Holmes** all that my house & Land Lying in Newport which I bought of **Henry Bull** To him and his heirs Bounded South by Land of **Francis Brindley** west by the Cove or salt water northerly by Land of Capt: **Nathaniell Paine** Easterly by the Streett or High way It being forty foott front Also I Give unto my Son and his heirs Two acres and three Quarters of Land Lying in Newport it being the westerly Part of my Land by Major Bliss mill which was formerly Called Common.
Also I Give unto my Son **William Holmes** and heirs a Lott of Land which I bought of the Town Bounded Northerly by a Two Rod highway Easterly by the Broad Streett Southerly by Land of **William Sanford** Westerly by Land of **John Balley** Said Land being four Rods and four fifths of a Rod in Breadth & Also I Give unto my Son William Holmes and his heirs all my Land Lying in Swandsey in the County of Bristoll Divided and undivided the Divided being three Hundred & Eighty acres Bounded south ward by Land of **Sam^ll^ Gardiner** westerly by the salt water or Cove northerly by Land of **Zachariah Luther** Easterly by Land of **Ralph Chapman** also I Give unto my Son Willm Holmes my Large Silver Tankard after my wifes Decease as also the other Half of my wareing Cloaths wollin and Linnen also my will is that my Son William Pay Unto my wife Mary Holmes Ten Pounds pr Year Dureing her Natural Life.
I Give unto my Daughter **Kathrine Gardiner** fifty Pounds in Money Besides the fifty Pounds before Given her by me.
I Give unto my Daughter **Frances Carr** Eighty Pounds in money Besides the twenty Pounds already I have Given her.
I Give unto my Daughter **Ann Peckham** Seventy Pounds in money Besides the Lott of Land I have already Given her in Newport Bounded South by a high way west by **John Ellerys** Land North by **Richard Higgins** Land East by **Freegift Coggeshall** Land –
I Give unto my Daughter **Deborah Holmes** one Hundred Pounds in Money
I Give unto my Daughter **Phebe Holmes** one Hundred Pounds in Money; the above said Legacies to be Paid within one whole Year after my Decease by my Executor hereafter named –
Further I Give unto my Loving Wife **Mary Holmes** my Dwelling house That now I Live in Dureing her Naturall Life, and the Lott of Land I Bought of Major **Nathaniell Coddington** and the one Third of all the Rest of my Moveable Estate that I have not Disposed of In Lieu of her Thirds.
The other Two Thirds of my Estate Undisposed of I Give Unto my two Sons and my two Daughters John and William and Deborah and Phebe Equally to be Divided amongst them; for my Executors are my wife Mary Holmes and my Son John Holmes and my Son William Holmes –
Further I Give unto my Son **John Holmes** at my Decease that Shop that now he works in and the house that now he Lives in and half the Garden and half the wharfe beelow the house untill he comes to Injoy my Dwelling house that

now I Live in and then that house and Land to Return unto my Son William – [*A line of large loops separates the document at this point*]

Whereas it hath Pleased God Suddenly to take our father out of this Life, before he had Put his house in order as the Law Directs, Yett notwithstanding we being sencable that the foregoing and above written was his mind and will which wee the Subscribers his Children by no means will alter change or make Void so far as it can be understood to be his True meaning & for the Explaining thereof according to our Conseption of the Premises wee all agree [*illegible*] to the Content and Receive as our full Legacies or Shares of our Deceased fathers Estate (vizt) **John Holmes** to have ye house and Land In Poynt Juda one acre and three quarters of Land in Newport four shares of the Town Wharf forthwith and the Dwelling house in which our said Father when Liveing Dwelt in and the Lott or Garden Bought of **Maj. Coddington** after his mother **Mary Holmes** Decease wch legacies are his full Proportion of the fee simple in s^{d} Estate and the Goods and Chattels as is Expressed in ye foregoing and above witten together with ye Shop he now works in.

And that **William Holmes** shall have as his full Proportion of our Deceased Fathers Estate all the houses and Lands in Swansey in the County of Bristoll which to sd Estate Did belong and that forthwith and the whole of that house and Land which our father bought of **Henry Bull** in Newport Saveing a Reserve of that Part of the House and Land, in and on which the said John Holmes Lives is to Remain in his Possession, and for his use untill he shall Come to Enjoy our said Deceased Fathers Mansion House and apurtenances and then the whole of said House and Land to appertain to said William Holmes and his heirs forever Together with one Lot bought of the Town, and Two acres and three quarters of the Land formerly Newport Common And also all the Chattels in our father's foregoeing Intended will mentioned and that out of the Remainder of our Deceased fathers Goods Moneys Rights or Creditts **Cathrine Gardiner** shall have and take fifty Pounds in money for her full Proportion or Legacie of the whole Estate aforesaid

And that **Francis Carr** shall have and Receive in full satisfaction out of the Said Estate as her Part or Legacie thereof the sum of Eighty Pounds money.

and that Ann Peckham shall have and Receive in full satisfaction of her Part or Legacie in said Remainder of said Estate the sum of seventy Pounds in money.

And that **Deborah Manchester** late **Deborah Holmes** shall have one Hundred Pounds in Money as her full Part or Proportion of said Estate and in which she takes satisfaction and content. And that **Pheby Holmes** shall have the sum of one Hundred Pounds in Money out of ye sd Estate which shee shall have and Receive as her full Proportion Legacie or Part thereof all which Parts or Proportions we Conceive the true Intent and meaning of our Deceased fathers will and which we Readily comply with, and for the Remainder of the Goods Chattels Rights and Credits belonging to said Estate and not Expressly Given in said will we unanimously agree that the same and Every Part thereof shall be Equally Divided between John Holmes William Holmes Deborah Manchester and Pheby Holmes as in said will is Expressed allowing Every article and Clause therein to Be Duely Observed by Each Person Concerned therein for the Complying therewith and the Performance thereof according to the true intent and meaning wee subscribe our hands and fix our seals this fourth Day of October in the Eleventh year of the Queens Reigne Annoqui Domi 1712

Signed Sealed [by] John Holmes William Holmes Joseph Gardner Nicholas Carr Ann Peckham John Manchester Phebey Holmes
In the presence of Weston Clarke [and] Nicho^s^ Lang
The subscribers acknowledged their signatures before Sam^ll^ Cranston Govr the same day, and witnesses Clarke and Lang attested them.
"Ordered that the same be Placed to Record in the Councell Book.
Attested by John Hammet Clarke of the Council, Newport Novemb^r^ the 12/1712. A true Coppy of the Will of Mr John Holmes Tacken out of the Town Councell Book of Newport N° 5 as also the True Coppy of the articles of agreement between the above Subscribers June the 15th 1716 attest Wm Coddington Clark Councell"

35A. 1713, December 5. The Will of Giles Slocum. [*This record was one of two Newport wills found in the Bristol County Registry of Deeds in Taunton, Massachusetts, in 1985, badly faded and torn, among a pile of original deeds. It probably relates to a Bristol County Court Case ca. 1729. This compiler has a photocopy; the original was turned over to the Bristol County Registrar of Deeds. The other will was that of Thomas Ward, No. 4A. This will was previously printed, along with revised genealogical information on Giles*^{2} *Slocum, in* Rhode Island Roots, *17 (1993), 7-9.*]

To all People To whom these Presents Shall Come Know Yee That I **Giles Slocum** of Newport in ye Collony of Rhoad Island and Providence Plantations in New England in America being by Gods Mercy of a Good Understanding and Perfect Memory but Very Sick and Weak in Body Do make and Constitute this my Last Will and Testament in Manner and form as followeth.

Imprimis. My Mind and Will is y^t^ all my Just and Lawfull Debts be Truly paid within Convenient Time after my Decease by my Exc^rs^ hereafter named

Item I Give unto my Two Sons **Giles Slocum** and **John Slocum** Equally To be Divided between Them and To their and To Either of their Heirs and assigns for ever all my farm now in ye Possession of **Jonathan Talman** which Lyeth att a Place Called ye Ware or Pascomansett River (in ye Township of Dartmouth in ye County of Bristoll) on ye West Side of Said River and four acres and one half on ye East Side of said River Together with ye forty acres of Land Lately Laid out on ye Westward of ye Said Farm and one Whole Quarter of a Share of ye undivided Land both upland and Meadow from y^e^

Division of the Eight Hundred acre Lotts, Together with ye Housings, Fences, Profitts and Priviledges Thereunto belonging.

Item. I Give to my son **John Slocum** To him his heirs and assigns for ever all my Orchard in ye Township of Portsmouth in ye Collony afforesaid.

Item. I give and bequeath To my Daughter **Elizabeth Earll** and To ye heirs Lawfully Begotten of her Body one and Twenty acres of upland already Laid out adjoyning To ye Land of her husband **Joseph Earle** in ye Township of Dartmouth afforesaid also I Give to my Daughter **Elizabeth** my Negro woman **Bess** and one Good pair of Sheets.

[*Page 2*] Item. I Give and bequeath To my Son **Joseph Slocum** and to his heirs and assigns for Ever my now Dwelling house and out houses, in ye Township of Newport with Fifty acres of Land in said Township on ye South Side of my Farm beginning att a Maple Tree standing in ye Wall att ye Westward of my Orchard below ye house, and To Extend Northward upon a Streight Line, Six Rods Westward of ye Well and Three Rodds Northward of ye Said Well beyond ye old Orchard and To Extend Eastward Through ye Farm up To ye Main or Great Road To make up Fifty acres of Land, also I Give unto my Said Son Joseph Slocum and To his heirs and assigns for Ever ye Two Eighteen acre Lotts, ye one Purchased of **Thomas Lyllibridge** and ye other of **John Easton**, also four acres and an half more Purchased of **Thomas Cornwall** and Eight acres more Purchased of **Jonathan Nickolls**, and three acres more Purchased of **Ephraim Bull** and his Sister **Mary Coggeshall** as by Deeds under all their hands & seals may more att Large appear and To Come into his Possession when he Shall attain To ye Age of Eighteen Years Together with all ye Profitts and Priviledges Thereunto Belonging, also I Give unto my Son Joseph Slocum Priviledge To Cut Firewood for his Own Use, in ye Swamp (herein Given to my Son Peleg) Dureing ye Space of Twelve Years and Priviledge to Carry of ye Same.

Item. I Give and Bequeath To my Son **Peleg Slocum** and to his heirs and assigns for Ever all ye Remaining part of my Farm in ye Township of Newport afores^d^, Being one hundred and Thirty acres of Land be It more or Less and To Come Into his Possession when he shall attain To ye age of Eighteen Years but If Either of my Two Sons Joseph or Peleg Dye Before they Come To Possess ye Said Land Given Unto y^m^ My Will is the Survivor Shall Enjoy all my Land In Newport and to be and Remain unto him, his heirs and assigns for Ever.

[*Page 3*] Item. Whereas my Wife Is now with Child and If It Shall happen to be a Son y^t^ y^n^ I Do Give and Bequeath unto him, his heirs and assigns for Ever, all my farm which Lyeth in ye Neck Commonly Called Nomquid Neck within ye Township of Dartmouth afforesaid and one whole Quarter of a Share of ye undivided Land Both upland and meddow from ye Last Divisions of ye Eight hundred acre Lotts Together with ye Housing Fences Profitts and Priviledges thereunto belonging But If It shall happen To be a Daughter, y^n^ I Give and Bequeath ye Said Houseing and Land with ye Profits and Priviledges Equally to be Divided Between my Two Sons **Joseph**

Slocum and **Peleg Slocum** & to their or Either of their heirs and assigns for Ever they paying To ye said Child If a Daughter Fifty pounds apeice when she shall attain To ye age of Eighteen years or Day of Marriage, which shall first happen.

Item. I Give unto my Daughter **Mary Coggeshall** ye Use & Benefitt of all my houseing and Land which Lyeth in ye Said Nomquid Neck for and Dureing ye Space of Ten years and to Begin as soon as ye Lease of Henry Howland be Expired.

Item. My Will is y^t^ my Two Sons **Joseph** and **Peleg** shall Pay unto their mother when they Come to Possess the Lands Three Pounds apeice in or Equivolent To money Yearly and Every Year Dureing her Natural Life, But If Either of my Two Sons Dye Before they Come To Possess ye Lands Given y^m^ y^n^ ye Survivor shall pay ye whole sum afforesaid.

Item. I give unto my Two Daughters **Martha Slocum** and **Ann Slocum** Forty pounds in money To be Lett out To use by my Exc^rs^ and Executrix hereafter named Untill my Said Daughters shall attain To ye Age of Eighteen Years or Day of their Marriage which shall first happen, and then To be Delivered unto y^m^ with ye Intrest also I Give unto my Said Daughters Martha and Ann all my Household Goods [*Page 4*] whatsoever to be Equally Divided Between them Except what Is herein Given unto my Loveing Wife, **Mary Slocum**, also I Give unto my Said Daughters Martha and Ann four Good Cows and Twenty Good Ewes Sheep Equally Between y^m^ and To be Delivered unto y^m^ Together with all ye Household Goods when they shall attain To ye age of Eighteen Years or Day of their Marriage by my Exc^rs^ or Exe^trix^, But If Either of my Said Daughters Martha or Ann Dye Before they attain To ye age of Eighteen Years or Day of Marriage ye Survivor shall Enjoy ye Legacy of ye Deceas^d^.

Item. I Give unto my Grand Children **Ann Whipple** and **William Almy** five shillings apeice to be Delivered within one year after my Decease.

Item. I Give unto my Grandson **Giles** [*over a name blotted out*] **Coggeshall**, Five Pounds to be Delivered unto him within one year after my Decease.

Item. I Give unto my Grandson **Giles Slocum** my Young Roan Mare.

Item. I Give To my Grand Daughter **Sarah Russell** Ten Good Sheep when she attains To ye age of Eighteen years If she Demands them.

Item. I Give and Bequeath To my Loveing Wife **Mary Slocum** all ye household Goods she Brought with her and my Indian Girls **Audry** & **Sarah** she Performing Their Covenant, also I Give unto my Wife ye whole use and Benefitt of all my housing and Land in ye Township of Newport with all my Goods and Chattles and ye Benefitt of my Two Indian Servant Boys as Long as she Remains my Widdow for her Support and Bringing up of my Children.

Item. What Is above mentioned Given unto my Loving Wife Is In Lieu of her Thirds.

Item. After all my Just Debts and ye Legacy herein Given are paid all ye Rest and Residue of my Personall Estate whatsoever I Give and Bequeath unto my Two Sons – **Joseph** and **Peleg**, to be Equally Divided Between them and To be Delivered unto y^{m} by Exc^{rs} & Exc^{trix} when they attaine To ye age of Eighteen Years But If Either Joseph or Peleg Dye before they attain to ye age affores^{d} my Will is y^{t} ye Legacy of ye Deceased be Equally Divided between my Two Daughters **Martha** and **Ann Slocum**.

Item. My Will is If my Wife **Mary Slocum** Marry before my four Children (Vizt) **Joseph, Peleg, Martha,** and **Ann Slocum** attain To ye Age of Eighteen Years, then my Son Giles Slocum whom I Do appoint and ordain my Exc^{r} with my Son Joseph Slocum, to this my Will, shall have full Power To Take Into their Possession all my Estate in Newport Given to my Children (Viz^{t}) Joseph Peleg Martha & Ann Slocum Together with my Indian Servants to Improve To ye Best Use and advantage for my four Children untill they attain To ye age of Eighteen Years.

Lastly I Do appoint and Constitute my Well Beloved Wife Mary Slocum my Exct^{rix} with my Son Giles and my Son Joseph Slocum to this my Last Will and Testament Dureing her Widdowhood, But If my Wife Marry her Executrixship to Cease & Determine and my Son Giles Slocum and my Son Joseph Slocum to be my Sole Exc^{rs} to this my Last Will and Testamunt and To See y^{t} It be Duly Performed in Every Article according To ye True Intent and meaning of ye same and I Do hereby Revoke Disannull and make Void all and Every other former Testaments & Wills by me in any Wise before this time named In Wittness y^{t} this is my Last Will & Testament I have hereunto sett my hand and seal this twenty fith Day of ye Tenth Month Called December in ye Year of our Lord one Thousand seven hundred and Thirteen 1713.

Witnesses were **Sarah Coggeshall** (who signed by mark *S*), **Hope Sanford**, and **Wm Sanford**. The two Sanfords appeared in Council (date not given) to attest their signatures before Richard Ward, Council Clerk. The copy of the will made 4 July 1729 by Wm Coddington, Council Clerk at that time, includes the notation that it was recorded in Newport Town Council Book No. 5, pages 6, 7, and 8.

36. In a deposition dated 12 March 1713/4 before Sam^{ll} Cranston, Govr, **Thomas Thurston**, aged 24 years or thereabouts, stated that he and "others Employed by **Jahleel Brenton** of Newport Esq. hath severall times in these last four years past mended up the partition fence between Brentons land called Rocky farme and **Fregift Coggeshalls** land, and severall times carted Railes and other Stuf there to mend the sd fence the Railes having many times been lost, which [I] doe believe were thrown down by gunners and all others comeing into the sd Brentons land, and carryed away with the tide in the creek, near which the sd fence is made, and . . . dureing the time aforesd . . . have severall times seen Abraham Coggeshall with his Gun and his Dogg or Doggs in the sd Rocky Farme."

On 1 April 1714 before Wm Wanton, Assistant, **Joseph Bell** aged 22 years or there about testified that he with other persons was employed by Jahleel Brenton of Newport, Esq., "has severall times since the month of March 1713 before the first of February last mended up the sd Brentons fence at Rockey Farme and Hammersmith Lands thereto adjoyning . . . has seen persons, unknown to him, in less than an hours time pull downe the fence so mended up, that some time the begining of the last Winter . . . Brenton sent one of his Servants to fetch up a sheep bitten by a Dogg or Doggs, which was allmost Dead . . . divers other Sheep bitten by Doggs . . . deponent has this last winter seen a great many persons going over Rockey Farme with their guns and Doggs . . . on the 27 day of Novmber last [he] and **Isaac Neebe** were ordered by the sd Brenton to drive about 60 Head of Cattle from Hammersmith to Rockey Farme, which accordingly they did doe, but the same day the sd cattle came back againe to Hammersmith, all over wett and dirty . . . this deponent thinks they run through the pond by the Marshes of Rockey farme . . . Isaac drove [them] to Rockey Farme againe on the thirtieth of November this Deponent and the sd Isaac went to Rockey Farme to fother the sd Cattle in Jefferys Neck and as they went thither they found one of the best and vantage heifers dead in the aforesd pond, and as they were driving the rest of the sd cattle to Jefferys Neck the cattle run back againe upon the sd Isaac, this deponent being at some distance . . . asked him what frighted the Cattle, he answered that Abraham Coggeshall with his gun and his dogg met them upon the end of the beach and frighted them back againe . . . on or about the fifth day of January Brenton sent severall persons to Rockey Farme to fetch home the cattle in order to put the heifers that were with calf, and others of the poorest of the cattle, amongst his cows att Hammersmith, which accordingly was done, and a little before noon on the same day Brenton ordered [him] and others to drive the rest of the cattle to Rockey Farme again . . . as [they] were driving the cattle . . . they saw three men in Brentons land one of them had a gun and an other of them had a pole, these three persons meeting the sd Cattle frighted them back againe, and the sd cattle run all the remainder of that day, two of them were quite tired and were left in the woods in Hammersmith, another of them being the largest two and vantage steer amonst them was allso tired and left in the evening near Rockey farme house and the next morning early was dead on the same place he was left the evening before . . . does believe that the heifer that was dead in the pond as aforesd was frighted in there by the guners . . .."

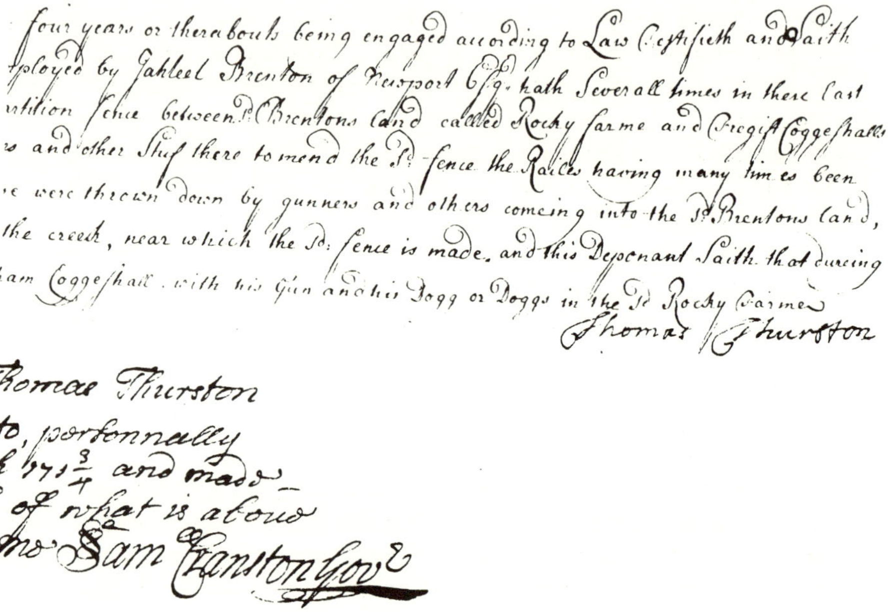
four years or thereabouts being engaged according to Law Certifieth and Saith
ployed by Jahleel Brenton of Newport Esq. hath Severall times in there last
rtition fence between sd Brentons Land called Rocky farme and Gregist Coggeshalls
s and other Stuf there to mend the sd fence the Railes having many times been
e were thrown down by gunners and others comeing into the sd Brentons Land,
the creek, near which the sd fence is made. and this Deponant Saith that dureing
am Coggeshall . with his Gun and his Dogg or Doggs in the sd Rocky farme
Thomas Thurston

Thomas Thurston
to, personnally
h 1713/4 and made
of what is above
me Sam Cranston Gov

Detail from Thomas Thurston's deposition

General Court of Trials — March 1714

37. **Stephen Hazard** of Kingstown, yeoman, and **Elizabeth** his wife, one of the children and daughters of **Rows Helme** late of Kingstown, yeoman, deceased, vs. Rows Helme of Kingstown, yeoman, executor of the will of Rows Helme, in action of detinue . . . to render goods and chattels to ye vallue of £23:14:9, it being one-sixth part of one-half part of the inventory of the deceased. Writ dated 1 February 1713/14; N. Blagrove attorney.

Copy of nuncupative will of Rows Helme: We whose names are here under written [**Mary Coggeshall** and **Ezek^{ll} Bull**] being present, wth Mr Rowse Helms of Kingstown late deceased a few days before his death, but while he was in his right mind, and heard him say how he would have his Estate setled which by reason of his wifes Death after his Will was made needed some farther Settlement, which was as followeth or to this purpose Viz^t -

That Considering the great help his wife would have been to the maintaining and Looking after of **William** (If she had Lived) wch now would lye wholly on his son **Rowse** (whom he ordered to take the Care and Charge of him) therefore his wifes part or right in the will he gave to his son Rowse, and some other things he setled by words at the same time.

The above evedances was tacken be foar me at Newport the 21st day of the 8th m^o 1713 . . . John Wanton Justice [recorded p. 187 of Kingstown Record Book 1, 9 November 1713, pr Sam^{ll} Fones, Town Clerk]

38. **Magdalen Fromoget** of Newport, executrix of the will of **Magdalen Royer**, widow, deceased, vs. **John Hardouin De Latouch** of Newport, gentleman, in an action of trover. Writ dated 6 July 1714.

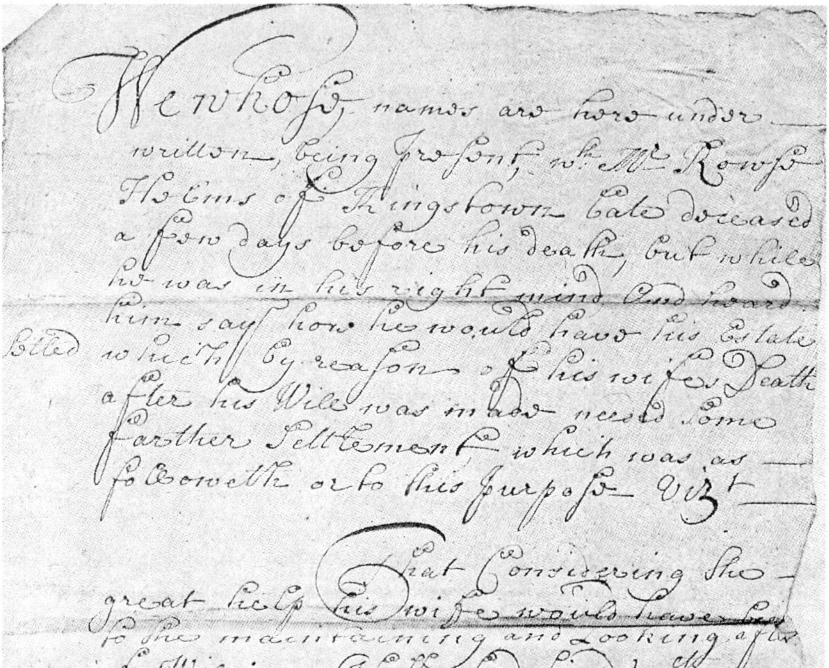

Wee whose names are here under written, being present, wth Mr Rowse Helms of Kingstown late deceased a few days before his death, but while he was in his right mind And heard him say how he would have his Estate Setled which by reason of his wifes Death after his Will was made needed some farther Settlement which was as followeth or to this purpose Vizt

That Considering the great help his wife would have bin to the maintaining and Looking after of William (If she had Lived) wch now would lye wholly on his Son Rowse (whom he ordered to take the Care and Charge of them) therefore his wifes part or right in the will he gave to his Son Rowse, and some other things he ~~gave~~ Setled by words at the same time

Mary Coggeshall

Ezek Bull

The above evidences was taken be fore me at Newport the 21 day of the 8 mo 1713

John Wanton Justis

Rowse Helme's nuncupative will, 1713,
attested by Ezekiel Bull and Mary Coggeshall [No. 37]

General Court of Trials — 1715

39. **George Stanton** formerly of y[e] parrish of Easeington in y[e] County of Hertford in the Kingdome of Great Brittain but late of Newport, gardner, and **Elizabeth** his wife daughter of the late **John Wetherhead** late of Hunslett in the County of York in y[e] kingdome aforesd, clothier, vs. **William Wood** of Newport, yeoman, y[e] only surviveing executor of the last will and testament of **Joseph Wetherhead** late of Newport, weaver, deceased, in action of trespass and ejection for withholding from the plaintiff the possession of a tract of land containing 43 acres or thereabout . . . arable, pasture and meddow land with all the houseing & outhouseing & fences . . . scituate in Newport . . . butted and bounded southerly partly by a highway and partly by land of **Henery Hopson**, westerly partly by land of **Thomas Rogers** and partly by land of Henerey Hopson, northerly partly by land of Thomas Rogers and partly by land of **Jeremiah Clarke**, easterly partly by land of **Robert Taylor** in possession of **John Taylor** and partly by land of Jeremiah Clarke. Writ dated 20 July 1715; N. Blagrove, Attorney (an earlier writ was dated 30 December 1714). Said land was of the estate of Joseph Wetherhead, whereof he died seized and by his last will & testament dated 16 September 1710 and proved before the Towne Councill of Newport did among other things give & bequeath unto his eldest brother John Wetherhead to him his heires & assignes for ever, all his houseing and lands in Newport containing by estimation 43 acres . . . and the sd John Wetherhead by his last will and testament dated 21 September 1711 and duely proved in the Prerogative Court in London 19 November 1712 . . . after y[e] giveing of severall summs of money as legacys the remainder of his estate both real and personal in New England in America and in Great Brittain or else where he gives devises & bequeathes unto his eldest daughter Elizabeth Stanton wife of George Stanton . . . . Nevertheless y[e] aforesd William Wood executor . . . alltho often requested . . . refuses to deliver . . . .

Letter from **George Clarke** dated at Hunslet, 23 June 1711 [*note on back:* "The Rev. Mr. George Clarke's letter to **Peter Marshall**]. "I receiv'd yours on Saturday last and have communicated y[e] contents of it to John Weatherhead and put him into a very agr[eable] surprize, and to several other substantial inhabitants in y[e] Town of Hunslet who in conjunction with me have agreed to make him all y[e] assistance we are capable of. He's reduc'd poor man to y[e] lowest ebb of fortune and his needy circumstances loudly call for relief. You have done S^{r} a generous act, for wch we think y^{w} worthy of our greatest commendations . . . . We think it very sham[?eful] y^{t} ye executors sd conceal his death [*torn*] and are apt to conclude they have no good design in view . . . . If you 'l be so kind as to consult with **Mr Honnyman** which method will be best for us to take on this occasion in order to recover ye estate."

Will of Joseph Wetherhead of Newport, weaver,

. . . being very weake in Body But of Perfect Mind & Memory thanks be Given unto God Therefore Calling to mind the Mortality of my Body knowing that it is Appoynted for all men Once to die Do make and Ordain this my Last Will and Testament in the following Manner and form

First and Principally I Recommend my Soule into the Hand of Almighty God that Gave it me, And for my Body I Recommend To the Earth To be Buried in Christian and Desent Manner according to the Discression of my Executors hereafter Named, and as Touching Such worldly Estate wherewith it hath pleased God to bless me in this Life I Give Devise & Dispose of as followeth

First after my Just Debts and funerall Charges be paid

Imp^{rs} // I Give and Bequeath to my Eldest Brother **John Wetherhead** to him his Heirs & Assignes for Ever all my Houseing and Lands in Newport aforesaid Containing by Estimation Fourty Three Acres be it more or Less Together with Twenty six Sheep and all my Househould Stuff Loomb and Implements whatsoever.

Item // I Give and Bequeath to my Loveing friend **Jane Nickolson the Elder** five Pounds in Money.

Item // I Give and Bequeath to my Loveing friend **Jane Nicholson the younger** five Pounds in Money

Item I Give and Bequeath to my Loveing friend **Joseph Ward** five Pounds in Money.

All the Rest of my Money and Bills Containing Two Hundred and five Pounds, I Give and Bequeath to my Aforesaid Brother John Wetherhead to him his Heirs and Assignes

Item // I Give and Bequeath unto **William Brown** Grandson of **Joseph Nicholson** my Gun.

Item // Of this my Last Will & Testament I Do Appoint Constitute and Ordain my Two Loveing friends Joseph Nicholson of Portsmouth, and William Wood of Newport to be my Executors to this my Last Will and Testament to see that this my Will be Truely Performed According to the True Intent and meaneing of the Same.

And for their Trouble and Paines I Give to Each of them fourty shillings a year yearely and Every year Out of the Estate aforesaid

Ratifieing Allowing and Confirming this to be my Last Will and Testament Revoakeing all Other Testaments and Wills Heretofore by me Made and Confirmed In Witness Whereof I have hereunto set my hand and seale this sixteenth Day of September In the year of our Lord One Thousand Seven Hundred and Ten *1710*

Joseph Wetherhead

Witnesses: John (mark I) Bayly, John Wood, William Sanford

Proved at Newport 2 October 1710, and copied out of Council Records 23 July 1712, John Hammet Clarke of the Councill

Deposition of **Jonathan Leathley** of Blossoms Inn in the Parrish of St. Lawrence Jewry London, Tapster, and **William Robinson** of Bricklane in Spittlefeilds in the parish of St. Dunstans Stepney in the County of Middlesex, Weaver, made oath 20 August 1714 that they well knew and for many years were well acquainted with John Witherhead late of Hunslett in the County of York, Clothier and that he dyed about two yeares since. Jonathan Leathley saith that he hath frequently heard from the said John Witherhead as from severall of his Relations & others that [he] had a Brother named Joseph Witherhead and that the said Joseph dyed in Rood Island in New England and left his estate to the said John Witherhead. William Robeison [*sic*] saith that he personally knew & was well acquainted with the said Joseph Witherhead the Brother of the said John . . . Joseph went beyond the seas many years agoe and dyed (as [he] has been informed) about four years since att Rood Island . . . & left his estate to his said Brother John. Both these Deponents say that they verry well know Elizabeth the now wife of George Stanton and have knowne her from her Childhood and say that [she] is one of the Daughters of the said John Witherhead borne in lawfull wedlock and is now of the Age of Two & thirty yeares or thereabouts . . . they have been credibly informed & believe that the said John Witherhead after having bequeathed by his last Will & Testament severall pecuniary legacies Gave by the same Will the Residue of his estate both Reall and Personall as well in New England as in Great Brittaine to his said Daughter Elizabeth Stanton . . . and made her sole Executrix . . . they are likewise well acquainted with the said George Stanton the husband of the said Elizabeth and have knowne him for severall years last past And say that the said George Stanton is a Short man of a pale complexion wearing his own Haire & having a Mole on his right Cheeck and is now of the Age of Thirty yeares or thereabouts . . . [he] went from London for Bristoll (about the month of August last past) In order to take ship there and saile for New England in quest of such estate as the said Joseph Witherhead dyed possessed of in New England . . . arrived in New England about the month of December last and is now att the house of Mr **Augustus Lucas** Merch^t^ in Rood Island.

Deposition of **Peter Marshall**, 6 September 1715, before **Nicho[s] Lang**, J.P.: deponent was well acquainted with Mr Joseph Weatherhead late of Newport deceased . . . had at several times discoursed with him concerning a brother of his named John Weatherhead that lived at Hunslett in Yorkshire . . . was a weaver by trade and he had been an apprentice to his brother John . . . doth not remember that any time he mentioned any brother except John . . . . At funeral of Mr Weatherhead Mr Nicolson one of the Executors of sd Joseph asked this Deponent if he knew Joseph & John Weatherhead and whether he knew the town where John Weatherhead lived to which this deponent answered that he knew Joseph very well and where he had lived in England - but pauseing a little to recollect . . . the sd Mr Nicolson went away as if not willing to take an answer whereupon this deponent believeing that [he] was not desirous to find out or send word to the said John concerning his brother Joseph's death he did some months after write to Mr **George Clark** minister of Hunslett in Yorkeshire giving him an account of said Joseph Weatherhead's death & devise of his estate . . .received an answer from Mr Clarke dated the 23[d] of June 1711 where in he wrote the said John was then alive . . .deponent doth verily believe that John Weatherhead the father of Elizabeth Stanton the present plaintiff was the same John Weatherhead to whom the said Joseph Weatherhead did bequeath his estate in Rhoad Island for that [he] hath heard the said Joseph say that his brother John had children . . . .

Joseph Cundall of Portsmouth, ffuller, signed a statement that in February twelve months last past he was at the Towne of Leeds in Yorkshire . . .in Company w[th] **Abraham Anthony** the Younger (who formerly liv'd at Newport in this Collony) and at the same time the second son of John Wetherhead of Hunslett near Leeds . . . was in Company wth them and ye sd Abraham Anthony was at that time indeavouring to purchase of ye sd Wetherhead all his right & Interest of a certain Estate w[ch] Joseph Wetherhead had left to his ffather John Wetherhead by will & in w[ch] Estate one **Willm Wood** . . . is at present in poss'ion in this Collony . . . was Inform'd that [Anthony] offer'd . . . £300 . . . But after [Anthony] brought an attorney to ye sd Wetherhead [he] heard some of ye people in the house say that the reason [Anthony] did not purchase [it] of the sd Wetherhead was because he could not make it out whether his Eldest Brother was dead or no and therefore could not make himselfe appeare to be right heir to ye said Estate (His sd Eldest Bro[ther] as this Depon[en]t has been told having some time before beene gone into the Warrs & not since heard of.)

Thomas Lillybridge signed [by mark] a statement before Nichos Lang, J.P., 8 September 1715 that "some time before the last sickness of Mr Joseph Wetherhead late of Newport . . . [he] had at severall times discourse with said Joseph Weatherhead concerning his Brother John Weatherhead then in England . . . told him his Brother John was a broad weaver and that he was a Yorkshire man and that he was formerly an apprentice to his said brother . . . and uppon some disgust left his said Brothers service some time before his apprenticeship was out . . . .

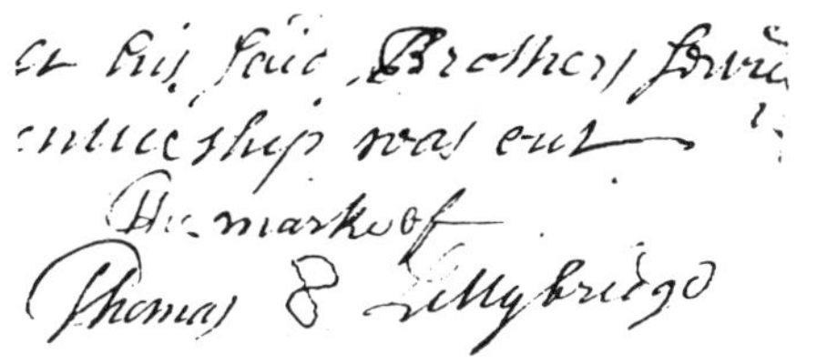

Indenture made 21 November 1676 between Joseph Weatherhead of Hunslett in ye county of Yorke and John Weatherhead of Hunslett aforesaid, clothier: Joseph to be apprentice to John, to be learned and taught in the Art and Mistery of a Clothier, etc. [*printed form used*]. Signed in presence of John Wetherhead Jr, Joseph Lambert, William Mann, and Joseph Powell.

In his answer, defendant William Wood of Newport, yeoman, the only surviving executor of the will of Joseph Wetherhead, pleaded not guilty, and said that John Weatherhead was named as the Eldest Brother to Joseph in the declaration but not in the writ; there are two John Wetherheads of Hunslett, Clothiers, and no John Weatherhead whatsoever was ever possessed of the premises so had no right to dispose of, etc.

The Stantons eventually won possession of the land sued for.

40. **Thomas Peckham** of Newport, house carpenter, vs. **John Scott** of Newport, house carpenter, in custody of sheriff, for not paying to the plaintiff £13:19:6 "for that **Elizabeth Scott** wife to ye sd John Scott did sometime in August last past desire the plaintiff to goe & seek after a mollatto man slave belonging to ye defendant wch had run away & deserted . . . sd Elizabeth Scott promiseing to pay all his expences he should be at . . . and allso to sattisfie [him] for his time & trouble . . . he did take two journeys and made diligent search . . . ." Writ dated 17 December 1714; N. Blagrove Attorney for plaintiff.

Benjamin Star, sheriff, testified at New London 2 September 1715 before **John Plumbe** Justice, that he had been desired by Thomas Peckham of Rhode Island some time in the latter end of the summer to go after some runaways. "We went to Colchester Glasenbary Weathersfield Hartford when we came to Hartford we herd of two Inden wommen at Winsser which we thought to be two of ye runawis we ware after & next morning we went to Winser . . . went to y^{e} **wedow Wolcots** whare ye Inden women war ye night before . . . but ware then gone they thought not above five or six ours so we searcht about ye town till about teen a Clock we then searcht ye madows betwen Winsor and Hartford but cold not heare of those Inden women any more Then we returned home to new london againe for which serves sd Packham paid me twenty eight shellings and paide forty shoueing my hors we ware gone about three days and a half." The bill shown included sums for two horses at Wethersfield, refreshment at Hartford, entertainment one night at Windsor, searching the meadows next day and entertainment that night at Hartford.

The answer of the defendant was that a wife's contract or promise "cannot in law bind and oblige her husband without his assenting to it; unless for victuals drinke & necessary cloathes and many a man might be ruined by his wife if such contracts are allowed . . . ."

41. **Sarah Purdy** of Newport, widdow and taverne keeper, vs. **Richard Wilburne** of Newport, barber, in custody of the sheriff, for debt of £3:6:4 due by note dated 25 June 1715 witnessed by **Thomas Bradford** and **Robert Currie.** Writ dated 1 July 1715; Nathaniel Newdigate attorney.

42. **Bathsheba Hart** of Newport, widow and administratrix of the goods of **Peter Bourse** late of Newport, merchant, deceased intestate, vs. **Stephen Mumford** of Newport, merchant, in custody of the sheriff, in an action of account for the time when he was bailiff of the said Peter Bourse, of 3/4 part of the sloop named *Bathsheba* and her cargo and the whole sloop named *Newport* and her cargo and half of the sloop *Elizabeth* and her cargo and of a division of goods left by Peter in his warehouse in April 1708, to the value of £500, and a Negro man named **Sandall** and a Negro woman named **Katherine**, and moneys [£400] received on the account of Peter Bourse for hire of the sloop *Bathsheba* at Port Royale in a former voyage in the service of the Collony of Rhode Island from **William Lemonte**, merchant, at the Island of Curacoa, to the value of 850 pieces of eight in Spanish money . . . ." Writ dated 15 June 1715; Nathaniel Newdigate attorney.

43. **Richard Mew** of Newport, merchant vs. **Josiah Summers** late of Bristol now or of late resident in Newport, ship carpenter, for £180 due for

goods sold and delivered from 6 January 1714 to May 1715. Writ dated 16 June 1715; Nathaniel Blagrove attorney. Bill included items: "**Daniel Pierces** bill . . . **Capt Mumfords** account . . . whip saw, ozenbriggs, [accounts of] **Daniel Ayrault, Thoˢ Leach, James Chadsey, Majʳ Sheffield, Williaᵐ Earle, Ephraim Hicks,** and **Samuel Holmes.**"

44. **William Champlin** of Westerly, yeoman, vs. **Zacheriah Allen Junr** of Westerly, husbandman, in action of trespass. Writ dated 22 June 1715; R. Robinson attorney. The plaintiff had been appointed a Justice of the Peace by Governor Samuel Cranston 16 May 1698 [several pages about his good name and character follow], nevertheless Zachariah Allen Junr "designing and malitiously intending [to bring] William into scandall, trouble, vexation and infamy amongst his neighbours, etc., on 7 April last past at Newport in the presence and hearing of divers faithfull subjects of our Lord the King . . . false words &c did utter and say that he William Champlin did some time before when he was a Justice of the Peace marry him ye sd Zachariah unto the woman who then cohabited with him and wᶜʰ he then did and still doth call his wife (meaning **Sarah Williams**) . . . William liable to be hurt and prosecuted . . . [the fine] for marrying persons not duly published being £5 for the first offence and £10 for the second." **Job Almy**, merchant [and **William Gibbs**, painter, crossed out] testified 8 September 1715 before Nicholas Lang, J.P., that on or about 7 April last past at the time when the court was held at Newport, he "heard Zacheriah Allen Junr publickly say [that Champlin had married him to his wife, etc.] and that if he had not married them why did he suffer them to lye together in his house." **Joseph Borden** swore to the truth of the statement. Verdict for the plaintiff, costs of court, with notation that full costs were to be allowed.

45. **Zachary Allen junʳ** of Westerly, husbandman vs. **William Davell** of Westerly, yeoman, in a case of trespass, charging that on 13 July 1715 he had assaulted, beat, etc., and imprisoned him for two hours. Writ dated 19 July 1715; Nathaniel Newdigate attorney. The defendant answered that he, as constable, was executing a judgment passed by the Justices against one **Sarah Williams** alias **Sarah Allen** at the suit of one **Pasavel Allen** . . . which Sarah Zachary Allen acknowledged as his wife.

46. **Samuell Clarke** of Westerly, yeoman, vs. **Samuell Dennison** of Westerly, husbandman, in custody of the sheriff, in an action of trespass concerning the possession of six acres in Westerly, part

meadow and part pasture land, bounded easterly, northerly, and westerly on a highway and southerly on land of **Edward Richmond**. Writ dated 21 July 1715; Nathaniel Newdigate attorney. The plaintiff claimed that in the year 1661 by order of the proprietors of Misquamacuck (now called Westerly), the land was laid out and given to **Joseph Clarke**, the plaintiff's father, it being the seventh lot; on 26 September 1694 he disposed of it by deed to one **William Hiscox** of the Towne of Newport who improved it for many years and when he died it descended to **Thomas Hiscox**, the son and heir of said William, who by deed dated 20 July 1715 did resign and reconvey it to Joseph Clarke, who afterwards on the same day deeded it to his son Samuell Clarke, the plaintiff.

47. **John Harris** of Newport, chirurgeon vs. **William Rouse** of Newport, blacksmith, in action of trespass, for £5 for sundry physick administered to him, and care and attention in his late sickness. Writ dated 25 July 1715; R. Robinson, attorney. Nihil dicet.

48. **Henry Gardener** of Kingstowne, yeoman vs. **James Bundy** of Kingstowne, cooper, in custody of the sheriff, in an action of trespass. Writ dated 25 July 1715; Nathaniel Newdigate attorney. On 28 October 1714 the defendant "with gun laden with gun powder and shott one gelding of sd Henry Gardeners of the price of £18 found and did shoot and wound soe that by reason thereof sd gelding did afterwards dye."

Depositions made 25 July 1715 before Christopher Allen, Justice: **Aaron Jacways** of Kingstown stated that "sumtime last fall in the year 1714 he did hear a gun goe ofe and did see a man run away which he judged to be James Bunday And sune after Henry Gardeners hors com up to the deponent's hous and put his head in to sd hous . . . see a wound in [his] flank . . . some time after Bundy tolde the deponent he had shot Henry Gardeners hors and beleved he would never Com in to his Ground any more . . . sd hors died within a fue ours after he was shot." **Samuel Jacways** testified that he heard James Bundy [confess]. **Nathan Jacways** of Kingstown deposed 31 August 1715 that he had heard Henry Gardener Junr offer 4to any two men "what would swear who killed his hors."

Depositions 5 September 1715 before Elisha Cole: **Abigail Bundy** of Kingstown testified that "some time last husking time she see Samuel Jacways Going Over ye field with a gunn on his Shoulder and quickly after heard a gunn go of and then he Came into ye house and said there was one of Mr Gardeners [horses] would never goe home as he believed . . . ." **Samuel Bundy** of Kingstown testified that he saw

Samuel Jacways "coming over James Bundy's field . . . went near som Horses belonging to Henry Gardiner . . . poynted his gun and fired and ye horses Run . . . came to me and said that Mr Gardner had one horse the Less for him." **Ebenezer Bundy** of Kingstown, between 16 and 17 years of age, stated he saw Samuel Jackways fire his gun, etc.

49. **Mary Rogers** of Bristoll, widow, relict, and executrix of the will of **Joseph Rogers** late of Newport, merchant, deceased, vs. **Samuell Pike** of Newport, taylor, for £5:1:2 for goods sold and delivered from 29 August 1709 to 20 January 1710/11. Writ dated 27 July 1715; Nathaniel Newdigate attorney.

50. **Samuel Holmes** of Newport, merchant, vs. **William May** of Newport, pavier, in custody of the sheriff, for £11:11:11 due for 49 days work of the plaintiff's Indian man **Cubit** and goods sold and delivered from 19 October 1714 to 29 November 1715 [*sic*]. Writ dated 28 July 1715; Nathaniel Newdigate attorney. Bill calls the defendant a payver; items billed include 49 days working Cubat ingen 3s pr day, bead cord, shugar, silk lace, jacott, hatt, hanchach, gals rum, pear sheres," and is signed by **Rebeckah Holmes**, who attested it 6 September 1715.

51. **James Fowler** of Newport, worsted comber, vs. **Joseph Sawdey** of Newport, mason, for £7:11:0 due for goods sold and delivered from 4 June 1708 to 24 March 1709/10. Writ dated 28 July 1715; Nathaniel Newdigate attorney.

52. **Timothy Holloway** of Dighton, yeoman, vs. **Christopher Almy** of Newport, merchant, for £6 due in March 1714/15. Writ dated 28 July 1715; Nathaniel Newdigate attorney.

53. **Oliver Arnold** of Jamestown, yeoman, vs. **Thomas Northrop** of Jamestown, ferryman, in an action of trespass concerning a messuage and dwelling house and piece of pasture land containing 4½ acres in Jamestown, bounded west by the sea, north by land laid out to **William Sandford**, east partly by land of William Sandford and partly by land of **Francis Brindley**, south by the highway that runneth across the Island of Cananicutt from the Eastern to the Western ferry [which] **Benedict Arnold**, Esq., Governor, by his will dated 24 December 1677 bequeathed to his son Oliver, the plaintiff's father, who by his will of 10 September 1697 bequeathed it to the plaintiff. Writ dated 27 July 1715; Nathaniel Newdigate attorney. **Thomas Parker** lately of Jamestown, deposed 3 September 1715 before Weston Clarke, Justice, and said that he had viewed the land in controversy and it was the same which he had formerly "hyred of Mr. **Jonathan Marsh** and

afterwards of Mr. **Robert Barker** . . . fence which was then the partition fence betwixt the land of Coll[l] **Peleg Sandford** and Mr. **Oliver Arnold** is now removed considerable to the southward of what it then stood." Mr. **Peter Parker** of Jamestown testified to the truth of that statement.

54. **James Bowdwin** of Boston, merchant, vs. **James Fowler** of Newport, weaver, for £28:14:8 for goods sold and delivered from 6 January 1613/4 to 15 June 1714. Writ dated 18 April 1715; **Nathaniel Newdigate** attorney. Bill included 2 dozen small ivory combs, "blew calico, neck cloths, pepper, ozenbriggs, permento, yarn stockings, codfish, inkhorns, bars [of] iron," etc.

55. **Robert Barker** of Newport, shopkeeper, vs. **John Dublin** of Newport, boatman, for £20 due by note dated 16 February 1714/15, witnessed by **John Wright** and **John Hammett**. Writ dated 6 May 1715; **Nathaniel Newdigate** attorney. **Joseph Barker Juner** of Newport testified on 16 June about going with John Dublin to Robert Barker to give him 4s as the full amount of an award of arbitration in a case concerning earnings from a boat named the *Ceser* belonging to Barker "which sd Dublin went in and Improved the last sumer." **John Pocock** made a similar deposition.

56. **Peter Marshall** of Newport, taylor, vs. **Danyall Pougher** of Kingstown, butcher, for £4:7:0 due "in consideration of a sorrell horss bought of the plaintiff 10 March 1714." Writ dated 15 July 1715. No answer in office; nihil dicet.

57. **Paul Collins** of Newport, merchant, vs. **Joseph Sawdy** of Newport, mason, for £2:5:0 due "for my Neges **Caesar** Jurney for 15 days work at 3 [s] pr day from 29 April 1714 till 9 April last." Writ dated 27 July 1715; **R. Robinson** attorney. No answer in office; nihil dicet.

58. **James Updike** vs. **James Thomas** in Justice's Court at Kingstown (Justices **William Hall** and **Daniel Eldred**) 19 March 1714/5 in action of trespass. **Thomas** had "fenced in land between **William Bentley**'s fence and a little brook that runs through Weathers' his field, & to the eastward of the country road." **Lodowick Updike**, aged 67 or thereabouts, in testimony dated 17 March 1714/15 before Dan[ll] Eldredge, Justice, stated that the "Path of the Pequit Road w[ch] I have knowne this 50 years or upwards went down from my Brook southwest nearest, [and] so to the house whare **George Thomas** now Lives and so by the upper part of the low Ground fenced in now by **Sam[ll] Phillips** and so by **Sam[ll] Eldreds** house now in possession of **Joseph Austen** and so to y[e] Plaine or Shuger Loofe hills [and] so to the

Graet Pond . . . ." **Abigail Fennix** aged 65 years or thereabouts testified on 25 March 1715 that she had "dwelt in the Narragansett Country 53 years and upwards . . . knew the New London Road or Pequot Path ran nigh to the dwelling house of old Samuel Eldred in Kingstown . . . the tann house of Samuel Phillips and "so northerly to the east of the place where William Bently Senrs dwelling house and inclosure now stands and extending still northward through the land now called **Priscilla Weathers** her land and over a small brook to the dwelling house of **Walter House** deceast and over another little brook whereon stood Wethers' land and extended northerly thence to a neck of land called [? Bemelicks] Neck and so northerly . . . . " **John Pinder** aged 31 years or thereabouts, deposed 28 March 1715, before **Daniell Eldredge,** Justice, that a "parcell of land now fenced in by **William Bentley** and **James Thomas** now in dispute is part of the farm lett out to my father **Jacob Pinder** of James Thomas by Mr. Updike for upwards of 20 years since." **Arthur Aylsworth**, aged 62 years or thereabouts, deposed 29 March 1715, that it "hath been upwards of this twenty years . . . Mr. **James Updikes** farm which was then in the possession of **John Thomas** rented to him by Mr. Updike . . . extended to the highway or country road that is now . . . [I] saw grow thereon Indian corn by the road . . . ." Judgement: defendant to remove fence and pay costs. [*See also No. 104*]

59. At a Court of Justices held at the house of the widow **Mary Nichols** 2 March 1714/5, **Weston Clark** and **Sam^ll^ Cranston,** Judges:

John Stephens vs. **Joseph Knolton** in an action of detainure for work done. Plaintiff testified that he and his son worked five days for the defendant, who owed him 5 shillings for himself and one for his son. **Daniell Westerton** of Newport, mason, deposed 30 March 1715 before **Sam^ll^ Cranston**, Justice, that he was "desired by **John Stephens** of Newport and likewise **Richard Walker** of the same town, to view a parcell of work done in a seller for **Joseph Knolton** of sd town, house carpenter . . . did and ackording to custom judged of sd work att 3s 6d per perch and likewise sd Stephens showed them a [? wall or well] he had stoned for Knolton and they judged that at 12s . . . . had heard sd Stephens say that he was to do all the stoning work of the sd house but whereas [he] was at work att some Earnest Work att home the sd Knolton imployed another man in his room." Judgement: defendant to pay 20s besides 10s already paid and costs, 8s more, and remain in custody of the constable until all be paid.

60. 1715, September 2, Depositions [*separated from case*]: "**Ann Powell** of Lawfull age . . . saith thatt she Lived with her former husband **John**

Lambe one the east side of Pacatuck River one **Roger Plastid** his Land: and did keepe posesion some years one s^d^ Land for s^d^ Plaistid by Building one & Improuving of s^d^ land above fifty years now past . . . . **Thomas Lamb** sun to the above named John Lamb & Ann Powell testifieth . . . that he well Remembers thatt he Lived with his father & mother when thay Lived one the East side of pacatuck river one Roger Plastids land . . . Ann Powell and Thomas Lambe both of Groton in the County of Newlondon . . . made oath to the truth of the above writen evidence: Groton September ye second 1715. . . . Nehemiah Smith Justice of Peace."

61. Note signed by **James Bundy**, dated "Kingstown November 5: 1715," to Capt. **Samuell Shewwill [Sewall]**: "Sir after my kind love presented to you these are to give you to understand that I have lived one the ministereal land a pretty while and have kept it from being stript of the wood which now there is one that lives on **Mr Brintuns** farm that joynes to it that cuts for him self and sels to other men and I cannot hinder him without you send me an order to stop him from destroying it and send it by the barer hereof a fue lines under your hand and aquaint Mr **Samuell Niles** with itt pray Sir if you have any opertunity no more at presant but your loving frind and servant . . . James Bundy." There are two notations on the back; the second is dated at Boston, March [*torn*] 1738/9, by **Jacob Wendell**, stating that "**Samuel Sewall**, Esqr of Boston Sonn of the late Honble Judge Sewall and GrandSonn of the late Honourable **John Hull Esqr** one of the originall Purchasers of Patequamsquet in Narrgansett appeared, and made Oath that he found this Paper, among his fathers papers, relating to the Narragansett affairs, and that the Instrument thereon, is in his fathers own writing." The instrument [note] referred to is "James Bundy about the Minister's Lot at Narraganset being pillaged. No. 28."

—March 1716 —

62. **John Thomson** of London in the Kingdom of Great Britain, merchant, and **Peter Ford** of the parish of Saint Mary Magdalen Bermundsay [*sic*] in County of Surrey, merchant, administrators of **Thomas Thomkins** late of London, broker, vs. **Daniel Hodgson**, late of London but now of Newport, mariner. Writ dated 28 January 1715/6. **Weston Clarke**, gentleman, and **John Wanton**, merchant, were sureties to a bond dated 28 January 1715/6 for the defendant to appear 2 February next to

answer the charge; **Abraham Redwood** and **Th^s Cranston** were witnesses. Capt. Daniel Hodgson, mariner, testified 25 March 1715 that sometime last winter he had a sloop that lay on the north side of **Thomas Pelham**'s wharf in Newport at the west end of **Charles Tillinghast's** wharf, and paid sd Thomas Pelham 6d. per diem for the wharfage of sd sloop.

Copy from Newport Town Meeting Book 1, page 29, shown: ". . . ordered that it shall be the Liberty of any man y^t hath Land abutting upon the water side to build a wharf upon before his own Land before his own propriety for houseing, craneage, sellering &c on which he may go Eight Rods to of seawards from hightide water marke of ordnary tides."

Henry Stanton and **Ralph Chapman** testified 1 April 1717 before Nathaniel Sheffield, Assistant, that they "well know and remember that **Samuel Banks** late of Newport, deceased, shipwright, who died about 4 or 5 years agoe layd logs along the shoar uppon the land hyred by him of **Edward Pelham** with peeces lett in for the security of sd loggs and filled a considerable part with chips according to the covenant betwixt them made 1 March 1705/6."

63. **George Stewart** of Boston . . . phisition, vs. **William Huckle** late of sd Boston now residing in Newport, surgeon, in custody of the sheriff, in action of promise. Writ dated 7 October 1715; Nathaniel Newdigate attorney. George at the special insistance and request of William did in September 1715 at Boston become bail for him to **William Dudley** Esqr sheriff of the county of Suffolk . . . for William's appearance at the Inferior Court of Common Pleas to be held in October 1715 to answer to **Rebecca Fowle** of Boston, widow and retailer . . . he did not appear and George was forced to pay Rebecca Fowle £3:17:6 debt and £2 costs of court.

64. **Peter Ford** of the Parish of St. Mary Magdaline, Bermondsey, in Co. Surrey, Great Britain, merchant, vs. **Daniel Hodgson** late of London now of Newport, mariner, for an accompt of goods. The defendant was a bailiff or factor to the plaintiff and in April and May of 1713 shipped on board the *John Galley*, otherwise *John of London*, whereof the defendant was master in the Port of London, goods which included a bail of linen, Holland cloath, cordage, etc. Writ dated 14 February 1715/16.

Peter Treby of Newport deposed 25 March 1716 before George Goulding, J.P., that he, being acquainted with **Richard Ford** of London in Great Britain who called him selfe mate of the ship *John*, Capt.

Daniell Hodgson master, heard Richard Ford say his uncle Ford was part owner of said ship.

65. **Job Almy** of Tiverton, yeoman, vs. **Jacob Queakin** of Newport, Indian and labourer, for money due by book from 1 July to 1 December 1715.

66. **Edward Mott** of Kingstown, husbandman, and wife **Penelope,** (widow of **William Tosh**, deceased), vs. **John Rose** of Block Island alias New Shoreham, yeoman, to recover Penelope's dower right. Will of William Tosh, proved 21 November 1699, named son **Daniel Tosh** and daughter **Penelope Tosh**.

– September 1716 –

67. **William Crawford** of Providence, merchant, eldest son & heir to **Gideon Crawford** late of Providence, merchant, deceased, vs. **Joseph Willson,** farrier, **Benjamin Willson,** hatter and **Mary Smith** widdow and relict of ye late **William Smith** formerly of Newport, taylor deceased, all of Newport . . . in action of trespass & ejectment for illegally witholding from the plaintiff the possession of a certain piece of land "containing halfe a quarter of an acre more or less (which was originally laid out for two lotts) with a dwelling house thereon standing scituate in Newport, butted and bounded southerly and southwesterly by a street or highway, westerly partly by land formerly ye land of **John Paine** now in ye possession of **Oliver Arnold** & partly by land formerly ye land of ye late **Major Isaac Martindale** decs[d], northerly partly by ye land of ye sd Martindale & partly by ye land formerly ye land of ye late **William Hanncock** decs[d] which sd land and dwelling house . . . William Smith in his lifetime was seized thereof in fee simple & being so seized did make over and binde unto ye aforsd Gideon Crawford in his lifetime for secureing ye payment of £54 cur[ren]t silver mony of New England to be paid at ye dwelling house of ye sd Gideon Crawford in Providence at or before 17 March 1702 as by one instrument in writeing under the hand & seal of ye sd William Smith bearing date 17 March 1701 . . . altho ye sd William Smith ye sd £54 in his lifetime or his heirs or any other person since his decease hath not payd either to ye sd Gideon Crawford in his lifetime or to his heirs . . . (whereby ye sd house and land becomes forfeited and doth now of right belong to ye plaintiff as eldest son & heir to ye aforesd Gideon Crawford . . . . £200 damages." Writ dated 25 July 1716. Nath[l]

Blagrove Attorney for plaintiff. On 5 September 1716, "There being no answer . . . plaintiff enters a nihil dicit."

Deposition of **George Belfour**, merchant of Kingstown, 3 September 1716 before **John Eldred**, Assistant, that at Providence in the year 1701 he did see "one **William Smith** of Newport, taillar, w[ch] sd Smith was afterwards killed at sd Kingstown by an accident: sign seal and deliver a mortgage deed unto Gideon Crawford merchant, late of Providence dated 17 March 1701" and the deponent had set his hand thereto as witness.

68. **John Pinder** vs. **Charles Hazleton**. Defendant allegedly stole a quilted saddle belonging to the plaintiff. **John Eldred Sr.** of Killingworth deposed 9 May 1716 that he had been in company with Charles Hazleton late of East Greenwich now residing in the Colony of Connecticut and "knowing y[t] one John Pinder of sd town had a suspition of [him] making away or felonosly taking a saddel of sd Pinders . . . tould sd Hazleton ye best way was to go to ye sd Pinder and mak it up . . . [he] replyed I intend to mak it up with him before I go out of this town . . . ."

Depositions at Woodstock 9 June 1716 before **John Chandler**, J.P.: **John Cady** of Canterbury deposed that the "quilted saddle which Charles Hazleton of Grenwich in the Narragansitt Country sold to **Jeremiah Plimpton** of Plainfield in October 1714, which sd Plimpton still hath and useth, was brought by sd Hazleton unto the dwelling house of the deponent on or about the beginning of June 1714 . . . was then a new saddle . . . ." **Thomas Williams** of Plainfield stated that he had been at the house of John Cady, etc. **Jeremiah Plimpton** testified that in October 1714 he bought a quilted saddle, which was then new, from Charles Hazleton, then of Greenwich, and had paid £3 and another saddle.

Rachel Bennett of East Greenwich deposed 11 October 1716 before **Thomas Fry**, Justice, that Hazleton had come to her house; she asked him about the matter and he said there was no truth in it . . . he had a saddle of John Pinder and had paid him. **John Nettleton** of Killingworth deposed 12 December 1716 and **Thomas Rutty** of Killingworth on 13 December.

Joseph Griswould of Killingworth deposed there 15 December 1716 before **Abraham Pierson,** J.P., that on 6 September 1714 "in y[e] Evining he being at the house of Capt. **John Griswould** of Killingworth . . . in company with **Thomas Rutty** and **John Nettelton** . . . saw **Charles Haselton** then of Grenwich in the Narragansit Country and discorsed with him."

At Killingworth 13 March 1717 a petition was signed by a group of men "acquainted with Charles Hazleton formerly of East Greenwich now of Killinworth for two years and upwards . . . during which time he hath followed the occupation of trader or merchant & in all his dealing among us . . . [we] have not heard or seen anything to the contrary, but that he hath ben honest & upright & that his good name hath not bene soilled by any misdemenior either in word or act . . . in all things his Life & Conversation hath bine honest peasable & quiet amongst us here in Killingworth . . . . [*Signed by*] John Lane, Solomon Davis, John Brooke, James Wright Senr, Robert Isbell, Daniel Kelsy, John Kelcey, Josiah Rosseter, Daniel Clark, Josiah Kelcey, Ebenezer Hurd, Roberd Hurd, John Shether, John Shether iuner, James Jordan, Jared Eliot, Samuell Buell Jus^t^, Capten John Griswold, Left. Samuel Be[w?]ll, Ins'n Joseph Willcox, William [?Well]man, Jonathan Lane, Joseph Kelcey, James Wright Juner, Samuell Willcocks, John Stevens, David buell, John Hull Ju^r^, Josiah Steevens, Nath^ll^ Parnall, Abraham Pierson Jus^t^.

Elisha Pain of Canterbury deposed on 28 March 1717 that he saw the saddle, etc.

69. **William Goddard** of Boston in ye County of Suffolk in ye Province of ye Massachusetts Bay . . . marriner vs. **Joseph Jones** of Newport . . . merchant who married with **Hannah Harvey** of Newport spinster . . . and the sd Hannah . . . in an action of Detinue per writt dated 19 May 1716, that they "tender to the plaintiff one good spangle gold necklace of ye vallue of £16 which they unjustly detaine from him [which] William Goddard sometime in ye month of June 1715 in Newport delivered to the sd Hannah whilst she was sole . . . to be safe kept and to him . . . when the sd Hannah should be thereunto required, to be redelivered . . . altho often required the aforesd Hannah when sole, or the aforesd Joseph Jones & Hannah since their marriage . . . the aforesd gold spangle necklace to . . . William Goddard have not delivered." Plaintiff by attorney N. Blagrove claims damages of £32.

Defendant **Joseph Jones** answered that he had been married to Hannah ever since the 14th day of September 1714 and therefore she could not be charged with a necklace delivered her [as] a sole woman in the month of June 1715. But in case the Court should "see cause to overule the aforesd plea and admitt a tryale . . . the defendants for plea . . .say they doe not detaine the said gold spangle necklace as the plaintiff hath declared." Nath^ll^ Newdigate attorney for the defendants.

70. Deposition dated 19 June 1716 by **John Hoxey** of Westerly [*Kingstown crossed out*] of lawfull age, before **Samuel Fones**, Justice [*in Fones's handwriting*] . . . that he and **Nicholas Young** of Kingstown were "both of them desired by **Thomas Wilcox** of sd Kingstown to goe with him the 18th day of June 1716 to se **William Gardner** of sd town cordwainer and his men & oxen at plow on the land that he the sd Wilcox claimed to be his . . . they did both goe with him the sd Wilcox the same day and did see sd Gardner and his men at plow and braking up of new ground to the southward of a celler where one **Francis Diviller** a frenchman did then live and also to the southward of the line run by **William Hall** of sd Town the 19th day of April last past . . . the sd Gardner and his men were at plow about twenty rods or something more to the southward of sd line & celler . . . sd Willcox did then forwarn him the sd Gardner and his men from working on or plowing on the sd land where they were then at worke . . . ." **Nicholas Young** of Kingstown testified to the truth of the above.

71. **William Dyre** of Newport shopkeeper vs. **Joseph Sawdey** of said Newport mason, in custody of the sheriff, for £3:5:5 owed for diverse goods sold and delivered at sundry times between 20 September 1714 and 22 December 1714 as shown by bill. Writ dated 25 July 1716; Nathaniel Newdigate attorney. Accounting includes "10 yd of Dammask by yr Daughter . . . 1 gal rum by **Negro Dick** . . . tobaco . . . knife & fork . . . nutmigs . . . 1 sash hankerchiff by yr self . . . 1 gal rum by Morss wife . . . 1 gall rum by **Negro George**. . . ."

72. Deposition [*separated from case*] of **Samuel Anthony** of Kingstown of lawfull age, taken in Newport 5 September 1716 by **Samll Clarke**, Assistant, that he "being in company with **Thomas Hassard** and **David Nicholls** both of Kingstown . . . sum time in July in the year 1716 at a place called and known by the name of Little Point Judah Neck in sd Kingstown nere the southard part of sd neck and thare see two Indian men mowing of grass and the sd Thomas Hassard then did aske said Indians who thay mowed for . . . thay answered and said for **George Mumford** then hee asked them what their names was one of them said his name was **John Perrey** and the other said his name was **Toby Wilson** then the sd Hassard did forbid them mowing or makeing any hay. . . ."

73. Deed, **John Eldred Senr** to **Samuel Holway**, 19 November 1716 [*loose in Miscellaneous Box, separated from case*].

Know all men by these pr[e]sents that I John Eldred Senr of Kingstown in the Colony of Rhoad Island and Providence Plantations for and in consideration of the Love and good will I do bare unto my Loveing friend Samuel Holway of y^{e} above said town and Colony Miller Have by these presents Remised Released and forever Quit=claimed and Resigned up unto the above said Samuel Holway all my Right Title Intrest, Whatsoever I have or Ought to have unto a Sertaine Tract of Land which the said Holway hath now within fence Lying and being in Kingstown aforesaid between the Country Rhod now in use and the antiant Pequit Path and is bounded as followeth on the East upon the said Pequit Path; on the west upon the said Country Rhod; on the South upon **William Bentlys** fence; on the North upon a Rhod; That Leads to **Joseph Smiths** Mill I do by these Presents for me my heires Execut^{r} Admin^{rs} Surrender up and give a Quit=claime of all my Right Title Intrest Whatsoever I have unto the said Tract of Land by Virtue of a Deed I had of y^{e} Committe – Impowered by said Colony to Dispose of y^{e} Vacant Lands in the Narraganset Country: Bareing date May the 25th 1709 I Do by these presents give a Quit=claime of all my Right Title Intrest Whatsoever I have unto the said Tract of Land by Virtue of Said Deed unto the above said Samuel Holway his heires Execut^{rs} Administ^{rs} & Assignes forever: In wittness whereof I have here unto sett my hand and seall this 19th day of Novemb^{r}: Anno Dom: 1716

[*signed*] John Eldred in the presence of **James Sweet** and **Larance Whaley**, and acknowledged 8 April 1717 before **Christ^{o} Allen** Jus^{t}

– 1718 – Miscellaneous –

74. In a deposition dated 8 March 1717[/8] before **Samuel Sewall J. P.** at Boston [*in Miscellaneous Box; separated from case*], the **Hon^{bl} Wait Winthrop Esqr** aged seventy three years stated ". . . that the old Road or Path he has many times Travelled in his Yonger Time in Company with several other Travellers between Pequitt (now New London) and Boston through the Narriganset Country was by the Great Pond from thence over the Long Hills or high Land above **Rouse Helms** his late Dwelling and Cross said high Land a slant to the lower Part of the Great Plain leaving ye bare Hills below the Plains which were then called the Sugar Loaf Hills a great Way to ye Eastw^{d} the Country being mostly clear so that we could see a long way before as we crossed the said Plain in a Direct Course as it seemed to me untill we passed the Brook that runs down East ward and in the Same direct Course the Path or Road led us near the Plain Field below where **Mr Updicke** now lives and this was Accounted the Pequit Road or Path and I never knew or heard of any other untill many years after we went by the Stone fort and so by old Mr **Eldredges** House and so by ye Town House to **Maj^r^ Smiths** now **Mr Updickes** which way is far eastward of the old Road which Leads directly from the Great Plain to the field abovesaid and which Path I believe is not so worn out but it may yet be seen to pass the Brook far to the Westward of ye sd To[w]n House"

75. **Job Carr** of Oyster Bay, Queens County, on Long Island, cordwainer, vs. **Deborah Hicks** of Newport (widow), vintner, for £29:19 due for hire of a certain messuage or dwelling house in Newport. Writ dated 29 October 1717; Jno Higgins attorney.

76. In a deposition dated 25 March 1718, **Abigail Fenix** of Kingstown, midwife, said that she "hath been for about 25 years acquainted with **Thomas Wethers** late of Kingstown, yeoman, deceased, and **Priscilla** his wife and in the month of July 1696 delivered sd Priscilla of **John Wethers** of sd Kingstown, yeoman and son of the aforesd Thomas Wethers, and that the sd John Wethers in the month of July last past did attain the age of 21."

77. At a Justices' Court 18 July 1718 at the house of **Edward Thurston** in Newport, **Ralph Chapman** and **Jonathan Thurston**, owners of the sloop *Tryall*, accused **John Langford** of having taken from Jonathan Thurston, who was master of said sloop, 18 shillings more than he ought to have for the entering and clearing of said sloop according to tables of fees stated by Act of Assembly of the Colony. Defendant acknowledged he had taken 26 shillings. He was ordered to pay the 18s and costs and remain in the constable's custody until the judgement was complete. He appealed to the September Court.

78. In a deposition dated 13 August 1718 before William Spencer, Justice, **Abigail fennix** of Kingstown, widow . . . an ancient inhabitant of sd town, stated that she was a "niar dweller unto **Samuell Eldred** father unto Captain **John Eldred** and well knew that he did live on and possess that place where his son Captain John Eldred now Liveth on 48 years or thereabouts . . . Samuel Eldred and Capt. John Eldred his son [were] possessed [of] sd place yt Capt. John Eldred now lives on ye abovesaid term of time without any hindrances or molestation from any person or persons." **Thomas Ayres** of Kingstown "likwise an ancient Inhabitant" agreed. These depositions were copied 12 April 1720 for another case.

79. In a deposition dated 4 September 1718 before Christopher Allen, Justice, **Ephraim Bull** of Kingstown aged 49 years or thereabout, stated that about four years since **Edward Mott** of Kingstown gave him leave "to cutt down some Ceder trees in a Ceder Swamp neare a Celler where one **Braman** lived some little before, & he implyed a man who cut down some Ceder trees in the said Swamp & split them into Bolts & carryed them to ye upland to the quantities of about a Cart load of Bolts, & ye place where ye said Bolts were Cut down, the sd Mott said was in Land in his possession, & which he Counted was his Land lords, by which he understood he ment his Land lord **Brenton**: Some Letle time after, he went to the place where he had some time before left ye Bolts But the Bolts were Gone and Afterwards he meeting with ye sd Mott: told him that ye aforesd Bolts were gone, & asked him how he should do for [the deponent Bull's] Labour bestowed on ye Bolts, to which [he] Replied, that he would get him some Bolts to his house."

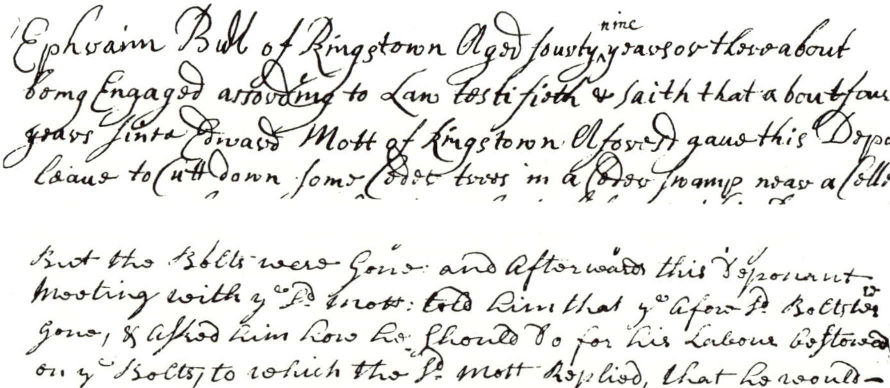
Ephraim Bull of Kingstown Aged fourty nine years or thereabout
being Engaged according to Law testifieth & saith that about four
years since Edward Mott of Kingstown Aforesd gave this Depon
leave to Cutt down some Ceder trees in a Ceder Swamp near a Celler

But the Bolts were Gone and Afterwards this Deponent
meeting with ye sd Mott: told him that ye aforesd Bolts were
Gone, & asked him how he should do for his Labour bestowed
on ye Bolts, to which the sd Mott Replied, that he would
get him some Bolts to his house. Ephraim Bull

Detail from deposition of Ephraim Bull, above [No. 79]

80. **James Hulines** of Newport, mariner, late mate of the sloop *Elizabeth*, was indicted in September 1718; Weston Clarke attorney [general]. It was charged that he "did by force of armes in Newport in a voyalent manner on 25 April last past Rescoue out of the hands of **Peter Easton** who was then constable an Indian man called **James Ahannah** who was then Arrested by sd Constable by vertue of a warrant under the hand of Samuel Cranston, Justice of the Peace . . . whereby Justis could not be done . . . with many threatts and bad words given sd Constable by sd James Hulines which Act of his is High Contempt of Authorety."

General Court of Trials – September 1718

81. **Thomas Bingham** of Newport, joyner, presented [by General Attorney Weston Clarke] "ffor that he being inexpert in the practice of physick, and taking upon him nevertheless, to administer physick to persons indisposed and grievously sick, did on or about the 22d day of June 1718 at Newport . . . administer & give to one **John Abbot** of Newport being then sick, three potions of physick vizt. 82 grains of Mercurius Dulcis in ye whole in venus treckle, wch sd potions the sd John Abbot then & there did take & drink, or swallow downe . . . caused the death of the sd Abbot, wch happened in a few dayes afterwards, s^{ch} is a great misdemeanour & deceit in ye sd Thomas Bingham, & ag[ains]t the peace of the King &c." Thomas was arrested by order of Gov. Samuel Cranston 30 June 1718, after "**Andrew Rowan, John Harris & ffrankland Mortan** Phisitians . . . viewed the corps of John Abbot, who deceased yesterday morning the 29th instant att the House of **William Brightman** in the Towne of Portsmouth . . . theire judgments is that the cause of the death . . . was by malepractice . . . ." Gov. Cranston added that "you may take £200 bail with good security." Bail was posted by bond of Tho. Bingham with Stephen Easton and Samuel Lyndon:

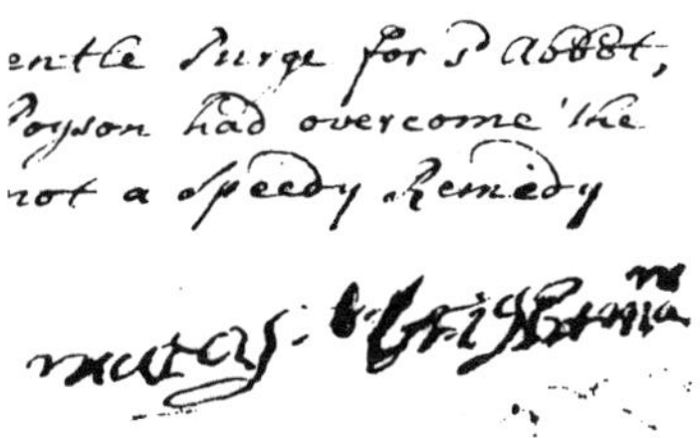
entle Purge for sd Abbot,
Poyson had overcome the
not a speedy Remedy
Mercy Brightman

Mercy Brightman wife to Wm. Brightman of Portsmouth, testified at Portsmouth on 1 September 1718 before Jonathan Nickolls, assistant, that "on the 22^{d} of June 1718, Thomas Bingham came Early in the morning to their house in Ports-

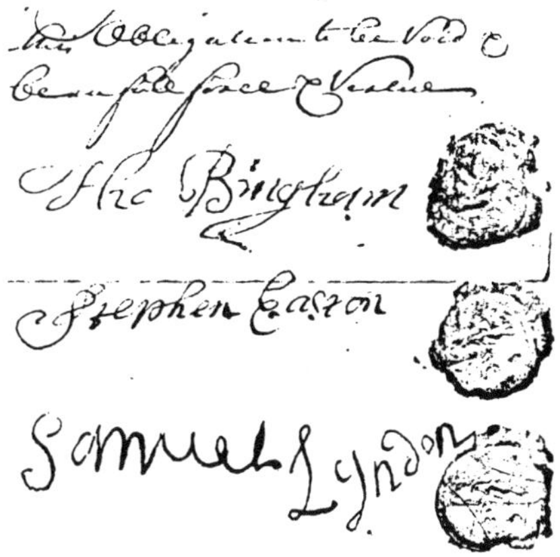
Tho Bingham
Stephen Easton
Samuel Lyndon

mouth not acquainting her of his business, but afterward she Perceived by John Abbot it was on his acc^{t}: he came in order to give him a Portion of Apsom=salt to Purge his Stomach . . . to prepare his body for the Operating by Physick, and the sd Bingham administred other Portions of Physick, as the said Abbot told her, which Portions not Operating according to Expectation, caused the deponent to ask Bingham the Resons . . . which [he] made very light of, Telling, the Reason of its not working was because the sd Abbot had heretofore worn a Quicksilver girdle and the whole Mass of his blood was corrupt, therefore what he administered was to draw the Distemper out . . . which would be effected in three dayes time . . . [and that] the sd Abbot was Impatient and afraid of laying out his money . . . . Abbot used this Expression saying this wretch hath deceived me and Poysoned me with his Physick, and then the sd Abbot ordered **Doct^{r} Tallman** to be sent for, who when he came ordered a gentle Purge for sd Abbot . . . and the sd Abbot further added that the Poyson had overcome the Physick, and he was a dead man, if he had not a speedy Remedy . . . ." **William James** of Portsmouth and **Mary** his wife [who signed by her mark] testified also on 2 September about the Quicksilver girdle and Bingham's attempts to treat Abbot by giving him physick to salivate him.

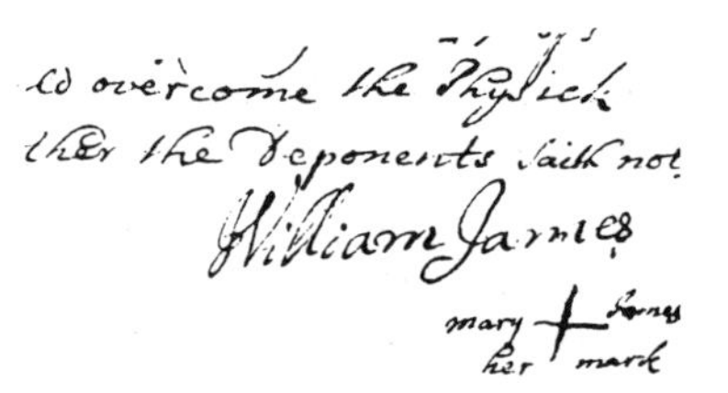
to overcome the Physick
ther the Deponents saith not
William James
mary + James
her mark

82. Petition of **Sarah Peters** wife of **John Peters** of Newport, physitian, late widow of **William Collins** of Newport, tanner, in behalf of her son **William Collins**, an infant. In 1717 her son was persuaded by the friendly speeches and insinuations of one **Thomas Markie** of Newport, tanner, with the consent of the petitioner who is his natural guardian, to become bound to sd Markie by indenture dated 16 November 1717 to serve 5 years . . . "having mett with great severity in his service he became weary of sd indenture and refus'd to serve any longer and thereupon apply'd to y^{r} petitioner that she might gett him freed . . . ." Markie put him in jail for several days in close custody.

83. **Samuel Kelton** of Providence, cordwainer, vs. **Benjamin Potter** of Providence, innholder, in custody of the sheriff, for £26:17:6 due by note dated 16 November 1717 witnessed by **Joseph Angel** and **John Yeats** Juner. **Nathaniel Newdigate** attorney.

84. **William Wilkenson** of Westerly, yeoman, vs. **William Valence** [signed Vallence] of Newport, tanner, in custody of the sheriff, for £20 due by note dated 28 April 1718, witnessed by **Charls Lee** and **John Stanton** Junr. **Nathaniel Newdigate** attorney.

85. **Ezekiel Bull** of Newport, innkeeper, vs. **Thomas Hill** of Newport, post rider, in custody of the sheriff, for £6 due on a bill dated 28 September 1717 for "keeping [your] horse and money lent you . . . use of my saddle . . . horse & saddle of the value of £14." Writ dated 6 June 1718. **William Cowel** of Boston deposed on 2 June 1718 that he delivered to Hill at Boston a brown horse with saddle and bridle, goods of the plaintiff, to be delivered at Newport.

86. **Job Almy** of Newport, merchant, vs. **Elkanah Pembrooke** of Newport, shopkeeper, in custody of the sheriff, for £57:16:0 due by note dated 11 September 1717 witnessed by **William Coddington** and **Joshua Raymond**. Writ dated 9 June 1718; **Nathaniel Newdigate** attorney.

87. **James Brown** of Newport, taylor, vs. **Thomas Moore**, resident in Newport, mariner, in custody of the sheriff, for £6:4:5 due by bond dated 12 June 1718, signed by mark and witnessed by **Saml Bissell** and **Jno Higgins**. Writ dated 13 June 1718; **Jno Higgins** attorney.

88. **John Hewlett** of Newport, merchant, vs. **Samuel Talbutt** of Taunton, boatman, for £7:19:0 due by book for a parcell of cordage sold and delivered in September 1717. Writ dated 15 July 1718; **Nathaniel Newdigate** attorney.

89. **Daniel Wightman** of Newport, house carpenter, vs. **John Langford** of Newport, gentleman, for £65:2:6 due by book. Writ dated 17 July 1718; **Nathaniel Blagrove** attorney. Bill included "timber planks & boards for frame of his house he now dwells in in Newport," 2 November 1717, and 1 May 1718, "frameing sd house, making window frames & finishing the carpenters worke . . . and mending an old cubboard since." **John Huling** and **Job Jonson** [or **Townson** ?] deposed 5 September 1718 before Jon^a^ Brown, Assistant, that "in March last when they was at worck near Mr. Lankfords house [they] heard [him] say to Mr. Daniel Whitman to do what work he said [and he would pay]. . . ."

[*Separated from the case*] "Artikels of agreement . . . July 10th 1717 . . .between J.L. & D.W. who for the consideration hereafter Exprest doth bargin with J.L. to build him an house as followeth to finde a frame of 25 foot frunt and 27 foot deep and to be set whare **Daniel Aros** [Ayrault's] Shop now is to be of the heith of **William Dyre** house the west side Joyne to Roes [Ayrault's] house to find plank for the out side and for the petitions and oke board for the rough finde seven gurt windows and three dormor windows & all belonging to them and doe all the Carpenters work as planking boarding clabord boarding, shingling it & make a Cornish and peint house on the front and make 2 dormonds on the front and 1 on the back side and divid sd house a crosse boath wayes above and below according to the draft & make 2 shops one the front part with 2 windows a peace and doors and Counters and Shelves in boath lay 3 floors throught the house one of which to be don [*illegible*] make 2 pare of stairs one into the Chamber and the other into the garrat make rough petitions as well in the seler with a door make one outsid door 7 framed doors case the posts case the windows make 2 seller windows seller stairs inside and out and out side seller door a floor in part of the seller for a kitchen and a petition across the seller and to be finished by [*blank*] In consideration whereof the sd J.L. doth promise to pay unto sd D.W. £55 viz £25 at raising £20 in goods & 5 in money £15 at Inclosing £15 at finishing and sd Mr Lanford to be at the Charge of raiseing Dinner, the whole £55 to be paid as followeth £30 in Bills of Creditt & £25 in Goods, the sd house is to have as Good work in every respect done in it as is done in Mr Ayrault or Mr Dyers houses. [*Both signed*]

90. **Charles Whitfield** of Newport, mariner, vs. **Ezekiel Bull** of Newport, victualler, for £32 due because Ezekiel had been a surety with **John Arnold** of Mansfield in the county of Hartford [Connecticut], farmer, as principal, dated 4 April 1717 and witnessed by **Daniel Pinder** and **Williamson Ford**. Writ dated 24 July 1718; **Nathaniel Newdigate** attorney.

— March 1719 —

91. **John Langford** of Newport, merchant, vs. **John Russell** of Newport, taylor, and **Aaron Milliman** of Newport, taylor, and **Aaron Milliman** of Canonicutt, taylor, for £40 due by note. Writ dated 31 January 1718/19; **Nathaniel Newdigate** attorney. Indenture, **John Russell** of Newport, tayler, and **Aaron Milliman** of Canonicutt, tayler, bound unto **John Langford** of Newport, merchant, in the sum of £40, due 6 March 1717/8 . . . conditional lease [*torn*]. Both signed. Witnessed by Mr. **Mathew Higgins** who attested it 28 March 1719. **Love^s^ Vaughan** and **Henry Bull** testified at Newport 2 December 1718 that they had been with John Langford, John Russell, and Aaron Milliman at the house of Mr **Edward Neregrass** in Newport on 16 July last, when John Langford produced a pair of leases of part of the house wherein he dwells in Newport . . . offered to execute his part but Russell and Milliman refused to sign or execute their part.

Lease shown, from **Daniel Ayrault** of Newport, shopkeeper, for yearly rent and covenent, set and to farm lett unto John Langford of Newport, merchant, a certain shop and two dwelling houses together with a piece of land adjoyning to the westward containing 45 feet in length and 24 in breadth, bounded easterly on Main Street, southerly by the house and land of **William Dyer**, westerly on the house of the **Widow Carr**, and northerly on a Gang Way going down to Carr's Wharf. Rent was to be £24 annually, and the leasor was to "oblige self to suffer all the tenants belonging to the Widow Carr to have free access to the Pump which stands on the land .. to supply themselves with water." It was signed by John Langford and witnessed by **Jno Chace** and **Charles Bardin Jnr**. A second indenture, dated 16 July 1718 but not signed, between John Langford and John Russell and Aaron Milliman, let a dwelling house in Newport wherein Langford dwells and a shop abutting to Mr. William Dyre, for five years at £28 yearly.

92. **Job Carr** of Newport, cooper, vs. **Henry Bull** of Newport, joyner, for payment of £147:16:0 due by book for sundry goods sold and delivered at several times in the year 1716. Writ dated 3 February 1718/9; **N. Blagrove** attorney. The accounting included "five barrels pr **Brinley Silvester**, building up three teers of wharfe for him, wharfedg of his Sloop 3 weeks . . . building his wharfe in ye year 1717."

93. For a case in which **Job Carr** was the plaintiff, and Mr. **Peleg Carr** his attorney, **Joseph Gardner** made a deposition 21 March 1718/19 before Edward Thurston, stating that he was "desired by **Samuel Carr** son of **John Carr** late of Newport, deceased, to give evidence what I know about the building of the wharfe that was his grandfather Mr **Caleb Carr** Esquires . . . know of [my] owne certaine knowledge [that it] was built out to the full width of the land from North to South and westward as farr as the West End of the warehouse that **Capt. Mumford** built upon the said Wharfe for above these 30 years . . . ."

94. **Kendall Nicholls** of Newport, mason, vs. **John Langford** of Newport, gentleman, in custody of the sheriff, for payment of £18:18:0 due by book for building a stack of chimneys in his house in Newport near ye widdow Carr's wharf and for lime & lathing & plaistering & other masons worke done in sd house in the year 1718. Writ dated 5 December 1718; **N. Blagrove** attorney. Defendant's answer was that at the time the writ was served on him, he was bound to England and sailed the next day, therefore had not time to provide for his defence; by his attorney **Nathaniel Newdigate**, he requested a continuation until September court and declared himself not endebted to the plaintiff.

95. **Benjamin Peckham** of Kingstown, cordwainer, vs. **Benjamin Hollway** of Westerly, yeoman, in custody of the sheriff, for balance due on debt for goods sold and delivered in February 1718. Writ dated 5 February 1718/19. "Benjamin having commenced a debt of divers particulars . . ." which included shoes and melacs [? molasses], credited with sum paid to **Frances Robinson** 16 February 1718 on Benjamin's account.

96. **Turne Humry** of Tiverton, cordwainer, vs. **Anne Larrose** of Portsmouth, widow and executrix of the will of **Peter Larrose** late of Swansey, husbandman, deceased, in custody of the sheriff. Writ dated 10 February 1718/19; **Nathaniel Newdigate** attorney. Turn Humry in December 1716 had sold and delivered to Peter Larrose "one black one Eyed horse at price of £3:10:0 to be paid on demand . . . ."

97. **Phillip Briggs** of Kingstowne, labourer, vs. **James Bundey** of East Greenwich, cooper, otherwise James Bundey of Kingstowne, for debt of £55:4:0 due by bond dated 23 March 1715/6; writ dated 17 February 1719. Bill, dated December 1717, **Joseph Sheffield** to James Bundy.

98. **Mordecai Dunbar** of Newport, taylor, vs. **George Lawton** of Newport, gentleman, in custody of the sheriff, for £3:9:0 due for goods sold and delivered 18 April 1718. **Jno Higgins** attorney. Bill for a holland Jacket & Breeches, £2:15:0 and a Swan Skin Jacket, 14s.

99. **Sion Arnold** of Newport, cooper, and **Mary** his wife and **Richard Ward** of Newport, gentleman, vs. **Thomas Potter** of Kingstown, yeoman, and **Sarah Potter** of Kingstown, widow, in an action of trespass. Writ dated 19 November 1718. The property sued for was described as one sixth part of a certain tract of land in Point Judith Neck within the township of Kingstown . . . about 640 acres, arable, pasture, meadow and woodland, and 3 messuages or dwelling houses, one barn or outhouse and one orchard thereon standing . . . part of the Pettaquamscutt Purchase, bounded easterly by the sea, southerly by the land of **Jahleel Brenton** in possession of **William Robinson**, westerly partly by Point Judith Ponds and partly by land of sd Jahleel Brenton in possession of **William Robinson**, and partly by land belonging to **Thomas Mumford**, into which **Thomas Ward** entered on 14 December 1682 by deed of that date under the hand and seal of **Samuell Wilson** . . . one sixth of his seventh part, excepting only out of the undivided lands in said great whole tract according to Proprietors 800 acres to be laid out to the heirs or assigns of **Benedict Arnold** and **Samuell Willbore**. On 9 June 1683 by his will Thomas Ward devised a two and fortieth part to his son **Thomas** and his heirs to the third generation, and the other half to daughter **Mary**, the now plaintiff, and her heirs to the third generation, and in case his wife **Ammy** should bear

one other son . . . if either of the children should die without heirs, the son should inherit. After the will was made, on 9 April 1689, **Richard Ward** the plaintiff, son of the aforesaid Thomas Ward was born of Ammy his wife; the testator Thomas Ward died in the year 1689 . . . and Thomas son of Thomas Ward died "in his none age" unmarried and without heirs. [*See No. 4A for transcription of will of Thomas Ward.*]

Deed in file: Samuel Wilson of Rochester in the Narragansett Country in King's Province, for £30 to **John Holmes** of Newport, one half share in one 14th part of all grantor's lands and meadow in Point Judith Neck in Narragansett in the Pettaquamscutt Purchase. Witnesses were Samuel Cranston, Weston Clarke, and Robert Little, and it was noted that the deed was copied [or dated?] in June 1688 from pages 363-364 of the Clasped Book of Land Evidences belonging to Providence Plantations.

On 7 September 1693 upon a division of lands in Point Judith Neck by the Proprietors, the aforesd land was laid out in the right of the aforesd Samuel Wilbore to such as could lawfully claim it.

Verdict for the plaintiff, reversion of former judgment.

– September 1719 –

100. **John Davis** of Kingstown, weaver, vs. **Thomas Phillips** of Kingstown, tanner, for £15:2:0 due for "cureing of 2 mares one in 1716 other in 1717 and for guilding of a colt in 1718 and for bills paid him by hands of John Davis ye plaintiffs Son 19 September last past." Writ dated 14 May 1719; Nathaniel Blagrove attorney.

101. Court of Inquiry held 13 November 1719 at the house of **George Thomas** to investigate a case of forceable entry and detainue between **Joshua Davis** of East Greenwich and **Thomas Phillips** of Kingstown. Defendant produced an indenture between **Samuell Phillips** of Kingstown, tanner, and **Thomas Phillips** son of said Samuell Phillips, tanner, dated 6 September 1719. Samuell for love and a covenant hereafter expressed leased to Thomas for seven years and six months a tract of land, swamps and uplands, 121 acres in Kingstown, bounded north partly on land of **William Smith**, partly on land of **William Havens**, east on land of **George Thomas** and partly on that of William Smith, west on land of Mr. **Samuell Boone**, and south "on the Ten Rood Highway that leads up into ye Country." Thomas was to pay £6 yearly on 25 March, and at the end of the time to deliver up peaceable and quiet possession to Samuell. Witnesses were **Nicholas Hutchinson** [signed by mark] and **John Ennis**. Copy compared 19 November 1719 pr Alexander Huling clerk. Verdict for the plaintiff.

– March 1720 –

102. Indictment of two Indians: "an Indian man called **Joseph**, an apprentice or servant to **Jobe Shearman** of the town of Portsmouth, who did some time in ye month of August in the year 1719 Brake open the Shop and warehouse of **Joseph Dennis** of sd town and stole out a Cask of Rum . . . about fourteen gallons of Rum and converted ye Same to his own use as will appear by his own Confession." Also of an Indian Lad called **James**, apprentice or servant to **Abraham Anthony** of Portsmouth. Note from **Thomas Cornell**, Assistant, to **William Coddington**, Sheriff, 17 9/mo:1719, "I send you herewith the Body of an Indian Lad James . . . with two other Indians about two or three months ago did break open a warehouse or shop belonging to Joseph Dennis and stole and carried away a Considerable Quantity of Rhum . . . I do constitute **Joseph Cook Jn^r^** a special Constable for the Execution of this precept." James, when examined, confessed that he was in company with **Joash** a free Indian and **Joseph** an Indian fellow (an apprentice to **Jobe Shearman** of Portsmouth), and "sayd he did not break open sd warehouse nor draw any of the Rum, but stood by one Corner of sd warehouse to watch If any body came out of the dwelling house of sd Dennis whilst the other two drawed the Rum and that they draw'd it in a swill pail which they found near sd house . . . ."

103. **Isaac Basson** of Providence, cordw[a]iner, indicted and charged with felony: he "in confederation with **Benjamin Wright** of Providence, labourer, and **Sam**, a negroe man servant or slave to **Danl Abbot** of Providence, on 22 January in the night of sd day . . . by wicked and evell instigation of each other did brake open ye shop of **James Dexter** shopkeeper in sd town of Providence . . . [and] take copper pennys and other goods, to [the] value of £20." James Dexter testified that "the morning after my shop was Brooken up I went to **Mr Hanses** the [*bargon?*] & asked them who was there the night before: **Henry** told me that Isaac Burson Abbots Shoe maker was theire tell about ten of the Clock."

104. **Samuel Holms** of Newport, mariner, vs. **Adolph De grove** resident in sd Newport, mariner, for debt of £21:8:3 due for sundry parcels of goods at Citty of New York sold and delivered to the defendant at sundry times beginning 21 May 1719 and ending 15 January 1719[/20].

105. **James Updike** of Kingstown, mariner, and **Daniel Updike** of Newport, mariner, vs. **William Bently** and **Benjamin Bently** both of Kingstown, curriers, in an action of trespass. Writ dated 20 January 1719/20; Nathaniel Newdigate attorney. Land in controversy was a "piece of arrable and meadowland in Kingstown . . . four acres . . . with a messuage or dwelling house, part of 800 acres which were bounded north on land of **Samuel Boone**, east on Narragansett Bay, south on Anaquetuckett River, and west on the country road; the four acres sued for were bounded north on land of Samuel Boone, east and south on land of **John Pinder**, and west by the country road. It was land of which Major **Richard Smith** died seized, and in his will dated 16 March 1690/91 bequeathed to Daniel Updike of London, mariner, and to James Updike, the present plaintiff, he bequeathed the other moiety [half]. Daniel Updike died leaving a will dated 9 February 1703/4 bequeathing his share to his nephew Daniel, the present plaintiff. Will entered in evidence; for full text, see Item No. 18, above.

Depositions were made 13 November 1719 before **Alexander Huling**, clerk of the court, by **Lodowick** and **James Updike** of Kingstown, that on the 4th instant November, they "being walking about a mile . . . to the westward of sd Lodowick's house . . . there see several men at work . . . viz. **Nich^{las} Hutchins Jn Eneas Wm Sterling Joseph Ceser** Negro **Joseph Pasco** Indian **Dick** and **Cato** Negres: some cutting hedge wood some carrying others making ye fence att a place where there was some iron ore dugg up . . . Mr **Thos Phillips** came to sd place to them and the deponents askt them no[?thing] but came away . . . ."

Extract copied from town records: at a town meeting held at the house of Left. **Benony Sweet** 22 April 1706, **William Bentley** was given "Liberty to set up a house convenient for carrying on of his currying trade on or by the road neare to **Sam^{ll} Phillips** his house and . . . have conveniancy of land for a Garden, and a place to dry his leather neare to his said house" (copied 27 August 1719 by Francis Willett, town clerk).

John Pender of Kingstown testified 27 August 1719 before William Hall, Justice, that his father **Jacob Pinder** and **John Thomas** together did hire the farm of Capt. James Updike which he now hires of Capt. James Updike and Daniel Updike, for several years together.

Depositions were made 24 March 1719/20 before William Spencer, Justice: **Thomas Phillips** of Kingstown testified that he was desired by

Benjamin Bentley to view the lease drawn between Capt. Daniel Updike of Newport and William Bentley, Benjamin's father; **Christopher Phillips** swore to the truth of his statement.

John Eldred Senr of Kingstown testified that he had been an inhabitant there upwards of 50 years and mentioned his honored father **Samuel Eldred**. **Mr. Thomas Eldred Sr** and **Mr Joseph Reynolds Sr** both Antient Inhabitants of Kingstown testified to the truth of the above.

The location of the Pequot Path became an issue; in the appeal, testimony from an earlier trial was entered [see No. 58, Updike vs. Thomas]. **Samuel Eldred**, 73 years of age, testified about the path 20 August 1714 before William Hall, Justice. Testimony was given 24 March 1714/15 before William Hall, Justice, by "an Indian called **grate plain James**" living in East Greenwich "being an inhabytant in the Naragansett Country this 66 years," who said that the "Anchant road called and known by the name of ye Pequot Path came by ye house of Samuel Eldred deceased some small matter to ye east of sd house . . . exstanded noth or northard over a brock called by ye Indians Namannoqatockett some small matter to ye east ward of y^t^ plain whareon Samuel Phillips tan hous now stands." **Mr John Gallup**, aged 70 years, deposed 25 March 1716 at Stonington before Nath^ll^ Chesebrough, Justice, that "in his younger time about 50 years ago, he travelled between Pequitt (now New London) and Boston through the Narragansett Country . . . ."

Depositions made at Stonington 21 June 1716 before Daniel Palmer, Justice of the Peace: **Nehemiah Palmer**, aged 79 or thereabouts, now living in Stonington, stated that about 60 years ago "I traveled the Road betwixt Rehoboth and Pequit often times and the Road I used to Travel in went by the Great Pond sid and from thence over the long Hill above where **Rowse Helmes** formerly dwelt and over the lower edge of the Great Plain & so over the Brook or River & so on a direct Course to **Maj^r^ Smiths** trading house . . . now **Lodowick Updikes** & this Road went above where **Mr Eldredge** dwelt a considerable distance or any of the Roads that has been troden since as I know of . . . there was noe English inhabitants after we came from Warwick to the Paucatuck River exepting Mr Smiths trading house. . . ." **Thomas Stanton S^r^** of Stonington, aged 78, testified that he travelled the path above 54 years ago.

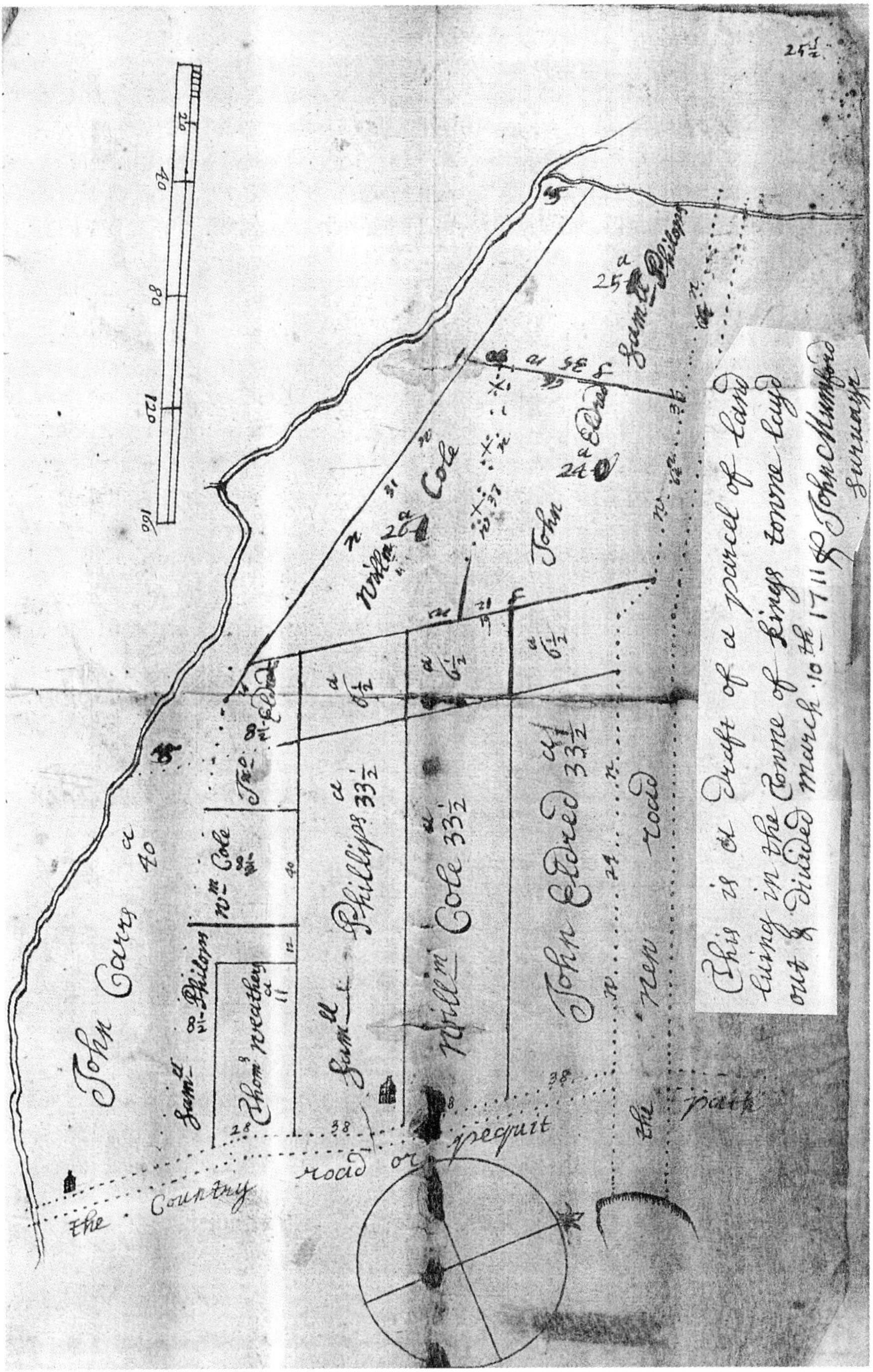

Plat showing location of property on Pequot Path

Records of a Justices Court, Rowse Helms, Assistant, and William Hall, Justice, 21 October 1717 were included. **Lodowick Updicke** of Kingstown, yeoman, charged **Samuel Holway**, cloather alias labourer, and **William Bently**, currier, both of Kingstown, with forcible entry into two parcels of land in Kingstown, one of about 12 acres enclosed by Holway, bounded west on the Country Road, north by a Brook or Crossway, east by Updike's land, and south by land fenced by Bentley; the other was fenced by William Bentley and contained 3 acres, bounded west on the Country Road, east and south by Updike land, and north by land of Holway. The court resolved that 24 good sufficient men of the town of Kingstown qualified according to law be called to inquire into the case. It was later noted that "William Bentley and Lodowick Updicke have agreed and sd Bentley Deeded Possession . . . of ye sd lands."

Lease shown, dated 23 October 1717, **Danl Updike** of Newport let to **Wm Bentley** of Kingstown a small piece of land . . . 2 acres . . . for one full year, rent to be 2 shillings and at the end of the time the land was to be delivered up; witnesses were **William Coddington** and **Richard Updike**; Bentley signed by mark, a curved W.

On 6 September 1720 Captain **Daniell Eldred** of Kingstown testified that upwards of 40 years past "there was two paths that went over the River near adjoining to the House of **Benjn Bentlys** in sd Kingstown that went by the names of Pequot Paths . . . one of which went through [my] father's land and the other through the land of **Samuell Eldred**s Brother which was the upper Path of the two . . . commonly called the old Pequot Path and that was the land now in Dispute between Mr James Updicke and Dan^ll Updicke . . . [land of] Benj: Bently lyes between those two paths and to the eastward of the Rhode that is now the Country Rhode."

On 8 March 1720/21, **Major Job Green** of Warwick deposed before John Wickes, Assistant, and said that he had been one of the first trustees nominated by **Ninigret** Sachem of the Narragansett Country. "I acted with ye rest of ye Trustees relating and setling ye Lands in sd Narragansett between this Colony and sd Sachem and the sd Sachem Ninigret did surrender up to sd Colony all his Right title and Claim that he then had or might have, to any of sd Lands excepting a certain tract settled on him and his posterity lying in ye Town of Westerly . . . wee never made any particular agreement wth ye sd Sachem concerning any more particular bounds or claim of the Lands . . . the Aincient Road formerly Deemed and called ye old Pequit Road went to ye

Eastward of Benjamin Bentleys house now in contest between sd Bentley and sd Updike . . . ."

An undated testimony by **William Wanton** probably belongs here: in court, before Wm Coddington, Recorder, William Wanton of Newport "saith that aout 15 or 16 years since, His Honour The Deputy Governour, He this deponent & others were Attorneys to **Ninegrett** Sachem of the Narogansett Country that was not Legally sold before, meeting with many Difficulties We (in the Name of the Sachem) Desired the General Assembly then Setting at Providence to take the matter into their Hands and to oppose the fforces & Injuries that were done to the Sachem, The said Assembly refusing our Petition, We thought that they were rather willing, That the Mortgage men whould have it, Then the Sachem & Colony, which very much disturbed us, Somtime after We mett in the Narogansett Country & Concluded to Sell Some of said Sachem's Lands, to Show the Colony said Sachem's Right, and accordingly we sold Severall Tracts of Land, And the said Sachem by & with the Consent of us his said Attornys Did give Deeds likewise of other Old Purchases — and all that bought of us holds under that Title. What we did in that affair proved very Successfull, For soon followed the Settlement of this Government & in that affair We the Attorneys often mett together to Consult for the peace of the same, We in all our Debates were willing & did agree (I think I may say as one man) That where there was a Difference or Dispute of any bounds to favour the proprietor & to Settle peace We did agree that the Country Road should be the Bounds against Capt John Eldridge and soe to the Northward as far as the Vacant Lands came to the Road . . . in all the whole affair never heard one man in the Assemblies once seem to desire that the Country should have any Right below the Road as it now runs in that place . . . .

Depositions 20 March 1720/1 before William Spencer, Justice: **Samuel Tifft** of Kingstown aged 77 years or thereabouts stated that the path ran to the "Eastward of ye ruens of an old house Belonging to Old Mr Eldred Father of ye now Capt. John Eldred and so to ye Eastward of Mr Phillips old Tannyard and from thence some Rhoads to ye Eastward of ye land now in possession of Benjamin Bentley which is in controversy. **Amy Gardner** aged 76 or thereabouts testified that she had known the Pequot Path upwards of three score years. **John Thomas** of Kingstown deposed and said that he "hath known the land this 2 or 3 and 30 years . . . never fenced till about 16 or 17 years ago." **Henery Knowls Senr** of Kingstown, aged 67 or thereabouts, deposed at the same time, and **Thomas Jakwise**, aged 41 years, testified that about 16 or 17 years ago he was "employed by John Thomas to help make fence to the westward of the Pequot path and the land to the eastward was in Benjamin Bentley's possession . . . there was never any fence between the country road and the Pequot Path before . . . ." **Dan^ll^ Eldredg** testified the same day before Elisha Cole, Assistant, James Updike being present, that upwards of 40 years ago his father built a frame for a house "and was agoing [to] raise it between the four peckit [Pequot] paths and the indians carried the timber to gether on the day it was to be raised and layd it one a heap [and] burned it to ashes because he would not set it one the est side of the lower path." **Stephen Northrup** of Kingstown, aged 61 or thereabouts, testified that he had known the Pequot Path these 48 years. **Henry Gardner Senr** of Kingstown, aged 76 or thereabouts, testified that he had known the Path upwards of three score years.

On 29 March 1721, **Richard Updike** of Kingstown testified before Richard Ward, recorder, that the land was "part of the farm **John Pinder** now lives upon . . . my Father let it to **John Thomas** up to the now Country Roade . . . afterwards leased it unto **Willm Bently** late deceased, who to my certain knowledge improved the same under ye said John Thomas and gave for Rent one pair of Shoes per annum."

106. **Thomas King** of the parish of St. James in the Island of Barbadoes, planter, and **Agnes** his wife formerly the wife and executrix of **Joshua Verin** late of sd Island deceased in her right vs. **Capt. Joseph Whipple** of Providence, merchant, in custody of the sheriff, in an action of trespass concerning two pieces of land in the township of Providence. Writ dated 13 March 1720/1; Benjamin Lynde attorney.

Will of Joshua Verein of ye Parish of St. James (Barbados) Planter, sick and weak . . . to Dear and Loving wife **Agnes Veren**, full half of the estate, the other half to such child or children she shall go with . . . if no child, then to the children of my cousan **Timothy Lindol** and the children of my cousan **Mary Williams** widdow equally divided they paying to the children of **John Belch** £5, to **Veren Parkman** £5, and £20 to my cousen **Dorcas Veren**. Wife to be executrix and worldly Friends Mr. **Wm Holder** and Mr **Francis McKennie** Trustees. Dated 21 May 1695. Witnesses **John Cole, John Ireland, John Batt**. Proved 12 December 1695. Copy compared 14 February 1721 by Richard Ward, Recorder.

Adam Justice, Clerk, Rector of the Parish of St. Peters Alsaints in Barbados, aged 42 years or thereabouts, testified 20 July 1720 that he knew Mr. Thomas King and Agnes now his wife formerly **Agnes Drake** widdow about 20 years and on or about 25 May 1701 did join them in the Holy State of Matrimony according to the Church of England. The Rev. **Thomas Napleton**, curate of the parish of St. Michael, aged 32 years or thereabouts, deposed 21 July 1720 that by the Registers of St. Michael, Joshua Veren and **Agnis Simson** were joined in matrimony 17 October 1694. **John Wright** of St. James parish now resident in Boston deposed that he "was well acquainted with Joshua Veren for 30 years and upwards, and heard him talk of an estate he had in New England and that he was a considerable Proprietor there and frequently offered some of his land to sale to [me] . . ." **John Fercherson** of St. James, aged 45 years, deposed that he "knew Joshua Veren [who] departed this life about 25 years ago . . . Agnes his wife afterwards Intermarryed with one **John Drake** late of sd Parish Glaizer who departed this life about 20 years ago and sd Agnes married Thomas King now of St. Thomas parish, planter . . . well knoweth [them] about 30 years . . . it was common report in the neighborhood that sd Joshua Veren gave his wife and her heirs half of all his estate . . . ." **John Wright** of the parish of St. James, planter, aged 50 and 4 years or thereabouts, gave similar testimony and said that he had known Thomas King and Agnes from his childhood . . . knew John Cole and his signature . . . Cole and John Ireland were both good substantial house keepers in sd Parish of St. James and persons of good credit and repute. **John Dunning** of the parish of St. James testified that he knew Thomas and Agnes King from infancy. **Mary Teange** of St. James, widow, aged 50 years, deposed that she knew Joshua Veren, and she had married **Thomas Ireland** who was the son of Veren's first wife and was very intimate in sd Veren's family. **William Moore** of the parish of St. Michael deposed that he well knew John Batt, planter, who was a man of good substance and of a fair character and reputation.

Mary Lindall, aged 70 years, deposed at Boston 20 October 1720 that she had lived in Barbados at the Black Rock with her father Capt. **Nathaniel Veren** and well knew her uncle Mr. **Joshua Veren** who lived there also . . . since his death her husband Mr. Timothy Lindall of Salem, deceased, acted in behalf of his and her own children and in behalf of the children of her cousin **Mary Williams** of Salem, and employed one Mr. **William Adams** of Barbados to receive the profit of the estate of her uncle . . . "He did send over to Salem Considerable goods and Effects on that account . . .," and about the year 1697

Joseph Whipple had a deed from John Whipple of Providence, tavernkeeper, dated 4 December 1707, witnessed by Thomas Olney Senr and Nathaniell Waterman Junr [*from Providence Land Evidence 2:97-98*]. Upon a rehearing, the verdict was for the defendant, the land sued for and costs of court.

107. **Othniel Tripp** of Newport, weaver, vs. **Jahleel Brenton** of Newport, Esqr., in custody of the sheriff, for £2:12:6 due by book for 15 days mowing in August last past in the farm of the defendant done by **John Fallace** then servant man to the plaintiff at 3s/6d per day. Writ dated 1 February 1719/20. **John ffals** deposed 13 June 1720 before Henry Bull, Justice, that he "was coming to town from his Master Trips house some time in Aug[t] last past, and was overtaken by Esq[r] Brenton agans Maj[r] Bulls ground . . . asked what [wages] his master askt a day, & told him [3s.6d.] . . . Esq[r] Brenton told him that he gave none of his men above 3s but if he could come the next day he would allow him 3s.6d. . . . which he did accordingly goe the next day and there work, to the number of 15 days with the 5 he had worked before." Warrant was sent by Mr. Joseph Chaplin, Constable for Newport, to notify Jahleel Brenton, Esq. that there "is an Evidence to be taken from John ffallis, this day at y[e] House of **William Mayes** twelve of the Clock relating to a case between [them], signed by Henry Bull, Justice; Brenton claimed he "had not timely notice and . . . could not come." Mrs. Mathew [**Martha**] **Church** testified 4 April 1720 before Edward Thurston, Justice, that she kept an account of "sev[ll] mens name & time of their Comeing to work att hammersmith in y[e] Summer 1719 amongs which is M[r] Trips man whose name is John . . . . on Aug. 17th old england man cam: cost 20:22 . . . Aug. 17 att night **Simon Sasimon** came cost 21 halfe a day . . . Aug. 18 the boy came in the morning . . . att night **iohn trips** man came . . . att night **i o briant** came cost 22 . . . Aug. 19: **Sam Wickam** and a nother man cam." **Jahleel Brenton** testified in court 8 September 1720 that he had agreed to pay John 3s. and the day following he [Brenton] and **Mr. Keys** went over the ferry together intending to go to New London. **John Tomlin** of Little Compton testified 2, 2 mo, called April, 1720, before William Anthony, Assistant, that he did work "at Jale Brenton's Esq[r] of Newport sum time in the month of August last past . . . man named John falles inquired what sd Esquire gave me a day . . . I answered 3s . . . ." **Joseph Emmery** testified in court 8 September 1720 that in the Spring of [*faded*] he bargained with Jahleel Brenton of Newport, Esq., to live with him a term of 6 months and did work there . . . was not absent one whole day before the

Saturday he went to Little Compton and on Tuesday night following he went to Hammersmith again . . . as he went by Othniel Tripp's house, John Follis called to him and told him if he would stop a while till he could get his things ready he would go with him . . . carried with him 2 scythes . . . never knew he went before except one day awashing sheep in June. Original verdict for plaintiff, reversed on a rehearing for the defendant.

108. **Moses Austell** late of London in the Kingdom of Great Britain now resident in Newport, merchant, vs. **Richard Mew** of Newport, merchant, in custody of the sheriff, for £1,916:15:6 and 3 farthings, the balance of an account settled 8 September 1716. Writ dated 21 December 1719; Nathaniel Blagrove attorney. Bill not in file.

109. **Oliver Arnold** of Newport, practioner of physick, and **Sarah Arnold** of Portsmouth, spinster, vs. **Mary Smith** of Newport, widow and executrix of the will of **Thomas Smith** late of Newport, shopkeeper, deceased, in custody of the sheriff, for £64:16:0 due by bond dated 14 August 1717 witnessed by **Caleb Clarke** and **James Akin**. Writ dated 8 February 1719; N. Blagrove attorney. Defendant pleaded she had not assets in her hands sufficient to pay the debt.

– September 1720 –

110. **William Gubbins** of Jamestown, cordwainer, vs. **Aaron Milliman** of Kingstown, taylor, otherwise of Jamestown, taylor, in custody of the sheriff, for £38 due by bond dated 5 September 1719, witnessed by **Nicholas Carr** and **Tiddeman Hull.** Writ dated 14 March 1719.

111. **Thomas Staples** of Newport, bricklayer, vs. **Richard Card** of Newport, bricklayer, in custody of the sheriff, for £20:11:7 due by book for meat, drinke and lodging for himself and his man and for money lent at sundry times since 16 July 1719. Writ dated 21 March 1719; Nathaniel Blagrove attorney. Bill included "cash lent to pay **Archibald.**"

112. **Capt. John Rogers** of Newport vs. **Henry Butler** of Newport, boatman, and **John Jeffers** of Newport, cordwinder, with warrant to arrest the defendant, who was charged with having taken a canoe last January. Writ dated 18 April 1720. Depositions of **John Ingraham, John Hedley, and Mary Stacey**, wife of **Joseph**, the last two stating that the defendants came and asked for a canoe. **Martha Rogers**, daughter of the plaintiff, deposed and said that "Henery Butler came to my

father's house in the evening, the last day of January 1719/20 inquiring for [him] but he was not within . . . he told my mother that he beleved the cannow which they had at ye crick or cove was Capt. Rogers . . . if Capt. Rogers desire they would bring her home tomorrow or the first opertunity to him but he thought it would be better both for them and the cannow to let her alone till thare come a snow for she would draw easier . . . ." The defendants claimed they informed Roger's wife about it. . . appeal allowed. Deposition of Mr. **John Toow (?Tew),** that he being at son-in-law Joseph Stacey's house, etc. . . . Depositions of **Joseph Stacey, John Ingraham** and **Thomas Peckham**, who found canoe on Eel Pond in Prise's Neck.

113. **Samuel Philips** of Kingstown, tanner, vs. **Samuel Whitehead** of Newport, cordwainer, in custody of the sheriff, for £13:18:8 due for severall parcells of tann'd Leather & Tann'd Skins sold from 11 September 1719 to 3 March 1719/20. Writ dated 6 May 1720, signed by Sam^{ll} Philips. Bill included charges for skins, sole leather, parcil of seal skins, etc.

114. **John Barbour** of Newport, mariner, vs. **John Jackson** of Newport, mariner, for £7:10:6 due by note dated 12 March 1719/20 due for service on board the [*torn*] *Friends Adventure*. Writ dated 16 June 1720. Note written at Boston by the defendant to Mr. **Cri^{ts} Ameny** to pay to John Barbour £7 on demand.

115. **James Brown** of Newport, taylor, vs. **Young Axton** of Newport, [?wheel]maker in custody of the sheriff, for £6:12:0 due by bond dated 1 April 1719 witnessed by **Edward Kirby** and **Samuell Darling**.

116. **Timothy Whitin** of Newport, vintner, vs. **Isac Nebe** of Newport, Indian man and labourer, in custody of the sheriff, for £6:1:2 due for victuals and drink sold and delivered from 5 September 1716 to 30 December 1717. Writ dated 27 June 1720; Nathaniel Newdigate attorney.

117. **Nicholas Power** of Providence, merchant, vs. **Isaac Ballard** of Providence, husbandman, in custody of the sheriff, for £12:6:11 due for goods sold and delivered from December 1712 to July 1713. Writ dated 28 June 1720. Bill included charges for "brandy, molasses, pr man's shoes and pr woman's shoes, nails, linin, pipes, salte, cardes, rum, cotton, a Juse harpe, flax, spoones, hollon & mohare, needles, shingels, 2 hogs . . . ."

118. **Edward Mott** of Kingstown, yeoman, vs. **Nathan Jackways** of Kingstown, husbandman, in custody of the sheriff, charging that the defendant, while "at his especial Instance and request lived in and improved a house and two acres of land of the plaintiffs scituated in Kingstown," bounded northerly and easterly by land belonging to **Jahleel Brenton**, Esq., southerly and westerly by land formerly of **Edward Greenman**, for the space of one year or thereabouts, destroyed or suffered ye fences about said two acres of land to be destroyed. Writ dated 12 July 1720; Nathaniel Blagrove attorney. **James Perry** of Kingstown deposed before **Rouse Helme**, Justice [*not dated*] and said that "when Nathan Jackways made agreement with Edward Mott at the house of Capt. **John Potter** (in Kingstown) about paying of money and cutting of oak and seder railes . . . I was a constable and said Jackways was then under an arrest and in my custody."

Depositions made 11 August 1720 before Rouse Helme, Justice: **Benjamin Peckham** of Kingstown [*separated from case*] stated that in the winter last past he was "at the house of Capt. John Potter in sd town and there being present Edward Mott and Nathan Jakques both of sd Kingstown in debate about some difference betwixt them . . . they came to an agreement . . . Jakques promised to pay Mott £3:8:0 for the month of June last past and also to cut two hundred Seder Rails or poles and deliver them to Mott at ye south side of the Great Pond in sd town and also to cut and split two hundred and fifty oak railes on Mott's farme where he now dweles . . . in winter last past Mott to find Jackques Provition while he is cuting oak railes." **Jonathan Turner** of Kingstown testified to the truth of the above and also said that "Jakques did promis to remove he and his family in ye month of June last past out of a house that he then lived in (which he hired of sd Mott)."

119. **William Dyre** of Newport, merchant, vs. **John Jackson** of Newport, mariner, in custody of the sheriff, for £5:11:8 due for goods sold and delivered from 14 October 1719 to 12 January 1719/20. Writ dated 18 July 1720; Nathaniel Newdigate attorney. Bill included charges for 7½ yds chellis, buttons, thread, pins, powder, sugar, etc.

120. **Cuthbert Campbell** of Newport vs. **James Browne** of Newport, taylor, in custody of the sheriff, for £23 due by bond dated 1 January 1719/20 witnessed by **Elkanah Pembrooke** and **Jonathan Chase**. Writ dated 19 July 1720; Nathaniel Newdigate attorney.

121. **George Wightman** of Kingstown, yeoman, vs. **Zechariah Jenkins** of Kingstown, yeoman, in custody of the sheriff, in action of trespass concerning 30 acres of pasture land in Kingstown. Writ dated 19 July 1720; Nathaniel Newdigate attorney. Land sued for was part of 450 acres which was part of the Great Tract of 1000 acres in the Pettaquamscutt Purchase. The 450 acre tract was deeded to the plaintiff 13 March 1693/4 by **John Wilbore** of Portsmouth, yeoman.

122. **Thomas Bradford** of Providence, yeoman, vs. **Stephen Easton** of Newport, yeoman, and **Nathaniel Dunn** of New Shoreham on Block Island, cordwainer, for £104 due by a bond dated 23 May 1715 witnessed by **James Cary** and **Samuell Goodspeed** [mark, S lying on side]. Writ dated 22 July 1720. Papers in file: receipt 13 November 1716 of **James Clarke** £12:10:0 in part of balance due; note dated at Darkmoth [*sic*] 12 June 1718 to "frind Thomas Bradford . . . be plesed to pay the bearer Stephen Easton £5:15 and in so doing you wold oblig youer frind & his resate shall be your discharg," signed by **Joseph** [or **Seth**?] **Gifford**; receipts signed by **Johannah Giffard** at Newport, 3 September 1718 received of Mr. Stephen Eston £5:15:0 on account of Thomas Bradford for my keeping a child for the sd Bradford, and "received of **Job Lawton** on account of Stephen Eston, £5." A receipt dated 1 June 1719 from Bradford to Easton for £3 refers to a bastard child.

123. **Charles Holden** late of Newport, cooper, now of Warwick, vs. **Emanuel Rouse** of East Greenwich, cooper, in custody of the sheriff, for £34:2:0 due by bond dated 11 April 1719, witnessed by **George Weastgeate** and **John Wickes**. Writ dated 25 July 1720; Nathaniel Newdigate attorney.

124. **Jahleel Brenton** of Newport, Esq. vs. **Edward Mott** of Kingstown, husbandman, in custody of the sheriff, for wrongfully withholding two farms or tracts of land and three lotts of marsh in Kingstown for one year after the term of a lease had expired. Writ dated 25 July 1720; Nathaniel Newdigate attorney. The property had been let to the defendant on 19 November 1709 for a term of seven years.

125. **Samuell Darling** of Newport, cordwainer, vs. **Ebenezer Sheppard** of Newport, taylor, in custody of the sheriff, for £33:16:6 due by book for boarding the defendant's servant **Henry Osborne** and for shoes and attending for himself and his servants at sundry times from 30 March 1719 to 31 July 1720. Writ dated 27 July 1720; Nathaniel Newdigate attorney. The defendant's plea was that Henry Osborne was the defendant's journeyman hired at so much per weeke, and no servant by indenture or other covenant. **Mordecai Dunbar** deposed 12 August 1720 before Henry Bull, Justice, and said that Osborne "boards at my house upon the account of Ebenezer Sheppard [who] hath engaged for the payment of the same . . . one **Davis** is there now upon the same terms." **Thomas Way** deposed 9 September 1720 that he was in Darling's shop two or three days before Darling arrested Sheppard, and **James Brown** testified at the same time. **John Cuthbertson** testified 10 September that he heard Henry Osborne say within the last year that he "workt by the week and had his diet found him by [the defendant]." Two notes in file from **Henry Joslen** dated 1 and 3 October 1718 to pay Samuel Darling 40s. on demand.

126. **James Arnold** of Newport, shipwright, vs. **Charles Whitfield** of Newport, marriner, in custody of the sheriff, for £55:18:1 due for sundry parcels of plank, timber, and ocum, and work done for the defendant from January 1718/19 to August 1719. Writ dated 27 July 1720; Nathaniel Newdigate attorney.

Depositions 6 September 1720: **Samuel Cranston Junr** of Newport, gouldsmith, testified before Henry Bull, Justice, that in the last fall of the year, about September or October, "**James Arnold** and **Daniel Lambart** both of Newport shipcarpenters came and desired me to walk with them . . . after some discorse they desired of me to write an agreement between them and Capt. Charles Whitfield . . . I took down a minnet of their agreement . . . but have lost it . . . to best of memory, Arnold and Lambert were to prepare a sloop of Whitfield's and to put in about fifty timbers . . . to fitt her of by the middle of fabruay Insuing . . . to have for their work and stuff £32. Before I had drawn the articles of agreement Arnold Came to me and inquired whether I had done the wrighting but I informed him I had nott . . . he told me I need not for Capt. Whitfield was gone to Connecticut . . . and would not return for some time and likewise said Whitfield was an honest man and would not wrong them." **Isaac Allen** made a deposition at the same time. **James Burges** deposed before Edward Thurston, Justice, the same day, and said that in the fall he had been with Charles Whitfield and Daniel Lambert at y^e^ *Angell and Crown* Tavern kept by **George Stanton** in Newport when they discussed terms. Arnold was asked to find the iron work also but refused. They agreed, "Joynd hands and Drank to Each other . . . said work was to be compleat^d^ and done in february now last past." **John Underwood Junr** testified at the same time that he had worked upon Whitfield's sloop with Arnold the last spring . . . "James Arnold worked by the Great and not by the day . . . some days did not work two hours or much more . . . ." Verdict for the plaintiff, reversed upon a rehearing, for the defendant.

127. James Browne of Newport, merchant, vs. **Joseph Chaplin** of Newport, joyner, in custody of the sheriff, for £7:17:4 due for sundry parcels of goods sold and delivered from 6 February 1716/17 to 15 November 1719. Writ dated 28 July 1720; Nathaniel Newdigate attorney.

128. Bill dated 1 June 1720 from **Henry Bull** of Newport to the Estate of **Mrs. Mary Cole** late of Kingstown, deceased, £58:4:6, for "sundries she had of my sister **Ann Bull's** estate after her death that belonged to me and my brother **Ephraim** deceased, to her entertainment from time to time, and in her sickness, until her death, with the attendance many hours; money to **Mr. John Coddington** for his charges, going to Kingstown to all her friends; **Mrs. Holt** for watching and attendance in her sickness; for a coffin, with the adorning; a winding sheet and other lining [linen]." **Anna Bennett,** widow, of Newport, deposed on 12 September 1720, that she did understand by **Ephraim Bull** that "all the cloathes and house goods (except one piece of homespun) of his sister **Ann Bull** deceased, did belong unto Ephraim Bull as his part and that accordingly shee was desired by Ephraim and did value or apprize them that sd Ephraim might know how to sell them; and that she did see a parcell of the above said cloathes lying on a bead w[ch] Ephraim said was for his **Aunt Mary Coale** . . . worth about £12 and that sd Mary Cole was to give her couzen Ephraim Bull £3 for the same he not being willing to displeas his Aunt Mary Cole as he then declared shee should have them att her own price by reason shee had bin kind to his sister . . . the truth to the best of my understanding it being so many years past" . . . signed **Anna Bennett. Capt. Henry Bull** being present allowed and approved of same.

129. Warrant, dated 19 August 1720, for arrest of **George Jackson** of Kittery in ye Province of Main[e], physician, to satisfy judgement received by **Stephen Easton** of Newport, yeoman, at the General Court of Trials in September 1719.

General Court of Trials - March 1720/21

130. Sarah Cutlove of Boston, widow and administratrix of the estate of **William Cutlove,** late of Charlestowne in the county of Middlesex . . . distiller, deceased intestate, vs. **James May** of Newport, late innholder now weaver, for £9 due for "a percell of strong waters sold and delivered on order 25 February 1718/19." Bill [*separated from rest of case*] "to Mr James May at ye Seven Seas in Newport," signed by Sarah Cutlove, dated 25 February 1718/19, is for "9 gals 1 qt & ½ of snake root, 9 gals 1 qt of clove, 9 gals 2 qts 1 pt & ½ of orange, and 3 [? Rinlet] at 3s/6d" each. Writ dated 8 February 1720; Nathaniel Newdigate, attorney.

131. **John Moon** of Portsmouth, weaver, vs. **George Thomas Ju^{r}**, carpenter, in an appeal from a judgement of a Justices' Court at the house of Capt **Willm Arnold** in Portsmouth on 13 12th mo 1720/21. It was charged that the sd George Thomas "did without any provication fall upon sd Moon the forth day of February 1720/21 at the house of Willm Potter in sd town and beat and abuse [him] . . . braking of his head in two places . . . afraid George Thomas would kill him . . . had stabbed sd Moon with a knife some time before. Moon was under bonds for his good behavior and dare not fight for to defend himself." In his complaint Moon had "desired a warrant perticular by itself for the brakeing of his walking stick." In court 13, 12 mo. 1720/21, **Prudence Potter**, **Elizabeth Chase**, and **Oliver Earl** testified about the fight, which involved a horn which Elizabeth Chase had taken "off from the shelf to give Oliver Earl to blow in to make the dogs howl." Moon had taken the horn, "laid it on his shoulder" and made remarks about a cuckold to George Thomas, who then struck him. They all saw Moon's walking staff lie broken on the floor, but didn't know how it got that way. **Susanna Potter** also testified, and said that [after the remarks] Thomas "being at the other end of ye house he Came to the fire where John Moon satt and gave Moon a blow with his fist and said that is ye first blow: then I . . . and Elisebeth Chase Run out of ye house and when we came in to ye house George Thomas Ju^{r} had John Moon down upon ye floore and was upon sd Moon Then I bid George Thomas Ju^{r} get out of ye house . . . when [they] parted there was blood on ye floore and Moons head was blooddy and Moons Cane lay broak on the floore . . . ." In the file is a statement dated 11 January 1720/21 by **Sarah Thomas**, wife of George Thomas Ju^{r} of "Porchmouth . . . haveing (as she saith) by her Husband's Instigation and Threatning Language bin forced, some time past to say (or) Intimate y^{t} the child with which she now goes, was got by John Moon of sd Town . . . but doth now upon her solemn oath, delcare that the sd child was got by her aforesaid husband George, and by noe other man," attested by Henry Bull, Justice. A paper signed by John Wanton and Elisha Cole, Assistants, at "a Justisis Cort held at Newport the 30th of the first m^{o} 1721 . . . Justis William Sanford playntif John Moon defend^{at} both of

porchmouth in an action of defamation that the sd Moon had notorously belyed the sd Sanford in the execution of his ofis the case being heard by us . . . and the fact being proved against the defendant but by reason of his mean surcumstancis in the world we pitied his Condition and Justis Cole advised him to acnoleg his fault to Justis Sanford which he redely did and was Discharged paying Cort Chargis."

– September 1721 –

132. **Nicholas Barber** of Newport, yeoman, vs. **John Rogers** of Newport, taylor, for "entertaining, keeping, and Employing" **Elizabeth Barber**, wife of the plaintiff, contrary to law . . . on 3 March 1718/19 knowing aforesaid Elizabeth Barber to be the wife of him Nicholas Barber, the defendant did receive sd Elizabeth at his dwelling house in Newport and did keep and employ her there from that time to 10 March 1720[/21], the date of the writ, against the will and consent of her husband, whereof Nicholas lost "not only the comfort and enjoyment of her company but sustained great loss in his household affairs and family not being taken care of," and claimed £500 damages; Nathaniel Newdigate attorney. The defendant answered that Elizabeth came to his house because he was her father and did complain of hard usages, outrages, and abuses committed by sd Nicholas and declared she was in fear and hazard of her life . . . on the same day Nicholas had made complaint to Weston Clark and Samuel Cranston, Justices, against the defendant for entertaining his wife; they heard the case and ordered that Elizabeth remain with sd John until otherwise ordered. In March last there was a full hearing by the Town Council of Newport, and Nicholas and John did agree that Nicholas should take care of his eldest child and deliver the household goods which were Elizabeth's before her marriage to her and that John would take care of her and the youngest child.

133. **Eunice Greenman** of Newport, spinster, vs. **Christopher Almy, Jnr.**, of Newport, gentleman, claiming £250 damages. Writ dated 14 July 1721; Jn° Read attorney. She declared that whereas she had "always from her childhood behaved herself soberly and virtuously and thereby gained ye good esteem and favour of her neighbours, and being thereby likely to obtain a reasonable preferment in marriage & secure a comfortable fortune in the World, the sd. **Christopher Almy**, know-

ing this, did sometime about the beginning of May 1715 at Newport make suit & pretended a marriage courtship . . . about the 25th day of March 1719 when under colour of the same . . . with many repeated protestations of his love and promises to marry he inticed and deceived her and begot her with child . . . and afterwards continued to pretend promises and courtship till on or about 25 September 1719 at Newport declared published Banns of Matrimony, yet afterwards deserted her and made suit to **Elizabeth Almy** of Tivertowne . . . banns [with Elizabeth] published 24 March 1719[20] or about the last day of April . . . whereby the plaintiff was brought to great shame and dishonour."

Jn° Brown, Ass't, testified that "Christofor son of **Capt. Job Almy** of Newport sum time in September 1719 came and desiared me to sine his publishment in order to be married to Eunice Greenman, and I sined it." **John Hammett** deposed about the same thing. Banns for Christopher Almy and Elizabeth Almy were exhibited, signed 24 March 1719[/20] by **Henry Bull**. An order dated 28 April 1720 forbidding marriage until the case be argued at the Court of General Tryalls was signed by **Henry Bull** and **Peleg Smith**, Justices. **Ruth**, wife of **William Wanton** of Newport, merchant, testified that she "knew Eunice Greenman for four years preceding the time of her having a child by Christopher Almy, . . . she had behaved herself very discreetly and soberly and kept [her]self reserved from company of any other man except sd Christopher." **Elizabeth**, wife of **John Scott** of Newport, merchant, testified that she knew Eunice when she lived at the house of **Coll. William Wanton** and she did live then a sober, retired life; she saw Christopher Almy often go to the house in the evening. **Leah Greenman**, daughter of **John Greenman** of Newport, testified 5 September 1721 that Christopher Almy owned the child born of her sister Eunice was his own. **Susanah Bayley** of Newport on 20 March 1722 testified that sometime in October John Greenman's wife called her to her house and said that she was afraid her daughter Unis would make away with herself . . . she went over to the Greenman house where in the chamber of sd house she saw the sd Unis sit upon the bed crying . . . heard John Greenman's wife ask sd Unis where her penknife was and she pulled it out and gave it to her mother. **Lewis [?Lois]** [*Greenman, crossed out*] **Mitchell** of Newport, deposed 26 March 1722 and said that [she] heard Christopher Almy Jr., son of Job Almy of Newport, merchant, say "about the time of the lying inn of her [*sic*] sister Uniss Greenman that the child that she had had was his child and that he would marry her but his father hindered him But for time to come he would marry her notwithstanding his father being against itt, about the same time he gave the child a pair of gold Buttons."

Verdict was for the plaintiff, £200 damages, but reversed, for the defendant upon a rehearing.

134. **John Stephens** of Killin[g]sworth in the county of New London [Connecticut], Black-smith, vs. **Joseph Willson** of Newport, mariner, in custody of the sheriff, for £20 worth of West India goods which he detaineth. Writ dated 5 April 1721; Henry Bull attorney. Defendant on 9 July 1719 had acknowledged himself indebted and promised to deliver in "West Ingey goods" before 9 September next, his note witnessed by **William Barber** and **John Chatfeilde**. A second note in the file from Willson to Stephens was witnessed by **Gideon Allen** and **James Jordan**.

135. **John Potter** of Kingstown, yeoman, vs. **Priscilla Withers**, widow, and **John Withers**, labourer, both of Kingstown, on a non-appeal. Writ dated 13 June 1721. At court in September last past Potter had won a judgement against Priscilla; she appealed but did not prosecute her appeal, and he therefore asked that the judgement be executed. In earlier case, John Potter of Kingstown, yeoman, vs. **Priscillah Withers** widdow and **John Withers**, labourer, both of Kingstown, in custody of the sheriff, for £17 due by bond dated 13 April 1719, witnessed by **William Browne** and **Christopher Allin**, signed by both defendants with marks, the last name spelled Weithers. Writ dated 12 July 1720.

136. **Thomas Burroughs** of Newport, boatman, vs. **John Pearce** of Prudence Island, yeoman, for debt due by note dated 13 Feb. 1720/1, due 13 July 1721, witnessed by **Preserved Pearce** and **John Davis**. Writ dated 17 July 1721.

137. **Samuel Snell** of Newport, vintner, vs. **Daniell ffairwater** of Newport, joyner, in custody of the sheriff, for £3:17s due for severall parcels of goods sold and delivered from 12 June 1720 to 1 June 1721. Writ dated 19 July 1721; Henry Bull attorney. Account included "drink and vittells at sundry times, flip, loging & brakforst, drink by **John Hicks**, biscake, punch, drink by **Elizbeth Vanham** [or Vauhan?], mugs of sider by wife," with credit in July 1720 for "mending one jont stool [and] mending one tabel," and in June 1721 for "glewing two joynts in tabels [and] mending whare house door."

138. **Stephen Brayton** of Portsmouth, blacksmith, principal, and **William Coggeshall** of Portsmouth, surety, bound in £100, by writ dated 18

August 1721, to answer charges of **Ambrose Brailey**, apprentice to sd Brayton, who claimed that he "hath divers times unreasonably abused beaten and also cripled the sd Brailey [so that he] is uncapable of following the trade for which he was put to sd Brayton to learn." The case was first heard by the Portsmouth Town Council at a Justice's Court held at the house of William Arnold, where Brailey accused his master of crippling him by flinging a stake at him which hit him on the hip and broke in three pieces which was the cause of his lameness . . . he was afraid to make it known that his Master had abus'd him . . . on Saturday last his Master stroke him with his fist and knock'd him down, kick'd and stamp'd upon him . . . the Monday following he stroke him several strokes on his back with a large Walnut Cudgel (which was produced much broken before the Town Council). It was determined that Brailey was wronged, and Brayton was ordered to appear at the next Court of Trials to answer charges.

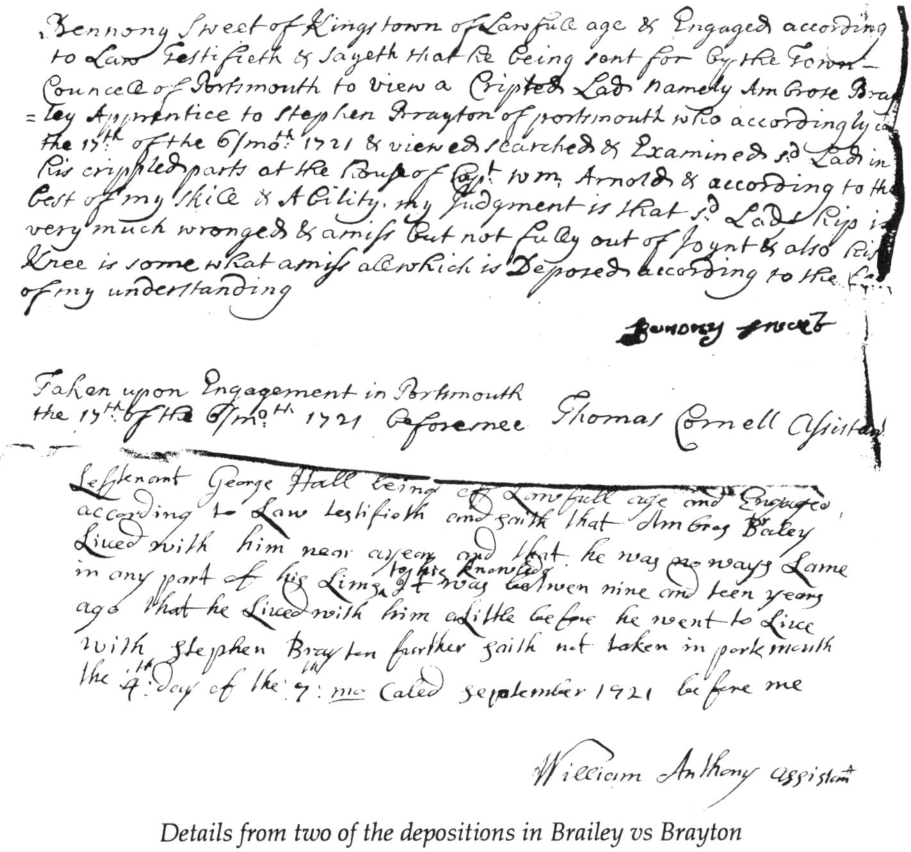
Bennony Sweet of Kingstown of Lawfull age & Engaged according to Law Testifieth & Sayeth that he being sent for by the Town Councell of Portsmouth to view a Cripled Lad namely Ambrose Bray=ley Apprentice to Stephen Brayton of portsmouth who accordingly [illegible] the 17th of the 6/mo 1721 & viewed searched & Examined sd Lad in his crippled parts at the house of Capt Wm Arnold & according to the best of my Skill & Ability, my Judgment is that sd Lads hips is very much wronged & amiss but not fully out of Joynt & also his Knee is somewhat amiss all which is Deposed according to the [illegible] of my understanding

Bennony Sweet

Taken upon Engagement in Portsmouth the 17th of the 6/mo 1721 before mee Thomas Cornell Assistant

Leftenant George Hall being of Lawfull age and Engaged according to Law testifieth and saith that Ambros Bailey Lived with him near a year and that he was no ways Lame in any part of his Lims to his knowledge It was betwen nine and teen years ago that he Lived with him a little before he went to Live with Stephen Brayten further saith not taken in portsmouth the 4th day of the 7th mo Caled september 1721 before me

William Anthony assistant

Details from two of the depositions in Brailey vs Brayton

Bennony Sweet of Kingstown, sent for by the town council of Portsmouth to view the cripled lad namely Ambrose Brayley apprentice to Stephen Brayton, 17th of 6th month [August] 1721, examined him at the house of **Capt. William Arnold**; his judgement is "that the lad's hip was very much wronged and amiss but not fully out of Joynt . . . knee also damaged." **Peleg Tripp** of lawful age deposed about Ambroce Brayley.

Ebenezer Shelley aged 24 years and upwards deposed that about two years ago he lived with **Stephen Brayton** of Portsmouth and "saw him take an ox gord out of his Apprentice's hand and struck him several blows; he said it was because he did not drive oxen so well . . . ." **Joseph Wilcox** of Tiverton aged 32 years and upwards deposed 4 September 1721 that when he lived in **William Potter**'s house near Brayton, he saw Stephen holding a plow and Ambrose driving oxen; Stephen left the plow and took the stick out of Ambrose's hands, etc. **Richard Joy** aged 21 and upwards testified the same day, that between three and four years ago Stephen Brayton and his apprentice Ambrose Brailey came to bring a cart laden with corn to be put into a boat . . . Stephen struck Ambrose, who seemed to mutter and be sassy and sd Brayton struck him again. Leftenant **George Hall** testified that Ambrose "lived with him near a year . . . he was in no ways lame in any part of his lims . . . it was between nine and teen years ago . . . a little before he went to live with Stephen Brayton . . . ."

Depositions 7 September 1721: **Preserved Braton** of Shawomit, Province of the Massachusetts Bay, deposed before Henry Bull, J.P., that some time in April last past Ambrose Brailey "was at my house and I observed him to go lame, and I asked of him how he came by his Lameness, his Reply was that he believed it to be the Gout, I told him I had heard that his Mast[r] had strook him with a stake and asked him if it were true, he answered no, it was a Lie, but if it was not the Gout it was done by catching a Stear. . . ." **Gedion Durfy** of Portsmouth, of lawful age, testified that about two years since he "was gowing by Steaven Brayton's shop in sd town and saw Ambrose Brayle heaveing of coles & complained to me of his masters beating of him & throwing of him down & stomping upon his breast & opened his cloaths and showed me his brest and it was sweled and brused black and blue . . . sd that his master had allmost killed him, for he could hardly fetch his breath. . . ."

139. **Henry Northup** of Kingstown, yeoman, vs. **John Eldred** of Kingstown, yeoman, in custody of the sheriff, in an action of trespass, for illegally

withholding from the plaintiff 14 acres of pasture, arable and woodland, part of 159 acres which is part of 844 acres, all in Kingstown. Writ dated 19 July 1721; Henry Bull attorney. The property was described as bounded northerly on the defendant's land and partly on Anockatucket River, easterly on the cove or harbour, southerly partly on land of **William Cole**, partly on land of **Thomas Eldred**, and westerly on land commonly called the Surplus of Boston-Neck. The 159-acre piece was bounded northerly by the Anockatucket River, easterly and southerly on land of **Thomas Place**, and westerly partly on the Country Road and partly on land of the defendant. The 14-acre piece was bounded northwesterly on a ditch, easterly on land in possession of the defendant, and upon all other sides by other parts of the 159-acre piece.

1710, March 12 [*found in Miscellaneous Box, separated from case*]: **John Cotton** of Boston, taylor, and **Sarah** his wife, and **Bethiah Wharton, Martha Wharton**, and **Dorothy Wharton**, all of Boston, spinsters, daughters, co-heirs and legatees of **Richard Wharton** heretofore of Boston, merchant, our late father, deceased, gave power of attorney to **John Nelson** of Long Island in y[e] township of Boston, Esq., to [sell] land in Boston Neck in the township of Kingstown in Narragansett County, occupied by **Henry Northup** and **Thomas Place** and **Stephen Northup**, devised by the will of **Richard Wharton.** Witnesses: **Benj[a] Simpson** and **Edward Weaver**.

The 844 acres were sold to the plaintiff and one Thomas Place by deed dated 21 October 1711 by **John Nelson** of the Town-ship of Boston in County of Suffolk in the Province of Massachusetts Bay in New England who was attorney to **John Cottan** and **Sarah** his wife formerly **Sarah Wharton, Bethia, Martha and Dorothy Wharton** daughters of **Richard Wharton** of Boston, merchant, who died seized thereof and by will dated 10 May 1689 declared that his Son should be excluded from all part or interest in any of his Estate whatsoever . . . the Estate to be divided amongst other children of whom the abovesaid daughters are the only survivors. The 159 acres did belong to the plaintiff . . . released to him by an instrument under the hand of Thomas Place 22 February 1716/7.

A copy of a Justice's Record in Kingstown was made 14 May 1720 by **William Spencer,** Justice, it being a deposition dated 8 August 1718 before **William Hall,** Justice, in which **William Burgis** of Kingstown testified that about 27 years ago he did make a piece of ditch for John Eldred of Kingstown where his fence on the southward side of his field now is . . . **Samuel Eldred** the father of the said John Eldred came to him when he was at work and told him said ditch was right in the line on the outside of his land. **Robert Green** of Canterbury in Connecticut, 46 years or thereabouts, testified the same day that he did "dwell on ye farme which **Thomas Place** and **Henry Northup** now dwell on untill neare 17 years of age. . . ." Deposition of **Rowland Jones** of 70 odd years of age that 35 years ago he came on to the farm of Mr. **Richard Wharton** with **Thomas Brooks** . . . farm **Henry Northup** now lives upon in ye surples of Boston Neck.

Thomas Place of Kingstown, Senr, deposed 5 July 1720 before Elisha Cole, Assistant, in the presence of **Capt. John Eldred, Robert, James, Samuel, and Anthony Eldred**, and **Robert Brownell**, and said that he upwards of 20 years in partnership with Henry Northrup did enjoy and possess all the land to the southward of the line run by **Malichai Rhodes** in the right of Mr. Wharton, part of which was now in controversy . . . . After we bought said Wharton's right . . . Capt. John Eldred would not allow Rhodes to run the line according to our draught directed us and bounded us himselfe to an oake tree marked IE and said he claimed no further to the southward. **Thomas Eldred** of Kingstown testified 7 July 1720 before Christopher Allen, in the presence of **Henry** and **Emanuall Northup**, that he had been with the proprietors about 30 years ago or upwards.

Depositions 1 September 1720 before George Hassard, Justice: **Samuel Holway** of Kingstown stated that he well knew a stone that stood in the dividing line between Northrup's and Thomas Place's . . . several rods to the northward of the ruins of an old fence which Thomas Eldred and Daniel Eldredg showed the Jury upon oath and said it was the northernmost bounds of Wharton's farm; **Samuel Kingsley** of Kingstown added that the land in controversy between Henry Northrup and Robert Eldred was never within fence for twenty years past and upwards nor improved . . . until Robert Eldred fenced [it]. **Benony Sweet** of Kingstown swore to the truth of Kingsley's statement.

140. **Henry Berry** of Newport, mariner, vs. **John Brewer** of Newport, mariner, in custody of the sheriff, in action of trespass, for that on 15 March 1720/21 "with force and arms to witt one wooden handspike uppon him at Cape Catoche in the Spanish West Indies . . . an assault did make and him did beat wound and evil entreat soe that of his life itt was even despaired and other enormety unto him did doe . . . ." Plaintiff claimed damages £150. Writ dated 24 July 1721; Nathaniel Newdigate attorney.

John Dunwell, mate of the vessel, in a statement evidently written at the time and sworn to at Newport 10 July 1721 before Henry Bull, Justice, described events on "March Wednisda the 15th:1720/21": "Turning up from Cape Cotoach to the [Water ?] Key we met with a two mast Boat Called the *Decoy* in which was Capt **Jonathan Thuston** and **Capt Hooper** and the Boat came on bord and put them on bord of us and then we bore up to the place wher Capt Thuston lay at Ancor and we ancored ther all night and while the two Gentlemen ware on bord our Capt Inquired of them Conserning Logwod whether it was Scarce or Plentiful to which they answared Scarce and our Capt said to Capt Hooper that he was the man that he Trusted too, to which Capt Hooper said that he would serve Capt Brewer as far as in him Lay: but Could not serve him till the rest of the vesils ware Loaded . . . then said Capt Brewer we must every man take an ax and go In to the woods and Cut wood ourselves . . . Henry Bary said he would not cut none and Capt Brewer said Dam your blood . . . many words passd between them conserning the mate and Capt brewer said that he would go and cut him selfe and the boy with him and that Henry Bary should Back it down too which he said that he would nither Cut nor Back then he said that he wold turn him on Shore . . . . still I said but little and Capt brewer went down into the Cabin and while he was ther Capt Thuston & Capt Hooper came to me and said that [I] should Incurrid the men to Cut and I answared them that I did not deni Cuting but I Expected Incurrigment and they asked me what . . . I tould them it was a tun of wood and they said that I should have it and beleved that Capt Brewer would not be against it and proffered to Oblige themselves that it should be so and then they went down to him and as I suppose tould what had passd betwen us and then they came up againe to me and began to talk of the matter againe but . . . up came Capt Brew in a pation . . . Called me a Sorrey nasty pimping Lowsy Dog . . . I said to him Capt Brewer don't put Your Selfe Into a pation but Lett It alone till such time that your pation is over and that we would talk . . . but it would nott apeas him . . . he ordered henry bary to hall the boat up which he did and begun to have words againe and Capt Brewer swore that he would beat his braines out with a handspoke and caught up the handspoke shure Enugh and Struck at him Severall times swaring that he would kill him and Punched him with the End of the handspok . . . which has don a grate deel of Dammig . . . I dont dout but that he had killed him iff I had not Steped to the Capt and hindered him . . . he swore he would doe as much to me so

Striveing to hinder him from Strikeing me with the handspoke in Strugeling toogather we baoth came to the Deck and som how or other his Coler of his Shirt was toore how I Know not and Capt Thuston and Capt Hooper came and took me from him and then Capt Hooper rund down Into the Cabin and Fetched up his gunn & Swore he would Blow my Braines out and had if the people had not hindered him and said I was a mutinear but I said I was not for what I did was to prevent Murder then the Capt ordered me In to the boat . . . and he abused me very much and Capt hooper struck me over my back with with the broad side of a Cutlash and made me go in to the Sloope again. . . ." The struggle continued, with Dunwell struck a "teribell blow upon my head that I fell to the Deck and the blood Ishewed out of the wound in abundance . . . [Brewer] still swore Reveng . . . and bid boath Hnry Bary and I begone about our Business from the vessill to that I said I would not without he Turned us away . . . he tould us that he had Ordered Capt Hooper to ti us to a tree and whip us when he Caught us which he promise to do . . . then have I written the truth of this barbarus Useage."

John Harris, Chirurgeon, testified that "on 16 March at Cape Catoach, Henry Berrey came on board the sloop *Ann*, Cornall John Cranston commander, and desired advice and assistance as to a hurt he had received . . . by a blow . . . viewed [the hurt] and by the Aplication of Proper Medicins the blackness went & I heard no more of it."

Capt. Brewer's defense was that the matter took place at Cape Catoach in the Spanish West Indies, a place not under the dominion or within the jurisdiction of our Sovereign Lord King George . . . .

– March 1721/2 –

141. 1721/2, March 22: **The will of Elizabeth Carr.**

In the name of God Amen I Elizabeth Carr of Rhode Island Widow being in good health and perfect memory and sound mind for which I bless Almighty God and knowing I must Certainly dye tho the Uncertainty of the time thereof I know not doe after haveing made with the Love & humillity an offering of my Soul to my Most Mercifull Creator through the alone Merrets of my blessed Redeemer Jesus Christ bequeath my body to buryed in the Church yard of Rhode Island in Joyfull hope of the Resurection from the dead And as Touching such Worldly Estate which in this life it hath pleased God to bless me with I give and bequeath as hereafter Followeth

First, My Will is that all my Just debts and Funiral Expences be duly Answered & paid

Item I Give & bequeath my Grandson **James Honnyman** all my land, & houses Whatsoeever and Whersoever Togeather with his Grand Fathers Silver hilted Sword and Seald Ring and all his Mothers Rings and half of all my plates and one of my Negroes which he shall choose, and the furniture of my best Chamber in my now Dweling house to be Enjoyed by my said Grandson when he shall come to Lawfull Age and after him to his heires but still saveing & Excepting the Reservation of what lands houses goods which are hereafter Mentioned which I otherwise Dispose of

Item I Give and bequeath unto my Grand Daughter **Elizabeth Dunbarr** all the Remainder of my Goods and Chattles whatsoever, and the lott of land lately built on by her husband **George Dunbarr** viz[t] his Dweling house & shop standing in the main Street being Twenty foot wyde from the north bounds of the said lott of land on M[r] **Robert Gardners** land to the way Goeing down to the Wharfe the South bounds & westward Towards the Watter being aout Sixty Six foot Joyning on my Old Dweling house

Item I Give to my Great Grandson **Robert Dunbarr** all my land and Interest at Block Island and to my Grand Daughter **Elizabeth Dunbarr** one half of the four acre lott taken out of the Commonage And if it should hapen that my s[d] Grandson James Honnyman should by any means or procurements prosecute or Disposses my Grand Daughter Elizabeth Dunbarr or her heires of her Fathers house and land Thereunto belonging in Newport or the lott of land Joyning to the East of it being Seventy foot in length and forty in bredth or of the house & shop lately built on the lott befor Mentioned then my Will is that in Compensation thereof I Give and bequeath unto my said Grand Daughter and her heires all the house and lands w[ch] M[r] **John Freebody** now Occupys and dwels in and if my s[d] Grandson James Honyman should dye before he comes to age or Without Lawfull Issue then my will is that my said Grand Daughter shall have all the houses and Wharfes from the main Street down to the end of the Wharfe or the head Thereof Besides the benifit of the way Leading up and Down said wharfe on which land stands her husband George Dunbarrs Dweling house, my Old Dweling house now the *Sign of the Swan* and all the store houses and shops on that side of the way to the Watters edge be Enjoyed by her and heires Lawfully begotten

And all the Residue of my Estate Real whersoever undesposed of I Will and Bequeath unto my kindred Viz[t] Maj[r] **James Brown**, **Esek Brown**, the now wife of **Edward Thurston**, Esq[r], **Job Carr** Cooper, the four Children of **John Hix**, Ship Carpenter Deceased and the late **Mary Hix** the now wife of **Ralph Earl** to them and the Survivers of them their & every of there heires Lawfully begotten to be Devided in equall parts amongst them but all the personal Estate I give to my Grand Daughter Dunbarr

And my will further is that the profits and Incoms of my Estate bequeathed unto my Grand Children shall be Improved Dureing their Minority for there bring[ing] up as farr as it will Extend and for noe farther Use.

Requesting and Impowering my Trusty and well beloved freinds Mr **Tho Cranston** Capt **George Lawton** & Mr **Jonathn Nichols** to be the Executrs of this my last Will & Testament or that I may Farther add allowing this and noe Othere to have any force or Effect and if either of my said Execurs hapen to dye before this my Will is Executed then the Surviveing two are hereby Impowered to Choose another and for their Trouble and charge in the premisses I will unto them Commissions at five pr Cent according to Coustom for Confirming this my last will and Testament I set to my hand and seal the Twenty Second day of March in the eighth year of the Reigne of our Sovereign Lord King George Annoque Domis 1721/2

Signed Sealed publisht
and Declared by the Testatrix — Eliza Carr (seal)
in the presence of John Freebody, Ann Kay, Nathll Kay

Proved 14 July 1724; recorded by Wm Coddington, Council Clerk, in Newport Book 6:19, 20, and 21. True copy 30 July 1724 attested by Wm Coddington, Council Clerk.

142. **John Wanton** Esqr, Deputy Governor of the Colony, vs. **Benjamin Ellery** of Newport, Esqr, in charge of defamation. Writ dated 29 November 1721. Plaintiff claimed that the defendant had damaged his good reputation by publishing and pronouncing false and scandalous lyes [saying] that he was proved in a false story or lye before his Honr the Governour.

143. **James Sands** of Oysterbay in Queens County in the Island of Nassau in the Province of New Yorke yeoman vs. **Nathaniel Dun** of Block Island alias New Shoreham in the Colony of Rhode Island, husbandman, in custody of the sheriff, in an action of trespass concerning a "certain peece of arrable meadew and pasture land in a place called the Corne Neck in Block Island," containing 18 acres. Writ dated 15 December 1721; Nathaniel Newdigate attorney. The land was bounded west on the highway, north partly on land of **Samuel Rathbun** and partly on land of **John Rathbun**, and partly on land of **Marcy Raymond**, east on land formerly belonging to **Thomas Terry** now in possession of **John Sands** and **Thomas Mitchel** in common, south partly on land of **Caleb Littlefield** and partly on land of **John Sands**, of which **James Sands** of Block Island, yeoman was in his lifetime seized and by will dated 18 June 1694 devised unto his son James, calling it his tract of land in the southeast called the Highland and Wogeskik . . . and one other parcel of mowing land or meadow in Corne Neck . . . about 18 acres. Defendant by his attorney Henry Bull pleaded quiet and peaceable possession for upwards of 20 years.

Evidence entered included: Copy of codicil of James Sands' will dated 24 February 1694[/5], from New Shoreham's Old Book of Records, pages 295-296. Record from same book, page 305: "Sarah Sands wife of James Sands deceased departed this life in the year 1708 whose will was provid June 13th 1709 - S. Raye Town Clerk." Deed dated 18 March 1715 from **Samuell Sands** of Cow Neck in the Colony of New York, yeoman, for £200 to **Jon^{a} Rogers** son of James deceased, both of New London, cordwinder . . . 80 acres in Block Island in the southeast at a place called Weikshik; witnessed by **Robert Sutton, Elias Clapp** and **Ann Sands** (copied 12 June 1716 from Block Island 1st Book:392 by Nathaniel Mott, town clerk).

S. Raye, Warden, testified 10 March 1721/2 that he knew that the same James Sands "that now lives in the township of Oyster Bay on the Island of Nassau is the Reputed son of James Sands of Block Island deceased." **Jeremiah Wilson** deposed 3 April 1722 before Job Lawton, Justice, that he was an apprentice to James Sands Senr of Block Island and after the decease of said James, his son Samuell Sands enjoyed the benefit of the land in controversy . . . "Josua Rayman occupied it in behalf of Samuell Sands who then lived att Cow Neck . . . Samuell kept a flock of sheep on Block Island and Raiman mowed the meadow land that James Sands now sues for . . . it was called Samuel Sands' land upwards of 20 years since." **Mrs. Marcy Raymond**, aged about 56 years, deposed on 8 June 1722 on Block Island before **Thomas Mitchell**, Deputy Warden, that she "heard [her] father James Saynds say he was much consarned for his son Samuell in that he hath not what he ought to have in a will I made when I was sick lastt But Senc the lord has ben pleased to bring me to my rightt mind I shall give to him my land in the necke part of my great Lot Lying on the East sid of the great path . . . and Emediatly had an inrement [instrument] Draun according to his Dezier and Raselution [and] Delivered it into my hand as in trust for him who capt the posesion of it till a Despsiall was made of it." **Peter Ball**, aged about 48 years or thereabouts, deposed 10 July 1722 on Block Island before Thomas Mitchell, Deputy, that "to my sarting knoledg Mrs Marcy Raymond had the land that Johnathan Rogers of new london sold to **Docter John Rodman** Jner of flushin on long island . . . it hath bin in Mrs Raymonds and my possession this twenty-five years or thereabouts . . . did formerly belong to Samuell Sand of Cow neck on Long Island in the Government of New York."

Verdict was for the plaintiff, land sued for and costs of court.

144. **John Scott** of Newport, merchant, vs. **John Holmes** of Newport, cordwainer, in custody of the sheriff, for £74:10:2 Sterling of Great

Britain . . . for time expended 28 August 1718 to 11 April 1720 and money expended at diver times within said space in defending as attorney to the defendant against an appeal before King and Council in Great Britain. Writ dated 12 January 1725; Daniel Updike attorney. Power of attorney dated 23 May 1718 from John Holmes, cordwainer, and **Thomas Martin**, taylor, both of Newport, to John Scott of Newport, gentleman, to represent them "before our Sovereign Lord y[e] Kings Majesty in Councill in Great Britain in an appeal brought against us by **Nicholas Carr** of Jamestown, gentleman, administrator of all the estate of **William Holmes** late of Newport, mariner"; witnesses were **John Walker** and **James Allen**, before Sam[ll] Cranston, with Colony seal attached. Accounting of John Scott in Great Britain from 27 August 1718 to 11 April 1720, "defending the cause of John Holmes against Nicholas Carr and compleating said affair . . . during which time I was at the expense of 8s Sterling per week for Board during the time I was resident in London which was for the most part, £74:10:2. Bill from **John Sharp**, in London, Mich[ael]mas 1719.

145. 26 March 1722: Deposition [*separated from case*] by **Daniel Arnold** of Providence, taken by Jonathan Sprague, Justice: deponent "in company with Insine **Thomas Man** and **Abraham Turtelow** at y[e] house of **John [--]oot** in Providence in December last past . . . did see [them] fight on[e] with y[e] other and Thomas Man strick y[e] above named Abraham Turtelow sevrall blowes that hit him upon y[e] head when thay was afighting . . ."

146. Deed dated 22 May 1722, from **Thomas Ward** of Middletown, Connecticut, and his wife **Elizabeth**, the daughter of **M[r] Thomas Starr** formerly of Newport, deceased, carpenter, "for the settling and ensureing a certain peice of Land with a house upon it: unto and upon our brother **Archable Greenfeild** of Newport . . . and for other good causes and valuable considerations hereunto moving and especially for the certain sum of thirty and five pounds . . . fifteen now in hand payed and twenty pounds to be payed at or before [21 August] next . . . quitclaim . . . all the right title . . . which we . . . now have or ever had or which we or oure heirs at any time here after may or ought to have of in or to a piece of land with a hous upon it lying and being within the said town of Newport which was granted by the proprietors of said Newport to oure said honoured father Thomas Starr and also by a deed bearing date January the:21:Day:1709: and according to said buttments and bounds as is expressed in said deed . . . ." Both signed; witnesses were **Ezekiel Rogers** and **Daniel Starr**. Thomas and

Elizabeth acknowledged the deed 3 July 1722 before John Hamlin, Assistant, and it was recorded in Newport Land Evidence Book 6, pages 424 & 425 on 26 August 1722 by Wm. Coddington, Town Clerk.

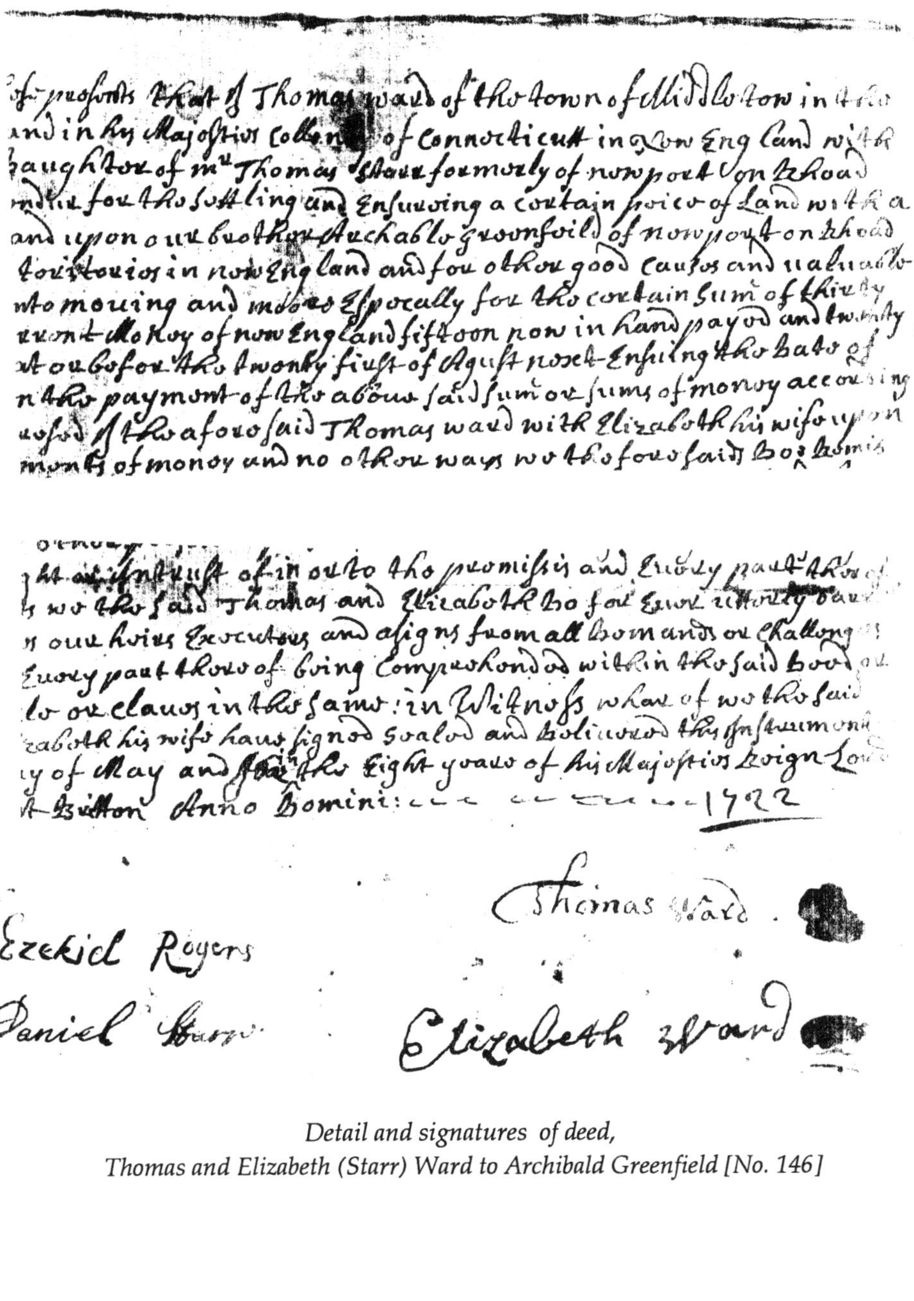
of presents that I Thomas Ward of the town of Middletown in the
and in his Majesties Colleny of Connecticutt in New England with
daughter of Mr Thomas Starr formerly of Newport on Rhode
make for the setling and Ensureing a certain peice of Land with a
and upon our brother Archable Greenfeild of Newport on Rhode
territories in New England and for other good causes and valuable
unto moveing and more Especally for the certain sum of thirty
current Money of New England fifteen now in hand payed and twenty
at or before the twenty first of Agust next Ensuing the date of
n the payment of the above said sum or sums of money according
posed of the aforesaid Thomas Ward with Elizabeth his wife upon
ments of money and no other ways we the foresaid Borgainers

ht and Interest of in or to the premisses and Every part there of
s we the said Thomas and Elizabeth do for Ever utterly bar
s our heirs Executors and asigns from all demands or Challenges
Every part there of being comprehended within the said deed or
le or clauses in the same: in Witness where of we the said
zabeth his wife have signed sealed and delivered this Instrument
y of May and in the Eight year of his Majesties Reign Lord
t Britton Anno Domini ------ 1722

Thomas Ward

Ezekiel Rogers

Daniel Starr

Elizabeth Ward

Detail and signatures of deed,
Thomas and Elizabeth (Starr) Ward to Archibald Greenfield [No. 146]

147. **Elisha Cole Esq.** made a complaint 20 July 1722 in Kingstown to **Francis Willet**, Justice, that "theire was Several Parsons In a Ryatous Manner A Diging and Indeavouring to Throw Down the Mill Damb belonging to [him] Upon Which Complaint I [Willet] Immediatly went to sd Mill Damb and Did theire find **Henry Northrup Ju^r**, **Nicholas Northrup, Laranc Whaly, Jeremiah Clarke** and **Jonathan Card Ju^r** all at the East Eand of sd Damb and Some . . . of them att Work in Diging &c and I heard Henry Northrup Ju^r say they Intended to Let the Water out or Drean it from his meadow theire . . . I Required all the Above named Parsons to fforbare . . . and for them to appear forthwith before Mee at the Hows of **John Bull** which accordingly they did all Appeare and after Som Debate & Consideration their In I did Order them all fforth with to appeeare at the Hows of Capt **John Eldred** in sd Town . . . ." At a Justices' Court at the house of **John Bull** the next day, 21 July, with **Jeremiah Gould**, Assistant, and Justices **Francis Willet, William Hall**, and **William Spencer** presiding, the defendants declared that "there Intent in Diging the Ditch att the East Eand of the Mill Damb belonging to Elisha Cole was to Draw the Water out of the Pond they being Imployed by **Stephen Northrup** . . . Wee the Subscribers haveing Viewed the Place and made Inquiry theirin by Evidenc are of the openion that the Proseadings of sd Parsons in this Case are a Breach of his majesties Laws . . . ." They were ordered to appear at the next Court of Tryals in Newport in September and "in the mean time to be of Good Behavior towards all his Majesties Subjects and More Espetially towards Elisha Cole Esqr or be forthwith Committed to his Majesties Gale in Newport . . . ."

148. 20 August 1722, at a Justice's Court in Newport, John Coddington and Dan^{ll} Updike, Justices: **Jonathan Bishop** of Rehoboth, Inholder, was arrested on complaint of **James Spurling** of Newport, mariner, in an action of Detennew [*sic*] for one gunn which sd Jonathan did receive in the beginning of last month . . . damages 40 shillings. **John Fairchilde** testified that he heard **Willm Harris** say he delivered the gun to Jonathan Bishop. **Sarah Harris** testified that a person came from Mr. Bishop's to her father William Harris for a gunn and "she see her father carry ye gunn down stairs." **James Cary** testified that he "heard in July last Jonathan Bishop tell James Spurling that the gunn in contriversy between them his Servant had and was Gon into the army." **Richard Ireson** gave similar testimony. The Justices ordered the defendant to restore the gun or render payment. He appealed to the September Court and won a reversion.

– September 1722 –

149. At the General Court of Gaol Delivery, the first Tuesday in September 1722, **Solomon Coomes** late of Dunstable in the county of Middlesex, labourer, was indicted; Daniel Updike, attorney general. It was claimed that on 28 February last past "in the silent Time of the Night . . . at Kingstown . . . he did feloniously take, steal, and convey away from the dwelling house of **Robert Potter** of Kingstown one Black Horse branded *C.D.* on the rear Buttock with one Quilted Saddle and one Snaffle-Bitted Bridle, valued at £15, of the proper goods and chattels of **Ephraim Gardner** of Kingstown, yeoman . . . the horse was fastened and secured."

The warrant for Coomes' arrest is dated 9 May 1722: ". . . one Solomon Coomes a Rogue who resided for about a fortnight there hard by att y[e] house of **Mr. George Webb** . . . without privity of sd Webb or his family eloped and departed from sd house in y[e] dead time of the verry night . . . took with him one Large Loose bodyed Coat Gray Coloured without any Cape having two holes burnt in y[e] foreskirt thereof and mended with y[e] same sort of cloath . . . belonging to sd Mr. George Webb . . . suspect is a tall fellow, somewhat slim, with a longe nose, thin visage, looks pretty pale and had on a homespun grayish coat without any lyning in y[e] back and y[e] foreskirt lined with blew shalloon . . . his breeches and jacket of y[e] same Cloath with y[e] outside of his Coat . . . had with him a pair of cherry derry breeches lined with ozenbrigs . . . ." The warrant was signed by Elisha Cole, Assistant, to **Benjamin Drake** of Kingstown, "constituted special constable to execute the precept." On 16 May 1722 at Groton, Massachusetts, **John Evans** appeared before Jonas Prescott, J.P., desiring [authority] to seize sd Solomon Coomes. He was apprehended and appeared before John Pynchon, J.P., at Springfield 22 May 1722, who reported: "Solomon Coomes says he knows nothing of one Ephraim Gardner of Kingstown . . . knew one George Webb of Kingstown but not his Crisen name . . . worked with him severall Days . . . knew Robert Potter of Kingstown a tavern keeper . . . there is two Robert Potters that keep tavern and he knows them both . . . never knew nor saw such a one as Ephraim Gardner . . . the Last night he Lodged in Kingstown was at one **George Gardners** who Lived ab[t]. a mile from one of sd Robert Potters . . . he bought a horse at Dorchester a Bay horse . . . went from Kingstown Latter End of February and thence to Dorchester afoot where he arrived first Saturday following at 10 of the Clock in the Morning where he bought the horse and saddle of a man and knows not his Name . . . stayed an hour or two and from thence to Wooborn the same day and stay'd there till Fryday following . . . thence to Dunstable [where he] has been ever Since till Evans brought him from there . . . the first place he went from Kingstown was Warrick . . . he bought the horse and coat honestly . . . ." On 26 May 1722, described as a "trantient person," he was examined before Elisha Cole, Assistant, and Rowse Helme, Justice. He said that he "rode on y[e] horse till he Came into Warwick Woods and there turned him loose and [he] was found and appeared with sd Coate on his back as Discribed in the Hue & Cry." He was found guilty.

150. ". . . two cases inter **Benj[a] Stanton** and **John Pike**, & **John Pike** and **Benj[a] Stanton**, now pending this Court, are by a Rule of Court refferred to the next Gen[l] Court of Trials, and M[r] **Arnold Collins, M[r] Tho[s] Richardson,** merch[t] & M[r] **Tho[s] Leach** are appointed to auditt & settle the s[d] Accounts and make their report . . . "

Documents in file: Bill, 21 May 1720: Note from John Pike [*signed by mark X*] to pay Maj[r] **Benj. Bull** £1:06:0 on demand for value received; witnesses **James May** and **Jethro Jeffers** [*his mark*]. Bill from Pike to Stanton dated 9 August 1722, for £47:02 due from 1 February 1720 to 4 April 1721 for "314 Dayes work att 3/ pr day, To working one Training Day which you promised to pay for with my fine, which time I have p[d] my self," and "To 10 Dayes work the Last Spring [April 1722] att 3/ pr Day." Bill from Stanton to Pike "for one barel of **Samue Buffume**" and "skins of **Richard Clarke**," in 1720. Another bill, three pages long, to Pike "for sundrys" beginning 1719, 6 day 4 mo and ending 1721, 3 day 1 mo: includes corn, "wood of **Haile**," cash paid **Joseph Allen**, cordwood, cordwood delivered to **John Dublin**, "an accombt paid **Ephraim Haris** for shoose," three pound paid **Maier Codington**, a horse one day, cloths of **Richard Mechel**, cash paid by a stiller, 13 pound of veal, cash he took for carting a chest, cash paid **Thomas Markses** man, an accombt paid **Stephen Bale**, one gallon of mullases, mutton, bread of **Thomas Richerson**, beef, carting pumkins, bill paid by **John Engorum** to **Becket**, salt, 286 pounds of beef on one occasion, one hog of **Isaac Peccom**, tallow, cash paid a woman for weaving, an accompt paid **Daniel Aro--**, wood for **Charles Holding**, cash paid Markses **Robert** for shoose, accombt paid **Joseph Wilson**, cash paid him by **Jeames Fowler**, a horse of Marks, wool, accombt paid **Nathaniel Dier** for meat, accombt paid **Ezekiel Bull**, milk of the

Widdow Eastion, accombt paid **Thomas Jones** for meat, 7s paid **Robert Nortgam**, accombt paid **John Tare** on **Ralf Smiths** accombt, 15s paid a Seconet man, 5s paid **John Jefors**, 9s 2d paid y[e] **Widdow Prat**, accombt paid **Jobe Laton**, 10s paid **Joseph Tiffene**, one bushel meslins, 6s paid **Thomas Davis**, 8 yards ozenbrigs, cash paid his boy, 1s paid **Docter Rodman**, 150 pounds of bull beef at 1d, a jacket and briches of **Richard Mechel**, ½ bushel beets, goods of **Lucas**, more beef, tallow, and corn, one barrel sider of **Rutenbark**, a 91-pound hog, another of 73 pounds, cash paid **John Gorge**, accombt paid y[e] French woman, wool of **Thomas Marks**, one skin of Marks, accombt paid **Thomas Stephens**, 10d paid **Thomas Jones**, accombt paid y[e] **widdow Bright**, more corn and molasses, and several payments of cash paid himself. Total, £60:16:4 3/4. Credit to John Pike, £49:8:0, for work in 1719: 111 days in one period, 11½ days in another, 8 months, and 24 days, all at 3s pr day. Signed by Benja Stanton, 15 day of ye 4 mo 1722. Another bill to Pike, from 1721, 8 day first mo, to 1722, 4 mo: rent I paid **Jacob Norten**, corn, cordwood, accombt paid **Gardner**, mulasses, veal, cash paid **Christophar Lidstone** on **Benj[a] Bulls** account, accombt paid **John Dennes** for **Judah Eirs**, cash paid Markses **Robert** for a skin for briches, 1½ bushels of meslings [twice], accombt paid **Pendor** of Nareganset, beef and tallow from Nareganset, a hog, cash paid **Otheniel Trip**, corn of **Gorge Tibbits**, cheese, more meslings and mulasses, accombt paid John Dennes for keeping a cow, one years rent for a house to **Sarah Peters**, cordwood **Burrus** brought, accombt paid **Ezekiel Bull**, corn of **John Dennes**, accombt paid y[e] **Widdow Pocock**, accombt paid **Garnery Dicker**, milk, goods of **Thomas Leach**, shoose of **Philip Weeden**. Credit to Pike for one years work, £32, and 20s worth of shoos of **John Jefors**, plus 12 days worke, and 2 days work of his boy, all in 1722.

Deposition of **Phillip Weedon** of Newport, 4 September 1722, before Peleg Smith, J.P., that he was at his house and John Pike came there some time the last year and told him that he was "hired by **Benjamin Stanton** by the year . . . to have thurtey pounds for a years servis . . . ." Deposition the same day by **Moses Stasey** of Newport that in January 1720/21 he was in company with John Pike who told him that "Benjamin Stanton had hired him by the year and that he was to begin his Servis the first of Febuary . . . was to have Thirtey Pounds or Two and Thurtey . . . ."

The three arbitrators found a balance of £12:0:9 due to Stanton.

151. **Thomas Lillibridge** of Westerly, yeoman, vs. **Edward Popplestone** of Westerly, husbandman, in custody of the sheriff, for £5:12:8 for goods

sold and delivered. Writ dated 1 April 1722; Wm Sheffield attorney. Bill for bed, beding, bolsters, iron pot, bushel apples, 5 bushels corn, cash, oats, charges of a horse; credit for several dayes moweing, a cow, a dayes work.

152. **John Tayer** of Newport, cordwainer, vs. **George Cook** of Newport, ship-wright, for £4:4 for work done and goods sold and delivered from 11 October 1718 to March 1722. Writ dated 2 July 1722; Daniel Updike attorney.

153. **Ebenezer Kinion** of Kingstown, husbandman, vs. **William Herrindeen** of Providence, yeoman, for £10 due by note dated 29 October 1720. Writ dated 29 June 1722; Henry Bull attorney. Defendant answered by attorney Nathaniel Newdigate, that action should be abated because his name was wrong in the writ; his father was **William Herington** and living in Providence, therefore he was **William Herington Jr.**

154. **Ebenezer Shepherd** of Newport, taylor, vs. **Samuell Shipwright** of Newport, taylor, for £21:6 due by note dated 30 May 1722. Writ dated 17 July 1722; Henry Bull, attorney.

155. **Joseph Place Junr** of Providence, husbandman, vs. **Elizabeth Tucker** of Providence, single woman, for £14:9:10 for entertainment, labour done, and goods sold and delivered from 14 November 1720 to 1721. Writ dated 23 July 1722; Henry Bull attorney. The defendant answered by submitting a bill to the plaintiff dated 15 November 1720 for four months service for nursing his wife when she lay in at 5s per week. **Elizabeth Perce** wife of **Daniel Perce** of Kingstown deposed 28 August 1722 before William Spencer, Justice, at Kingstown, that she had one Elizabeth Tucker of Providence in her service for one year in the year 1720 . . . "in the same year Joseph Place and his wife both of Providence came to ye house . . . did persuaid Elizabeth out of her sarvice telling her that she should take his house for har home and . . . stay as long as she plesed she should be welcom." **Thomas Taylor** of Providence deposed and said that Joseph Place and his wife and Elizabeth Tucker came to his house in the fall of 1720, from the house of Daniel Perce in Kingstown . . . asked Elizabeth Tucker "if she had Don living with her Unkel Perce and she said she had . . . said Place answered and said she was not weel and was agoing to live with him and take his house for her home as long as she saw cause to stay . . . should not caust har a farding . . ."

156. Receipt [*separated from case*] signed by **Wm Brock** at New York Aprill ye 10 1722, to **Gideon Raye** of Block Island, for £5:11:7 "which at my

Intreaty he supply I haveing a grate Nesessety for the same." Witnesses were **Silvester Sweet** and **Joseph Bennett**.

157. **Job Carr** of Newport, shopkeeper, vs. **John Viall** of Newport, boat builder, for £15:5:0 due for sundry parcels of goods sold and delivered from 11 June 1720 to 15 July 1722. Writ dated 17 July 1722; Nathaniel Newdigate attorney. Bill included some ginger, starch, indego, allspice, and tobakar, but most of it was for frequent and regular deliveries of "cakelet" [?chocolate] and sugar.

158. Deposition [*separated from case*] by **Mr Solomon Paine** of Providence, taken 27 August 1722 by Richard Waterman, Justice, that "sum time in the fall of the yeare last past: **Richard Gurney** Liveing with him came home one day and said that he was undon: I asked him how: he said Potter had got the forty shillings . . . I asked him if Potter had got the note he said no but he had a Receipt: asked if he had sett his hand or made his marke to it . . . he said had made his marke . . . Gurney said Potter would a had a Cupple of Girls sett there hands to said Receipt as witnesses but they Refused for they said they was not used to Writeing and so they did not Care to doe it."

159. **Eseck Brown** of Swansey, yeoman, vs. **Joseph Knight** of Providence, yeoman, in action of trespass; Nathaniel Blagrove attorney. Deed dated 10 May 1722, acknowledged 6 August 1722: **Samuel Gardner** of Swansey, yeoman, sells for £2 to **Esek Brown** of Swansey, yeoman, his right in land divided and undivided in Wesconoak Purchase in Providence Plantations, it being his by virtue of the will of **Daniell King** late of Freetown in the County of Bristoll shipwright, deceased, dated 21 April 1688. Wife **Hannah Gardner** released her right of dower. Witnesses were **James Green** and **Patiance Cranston**. Copy of will of Daniel King in file, copied from Bristol Probate Book 1.

160. **James Whipple** of Providence, yeoman, vs. **John Whitman** of Providence, yeoman, in an action of trespass. Writ dated 24 June 1722; Henry Bull attorney. In April last past the defendant with force and arms in Providence "did malitiously unlawfully and willingly Drive and cause to be Drove in the meadows called Lokisquisett meadows two neat cattle of the plantiffs and them thare in Did mire, and would have therein Dyed, if not Releived, by the Neibours, and other Enormities against him then and there did Doe . . . ."

161. **Robert Hannah** of Kingstown, yeoman, vs. **Daniel Greenall Jr.** of Kingstown, labourer, for £29 due 19 July 1722 by note signed by mark

and witnessed by **John Shelden** and **Joseph Sheffield**. Writ dated 23 July 1722.

162. **John Philp [Phelps]** of Warwick, husbandman, vs. **Joseph Tiffany** of Newport, carter, in custody of the sheriff, for [an accounting of] time he was bailiff of the plaintiff in Newport, for 7 barrels of tar sent to sell on his account in the fall of the year 1716 by **Daniel Briggs** of Greenwich, boatman. Writ dated 15 June 1722; Nathaniel Newdigate attorney. Deposition of **Daniel brigs** of East greenwich, boteman, 3 September 1722 before John Nickioles, justice, that in the year 1717 he did transport from Worwick to Newport some barrels of tar which belonged to John Phelps of Worrick . . . delivered to **Joseph Sisen** of Newport then living upon [*illegible*] whorf.

163. 1722, August 24: Depositions [*separated from case* ? **Brenton vs. Brown**]: **John Smith** aged 77 or upwards; on 3 September 1722, **Peleg Mumford** of Kingstown, aged 63 years, **Mary Gardner** of Kingstown, aged 77 years, and **William Knowles** of Kingstown, aged 75 years.

164. **Thomas Jones** of Newport, butcher, vs. **John Weston** of Newport, cooper, in custody of the sheriff, for £3:14:4 due for meat [mutton, sheeps heads, etc.] sold and delivered from 14 June 1721 to 19 June 1721. Writ dated 9 April 1722; Henry Bull attorney.

165. **Jeremiah Wilcocks** of Dartmouth, yeoman, vs. **George Jeffers** of Fishers Island in the province of New York in America, weaver, in custody of the sheriff, for £10:2:6 due for arrears in rent. Writ dated 5 July 1722; Nathaniel Newdigate attorney. On 12 February 1719/20 at Newport the plantiff let to George part of one messuage and tenement and dwelling house there . . . for one whole year . . . as long as both parties should please . . . paying quarterly. Arrangement lasted until 12 March 1722. Note dated 30 March 1722 from "**Marcey Jeffers** wife of George Jeffers of Fishers Island in the colony of Connecticut clothier . . . forthwith Intending to go to my said Husband These are to acknowledge that I have dwelt in a Certain Dweling House in Newport on Rhode Island belonging to Jeremiah Wilcox of Dartmouth, yeoman, for the space of Two Years before the [12 February] last past . . . of which said House [I] am now possessed." Witnesses to the note were **Sarah Bliss** and **Isaac Anthony**.

166. **Peter Crandell** of Westerly vs. **Ebenezer Kinyon** of Kingstown, husbandman, in custody of the sheriff, for £30 due by note dated 18 August 1720, witnessed by **James Kinyon** and **Mary [Fordice ?]**. Writ dated 6 April 1722; Henry Bull attorney.

167. Depositions [*separated from case*]: **Thomas Peckham** on 29 August 1722 testified before Randall Holden, Assistant, that he had bargained with **Elisha Green** of Warwick to "stone one Cellar for one frame of twenty-six feet long and twenty five feet wyde and to make the Wall six feet and a half high .. and for the same to have [£4:5:0] . . . Green to pay all charges both goeing and comeing and to find attendance for sd work and to find me dyett and lodging and horse keeping dureing sd worke." **George Weastgeate** deposed 31 August 1722 before Randall Holden, Assistant, that "som time since Thomas Peckham had stoned a seller for Elisha Green . . . sd Green desired my self and **Joseph Cahoon** to go and heare him talk with the sd Peckham for he said the seller was not Dun according to Bargin and when theay came togather after . . . sd Peckham did prommis . . .to goe forthwith and finish the seller . . . according to Bargin." **Joseph Cahoon** testified at the same time.

168. Deposition of **John Hicks** of Newport [*separated from case, which was possibly in March 1723*], dated 6 September 1722 at Newport, that he "heard **Jobb Carr** of Osterbay in Government of Newyork say that y[e] Shuffel board Table in the house of **Samuel Snell** called *The Sign of y[e] Ship* in sd Newport was his for abought ten years past and he never knew sd Jobb Carr sold it ... it was Jobb Carr's table still." **Young Axton** of Newport added that Snell had bought Carr's house.

1723 - Miscellaneous Documents

169. Examination of **Elisabeth Ellis,** wife of **Robert** of Newport, 15 February 1722/3, concerning her stealing from **Maj**[r] **Brown,** etc. [She] gave to **Mrs. Waye** some muslin to make the border of a cap to [for] her daughter **Mary Mumford.**

170. Indictment, last Tuesday in March 1723, of **Johanna Chapman,** wife of **John Chapman** of Newport, mariner, charging that in October last at Newport she did receive of **Lambo,** a Negro servant belonging to **Robert Tayler** of Jamestown, shipwright, 14 bushels of Indian corn in Ears to the value of 30s, of the proper goods of **Samuel Clarke** of Jamestown.

171. Indictment, last Tuesday in March 1723, of **Jeremiah Child** of Newport, cooper, for having received stolen goods from the hands of Negro **Jack,** a servant to **Samuel Clarke** of Jamestown, on 24 December [1722].

172. **Robert Barker** of Newport, merchant, vs. **William Maccomber** of Darkmouth [*sic*], yeoman, for witholding from the service of sd Robert for part of two days in the present month, a certain Negro woman which he lawfully possesses, called by the name of **Bess.** Writ dated 14 December 1722. Defendant pleads that sd property is in the estate of **Abial Macomber,** his brother, deceased.

At a Justices' Court 14 December 1722, Nicholas Easton, Peleg Smith, and John Coddington, Justices, William Macomber was ordered to pay the plaintiff Barker 5s and costs, "it appearing that sd Negro was Legaly Possest by sd Robert . . . William hath not Proven y[t] [she] was the Estate of the sd Abiell."

Depositions made 24 December 1722 before Peleg Smith, J.P.: **Stephen Easton** deposed and said that Bess was always deemed the estate of Abial Macomber. **John Burch** [outside of file calls him John Church], mariner, testified that he lived with his mother **Ellener Phillips** at the Island of Antigua when she "sold to Abial Mackmore [*sic*] a Negro garl named Bess," who was the same girl. . . . **Peleg Chamberlin** of Newport testified that he "made Abi: Mackmore shoes for severall years and allso for a Negro garl named Bess . . . Abi: Mackmore paid for the shoes."

Will of Abial Macomber attached [*see Item No. 33 for full transcript of will*], copied by Wm Coddington, Clerk of ye Councill and attested by

Richard Ward, recorder. Two of the witnesses, **Ann Brewer** and **Jerem: Childs** appeared in Councill and declared that they Put their hands as Wittnesses to the [will] but it was soe long since that they cannot Remember how it was done . . . taken in Councell January 7th 1722. Verdict for the plaintiff.

173. **Peter Crow** of Kingstown, cordwainer, vs. **Ephraim Gardner** of Kingstown, yeoman, for rent due and damages. Writ dated 21 January 1722[/3].

174. **Samuel Snell** of Newport, vintner, vs. **Adrian English** of Newport, mariner and **Patience** his wife otherwise **Patience Hart** widdow of Newport, for £17:10:0 due by an obligation of Patience Hart together with **Mathew Read** of Newport, mariner, dated 17 November 1720. Writ dated 8 February 1722[/3]; Nathaniel Newdigate attorney. Note is signed by Pathant heart, her mark, and witnesses **John Jackson** and **Thomas Stevens**.

175. **Mary Borden**, late of Portsmouth, now residing in Tiverton in the County of Bristol in the Province of the Massachusetts Bay, widow, vs. **Gideon ffreeborne** of Portsmouth, Esq., in an action of trespass and ejectment for illegally entering and unjustly withholding "one piece of meadow and pasture land lying in Portsmouth, containing 20 acres, bounded easterly by land formerly common but now or late partly in possession of **Nathaniel Hall**, southerly by land formerly common now in possession of the defendant, northwardly partly by land that formerly belonged to **James Sands** now in possession of the defendant, westwardly partly by land formerly **William Freeborns** now in possession of the defendant and partly by land that formerly belonged to **James Sands** and his wife **Sarah Sands**, where was a path formerly called the Mill Path . . . which came to them by the will of **John Walker** . . . of which land John Walker formerly of Portsmouth, yeoman, deceased, dyed seised in fee simple having before made his last will & testament proved 18 March 1647 & therein did devise and bequeath the sd piece of land to his daughter **Mary Walker** mother to the now plaintiff . . . Mary Walker took to husband and became the wife of **William Earle** of Portsmouth yeoman . . . and some time after dyed intestate leaving the present plaintiff her only child surviving whereupon the aforesaid piece of land accrued to the sd William Earle as tenant by the courtesie of England for term of his life, the reversion in fee to the said Mary the now plaintiff after the death of the sd William Earle descending . . . in or about the year of our Lord 1714 the aforesd William Earle dyed whereby the [land] did fall and descend to the now plaintiff in fee simple. . . ." Writ dated 9 February 1722; Nathaniel Newdigate attorney. On the bottom of the writ is noted: "The Defendant admitts the land sued for to be old John Walkers."

Birth record filed: **Richard Borden** son of **John Borden** and **Mary** his wife of Portsmouth, born in the town of Portsmouth upon ye 24th day 8th month, 1671; copy taken out of the Records of Friends by **Thomas Rodman**, clerk.

On 19 August 1721, before Wm Sanford, Justice, **Mary Gatchel** of Tiverton, formerly the wife of **Jonathan Gatchel** of Portsmouth, deceased, aged 77 years, deposed in Portsmouth that she "had remembrance of one John Walker of sd Portsmouth . . . more Especially of Katherine his wife who survived him . . . when she used to go from Portsmouth to the Watermill of **William Freeborn** she used to leave the house of John Walker to go to the said Freeborns on the right hand . . . said Walkers land as was called lay to the southward of the land of **Robert Hassard** . . . said Mill was to the Southward of the said Walkers land . . . [which] extended westward to the sea or salt water and Eastwardly up to the Common, and the white Rocks to the Northward of the Corner thereof. . . . as she used to go by water to the sd Mill in a Canoe she hath often heard the People with her say when they were against the lands butting upon the sea that there is Brownells land &ct and there is goodman Walkers land &ct. . . . Mary Walker (the Reputed daughter of sd John Walker and Katherine his wife) who afterward became the wife of **William Earl** of Portsmouth had but one only daughter as this deponent was Informed by **Jone Earl** who as she said was present at the Childs birth who was called **Mary Earl**, The which said Mary Earl between the age of 16 & 17 years became the wife of **John Borden** of sd Portsmouth, the said Mary now widow of sd John Borden being 66 years of age some time in the fall of the year last past, which [she] saith she hath known ever since she was about a month old . . . the said William Earl after the death of Mary his wife, lived at her fathers house, and [he] having been abroad, was ask'd why he stay'd so long abroad, his answer was that he had been selling his land, and that her father or mother told him he could not sell the land for it was his brother Ralph's, his Reply was that it was not that land . . . believed he said it was his father Walkers, or that, that came by his wife . . . the deponent's father and her uncle **Lot Strange** and her Aunt Strange and some others told him he had nothing to do to sell it for it was his Childs land and it would wrong the Child and his Reply was that he had sold it to **James Sands** and they might keep it so long as they Could, which after said sale the Gen^{ll} discourse amongst People was that he had very much wronged his Child thereby. . . . and further saith that **Ralph Earl** father to the sd Wm Earl manifested his dissatisfaction therein to that degree that he would loose all that he had before the Child should loose her land."

Mary Grinnell of Little Compton, widow, aged 81, deposed 31 August 1721 and said that she remembered **John Walker** and his wife, who survived him, formerly of Portsmouth. They had "two children and noe more, two dafters" . . . **Sarah** became the wife of **James Sands**, and **Mary** the wife of **William Earle**. Mary was delivered of only one daughter and soon after died; her daughter **Mary** before she was 20 years old became wife of **John Borden** . . . "[she] was younger than I att least 12 or 14 years." She testified also about land that had been **Thomas Cornell**'s and later Robert Hassard's. **Martha Dyer**, widow of Portsmouth, aged 74 and upwards, gave the same testimony.

Robert Brownell of Little Compton aged "70 years past," deposed and said that he formerly lived in Portsmouth and had knowledge of a piece of land which "was called **John Walkers** Land and **James Sands** Lived upon the Lower part of itt next the sea, which sd Land Lay between the Land of **William Freeborn** and the Land of **Thomas Brownell** the deponents father, joyning Northward on sd Thomas Brownells Land which afterwards was **Robert Hazards** Land . . . there was a Water Grist Mill which stood on the southward side of sd Walkers Lands or near it . . . Walkers Land extended westward to the sea or salt water and eastward up to the common and joyned northward the lower part thereof on the sd Brownell . . . the upper part thereof on the Common near the white Rocks . . . before Philips Wars the uper End of sd Walkers Land was fenced a cross the Head from the Corner a Little above or to the southeastward of the White Rocks, to the Corner next to where **Tiler & Grinell** Lived with a Wooden fence but in or soon after Philips Wars **Gideon Freeborn** by two Indians erected a stone wall across the Head of sd Walkers Land from Corner to Corner att or near where said Wooden fence stood, the sd stone wall hath so remaind to this Day . . . the deponent saith that to his knowledge his Brother in Law Robert Hazard and James Sands made an exchange of some Land, which the sd Sands past and conveyed to the sd Hazard being a Gore of Land out of that which was Walkers Land next the Sea beginning at or near the Mill path so called for a piece of Land which sd Hazard passed and conveyed to Sands out of the upper part of his Land. . . ." **Mary Hassard** of Kingstown, aged 80 years past, deposed 2 September 1721 and said that she knew

John Walker and his wife, who lived on their own land . . . "the house stood a little to ye westward of an olde path which led from [the deponent's] ffathers land which was afterwards her Husbands **Robert Hassards** land . . . a cros sd Walker's land to a grist mill which was kept som time by **Thomas Stafford** and som time by Jeames Sands and som time by **William ffreeborn**. The path that then led from the aforesaid Robert Hassard's house and land and across to Walkers' land to the aforementioned grist mill was always called the mill path." **Martha Dyer** also made a deposition about the land of her father which afterward belonged to **Robert Hassard**.

176. **Dan^{ll} Smith** of Burlington in West New Jersey, merchant, vs. **William Sheffield** of South Kingstown, carpenter alias joyner, in custody of the sheriff, for £4:06:07 current money of the county of Burlington for sundry goods sold and delivered from 17 October 1713. Writ dated 3 April 1723; H. Batty attorney. Bill dated 1713 at Burlington is for "yards of stuff, buttons, mohair, bucrum, linen, bucalls, gartering, muslin, thread, gloves, bottles and sundry small things . . . Willim Shiffeld please to pay ye above amount to **Clarke Roodman** which is Impowered to receive and discharge ye same." Daniel Smith attested the bill in Burlington County before John Allen and Thomas Hunlocke, Justices of the peace.

177. **John Chapman** of Newport, schoolmaster, vs. **Nicholas Migood** of Newport, ship carpenter, in custody of the sheriff, for £26 for "bord, washing & lodging, makeing of shirts & licor sold & delivered & done at sundry times beginning 3 April 1722 & ending 10 April 1723." Writ dated 15 April 1723. Accounting signed by **Joanna Chapman** includes items as stated and also "my dawters makeing shirt & mending sundry linin cloathes." Credit included cash on account, cheese, making a casement, tobacco, work in gardening, and cash "pd my dawter."

178. **Joseph Bryant** of Newport, marriner, vs. **Joseph Sanford** of Newport, marriner, for £15 damages concerning the delivery of 552 feet of pine boards sold and delivered in Marteneco in July 1722. Writ dated 19 April 1723.

179. **Jeremiah Wilcox** of Dartmouth, yeoman, son and heir to **Mary Sandford,** deceased, formerly wife to **Thomas Mallett** of Newport, deceased, and then wife to **John Sanford** of Newport, butcher, vs. **James Akin** of Newport, innholder, in action of trespass, claiming damages of £600. Writ dated 18 July 1723. The defendant claimed that:

1. The will of Thomas Mallet devised remaining estate to wife Mary but did not say that the house and land were part of the remainder. 2. Sd Mary entered the premises and died about 15 January 1721, leaving the plaintiff her oldest son and heir then surviving. 3. [Plaintiff's claim] did not recognize that Mary Mallet left a daughter Mary then married to **Capt. Thomas Brooks** of Newport, who [Mary] is lately dead and hath left behind her severall children, so therefore the plaintiff did not have right to sue for the whole estate.

A note dated 15 February 1721/2, signed by John Sandford: "James Akin to deliver up the house and land I now live in in Newport unto Captⁿ Thomas Brooks, Mr. Jeremiah Willcocks or their order, on or upon the 20th day of Aprill next by order from me . . ." witnessed by John Stanton Junr and Weston Clarke [*separated from the case*].

Copy of the will of Thomas Mallet of Newport, innkeeper, very sick and weak, dated 8 December 1704 [*for details of will, see No. 21*]. On the back of the will is noted "15 Day of Jany 1721 Mary Sanford Dyed."

180. **Zerobabell Wastcote** of Kingstown, yeoman, vs. **Daniel Greene** of Kingstown, yeoman, and **Daniel Greene Junr** of Kingstown, husbandman, in action of trespass, to recover four acres at Quidnesset, part of a tract of 159 acres bounded northerly partly on land purchased by the plaintiff's father, **Robert Wastcote**, of **John Greene**, deceased. Robert died in the year 1675 and the property descended to the plaintiff as his eldest son and heir. **Nicholas Spink** aged 50 years or thereabouts, **James Green**, aged 68, **Arthur Aylesworth**, aged 69, and **Edward Green**, aged 60, made depositions on 26 January 1722/3. **John Mumford** deposed on 5 February 1722/3 that he had surveyed the property at Zerobabell Wastcote's request.

181. In a deposition dated 26 March 1723 before Wm Sanford, Justice, **Jeremiah Clarke** of Newport stated that he "with **Thomas Dungan Clement Weaver Latham Clarke & John Crandall** from this Island and **Samuel Reap** from Petuxet some time in the year [1675] went up to a place called and known by the Name of Mescanauge Purchase lying and being in the Narraganset Countrey, and that the then Proprietors of sd Tract of Land did then agree to Receive in the sd **John Crandall** & gave him a half share of the aforesd Purchase for his going up with them and in order to settle one **Nicholas Utter** upon sd Purchase and accordingly they sett up a Shelter for themselves and sd Utter and left the sd Utter in Possession of sd Shelter which was Erected on sd Purchase . . . Utter Improved half an acre of land in the sd Purchase by planting thereon."

– September 1723 –

182. **Peter Boss** of Kingstown, yeoman, vs. **Christopher Champlin Ju**r, Esqr and **James Hall**, husbandman, both of Westerly, in custody of the sheriff, in an action of trespass, charging that on 23 April 1723 the defendants "with force and arms the close of him the sd Peter in Kingstown did break and enter and two cows and one calf of the price of £14 there being did take and drive away unto places to the plaintiff unknown," claiming damages of £30. Writ dated 6 May 1723. The defendant's plea was that James Hall was called son of the late deceased **Henry Hall** and elsewhere James Hall, husbandman . . . the cattle in question were in the estate of Henry Hall, deceased, late of Westerly . . . **James Covey**, town sergeant of Westerly directed them to take the cattle. Christopher Champlin at the time was a member of the General Court of Assistants of the Colony and therefore protected from any arrest by statute.

183. **Zechariah Allen** of Westerly, yeoman, vs. **Samuel Perry** of Westerly, yeoman, for trespass, concerning 40 acres in Westerly hired by the defendant from **Zechariah Allen** Junr by lease dated 5 August 1721. The defendant protested, "the father shall allow his son to act as his Bailiff or Steward and let his lands out and grant Leases in his own name and receive the Yearly Rent beforehand as in this case . . . and then the father shall bring action of trespass against the tenant . . . [it] appears a design'd thing . . . both father and son to cheat and defraud." Deposition of **Peter Allin** that sometime since in the year 1723 he was at the house of **Samuell Perry** in Westerly when Samuel told him his [deponent's] father had sued him for possession of land now in controversy between **Benjamin Wing** and Samuel Perry and his Father had received judgement and said Perry had paid deponent's brother Zachariah Allen the money for rent beforehand and was about to sue Zachariah for sd money and then his father agreed. . . Deed: Westerly - Edward Larkin to Zachariah Allen of Dartmouth.

184. **Thomas Jones** of Newport, butcher, vs. **George Palmer** of Newport, butcher, in custody of the sheriff, for £15:12:08 due for meat sold and delivered at sundry times and money paid to sundry persons at several times from 20 September 1722 to the month of November 1722. Writ dated 18 June 1723. Persons named in the accounting: **Thomas**

Huxham, David Dure, Pearce Rogers, Wm Swan, George ffitch for house rent, and **Richard Joy.**

185. **Stephen Northop** of South Kingstown, yeoman, assigne of **Richard Wharton** late of Boston, Esq., deceased, vs. **Thomas Mumford** of South Kingstown, yeoman, otherways of Rochester in the King's Province, in custody of the sheriff, in an action of covenant concerning the keeping of a writing dated 6 October 1686 between Richard Wharton of Boston, Esq., and Thomas Mumford that they should "have and peacebly enjoy the liberty and freedom of a half part of the Brooke or Stream running by the land of Richard Wharton on Boston Neck, called Mattatuxett . . . to sett up a mill make a mill dam and joyn it to land of sd Wharton . . .." [*For transcription of Articles of Agreement, see No. 8.*] Writ dated 4 July 1723; Henry Bull attorney.

Agreement dated at Pettiquamscut, March 18th 1693/4 [*separated from case*], between **Thomas Mumford** of Pettiquamscut as guardian to **James Wilson** and in his presence and by his consent, **Robert Hanah** and **John Potter** in behalf of themselves and **Jeremiah Wilson** orphan and brother to sd James Wilson on the one part and **John Smith** of Newport on Rhode Island in behalf of **Amy Collins**, Executrix of **Thomas Ward** of said Island deceased. Thomas Ward did in his lifetime purchase of **Samuell Wilson** since deceased a part of several undivided lands in y[e] Pettyquanscut Purchase.

Depositions at Kingstown 17 March 1722/3 before Stephen Hassard, Assistant: **Henry Gardner** of Kingstown, 77 years of age, testified that "the first mill known or cald by Petysqamcut Mill was built by **Luke Brumley** 60 years past and the mill now standing which was built by Thomas Mumford and Cumpany the greateth part of the main Fabrick is now Standing and the Distance between the first and that now Standing is about 20 Rods but both upon one Stream . . . There was a Mill built by **George Palmer** where the Dam now stands which was bornt down in the Indian Warr." **Joseph Case** of Kingstown, aged about 68 years, stated that he "has known the mill that now belongs to Elisha Cole . . . ever since it was built by Thomas Mumford & Co. . . . I haveing viewed sd mill do testifie that the principall part or maine fabrick of sd mill is now standing . . ." **Moses Barber**, being upward of 70 years of age, stated that he "helped to get the Timber for the Roof of the mill . . .." **Alexander Huling** of Kingstown, being in his 57th year, testified that upward of 30 years past he received of **Thomas Mumford** £10 in money on the account of **M[r] Wharton** of Boston ". . . for the Priveledg of Daming for a grist mill upon sd Whartons land." **Samuel**

Tifft of Kingstown, aged about 76 years, deposed and said that he had worked with **Luke Brumley** in the building of a mill on the stream which now belongs to **Elisha Cole** in Kingstown, but about 20 rods to the northward of Cole's mill, upwards of 60 years since . . . last mill now standing which was built by **Thomas Mumford & Co.** . . . viewed . . . main fabrick now standing. **George Palmer** built a mill on sd stream where the dam is now . . . was burnt down in the Indian War.

On 21 March 1722/3, **Peleg Mumford** of Kingstown stated that about 37 or 38 years since, he was "att worke upon the boulding of the mill . . . then come Richard Whorton of Boston, & Maj G[ll] Rich[d] Smith of Kingstown and by vertue of an athority Comanded my Brother Tho[s] Mumford who was then att work with me to go along with them to ye sd Maj G[l] Smiths house . . . when we came there we was Constrened by threttening that if he would not leave of working upon ye sd mill or pay ye sd Wharton £10 for the streem that ye sd Mill stood upon with some other previleges, as to ye Diging of Stones, & Gravill & cuting of brush on sd Whartons land for Daming ye sd Streem, to which ye sd Tho[s] Mumford agread to & did pay . . . I ye Deponent & others that was concerned in sd mill Refused & did not pay any part . . .."

Depositions 24 March 1722/3: **Larance Whaley** and **Beiaman Smith** both of Kingstown, of full age, stated that they knew there "had been a Reparcation of the sd grist mill now in the possession of **John Bull** of Kingstown . . . viz. to new posts & planks in the fore bridge at the head of the mill to new brest against the watter at the head of the mill To a new flore under the watter wheale and stone worke now repared one each sid of the watter wheale To two small peces that hold up the hopper and a new flud gate To a new shaft and watter wheale and cogg wheale and two new mill stones To two new [*illegible*] blocks that bares up the water wheale To two corner posts on the east side of y[e] sd mill part gone and made up with stones To four peaces of timber that the mill stones lye on in part To two new posts about nine foot long and a new beame framed . . . one post about four foot long In to them on the west side of the mill stones and a new girt to the same To a new sill the full length of the sd mill . . . sd Benjamin Smith tended y[e] sd grist mill between three and four year by times . . . above sd Larance Whaley lived att or nere y[e] above sd mill fourteen year." **James Baker** testified that he knew there had been a "Reparasion of ye grist mill," and added a detailed description. **Samuel Hollway** of Kingstown stated that "I . . . did Erectifye or mend the Grest mill now In ye Position of John Bull," adding details.

The file contains three earlier depositions, two dated 16 July 1718 before Silas Greenman, Justice: **John Bull** of Kingstown stated that he "did Erectifie and mend ye Grist Mill now in my possession," and explained what he did to it. **Jeremiah Hassard** testified that he "being at the house of John Bull of Kingstown, carpenter, on 8 July 1718 and having sum discourse with sd Bull concerning the mill that he now tendeth which stands on the River that runs into the Salt Water called Petequanscut River . . . Bull declared that the mill was useless in the winter last past."

On 1 September 1722 **Thomas Northup** of Jamestown testified before John Watson, Assistant, that he was "at the mill that now belongs to Elisha Cole and in the possession of John Bull when the sd Mill did belong to **Joseph Smith** late of Kingstown . . . did help sd Smith Raise and put into sd mill a stick of timber of 16 foot long and 10 inches one way and 8 inches the other way which lieth A Cros the est end of sd mill which stick of timber seports several princeble sticks of timber in sd mill. . . ."

[*The following deposition is in the file, but probably belongs elsewhere*]: Deposition of **Thomas Mumford** of Kingstown, dated 27 March 1721, that he was with **John Smith**, surveyor, at the laying out of the thousand acre farmes, in the Pettaquamscut Purchase and "to my knowledge, **John Willbur** of Porchmouth was nott at the Laying out of the bounding of said farme. . . ."

186. **Charles Dickinson** of South Kingstown, yeoman, vs. **Ebenezer Perry** of South Kingstown, Doctor, in custody of the sheriff, for £279:19:06 due 6 September 1722 by bond, witnessed by **Abiel Sharman**, who testified 22 August 1723. In the bond, Dickinson was called of Bostone neck. On 30 August 1723, **Dorcas Fry** of Newport testified that "sometime in February or March last Doct^r Ebenezer Perry came to **John Dickinson's** house in Newport and said he wanted the key of Dickinson's store where his Pease was . . . [he] went in . . . delivered the key to Dickinson's wife and told her he had got all his Pease out of the store and offered [her] a half peck of pease . . . told her there was the sweeping of the peas in sd store [and] if she should accept of them she should be welcome." On 31 August 1723 at Newport **Peter Williams** of Groton in the Colony of Connecticut testified that some time in the latter end of November last past, "I brought a parsell of Pease unto Rhoad Island from Harford for Docter Ebenezer Perry then belonging to Kingstown & [he] putt in 20 bushells of Peas into John Dickensons stoar in Newport & no moor to the best of my Remembrance." On the same day, **Elionor**, wife of **Valentine Sweet** of Newport, testified that Dr. Ebenezer Perry "was in the house her husband hires of Mr **Daniel Ayrault** . . . some man came and asked to buy peas and Dr Perry got the key," etc. On 2 September 1723 at East Greenwich, **Thomas Rodman** of South Kingstown testified that "about the 17th day of the last month he heard Doct[r] Perrey of sd town and John Diskingson of Newport discorse concerning a parsell of Peese which sd Perry had sued Diskingson for at the next Cort at Newport . . . sd [Dickinson] put the Question to sd Perry wheither he could look him in the fase and say he had not fetched some of those pees out of his warehouse that he had sued him for and said Perry made a little pause and said that he had fetched some once . . . [Dickinson] put the Question again, and sd Perry answered that he did not know but he did fetch some once more . . .."

187. **Thomas Jackes**, late of Boston, pedler, vs. **W[m] King** of Westerly, husbandman, and **Anna** his wife, in custody of the sheriff, for £3:08:08 current money of New England due for sundry goods sold and delivered in September 1721. Writ dated 6 July 1723.

— March 1724 —

188. **Adam Powel** of Newport, merchant, vs. **Freegift Coggeshall Jun[r]** now of Newport, mariner, in custody of the sheriff, for that he "did deliver to the plaintiff one Barrel of Starch, 2½ barrels of gun powder, one barrel of Raisens and one Caske of Allum wet with salt water and damnified whereas he should have delivered said [goods] in good order and well conditioned." Writ dated 22 November 1723; Daniel Updike attorney. On 30 October 1723 the defendant received of the plaintiff on board the sloop *Tryall* then lying at Boston, whereof he was then master . . . to be delivered at the Port of Newport in good order (the Danger of the Seas only excepted) . . . he arrived on or about 15 October 1723 safely . . . immediately haled his vessel to the wharf commonly called Pelham's Wharf and there for some Days . . . did leave sd Vessel [and] for want of People on Board to take due Care she was filled with water and the cargo damnified."

In a Protest registered with Richard Ward, Notary Public, 18 November 1723: Freegift Coggeshall, "master of the sloop *Trial of Connecticut*, burthen 38 tonns, navigated with 3 men, being laden with dry goods, bound from Boston to Newport on Rhode Island and Connecticut," stated that "in Newport Harbour at the Wharfe of **Thomas**

Pelham on the 17th Instant . . . had a violent hard Gale of Wind at the North West which beat the sloop so hard and heavily against the wharf it caused her to spring a Leake whereby she had several feet of water in the Hold . . . Cargo much Damnified thereby."

John Borden deposed 26 9ber [November] 1723 before Joseph Borden, J.P., that "passing upon the wharf [I] saw Capt. Freegift Coggeshall's sloop lay with her stern something higher than [I] thought was common . . . told sd Coggeshall his sloop as he thought lay very ugly. He answered he thought shee was aground. Shee had no list as he minded and lay with her Starboard side next the wharf." At the same time, **Ralph Chapman** of Newport testified that he was desired by Freegift Coggeshall to "view the sloope she being then on the Careen after she had been filled with water upon the Star Board side about midship in the first and second streake from the keel between two floar timbers . . . the planke was so broak and shattered . . . sufficient to sinke her in a very short time. **Jeremyah Clarke** and **Capt. William Barn** testified to the truth of the above and said that Clarke had taken "a sticke to try the Breach and thrust it into the hole."

James Coden now resident in Newport, mariner, testified 2 January 1723[/4] before Samuel Cranston, Governor, that at the end of November last past he was at the house of Mr. **John Channing** in Newport and saw two of the sailors belonging to the sloop then lying at Pelham's Wharf . . . "and speaking to [them] told them he did believe their sloop would receive damage . . . she lying on some sunken logs at the end of the wharf . . . asked them where their master was . . . they told him they knew not but believed he was at Meeting it being Sunday . . . [he] told them they should carry an Anchor of[f] . . . they answered they could not, then he told them he would lend them his boat & people to assist them, that the sloop would certainly take damage at low water . . .."

The bill of lading includes also wine, pipes, 37 iron pots, a dozen tinderboxes, 6 quart tin pots, and a cask of iron ware, in addition to starch and allum sent by **Josias Byles** of Boston.

189. **John Coggeshall** of Portsmouth, yeoman, great grandson and only lawful heir of Major John Coggeshall, vs. **Freegift Coggeshall, Benjamin Coggeshall, and Abraham Coggeshall,** all of Newport, yeomen, and **John Proud** of Newport, watchmaker or watchmender, in an action of trespass for four messuages or dwelling houses and "a certaine great peece or tract of land with appurtenances in Newport . . . arrable, pasture, meddow, salt marsh, and woodland" . . . 600 acres, bounded easterly partly by land of **John Mumford** and partly by the sea, southerly by the sea and partly by land of **Jahleel Brenton,** westerly partly by Brenton and partly by **John Stanton Jun**r, north and northwesterly partly by the highway or lane and partly by John Stanton Junr. Writ dated 10 January 1723[/4]; Nathaniel Newdigate attorney. John Coggeshall died in 1708 intestate leaving John Coggeshall his grandson, eldest son of John Coggeshall of Portsmouth, deceased, who was the eldest son of Major John Coggeshall . . . the grandson died in or about 1711 leaving the plaintiff his eldest son. The defendants' plea, by attorney N. Blagrove, was not guilty, that Major John Coggeshall had left a will; the plaintiff had not sued all the tenants; and **Mary Coggeshall** "so-called" was in possession of a certain dwelling house and land within the 600 acres. [*See will of John Coggeshall, Item No. 24.*]

190. **Matthew Randel** of Stoneingtown in Co. New London, Colony of Connecticut, yeoman, vs. **Jeffery Hazard** of South Kingstown, yeoman, for £110 due by note dated 29 January 1723/4.

191. Execution of judgement received at September 1723 court by **Abigail Burroughs** of Newport, widow and administratrix of **Thomas Burroughs** late of Newport, boatman, deceased, against **Hubbart Stanbrough** of Newport, mariner, for £9:6; receipt signed 17 December 1723 by **Ezekiel Burroughs** "for the account of the within named Abigail Burroughs."

192. **Matthew Newton** of Stonington, taylor, vs. **Daniel Wilcocks** [signed Willcocks] of Westerly, yeoman, otherwise of Shanick [Shannock], in the Government of Rhode Island, yeoman, for £100 due by note dated 29 July 1723, witnessed by **John Shelden** and **Lionel Udall**. Writ dated 11 February 1723/4; Nathaniel Newdigate attorney.

193. **Samuel Cranston** of Newport, Esq., vs. **James Brown** of Newport, taylor, for money due for goods sold and delivered since 10 September 1716. Writ dated 17 December 1723; Nathaniel Blagrove attorney. Bill signed by **Judeth Cranston** (called Madame Judeth Cranston elsewhere in file), and was mostly for various yard goods and "chocklatt," and a sum "to **Bartholomy West** by yr order."

194. Deposition of **John Cook** of full age, 29 August 1724 at Little Compton, for case *Snell vs. Almy,* that sometime in year 1720 he gave Mr. **Sam**ll **Snell** a bill to pay him £7 on demand and at same time Snell gave sd bill to his brother **Jobe Almy** and said to Cook that when he had got the money he might pay it to sd Almy and within a month after that he had paid it. Note from Samuel Snell of Tiverton, tanner, to **Job Carr** of Oyster Bay, Queens County, New York, cordwainer, for £200, dated 15 April 1718, endorsed by Job Carr to **Capt. Jos. Whipple** of Newport, merchant, on 23 May 1719.

195. **Benjamin Smyton**, infant, and grandson and heir of **William Smyton** formerly of Portsmouth, deceased, by **Nathaniel Byfield** of Bristol, Esq., his guardian, vs. **Thomas Borden** of Portsmouth, yeoman, in action of trespass concerning eight acres in Hog Island within Portsmouth, bounded east on lands laid out to **John Borden**, father of Thomas. Writ dated 20 July 1724; Nathaniel Newdigate attorney. "Plaintiff saith his grandfather William Smyton dyed A.D. 1671 seized of freeholds in Portsmouth and by his will dated 13 June 1671 devised his real estate to his wife **Sarah** for life. Sarah died in or about the month of April 1709, and the rights descend to plaintiff as grandson and heir, viz[t] eldest son of Benjamin Smyton then deceased who was eldest son of William Smyton." A lot of four acres was laid out 24 April 1700 by **John Albro, George Brownell**, and **George Sisson**, to Benjamin Smyton on the right of William Smyton for tenant Sarah. On 12, first month 1713/4, another lott of eight acres was laid out on the right of William Smyton to **Thomas Brownell**, for the use of the heirs of William Smyton, sd. Sarah being then deceased.

Documents dated 13 February 1723: (1) statement that **Benjamin Smiton**, son of Benjamin Smiton of Wapping in the Parish of St. Dunstan's Stepney, Co. Middlesex [England], mariner, and of **Elizabeth** his wife, was baptised at St. Dunstans, Stepney aforesaid, 18th November 1705, and (2) that **Benjamin Smiton** and **Elizabeth Bonham** of Wapping "back of St. Paul's Shudwell" were married in the Parish Church of Trinity in the Minories 7th December 1693. **Samuel Bonham**, Sen[r] of the Parish of St. Dunstan's Stepney, merchant, and **Henry Wotton** of the Parish of St. John's Wapping, merchant, deposed and said that the certificates were correct, and that sd Benjamin Smiton was the reputed son of **William** and **Sarah Smiton** heretofore of ye Town of Portsmouth, Rhode Island in North America, deceased; dated 10 February 1723, sworn before **Sir Peter Delme**, Lord Mayor of the City of London. **Weston Clarke** of the age of 75 years deposed at Newport, 3 September 1723, and said that he was well acquainted with Will[m] Smyton formerly of Portsmouth in Rhode Island, mariner, and [knew that] about 50 years ago [he] did live upon a farme in sd Portsmouth between the eastern road and a place called the Swamp, which sd Farm and house thereon was called his, sd

Smiton's, farme, and some years after the sd William Smiton's death, one Benjamin Smiton who was by all persons deemed the sonne of sd William Smiton came over from England and came to this deponent being then Recorder of sd Colony and desired him sd Clarke to goe with him sd Benjamin Smiton to hear some discourse between him and his sister Brownell the wife of **William Brownell** concerning his sd Father's Family and Estate . . . after discourse sd Benjamin left the Farme with her to improve in his absence being then bound to Sea.

196. **Benjamin Smyton**, infant, and grandson and heir of **William Smyton** formerly of Portsmouth, deceased, by **Nathaniel Byfield** of Bristol, Esq., his guardian, vs. **Stephen Brayton** of Portsmouth, blacksmith, in action of trespass, to recover a house and 40 acres of land in Portsmouth, bounded north by the defendant's land, east on a highway, south on land of **Thomas Durfee**, and west partly on land of **Samuel Anthony** and partly on a highway, by virtue of a deed of sale dated 24 June 1667 under the hand of **Peter Toleman**, attorney to **Samuel Hagburne** of New London . . .

The file contains a copy of the deed from Peter Talman of Portsmouth by power of attorney dated 20 April 1666 from Samuel Hagburne of New London . . . Connecticut . . . selling for £120 to William Smyton, now inhabitant in Portsmouth, 28 acres there, bounded north by land of **John Archer**, southeast by a highway, southwest on land of **Thomas Ginnings**, and northwest by the Common, with a dwelling house and all other houses thereon standing. Witnesses were **John Tripp, John Anthony,** and **John Sanford**. There is also a quitclaim deed confirming the sale by Samuel Hagburne dated 9 July 1667.

Included is a copy of the will of William Smyton dated 13 June 1671, witnessed by **Symon Cooper** and **William Correy** [*see No. 2 for the full text of the will*], and the administration to Sarah 7 July 1671, Wm. Baulstone Assistant. A letter dated at Newport 12 December 1696 [*left side badly torn*] to [Sara]h Smyton from "your loving Freind **Francis Brinley** . . . to [ac]quaint you that the town of Portsmouth laid out a great Part of their Common . . . to each proprietor of lands 12 acres . . . 12 acres your due . . . [proposes selling it for her] for delays are dangerous in this case."

On 3 October 1723, before Sir Gerard Conyers, Lord Mayor of London, depositions were made by **Samuel Bonham Senr** of the parish of St. Dunstan's, Stepney, County of Middlesex, merchant, **Mary Wotton** of Wapping Stepney, widow, **Mary Moore** wife of **Jos^{a} Tho: Moore** of the same, mariner, **Margaret Keddick**, and **Hannah**

Robinson, both of the same. Bonham, Mary Wotton, and Mary Moore stated that they were very conversant and well-acquainted with **Benjamin Smyton, Senr**, late of Wapping, mariner, and **Elizabeth Smyton** his wife, both deceased, and well knew Benjamin Smyton Junr, [their] eldest son who is now, they are informed, att Rhode Island in New England. Samuel Bonham and Mary Wotton testified that they were own brother and sister to the said Elizabeth Smyton; Mary Moore testified that she was own sister to Benjamin Smyton now of Rhode Island. Margaret Keddick and Hannah Robinson testified that they knew Benjamin Smyton Senr and Elizabeth; Margaret was the midwife who delivered Benjamin Junr, and Hannah was present at the birth 12 November 1705 between the houres of 12 at Night and One in the morning and present when he was baptised 18th of the same month; both signed.

197. Bond dated 26 September 1724, signed by **Edward Boss** of Newport, principal, and **Nathan**^{ll} **Niles Ju**^{er} and **Robert Hannah**, both of South Kingstown, suretyes, for Edward Boss's administration on the estate of his father Edward Boss, deceased. Witnesses **Robert Potter** and **Susanah Potter**; all original signatures.

— March 1725 —

198. Indictment of Indian **Dick**, a servant of **Peleg Smith**, Esq., for having made an assault on **John Davis** of Newport, baker, 25 December 1724 in the house of one **Mary Silverwood** in Newport and wounded him in the left hand with a sharp knife so that he was greatly disabled, &c; Daniel Updike, attorney. John Davis stated that he was passing by the house of Mary Silverwood, and "was desired to go up into her Chamber and suppress anoyes and Disturbance there . . . [when he] came up there was Dick an Indian belonging unto Peleg Smith Esq. and **Boston** an Indian belonging to Mr. **Peter Treby** and **Worwick** an Indian belonging to **Edward Thurston**, Esq. . . . wass some Squas in the Chamber which I did not know . . . Dick struck att me with a knife and cutt me acrose the hand and rist of ye aposite hand." Dick, in his statement, said that he was quarrelling with **Tom**, a Negro belonging to **Major Brown** about a squaw and mistook Davis for Tom. **Tom** stated that the "week before last I sea Mary Silverwood by the Watch house and she asked me to come to her house on Cristmas Day night." **Boston** under examination said that they "had ale and punch at Silverwoods and [he] spent 3*s* . . . took a knife away from Dick . . . did not know Mr. Davis was cutt until this morning . . . there was **Alce Frye** and **Judey** that lives with **James Brown Jn^r^**." **Toney**, a Negro belonging to Mr. **Daniel White**, was questioned and said that he was at Mary Silverwoods last Friday night and Tom and Dick quarrelled about squaws . . . "Mrs. Silverwood desired **James Cadman** a free Negro to walk up in the chamber and prevent there quarriling . . . sd James belongs to **Mr. Rodman**. We Disired them to walk Down but they would not and Mr. Rodmans Negro tuke of Dicks hatt and Run down Stayors and the Indian follow . . . Dick said he would not go Down so James Cadman went to Putt him Down Stayors . . . James was Cutt . . . Mr. John Davis came up and the Candell I think was out when Mr. Davis was Cutt . . . I went away presently after to **John Butmans** a Negro. . . ."

199. **William Bently** of Westerly, cordwainer vs. **Stephen Wilcox** of Westerly, yeoman, in custody of the sheriff, for £63:7:0 due by note dated 15 January 1721/2, signed by mark W and witnessed by **Jeremiah Boss** and **ffran^s^ Colegrove Ju^r^**. Writ dated 2 September 1724; Daniel Updike attorney.

200. **William Pinneger** of Newport, hatter, vs. **John Tennant** of Jamestown, mariner alias labourer in custody of the sheriff, for £4:11:0 due for goods sold and delivered sundry times between 14 August 1721 and 10 June 1722. Writ dated 16 September 1724. Bill includes a beaver hat on 14 August 1721 for 30*s*, on 10 June 1722 another beaver hat for 36*s* and a caster hat for 25*s*.

201. **Joseph Whipple** of Newport, merchant, vs. **Thomas Baley** of Newport, fellmonger, and **Rebeca Baley** of Newport, spinster, executor and executrix of the will of **Stephen Baley**, their father, late of Newport, deceased, for a debt due for rum and sugar delivered in August 1724.

202. **Thomas [Cranston**; *see below*] a Molatto man of Newport, servant to **Simon Pees** of Newport, merchant, vs. **Edward Cain** of Newport, mariner, for £18:13:0 due for the services of **Godfrey Jesper** a Molatto man (belonging to the plaintiff) performed on board the brig *Leopard* of which the defendant was then master, from 26 June 1724 to November 1724. Writ dated 2 January 1724[/5]; Henry Bull attorney. The file contains an account dated at St. Eustatia 24 November 1724, to **Charles Mackey**, debtor to **Joseph Simpson** for eating and drinking, £1:12:9 . . . Edw[d] Caine master of the brig *Leopard* to pay.

Joseph Brock of Newport testified 30 December 1724 before John Coddington that he was with Capt. Edward Kaine [*sic*] on board the brig *Leopard* at Martineco in or about November last past . . . "**Joseph King** came on board . . . one of Caine's men went on board of **Capt. Potter** [and] changed their berths by consent of the captains . . . King came in room of **Jonathan Lea** . . . no person shiped in Roome of Godfrey Jesper. When we were worping out of Martineco Capt. Cain sent a letter or paper on shore and said that this is what sels Jasper . . . we went on Shore at Martineco by order of Capt. Cain with a french man to look for Jasper but could not hear anything of him for the french man was drunk and fired at a connew whereby we had like to have lost our Lives . . . Capt. Cain carryed sd Jasper on Shorr on Asabeth Day to play on the viallin to Plesure him and he came on board after that night and brought the viallin on board again but we never seed sd Jasper afterwards but we lay att the Place 7 or 8 Dayes after he went on Shore." **Thomas Jarrat** swore to the truth of Brock's statement. **Joseph King** of Newport testified that he came from Martineco in the brig *Leopard* in Rome [room] of Jonathan Lea, etc., and "I agreed with Capt. Cain that he should give me £8 for the run from Martineco home to Newport."

A receipt was shown dated 3 January 1725 and signed by **Thomas Cranston** by mark +: ". . . of Capt. Edward Cain Indenture for Godfrey Jasper to me."

Depositions were made 26 July 1725 before Job Lawton, J.P, in the presence of **Thomas Pease**: **Stephen Remington** of Newport, mariner, stated that on the "last voyage I made to Martainneco some time in February last past I caried a Letter from Capt Edwd Caine to **Mr. Henry Allan** of sd place . . . askt him whether he had got the indenture of Jaspers . . . He said no but he had sent for it . . . some time after I see **Rich^{d}. Rice** of sd Place and he told me he had sent [it] to Mr. Allan and Jasper did Run away from Capt Caine and that he waited Severall days to find him and after which I see Henry Allan . . . did hear **Benjamin Smith** aske Jasper what made him Run away . . . he answered he had no mind to come Home that time of the year for he Had Rather Stay with the french. **Benj^{a} Smith** of Newport, mariner, stated that "Caine left the indenture with **Richard Rice** of Martineco . . . asked Jasper [why he ran away]. . . he made little or no answer but signified that he had a mind to seek some better fortune. A little time after Mr Allan told me he had the indenture . . . did send for it because he had strock sd Jasper and the authority was a going to Lay Hold of him for it." **William Bell** of Newport, mariner, stated that when he was last at Martineco, he "mett Mr Henry Allan one morning and he seemed in a Great Passion . . . had just been Licking the malattow fellow that Run away from Capt Edward Caine Last voyage . . . said he was in Prisson . . . [I asked] how he came there . . . he answered he was Taken in the Barbadoes Sloop by the Gard . . . I asked him how he Diard to Strike a Kings Prisoner and he said he did not mind for he had his Indenture and should take care of him and Did Design to Send him Home."

Decision was for the plaintiff, a reversion of an earlier decision.

203. **Edward Boss** of Newport, yeoman, vs. **Henry Knowles Jr.** of South Kingstown, yeoman. Writ dated 2 January 1724[/5]; Henry Bull attorney. The defendant had received 10 neat hides at South Kingstown from **Joseph Powers** to be tanned and returned to the plaintiff. **Job Jenkins** of North Kingstown deposed 29 March 1725 before Rowse Helme and said that he had been employed the year last past by Henry Knowles Jr. and in September or October last he carted 9 sides of leather from Kingstown to Joseph Powers and delivered them to Powers' wife to keep in his "wairhouse for Edward Boss till he come over."

204. **John Sabeer** of Newport, merchant, vs. **James Tilley** of New London, rope maker, for £57:10:2 for sundry parcels of goods sold and delivered and cash paid in July and August 1724. Writ dated 23 January 1724; Nathaniel Newdigate attorney. Bill was for "goods of Mr **MordyCay dunbar** paid for . . . black silk delivered to Mr MordyCay dunbar for you . . . ."

205. **Hannah Carr** of Jamestown, widow, vs. **George Thomas** of Jamestown, weavour, in custody of the sheriff, in action of trespass. Writ dated 25 January 1724[/5]; Henry Bull attorney. Plaintiff charged that in November last past, the defendant "into [her] land did enter and 28 tame geese of the plaintiff did yard and Impound and . . . by catching and frightning did cause to run away so that thereby sd geese are Lost." Depositions were made 8 February 1724/5 in Jamestown before Teddeman Hull, warden: **Sarah Carr** wrote her statement, embellishing her signature, and said that "Ye 26 day of November Last 1724 . . . I see George Thomas driving my mother's geese up to a yarde that he had maide in my mother's Ground and I see theme in the yarde and he was thare a Catching them and I see him throw them out of the yarde and I see them runing from the yarde Tords the salt Water as far as I could see them and I tould my mother of it and shee went to him and that is the Last that wee can find of 28 Geese that has been gone ever Sence that time. Ye 3 day of december Last I heard my Mother demand Sattifaction for her Geese of George Thomas and he tould her That She Should have nothing but what she Could geet by Law."

John Weeden testified that his mother Hannah Carr had desired him to go with some others to look for her geese and they could not find nor hear of them. **James Gould** testified that some time "in the Latter End of November last past" he was walking from his School-house towards the house of Mr. John Carr, and in Mrs. Hannah Carr's Ground he "see George Thomas had got some geese up in a small yard, whereupon he asked sd George Thomas if he was yarding his geese . . . he answered and said he was yarding some of Mrs. Carr's [geese] . . . ."

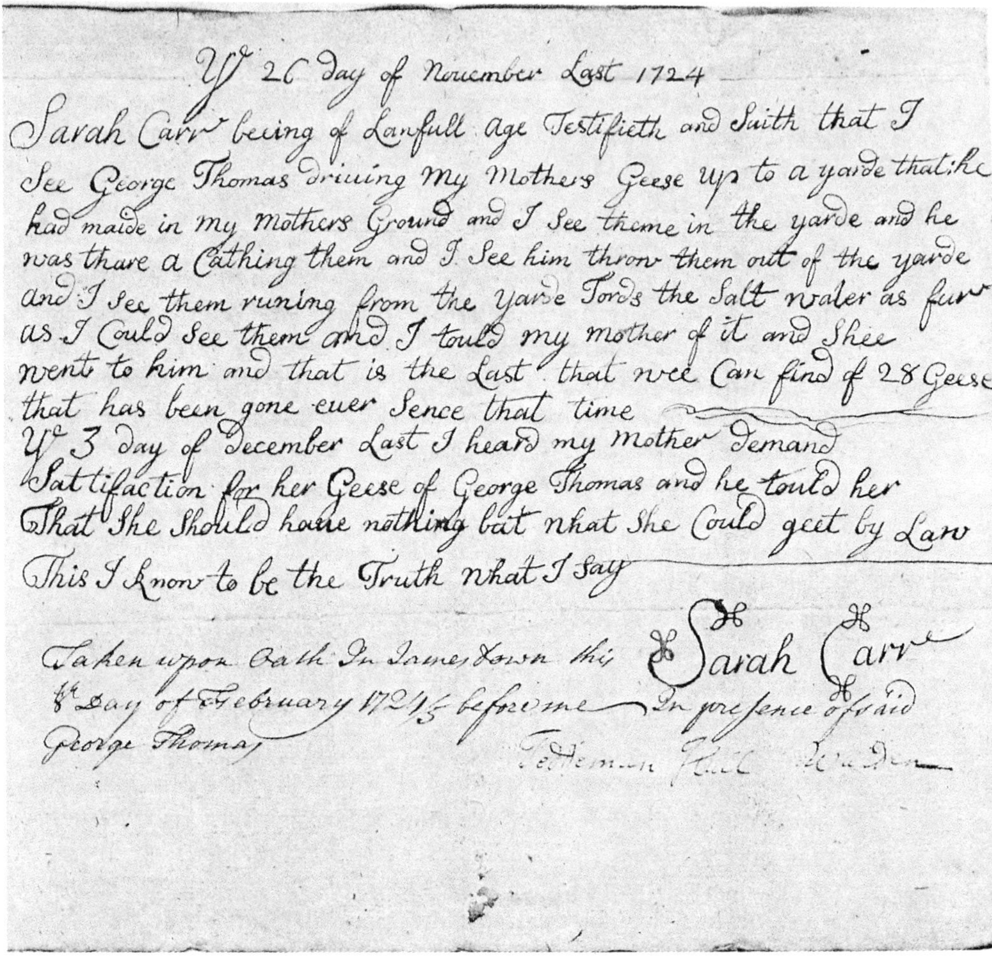

Ye 26 day of November Last 1724
Sarah Carr beeing of Lawfull age Testifieth and Saith that I
See George Thomas driuing My Mothers Geese up to a yarde that he
had maide in my mothers Ground and I See theme in the yarde and he
was thare a Cathing them and I See him throw them out of the yarde
and I See them runing from the yarde Tords the Salt water as fur
as I Could See them and I tould my mother of it and Shee
went to him and that is the Last that wee Can find of 28 Geese
that has been gone euer Sence that time
Ye 3 day of december Last I heard my mother demand
Sattifaction for her Geese of George Thomas and he tould her
That She Should haue nothing but what She Could geet by Law
This I Know to be the Truth what I Say

Sarah Carr

Taken upon Oath In Jamestown this 8th Day of February 1724/5 before me In presence of said George Thomas

Peddeman Hull Warden

Sarah Carr's deposition, 1725 [No. 205]

James Carr testified that on the first day of December 1724 his "mother sent for George Thomas and asked him whether he would go and look for her geese that he caused to go away. He told her he would go over to Goold Island if the wind did not blow to Hard . . . [she] sent for [him] the Second Time and then he said that he yarded [her] Geese and catch[d] one that he said was his Gander & was going to catch another, and after that, the Depon[ts] mother Demanded satisfaction . . . for the Geese, and Made Search and Enquiry after them but could not find them nor hear of them . . . ."

On 18 March 1724/5 before Nicholas Carr, warden, **John Goddard**, about one and twenty years of age, testified that he was at Hannah Carr's on the day in question, and gave a similar account of the events. Verdict was for the defendant, who in his plea had stated that the case was not valid because the plaintiff had failed in her writ to set a value on the geese.

206. **James Honyman** of Newport, clerk, vs. **Jonathan Nickols** of Newport, Esq., **George Lawton** and **Thomas Cornell**, both of Portsmouth, gentlemen, executors of the will of **Elizabeth Carr**, late of Newport, widow, deceased, in an action of debt for £500 which Elizabeth in her will dated 8 July 1714 had acknowledged herself bound to sd James. Writ dated 26 January 1724[/5]; Nathaniel Newdigate attorney. Case went to arbitration: the referees reported that "£500 charged is Mrs. Carr's accompt, for building Mr. Honyman's dwelling house, which clearly and fully appearing to sd Referees to be Built upon her Daughters Land . . . dwelling is his own Right and Property," and the debt therefore was to be cancelled. [*For transcription of the will of Elizabeth Carr, see Item 141.*]

207. **Mary Goslin** of South Kingstown, widow, otherwise called Mary Goslin, Relict of **Tho[s] Goslin**, deceased, innkeeper, vs. **Pasco Whitford Jn[r]** of North Kingstown, husbandman, in custody of the sheriff, to recover a debt of £20 due by bond dated 8 August 1724 witnessed by **Danel Smith** and **Jn[o] Lilly**. Bond is signed by Paske Whitford, and a fingerprint on the seal. Writ dated 1 February 1724[/5]; Henry Bull attorney.

208. **William Wood** of Little Compton, glazier, vs. **Benjamin Sawdey** of Newport, bricklayer, in custody of the sheriff, for £20 due by note dated 21 March 1721/22, signed Benj[a] Sawdey and witnessed by **Joseph Bennett** and **James Cary.** Writ dated 2 February 1724[/5]; Nathaniel Newdigate attorney. Sawdey was arrested the same day by William Pinniger, Constable.

209. **Gideon Freeborne** of Portsmouth, Esq., vs. **Thomas Goodfellow** of Portsmouth, trader, in custody of the sheriff, for trespass. Writ dated 3 February 1724[/5]; Henry Bull attorney. Freeborne charged that the defendant had illegally entered into and withheld from him 2 lotts of land amongst the small lotts on the south side so-called of Portsmouth, numbers 71 and 72, containing 2 acres or thereabouts with the dwelling house and other buildings thereon standing, bounded north, east, and south upon highways, and westerly on the 51st lot, which land Thomas deeded to him 14 December 1723. Copy of the deed, from Portsmouth "3rd Book of Land Evidence No. 2," pp. 463 & 464, whereby Thomas Goodfellow with free and full consent of his wife **Elizabeth** (who also signed) [mortgaged] the lots to Freeborne; witnesses were **Wm Anthony, Junr** and **William Anthony** [*sic*]. Verdict for plaintiff, "land with housen thearon sued for."

210. **James Honyman Ju^r^**, Infant and heir in Taile generall to his grandfather **Robert Carr** late of Newport, merchant, deceased, by **James Honyman** of Newport, clerk, his father and guardian, vs. **George Dunbarr** of Newport, shopkeeper, in custody of the sheriff, in an action of trespass. Writ dated 5 February 1724[/5]; Nathaniel Newdigate attorney. The property concerned was described as "one certaine wharf, one Warehouse or part of sd Wharfe lying in Newport," bounded northerly partly on a house, yard and warehouse in possession of **Dr. John Harris**, partly on the wharf in possession of the defendant, partly on a wharf in possession of **Job Townsend**, partly by a house in possession of **John Studley**, partly by a house in possession of **John Jackson**, partly by a house . . . of **William Cook**, partly by a wharfe belonging to **Robert Gardener** and partly by the salt water; southerly partly by a stable, wharf and warehouse belonging to **William Dyre**, partly by a house, wharf and warehouse belonging to **John Dickinson**, partly by the salt water; westerly on the salt water or harbour of Newport; easterly partly on a paved way that leads down from Main Street to the Wharfe and partly on land of **John Freebody**. Robert Carr Senr of Newport, great grandfather of the plaintiff, in his will dated 20 April 1681 left the property to his son Robert who died in 1703 leaving only one son named Robert (the plaintiff's uncle), and one daughter, **Abigail Carr** (the plaintiff's mother), who died 18 March 1709 leaving the plaintiff her only son. His uncle was seised of the property and died 20 September 1710 without issue . . . the property therefore descended rightfully to the plaintiff.

Copies of documents entered in the file: A deed dated 1 August 1687 from **Eseck Carr** and **Susannah** his wife of Little Compton in the

County of New Bristol, for £20 to **Robert Carr** of Newport, for half an acre in Newport bounded easterly on land of Major **Peleg Sanford**, southerly on land in possession of Mr. **Francis Brinley** and Mr. **Caleb Carr Sen**[r], northerly by land of sd Robert Carr and land now or late in possession of **Samuel Gardner**, westerly on the highway or Common Road leading through Newport Town into the Neck. The deed was witnessed by Samuel Gardner, **John Tillinghast**, and **Weston Clarke**, and acknowledged 30 Nov. 1687 before Joseph Church, J.P.

Writ of Execution and Recovery from the General Court of Trials, March 1715 to William Coddington, Sheriff, 12 November 1716: whereas **William Bright** of Newport, vintner, at the General Court of Trials the last Tuesday of March 1715 had received a judgement against Elizabeth Carr, executrix of the estate of her son Robert Carr, late of Newport, gentleman, deceased, for £9:19:7, [you are] to "value all [her] goods in your Bayliwick." Elizabeth had been dissatisfied with the verdict, the case was reheard and the judgment confirmed in September 1715, and an order was issued to "seize all goods and chattels of Robert Carr (ye horses and Beasts of ye Plough excepted) in the hands of Elizabeth Carr to be administered and also ye moiety and half part of all [his] lands and tenements in your Bayliwick." An Inquisition at Newport 14 November 1716 before William Coddington, on the property of Elizabeth Carr, executrix of Robert Carr, found her "seized in her Demesne as of fee of ye Estate of ye sd Robert Carr of and In one stone house in ye Possession and Tenour of **George Stevens**, £120 value, yearly value £6, one Warehouse in possession of Mr. **Augustus Lucas**, value £80, £5 annually, one house, shop, &c. in the possession and tenour of Dr. **Daniel Ayrault**, value £200, £11 annually, given to Robert Carr by the will of his father Robert Carr . . . ."; jurors on the inquisition were Stephen Mumford, Henry Bull, Benj: Norton, Tho[s] Brookes, Tho[s] Millis, Ralph Chapman, John Franklin, W[m] Gibbs, Ben: Bull, David Wiatt, Nath[ll]. Coddington Jun[r], and William Rouse.

A lease dated 12 October 1720 from Elizabeth Carr of Newport, widow, to Capt. George Dunbar of Newport, shopkeeper, for a wharf in Newport, 30 by 18 feet, bounded west, north, and east on the remainder of the wharf, and south on a Partition Line between the widdow Carr and assigns of Robert Carr, shipwright, for £3 per year; witnesses **Daniel Ayrault** and **Peter Money** [?Morey]. Another lease dated 10 January 1721 between the same parties, for a wharf between the land of Mr **Robert Gardner** and Mr. William Dyre, for £15 annually, witnessed by **George Goulding** and **John Hammet**.

The will of Robert Carr, Esq., probated 5 February 1704, copied from Council Book, p. 159. [*for full transcript of will, see No. 17*]

211. **Jeremiah Wilson** of Newport, brother and heir of **James Wilson** of Kingstown now called South Kingstown, yeoman, deceased, mariner, vs. **George Webb** of South Kingstown, husbandman, in action of trespass. Writ dated 7 February 1724/5; Nathaniel Newdigate attorney. The property in controversy was described as a dwelling house and stable with a tract of land (250 acres) adjoining at a place called The Thousand Acres, bounded east by the highway, south by land of **Robert Potter**, west by Chepucksett River, and north by land of **Jahleel Brenton**. It was possessed by **Samuel Wilson** of Kingstown, yeoman, who died in or about 1680 intestate, then descended to Samuel his eldest son and heir, brother of the plaintiff, who died about 1690 intestate leaving no issue, whereupon it descended to James, brother and next heir, until **Robert Hannah** of Kingstown, yeoman, entered and disseized him. James Wilson died without issue in or about February 1705/6 and it then descended to the plaintiff. Verdict for the plaintiff, land sued for and costs.

212. **John Ingraham** of Newport, cooper, vs. **Samuel Holway** of Westerly, husbandman, for £13:12:1 due for goods sold and delivered in 1722. Writ dated 10 February 1724[/5]; Henry Bull attorney. Bill included 1 hogshead of "malas at 2s pr galen" (103 gals) and £3:6:1 worth of rum at 4s gal. Constable **John Webster** attached a "puter" porringer when sent to arrest the defendant.

213. **Samuel Lewis** of Westerly, yeoman, vs. **John Boarman** late of Westerly, bloomer, for £16 for one mare sold and delivered in May 1720 and two steers in June 1720. Writ dated 12 February 1724/5; Nathaniel Newdigate attorney.

214. **Thomas Rogers** of Westerly, yeoman, and **Anne** his wife, one of the daughters of **Peleg Trip**, late of Portsmouth, yeoman, deceased, vs. **Job Shearman** of Portsmouth for illegally witholding land in Portsmouth. Writ dated 12 February 1724; Henry Bull attorney. The land was described as one third part of 12 acres, woodland and pasture land, bounded south and west by highways, north by land of **William Wood**, and east on land of **Adam Lawton**, being undivided land held in common with other tenants, which Peleg Tripp in his will dated 6 November 1713 had left to his daughter Ann, as the rest of his right in the common or undivided land not disposed of. **Job Tripp**, brother of Ann, received two-thirds of the property. The plaintiff claimed damages of £160 to himself and wife **Mary** [*sic*].

Deed from **George Sisson** of Portsmouth, yeoman, in consideration of a mutual exchange, 7 April 1677, of 3 eighth parts of a share of land in Dartmouth in the Colony of New Plymouth, between himself and Peleg Tripp of Dartmouth and 32 acres in Portsmouth [bounds as above], witnessed by John Sanford, Benja Congdon [*mark like a backwards S*], copied from Clasped Book, page 141, by William Sanford, town clerk, 3, 4m, 1725.

Agreement between Peleg Tripp, yeoman of Portsmouth, and his wife Ann, and "our son Job Tripp of Portsmouth," dated 6 March 1702/3, signed by all three: for "a certain sum of silver money . . . all our farm where wee now dwell in Portsmouth . . . bounded north on land of **Latham Clark**, east on a highway, south and west on land of **Adam Lawton**, and west on land of **Jeremiah Lawton** . . . reserving our dwelling house . . . a third part of the Great Orchard and garden during our natural life . . . as for the Little House Job is to have it to dwell in together with the remaining orchards, woods, waies, claims, priviledges and appurtenances [*the last word underlined, probably at the time of the court case*] . . . Job to enter into a bond [to bear the same date] for payment of £30, half to our daughter **Priscilla Tripp**, the other half to our daughter **Sarah Tripp**." Witnesses were John Rogers [*mark I-*], Richard Tripp [*mark R*], and Elias Williams; acknowledged 3 March 1707[/8] before Thomas Cornell, Assistant, and recorded 19 11m 1713/14. "Extracted 4 3d 1725 from Portsmouth LE 3 #2."

The will of Peleg Tripp: I Peleg Tripp of Portsmouth in the Colony of Rhode Island and Providence Plantations &c Yeoman being but weakly in body, but of good Memory praised be God Therefore, calling to mind the Mortality of my body, and for the preventing of future trouble amongst my wife and Children, do make and ordain this my last Will and Testament in manner and form as followeth.

Imp^{rs} My mind and Will is that all my Just and lawful debts be paid by my Executrix hereafter named.

2^{ly} I give and bequeath to my well beloved wife **Anne Tripp** my now dwelling house and one third part of the great orchard and my Garden during her natural life. Also I give and bequeath to my well beloved wife eighteen pounds a year to be paid unto her yearly and every year during her natural life by my son Job Tripp.

3^{ly} I give to my daughter **Priscilla Tripp** fifteen pounds in Currant silver money of New England.

Item: I give to my daughter **Sarah Rogers** fifteen pounds in Currant silver money of New England.

Item: I give and bequeath to my son **Job Tripp** all the rest of my land where I now dwell to him his heirs and assigns for ever (he my s^{d} son Job Tripp paying the aforementioned Rents unto his s^{d} Mother, and the aforementioned legacies unto his said sisters. also I give unto my s^{d} son Job Tripp to him his heirs and assigns forever two thirds of my Right of the Common or undivided in Portsmouth, a foresaid. Also I give to my son Job Tripp my great Scales and weights with the beam and the Cabbin bedstead whereon I lodge after the decease of my wife.

Item: I give to my son **Peleg Tripp** five shillings in or Equivalent to money to be paid by my Executrix within one year after my decease.

Item: I give to my daughter in law **Sarah Tripp** one shilling if she demands it.

Item: I give to my daughter **Mary Smith** ten shillings in money.

Item: I give to my daughter **Anne Rogers** all the rest of my Right in the Common or undivided land (which I have not herein disposed off), in Portsmouth aforesaid to her her heirs and assigns for ever. also I give to my daughter Anne Rogers ten shillings in money.

Item: I give to my daughter **Mehetabel Thurston** ten shillings in money.

Item: I give to my daughter **Priscilla Tripp** one good feather bed, bolster and pillow, one good Coverlet and a p^{r} of blankets and a bedstead and a small Iron kettle to be delivered by my Executrix.

Item: I give and bequeath to my well beloved wife Anne Tripp to her, her Executors, Administrators or assigns fourteen acres of land with the allowance scituate lying and being on the westward side of Ponaganset pond in the Township of Dartmouth within the County of Bristol. but if my son **Richard Tripp** shall do well and truly pay unto his Mother Anne Tripp six pounds in Currant money of New England in two years first after the date hereof, and six pounds more in like Currant money as above[*torn*] [*page* 2] within two years after the first payment. That then the said fourteen acres of land with ye allowance shall be and remain unto him the said Richard Tripp his heirs and assigns for ever.

Item: I give and bequeath to my son **Richard Tripp** his heirs and assigns forever all my Right of land in the Township of Dartmouth within the County of Bristol both divided and undivided (which I have not herein disposed off) he my said son Richard Tripp yielding and paying therefore unto his Mother Anne Tripp five pounds a year in Currant money some time in the first week in May yearly and every year during her natural life. but in case my wife marry again, my mind and Will is that my son Job Tripp shall pay unto his mother Anne Tripp but twelve pounds a year in lieu of the aforesaid eighteen pounds a year. And also my Will is that if my wife Marry that then my said wife shall pay unto my daughter Mary Smith five pounds, and to my daughter Anne Rogers five pounds, and to my daughter Mehetabel Thurston five pounds, and to my daughter Priscilla Tripp five pounds, and to my daughter Sarah Rogers five pounds being in all twenty five pounds to be paid in or Equivalent to Money.

Item: I give and bequeath to my loving wife **Anne Tripp** all the rest of my moveable Estate whatsoever which I have not herein disposed of, as

Money Cattel Sheep Swine and houshold goods. likewise bills and bonds. And whatsoever shall be remaining of my Estate at my wifes decease undisposed off shall be Equally divided into five parts between my five daughters.

Lastly I do hereby make and ordain my loving wife Anne Tripp my full and sole Executrix to this my last Will and Testament, making void all former Wills and Testaments whatsoever by me made. And do hereby nominate and appoint my kinsman **William Sanford** to be my overseer and for his trouble and care my Will is that he be paid twenty shillings by my Executrix.

In Witness whereof I have hereunto sett my hand and seal the sixth day of the ninth month called November Anno Domini one thousand seven hundred and thirteen 1713.

Witnesses:

Thomas Cornell Junr [signed] *Peleg Tripp* (seal)

James Clarke Junr

William Sanford

The will was proved 8:12mo:1713/14 and recorded the next day by John Anthony, Portsmouth Town Clerk. It was copied from Portsmouth Council book 2:208 on 2:2mo:1725 by Wm Sanford, Clerk of the Council.

Receipt dated 14:6mo:1714 from **Abraham Anthony, Isaac Lawton, Benjamin Hall** [*mark B*], Thomas Cornell Ju^{r}, **George Lawton,** and **Samuell Clarke,** "chosen committy at a meeting of the free inhabitants of the town of Portsmouth 12:1 mo:1713/14 . . . fully impowered to lay out all undivided land in sd town . . . acknowledge receipt of 24s of **Job Tripp** of Kingstown in the Narihagansit . . . whereof wee have granted and laid out . . . 12 acres of land be it more or less by virtue of a ffreehold in the town of Portsmouth given to sd Job Tripp by his deceased ffather **Peleg Tripp** . . . ."

Depositions were made 13 March 1725 by **Benjamin Hall, Abraham Anthony, Isaac Lawton,** and **Thomas Cornell,** all of Portsmouth, before William Anthony, assistant, stating that they had been on the Committee of the town of Portsmouth for the disposing of all the undivided land or common in said town, and that Thomas Rogers who had married Peleg Tripp's daughter came to them and asked that some part of the common land be laid out for him, but they judged he had no right.

215. **Richard Sherwin** vs. **Rowland Robinson**: whereas **Richard Sheran** late of Boston, butcher, deceased, in his will nominated his widow **Sarah** (since **Bull**) executrix; she also deceased without administering

the will [another document in file gives date of death of Sarah, wife of **Job Bull,** 27 August 1715]. Will of Richard Sherwin dated 19 October 1710 names children **Richard** and **Jane.** An accounting dated 7 June 1712 mentions **Jane Sherrin,** amounts for schooling, etc. Permission given to Job Bull and widow Sarah to sell real estate of Richard Sherwin. On 30 August 1715, **Richard Sheren,** an orphan and only surviving child, requested a guardian. A letter from Richard Sheren dated at Boston 15 July 1723: "your father Mr. Rowland Robinson . . . £250 silver money borrowed of my father Mr. Richd Sheren, victualler, in the year 1710 . . . found by chance in looking over a bundle of papers." Deposition at Boston 23 March 1725 by **Barth^{o} Greene** that he "heard **Richd Sherwin** say he had a bond by him of considerable value signed by **Roland Robinson** of Pt. Judah to his father Richd Sherwin, and did not demand it because he was afraid that Mr. Robinson had a receipt to Cutt or Satisfy sd Bond . . . asked him two years ago July when he went to Rhode Island to find sd W^{m} [*sic*] Robinson to get an answer." **Thomas Manchester** deposed 28 March 1725 at Portsmouth, signing by mark, T, before Giles Slocum, Assistant, testifying that he was "at ye house of **Richard Shearing** of Boston, butcher, About ye latter end of December or beginning of January in ye year 1700 And **Rowland Robinson** being theire was then makeing up Accompts with said Shearing and **ffreegift Coggeshall** did Assist them . . . the deponent very well remembers theire was noe Bill for money Lent brought into ye Account nor any booke or pockitt booke produced . . ." and he saw Richard Shearing pay money due to sd Robinson. Verdict for the defendant; bond declared fraudulent.

216. **John Thayer** [Tayer in declaration] of Newport, cordwainer, vs. **James Peckham** of Newport, house carpenter in custody of the sheriff, in a case *sur trover,* charging conversion and "disposicion of twenty and two neat hydes" valued at £15, of which the plaintiff was possessed at Newport on 14 August 1724 and on that day did lose, etc. . . . on 11 December 1724 the defendant converted them to his own use . . . damages £30.

Deed dated 13 August 1724 from **Joseph Wight** of Newport, tanner, mortgaging for £39 to James Peckham of Newport, house carpenter, "all my hides, skins, whatsoever in the tanyard in Newport which I have hired of **Hannah James** of Newport, widow, and also in every other place. . . ." Condition of the mortgage was that Wight was to discharge within three months a bond of £29 wherein he and Peckham were bound to **John Pain** of Jamestown, yeoman, and one that Peckham and **Samuel Allen** of Newport, cordwainer, owed to **Richard Ward** of Newport, gentleman. Witnesses were **Ezek**^{ll} **Bull**, who was sworn 30 March 1725, **Peleg Smith**, J.P., and **John Bennitt**. [The back of the mortgage was evidently used as a pen trial page by someone writing the words London, Commandement, New london, Newfoundland, and Newengland several times randomly.]

On 12 March 1724/5 before Job Lawton, J.P.: **John Bennett** of Newport, felmonger, deposed that James Peckham had desired him to take the hides "out of the tan fatts that was once in possession of Joseph Wight late of Newport, tanner and dress them . . . did so and delivered to James Peckham . . . they were marked † + T . . . I tanned large hides for 9*s* apiece and small ones for 8*d* . . . didn't know who they belonged to." At the same time, **William Risbey** of Newport, courier [?currier], testified that he had been at the house of James Peckham in Newport where he "did see aboute 20 tan'd Hides and some marked † T and some † + T with two punch holes . . . ." On 17 March 1724/5 before Job Lawton, **Thomas Bayley** of Newport, tanner, testified that he and Joseph Wight "had some conserns together in taning of leather in June last past . . . in 1723 [he] assumed Wight received of John Tayer 22 hides to tann . . . went up to the tanyard and there was **W**^{m} **Bennett** and John Tayer and **John James** . . . Tayer said to [me] what he Should do for his Leather . . . [I] replyed he had no conserns with it . . . Wm Bennett said 'whie should we stand here Lett us Hall up the Leather' and accordingly we began and did Hall up several hids and in the Intrem James Peckham appear'd . . . and forbed them medleing . . . he had got power of attorney from Joseph Wight . . . ." On 5 April 1725, before John Coddington, J.P., **William Risbey** of Newport testified again, that "on or about August last past at the tanyard Joseph Whight worked in before he Ran away . . . sundrey persons was there helping Draw the tan fatts of what Leathers there was in [them] & James Peckham was Present & tuck an account . . . ." **William Bennett** testified at the same time to the same thing. **Daniell Vaughan** and **Jonathan Sabin J**^{r} swore to the truth of their statements and said they had been present at the time and place ". . . Peckham bid them not to draw [leather] until he came and none was drawn . . . only one calves skin and two sheep skins . . . ."

Verdict was for the plaintiff, the hides sued for and costs of court.

217. **William Swan** of Newport, vintner, vs. **George Metchelf** [? Mitchell] of New Shoreham, husbandman, for debt due by book.

– September 1725 –

218. **Peter Coggeshall** and **Benjamin Coggeshall** had sued each other, and in September 1725 agreed to arbitration, by Job Almy, late of Tiverton, Robert Barker, and Joseph Borden. On 20 7ber [September] 1708 Benjamin Coggeshall, yeoman, and Peter Coggeshall, carpenter, both of Newport, signed an Articles of Agreement. Peter agreed to build a "House below my Father's gate of 30 foot long and 20 foot wide and 16 foot studd with a Leanto at the End of the Chimney 20 foot wide and 12 foot long and to find and do all (except the Masons work) upon [my] own proper cost and charge for the same £110 . . . workman like to the Turning of the Key . . . [to be done] 1 July next." Witnesses were **John Rogers** and **John Carr**. The file includes a bond, Peter Coggeshall of Newport, mariner, as principal, and **Baulston Coggeshall** of Newport, mariner, surety, bound to Benjamin Coggeshall of Newport, yeoman, for £40, dated 6 October 1720, witnessed by **Joseph Coggeshall** and **Christopher Townsend**.

Benjamin Coggeshall made a statement "to inform the arbitrators I am damnyfied at least £20 by reason my house was not done workman-like . . . no cellar beams . . . ruff [roof] in danger in a storm . . . end ruff so weak I was forced to prop it up . . . I have been forced to gitt a Lader & nale & patch [clapboards] while I was a wary [weary], & still it wantes more still, & so it will Yearly - one of the main posts was of my timber, because I can see where it was heaved & scored in, which [? while] tother was sawed . . . ."

Peter's account to Benjamin included charges for "a bedsted, cradel, large ovell tabell, doughtrofe, meatrofe, small ovell tabell, pc silke, sundreys done to his house over my Bargin, dubell flore witch, flore of gyce [? joysts] in the ticken wick [?kitchen wing]. . . to be now seller sow was forste to get a Large gurte to gow across . . . Mapel planke steps fore the dore In stide of Pine . . . ." [Benjamin's various writings are unusually neat and carefully lettered, in contrast to Peter's evident careless style.]

Depositions 29 August 1725 before Jn° Coddington, J.P.: **John Pocock** of Newport testified that he had been desired by Benjamin Coggeshall to view the clapboarding of the house and it was not done workmanlike. "About the year 1710 I and my brother **L[*blot*]ey** made [*illegible*] to sd Coggeshalls great Lower Room of his house in Newport." At the same time, **Samuel Easton** "upon Affirmation" testified that he was employed by Benjamin Coggeshall to do work about the house in 1710

. . . "put Lifts Round the Great Room . . . for Chears to Lean ag^{t} . . . I put the Corner board about the house . . . made shelves for one of the Cosets [*sic*] and did some work to one of the Mantletrees Shelves and put one Window to ye sd Closett and . . . putt Weather Boards to 3 windows of sd House there was Capps to the Windowes but they were not tight & the Clapboarding was not clapped as it should be . . . not Lap't well nor nailed well." **Ezekiel Burroughs** of Newport testified that he was desired by Benjamin Coggeshall "to goe and look at ye Clapboarding of his house to See if it was done Workman Like . . . went on ye 27th Instant . . . several places in y^{t} house I see the Plank by Reason the Clapboards was not Large Enough no[r] are they Nailed Enough to be done Workman Like . . . four or five Planks y^{r} was bare . . . ." **Joseph Bennet** testified 31 August 1724 before Peleg Sanford, J.P., and said that in the year 1709 he was employed by Peter Coggeshall as a carpenter "to help build ye house y^{t} Benjamin Coggeshall now lives in . . . clapboarded the East End up to the Plank and the grater part of the South Side and all done workman like . . . ." In a second deposition 15 September 1725, Bennet added that he "dont remember [I] ever heard Peter say he did any over plush work . . . or that Benjamin Coggeshall was to keep horses for him clear of charge . . . Peter had divers horses whilst we ware at work upon sd house." **Richard Coggeshall** of Newport testified 17 September 1725 before John Coddington, J.P., that he "was a prentice unto Peter Coggeshall when [he] built the house . . . **Daniell Coggeshall** then worked with me being prentice the same time . . . Raked part of the day upon the Marsh . . . don't remember we helpt Rake or make hay any oather time for Benjamin Coggeshall." **Ebenezer Shepherd** testified 23 September 1725 before John Coddington, J.P., that he worked with **Elexander Young** of Newport, taylor, about 16 years ago and "made a sute of cloths for Benjamin Coggeshall . . . about 8 yards of narrow Pershon putt into the sute . . . which Persian was spoted or Damnified [? because of the roof leaking]."

219. **Samuel Snell** of Newport, vintner, vs. **John Carr** of Jamestown, yeoman, in custody of the sheriff, for £2:18:2 due for drink and entertainment at the plaintiff's house at sundry times from 8 February 1722 to January 1724. Writ dated 18 February 1724[/5]; Daniel Updike attorney. Account includes "a Chary dram . . . orring dram . . . drink, punch, sugar dram, surrup dram, liquors . . . ."

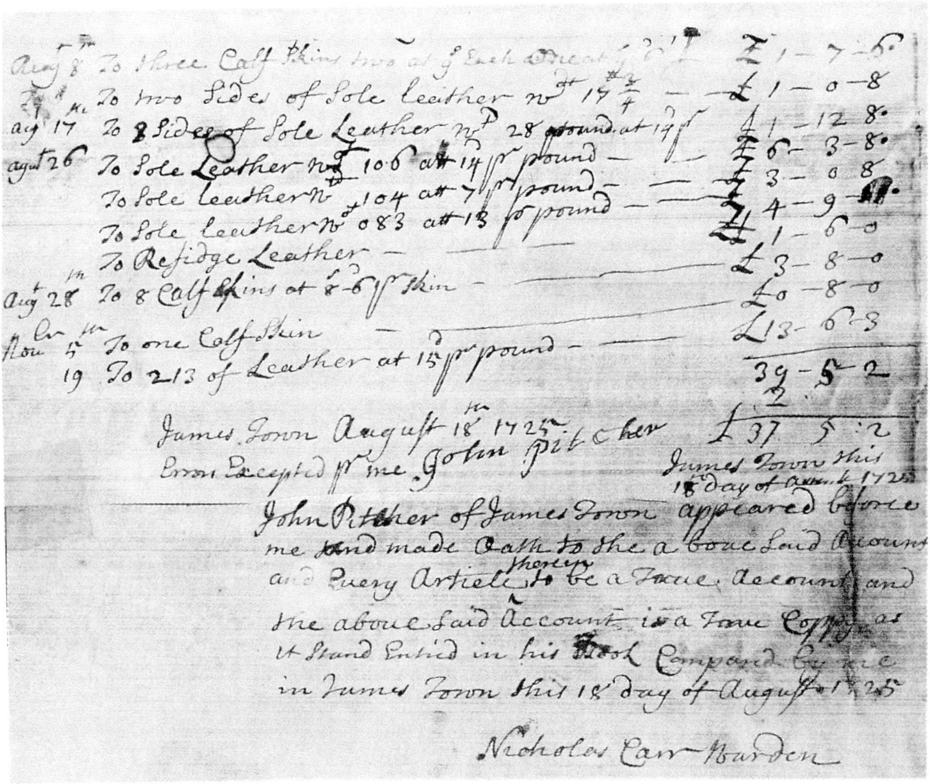

Aug 8th	To three Calf Skins two at 9s Each one at 9s 6d	£ 1 – 7 – 6
	To two Sides of Sole leather wt 17 3/4	£ 1 – 0 – 8
aug 17	To 8 Sides of Sole Leather wt 28 pound at 14d	£ 1 – 12 – 8
augt 26	To Sole Leather wt 106 at 14 pr pound	£ 6 – 3 – 8
	To Sole leather wt 104 at 7 pr pound	£ 3 – 0 – 8
	To Sole leather wt 083 at 13 pr pound	£ 4 – 9 –
	To Refidge Leather	£ 1 – 6 – 0
Aug 28th	To 8 Calf Skins at 8s-6d pr Skin	£ 3 – 8 – 0
Nov 5th	To one Calf Skin	£ 0 – 8 – 0
19	To 213 of Leather at 15d pr pound	£ 13 – 6 – 3
		39 – 5 – 2
		2
		£ 37 5 2

James Town August 18th 1725
Error Excepted pr me John Pitcher

James Town this 18 day of August 1725
John Pitcher of James Town appeared before me and made Oath to the above said Account and Every Article thereof to be a True Account and the above said Account is a True Coppy as it Stand Entred in his Book Compared by me in James Town this 18 day of August 1725

Nicholas Carr Warden

John Pitcher's account with Peleg Rogers [No. 220] is a typical example of bills found in the court files

220. **John Pitcher** of Jamestown, tanner, vs. **Peleg Rogers** (son of **Thomas Rogers**) of Newport, cordwainer, in custody of sheriff, for debt of £39 due by book for sundry parcels of leather sold and delivered to the defendant at sundry times between the month of July and 19 December 1724, and £50 claimed damages. Writ dated 26 February 1724[/5]. Account commencing with July 1724, signed 18 August 1725 at Jamestown, lists various sales of calfskins and sole leather, and credits Rogers with two payments of £1 each, the second "Reseved of your Jurny man," and "three pair of shoose for **Thomas Astin** . . . one paire for **Andrew Pitcher** [*and*] one paire for my Self."

221. **William Hall** of Providence, cordwainer, vs. **Thomas Gage** [signed **Gaige**] of Freetown . . . Province of Massachusetts Bay . . . inholder, in custody of the sheriff, for £3 due by bond dated 28 December 1723 witnessed by **Joseph Brownell** and **Samuel Forman**. Writ dated 20 April 1725; Henry Bull, attorney.

222. **James Winslow** of Freetown, cordwainer, vs. **Morrice Tucker** of Westerly, yeoman in custody of the sheriff, for £9:8:0 for goods sold and delivered and work done from 8 October 1720 to June 1722. Writ dated 8 July 1725; Daniel Updike attorney. Account was for tackling, chain, bushels of corn, wheel hoops, a load of hay, sheep shears.

223. **Kathrine Bowin** of Swansey, singlewoman, vs. **James Nichols** late of North Kingstown, husbandman, in custody of the sheriff, for £5:1:10 due for work done, goods sold, and money lent, in 1723. Writ dated 17 July 1725; Henry Bull attorney. Accounting beginning February 1722/3 and ending March 1723/4 included "making hollen shirts . . . orsonbrigs shirts . . . niting 2 caps . . . spinning and niting 2 pr stockings . . . spinning 3 pounds of coton . . . weaving . . . 10 pounds of wool . . . washing your cloes a year . . . mending [ditto]. . . ." On 26 July 1725 before William Hall, Justice, **Elizabeth Bates** of North Kingstown testified that "the same year Kathrine Boen charges James Nickols for work done . . . [she] was hired to **Margaret Bates** from some time in February . . . untill May . . . [his] cloths were not at the house where sd Boen dwelt . . . the deponent dwelt at sd house the same time." **Margaret Bates** of North Kingstown swore to the truth of that, and added that "his clothes was not at our House, nor washed or mended here . . . ." On 30 August 1725, **Samuel Anthony** of South Kingstown deposed before Wm Robinson, J.P., that some time in November 1723 he "hired James Nickols of North Kingstown for one whole year from the time . . . and he was by agreement to wash and mend all sd Nic-

kols cloaths for the full time which he did performe . . . do not no that he had any cloaths washed or mended any other waies than what I did." His wife **Mary Anthony** made oath to the truth of his statement. On 1 September 1725, **James Hyums ju^r^** testified before William Hall, J.P., that he was well acquainted with James Nichols of North Kingstown, labourer, for several years last past and often in his company . . . but in the year 1723, sd Nichols was "gone out of these parts . . . I neither saw him nor heard of his being in Kingstown nor in these parts of New England from about the middle of the month of May until some time in September or October following." **David Vaughan**, son of **John Vaughan** of Kingstown, swore to the truth of that, and added that he "had sd Nickols his cloaths in keeping from some time in May until September or October . . . ."

Verdict was for the plaintiff, the amount sued for and costs of court.

224. **Elisabeth Pratt** of Newport, widow and shopkeeper, vs. **Stephen Easton** of Newport, yeoman, in custody of the sheriff, for £3:6:0 due for sundry goods sold and delivered from 14 November 1723 to 10 September 1724. Writ dated 21 July 1725. Accounting, signed by Elizab. Pratt, includes "yarn stockings, worsted stockings, a brockadow'd girdell, 2 speckled shirts."

225. **Henry Davison** of Westerly, school-master, vs. **Isaac Thompson** of Westerly, merchant, for money due for services done and money advanced, £20:15:8, and damages £40. Writ dated 3 September 1725. Bill presented for 1723/4 for "posting books . . . making and erecting of two very large Vertical declining Dials upon yr house, £3 . . . attending yr Son during his Sickness by y^r^ order . . . schooling yr children at several times . . . cash received of **Edward Larkin** for my attendance at court." Deposition of **William Champlin Junr** of lawfull age who said that "somtime last fall or ye later end of ye sumer I saw the Dyall that now stands upon my father Thompsons house amaking att ye house of **Roger Oldersons** by **William Dee** a joyner of Westerly and that [I] did helpe to plaine sum of ye boards of [my] father **Thompsons** and sd Dee said he was amaking itt for the sd Thompson . . . to [my] knowledge **William Thompson** made all the Irons for sd Dyall and **Henery Davison** did nothing to sd Dyall but paint itt make ye figers and sett ye Irons and fix itt open [upon] sd Thompsons house and [I] meshured itt it being about three feet and 1 inche square each part." Deposition of **William Thompson,** the same date: "the dyall that now stands upon my father's house I saw **William Dee** amaking of itt att **Roger Eldertons** house, he being a Joyner of Westerly . . . was to have

7 shillings for ye making . . . [I] made the Irons for sd Dyall." Deposition 11 September 1725 of **Joseph Sheffield** of South Kingstown, stating that he was in Westerly in the fall of 1724 and was "desired by Mr. **Isaac Thomson** of sd Westerly to visit his son William Thomson of sd Westerly (whoe was then sick) as a doctor and accordingly did and was his doctor in sd sickness . . . I then understood sd William Thomson had been sick but a fue days . . . did not then keep his bed constantly, and in less than a month afterwards [I] saw him abroad according to the best of my memory . . . did not understand that **Henry Davison** of Westerly attended [him] or [came] to look after him more than as a neighbour . . . at the same time I saw one **Marcy Babcock** there whoe attended [him] as a nurs . . . I left medisons in charge with [her]."

226. **John Chapman** of Newport, schoolmaster, vs. **John Fling** late resident in Newport, mariner, in custody of the sheriff, for £14:19:4 due for victuals, drink, and boarding of himself and others by his order and money lent and goods sold in December 1724. Writ dated 19 April 1725; Nathaniel Newdigate attorney. Other persons listed in the bill are **John Mathews** and **Elitt**; includes "6 meals more to your mean gouing with you to the Bay . . . Brandy . . . **Anah Holmes** account . . . **Sarah Cogshalls** account . . . cash lent you sent pr **Caleb Clarks** boy . . . cash by **John Lovering** . . . 2 Qts mustard seeds . . . razor." Credit: 26½ yds silk, &c. Bill signed by **Joanna Chapman.** Defendant John Fling's answer was that the writ called him late resident in Newport, mariner, whereas the plaintiff was a transient person, no free holder, and there was no bond given for him [i.e., his settlement — therefore he had no right to sue].

227. **Edward Rossam** of Newport, sadler, vs. **David Ingersole** of Springfield, County of Hampshire, Province of Massachusetts Bay, horse jockey, in custody of the sheriff, for £18 due for goods sold and put on board the sloop *Mary*, **George Lemote** master, 27 November 1724 by order of the defendant. Writ dated 3 June 1725; Nathaniel Newdigate, attorney.

Depositions made 2 September 1725 before Daniel Updike, Assistant: **William Green** and **Richard Billings** both of Newport stated that they were present in November last past when Edward Rossam sold three saddles and three bridles to one David Ingersole and at the same time he ordered said saddles and bridles to be put on board of a sloop. **Thomas Huxham** of Newport stated that in May last Ingersole "ordered me to pay £18 to Rossam but it fell through and I never paid, but answered the same to Ingersole himself and one **Kelly** to whom I owed it." Receipt dated 27 November 1724 from George Lemote for 3 breasted saddles, 2 plain and one quilted, upon account and risque of David Ingersole of Springfield to be delivered at Hartford. Verdict for the plaintiff.

228. **Charles Brown** of Newport, yeoman, vs. **Nicholas Young** of North Kingstown, husbandman for £16:2:6 due by note dated 10 September 1717, signed by mark **N** and witnessed by **Samuell Casey** and **John Wels**. Writ dated 22 June 1725.

229. **William Swan** of Newport, vintner, vs. **Samuel Cross** of Newport, miller, for £29:10:10 due for goods sold and delivered from July 1721 to June 1725. Writ dated 1 July 1725; Henry Bull, attorney. Bill is all for "licker."

230. **Stephen Wilcox** (son of **Thomas**) of North Kingstown, yeoman, vs. **John Case** (son of **Joseph**) of South Kingstown, yeoman, for £21 due by bond dated 8 February 1724, witnessed by **Joseph Renolds** (mark +) and **Comford Baker**. Writ dated 5 July 1725; Daniel Updike, attorney.

231. **Francis Gilburt** late of Newport, vintner, vs. **Stephen Easton** of Newport, yeoman, in custody of the sheriff, for £46 due by bond dated 22 April 1724, witnessed by **William Bennett** and **Mary Willson**. Writ dated 9 July 1725; Henry Bull, attorney.

232. **Martin Howard** of Newport, clothier, and **Ann** his wife, **Sarah Collins** of Newport, spinster, and **Elizabeth Collins** an Infant by **Daniel Whitman** her guardian of Newport, house carpenter, three of the daughters and children of William Collins of Newport, deceased, and coheirs to **William Collins** their brother late of Newport, mariner, deceased, vs. **William Tippets** of Warwick, husbandman, in an action of trespass concerning 105 acres in Warwick, part of one of the Five Farms called Wechocheconet, No. 3, laid out to **John Smith**. Tried first at General Court of Trials, September 1720 and appealed. [*Copy of case; extremely faded and burned around the edges, thus partly illegible.*]

The defendant claimed right by deed of gift from **Eliza Collins** to his two sons **Eliza** and **William**; Eliza the son died in 1688, under 21 years of age, and his right descended to William, father of the plaintiffs, but **Thomas Collins**, elder brother of Eliza and William was still living and his right was not mentioned in the suit; Nathaniel Newdigate attorney for defendant.

Birth record: **Thomas Collins** son of Leiu^{t} Eliza Collins & Sarah his wife was born in Warwick October ye 26th 1664 / Eliza Collins son of Lieu^{t} Eliza Collins & Sarah his wife was born in Warwick June ye 11th 1666 / Willm son of Lieu^{t} Eliza Collins & Sarah his wife was born in Warwick March ye 8th 1677 . . . pr John Wickes Town Clerk.

"A True Copy of the Original Deed of Purchase of The Plantation of Warwick, attested by Samuel Gorton, Town Clerk": Deed from **Myantonomy** Chief Sachem of the Naraganset to Randall Houldon, John Green, John Wickes, Francis West, Samuel Gorton, Richard Waterman, John Warner, Richard Carder, Samson Shollen, Robert Potter, and William Wuddall, for a parcel of land "with all the rights and privileges thereof whatsoever lying upon the west side of that part of the Sea called Sowhomes Bay from Copescuatuxet over against a Little Island in sd Bay being the North Bounds and the outmost point of that Neck of Land called Showhomet being the South bounds from the Sea Shore of each Bounder upon a Strait Line westward twenty miles, I say I have truly Sold . . . for 144 fathom of Wampom-peague, the twelfth day of January 1642." The Indians signed by specific, detailed marks: Myantonomy with a bow and arrow pointed vertically, Sotanoman with a musket-type gun pointed vertically, Pum Homm with a pipe, and Jans with a bird. John Green Junr signed for the grantees.

Whereas **John Smith**, Deputy, of Warwick deceased intestate, the Town Council by the Law of the Colony appointed in such cases to make a will on 14 September 1663 appointed Mrs. **Ann Smith**, widow of John Smith, executrix. "It doth appear that her son **Eliza Collins** hath due to him £200 as a Legacy formerly given unto him and his sister **Ann Collins** which sister being dead the whole sum is due to him . . . Ann Smith executrix is ordered to make over all the housing and lands in Warwick of John Smith, deceased, unto her said son Eliza Collins for security that his portion may be duly satisfied . . . Ann Smith shall enjoy sd property during her Life. If any heir of sd John Smith be living and present them selves we bequeath unto him or them 5 shillings apiece if demanded . . . ." It was signed by Samuel Gorton Senr, John Wickes Senr, John Greene, Randall Holdon, Walter Todd, and Richard Carder.

Copy of Purchase of Mishowomet, 13 February 1672, included, with map showing original lots and owners.

Deed from **Eliza Collins** and wife **Sarah**, inhabitants of town of Warwick, to **John Green Senr** of same, 2 June 1675, witnessed by

James Greene and **Anna Smith**; taken from Warwick records . . . half a purchaser's shares . . . ref. to deed of grant 25 March 1675.

Deed from Eliza Collins of Warwick, dated 27 March 1677 and acknowledged 1 May 1677, or £50 to **John Smith** and **Philip Sweet** both of Prudence Island and with consent of aged mother Mrs. **Ann Smith** and wife **Sarah Collins** . . . one whole purchaser's share of land commonly known by the Purchasers Rights to the Plantation of Mishawomet . . . in which parcel my father-in-law Mr. John Smith had three shares by right of purchase . . . one of which I now sell . . . the 6th . . . . all signed; witnesses were **John Sweet Senr** [*mark IS*] and **Edmund Calverly**.

Deed from Eliza Collins and wife Sarah of Warwick to **Robert Malins** of Newport for part of tract of 2000 acres, dated 2 April 1677, witnessed by **Peter Green** [*signed by mark X*], and **John Allin Jun.**, recorded 14 May 1677.

Copy of deed from Elisha [signed Eliza] Collins of Warwick for great love and good affection towards his sons Eliza and William Collins both of Warwick, dated 3 April 1681, witnessed by **John Potter** and **Amos Westcott**, who attested it 6 November 1683.

Power of attorney from William Collins of Coweeset to his beloved friend and brother **Samuel Gorton jun^r^** of Wickecheconet in the township of Warwick, dated 17 May 1696, witnessed by **Anthony Sadler** and **Nicholas Lange**.

Deed from **Philip Sweet** and wife **Elizabeth**, 6 July 1703 to **Jonathan Hill** of Prudence Island in township of Portsmouth, witnessed by **Robert Westgoate** and **Sam^ll^ Gorton**.

Copy of the will of William Collins of Newport, very sick and weak, dated 18 January 1711/12 and witnessed by **William Martin, James Allen,** and **John Hammett**. [*See No. 33 for full text of will.*] It was proved 4 February 1712 by witnesses John Hammett and James Allen, and recorded 6 February 1712 by Richard Ward, Clerk of Council.

Deposition 16 June 1720 before John Burton, Justice, by **Robert Potter** of Providence, that in 1697 he was put into possession by William Collins of Newport, tanner, of his farm in Warwick . . . Wequachockonet . . . he continued nine years and then resigned it up to William Collins again. Deed entered in evidence: dated 16 January 1720/21 from **Jonathan Hill** [*signed by mark* **O**] of Prudence Island "in the township of Pourchmouth, yeomon, for ye love and in consideration of the good will and affection that I bare towards my beloved son **Thomas Hill** of ye town of Swansey ales Barrinton in ye County Bristol in ye Province of ye Masitusets Bay . . . make over unto him . . . a sartain parsel or tract of land lying in the township of Warwick . . . commonly called and known by the name of Wecacheconet Lands be estimation one hundred and five acres be it more or less it being one quarter part of a farme that belongeth unto me ye sd Jonathan Hill **Mr Rice** and [??] **Smith**. . .," witnessed by **Joseph Carpenter** and **Mathew Allin**; recorded page 17 in the "Great Book called the [? Warwick] Towns and Proprietors Book" by George Weastgate, town clerk.

Edward Gorton of Warwick deposed 16 August 1725 that three years ago he was cutting wood . . . "Rice came and asked whether I cut that wood there to hold Possession for my Aunt and Cousins and I answered No I did not cut for any such Thing . . . sd Rice told me If I did do it upon that account he should trouble me Because He said he claimed that Land . . . some time after I having occasion for some Cribb poles I asked Capt Rice leave to cutt some Poles and he told me I might cut as many as I had Occasion for, and accordingly I did . . . near to a Place called Bald Hill which sd Farme is now in Controversy . . . ."

John Reynolds of North Kingstown, carpenter, deposed 24 August 1725 before Benja. Nichols, Justice, that "ten or twelve years ago he was cutting of timber with **Thomas Tibbets** in a farme and northwest of **Rebecca Tibbets** house at Wecocheconet . . . **John Rice** Secundus came and asked upon whose account . . . said they had leve from **John Sweet** and **Jonathan Hill** . . . Rice said if they cut on their account it was well But if they cut on Collins's account He must put them to Trouble . . . ."

William Allin Senor of Prudence Island deposed on 28 August 1725 before **Dan^ll^ Pearce**, Justice, that he was hired in 1702 or 1703 by Jonathan Hill to fence, etc. **Rebekah Tibbits** deposed 3 September 1725 and said that about 19 years ago she came to Warwick to dwell and "dwelt ever since on the farme [I] bought of **Robart Potter** which lyeth near the farme now in contest between John Smith of South Kingstown and partners and the children of **W Collins**, deceased." **Elner Burllingame** of Providence deposed 22 October 1725 and said that "to her sertain knowledg Eliza Collins son of Eliza Collins of Warwick and brother to **William Collins** of Newport, tanner, deceased, died before he attained to age of 21 years and was then in his apprenticeship to **Thomas Hopkins**, carpenter." **John Burlingame** of Providence testified to the same effect.

On 9 November 1725 **Immanuel Rouse** of East Greenwich deposed that in 1716 he was employed to make staves out of timbers cut off the farm in dispute between Martin Howard and William Tibbets by Samuel Gorton of Warwick, son of John Gorton . . . "nobody molested us . . . about two years after the deponent was at work for **John Rice** getting of Cooper Stuff . . . shewed John Rice some good trees for their use . . . Rice sayd 'them trees grows on Collins his land' . . . deponent said 'Let us cut them,' 'no,' sayd Rice, we dare not . . . ."

Robert Potter of Providence, aged 60 or thereabouts, deposed at Warwick 12 November 1725 before John Wickes, Assistant, that he lived at Warwick many years and was very well acquainted with Eliza Collins Senior and well remembered the talk of sd Collins' selling the Purchase Rights in Warwick to John Sweet and Philip Sweet . . . they had possession by virtue of a deed near 40 years.

Deed dated 18 November 1725 from **John Rice** for love and affection to son **John Rice**, yeoman . . . "right in Farm I hold with **John Sweet** and **Jonathan Hill** and his son **Thomas** . . . one quarter part of sd Farm . . . same I bought of **George Vaughan** of East Greenwich . . . originally belonging to **John Sweet** formerly of Warwick, deceased . . . same **John Sweet** and **Philip Sweet** bought of Eliza Collins"; witnesses **John Spenser, John Wickes**.

Major **Job Green** of Warwick deposed 6 December 1725 before John Wickes, Assistant, that he "being at his father's house in Occapasetuxet some short time after **William Collins** of Warwick was out of his Apprenticeship which he concludes to be upwards of 30 years past did then and there hear the sd Collins propose to make an Exchange with his Father Major **John Green** . . . to exchange the half of the same his father Mr **Eliza Collins** gave to him and his brother **E[liza]** in that part of the Warwick Purchase called by the Indians Wecocheconet for his half right which sd Eliza Collins had formerly sold to his father the sd John Green in the Land called Seven Mens Land in sd Purchase . . . sayd he understood there was not a Sufficiency to make up one full Purchasers Right to **John Sweet** and **Philip Sweet** . . . went away and never completed same . . . ."

On 19 February 1725/6 **Henry Tibbits** of Warwick deposed that some ten years past Samuel Gorton "came and forewarned me for cutting any timber on sd farme." On 21 February 1725/6 **Thomas Hutson** of Providence deposed that he was "at work with **John Willson** of East Greenwich agetting Frame on the Farm belonging to the Gortons . . . Capt. John Rice being in company did say [that] next farme to the south did belong to William Collins deceased and just to the north [was] the farm belonging to Rebeccah Tibbits."

In March 1726, the court's opinion was that if the deed to John and Philip Sweet by Eliza Collins, Ann Collins, and Sarah Colins was not acknowledged, verdict should be for the defendant, but if it was good in law then the plaintiffs should have the land sued for and costs of court. The court judged the deed good in law, but ordered that the defendant was to have his costs. The case was reheard in September 1726. **John Burton** testified 2 September 1726 before Randall Holden, Assistant, that **Sarah Peters**, formerly wife of William Collins of Newport, tanner, deceased, "came to my house and desired me to take an evidence of Robert Potter and his wife concerning a difference about some Land, which difference still continues between **John Rice the Second** and Partners and **Martin Howard** and Partners . . . now depending at court. Some time in February last **Sarah Collins** daughter of the abovesd William came to my house and desired me to grant notification to Capt. John Rice and William Tippets to appear at the house of the abovesaid Robert Potter to see Evidence taken which Concerned them . . . Evidence was taken but Rejected at Court." On 23 September 1726, **Robert Potter** of Providence testified at court about the same situation. **William James** of Newport, mariner, testified that in the year 1722 he was at Port Royal, master of a Vessell [*faded*] . . . one of the hands on sd Voyage was William Collins of Newport . . . I understand to be the son of William Collins of Newport, deceased . . . sd William died at Port Royal and was carried off and according to custom there was buried in the Sea after which I took care of his Chest and Cloaths and brought them home and sent them to Sarah Peters his mother by a man she sent for them. **Philip Basil** [signed **Basan**] of Newport, mariner, testified to the truth of James' statement except the part relating to sending the clothes, he being with sd William James in sd voyage. Upon this rehearing, the plaintiffs received land sued for and costs.

233. **Major Job Green** of Warwick, yeoman, vs. **Jeffery Hazard** of South Kingstown, otherwise Jeffery Hazard of North Kingstown, yeoman, for £160 due by note dated 30 September 1723 with **John Wilcox** of Westerly, yeoman, witnessed by **Othniell Gorton** and **Samuel Greene**. Note is signed John Willox and Jeffery Hassard. Writ dated 14 July 1725.

234. **Jeremiah Wilson** of Newport, vintner, vs. **Philip Sherman** of Portsmouth, weaver, in custody of the sheriff, for £2:1:7 due for Liquor had at the plaintiff's house at sundry times between July 1724 and 24 March following. Writ dated 15 July 1725; Daniel Updike attorney.

235. **Benjamin Cary** of Bristol . . . Province of Massachusetts Bay . . . yeoman, vs. **William Brightman** of Newport, yeoman, in custody of the sheriff, for £14 due for a "pair of stears" sold and delivered 25 August 1724. Writ dated 17 July 1725; Henry Bull, attorney.

236. **Benjamin Allin** of North Kingstown, yeoman, vs. **David Nichols** of North Kingstown for £23 due by note dated 19 June 1725, witnessed by **David Vaughan**. Writ dated 18 July 1725.

237. **Henry Knowles Jun**^r of South Kingstown, yeoman, and **Susannah** his wife, daughter of **Edward Boss** late of South Kingstown, yeoman, deceased, vs. **Edward Boss** of Newport, marriner, for £140 due for their fifth part of a "certain peece of land being the homestead of said Edward Boss" . . . about 154 acres, part in South Kingstown and part in Westerly. Edward Boss had been seized thereof in or about August 1724 when he died intestate leaving three sons, the eldest **Jeremiah**, and **Peter** and one daughter, **Sussannah**, the plaintiff. The Town Council of South Kingstown on 11 January 1724/5 had ordered that Edward Boss, mariner, should have all the land, he paying to the rest of his Brethren and Sisters their Proportionable parts according to Inventory. Copy of inventory and town council records included. Writ dated 19 July 1725; Nathaniel Newdigate attorney. Verdict for plaintiff, money sued for and costs of court.

238. **Arnold Collins Jun**^r of Newport, merchant vs. **Stephen Wilcox** of Westerly, yeoman, in custody of the sheriff, for £4:16:0 for three Beaver Hatts sold and delivered 30 March 1721. Writ dated 19 July 1725; Daniel Updike attorney.

239. **Joseph Maxon Jun**^r of Westerly, husbandman, vs. **Hezekiah Wilcox** of Westerly Black-smith, in custody of the sheriff, for £26 due by note dated 27 March 1724 witnessed by **Sarah Renalls** (mark S) and **John Maxson ye second**. Writ dated 20 July 1725.

240. **Caleb Carr** of Jamestown, yeoman, eldest son and heir of **Caleb Carr** who was the eldest son and heir of **Robert Carr** late of Newport, deceased, yeoman, vs. **Daniell Updike** of Newport, Esq. (now tenant in possession to the Executors of **Elizabeth Carr** late of Newport, widow, deceased) in action of trespass concerning a lot of land with house and buildings thereon in Newport, about 100 feet in length and 40 feet in bredth, bounded north on land of **Jahleel Brenton**, Esq., easterly on land of Maj^r **James Brown**, southerly on Church Street, westerly on Thames Street. Writ dated 30 July 1725. Robert Carr was possessed of the property when he died on or about 1681 intestate; it

descended to his son Caleb Carr who died on or about 1689/90 when it descended to the plaintiff. The defendant answered that he and those under whom he holds the premises have enjoyed peaceable and quiet possession upwards of 20 years . . . "the manner of the writ is an Indignity . . . vicious and obnoxious."

241. Two cases, **Josiah Arnold** of South Kingstown infant by **Wm Gardiner** of South Kingstown his father-in-law and guardian vs. **Benedict Arnold** of Jamestown, yeoman. Both writs dated 20 July 1725; Henry Bull, attorney.

The first is an action of trespass. The defendant had on or about 1725 entered on land devised to Josiah by the will of his father Josiah Arnold, deceased, and did "cutt down and carry away about fourty cord of wood . . . to the value of £20." Copy of will of Josiah Arnold, dated 23 September 1721. Copy of guardianship dated 23 February 1724/5, Jamestown; Josiah Arnold made choice 18 February of William Gardiner his father-in-law (copied from Jamestown TC 1:331).

Depositions 13 August 1725 in Jamestown: **Hannah Curtis** of Newport testified that "in March 1725 and several other times I hird William Gardiner of Boston Neck in South Kingstown say to Benedict Arnold why do you not fetch away that wood that was cut on Josiah Arnolds part of the farme . . . ." **Jeremiah Mott** of Jamestown also testified that he heard William Gardiner and his son-in-law Josiah Arnold give Benedict Arnold leave to cut and cart wood. The defendant answered that the greater part of the wood was cut in the lifetime of Josiah's father.

In a second case, the plaintiff charges the defendant with "retaining and keeping an Indian servant man known by the name of **George**" left to him by his father's will as cited above. According to the terms of the will, Josiah was to have "my Indian slave called George to serve until he attain the age of thirty four years" but the defendant refused to deliver him.

242. **John Holmes** of Newport, cordwainer, eldest son and heir of John Holmes, late of Newport, cordwainer, deceased, vs. **Alice Wilson** of Newport, widow and executrix (with **Joseph Smith** late of Kingstown) to the last will of **James Wilson** late of Kingstown, husbandman, deceased, who was the eldest brother and heir surviving to **Samuel Wilson** late of Kingstown, yeoman, deceased, for £100 due by bond dated 24 May 1687 whereby Samuel Wilson guaranteed to maintain John Holmes and his heirs in peacable possession, etc., of half a share or 14th part of the land in Point Judith Neck in Narraganset which

John Holmes purchased of Samuel Wilson. Writ dated 26 July 1725; Henry Bull attorney. The plaintiff charged that the bond was forfeit because the promise had not been made good, [because] in November 1718 **Sion Arnold** of Newport, cooper, and **Mary** his wife with **Richard Ward** of Newport, gentleman, did by writ of ejection 19 November 1718 arrest **Thomas Potter**, the tenant in possession to the plaintiff of said lands and finally at the Court of Trials in March 1720 received a judgement for the sixth part.

Deed dated 24 May 1687, from Samuel Wilson of Rochester in the Narragansett Country or Kings Province, for £30, to **John Holmes** of Newport . . . one half share, it being a 14th part of all lands and meadows in Point Judith Neck in the Pettaquamscutt Purchase in Narragansett. Witnesses Samuel Cranston, Robert Little, and Weston Clarke. Recorded on pages 363 and 364 of the Clasped Book of Land Evidence belonging to Rhode Island Kings Province and Providence Plantations June 1688.

The defendant's plea by her attorney Nathaniel Newdigate was that her husband had left no estate to be administered, and she could not be held responsible for the bond. Verdict was first for the plaintiff, the money sued for and costs, but upon a rehearing, it was reversed: for the defendant, the bond sued for and costs of court.

243. **Peter Green, John Green,** and **William Green,** all of Warwick, yeomen, executors of the will of their father **Capt. Peter Green** late of Warwick, yeoman, deceased, vs. **Elisha Green** of Warwick, mariner, in custody of the sheriff, for £40 due to them as executors. Writ dated 28 July 1725; Daniel Updike attorney. File includes a copy of the will of Peter Green, dated 16 May 1718, in which he named four of his sons, Peter, John, **Stephen**, and William executors, of whom the plaintiffs at the death of the testator were the only surviving. Elisha Green borrowed £40 of Peter Green in his lifetime and now owes the estate.

Will of Peter Green: In the Name of God amen I Peter Green of Warwick in ye Colony of Rhoad Island & Providence plantations in New England being antient but of Perfect mind and memory thanks be given to God therefore: and Calling to minde ye mortallity of my body and knowing that it is appointed for all men once to Dye & being willing to sett my [*illegible*] in order whilst it hath Pleased God to give me ability and understanding Do make and ordaine this my Last will and Testament In manner and form following: viz first and Principaley I Recommend my Soule into ye hands of ye allmighty God that gave it hoping for Salvation through ye merrits of our blessed saviour Jesus Christ; and as for Worldly and Temporall Estate it hath pleased God to bless me with in this Life I Give and bequeath my body to ye

Earth to be Deacently buried in Christian Like manner at ye Discretion of my Executor hereafter named and for as much as it hath pleased God to Visit my well beloved Wife **Elizabeth Green** with a Distemper for this many years past where by she is not in her Right sences & howlong it may pleas God y^t ye same be Continued there fore for ye tender love I have to her I appoint y^t my Executor hereafter named Carfully keep & maintain her During her naturall life with sutable & sufitient meat Drink Washing Lodging and all other nessessaries which may be sutable and Convenient both in sickness and in helth as well as they can & are obleged to in Duty to her and myself: Item I Give and bequeath to my well beloved son **Peter Green** my homestead farme & mantion house and housings buildings and Edifices thereupon in Warwick where I now Dwell: onley Excepting what I shall hereafter Reserve out of sd farme: to be to my sd son to him his heirs & assigns to have and to hold forever also i give to my sd son Peter Green my lot in Warwick which i call ye Rockey farme and also one shear of Bog meadow which I bought of my Uncle **Tho^m Green** lying at ye south end of Mashapoge pond & also Twenty acres of my lott in Warwick Neck & sd twenty acres to be taken of on ye south side of sd lot to be ye whol length of sd lott ye which lott was Given to me by my honoured father Maj^r **John Green** ye sd Twenty acres to be to my sd son his heirs and assigns for ever I also Give to my sd son Peter Green one quarter of a right or one quarter of a seventeenth of all ye undevided Lands in ye TownShip of Coweasett; that is to say: to ye westward of ye south-pranch that Runs Down by John Greens to him his heirs and assigns for ever

Item I Give and bequeath to my well beloved daughter **Sarah Arnold** one Negro Garl named **Raney** I having given her a Portion already. Item I Give and bequeath to my sd six sons namly **Peter John Stephen $Will^m$ Elisha & Barlo Green** all my Right Title and Interest that I have in the Lands lying to ye Eastward of ye farms Laid out in Coweasett both Devided and undevided as well below ye path as above to ye sea as also my Right in ye Island Called Chippenexet to be Equally Devided amonst mysd sons to them and their heirs & assigns for ever;

Item I Give and bequeath to my Well beloved son **Barlo Green** for an adition to his Portion all my Right and Title in ye Eastward part of ye lands which are Called ye Seven mens lands which I Reserved in ye Deed of Gift which I gave to my sd son to be in him his heirs and assigns for ever: as also Twelve pounds in or as money to be paid by my Executor hereafter named within two years after my Decease

Item I Give and bequeath to Each of my Grand Children that shall be living at my Decease one bible of ten or twelve shillins price to be paid by my Executor here after named

Item I Give and bequeath unto my well beloved son **Elisha Green** for an Addition to his Portion twelve pounds in or as money to be paid by my Executor within two years after my Decease

Item I Give to my Negro Woman named **hager** ten shillings and to each of her Children five shillings which may Induce her to be kinde to my Wife and also my Will is y[t] my sd Negro Woman named **hager** be keept in my house to be for ye use of my sd Wife During her life and in case she should outlive my sd wife to be to my Executors here after named

Item I Constitute and appoint my four well beloved sons Peter John Stephen and Will[m] Green to be my Whole and sole Executors to be coEqual in ye Execution of this my Last Will and Testament To whome I Give and bequeath allye Rest my Lands and Meadows not allready Disposed of be it What or Where so ever or of What kind or Nature soever either in Providence or Warwick or else whare to them their heirs and assigns forever as also all my Movable Estate let it be what or where so ever; the which I Give ye beter to Inable them to Execute this my Last will and Tstament for ye Carefull attendance on there mother as I have above ordred and for my Interment and paying my Just Debts: and this I make my Last will and Testament Uterly Revoaking all Wills and Testaments here tofore by me made Ratifying and Confirming this and no other to be my Last Will and Testament In Witness Whereof I have here unto sett my hand and seal this 16th Day of May 1718

[signed] *Peter Green* (seal)

Witnessed by Sam[ll] Green, Thom Stafford, and John Wickes; proved 14 September 1723 and recorded Warwick Council Book folio 195 & 196 by John Wickes, Town Clerk.

Maj[r] **John Green** of Warwick deposed 9 August 1725 before **John Wickes**, Assistant, that "his cussen Elisha Green came to his house some short time after the death of his father Capt. Peter Green in August 1723 sum fue days after the will was opened . . . said there was very little gave to him . . . that he was hardly delt with by Reason he had heard his father say he would give him part of a Comonage and ten acres in Warwick . . . I told him his father had done Considerable for him, by Deed of Gift and Put him out when young to a Good Trade . . . but Elisha showed himself very much Dissatisfied about it."

244. **John Rogers** of Newport, town treasurer vs. **Thomas Peckham** of Newport, house-carpenter late constable for Newport for £16:4:0 due from rates [taxes] that he was to have collected when he was constable. Writ dated 26 July 1725; Daniel Updike, attorney.

245. **Isaac Thompson** of Westerly, merchant, vs. **Henry Davison** of Westerly, schoolmaster, in custody of the sheriff, for £3:0:3 due by note [evidently for goods received] dated 4 July 1722. Writ dated 28 July 1725; Nathaniel Newdigate, attorney. Accounting includes "remains of ye stockins, 6 2/8 of Cherry Derry, 2½ doz. buttons . . . thread . . . handkerchief."

246. **John Coddington** of Newport, Esqr vs. **Jonas Belton** of Newport, trader, in custody of the sheriff, in an action of deceit. Writ dated 28 July 1725; Henry Bull, attorney. In July 1725 at Newport the defendant did fraudulently and maliciously in the sale of a certain horse to him deceive him . . . horse had Infirmity in his Back . . . said Horse being a broken back Horse. Claimed £30 damages. Defendant answered that his name was **Joseph Belton**, not Jonas, and the suit should therefore be abated.

– March 1725/6 –

247. **John Stephens** of Newport, stone-cutter, vs. **Thomas Baley** of Newport, tanner, in custody of the sheriff, for £14:6:0 due for "one tomb stone and the cuting a coat of armes thereon and for the erecting the same over his Father's Grave in the month of March last past." Writ dated 7 December 1725; **Daniel Updike** attorney. Bill signed by **John Stevens**, for tombstone, £10, for cutting coat of arms, £2, for 300 bricks, 15*s*, carting, setting up, etc.

248. **Edward Ashby** of Groton in the county of New London, Connecticut, husbandman, vs. **Ichabod Potter** of South Kingstown, husbandman, for £17:10:0 due by note dated 13 February 1722 for a horse bought from him that day, with promise to pay on 1 May next, signed Ichabod Potter Junr. Witnesses: **David Dodge, James Ashby**. Writ dated 29 December 1725.

249. **John Ingraham** of Newport, cooper, vs. **John Webster** of Westerly, husbandman, in custody of the sheriff, for not executing according to law one writ dated 10 February 1724 against **Samuel Holway** . . . defendant was then town sergeant. Writ dated 6 January 1725.

250. **John Julian** of Newport, hatter, vs. **Edward Pelham Junr** of Newport, gentleman, in the custody of the sheriff, for £79:14:11 due by book for sundry parcels of goods and money lent and work by the plaintiff's Negro for the defendant beginning 17 January 1710/11 and ending 19 September 1719. Writ dated 17 January 1725/6; **Nathaniel Newdigate** attorney. Long bill with many items, torn and faded, includes "cash paid your self for **Capt. Chapman**, 3 pr clothing dyed black, cash lent when going to Boston, dying leather breeches, long plank to make a slead, beaver hat for your father, 4 lbs chocolat, cash paid **William James** for mending the gunns, cash lent yourself at **James Hakins** house, 2 large deerskins dressed, 12 days work of my Negro **John**, 2 beaver hats delivered to **Captn William Wilkson** pr your order, cash lent your self upon the Beach. *Credit*: cloth, pasturing of horse, hay, beef, rum, one double pistol . . . ." Auditors **John Coddington, Wm. Dyre** and **Samuel Wickham** on 5 April 1726 found a balance of £5:18:0 due to Edward Pelham.

251. **John Mason** of Stonington, gentleman, and **Anne** his wife (one of the daughters of **Peleg Sandford** late of Newport), **Job Almy** of Newport, gentleman, and **Brigit** his wife (one other of the daughters of Peleg

Sandford, etc.), and **Thomas Noyes** of Stonington and **Elizabeth** his wife (one other of the daughters of Peleg Sandford, etc.), vs. **William Robinson** of South Kingstown, Esq., in action of trespass, to recover 1200 acres of land in South Kingstown laid out to **William Brenton** late of Newport, Esq., deceased, as part of his one-seventh part of the Pettaquamscutt Purchase, and 600 acres in Point Judith, bounded north by **Thomas Potter**, east by the sea, south partly by land in possession of **Daniell Mackoone**, partly by **Stephen Haszard**, partly by **Ichabod Potter**, and partly by land belonging to **George Haszard**, and west by Point Judith Ponds, including a mansion house.

252. **Elizabeth Mitchel** of Newport, widow, vs. **John Overbeck** late of Newport, practioner of Physick, for debt of £10:12:4 due 2 April 1725 for lease of her house in Newport at £25 per annum. Declaration signed [with particularly fine signature] Eliz^th^ Mitchell.

253. **George Brownell** of Little Compton in the province of Massachusetts Bay, yeoman vs. **Ichabod Potter Junr** of South Kingstown, yeoman, for £40 due by note dated 3 April 1722, witnessed by **N. Blagrove**, wherein the defendant had promised to pay to the plaintiff £40 in good Barbadoes Rum at 3s. 6d. per gallon and £8 in money on or before 30 June following. Writ dated 28 January 1725; **Nathaniel Newdigate** attorney.

254. **Daniel Mackoon** of South Kingstown, yeoman, vs. **Ebenezer Niles** of South Kingstown, husbandman, in action of trespass, to recover 20 acres there which were part of 250 acres which **Samuel Wilbour** late of Portsmouth by will dated 21 August 1678 bequeathed to his cousin **William Wilbour Senr** upon a division of land in the Narragansett Country. William Wilbour Sr. by a deed of gift dated 11 May 1705 gave it to his grandson **Samuel Wilbour** son of his son **Thomas**; Samuel by deed dated 9 September 1715 deeded it for £550 to Daniel Mackoon, the present plaintiff. Writ dated 1 February 1725. The property was bounded north on the defendant's land, east on the Saucatucket River, south on the plaintiff's land, and west on land in possession of the plaintiff. **Nathanael Niles Junr** of South Kingstown deposed and said that land his Hon^rd^ Father bought of **Samuel Arnold** was laid out by the surveyor which he, the deponent, was informed was **James Carder.** Deposition of **Stephen Hazard** of South Kingstown aged 58 years and upwards, 3 September 1725, that he being desired by **Capt. Caleb Arnold** of Portsmouth, deceased, and others to go and see a certain parcell of land laid out on Westerly side of Pawcutucket River near to the house of **Capt. Nathaniel Niles** . . . land was laid out in

right of **Samuel Arnold** of North Kingstown, son to sd Caleb Arnold, as land given to him by his grandfather **Samuel Wilbour** of Portsmouth . . . laid out by Capt. James Carder of Warwick, **John Wilbour** son to sd Samuel Wilbour being present, and several other men to the best of my remembrance . . . [land] was laid out near 30 years agon and hath been improved by Capt. Niles and his sons upwards of 25 years past by fenceing part or all of sd land. Lieut. Col. **George Hazzard** aged 61 years and upwards, presented to the court a plat of the above land.

255. **Christopher Almy** of Newport, merchant, vs. **Daniel Dunam** of Newport, chaies maker, for £10:13:0 due by book for one hogshead of molasses sold and delivered in February 1722/3. Writ dated 3 February 1725; **Daniel Updike** attorney.

256. **George Rounds** of Newport, mason, vs. **Wm Pinigar** of Newport, feltmaker, for £12:11:9 due by book for work beginning 1 August 1725 and ending 8 November 1725. Writ dated 7 February 1725; **Henry Bull** attorney. Bill includes "making two chimneys att £2/10 per funell. . . building a ash hoale and oven. . . 58 yds of plaistering at 10*d* pr yd. . . hanging yr warping kettell twice. . . laying yr two hearths. . . splitting and shaving of laths." Defendant showed a contrary bill for liquor, to be taken off what he owed. Case went to referees.

257. **William Dival** late of Westerly vs. **John Haley** of South Kingstown, weavour, for £28 due by note dated 3 August 1724, witnessed by **Thomas Bennett** and **J^{o}/n Case**. Writ dated 10 February 1725; **Henry Bull** attorney.

258. **John Vaughan** of Newport, yeoman, vs. **Thomas Weaver** of Newport, yeoman, for £160 due by bond dated 1 March 1710/11, the condition of which was that the defendant was to pay to the plaintiff £80 in silver money when his children came of age or married. Writ dated 10 February 1725[/6]; **Nathaniel Blagrove** attorney. The children of John Vaughan were two sons: **John**, who arrived at age 21 in November 1723, and **Daniel**, who arrived at age 21 in March 1724/5. **Lawrance Clark** of Newport deposed 28 January 1723/4 before Peleg Smith that "some time in December last past he did hear Vaughan say that his Unkle Thomas Weaver could not Read nor Wright and that his Son John had not bin at the Colledge for nothing and that he had Put his Busness into his Sons hands conserning the Intrust of that Money in sd Weavers hands." **Stephen Bayley** deposed 29 June 1724 before John Coddington, J.P., that he saw Thomas Weaver Sr. of Newport pay unto John Vaughan of Newport Senr the interest of a bond of £80 and Vaughan declared himself fully satisfied. **Lov[s] Vaughan** of Newport testified 19 February 1725/6 before Nicholas Easton, Justice, that he was at the house of Mr. Stephen Bayley and saw Thomas Weaver pay John Vaughan in the year 1723. **Isaac George** and **Joshua Clarke** of Newport testified 24 March 1725/6 before Job Lawton, J.P., that some time in December 1723 at the house of **Caleb Clarke** in Newport they saw Weaver tender to John Vaughan Jr. £12:10:0, saying this was in full [payment] of the bond. **Stephen Easton** deposed at the same time that in June last past he was with Thomas Weaver and John Vaughan Jr. and his brother Daniel at the house of **Sylvester Sweet** in Newport, and saw the money paid, etc., and Vaughan agreed that it was in full satisfaction for the bond given him by his Granfather. The bond was signed by Thomas Weaver with a mark, W, and witnessed by **Jonathan Sabin** and **Thomas Peckham**. Verdict for the defendant, costs of court.

259. **Daniel Grinnel Ju[r]** of South Kingstown, yeoman, vs. **Nicholas Young** of North Kingstown, husbandman, for a debt of £6:3:0 due by note dated 11 January 1725, witnessed by **Jane Lewis** and **Israel Lewis**, signed by mark **N**. Writ dated 12 February 1725[/6].

260. **Henry Wright** of Newport, bricklayer, and **Hannah** his wife vs. **Thomas Plats** of Newport, bricklayer, in custody of the sheriff, for payment of £50 due Hannah by the will of her former husband, father of the defendant. Writ dated 14 February 1725[/6]; **Henry Bull** attorney. "Whereas the 30th Day of June AD 1710 Thomas Plats late of Boston . . . Butcher deceased (former Husband to ye sd Hannah and father to ye Defend[t]) by his Last Will and Testament . . . among other Devices and Bequests in said Will did in these words following bequeath (viz) Also I give to my said Wife one hundred Pounds money to be Paid by my two sons **Thomas & John Plats** equally when they come of Age . . . Plaintiffs now of age but hath not yet paid . . . ." Copy of portion of will in file continues, "Lastly I give and bequeath unto my said two Sons Thomas & John Platts my Housing Lands & Estate Real & Personal Equally betwixt them to be Divided when they shall come of Age . . . if either of them dye . . . without lawful Issue his part of the Estate shall be equally Divided betwixt the Surviving Son and his Sister **Hannah** aforesaid. . . M[r] **Richard Draper**, M[r] **Henry Bridgham** and my wife **Hannah** the Executors of this my last Will . . .," signed by **Thomas Platts** in Boston 13 June 1710.

261. **Samuel Boon** of North Kingstown, merchant, vs. **Samuel Sweet** late of North Kingstown now of Newport, innholder, in custody of the sheriff, for debt of £42 for rent of a dwelling house and 50 acres of land in North Kingstown which he occupied from 11 April 1722 to 11 April 1725 at £14 per year. Writ dated 14 February 1725/6; **Nathaniel Newdigate** attorney. **Capt. Bennoni Sweet** of North Kingstown testified there on 1 March 1725/6 that he heard Samuel Sweet hire the house of the plaintiff. **William Underwood** of Newport, late of North Kingstown, ferryman [signing by mark **V**], testified before **Job Lawton**, J.P., at Newport 4 March 1725/6, that he had lived near to Samuel Sweet in North Kingstown. On 14 March, **Benony Sweet** of North Kingstown testified at Newport before Job Lawton, J.P., that sometime after his brother Samuel Sweet had hired the farm of Samuel Boon, he had been in company with them and Boon showed them his line of fence which leads to Rig Hill. On 28 March 1726 **James Green** of North Kingstown testified before **William Hall**, Justice, that he had been in the company of Boon and Sweet and heard them come to the rental agreement. On 29 March 1726 before **Francis Willett**, J.P., **Silvenus Justin** of North Kingstown deposed and said that the first year Samuel Sweet came to live on the farm belonging to Samuel Boon, he being in company with Boon and Sweet and his brother **Martin Justin**, he agreed with Boon to make him some stone wall and a ditch in the line between his farm and land in possession of **William Underwood** if Boon and Underwood could agree to change the end of their fence . . . they did not agree . . . "we made neither. . . ." Later Boon agreed with him to make a double ditch at the other end of the line. **Benjamin Congdon** testified at the same time about the ditch, and **Martin Justin** of North Kingstown also testified. **Jonathan Mott** of North Kingstown deposed 30 March 1726 before Francis Willett, J.P., that in April 1722 he assisted Samuel Sweet in moving his household goods from the house of **Thomas Joslin** to the house of Samuel Boon in North Kingstown . . . Sweet lived in said house three years and upwards. Several receipts in the file. One from "Samuel Boon to Mr. Samuel Sweet, £3:3:4½ part for rent, part for paying of a glays for glasing of ye hous . . . allso ye carpenters for making 2 casements," dated at Kingstown 14 July 1723.

Judgement was for the plaintiff, £8 "besides what he had received" and costs.

262. **John Plats** of Newport, butcher, vs. **Thomas Plats** of Newport, bricklayer, in the custody of the sheriff, for an account of the time he was

receiver in Boston of money of the plaintiff. On or about April 1725 Thomas had a power from John to sell or dispose of a certain estate in Boston belonging to the said Thomas and John . . . he did so for a certain sum of money unknown to the plaintiff, half of which belonged to him. Writ dated 14 February 1725. **Richard Mew**, constable, attached goods of Thomas's: one shovel, one spade, two hodze, a sive and five trowels on 17 February.

263. **Jedidiah Jenkins** of North Kingstown, house carpenter, vs. **Stephen Northup** of North Kingstown, yeoman, in custody of the sheriff, for debt of £18 due by bond dated 26 June 1725 witnessed by **Benjamin Mory** and **Jeremiah Baker**. Writ dated 15 February 1725[/6].

264. **Caleb Kinnion** so called of Newport, mariner, vs. **John Webster** of Westerly, cordwainer, in custody of the sheriff, in an action sur trover concerning the conversion and disposition of one certain indenture or covenant by the defendant executed . . . and made with the plaintiff of the value of £10. Writ dated 6 February 1725[/6]; **Daniel Updike** attorney. Caleb in August 1722 at North Kingstown was possessed of the indenture or covenant as of his own proper writing which was his security for a horse and a suit of clothes when he should attain to the age of 21 years . . . about the month of September 1722 he left [the indenture] at the house of **Peter Boss** in North Kingstown . . . was casually lost . . . afterwards about the last of September 1722 [it] came into the hands of the defendant who refuses to give it back. Webster's answer by his attorney **Nathaniel Newdigate** was, that on 16 June 1722 Caleb became bound to him by an indenture for 2 years and 5 months as an apprentice during which time he was to serve faithfully & truly . . . but soon after running away from him and takeing away some of his goods & proving so bad that the defendant could not keep him. Defendant and plaintiff agreed that the indenture should be delivered up to the defendant and sd Kinyon on 3 October 1722 with the consent of his father **Benjamin Rood** and his mother **Phebe Rood** by a new indenture bound himself to one **Zacharia Allen** and left the defendant's service, thereby making the indenture with the defendant utterly void.

Evidence entered: Document dated 16 June 1722, signed by **Robert Willcocks** [mark *R*], of Kingstown, masson [*sic*], witnessed by Peter Boss and **Israel Lewis**, assigning to John Webster of Westerly cordwinder "all my power right and Intrust authority and Consern that I have to Caleb Kinyon ye son of Phebe the Wife of Benjamin Rude of Westerly by vertue of any Indentures made to me before the

Date of these presents . . . ." A similar document signed by John Webster, witnessed by **John Hall** [mark *J*] and **Joseph Hull Junr** dated 29 September 1722, transferring his right in Caleb to Zachariah Allen Junr of sd Westerly, yeoman. Indenture dated 3 October 1722, whereby Caleb Kinion bound himself unto Zachariah Allen Junr for the term of 2 years and 17 days . . . with consent of his father Benjamin Rood and his mother Phebe Rood . . . in consideration of £10 paid John Webster, Caleb's former master; Caleb signed by mark [S], Benjamin Rude signed his name, and Phebe [*d*] and Allen [*A*] made their marks; witnesses were **Jean** [no surname given] and **Elizabeth Sunderlin** [mark *E*]. This is followed by a document dated 28 August 1723 at Westerly, signed by Justices **John Babcock, Joseph Stanton,** and **John Saunders,** recording that one Caleb Kinyon was brought before them that day "by Virtue of Hue & Cry by **Soloman Carpenter** Town Sergent of South Kingstown . . . the young man owned he run away for no just Grounds but was perswaded by one other young man so to do our Judgement is that the Servant Caleb Kinyon So called Shall make up his lost Time which is Six Weeks and two Days and pay the present Charge which is £2:19:0." The charges included paying Esqr **Helm** for a hue & Cry, to Constable **Mumford,** to Soloman Carpenter, to "the Man of Norwich which infor'd ag^st^ him," and to the justices for time and trouble. This is followed by a bill of sale dated 6 September 1723 whereby Zachariah Allen for £8 assigned him rights in Caleb to **Capt Joseph Whipple** of Newport, merchant, signed by both Allen [mark *A*] and Kinion [mark like a *9* at a 45 degree angle]; **Job Lawton** and **John Holmes** were witnesses. A memorandum dated 20 September 1725 signed by Justices D. Updike and John Coddington stated that "Caleb Kinion *Mustee* . . . who had deserted his Master Mr Joseph Whipple for Some Space" was brought before them. "We find that [he] hath put his said Master to great Charge in apprehending him and therefore order that he serve his sd Master for the Space of One Year and Eight months from [this date]."

Zachariah Allen Junr testified 9 October 1725 before John Hill, Justice, that "I went Downe to Peter Bossis of Kingstowne with John Webster . . . sd Boss did then by ye perswation of sd Webster Deliver an Indenture to sd Webster and he promised sd Boss to seave him harmless sd Indenture being then read in my hering . . . Webster was to give his aprentice Caleb a horse and a suit of cloths when he came to ye age of 21 yeares . . . I did then persuade Webster to putt sd Indenture in to Joseph Hills hands for itt was ye boys security but he refused [*blotted*] . . . . **Joseph Hull** deposed the same day that he saw the indenture at the house of Peter Boss. Peter Boss of North Kingstown testified 3 February 1725/6 before William Hall, Justice, that "he had the indenture in his keeping until Webster came to sd Deponant and Zachariah Allen Jun[r] with him, and told him that he had sold sd Caleb to sd Allen and urged to have sd Indentur delivered, but sd Deponant saith he was loath to deliver [it] but after much perswasion, and sd Webster promised that sd Deponant nor sd boy called Caleb, should neither of them be damnified, sd Deponant saith he did deliver [it]." **Isrell Lewis** was interrogated 23 March 1725/6 before John Richmond, Justice, at Westerly, John Webster being present, and testified that he wrote the indentures at the request of the two parties, and that he heard Kinion had run away before his time was served. **Phebe Rude** deposed 25 March 1726 before **John Hill**, Justice, that sometime in September 1722 "we were all agreed that Caleb should go to Live with Zachariah Allin jun[r] of Westerly wherupon the [he] with my Consent and my husband agreing therunto did desier sd Zachariah Allin to go with John Webster in our behalf to M[r] Petter Boss and Desier him to Give up that indenture which we delivered to him to keep and to let the sd Webster have it as it did belonge to him by our aforesd agreement . . . John Webster had Received much Damage by sd Calebs miscarages and by his absenting himself from his masters service for which they made the aforsd agreement." In a second deposition Phebe said that to "her sertain knowledge theire was but one Indenture Between John Webster Master and my son Caleb Kinyon his aprentiss." John Hill noted that the adverse party [Webster] "Living above Ten miles from my house wher the above writtin evidence was Taken . . . was the Reson he was not notified." Benjamin Rude gave testimony almost identical with his wife's. Verdict was for the defendant, costs of court.

– September 1726 –

265. **John Coleman** of Weathersfield, Connecticut, yeoman, vs. **Anthony Negro**, resident in East Greenwich, labourer, otherwise called Anthony Negro formerly servant to **John Ward** of Weathersfield, in custody of the sheriff, for £20 due by note dated 25 August 1722. Writ dated 21 April 1726; **Nathaniel Newdigate** attorney. Plea of the defendant was that he was born a slave and was still liable to slavery,

the freedom he now enjoys only depending on the Will of his master . . . can't be liable or sued since he is not enjoying the privilege of a subject.

266. **Barak Coles** of the City of New York, vintner alias merchant, vs. **Lewis Sharp**, resident in Newport, mariner, in custody of the sheriff, for £8:9:1½ of New York money due by book for diet, lodging, and drink at the plaintiff's house in the City of New York in 1723/4. Writ dated 25 April 1726. Bill included sums for several weeks at a time, "Connecticut money rec'd of Mr. Langford . . . one week deducted for your absence in the country, assig. on **John Langford** . . . ."

267. **Nicholas Carr** of Jamestown, Esq. vs. **Richard Robinson** of the City of New York, mariner, in custody of the sheriff, for non-peformance of promise: about May 1725 at Newport the defendant received on board a sloop whereof he was then master one cask of molasses containing 50 gallons to be delivered to **Hannah Carr** at Oyster Bay in Long Island, she paying reasonable freight for it; the molasses was spilt and lost. Writ dated 27 April 1726; **Nathaniel Newdigate** attorney. **Micajah Townsend** testified at Newport 26 April 1726 that some time last spring, he believed it was in April, **Jacob Townsend** "told me one of the Carrs would send a cask of melasses to Hannah Car and desired me to call at **Pealick Cars** where I put my goods on board of Richard Robersons sloop . . . as we was agoing home Roberson went into Greenwich harbour to on load some goods for **John Hull** and Roberson had a mind I should take part of my goods out there . . . I being desired by Jacob Townsend to take some cear that it should be landed conveniant for her their being a small boat at that place that was agoing to Oyster bay . . . as they were hoisting the said cask out of the hold the head whops [hoops] was stript of against the comeings of the hatch . . . and as they loared it on the land or shoar, the head burst out and lost all excepting a few gallons which Roberson had a mind to send to the said Hannah Carr . . . I put it in my brother's seller and told Hannah Car of it . . . she wold not receive it . . . could not find any nales nor pins to stay the whoops on said cask . . . ."

268. **Christopher Almy** of Newport, merchant, vs. **Benjamin L'Homedieu** of Southold in Long Island in the province of New York, mariner, now resident in Newport, in custody of the sheriff, for non-performance of promise. Benjamin L'Homedieu, father of the defendant, late of Southold, in his lifetime in March 1716 was indebted to Christopher Almy for £26:7:0 for goods sold. Writ dated 28 April 1726. Bill: to Benjamin l'homedieu of South Hole Longe Island, for 220 gall rum @ 30s, sugar, molasses, etc. Credit: "cash rec'd of your wife." **Joseph Borden** of Newport, Esq., deposed and said that he was with Capt. Christopher Almy on Long Island at the house of Benjamin L'homedieu and heard the son promise to pay his father's debt. **William Almy** swore to the truth of that. **Mary Almy** wife of Capt. Christopher Almy testified about the bill. Judgement was for the plaintiff, balance sued for and costs of court. Plea of the defendant was that the promise had been made in 1716 and it was "near 10 years" to the taking out of the writ and therefore within the statute of James I and 21st Chapter the 16 . . .

269. **Christopher Fell** of New York, gentleman, vs. **Weston Clarke Junr** of Newport, merchant, for £7:5:0 in New York money due by note dated 11 March 1722, witnessed by **Charles Man** and **Th^o Michell**. Writ dated 19 May 1726; **Henry Bull** attorney.

270. **William Pinnigar** of Newport, hatter, vs. **Edward Richmond Jr.** resident in Newport, labourer, in custody of the sheriff, for £4:16:2 due by book for victuals, drink, horse hire, and use of the plaintiff's servant at sundry times from 7 May 1725 to 28 February 1726. Writ dated 1 June 1726; **Daniel Updike** attorney. Defendant did not answer; plaintiff declared nihil dicet.

271. **Samuel Sweet** of Newport, vintner, vs. **George Rounds** of Newport, mason, in custody of the sheriff, for £9:18:7 due by note dated 9 December 1725. Writ dated 1 June 1726; **Daniel Updike** attorney. No answer; nihil dicet.

272. **Thomas Coggeshall** (son of **Freegift**) of Newport, yeoman, vs. **Dan^{ll} Lambert** of Newport, shipwright, for £4:16:0 due for 12 days work of his man at 8 shillings per day in AD 1726. Writ dated 9 June 1726; **Henry Bull** attorney.

273. **Elizabeth Little** of Newport, spinster, feoffee in trust to **Rebecca Lawton**, wife of **George Lawton** of Portsmouth, yeoman, son of George Lawton of Portsmouth, yeoman, son of George Lawton of Portsmouth, deceased, in action of annuity to recover £12 in arrears which George oweth. The General Assembly at Newport 13 June 1721 had directed George Lawton to pay yearly to **Henry Bull** of Newport, feoffe in trust to said Rebecca and for her use £12 commencing 15 June 1721 during the time of their living apart or asunder . . . Henry Bull had refused to proceed any further and on 5 May 1724 the General Assembly had empowered Elizabeth to receive the money. Writ dated

8 June 1726. Receipt dated 31 March 1726 from Eliz^{bth} Little to **Job Lawton** on account of his brother George Lawton towards the maintenance of his wife Rebecca. Defendant's answer was that he was ready to receive his wife and desired to cohabit with her and would maintain her if she returned to him. Judgement for the plaintiff, money sued for and costs.

274. **Joel Chaffee** of Barrington, county of Bristol, Massachusetts Bay, cordwainer, vs. **Benjamin Smith** of Newport, yeoman, in custody of the sheriff, for £15 due by note dated 6 February 1724/5 to **Thomas Brown** of Newport, yeoman, witnessed by **Joseph Allen** and **Sam^{ll} Haydon Jr**. Writ dated 9 June 1726; **Daniel Updike** attorney. Defendant's plea was that Thomas Brown was called of Newport in the declaration and is now of Bristol County . . . a felmonger.

275. **Thos Jones** of Newport, butcher, vs. **John Vial** of Newport, boat builder, for £10:17:9 and 3 farthings due for provisions sold and delivered between 3 April 1725 and 6 June 1726. Writ dated 30 June 1726; **Henry Bull** attorney.

276. **Arnold Collins Jr** of Newport, merchant, vs. **Christopher Phillips** of North Kingstown, tanner, administrator of the goods of **Thomas Keeling** late of Newport, mariner, deceased, in custody of the sheriff, for £52:10:8½ due by book for goods delivered in the lifetime of said Thomas Keeling and at his request to **William Brock** his brother, from 10 April 1723 to 18 July next. Writ dated 6 July 1726; **Daniel Updike** attorney. Bill included "7 yds Mantua silk 20/4, 1 bagg gold buttons £7:3:4, 1 bagg silver buttons £5:10:0, snuff, flowered sattin @ 22s yd, persian @ 14s, ferrit, 4s, ribbon, 12d, a beaver hat, 50s, a red trunk, 20s . . . ." Judgement for plaintiff, money sued for and costs.

277. **Samuel Boon** of North Kingstown, merchant, vs. **Thomas Jackwise** of North Kingstown, yeoman, and **Joseph Gardner** of East Greenwich, yeoman, in the custody of the sheriff, for debt of £25:11:6. Writ dated 11 July 1726; **Nathaniel Newdigate** attorney. For want of the body of Thomas Jackwise, **Imanuel Northrup**, town sergeant, on 13 July attached a pewter plate belonging to him.

278. **Samuel Boon** of North Kingstown, merchant, vs. **Samuel Barber** of South Kingstown, husbandman, in the custody of the sheriff, for £16:12:0 due by note dated 7 March 1723/4 witnessed by **James Eldred** and **Joanna Sweet**. Writ dated 11 July 1726; **Nathaniel Newdigate** attorney.

279. **Samuel Boon** of North Kingstown, merchant, vs. **Benjamin Holway** of Westerly, otherwise of South Kingstown, for debt of £35:0:8 due by note dated 14 January 1723/4 witnessed by **John Sweet** and **Alexander Brown**. Writ dated 12 July 1726; **Nathaniel Newdigate** attorney.

280. **Peleg Carr** of Newport, merchant, vs. **Edward Rossam** of Newport, sadler, in action of trover in the conversion or disposal of a piece of gold, a Spanish coin valued at £2:10:0 in November 1725. Writ dated 14 July 1726; **Daniel Updike** attorney. On 16 August 1726 before **Job Lawton**, J.P., **Richard Mew** of Newport testified that when he had taken up **John Hammett**'s Negro called **Ned** for breaking into Capt. Peleg Carr's house and stealing several pieces of gould [*sic*], Ned said that Rossam's lad had taken up a piece which he had lost and he was afraid to ask him for fear he should be discovered. **Daniel Clarke** testified that he had had some discourse with **Peter Stanbury** who lived with Mr. Rosham about a piece of gold he had found . . . Peter "told me he had found it up town by **Thomas Peckham**'s pound and after that he told me he found it down town between **Cooks** and **Greenmans**. He took it up the same day that I found a piece of gould between **Trips** and **Stantons**." **John Hammett** of Newport [in a statement that is a page and a half long] declared that last spring he went to Edward Rossam and said unto him, "I understand one of thy apprentices has found a piece of gold that my boy stole from Peleg Carr and that thou had it in thy keeping I hope thou intendest to give it to him again." Rossam said he didn't know whose it was. There had been aggravated words between Rossam and Carr . . . Rossam said that since Carr had "so abused him he was resolved he should not have it unless he gott it by Law . . . His wife said she was sorry her husband was such a passionate man . . . seemed much concerned about it . . . suggested he deliver it to the Governor and the deponent [Hammett] would engage to prevail with Carr to withdraw the action . . . Rossam replied he had delivered it to the boy again . . . ."

281. **Adam Haydon** of Kingstown in the county of Ulster, government of New York, sadler, vs. **Thomas Stafford** of Warwick, yeoman, for debt of £15 due by note dated 27 May 1725 witnessed by **Jon[a] Nicholls** and **John Wickes**. Writ dated 15 July 1726; **Nathaniel Newdigate** attorney.

282. **Robert Gibbs** of Providence, apothecary, vs. **William Olney** of Providence, tanner, for £33 due by note dated 17 February 1726 witnessed by **Thomas Olney** and **William Turpin**. Writ dated 17 July 1726; **Nathaniel Newdigate** attorney.

283. **John Beere** of Newport, shipwright, vs. **Benjamin Smith** of Newport, boatman, in custody of the sheriff, for £20:17:0 due by book for money lent and goods sold and delivered from September 1724 to 20 September 1725. Writ dated 18 July 1726. A credit account presented included "5 sticks received on account of **William Hack** . . . one keele pc 50 foot long, one waile pc 52 foot long, towing two stiks . . . one keele pc 44 foot . . . one waile pc 42 foot . . . one p^{s} for a kilson . . . towing . . . ."

284. **John Raynolds** of North Kingstown, yeoman, vs. **Thomas Collins** of East Greenwich, for non-performance of promise to deliver £5:5:0 in good and passable pitch pine boards at market price upon the last of April next . . . in year 1725 . . . for value received. Writ dated 18 July 1726. No answer; plaintiff declared nihil dicet. The note calls the defendant **Thomas Collins Jn^{r}** of East Greenwich, house carpender.

285. **Robert Dennis** of Tiverton, yeoman, vs. **Zachariah Allen** of Westerly, yeoman, for debt of £31:4:0 due by note dated 6 September 1723, witnessed by **John Cook** and **Wm Brown**. Writ dated 19 July 1726; **Henry Bull** attorney.

286. **Joseph Hockeday** of Newport, late mariner on board the ship *Brumley*, **Capt. Wm Herbert**, master, vs. **Samuel Holmes** and **Thomas Richardson** of Newport, merchants and part owners of the said ship, for £6:3:9 due for service and labor aboard said ship from 14 February 1725 to 25 April 1726. Writ dated 19 July 1726; **Henry Bull** attorney. File includes testimony by Samuel Holmes on 1 February 1725/6, before **Samuel Cranston**, Governor of the Colony, and **Nathaniel Kay, Esq.**, Collector and Principal Officer of his Majesty's Customs, that the *Brumley of London* was of the burthen of about 100 tons, built at Newport this present year [1725]; the deponent together with **Edward Hanken, John Payne** of London, and **Thomas Richardson** of Newport at present are owners thereof . . . no Foreigner directly or indirectly hath any part nor interest therein. On 8 September 1726 before Job Lawton, J.P., **James Davis** and **Thomas Hows** [Hows signing by mark] testified that in April or May last "Capt. William Herbert came to Joseph Hockeday in his majesty's gaol . . . promised to take him out of gaol and bid him be of good hart and also gave him 2 shillings sixpence upon account and told him he would not send his cloathes ashore by reison he did intend he should goe the voyage with him." Bill to "Homes & Richardson" for wages, 2 months and 8 days at £2:15:0 per month.

287. **Noah Whipple** of Providence, yeoman, vs. **Thomas Arnold** of Providence, yeoman, in action of *quod permittat*: that without delay he permit the plaintiff to bring back and turn a certain brook or stream of water in said Providence commonly called Absolute Brook into its true and ancient course. The defendant by digging a ditch or drain in his own land within the last three years had drawn off and diverted it through his own land. Writ dated 19 July 1726; **Daniel Updike** attorney. Depositions were made 30 August 1726 by **Mr. John Smith, Capt. James Olney,** and **Mr. John Browne,** all of Providence, who "went this present day to take a view of the place in controversy . . . found a dam . . . an eight foot ditch . . . an old ditch [we were] informed was dug by **Capt. Richard Arnold**, deceased." **Mr. Christipher Smith** of Providence, aged about 50 years and upwards, testified the same day, along with **Edward Smith**, aged about 57 years. On 3 September, depositions were made 3 September by **Mr. Daniel Angel** of Providence, aged about 45 years, and **Mr. Hope Angel** of Providence, who said that he "hath had knowledge of the swamp called the Absolute Swamp about thirty years . . . niver knew any natyurall corse of water run out of said swamp but what run out at the southern end . . . of the opinion Mr. Thomas Arnolds depriving [the defendant] of [it] hath bin a greate damage . . . ." **Mr. Jonathan Whipple** and Mr. **Thomas Whipple** of Providence testified that at the request of Noah Whipple they went with him to Thomas Arnold's to hear the debate on the matter. . . Arnold proposed to Noah Whipple and his partner [**Thomas Olney**] being one of the guardians of **Obadiah Olney** that they might dig a dreane into his ditch and take away what water they could that way. On 5 September **William Olney** of Providence, blacksmith, aged about 23 years, testified that he "saw one of Thomas Arnold's sons and his man that lived with him at work at the dam that floated said swamp with a teem . . . Noah Whipple improved said water in floating a swamp sum years agoe . . . ." **William Potter**, aged 27 years, testified the same day.

288. **Clement West** of Westerly, labourer otherwise yeoman, vs. **Benjamin Mory** of North Kingstown, yeoman, and **Ichabod Potter** (son of **Thomas**) of South Kingstown, weaver, for £200 due by note dated 20 March 1723/4 witnessed by **William Hall** and **Thomas Jackwies**. Writ dated 19 July 1726.

289. **Samuel Mott** of Newport, victualler, vs. **John Vial** of Newport, boat builder, for £5:3:5 due for victuals sold and delivered from 29 April to 16 June 1726. Writ dated 20 July 1726; **Nathaniel Newdigate** attorney. The bill included calf's head, several sheep's heads, quarter lamb, &c.

290. **William Hall, William Spencer,** and **Benjamin Nichols,** all of North Kingstown, Esqrs., vs. **James Nichols** and **Francis Bates,** both of North Kingstown, husbandmen, and **Samuel Anthony** of South Kingstown, husbandman, in the custody of the sheriff, for £100. The defendants had bound themselves in that penal sum on 31 January 1723 on the condition that James Nichols fulfill an order made by the Justices above-named, dated 31 January 1723, concerning maintenance of a male child born of **Kathrine Bowin** at the rate of 2/6 per week, to be paid quarterly. Writ dated 21 July 1726; **Henry Bull** attorney.

291. **Comfort Baker** of North Kingstown vs. **Ezekiel Whitford** of North Kingstown, weavour, for debt of £28:15:0 due by note dated 7 February 1725/6 witnessed by **William Hall** and **Sarah Hall** [her mark]. Writ dated 21 July 1726.

292. **Caleb Claggett** of Newport, baker, vs. **Samuel Sheffield** of Newport, mariner, for non-fulfillment of promise made 27 December 1725 at the Bay of Honduras to pay £60 of Rhode Island money drawn on the account of **Major Nathaniel Sheffield** of Newport to **Messrs Westbeere & Rowden**. Writ dated 25 July 1726; **Daniel Updike** attorney. Memorandum to **William Rowden** at Eaton Town in North Carolina. Judgement for the plaintiff, bill sued for and costs of court.

293. **Capt. Ichabod Palmer** and **Rufus Minor** both of Stoningtown [Connecticut], yeomen, vs. **Joseph Case** of South Kingstown, yeoman, for £50 due by note dated 11 October 1725. Writ dated 26 July 1726. Note: ". . . pay £50 for 10 head of cattle sold and delivered by said Palmer and Minor at my next return from Boston," acknowledged at Newport 7 September 1726 before **Samuel Cranston,** Governor.

294. **George Lyte** and **Robert Shelton,** of the parish of St. Michael in the Island of Barbados, merchants, vs. **Edward Coddington** of Newport, mariner, resident in the Island of Barbados, for debt of £524:11:8 of lawful money of Barbados. Writ dated 26 July 1725; **Daniel Updike** attorney. Letter from Geo: Lyte to Freind Almy [**Job Almy**], from Barbados 2 November 1719, "have advised my father to put this affaire of ours in your hands." He explained that a note of Edward Coddington's had been drawn on his father, **Major Nathaniel Coddington,** for proceeds "'of a hogshead and a teirse of rum which he left in his father's hands of ours . . . his father sold it at 4/6 . . . 167 gallons . . . [and] has drawn commission." He desired Almy to "if possible ship in staves otherwise what you think will answer best here." Edward's bond was witnessed by **John Reed** and **Benj[a] Dawson,** and bill of sale

dated 26 October 1719 for 10 hogsheads of rum and 5 of molasses "shipt from Antigua to Boston and Rhoad Island for account of George Lyte and Robt Shelton . . . 850 gals. sold at Boston for £291:6:6." Judgment for the plaintiff, breach of covenant; £6 damages and costs.

295. **Samuel Mott** of Newport, victualler, vs. **Samuel Haydon Junr** of Newport, blacksmith, for £31:14:9½ due by book for victuals sold and delivered from 21 April 1725 to 8 December 1725, including beef, veal, mutton, lamb, tongue, etc. Writ dated 27 July 1726; **Nathaniel Newdigate** attorney.

296. **Samuel Sanford** of Newport, hatter, vs. **Wm Wood** and **John Allin**, both of Newport, husbandmen, in action of trespass to recover 150 acres in Portsmouth, bounded north on land of **John Sanford**, east on the Bay or salt water, south on land of **George Lawton**, and west on the highway. **Mr. Jeremiah Clark** aged about 84 years deposed 10 January 1726 before **William Barker**, Justice, and said that he "well remembered lands at the place called Black Point where John Sandford, William Wood, and John Allin now improve and occupy was in the lifetime of Mr. John Sandford grandfather to said John Sandford deemed to be . . . understood said John Sandford gave it to six of his sons -- **Samuel Peleg Rescum William & Elisha** . . . deponent was well acquainted with all except **Isborn** who departed . . . understand he was a married man before he died . . . rest of the sons all lived to be above 21 . . . ." Defendants won costs of court.

297. **Mary Sanford, Margaret Sanford,** and **Grizzel Sanford**, infants, children and co-heirs of **William Sanford** late of Newport, gentleman, deceased, by **Nathaniel Cotton** of Bristol, province of Massachusetts Bay, clerk, and **Grizzel** his wife their mother and guardian, vs. **Samuel Pike**, taylor, **John Cranston**, mariner, **Samuel Holmes** and **Thomas Richardson**, merchants, all of Newport, in action of trespass to recover one small piece of land with one shop and two warehouses and a wharf thereon in Newport, bounded east at the front 12 feet upon Strand Street otherwise known as Thames Street, south on land in possession of John Cranston, north on the plaintiff, and west on the harbour, whereof William Sanford, deceased, father of the plaintiffs, was seised at his death on or about April 1721 intestate. Writ dated 28 July 1726; **Nathaniel Newdigate** attorney.

The very large file includes a copy of the will of **John Sanford** of Portsmouth. Lease: **Sam^{ll} Pike** of Newport, taylor, "having hired of Wm Sanford of Newport aforesaid a small piece of land on which my shop now stands . . . for an entire year from 1 March 1714/5 . . . east on the main street of Newport . . . north on **Jn° Stanton** his butcher's shop . . . west on Sanford . . . south on the house of **Coll. Jn° Cranston** now in possession of **Jn° Chambers** . . . acknowledged as tenant from 1 September 1712"; signed 2 March 1714/15 and witnessed by **William Norton**.

298. **Benjamin Smyton** infant and grandson and heir of **William Smyton** formerly of Portsmouth, by **Nathaniel Byfield** late of Bristol now of Boston, Esq., his guardian, vs. **William Potter** in action of trespass. Writ dated 21 July 1726; **Nathaniel Newdigate** attorney. Deed shown, whereby **Thomas Brownell** of Tiverton, husbandman, on 24 11th month called January 1718/19 for £300 deeded to **William Potter Jr.** of Portsmouth, mariner, a dwelling house and 40 acres in Portsmouth, bounded northerly by land of Stephen Brayton, easterly by a highway, southerly by land now in possession of **Thomas Durfie**, westerly in part on land of **Samuel Anthony** and part on the highway leading to the spring. Witnesses: **Abiel Tripp, Benjamin Hall Jr.**, from Portsmouth Land Evidence 3:256.

Defendant answered that the plaintiff had not considered "my lawful conveyance from **Peter Talman** attorney or **Samuel Hagburn** principal to **William Smyton** which is the foundation of my title," and questioned the plaintiff's title on grounds that Smyton's will directed his wife to pay his debts and after her death whatever remained undisposed of was to go "to my children as my wife shall see cause." He added that the defendant was now of full age and could not therefore sue by his guardian; he said also that he had been in quiet and peaceable possession of the premises for more than 40 years and the statute of limitations should take effect. Judgement was for the plaintiff, land sued for and costs; appealed.

299. **Philip Shearman** of Portsmouth, weaver, vs. **Joseph Wilcox**, husbandman, of Portsmouth, alias yeoman, for non-fulfillment of promise. On 15 March 1721/2 at Newport, Shearman had paid **William Coddington**, Esq., Sheriff, £1:10:0 to discharge Wilcox from gaol, plus £48:3:0 to satisfy a debt that Wilcox owed to his brother **Daniel Wilcox** of Dartmouth, yeoman, on whose suit he was in gaol. William Coddington testified 8 September 1726 as to what he remembered: Philip Shearman told Joseph Wilcox that "he hoped he would not be a Rogue but that he would pay him again . . . I believe Mr. Brenton was there when he was let out . . ." Receipt from Benjamin Durfee at Freetown 8 August 1726: "Philip Shearman pd me 47/3 due from Joseph Wilcox to

his brother Daniel Wilcox." On 6 September 1726 **Lieut. Benjamin Hall** of Portsmouth testified that at the latter end of May a year since, or the beginning of June, he "being at work at the dwelling house of Philip Shearman in Portsmouth . . . in discourse heard **Hannah** the wife of Philip say her husband had paid the money for Joseph Wilcox, and to his certain knowledge he had seen Philip Shearman in the town of Portsmouth once in two or three weeks or thereabouts ever since he wrought in the town of Dartmouth, and heard him say that Portsmouth was the proper place of his dwelling." Hall and **Capt. Samuel Cornell** of Dartmouth testified about conversations that had taken place at the house of **Widdow Hannah Arnold** on Rhode Island in January last past.

300. **John Sabeer** of Newport, merchant, vs. **Nathaniel Dyer** of Newport, tallow chandler, for £40:16:5½ due on account to sloop *Nimrod* which the defendant did on 10 November 1723 assume for his son-in-law **John Wallen** of Newport, mariner.

301. **Caleb Carr** of Jamestown, yeoman, eldest son and heir of Caleb Carr, his father, late of Jamestown, yeoman, deceased, who was Eldest Sonn and Heir of **Robert Carr**, his grandfather, yeoman, deceased, vs. **Daniel Updike** of Newport, Esq., in a charge of trespass concerning land and house in Newport.

Plaintiff claims property descended to him by death of Robert Carr who died in the year 1681 intestate. Defendant answers that he is tenant under **James Honeyman Junr**, infant son of **Rev. James Honeyman** of Newport, clerk, whose heir he is, and has enjoyed uninterrupted and peaceable possession above 40 years.

– March 1726/7 –

302. **John Belitho** and **John Malem** of Newport, distillers in partnership and company, vs. **Scipio** a Negro man of Newport, carrier, in custody of the sheriff, for not delivering in good order one hogshead of molases containing 101 gallons, worth £15:3:00, to the plaintiffs belonging. Writ dated 15 November 1726; **Henry Bull** attorney. The defendant had taken the molasses into his possession 14 November 1726 at Newport and was to transport it from the wharf belonging to Joseph Borden at the Point to the stillhouse of the plaintiffs in Newport . . . it was spilt and lost by means unknown to them. **Isaac Anthony** of Newport testified 30 November 1726 before John Coddington, J.P., that "some time in this month I was walking over the brige or crossway from the Point and I see Sypeo negro man belonging to Newport Driveing a truck Cart with one hogsh[d] in itt & as he Drove the head of the Hogs[d] flue out & I observed [it] was Severall Inches from the Wheele of the truck so that the Wheel could not touch it & the carter Drove to the best of my Understanding slow anogh & cairfully & as I understand itt was the first hogs[d] that was stove in the trucks that Day. . . ." **Capt. Elisha Gibbs** of Newport gave similar testimony.

Depositions 30 March 1727 before John Coddington, J.P.: **Nathan Townsend** of Newport testified that "John Belitha being at my Shoop in Newport a fue days after Sippeo had been acarting molasses [he] said to Sippeo Why do you not take cair of that molasses for he would not . . ." **William Hannah** of Newport testified that when Scipio brought the molasses "stove in his cart Belitho and Malem would not receive it." **Daniel Kinnecot** testified that he "trimed the hogshead of molasses that John Belitho and John Malem sueth Scipio a negro for which was stove in sd Scipio's cart last November . . . was well trimed and nailed and fitt for trucking or shipping." Verdict was for the defendant, costs of court.

303. Summons dated 14 February 1726[/7] for **Jonathan Nicholls** of Newport, Esq., **Thomas Cornel**, and **George Lawton**, both of Portsmouth, Esqrs., executors of the will of **Elizabeth Carr**, late of Newport, gentlewoman, deceased, to answer a complaint of **Samuel Haydon** of Newport, blacksmith at the General Court of Trials in March next. Long accounting from Haydon to Madam Elizabeth Carr, beginning 2 October 1712 and ending 24 February 1719. Items include: "rent of her house . . . linnen cloth for a shift for **Moll**, making [shift], thread,

sundry bonnets for M[rs] **Slocumb**, tobacco, cash pd M[r] **Eseck Browne**, irons for four casements, 5 turnbuckles and squares, 10s to clerk for the year 1713 by M[r] **Lillibridge**, cash pd M[r] **John Langford**, **Joseph Fry** for glaseing windows, cash pd her by Cap[t] **Friend** [and] **George Westgate**, cash pd by my wife to y[r] granddaughter, setting a lock on y[e] Pew Doore, pair of doggs, mending tongs, 2 heaters, 2 almanacks for the year 1715, chimney barrs, hooks, hinges, spikes, &c, half a pigg to **M[r] Holley**, 2 bushels of Indian meal, seathing a wheelbarrow, wheat, deck nailes for **M[r] Dunbar**, axes to **Harry**, sett curtin rods and hooks, 3 ring bolts for the wharfe, mending the pumpbrake . . ." for a total of £87:9:3, signed by Samuel Haydon. Credit for "hire of her house from 27 April 1711 to 27 January 1716 is 5 years @ £14 per annum . . . 9 months more . . . worke done [June 1720] by your Negroe man." The original accounting is beautifully written; the file contains also a carelessly-written verbatim copy.

304. **Cuthbert Campbell** of South Kingstown, merchant, vs. **Stephen Wilcox** of Westerly, yeoman, for £27:7:8 for goods delivered from 26 July 1726 to September 1726, including fabrics, ivory comb, paper of pins, gun powder, rum, handkerchief, fan and velvet mask, looking glass and snuff box full of snuff, horse whip, women's black silk gloves and necklace, and sewing thread. Also an item for "rice received by **Mr. Randall** for yr daughter's use when she was sick." Writ dated 16 January 1726[/7].

305. **John Warner** of Warwick, Esq., vs. **John Gereardy** of Warwick, weaver, in action of trespass, for possession of a dwelling house and ten acres in Warwick, partly an orchard and the rest arable, pasture, and meadow land, formerly the house lot of **Ezekiel Hollyman** late of Warwick, yeoman, deceased, great-grandfather of the plaintiff. The property was bounded northwesterly by the main street that leads through the town, southwesterly by the highway that leads into the neck, southeasterly by a highway, and northeasterly partly by the river, partly by land in possession of the plaintiff. Ezekiel Hollyman died in the year 1659 intestate and the Town Council of Warwick on 27 September 1659 did approve **John Warner** one of the grandchildren and father of the plaintiff, to be heir of all the housing and lands belonging to the said Hollyman at his death in the town of Warwick. Said John Warner died in or about the month of April 1712 intestate and right to the property descended to the plaintiff his eldest son and heir. Writ dated 2 February 1726[/7]; **Nathaniel Newdigate** attorney. Defendant answered that the Town Council's action [in making a will] was absurd and contrary to law.

The file contains copies of several depositions made years earlier. On 24 April 1695 **James Sweet, Sr**, aged about 73 or 74, of Kingstown, signed his mark to a statement about the town lot which John Gereardy of Warwick bought of Ezekiel Holliman. **John Rice** also deposed. On 30 August 1708 **Samuel Gorton** of Warwick, aged 88 or thereabouts, and Lt. **Amos Stafford**, aged 52 or thereabouts, made depositions, and on 18 April 1724 **Hugh Stone** aged 76 or thereabouts, did so.

306. **Jeremiah Wilson** of Newport, yeoman, vs. **John Watson Jr.** of South Kingstown, yeoman, in custody of the sheriff, for trespass, to recover one-seventh part of a tract of 18 acres in South Kingstown, bounded easterly partly on the Pettaquamscutt River and partly on the marshes, southerly on the defendant, westerly and northerly on highways. **James Wilson** late of South Kingstown, yeoman, deceased on or about 1703 seised of the property as tenant-in-common with other proprietors in the Pettaquamscutt Purchase. By his will of 8 February 1705 he devised it to his brother Jeremiah Wilson's children to be equally divided . . . children were **Mary** and **Ann Wilson**.

Will of James Wilson:

In the Name of god Amen The Eighth Day of February 1705/6 I James Wilson of the Town of Kingstown in the Colony of Rhode Island and Providence Plantations in New England &c Husbandman being very sick and weak of body but of perfect mind and memory - Thanks be given unto God therefore calling unto mind ye mortality of my body and knowing that it is appointed for all men once to die do make and ordain this my last will and testament that is to say Principally and first of all I give and recommend my Soul unto ye Hands of God that gave it and my body I recommend to ye earth to be buried in decent Christian burial at ye discretion of my executors nothing doubting but at ye general resurrection I shall receive ye same again by the mighty power of God and as touching such worldly estate wherewith it hath pleased God to bless me with in this life I give demise and dispose of ye same in ye following manner and form.

Imprimis I give and bequeath to **Alice Wilson** my dear beloved wife and to her son **Samuel Wilson** and his heirs my now dwelling house with ye lot it is on and halfe ye farm thereto belonging with that lot also bought of **Thomas Mumford Senr** together with all other priviledges and appurtenances thereto belonging with all my moveables for ever immoveables to be peaceably enjoyed and possessed by them or either of them during the full term of their lives and if in case her son Samuel Wilson dye without lawful issue then ye land return'd to my loving brother **Jeremiah Wilson** or his heirs.

Furthermore It is my will and desire that Mr. **Joseph Smith** shall be my only and sole executor to this my last will and testament together with **Alice Wilson** my wife whom I also appoint my only and sole executrix.

Item I give and bequeath unto my loving brother in law **Daniel Sabeer** of Newport two hundred acres of my land to be laid out in some convenient place which I give and bequeath to him his heirs execut^ors^ administrat^ors^ and assigns for ever And as for ye remaining part of my lands I give and bequeath unto my brother **Jeremiah Wilson**'s children to be equally divided amongst them when they come to twenty one years of age and I do hereby utterly disallow revoke and disannul all and every other former testaments wills legacies and bequests and executors by me i any wise before named willed and bequeathed ratifying and confirming this and no other to be my last will and testament i witness whereof I have hereunto set my hand & seal ye day and year afores^d^.

Signed by James Wilson with his mark, and by witnesses **Benjamin Mory** [his mark *X*], **Joseph Case** [mark *IC* turned on side], and Mercy Culver, who wrote her name; proved 23 February 1705/6.

On 16 March 1705[/6] the guardians of **Henry Bull** who was then a minor brought legal process to evict the tenants. Warrant in file, attested by **Aaron Jacways**, town sergeant, not dated: "According to the precept on the other side the force was removed by laing open the fence on the northeast part of the said lands near Mr **Belpheres** house into the plowd ground and also on the southwest side of the said lands into the grass ground and the said **James Coggeshall** and **Ezekiel Bull** led in upon the said lands and all other persons commanded off and possession gave to them the said guardians to Henry Bull a minor in the Queens name by me."

It was noted that Jeremiah Wilson's daughter Mary took to husband **Edward Robinson** and Ann took to husband **Nathaniel Raye**; Nathaniel died on or about 1722; Mary and Edward and Ann on 14 December 1724 quitclaimed the property to Jeremiah Wilson. Writ dated 7 February 1726/7; **Henry Bull** attorney.

307. **John Chadwick** of Newport, mason, vs. **Martin Howard** of Newport, clothier, in custody of the sheriff, in an action of trespass, concerning land in Newport measuring 52 by 80 feet with a dwelling house, bounded west on the street, north on land belonging to the Family of the **Pearces**, east on land of the Sanfords, south on a tannyard lately belonging to **William Collins** late of Newport, deceased, tanner. Martin Howard and his wife by a deed dated 31 December 1725 [mortgaged it] to the plaintiff for securing a payment of £27:10:0 on or before 30 December next and had not paid. Deed is signed by Martin

and **Anna Howard**, witnessed by **Mehetabel Treby** and **Anstis Updike.** Writ dated 8 February 1726[/7]; **Daniel Updike** attorney. No answer; declared nihil dicet. An endorsement on the deed indicates that the mortgage was discharged 28 April 1727.

308. **Samuel Snell** of Newport, vintner, vs. **Thomas Huxham** of Newport, butcher, in the custody of the sheriff, for £17:2:9 due by book for money paid, wood, and drink sold and delivered and work done by the plaintiff's son and servant **Sam** at sundry times beginning 16 October 1725 and ending 14 September 1726. Writ dated 16 February 1726[/7]. Accounting dated 8 March 1726/7 included a cord of walnut wood at 12s, money "paid **John Platts** on your account . . . my son Samuel helping you," etc. Credit: mutton, veal, beef, etc. Several bills in the file.

309. **Robert Wilcox** of North Kingstown, yeoman, vs. **Palmer Cleveland** of North Kingstown, tailer, for damage done to his property by livestock of the defendant. Wilcox had impounded five swine belonging to Cleveland on 12 October 1726, and submitted a bill which included charges for bringing the suit. On 12 October 1726 before **William Hall,** Justice, **Job Tripp** and **Jeremiah Austin** testified that they were fence viewers of North Kingstown and were called by Palmer Cleveland to view the fence of Robert Wilcox which enclosed his cornfield and found it not to be sufficient. On 17 October 1726 before **Francis Willett,** Justice, **Jeremiah Fish** of South Kingstown testified that he "being often this fall near a field of corn belonging to Robert Wilcox son of **Stephen** divers times seen horses in said field and once a yoke of oxen . . . same field where **Samuel Davis** and **James Braman** apprised damage. . . ." **James Braman,** mason, and **Samuel Davis,** cooper, both of North Kingstown, testified that they had been employed by Wilcox to appraise the damage . . . "some done by horskind . . . cattle and swine . . . the farme which Wilcox hireth of **Jeffery Haszard.**"

310. **Thankful Collins** of Warwick, yeoman, otherwise known as husbandman, executor of the will of **Thomas Collins** late of Warwick, deceased, vs. **Thomas Collins** of East Greenwich, yeoman, otherwise housecarpenter, for £118:16 due by bond dated 5 February 1724/5 [to his father]; bond originally given to **Randall Holden** of Warwick. Witnesses to note were **William Ford** and **Amos Lockwood**.

311. **Mordecai Dunbarr** of Newport, taylor, sued **John Pitcher** of Jamestown, tanner, for debt: £55:9:2 for labour done and sundry goods sold and delivered in 1726 and 1727. The accounting "with Mr John Pecher" includes "making your suite, two pare of trousers, one pare fine D° for your brother, and a duffel coat for **John Cary**."

312. **Joseph Bennit** of Newport, house carpenter, vs. **John Easton Jr.** of Newport, glazier, for 47*s* 4*d* due by note dated 23 March 1724.

313. **Samuel Perry** of Westerly, yeoman, vs. **Penelope Holway** of South Kingstown, widow and administratrix of the estate of **Benjamin Holway** late of Westerly who died in South Kingstown, for debt due by note dated 14 February 1725 in the lifetime of sd Benjamin. **Thomas Baker** of Westerly deposed 1 April 1727 about a warrant for the [ar]rest of the widow of **Esqr Helms** . . . **Sam^ll^ Perry** and his uncle **Benjamin Perry** . . . deponent had to watch the prisoner. **Phebe Mott** of Westerly, being about 15 years old, deposed and said that she was at the widow Holway's . . . widow Holway was a prisoner.

314. **Peleg Rogers** of Westerly, cordwinder, vs. **Daniel Willcox** of Westerly, blacksmith, for assault, charging that on 3 August 1726 the defendant struck him with a cutlass on his face, in South Kingstown. **Isaac Fowler** of South Kingstown deposed and said that both men were drunk, and had had a dispute over the spilling of a dram and Willcox had a glass in his hand and struck Rogers with it. Daniel Willcox, son of **Stephen Willcox** of Westerly, appeared in court 12 August 1726 and acknowledged that he had broken the peace . . . signed by mark X.

315. **James Forth** of Newport, barber, vs. **Peter Treby** of Newport, sailmaker, for £6:15:4 due for wigs and razour sold, cash lent, and shaving the defendant at sundry times between 9 April 1724 and 3 July 1726.

316. **Peleg Tripp** of Newport, butcher, vs. **John Dunwell** of Newport, mariner, for debt, for a quarter of beef delivered 20 November 1725.

317. **Sarah Tew** of Newport, widow, vs. **John Willcox** of Westerly, yeoman (son of **Stephen Willcox**), for £108 due by note dated 3 February 1721.

318. **Joseph Fones** of Jamestown, mariner, made a deposition in May 1727 that he was late master of the sloop *Concord* on a voyage to and from the Bay of Honduras.

319. **Samuel Collins** of Newport, blacksmith, vs. **Joseph Clinton** of Newport, cordwainer, for debt: £5 due by book for "the hyre of two horses about the beginning February 1726 . . . did ride or cause to be ridd to Boston and . . . from the plaintiff did detain for the space of three weeks and odd days . . . until 26 February 1726."

320. **Joseph Tefft** vs. **Capt. James Babcock**; appeal from judgment given 13 October 1726 at house of **Ezekiel Gavit** in Westerly, when Tefft vs.

Babcock for illegally impounding a gray horse belonging to him. **Sam^{ll} Slack** testified that on the 4th day of September last he was "desired by Capt. James Babcock to goe into his barne meadow to looke upon a gray horse which was in his meadow afeeding . . . deemed to be Tefft's horse." **George Brown** and **Ezekiel Gavit** testified 13 October 1726 about damage done by the horse. **Sam^{ll} Babcock** testified on 4 October 1726 that he was "desired by my father Capt. James Babcock on the 3rd day of September a little before Sun Rise to stop the gray horse now in controversy . . . then in my father's pasture and going to breake out of sd pasture . . . did then rub downe one of the bars but I stopped him . . . putt him in the cow yard."

The file includes a copy of a Westerly town record dated 11 October 1726 showing that Mr **George Brown**, Mr **Ezekiell Gavett**, and **Sam^{ll} Babcock** were admitted freemen.

321. **Bartholomew Gidney** of Boston, shopkeeper, vs. **Zechariah Allen Junr** of Westerly, yeoman, for debt: £14 for boarding the defendant's sons beginning ye 21st February 1720 and ending ye 27 November 1721. Writ dated 13 November 1726. Accounting includes items: an accidence and Inkcase, catachism, gloves, Bible, cash for a pair of shoes and mending a pair, comb, handkerchiefs, thread, boarding and schooling, and one ounce of nutmegs for wife.

322. **Daniel Ayrault** of Newport, shopkeeper, vs. **Stephen Easton** of Newport, yeoman, for £4:5 due by note dated 15 August 1726, "it being to Ballance the accompts between us from the Beginning of the World to this Day." Witness: **John Easton.**

323. **John Ingraham** of Newport, cooper, vs. **Jahleel Brenton Junr** of Newport, Esq., Sheriff, for Defects and Misdoing in serving a writ contrary to law (by **John Webster** of Westerly who was deput[iz]ed by the plaintiff to execute the same at the suit of Ingraham upon **Samuel Holway**).

324. **Edward Sanders** of Westerly, yeoman, vs. **John Haley** of South Kingstown, weaver, for £26 due on note dated 5 July 1725.

325. **Samuel Cooper** of East Greenwich, weaver, otherwise Samuel Cooper of North Kingstown, boatman [mark *X*] vs. **Benjamin Morse** of North Kingstown for £18 due on note dated 6 November 1725, witnessed by **William Haxstun** [mark *X*] and **Elebeth Haxstun** [mark *O*].

326. **Michael Spencer** of East Greenwich, yeoman, vs. **Stephen Potter** of Providence, cordwainer, for £24 due by note dated 19 November 1718; witnessed by **Phebe Greene** and **Thos** [*illegible*].

327. **Mordecai Dunbar** of Newport, taylor, vs. **Roger Elderton** of Westerly, boatman, for £15:19:6 due for sundry goods sold and delivered in 1726 and 1727. The accounting included several lots of "shegar," gallons of "sperats," and a small cask.

328. **Daniel Ayrault** of Newport, merchant, vs. **Samuel Allen** of Newport, cordwainer, for debt due for goods delivered sundry times beginning 5 October 1725 and ending 20 July 1726, including nails, sugar, spriggs, linnen, muslin and starch, and fish hooks to y[r] boy. The credits included a pair of shoes.

— September 1727 —

329. Indictment of **Jeremiah Wilcox** of Westerly, labourer, on charge that on 8 August 1727 he did feloniously and wickedly contrive and effect (with sundry other persons) the Breaking open of His Majesty's Gaol in Newport, whereby **Daniel Wilcox, John Richardson, William Grant,** and **Samuel Northup**, Felons made their Escape. **Daniel Updike**, Attorney General. On the back of the file is the notation "Ignoramus" ["we are ignorant"], signed by **Thomas Weaver, Benjamin Coggeshall, George Babcock, William Lawton, Adam Lawton, Peter Easton, Cuthbert Campbell, Abraham Coggeshall, William Allin, Fones Greene, Peleg Spencer, David Vaughan, Robert Gibbs, Job Harris,** and **Daniel Sabeere.**

330. **William Blye** of North Kingstown, yeoman, vs. **Benjamin Morse** of North Kingstown, labourer, for £10 due by note dated 26 November 1726, signed by mark X, witnessed by **Peter West** and **Benjamin Morey**. Writ dated 3 July 1727; **Daniel Updike**, attorney.

331. **Phillip Gray** of Tivertown . . . Province of Massachusetts Bay, yeoman, vs. **Turn Humery** now resident in Portsmouth, cordwainer, for £10:12:0 due by bond dated 25 March 1727, signed by mark X and witnessed by **Samuel Crandall** [whose signature matches script of the note] and **Ebenezer Taber**. Writ dated 5 July 1727; **Henry Bull**, attorney.

332. **Daniel Willcocks**, son of **Stephen**, of Westerly, accused of stealing a horse from **M[r] Jeffery Hassard** of North Kingstown, yeoman. Upon examination, 10 February 1726/7 at North Kingstown, he owned that he "took the horse, saddle and bridle from a stake as he was tyed in the highway by the dwelling house of **Robert Potter** in South Kingstown on Saturday Evening which will be two weeks tomorrow and

went that night to one **Mattasons** neare Providence the second night to Killingsley and lodged at one **Capt. Cadys** and from thence the next day he rid to Brookfield and lodged in a private house one **Jennengs** by name and from thence to Hadley where he left the horse bridle and saddle with the tavernkeeper for him to keep till [he] should call for them but has forgott the mans name from thence he returned on foot to Springfield and from thence to Infield and thence to Glasenbery where he tarryed untill Munday last and from thence to Colchester and from thence to Norwich where he was taken . . ." He was indicted the last Tuesday of March 1727; the charge was that on or about 28 January 1726 he took one Bay Stone-horse of the price of £60, a bridle and saddle. **Daniel Grinnell Jr** made a deposition.

333. At Justices' Court in North Kingstown 8 June 1727 at the House of **George Thomas**. "Order of Francis Willett Assistant and William Spencer Justice of the peace for North Kingstown . . . for the release of said Town in the Keeping of **Catharine** a Bastard Child begotten by **Caleb Green** late of said Town Deceased on the body of **Martha Card** Single Woman of the same Town &c. Upon the Examination of the said Martha Duly Taken we do finde that the said Caleb Green is Charged to have had Divers times Bodyly and Carnell Knowledge of her in July and August last Past . . . Therefore we do order and Adjudge that the said Caleb was the Reputed father of said Bastard Child which was born the 19th day of April Last as by her Oath Appears. . . . And that In as much as the said Caleb Green Departed this Life the 20th of April Last and Leaving a Considerable Estate we do order that **Daniel Green** his surety and Likewise Administrator . . . pay into the hands of one of the Overseers of the poore . . . towards the Releafe of said Child. . . ." Martha, ordered to pay a fine of 40s "or be whiped on her naked back ten lashes," paid her fine.

Daniel Green Junr of North Kingstown, yeoman, was summoned in November 1728 to answer the complaint of Martha Card for refusing to pay to her one Quarter of a years pay out of the estate for the support of Catharine, and at a Justices' Court 28 November 1727 held at the house of **William Havens**, Daniel was ordered to pay 26s for the second quarter, plus 18s costs of court.

334. **Sarah Barton** of Newport, widow, vs. **John Carr** of Jamestown, yeoman, for £4:13:5 due for sundry liquors sold and delivered sundry times in the year A.D. 1727. Writ dated 14 July 1727; **Henry Bull** attorney. The accounting, to Mr. John Carr of Conanicut, listed "Sundry Liq^{rs}, Meals, Victuals, Lodging &c to May 31:1727," and was signed by Sarah Barton.

335. **Francis Brinley** of Boston, gentleman, vs. **David Green** of Jamestown, yeoman, in an action of trespass. Writ dated 17 July 1727. Deposition 4 September 1727 by **Daniel Mackoon** of South Kingstown, before Tedeman Hull, warden, that to his "certain knowledge he being bread in Jamestown . . . and being this Day upon a Cartain Spot of Land, which ffranscis Brindley of Boston hath sued David Green of Jamestown for . . . David Green aforesaid hath lived in the actuall Possession of sd Lot of Land upwards of 23 years. . . ."

Deed, dated 5 April 1687, signed by **Francis Brinley** of Newport on Rhode Island, and **Hanah Brinley**, for "one parcel of land granted in exhange unto me" containing 120 acres . . . in the North end of the Island of Conanicut alias Jamestown . . . bounded easterly, northerly, and westerly by the Bay or salt water, southerly by lands of Francis Brinley . . . **Peleg Sanford** of Newport and **Mary** his wife have granted in exchange two certain parcels of land in Jamestown . . . one scituate in a place called the Township containing 87½ acres, the other in the westward side of the Island adjoining the northward part of the land of Peleg Sanford called the Great Farm, 16½ acres. Deed witnessed by **John Paine** and **John Odlin Jr**., acknowledged same day; recorded 6 September 1701; copied 8 September 1727 from Newport Land Evidence 3, page 336, by William Coddington, Town Clerk.

Deed dated 16 February 1708, **Francis Brinley** of Newport, "for good causes and considerations" to **Capt. Josiah Arnold** of Jamestown on the Island of Quonanaquit . . . land on sd Island called the Township . . . about 1/5 acre, "a proportionate part of [*blank*] acres and better which I reserved for myself (when I sold the rest of my Land in sd township unto Co^{ll} **Peleg Sanford**) with a full intention to build a house thereon in time, wch sd piece of land lies in common with lands of other persons not yet particularly divided." Witnessed by **Nath^{ll} Coddington** and **Francis Brinley Junr**; copied 6 February 1709/10 from Jamestown Land Evidence, page 131. Pages from the records of the Proprietors of Jamestown, dated 22 April and 19 May 1712 at the house of Mr **Nicholas Carr** in Jamestown, and 24 June 1712 at Newport, entered in evidence.

The defendant's answer to the charge, by his attorney **Henry Bull**, was that "persons who have for the space of 20 years had peacable and quiet possession of any land shall . . . to such possess a good title."

336. **John Dexter** of Providence, yeoman, vs. **Margaret Fuller** of Providence, singlewoman, labourer, in custody of the sheriff, for £12:8:0 for boarding and keeping her child 18 months, a pair of shoes

sold her and making and mending of clothes in the year 1726. Writ dated 25 July 1727; **Daniel Updike** attorney. The account is for "keeping yr daughter **Elizabeth.**" **James White** deposed 15 August 1727 before Richard Waterman, Assistant, and said that "on or about 14 July last past [I] being at the dwelling house of Margarett Fuller in Providence there came John Dexter and said Pegg I am come to you about your garll and shee said to Mr. Dexter what about ye Garll he answered ye case is altred with me I can not keep her y^{n} answered sd Margaret, called Pegg, send her home for I can have anough that will keepe her — next day after I saw ye garll at her mother's house ... her mother told her shee must goe to her mastors sd Dexter and fetch her clouse . . . ." **Richard Waterman Junr** deposed 4 September 1727 before William Jenckes, Justice, that "I heard Mr George Pigot - minister: publish the Intention of marraige betwixt James White and Margret ffuller: before the sd James White gave Evidence before me; in the Case that is depending betwixt the sd Margaret Fuller and John Dexter of Providence." Verdict for the defendant, costs of court.

337. **Christopher Phillips** of North Kingstown, tanner, vs. **John Grantland** of Newport, cordwainer, in custody of the sheriff, for £6:2:8 due for a parcel of leather sold and delivered in 1726. Writ dated 26 July 1727; **Daniel Updike** attorney.

338. **John Coddington** of Newport, Esq., vs. **Robert Northam** of Newport, caulker alias barber, for trespass concerning land and a dwelling house in Newport. Deed from **Nathaniel Coddington** of Newport, 20 July 1721, for love to son **John Coddington,** land in Newport bounded easterly on the Great and Long Street, 54 feet in width, 308 in length, northerly on land of **Thomas Richinson** as the land with the wharfe runing into the Sea Cove or Harbour, westerly on the salt water and Harbour, southerly partly on upland and the cove of sd Harbour, with buildings thereon. Witnesses **Joseph Rogers** and **Paul Unis**; acknowledged by Maj. Nathaniel Coddington 7 August 1721.

339. 25 September 1727: Order to arrest or attach property of **Ezekiel Bull** of Newport, innholder, to satisfy a judgment received against him at March court by **John Wanton** of Newport, gentleman [suit was for £100 due by note dated 30 August 1725]. Sheriff **Jahleel Brenton** wrote on the order: "There is no estate for the within named Ezekiel Bull to be found and the Body is Dead."

340. Deposition [*separated from case*] by **Thomas Jones** dated 8 September 1727, that he lived four years "with my master **John Stanton** and I have ever since lived with him every year . . . saw **Squire Brinton's** fences ly Down at times . . . Brintons sheep in my master's land and vice versa."

– March 1727/8 –

341. **Nehemiah Ward** of Attleborough, carpenter alias housewright, vs. **Daniel Squire** of Norwich in the county of New London, Connecticut, yeoman, in custody of sheriff, for £16:17:0 due by promise made 26 July 1727 when plaintiff gave bond for **Eleazer Newell** of Roxbery in lieu of sd sum for which he received of the plaintiff a horse, bridle, and saddle. Writ dated 3 August 1727; **Daniel Updike** attorney. **Rachell Leonard** deposed at Norton, Bristol County, Massachusetts, on 19 February 1727/8 before George Leonard, Justice of the Peace, that "on or about 26 July last past Daniel Squire of Norwich was at our house and there he sold a bond which he had of one Elezer Newell of Roxbery to Nehemiah Ward of Attleborough . . . went out of dores to deliver to sd Squire a horse." **George Leonard** also testified. Bond [*not in file*] was dated in January 1718/19.

342. **Thomas Phillips** of North Kingstown, shopkeeper, vs. **William Hazleton** of East Greenwich, husbandman, in custody of the sheriff, for £10:10:8 due by book for goods sold and delivered in 1727. Writ dated 19 September 1727; **Henry Bull** attorney. Accounting included 3,500 clapboard nails (£2:12:6), knife, pins, thread, leather briches, yds of duffles, plums, nutmegs, ticking capp, etc.

343. **Silvester Sweet** of Newport, vintner, vs. **Israel Chapman** of Newport, house carpenter, in custody of sheriff, for £7:12:7 for sundry liquors sold and delivered at sundry times in 1726. Writ dated 28 November 1727; **Henry Bull** attorney. Accounting included dram of tancy, 8s, etc. *Credit*, cag [keg] of tancy from **Gidley**, £5:13.

344. **Daniel Abbot** of Providence, yeoman alias merchant, vs. **Benjamin Tillinghast** of Providence, mariner, in custody of the sheriff, for £22 due by book for hogshead staves and heading sold to him in December 1727. Writ dated 28 December 1727; **Daniel Updike** attorney. **James Mitchell** of Providence, "marraner," deposed 4 September 1728 before Richard Waterman, Assistant, and said that "he ware one of the hands belonging to the sloop *Providence Friend* her first voyage she made to the West Indies." Benjamin Tillinghast was master and Capt. Daniel Abbot half owner. They arrived at Providence at their return the first part of September 1727 . . . "came at sd Abbot's wharfe where they hoised out the rum all upon the wharf . . . only five hogsheads in controversy between Tillinghast and Abbot . . . Abbot to return to Tillinghast seven or eight gallons." **William Potter** of Providence deposed the same day and said that he was summoned by Justice Waterman at the request of Daniel Abbot . . . he had ventured part of a share in sd vessell . . . some small quanitity of rum was due sd Potter from Tillinghast . . . Tillinghast loth to break a hogshead but sd there was seven and a half gallons due from Daniel Abbot and desired me to request it of sd Abbot and he would let me have the remainder in a littel time . . ." Accounting from Tillinghast to Abbot, dated "Newport January 6 1727, April and October . . . cash lent you traviling . . . **Frank** a day's work . . . sugar, rum, half a manger cloath . . . waiges . . . tarr . . . **Thomas Jones** bill." **Joseph Randall** testified that he was employed by Capt. Daniel Abbot to "coak [caulk] and grave [his] sloope after her first voyage to the West Indies . . . Abbot and Tillinghast being the chief owners . . . half a barrill of tar left for the work . . . sum little time after Abbot employed me to grave the sloop *Endeavour*, himself part owner and there being occasion for more tar . . . Abbot desired me to judge the quantity left as above and said he sould use it it being in his hands although he had charged it to the account of Tillinghast and would give Tillinghast credit . . . about half a barrell." Bill of lading: dated in Antigua 17 August 1727, the *Providence Friend* now riding at anchor in Harbour of St. John's entry bound for Rhode Island . . . 16 hogsheads of rum, one barrill of sugar, one peace of Renburongs?, one peace of garlick one peac of sear goes consigned to sd Abbot and Tillinghast."

345. **Martin Howard** of Newport, clothier, vs. **John Phillips** of Newport, husbandman, (son of **William Phillips** late of Newport, husbandman, deceased), in custody of the sheriff, for £2:5:0 due by note dated 9 October 1727, witnessed by **Lawrence Clarke** and **Jn° Moore**. Writ dated 9 December 1727; **Henry Bull** attorney. Warrant signed by defendant with mark, X.

346. **Samuel Boone** of North Kingstown, merchant, vs. **John Moot** son of **Edward Moot** of Westerly, husbandman, in custody of the sheriff, for £5:7:1:3*f* due by book for goods sold and delivered in October 1722, January 1723, June 1725, and July 1726. The account spells the defendant's name **Mott**, and lists nails, a frying pan at 8/6, wool cards, "puter, quart bottle, spike gimblet, blew calico, one testament, long syth, worsted cap, indego, knife and fork, 4^{ll} redwood, flax, pipes,

nuns thread, silk ferit, one primmer, and musling," and credits money by the hand of **Caleb Randle**.

347. **Thomas Townsend** of Newport, goldsmith, and wife **Abigail**, lately when sole named **Abigail Wilson**, vs. **John Hutton** of Newport, goldsmith, for £105:6:10 due by book for "sider and silver sold and delivered by Abigail when she was Abigail Wilson sundry times between 13 September 1726 and 18 April 1727. Writ dated 10 January 1727[/8]; **Daniel Updike** attorney. The account is for 80 ounces of silver at 14/5 and shows credits for a gold ring, cash, bedstead, milk, fish, rent of a chamber one month at 7/6, butter, two tubs for washing, one case of bottles, two days washing "of your Indian woman," hire of a bed 26 weeks and 4 days, and 16 weeks board." The defendant responded with a bill of her own showing credit due for "silver, house rent while living in my house, 16 weeks board at my house at 14/ pr week, Japanned case and bottles, my Indian woman's work 2 days (5s), use of shop and tools, borax . . . sold to his wife before her marriage."

348. **William Hack** of Taunton, yeoman, vs. **Robert Fish** of Portsmouth, blacksmith, for £28:9:0 due for 975½ bushels of "charcole" sold and delivered on 25 November 1727. Writ dated 12 January 1727/8; **Jon[a] Wilson** attorney. The account dated 20 May 1726 states, "bargined with william hack of taunton for a parsel of charcole to be delivered at the shore against the land of **pelig Shearmon** of Portsmouth . . . did promise with in one month time and at 6*d* per bushshel . . . I paid to hack £1 in earnest." Included are sums paid to **pittiface**, **barnot hale**, and **Thomas burden**. **Stephen Brayton** of Portsmouth, blacksmith, deposed 21 March 1727[/8] before William Anthony, Assistant, that he "bought of William Hack several hundred bushels of cole . . . [he] agreed to diliver it at his shoop at 6d per. . . ." Verdict was for the plaintiff, £3:6:3½ and costs of court.

349. **William Gibbs** of Newport, painter, vs. **Samuel Haydon Jr.** of Newport, blacksmith, in custody of the sheriff, for £12 due by book for oil colouring and labour. Writ dated 15 January 1727[/8]. Accounting dated May 1725, for painting outside of house.

350. **Thomas Phillips** of North Kingstown, shopkeeper, vs. **William Bly** of North Kingstown, husbandman, in custody of sheriff, for £11:8:9 for sundry goods sold and delivered at sundry times beginning in 1726 and ending in 1727. Writ dated 16 January 1727[/8]. Accounting for various fabrics, thread, needles, etc., "iron kittle, frying pann, malasses, bridle bitts, goods **John Raynolds** had by yr order, brimstone," etc.

351. **Samuel Swan**, resident of Newport, late of Portsmouth in New Hampshire, glovier [*sic*], vs. **Jeremiah Fish** of South Kingstown, yeoman, in custody of the sheriff, for £20 due by note dated 16 November 1727. Writ dated 23 January 1727.

352. **Mordecai Dunbar** of Newport, taylor, vs. **Timothy Caswel** of Newport, husbandman, in custody of the sheriff, for £6 due for work done and money lent in 1726. Writ dated 23 January 1727[/8]. Accounting included Holland jacket and breeches. Credit, 17 yds homespun @ 4s. Town sergeant **Peleg Rogers**, for want of the body of the defendant, etc., attached a pewter spoon of his estate.

353. **Nathaniel Newdigate** of Newport, gentleman, vs. **Joseph Tifft** of Westerly, innholder, in custody of the sheriff, for £5:16:2 due by book for the plaintiff's care and money expended in sundry actions for suits of law for the defendant beginning in August 1726 and ending April 1727. Writ dated 30 January 1727. Accounting included a writ for suit against **James Freeman** and an appeal from a judgment against **Capt. Babcock**.

354. **William Pinnigar** of Newport, hatter, vs. **Joseph Tift** of Westerly, tavernkeeper, for £3:5 due for a beaver hat sold and delivered 2 April 1727. Writ dated 1 February 1727[/8]; **Daniel Updike** attorney.

355. **David Allen** of Rehoboth, husbandman, vs. **Benjamin Luther** now resident of Newport, shipwright, in custody of the sheriff, for £3 due by note dated 29 December 1727. Writ dated 2 February 1727[/8]; **Jno Wilson** attorney.

356. **Edward Wilcocks** of Westerly, yeoman, vs. **Caleb Church** of Westerly, bloomer, in custody of the sheriff [arrested by **John Webster**, sheriff, 8 January] for £100 due by note dated 5 November 1726 witnessed by **Joseph Stanton** and **Edward Hall**. Writ dated 5 February 1727[/8].

357. **John Fones** of North Kingstown, yeoman, vs. **Robert Wilcox Junr** [signed Willcox] of South Kingstown, yeoman, in custody of the sheriff, for £400 due by bond dated 6 February 1722/3 witnessed by **Michael Harris** and **Jo^{s} Sheffield**. Writ dated 5 February 1727[/8].

358. **Silvester Sweet** of Newport, vintner, vs. **Peter Easton** of Newport, tanner alias butcher, for money due for liquor sold and delivered in 1726 and 1727. Writ dated 5 February 1727[/8]. Accounting included 2 gall. vinegar at 3/6*d*.

359. **Loveless Vaughn** [*sic; elsewhere in file Lovelace Vaughan*], of Newport, currier, vs. **Joseph Whipple** of Newport, merchant, in custody of the

sheriff, for £202:2:6 due for sundry goods sold and delivered and money advanced from 1719/20 to 1725. Writ dated 5 February 1727; **Henry Bull** attorney. Account of Capt. Joseph Whipple includes "milk, 2 journeys horse ride to Providence, horse hire to Portsmouth double, keeping horse, halters your brother had, your account to **Thomas Lawton**, paid **Jeremiah Weeden** for hay for **Newton's** vessel, sugar and spice at your kinsman's funeral, beef, oats, one gray horse in the Farm, one small bay horse I had of **Goulding**, one gray horse I had of **Howard**," etc. Credit includes rum "of **John Morehouse**, hay for 13 horses in Newton."

360. **Sarah Tew** of Newport, widow, vs. **Thomas Bayley** of Newport, innholder, in custody of the sheriff, for non-performance of promise. Writ dated 9 February 1727[/8]; **Henry Bull** attorney. On 25 July 1724 the defendant had promised to "repair all the outside Fences and ye Division Fence between the two lotts and repair the house where ye Defendant then Liv'd and to pay the plaintiff at ye Rate of £25 per Year for the time he should dwell in sd house . . . which sd House and Fence are now in ye possession and occupation of **Robert Wrightington, John Dommett** and others in Newport." The defendant by his attorney **Nathaniel Newdigate** answered that the dwelling was in possession of **Stephen Bayley**, his father, "when he dyed in the month of October 1724 . . . the defendant and his sister **Rebecca Bailey** being his executors had right to remain in the house for a time then to come. . . ." The case went to referees Samuell Warkman, Daniell Sabeere, and Samuel Lyndon, who decided 22 March 1728/9 that Bailey was to pay Sarah Tew £3:8:0 and costs of court.

361. **Jeremiah Wilson** of Newport, mariner, now living in South Kingstown, vs. **Nathaniel Niles** of South Kingstown, yeoman, in an action of £200 debt due by note dated 13 February 1724/5. Writ dated 9 February 1727/8; **Henry Bull** attorney.

Deed of quitclaim, dated 12 March 1705/6, witnessed by **James Fitch, Jedediah Fitch, Nath: Niles,** and **Nathaniel Niles Jn^{r}. Jeremiah Wilson** now of Block Island alias New Shoreham, "for divers good causes and considerations and for the future maintaining of Love and Good will between my selfe and neare relations . . . as part of the Portion or Dowry which did fall to my sister Mary the wife of **Robert Hannah** and daughter of my Honored father **Samuel Wilson** deceased . . . all of Kingstown . . . had certain land fall to them by a . . . deed of partition 15 March 1693/4 . . . 448 acres . . . part of a grand allotment by **Yoacock** . . . enjoy by deed under hand of my Elder Brother

Samuel Wilson deceased. . ."; copied 26 March 1728 from North Kingstown Land Evidence, 2:159-160. On 13 February 1724/5, **Jeremiah Wilson** of Newport, mariner, for £100 paid by **Nathaniel Niles Jn**[r] of South Kingstown, yeoman, quitclaimed all rights to a parcel of land in South Kingstown, 448 acres, originally belonging to **Samuell Wilson** formerly of Kingstown, one of the Proprietors of the Pettaquamscutt Purchase, "father to me. . .," bounded northerly by land laid out to **John Potter** late of Kingstown, easterly part on two ponds and partly on the Chepuxet River, southerly partly on land belonging to **Jahleel Brenton** and partly on land belonging to **Robert Wilcox**, westerly partly on land of **Moses Barbor** and partly on a Pond and partly on land laid out to **John Potter**; witnesses were **William Heffernan** and **Josias Lyndon**. The same day, with the same witnesses, **Nathaniel Niles** [signed Jn[r]], yeoman, of South Kingstown, gave a note for £200 to **Jeremiah Wilson** of Newport, mariner, to be paid half by 15 October next. The defendant, by his attorney **Daniel Updike**, claimed that the bond was fraudulently obtained. judgment was for the defendant upon rehearing, confirming a former judgment.

362. **John Tillinghast** of East Greenwich, yeoman, vs. **Joseph Cahoon** of Warwick, in custody of the sheriff, for £6:4:6 due by book for sundry things sold and delivered in March 1719 and for four years after. Writ dated 10 February 1727[/8]. Accounting included sums for "cash lent, cards at **James Browne**['s], indigo at Mr. Browns, bushel of rye, beefe by yr wife, ry by **Danell Brigs**. *Credit*, for freight to Newport," etc.

363. **George Tibbitts** of North Kingstown, yeoman, vs. **William Hambleton** of East Greenwich, labourer, in custody of the sheriff, for £80 due by note dated 15 May 1727 signed by William together with **David Hambleton** of Lebanon in Connecticut, yeoman, witnessed by **Henry Joslin** and **Josep Nickos.** David signed; William made his mark, *W*.

364. Deposition dated 8 March 1727/8 [*separated from case*] by **Rebecah Werden** late of Westerly, now resident in Stonington, that some time in the winter of the year 1726 she was at her own house in Westerly, and in came **John Gorton** and **Josiah Hill** and [they] exchanged oxen . . . her husband **Judah Werden** wrote a bond for y[e] £5 bond that Gorton was to give to Hill, and Judah and herself signed it as witnesses.

365. **Major Fairchild** of Newport, butcher, vs. **Christopher Penny** of Newport, mariner, in custody of the sheriff, for £3:7:4 due by book. Writ dated 6 February 1727; **Henry Bull** attorney. Accounting dated 25 July 1727, included a quarter of a lamb, sheeps heads at 4*d* each, shin beef, mutton @ 5*d* lb., beef @ 4½ and 5*d* lb., etc.

[*Also, in separate case*] **Major Fairchild** of Newport, butcher, vs. **Joseph Bennet** of Newport, house carpenter, for £7:15:5 due by book for provisions sold and delivered beginning April 1726 and ending the same year [in September]. Writ dated 6 February 1727; **Henry Bull** attorney. Accounting was all for meat.

366. **Daniel Updike** of Newport, gentleman, and **Anstis** his wife, lately when sole called **Anstis Jenkins** of Newport, spinster, vs. **Abigail Pelham** of Newport, widow and executrix of the will of **Thomas Pelham** late of Newport, gentleman, deceased, for £108 due by bond dated 28 March 1722, witnessed by **Stephen Mumford** and **Wm Coddington**. Writ dated 6 February 1727[/8]; **Daniel Updike** attorney. Bond was signed by **Edward Pelham** and Thomas Pelham, gentlemen, to Anstis Jenkins, spinster.

367. **Thomas Gould** of Newport, yeoman, vs. **Samuell Holmes** of Newport, merchant, in custody of the sheriff, for refusing to make and maintain 85 rods of fence between the lands of plaintiff and defendant. Writ dated 12 February 1727[/8]; **Henry Bull** attorney. Defendant was responsible for half of the line, or £54:6:0, according to return of the fence viewers citing an act of 18 Charles II for regulating fences throughout the Colony. Defendant's plea was that his land was fenced in by a stone-wall and ditch erected upwards of 30 years since and continued ever since to be the dividing line and fence. Report of **Thomas Cornell** and **Giles Slocum**, fenceviewers, dated 28 May 1728: Holmes to immediately maintain one full half of the fence . . . Gould to have first choice of one half, not choosing any part which Holmes has already maintained.

368. **John Cook** of Portsmouth, husbandman, vs. **Jeremiah Fish** of South Kingstown, yeoman, for £80 due by note dated 12 June 1727 witnessed by **Wm Brown** and **Josias Lyndon**. Writ dated 12 February 1727[/8]; **Daniel Updike** attorney.

369. **Godfrey Mallbone** of Newport, merchant, vs. **Joseph Hodges** of Newport, joiner, for £21:6:1 due by book. Writ dated 12 February 1727[/8]; **Daniel Updike** attorney. Accounting included feet of slittwork, boards, freight from Boston in **Scott's** [boat], sugar, molasses, rum, corn, rye, 2½ feet of wooden dishes @ 12*d* ft., rum and molasses at stillhouse, etc. Hodges' credit included an "advance on 179 days work at your New Houses at 1/6 per day per agreement, carrying up the staircase, done of nights after time of working, 10*s*, a double Rose Card, 5*s*, 2 nights work finishing doors and glewing of pannels for the

Great Room by me and my servant **Burgis Copner [? Cooper]**, strengthening the flour and puting up a chimney piece, and other odd things in your old House," for a total of £14:18:9, and note accepted from **M^{r}** Munday, £6:12:6.

370. **Thomas Jones** of Newport, butcher, vs. **Mark Maylem** of Newport, cooper, for £16:7:0 due for provisions sold and delivered in 1726 and 1727. Writ dated 13 February 1727; **Henry Bull** attorney. Accounting included mutton, veal, lamb, beef @ 6*d* lb.

371. **James Allen** of Newport, butcher, vs. **John Place** of Newport, shipwright, in custody of the sheriff, for £10:1:4 due by book for meat sold and delivered from September 1726 to November 1726. Writ dated 13 February 1727.

372. **Jonathan Marsh** of Newport, shipwright, vs. **Job Carr** of Newport, shopkeeper, in action of trespass, concerning a lot in Newport of "part beach and part water'd land containing 50 feet bredth and 80 feet in length in Newport, No. 104 . . . of which Jonathan Marsh late of Jamestown, deceased, father of the plaintiff, on or about 1703 was seized as tenant in common with **Benjamin Newbury** late of Newport, merchant, deceased, and in his will dated 9 June 1704 left to his sons **Jonathan** and **William** . . . land on Rhode Island which he bought of **Ann Bull** . . . to be equally divided." Paragraph from will of **Nicholas Easton** entered in evidence: "to my Loving wife **Ann Easton** and her heires and assigns forever . . . all the peice of parcel of Land . . . within the precinct of the town of Newport . . . 60 acres . . . bounded south by land now or late in possession of **William Coddington**, on the east by a highway, northerly by land now or lately in possession of **William Dyre**. . . . copied from Newport Town Council and Probate 1:132, 4 September 1728 by William Coddington.

373. **Henry Holland** of Plainfield, Windham County, Connecticut, yeoman, vs. **Jonathan Mott** of North Kingstown, labourer, in an appeal from an earlier judgment. Accounting from Holland to Mott dated March 1726/7, "to 20 weeks dressing of victuals, washing and lodging for two men at 2*s* 3*d* per week each . . . three weeks of two men . . . 100 quarts of milk at 2*d* per quart . . . one gallon of molasses at 4*s* . . . chintz, blew calico, silk crepe, one pair of Jewels, Silver Ribbon, muslin, &c . . . 2 wine glasses . . . stockings. Credit shown for lodging, &c.

374. **James Allen Ju^{r}** of Newport, butcher, vs. **John Pitcher** of Jamestown, tanner, for £233:15:9 due for hides and skins sold and delivered at sundry times from 2 September 1726 to 6 January 1727/8. Writ dated 13

February 1727; **Daniel Updike** attorney. Long bill, mostly for calfskins, valued by weight, usually at about 3*d* lb.

375. **John Bennett** of Newport, tanner, vs. **John Wamsely** of Newport, "a Negroe," for £3:8 lent to him sundry times in 1727.

376. **Ann Clagget** of Newport, widow and executrix of **Caleb Clagget** late of Newport, baker, deceased, vs. **Daniel White**, late of Newport, shopkeeper, in action of debt.

377. **Peleg Trip** of Newport, butcher, vs. **James Jackson** of Newport, currier, in custody of the sheriff, for £2:17:½ due for provisions sold and delivered in 1727. Writ dated 14 February 1727[/8]; **Henry Bull** attorney. Account includes "mutton, beef, bellies."

– September 1728 –

378. At General Court of Trials and Gaol Delivery, Indictment of **Peter Morrow** of Newport, brasier: on 16 August 1728 "in the Dark Time of the Night with force and Armes in company with **Daniel Todd** of Newport, Book-binder, he did enter the dwelling House of **Nathanael Coggeshall** and carry away six silver spoons valued at £9:16, a silver Sissers-Chain valued at 20*s*, 5 silk stockings, £5, and one pair of worsted and one pair of thread stockings, £1. In an examination 26 August 1728 before Samuel Vernon and John Coddington, Justices, Morrow was asked "whare did ye Lodg ye Last fryday night . . . & who Lodgd with ye?" He replied that he did "Lodg in my Shoop . . . Todd with me . . . came in about half an hour past ten . . . nor had I any beding but a blew Coat that hanged in the Shoop . . . Todd was Disguised in Lickoer very much . . . [he] woke about 9 of the clock . . . Todd stayed in the shoop untill I went to brakefaste & came back againe. . . ." Morrow was found guilty.

379. Execution of judgment, **Philip Tillinghast** of Newport, mariner, vs. **John Carr** of Newport, mariner, received at General Court of Trials at Newport on last Tuesday in March 1724, £42:10:0 and costs of court. "And afterwards the said Philip hath come into the said Court and hath chosen that all the Goods and Chattels of the aforesaid John (except the Oxen and Beasts of his Plow) be delivered to him and likewise the Half of all and Singular the Lands and Tenements of the aforesaid John according to the . . . Statute in said Case made and provided until the Debt and Cost aforesaid and Damages shall thereof be fulled levied." Warrant to appraise the property. 25 November 1728:

Inquis[it]ion Indented and Taken at Newport . . . before Jahleel Brenton Sheriff of the Colony . . . upon the Oaths of Sam[ll] Thurston Jun[r], Richard Mumford, Peter Bours, Job Bennet, Jeremiah Clark, Edw[d] Thurston, Phillip Wanton, Edw[d] Boss, Nath[ll] Hatch, Tho Coggeshall, Francis Sanford & W[m] James . . . that **John Carr** of Newport marriner in sd writ mentioned, was on the first day of Jan[y] 1727 seisd of an Estate lying and being in Newport now in the Tenure and occupation of **Sam[ll] Carr** of Newport, gunsmith, **William Tedder** of Newport, taylor, and **John Chaning** of Newport, vintner, containing by estimation on the south side or front 54 feet north 65 feet and at the East End 45 feet and in length east and west 70 feet or thereabouts haveing thereon two tenements, and all of the value of £350 and half of the yearly value of £10:10s . . . all which half part of sd Houses and land I the sd Sheriff have diliver'd to **Phillip Tillinghast** in sd Writ mentioned . . . as the sd writ doth require. . . . [*all 12 jurors named signed; original document in file*].

380. **Mercy Chadwick** of Newport, widow, administratrix of the goods, etc., of **John Chadwick** late of Newport, mason, deceased, vs. **David Nichols** of North Kingstown, yeoman, in custody of the sheriff, for £66 due by note dated 18 January 1726, witnessed by **Daniel Updike** and **Peter Mony**. Writ dated 10 July 1728.

381. Warrant for the arrest of **Ralph Allen** of Portsmouth, weaver, to satisfy a judgment won against him by **Josiah Tilton** of Chilmarke in Duke's County . . . Massachusetts, in March 1727 for £31:1:5 plus costs, issued 16 May 1728. On 1 September 1728 John Freeborn, town sergeant, noted on the warrant that neither body nor estate of Ralph Allen was to be found.

382. **Christopher Townsend** of Newport, joyner, vs. **Richard Durfey** of Newport, mariner, for non-performance of promise. Writ dated 2 March 1727[/8]; **Henry Bull** attorney. Richard on 1 March 1727 did assume [i.e., promised] to pay Christopher for making a desk and an oval table "such a price as should be sett thereupon by **Samuel Lyndon** of Newport, he being appointed for the same purpose by [both]." Samuel estimated £14:17:0 after deductions for mahogany found and procured by the defendant, yet Richard refuses to pay. The defendant in his plea by attorney **Jon[a] Wilson** stated that it should be admitted that the plaintiff had the desk and table, yet Lyndon did put a value on the making of them.

383. **Thomas Gardner** of Newport, shopkeeper, vs. **John Strowbridge** of Newport, mariner alias coaster, in custody of the sheriff, for £12:18:10 due for goods sold and delivered from 3 April 1727 to 8 February 1727/8. Writ dated 20 March 1727[/8]; **Daniel Updike**, attorney. Account includes charges for "Indian corn, meal, mugg, molasses, pins, sugar, cash lent, trousers for your Indian man, buttons, sticks of mohair, pipes, powder, felt hatt for your Indian man, raisons, shot, thread, rum, pad lock, drinking glasses." Credit: "cash of your wife."

384. **Samuel Sweet** of Newport, Inn-holder vs. **William Wilson** of Newport, mariner, in custody of the sheriff, for £7:18:5 due by note dated 23 March 1727/8 [no witnesses]. Writ dated 22 March 1727/8.

385. **John Kynion** of South Kingstown, yeoman, vs. a Molatto or Indian woman called **Betty Daniel** of South Kingstown who now lives with **Thomas Rodman**, in custody of the sheriff, in action of trespass . . . some time in AD 1727 she did ride a horse of sd Kynion's without leave or license and did then bruse and gaul sd Horse so that he died therewith. Writ dated 23 March 1727/8; **Henry Bull** attorney.

386. **Thomas Salter** of Newport, sadler vs. **Nathan Marrow** on Nassau Island in the province of New-York, marriner in custody of the sheriff, for £15 due for goods sold and delivered from 16 February 1726/7 to 6 May 1727. Writ dated 12 April 1728; **Daniel Updike** attorney. Bill to Nathan Marrow of Long Island, included charges for a "brested saddle, a quilted saddle, a plane saddle, hunting crub bridle, cash lent you at Mr. **Chase**'s, wash leather side sadle, hunting sadle," credits for wheat, "foullss," butter, etc.

387. **Thomas Baxter** of Newport, cordwainer, vs. **James Lipscombe** of Newport, book-binder in custody of the sheriff, for £3 due by note dated 19 April 1728. Writ dated 14 May 1728; **Daniel Updike** attorney.

388. **William Cook** of Newport, weaver, vs. **Peter Easton** of Newport, tanner, in custody of the sheriff, for £3:13:10 for work done in August 1727. Writ dated 16 May 1728; **Daniel Updike**, attorney. Account includes "Diging Grave to bury yr Child & Inviting People, 8s., Weaving [two pieces] of cloth. . . ." Credit for veal.

389. **John Rodman** of Burlington in the westerly division of the Province of New Jersey, physician, otherwise John Rodman Junr of Flushing, Queens County on Nassaw Island in the Province of New-York vs. **William Brightman** of Portsmouth in the Colony of Rhode Island, yeoman, in custody of the sheriff, for £300 of New York currency due

by bond dated 29 May 1723. Writ dated 17 May 1728; **Daniel Updike** attorney. The bond was from **Richard Dunn** and William Brightman of Portsmouth and **Nath^ll^ Dunn** of New Shoreham, to Doct^r^ John Rodman Junr of flushing, witnessed by **Stephen Bayley** and another signature that has been torn off.

390. **John Dickinson** of Newport, merchant, vs. **Stephen Jackson** of North-Kingstown, vintner, in custody of the sheriff, for £96 due by bond dated 25 October 1727, witnessed by **Margaret Ellis** [mark *M E*] and **Samuel Sweet**. Writ dated 20 May 1728.

391. **Ephraim Kettle** of Jamestown, labourer, vs. **Robin Scooner** an Indian late of South Kingstown in custody of the sheriff for £2:10:0 due by note dated 8 November 1727, signed Robart Sconer [mark, reverse C] and witnessed by **Richard Spencer** and **Joseph Havens**. Writ dated 22 May 1728; **Daniel Updike**, attorney.

392. **John Channing** of Newport, vintner, vs. **Thomas Plats** of Newport, mason, for £3:16:8 due for liquor sold and delivered in April and July 1726. Writ dated 27 May 1728; **Nathaniel Newdigate** attorney.

393. **Thomas Hassard** of South Kingstown, yeoman, vs. **John Kinnion** of South Kingstown (son of **John Kinnion**), yeoman, in custody of the sheriff, for £177:16:8 due by bond dated 13 January 1725/6, witnessed by **Solomon Carpenter** and **Ephraim Bull**. Writ dated 5 July 1728; **Daniel Updike**, attorney.

394. **Thomas Hassard** of South Kingstown, yeoman vs. **Joseph Mumford** of South Kingstown, yeoman, for £930:14:0 due by bond dated 8 February 1726, witnessed by **Edward Semon** [mark E] and **Ruth Robinson**. Writ dated 5 July 1728; **Daniel Updike**, attorney.

395. **Robert Gibbs** of Providence, merchant, vs. **Nathan Place** of Providence, husbandman in custody of the sheriff, for £53 due by bond dated 9 February 1725/6, witnessed by **Jeremiah ffield** and **Nathanel Carpenter**. Writ dated 8 July 1728; **Daniel Updike** attorney.

396. **William Smith** of North Kingstown, yeoman, and **Patience** his wife, sister to **Andrew Harris** late of Providence, deceased, vs. **Toleration Harris** of Providence, yeoman, administrator of the goods of Andrew Harris. Writ dated 9 July 1728; **Daniel Updike**, attorney. Andrew Harris deceased in or about December 1725 at Providence, intestate and unmarried, having personal estate valued at £927:1:6; he had only one brother and three sisters or their representatives as next of kin surviving . . . Patience had right to one fourth of the estate. The defendant claimed that the intestate estate was to be divided by the Town Council and this had not yet been done. Verdict for the plaintiff, money sued for and costs of court.

397. Ezekiel Johnson of South Kingstown, cordwainer, vs. **John Roy** of South Kingstown, cordwainer, for £26 due by note dated 29 May 1727, witnessed by **Jeremiah Brown** and **Ephraim Gardner**. Writ dated 10 July 1728; **Jon[a] Wilson**, attorney. John Roy signed the note by mark, A with elongated ends that curve outward.

398. John Powel of Boston . . . Province of Massachusetts Bay, merchant, vs. **Thomas Hicks** of Newport, labourer, and **Sarah Tiffeny** of Newport, widow, in custody of the sheriff, for trespass. Writ dated 10 July 1728; **Daniel Updike** attorney. Property concerned was one lot with dwelling house in Newport, the 56th lot at Easton's Point, bounded northerly and easterly on streets or highways, southerly on land of Samuel Clarke (Lot 54), and westerly on land of Samuel Holmes (Lot 42), measuring 53 feet in front and 100 feet in depth, whereof **Richard Morris** late of Newport, weaver, was seized and conveyed by deed of mortgage dated 16 August 1726 to the plaintiff. The deed, witnessed by **Richard Ward** and **Thomas Ward**, was copied from Newport Land Evidence 7:344-345. Verdict was for the plaintiff.

399. Peter Easton of Newport, tanner alias butcher, vs. **William Pollard** now resident in Newport, goldsmith in custody of the sheriff, for £25:6:0 due for "bording and attend[ts]" in 1727. Writ dated 10 July 1728; **Henry Bull** attorney.

400. Cap[t] Sylvanus Scott of Providence, yeoman, vs. **Solomon Carpenter** of South Kingstown, yeoman, in custody of the sheriff, for £220 due by bond dated 24 February 1726/7 with **Jeremiah Fish** [signed Jeremizah Fish], also of South Kingstown, yeoman. Writ dated 11 July 1728; **Henry Bull** attorney.

401. Peleg Rogers of Groton [Connecticut], cordwainer, otherwise of Westerly, vs. **John Wilcox** of Westerly, house carpenter, for £53:6:0 due by bond dated May 1728, witnessed by **Job Rogers** and [*as signed*] **Jaramylah Willcox**. Writ dated 15 July 1728.

402. Samuel Boon of North Kingstown, merchant, vs. **Richard Robbins** of North Kingstown, husbandman, for £7:7:0 due by bond dated 8 November 1727, witnessed by **James Eldred** and **Hannah Rhodes**. Writ dated 15 July 1728; **Nathaniel Newdigate** attorney.

403. Samuel Boon of North Kingstown, merchant, vs. **Jeremiah Sweet** of Westerly, yeoman, in custody of the sheriff, for £20:15:8½ due for goods sold and delivered from 20 April 1727 to 16 March 1727/8. Writ dated 15 July 1728; **Nathaniel Newdigate** attorney. Accounting includes charges for "cotton checks, silk handkerchiefs, blew callaco, brimstone, 2 scains of nuns thread, ribon, garlix, ivory comb, 3 yds blew rusel, sewing silk, allam, tape, worsted caps, raiser, 2 felt hatts, 1 bocket book, ½ bushel buckwheat, scyths, nails, ozingbrigs. . . ."

404. **John Rhodes** of Newport, cordwainer, vs. **Joseph Bennet** of Newport, house carpenter, for £4:7 due for sundry goods sold and delivered sundry times in the years 1727 and 1728. Writ dated 16 July 1728; **Nathaniel Newdigate** attorney. Account is for "Bakers Bread at divers times and 5 small Cheses."

405. **Timothy Whyting** of Newport, vintner, vs. **George Johnson** of Newport, gentleman in custody of the sheriff, for £10 due by note dated 23 December 1727 [no witnesses]. Writ dated 16 July 1728; **Daniel Updike** attorney.

406. **Benjamin Congdon** of North Kingstown, yeoman, vs. **Richard Updike** of North Kingstown, yeoman in custody of the sheriff, for £60 due by bond dated 5 March 1727/8 witnessed by **Francis Willett** and **Daniel Green Junr**. Writ dated 16 July 1728; **Henry Bull** attorney.

407. **Dan^{ll} Peck** of Attleborough . . . Province of Massachusetts Bay . . . yeoman, vs. **Thomas Hammond** of Newport, labourer, otherwise Thomas Hammond of Attleborough, yeoman, for £17:12:0 due by bond dated 11 November 1723, witnessed by **Seth Paine** and **Ichabod Peck**, in which he is "of Attleborough now resident in Newport." Writ dated 19 July 1728; **Jon^{a} Wilson**, attorney.

408. **Benjamin Ellery** of Newport, merchant, vs. **Benjamin Smith** of Newport, boatman, for £5:5:0 due for goods sold and delivered 10 October 1726. Writ dated 19 July 1728; **Daniel Updike**, attorney. Account included charges for 20 bushels of salt, one ironbound [?cask]; credit for "fraite of pork from New London."

409. **Thomas Coggeshall** of Newport, Esq., administrator of the estate of **Joshua Coggeshall** late of East Grinwitch, yeoman, deceased, vs. **David Nichols** of North Kingstown, yeoman in custody of the sheriff, for £33:14:0 due by bond dated 30 April 1726 witnessed by **Elizabeth Uderweed** and **John Olin** [mark *O*]. Writ dated 19 July 1728; **Henry Bull** attorney.

410. **Joseph Sheffield** of South Kingstown, yeoman, vs. **Jeremiah Sweet** of Westerly, yeoman, for £12 due by bond dated 28 December 1727, wit-

nessed by **Wm James** and **Stephen Willcocks of daniel** [signed by the defendant with a mark like a double *H* or a crossed *I* laid horizontally]. Writ dated 22 July 1728; **Nathaniel Newdigate** attorney.

411. **John Tillinghast** of East Greenwich, yeoman, vs. **Ezekiel Long** of East Greenwich, yeoman, for £23:16:6½ due for balance of accounts settled 13 February 1727/8. Writ dated 22 July 1728; **Daniel Updike**, attorney. Accounting includes charges for indigo, logwood, and sawing planks, boards, timber, and 7 logs for bedsteds at 3*s* each.

412. **Thomas Huxham** of Newport, butcher, vs. **Lawrence Clarke** of Newport, yeoman, for £5:19:6 due for goods sold and delivered from 20 September 1726 to 12 November 1726. Writ dated 23 July 1728; **Daniel Updike**, attorney. Account included mostly beef, and "after Grass, of my **Mother Wrightingtons** Land wch I hired £1:5," signed by the plaintiff.

413. **John Manton** of Providence, yeoman, vs. **Daniel Abbot** of Providence for £505 due by bond dated 13 November 1727 witnessed by **James Westgate** and **Nathan Waterman**. Writ dated 23 July 1728; **Daniel Updike** attorney.

414. **Henry Headly** of Newport, brewer, and **Ann Headley**, widow and executrix of the will of **John Headly**, late of Newport, brewer, deceased, vs. **Christopher Almy** of Newport, merchant, for £258:2:7 for sundry goods sold and delivered in the lifetime of John Headley, at sundry times from 1714 to 1717. Writ dated 24 July 1728; **Henry Bull** attorney. The defendant entered a counter suit the following day; **Daniel Updike** attorney, for £89:16:0 damages, asking that the Headlys produce their account books.

415. **Richard Berry** of South Kingstown, cordwainer, vs. **Elenor Berry** of North Kingstown, widow and administratrix of **Elisha Berry**, late of North Kingstown, weavour, for £14:6:9 due for cash lent and received by sd Elisha in his lifetime beginning in 1723 and ending in 1727. Writ dated 24 July 1728; **Henry Bull** attorney.

416. **Samuel Rogers** of Newport, baker, vs. **Peter Easton** of Newport, tanner, for £7:2:11 due by note dated 12 April 1728, witnessed by **Jo^{s} Chaplen** and **William Sanford**. Writ dated 24 July 1728; **Jon^{a} Wilson**, attorney.

417. **Henry Barzee** of Newport, labourer, vs. **Job Bennet** of Newport, carpenter, for £66 due by bond dated 2 November 1726 with **William Bennet** of Newport, butcher; names of witnesses cut off. Writ dated 24

July 1728; **Daniel Updike,** attorney. [*Seal used by William Bennet is unusual: head of a figure.*]

418. **James Brown** of Newport, merchant, vs. **John Hedges** of Newport, joyner , for £2:1:10 due for goods sold and delivered 8 April 1728. Writ dated 24 July 1728; **Jon^a Wilson** attorney. Accounting includes charges for grindstone, ax, saw, plow irons, hammer, etc.

419. **John Beer** of Newport, shipwright, vs. **Mark Maylem** of Newport, cooper, for £9 due for rent. Writ dated 25 July 1728; **Daniel Updike,** attorney. Plaintiff on 8 January 1727 let to the defendant a dwelling house and land in Newport for the term of one quarter year to go from quarter to quarter as long as both parties should please . . . rent in arrears.

420. **Jeremiah Child** of Newport, baker, vs. **Samuel Snell** of Newport, vintner, for £3:12:4 due for goods sold and delivered from 23 August 1727 to the year 1727/8. Writ dated 25 July 1728; **Daniel Updike** attorney. Accounting is for bread on a regular basis, usually at 6d. or 1s. per pound, and "bisket" once or twice; credit for "a 26 foot board, 1 qtr veal." The defendant filed a countersuit the same day, **Jon^a Wilson** attorney, calling the plaintiff, Jeremiah Child a cooper, and claiming £6:14:0 for veal and a board and money. **John Lyon** of Newport deposed 5 September before Wm Wanton Jr. and said that he was in the house of Jeremiah Child in Newport in company with Child and Samuel Snell came in and desired to settle accounts and acknowledged himself in Child's debt. Verdict for the defendant, costs of court.

421. **Samuel Snell** of Newport, vintner, vs. **Samuell Carr** of Newport, gunsmith, in action of trespass. With force and arms on 25 July 1728, the defendant entered land belonging to the plaintiff, bounded westerly by land of **Jeremiah Childs,** northerly by land of **Stephen Mumford,** easterly partly by land of **Peleg Carr** and partly by **Job Carr,** southerly by a highway and partly by land in possession of Jeremiah Childs, and 54 cabbages then and there standing and growing . . . of the value of £10 did cut up by the ground kill and destroy and other Enormities then and there did do Contrary to the Peace of our Sovereign Lord the King his Crown and Dignity. . . . Writ dated 25 July 1728; **Jon^a Wilson,** attorney. Defendant pleaded not guilty. Verdict, for the plaintiff one shilling and costs of court. Depositions: on 28 August 1728 **Deborah Whipple,** aged about 55 years, deposed that "about 1710 or 1711 she lived in the house that Samuel Snell now dwells in and she then improved the land on the north side of the house and as far westward as the chimney of the house Jeremiah Child now dwells in and improved the same until Samuel Snell came to dwell there . . . as the right of Job Carr who she hired the house of." On 10 September 1728 **Thomas Peckham** "of lafull age" testified that "twenty years or thear about past I . . . did buld a shop for **Joseph Gardner** one **John Carrs** land one the fore wharf and that **debra hix** did live whear **samuel snell** now dwells and thear was a hous of ofes about one rood bee low the west End of the said hixes hous and the wida hix mad yous of said Land to the said litel hous and . . . she hiered it of mr **Job Car** and about 4 years past I was at work for **Capt mumford** and sd Snell did say wee did set Capt mumfords hous one his Land but Capt mumford & snell did agree and I made fence for Capt mumford and snell gave Mumford leave to sett posts for brasing to ceep up said fence & the sd posts stood one snells land as brases to sd fence and are now standing. . . ."

422. **Joseph Borden** of Newport, Esq., General Treasurer of the Colony, vs. **Edward Mitchell** of Providence, husbandman, for £12 due by bond dated 4 January 1726, witnessed by **Nathan Waterman** and **James Yeats.** Writ dated 5 August 1728; **Daniel Updike**, attorney.

423. **Letitia Shippy** of Roxbury, in County of Suffolk, etc., widow and executrix of **John Shippy** late of Roxbury, innholder, deceased, vs. **John Brown** of Newport, ingraver, for £3:8:10 due for sundry things sold and cash lent in the year 1726 in the lifetime of sd John. Writ dated 22 August 1728; **Nathaniel Newdigate** attorney.

424. **Sarah Clarke** of Jamestown, spinster, vs. **Jeremiah Yeats** of Newport, cordwainer, for £5 due for money lent in September 1727. Writ dated 22 May 1728; **Henry Bull** attorney.

425. **Joseph Morss** of North Kingstown, husbandman, vs. **Ichabod Potter** of South Kingstown, yeoman, in an action of trespass, at Justices Court held in South Kingstown 6 September 1728 at the house of **Ichabod Sheffield** at ten of the clock in the forenoon. Warrant under hand of Christopher Allen, Justice, 4 September 1728. The complaint was that Potter on 30 August last past "brake the Cloos of him the sd Joseph Morss in North Kingstown . . . also Turned his horse in to the grass that Belongs to sd Morss the Grass was Growing on the Land in the possession of sd Morss . . . Lying and Being in North Kingstown . . . is butted and bounded . . . Northeasterly by the Land in the possession of **Joseph Reanolds** Southeasterly by a Laine that Runs Northwesterly

Between the Lands in the Possession of the sd Joseph Reanolds and **Sam^{ll} Arnold**" . . . westerly by land of the plaintiff, and southerly by land of Samuel Arnold. Plaintiff claimed 40s damage.

Several depositions were entered that had been taken by Rowse Helme, Assistant, 22 July 1728, Joseph Reanolds being present: **John Earl** of North Kingstown stated that Joseph Morss "hath Improved the Land on the south side of sd fence . . . about two years . . . and three or four or five years agoe the Land where sd Morss now Improves on the South side of sd fence Lay Common & was a Laine and **Robert Spencer** told this Deponant that said Laine was Left out for Jo:^{s} Rennolds Conveniancy and the sd fence which hath been Lately taken away hath of Late been maintained by sd Rennolds. At the same time, **James Haxton** of North Kingstown testified that "to his knowledge there hath been a fence two years Last Spring Standing Between ye Meadow of Joseph Reanolds and ye meadow now Improved by Joseph Morss . . . a part of the same is Taken away & Seemes to be Lately done." At the same time, **Samuel Arnold** of North Kingstown deposed about the fence, saying that it had been there "seven or eight years past and from thence quite to the Cherry Treese that stand near to said Joseph Reanolds house & the Land to the Southward of said fence hath been Improved by Joseph Morss by Mowing this three Seasons past. . . ." **Joseph Arnold** of North Kingstown deposed to the truth of the above evidence of Samuel Arnold and "saith further that to his Certain Knowledge ye sd Joseph Morss hath Improved ye Land that Lies on ye South side of the . . . fence three years Last Spring past & that he hath seen sd Joseph Reanolds people amending of ye said fence where it is Lately Taken away."

Samuel Arnold appeared before Rowse Helme, Justice, again 29 July 1728 and declared that he had "further Regulated his Memory & saith that ye sd Joseph Morss hath been in actual Possession of sd Land . . . three years Last Spring and the Next fence to ye Southward of sd Land . . . hath Been made and Maintained by sd Morss & Arnold Ever Since."

Samuel Arnold again testified, in court 6 September 1728, that on 30 August last he saw Ichabod Potter Junr throw down Joseph Morss' fence "and Jumped his horse into sd Morsses Land and Left him there feeding . . . while he . . . went to Joseph Reanolds house . . . when sd Potter Came back againe . . . he Took his horse againe and Rid away and Left sd Morsses fence Down." **Joseph Arnold** testified to the truth of evidence given by his father, Samuel Arnold, he being also present, and added that the "very strip of Land wch Morss hath arrested Ichabod Potter for Tresspassing upon is the Land that himselfe and Sam^{ll} Arnold hath sworn to ye possession of with Severall other Testimonies now produced in this Court." **John Weles** of North Kingstown testified that about 20 or 25 "years agone . . . Joseph Reanolds had the possession of a peace of Land Lying in North Kingstown which is Contained Within ye bounds as is Set forth in a Warrant brought by Jo^{s} Morss against Ichabod Potter son to Ichabod Potter Senr . . . doth not know who hath had the possession of the abovesd Land for this four or five years Last past."

The Justices, Christopher Allen, William Robinson, and Jo^{s} Mumford, "do find by Evidence & sd Potters own acknowledgment that sd Potter did Committ said Trespass . . . shall pay to said Joseph Morss five shillings Damages and also pay two shillings as a fine to ye Colony and the Lawfull Cost of this Court."

— 1729 - Miscellaneous —

426. Indictment of **Elizabeth Hopkins** in December 1728 concerning three deeds made to **Joseph Woodward** deceased, several bonds, one pocket book, and about £18 in paper money and 30 oz. silver money, all to the value of £100.

Warrant 7 January 1728/9 for arrest of **Elizabeth Hopkins,** singlewoman, of Providence for fraudulently concealing silver money, etc., from the estate of **Ruth Woodward,** widow of **Joseph,** of which **Joseph Arnold** of Providence is administrator. Defendant examined 14 January, because of extremity of weather adjourned to 3 February. When asked if anyone besides herself had knowledge of who Ruth Woodward had delivered deeds and bonds to, she answered that her sister **Ann** did. Bond of recognizance for Joseph Arnold to appear 17 February 1728/9. **Nathan Place, Nathaniel Jenks Jr.** witnesses. **John Whitman** of Providence on recognizance to appear, showed inventory of Mr. **Joseph Woodward** of Providence who departed this life 26 February 1725/6, taken 14 March.

On 8 January, under examination, Elizabeth Hopkins stated that she: "had deeds of Widow Woodward on condition I not deliver them again unless the Arnold and Lovets children would give her children that which her husband gave her." Search was made by **John Whitman**, constable, 8 January 1728. Mention was made of Elizabeth's brother **William Hopkins. Thomas Arnold** said he recognized his grandfather Woodward's pocket book in the house where Mr. **Thomas Hopkins** deceased dwelt. February 17: Recognizance by **Joseph Arnold Junr** of the Towne of Providence, yeoman, owning himself to be justly indebted unto the Kings Majestye in the sum of £100 to be levied upon "our severall lands goods cattle and chattles"; the condition being that Joseph Arnold was to appear at the next General Court of Tryals to be held at Newport in March next and there in His Majesty's behalf prefer a bill of indictment against **Elizabeth Hopkins** of Providence, single woman, and prosecute the same. Signed by **Joseph Arnold Junr** and **William Arnold;** witnessed by **Nathan Place** and **Nathaniel Jenks Junr,** before **Richard Waterman,** Assist. and **Elisha Knowlton,** justice.

427. Deed dated February 1729 [*separated from case*] from **Job Carr** of Oyster Bay, Queens County, Long Island, New York, cordwainer, for £600 to **Samuel Snell** of Tivertown, tanner, for a dwelling house commonly and known by the name of the *Ship Tavern,* now in occupation of **Deborah Hicks,** widow, and also one other dwelling house adjoining, now in occupation of **Jacob Axton**, in Newport near the old Ferry Wharfe, bounded easterly by land of **Nicholas** and **Peleg Carr**. Grandfather **Caleb Carr,** deceased, left it by will to the grantor 14 April 1718. From Newport Land Evidence 6:60-61.

428. Indian **Sarah Faraoh** indicted for murdering her child, which was found 15 March 1729 on **Col. Christopher Allen's** land by **Benjamin Lad, Ichabod Sheffield, Jr., Samuel Potter**, and **Nath^ll^ Sheffield**, all of South Kingstown. **Indian Hannah** "who commonly lives with **Robert Potter** in South Kingstown being an old Indian Woman," was called to testify and on 18 March 1729 declared that "Sarah Faraoh come to her . . . in the latter part of last mowing time and told her y^t^ she was not well and was much out of order and desired s^d^ Hannah to get some roots for her to take but s^d^ Hannah . . . told her she thought she was with child and if so the taking s^d^ roots would kill ye child and she must be hanged for it . . . she further says y^t^ Indians often use y^t^ sort of roots when they are in travil which soon cause y^m^ to be delivered." Taken in South Kingstown . . . before Rowse Helme Assis^t^ and Christ^o^ Allen Justice of the Peace.

Mary Sambo of South Kingstown, Indian woman, also made a deposition.

429. Warrant dated 5 October 1729 for the arrest of **Emmanuel Clark** of South Kingstown, husbandman. **William Gardner** of Boston Neck in sd town, yeoman, declares that in the night last past he had a dwelling house in sd Boston Neck burnt and consumed to ashes . . . he hath manifest cause to suspect it was sett on fire by Emmanuel Clark of sd South Kingstown . . .

The examination of **Emmanuel Clark** of South Kingstown . . . taken 5 October 1729 by **Rouse Helme,** Assistant: "First he Declares that on the 4th Day of October 1729 he was at **Joseph Powers** in ye Evening till Nine or Ten a Clock & then went in Company with **Eliezer Colegrove** Home and after he had bin to Supper Went Directly to bed and Did Not Goe out of ye House A Gaine till Mornning; But Upon further

Examination he Declared y^t^ he Did Goe out of ye House to Turn out a Travillers Horse in the Night After he had bin to bed Some Time."

Depositions taken at South Kingstown 5 October 1729 by Rouse Helme: **Larrance Whaley** of North Kingstown, of lawful age, stated that he was in company with **Emmanuel Clark** on 4 October 1729 "an hour before son sett and Clark told him y^t^ some of his hogs were killed, and supposed it was done by **William Gardner** or some of his people and seemed to be in a great rage about it but after ye deponant had advised him to be more moderate he sayd he would indeavour to overcome evil wth good or he said he would indeavour to overcome good with evil, but afterwards he said he would be even with Gardner within eight days time." **John Lilibridge** of South Kingstown, of lawful age, deposed that **Larrance Whaley** "came to the **widow Joslens** on Satterday ye 4th of this instant (October) and told this deponant y^t^ there was a war broke out in Boston Neck between **Emmanuel Clark** & **William Gardner** and he believed there would be a fire before morning higher than a house; sd Whaley being present acknowledged the same and said he guessed at it from sd Clarks discorce."

Depositions taken 6 October 1729 by Rowse Helme, Assistant, and George Hazard, Justice of the Peace, Clark being present: **Benjamin Allen** of North Kingstown deposed and saith "he being at **Joseph Whitford's** husking in North Kingstown in the evening of the last Saturday past a little after the moon rose & being out a doors saw a great light wch he supposed to be on Boston Neck and . . . then went into sd Whitford's house and declared what he had seen and there being in sd house **Freelove Smith** daughter to **Ephraim Smith** late of Sth Kingstown deceas't and also **Barsheba Smith** daughter to **John Smith** of sd S^th^ Kingstown and upon their hearing this deponent tell the same, they were both of them much surprised and went outadores & sd Freelove said the Lord have mercy upon her yonder is Gardners house or barn afire for I heard **Emanuel** sware that he would burn either Gardners house or his barn, for Gardner and Emanuel have had diffreance for Gardner has killed his hogs. . ." **Thomas Brown** of South Kingstown swore to the truth of **Benjamin Allen's** statement, and said he was present at the same time. **Lawrence Whaley** of North Kingstown, of lawful age, and being at sd Whitford's at husking at the time and place with the two deponants **Benjamin Allen** and **Thomas Brown**, testified that he was out of dores and saw a great light and said that he did believe it to be Gardner's house or barn afire and **Freelove Smith** beforementioned being present seemed to be much surprised and said that she did believe that **Emmanuel Clark** had bin at work this night for she heard him say that he would burn Gardner's barn in a night or two.

George Gardner of East Greenwich, of lawful age, testified that he was at husking at **Joseph Whitfords** in North Kingstown and about ye moon rising saw a grate lite which seemed to be in Boston Neck and I heard **Freelove Smith** say y^t^ she was afraid it was her **father Clarkes** house but did not heare her say that her father threatened to burn Gardners house or barn.

At a Justices Court held in South Kingstown 8 October 1729 **Emmanuel Clark** was brought before **Rowse Helme,** Assistant, and **Chris^to^ Allen,** Justice of the Peace, to be examined concerning a burning of a dwelling house in sd town which did belong to **William Gardner** of Boston Neck. . . . We considering the premises do order & adjudge y^t^ the sd Emmanuel Clark shall forthwith find sufficient suretys as well for his good behaviour toward his Maj^tie^ and all his . . . people as for his appearance at ye next Gen^ll^ Court of Tryalls & Gen^ll^ Goal Delivery to be held in Newp^t^ on the last Tuesday of March next ensuing hereof and that sd Gardner give bond to prosecute said compl^t^ at sd Gen^ll^ Court.

– March 1728/9 –

430. **Katherine Sheffield**, widow, and **James Sheffield**, shipwright, executors of the will of **Nathaniel Sheffield,** late of Newport, deceased, vs. **Mays Nichols** of Newport, vintner, for debt due by note dated 28 January 1727/8.

431. **Benjamin Wing** of Dartmouth, yeoman, vs. **Samuel Perry** of Westerly, yeoman, in action of trespass, to recover 50 acres in Westerly which **Zechariah Allen** late of Westerly, yeoman, on 28 June 1725 deeded by gift to his two sons, **Peter** and **Oliver Allen**. Oliver deeded his part 5 June 1727 to his brother Peter, and Peter on 30 March 1728 deeded it to **Benjamin Wing**. The land was described as bounded North by a pond and land of the defendant, east by the line between Westerly and Kingstown, south by a creek that runs out of the pond into the sea.

432. **Norbert Vigneron** of Newport, physician, vs. **William Hamilton** late of East Greenwich, labourer, for £8 due by note dated 2 February 1727, signed by mark W made like a double, overlapping V [*no witnesses*]. Writ dated 5 November 1728.

433. **Abigail Smith** of North Kingstown, widow, vs. **Job Jenkins** of East Greenwich, yeoman, and **Stephen Gardner**, both of North Kingstown, for debt due by note dated 20 Jan 1727/8.

434. **Richard Mortimer** of Boston, Perry-wigmaker, vs. **Hugh Wells** now resident in Newport, mariner, for £10:1:4 due for goods sold and delivered at sundry times in 1728. Writ dated 20 September 1728; **Henry Bull** attorney. Bill was for one wig in June 1728 and one in July, at £5 each.

435. **Constant Devotion** of Boston, hatter, and **Pricilla Devotion** of Newport, widdow, adminstrators of the goods of **John Devotion** late of Suffeild in the County of Hampshire . . . Province of Massachusetts Bay, merchant, deceased intestate, vs. **John Ingraham** of Newport, cooper, for an accounting of the time he was bailiff of the deceased at sundry times in the latter end of the year of Our Lord 1723. John Devotion had delivered to the defendant 900 and one-half good merchantable Iron [?bars] valued at £4 sterling pr 100, and 18½ bushels of

good merchantable Peas at 8s per bushel, all to the value of £26:17:6, to be sold for him.

436. **John Baggs** of Newport, cordwainer, vs. **John Phillips** of Newport, husbandman in custody of the sheriff, for £72 due by note dated 15 August 1728. Writ dated 20 November 1728; **Henry Bull** attorney. Bond signed by John Phillips [mark X] of Portsmouth, witnessed by **Samuel Rogers** and **Roger Hurrell; John Baggs** signed it over to **Richard Sanford** of Portsmouth 11 January 1728[/9].

437. **Wm Pinnegar** of Newport, hatter, vs. **Jeremiah Peckham** of Newport, housecarpenter in custody of the sheriff, for £17 due by bond dated 1 February 1727 witnessed by **Richd Ward** and **Th^{s} Ward**. Writ dated 21 November 1728; **Daniel Updike** attorney.

438. **John Tillinghast** of East Greenwich, yeoman, vs. **Caleb Church** of Westerly, bloomer, in an action of promise, concerning a debt of £5 due from **Joseph Pitts** of Westerly, bloomer, to the plaintiff for labor of the plaintiff's Negro servant. Writ dated 26 November 1728; **Daniel Updike** attorney. **Joseph Phillips** of South Kingstown deposed 9 September 1728 before William Robinson, J.P., and said that about the last of December or first of January last past, he was at the house of **Mary Josslen** in South Kingstown in company with John Tillinghast and Caleb Church . . . heard Church promise to pay the sum on behalf of Joseph Pitts . . . for one month's work of a Negro at making of iron ore . . . understood that Church had some time before received of **Job Rogers** two loads of hay upon Pitts' account.

439. **Thomas Salter** of Newport, sadler, vs. **James Morgan** of Groton [Connecticut], yeoman, for £2:18:0 due for boarding him two weeks and six days and his wife one week and five days in 1728. Writ dated 3 December 1728; **Daniel Updike** attorney.

Isaac Smith of Groton deposed before James Avery, Justice of the Peace, that last fall he had been an apprentice to Thomas Salter and was taken sick on a Saturday so "was not able to work and went to bed with a very bad fever which held me all that day and the next and Monday which was a very stormy day and Salter made me go up to the bowling green twice that day in the rain to get some wormwood and when I came back I was a great deal worse whereupon I went to bed again in a cold garrett where nobody would come near me to tend me except it was a girl about 14 or 15 years of age who very often when she came upon the garret stairs if I called her she would not give me any answer or come near me . . . and after[wards] Justice Morgan and his wife and my mother came down. . . ." **James Morgan** testified that "my brother-in-law Isack Smith was very sick and that my one [own] brother **Youngs Morgan** could hardly go from hous to shop yet was forced to work . . . my father and my mother-in-law came down and prevailed on [Salter] to bring him to a chamber which had a fier. . . ." **Dorothy Fish** of Groton testified 8 March 1728[/9] that she "had a son who was apprenticed to Thomas Salter taken sick in November last and Justice Jeams Morgan had a son bound an aprentis . . . went down to see them . . . there about three weeks. . . ." She gave details about the boys' diet and her own. **William Hawkins** deposed 18 August 1729 before William Wanton, J.P., and said that when the apprentices were sick, "I being the opposit naibor went several times to see them . . . master and mistris were very kind to them . . . had the same Docter to them that M^{rs}. Salter had. When Youngues Morgan was Ded I was sent for by ye sd father to lay him out and I took him out of the same bed above mentioned and the other Printis lay in another bed in ye same room." **Henry Hooper** of Newport, phisitian, testified 19 August 1729 as Lipscombe [*see below*] about the comfort and his attendance on them. **James Lipscombe** of Newport, bookbinder, testified 21 August 1729 before William Wanton, J.P., that in November last past he was "several times at the house of Thomas Salter . . . when Isaac Smith and Young Morgan apprentices of [his] were sick of a violent Feavour . . . they lay in a warm comfortable room in the Garrett being enclosed, and the Joynts in the Partition Boards pointed . . . had a young woman to attend upon and take care of them who was a Sufficient Nurse (with the help of Watchers for the Night Season (the sd Salter's wife having no other nurse when she was sick of a violent feavour a little before . . . they were soon removed from the Garrett into the Lodging Chamber of sd Salter and his wife . . . the bed they lay upon in their sickness was a vry good one . . . same the deponent lay on when he boarded at sd Salter's house. Salter and his wife in the deponent's apprehension were very tender and careful of them and did not Spare any Pains or Costs to effect their Recovery . . . kept a good Table having both Fresh Meat and salt provided and very often poultry in the season . . . seen James Morgan and his wife eat at sd Salter's house and always understood sd Morgan was to make

Salter satisfaction . . . after Salter had arrested James Morgan he sent his son-in-law **Capt. Samuel Gallopp** to agree and make up [offered 40s. for charges, which Salter refused] . . . afterwards the deponent was in company with Gallopp at the house of **John Channing** being the Sign of the Union Flagg in Newport. The deponent did for a considerable time work in Salter's shop, always in cold weather . . . had a good Charcoal Fire." **Mary Jackson** testified that she was living in the house of Thomas Salter when Isaac Smith and Young Morgan were there sick and was employed to attend them as she had formerly attended Salter's wife. Verdict for the defendant, cost of court.

440. **Robert Trip** of Dartmouth, tanner, vs. **Olliver Allen** late of Dartmouth, labourer in custody of the sheriff, for £11:13:0 due for money lent and advanced and goods sold from October 1726 to April 1727. Writ dated 11 January 1728[/9]; **Daniel Updike** attorney. Account includes "money in hand, pd to **Zoeth Howland**, bridles, saddles, to Boot between Horse kind. . . ."

441. **Daniel White** late of Newport, shopkeeper, now of Philadelphia in the province of Pensilvania vs. **Negro John** alias **John Brightman** of Newport, a free Negro and labourer, for £9:12:2 due for sundry goods sold and delivered beginning in May 1727 and ending 4 October following. Writ dated 27 January 1728[/9]; **Nathaniel Newdigate** attorney. Account included a pail, thimble, various kinds of fabrics, making a gown, thread, tobacco, sugar, molasses, bisket, pair of scissors, etc., and mentions defendant's wife **Betty**. Partial payment of £6 on 5 July noted.

442. **Thomas Phillips** of North Kingstown, shopkeeper, vs. **Wm Kaies** [Keaise on bill] of South Kingstown, schoolmaster, for £5:2:3 for goods sold and delivered at sundry times in 1727. Writ dated 28 January 1728; **Henry Bull** attorney. Account was for "duroy, shalloon, waddin, mohair, coat buttons, buckram, ozenbriggs, silk, thread, tape, needle," all in February 1727.

443. **David Austin** of Westerly, labourer, vs. **John Phillips** of Newport, labourer, son of **William Phillips**, for £18:2:6 due for oxen sold and delivered and horse hire in September 1728. Writ dated 31 January 1728[/9]; **Daniel Updike** attorney. Account dated 20 September 1728 at Westerly, to John Phillips of Rh^{d} Island, signed by David Austin [mark].

444. **Ann Philips** of Philadelphia in the Province of Pennsylvania, widow, otherwise called Ann Philips of Newport, executrix of the will of Mr. **Richard Philips** late of Newport, husbandman, deceased, vs. **Jeremiah Peckham** and **James Peckham**, both of Newport, house carpenters, for £9 due by note dated 16 November 1728 witnessed by **Nathaniel Newdigate** and **Richd Mumford**. Writ dated 3 February 1728; **Nathaniel Newdigate** attorney.

445. **Arnold Collins Junr** of Newport, merchant, vs. **Nicholas Otis** of Newport, tailer, for £15:16:3½ due by book for sundry goods sold and delivered sundry times from 20 December 1727 to 3 May 1728. Writ dated 5 February 1728[/9]; **Daniel Updike** attorney.

446. **Thomas Staples**, mason, **Charles Barden**, confectioner of Newport, and **Henry Whitton** of Boston, wine cooper, filed an appeal 17 March 1728[/9] in case against them by **Samuel Carr** (wherein the writ was dated 6 August 1728), pleading that they were called by the plaintiff assignees of **Alexander Mason**, late of Newport, vintner, whereas the land in controversy [14 ft. square] had been leased to **Robert Mason** on 28 May 1715 for 14 years, then transferred in December 1715 with the shop thereon to **James Brown** of Newport, taylor; another piece had been leased to **John Channing** by the defendants. A lease was shown, dated 24 September 1716, between Alexander Mason of Newport, vintner, Thomas Staples of Newport, mason, Charles Barden of Newport, vintner [*sic*], and Henry Whitton of Boston, wine cooper, referring to an earlier lease dated 20 January 1707 whereby **John Carr** late of Newport, yeoman, leased to Alexander Mason a piece of land in Newport then fronting and lying before the dwelling house of the sd lessor, from 1 January for 21 years, Mason promising to erect on the southwest part of the land a good substantial structure, edifice and dwelling house according to dimensions given in sd deed and to pay 20s every year except the first; witnesses were **John Scott** and **Richard Ward**. On 11 June 1717 Charles Barden granted a lease to Thomas Staples, witnessed by **Mordecai Dunbar** and **James Brown**. A deposition by James Brown of Newport, taylor [*apparently misfiled with case of James Brown, merchant, vs. John Hedges*] taken 13 March 1728/9 by John Coddington, J.P., states, "some time before my leas was up in the Shoop I now work in I asked **Sam^ll Carr** whether I should take of my shoop of the Land and he said if I did not take [it] before the Leas was out I should not take itt of attall and he Likewise said I should as Soone have the Shoop of him as anybody Elce and [he] forbid me surrendor the said Land unto Tho[s] Staples. . . ."

447. **Henry Whitton** of Boston, county Suffolk, province of Massachusetts Bay, wine-cooper, vs. **Sylvester Sweett** of Newport, vintner, for £110 due for goods sold and delivered per order in 1727 and 1728. Account is mostly for pipes of madeira and molasses. Writ dated 27 October 1728; **Henry Bull** attorney.

448. **Timothy Whiting** of Newport, vintner, vs. **Richard Durfey** of Newport, mariner, for trespass. Writ dated 19 November 1728; **Henry Bull** attorney. On or about 14 October 1728 the defendant came into the plaintiff's house and insulted him therein and did terrify and great indignities did do by spitting several times in his face. . . . judgment for the plaintiff, £5 damages and costs of court.

449. **Christopher Almy** of Newport, merchant, vs. **James Holland** of Newport, mariner, for £1:15:6 due by note dated 28 March 1728, witnessed by **R. Baker**. Writ dated 21 November 1728; **Daniel Updike** attorney. Defendant had been a mariner in a vessel belonging to the plaintiff, of which **Richard Gill** was master, in the Island of Antigua, when he borrowed £1:15:6 of the plaintiff's money, "Gill having directions to supply any of his people that wanted at said place or any other." Plea of the defendant, who called himself "late of Newport," was that the note was obtained from him by duress.

450. **Tho[s] Ingersole** of Springfield . . . Province of Massachusetts Bay, yeoman, vs. **Daniel Abbott** of Providence, gentleman in custody of the sheriff, for £13 due by note dated 29 April 1727 in which defendant promised "to pay in rum at the market price sum time in July next." Writ dated 26 November 1728; **Daniel Updike** attorney.

451. **W[m] Swan** of Newport, vintner vs **James Osborn** of Newport, mariner, for £22:0:8 due for liquor and diett in the year 1728. Writ dated 2 December 1728; Daniel Updike. Names on the account were spelled Oysburn and Swann.

452. **Samuel Pike** of Newport, taylor, vs. **Joseph Hedges** of Newport, house carpenter alias house joyner, for £14:7:0 due by book for sundry goods and merchandise and work for him done and three weeks dyet for his boy at sundry times beginning in April 1727 and ending in June

1728. Writ dated 3 December 1728; **Nathaniel Newdigate** attorney. Account addressed to Mr. Jopeth Hogges, includes "diet for your boy when you was in Boston . . . turning your coat . . . buttons, buckram, making your son coat . . . ."

453. **Timothy Whiting** of Newport, vintner, vs. **James Lipscombe** of Newport, bookbinder, in action of promise, concerning a note Whiting had given to **Jahleel Brenton**. Writ dated 18 December 1728. On 14 September 1728 at the request of the defendant, the plaintiff paid to **Robert Duncan** of Newport, taylor, £15:0:4 which was a debt due from the defendant to said Robert. Duncan gave a receipt and note, both witnessed by **Thos Staples** and **Nehe: Lambert**, "I promise to Deliver to Mr. James Lipscombe on his order, all his working Tools, Chairs, pictures, and whatsoever else I have of his in my hands on Demand." File includes a letter dated at Newport 22 August 1728 directed to Mr. James Lipscombe Bookbinder At New Yorke, from Timothy Whiting, addressing him as "Friend Lipscombe," informing him that his creditors are willing to give him time to pay his debts and "I do think it more advantageous for you to return than remain where you are, for Mr. Duncan is resolved not to send you your tools." A P.S. signed by **Francies Whiting** informs him that "Yr Man **Tod** is in prison on suspicion of Theft in Company with a Brasier." Robert Duncan deposed that he had attached the goods of the defendant.

454. **Benjamin Quithel** of Dighton, yeoman, vs. **Wm Godfrey** late of North Kingstown, house carpenter, for £50 due by note dated 11 September 1721, witnessed by **Rebackah Stevens** and **Josias Lyndon** agreeing to pay £20 in good merchantable goods at Newport on or before 11 May next. Writ dated 19 December 1728.

455. **John Mumford** of Newport, yeoman, vs. **George Lewis** of North Kingstown, husbandman in custody of the sheriff, for £156 due for goods sold and delivered in the year 1728. Writ dated 31 December 1729; **Daniel Updike** attorney. John Mumford's accounting to "George Luis" includes, 17 August 1728: a tars of rum 84 galons, a barle of shuger 212 lb, 64 pound of lead, 5 bushels of salt, 4 calf skin & a side of sd leather, 2 glass botels & 13s in money for [Nell? or Will?], on 18 August: a quarter of beef 132 lb **Robard Hopkins** had, 21 lb of beef & a bull hide; in September: more beef, cow hide, rum, and salt; October: a hogshd of molasis, 94 gals, a baril of pips, 12 pound of shot, and a cow hide; November: more molasses and salt, leather of **C: Philips**,

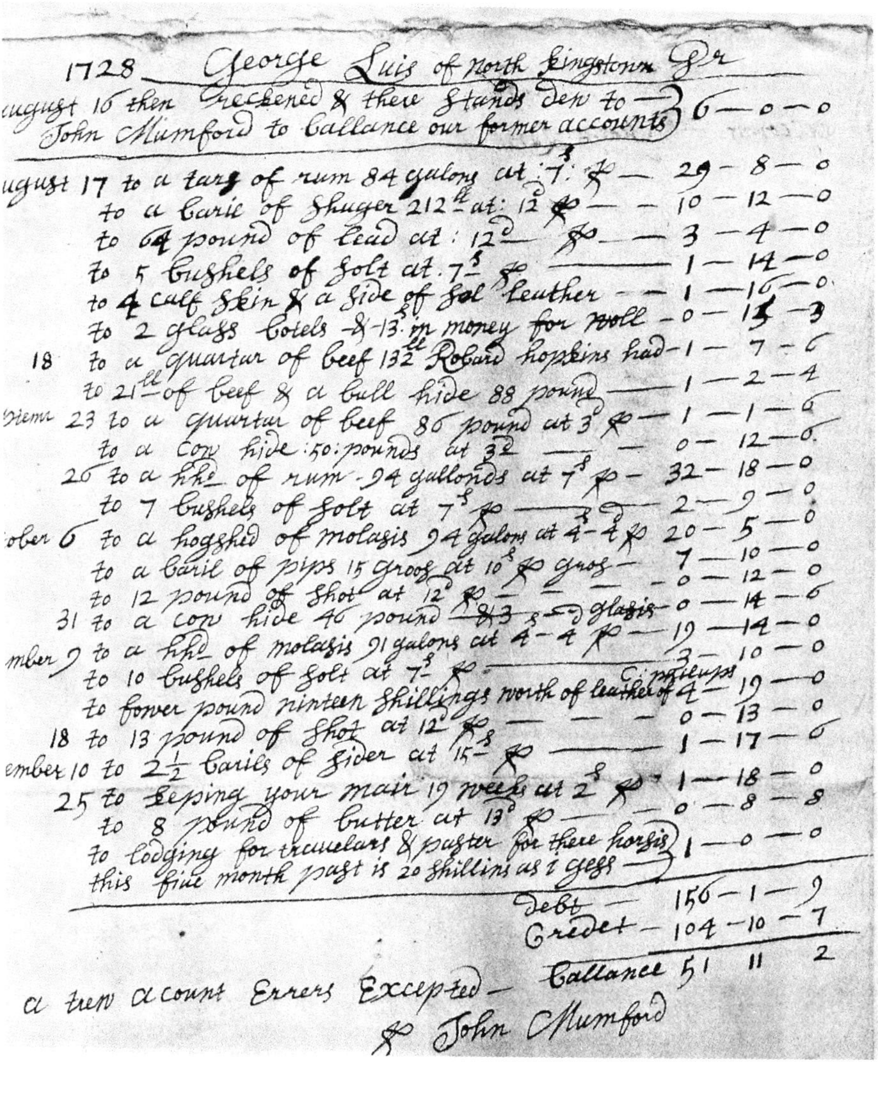

1728 George Luis of North Kingstown Dr

[A]ugust 16 then reckened & there Stands dew to John Mumford to ballance our former accounts — 6—0—0

[A]ugust 17 to a tars of rum 84 galons at 7s p — 29—8—0

to a baril of Shuger 212 ll at 12d p — 10—12—0

to 64 pound of lead at 12d p — 3—4—0

to 5 bushels of Solt at 7s p — 1—14—0

to 4 calf Skin & a Side of Sol leather — 1—16—0

to 2 glass botels & 13s in money for woll — 0—15—3

18 to a quartur of beef 132 ll Robard hopkins had — 1—7—6

to 21 ll of beef & a bull hide 88 pound — 1—2—4

[Se]ptem 23 to a quartur of beef 86 pound at 3d p — 1—1—6

to a cow hide 50 pounds at 3d — 0—12—6

26 to a hhd of rum 94 gallonds at 7s p — 32—18—0

to 7 bushels of Solt at 7s p — 2—9—0

[Oct]ober 6 to a hogshed of molasis 94 galons at 4s 4d p 20—5—0

to a baril of pips 15 groos at 10s p groos — 7—10—0

to 12 pound of Shot at 12d p — 0—12—0

31 to a cow hide 46 pound ~~&3~~ glasis — 0—14—6

[Nove]mber 9 to a hhd of molasis 91 galons at 4—4 p — 19—14—0

to 10 bushels of Solt at 7s p — 3—10—0

to fower pound ninteen Shillings worth of leather of [illegible] 4—19—0

18 to 13 pound of Shot at 12d p — 0—13—0

[Dec]ember 10 to 2½ barils of Sider at 15s p — 1—17—6

25 to keping your mair 19 weeks at 2s p — 1—18—0

to 8 pound of butter at 13d p — 0—8—8

to lodging for travelars & paster for there horsis this five month past is 20 shillins as i gess — 1—0—0

Debt — 156—1—9

Credet — 104—10—7

Ballance 51 11 2

a trew acount Errers Excepted — p John Mumford

Detail from John Mumford's account with George Lewis [No. 455] and shot; December: 2½ barils of sider, "keping your mair 19 weeks," 8 lbs of butter, and "lodging for travelars & paster for there horsis this five month past." "Contrary Credet" included "4 days time about the arbetrashon, 4*s* of **Clemont West**, drink the commishoners had when they run the coloney line . . . sundry small things i had of you & litel debts you payd for me taken out of your day book; £3:14*s* you payd to **Richard Robins**, £3:12*s* you payd to **John Butler**, 40*s* you payd to Mr **Cook** for honey & wax, 42*s* you payd to **Ben^en Rathbon**, 40*s* you payd to **Thomas Rathbon**, [cash] you payd to **Robard Havens** . . . sundry goods I have had & severall other parsons on my acount taken out of your day book." On 28 December: "a count of the goods left in the hous when **George Luis** run a way which was returned to me again: molasses, rum & water togeather, 72 lbs shuger, a payl of molasis shuger, lead, shot, pouder . . . 13 gross of pips." On 6 January 1728[/9]: "a count of the goods that ware seased or atached by the Sheref or his dep^ty John Rathbon: barils of beef, 8 neat hids, 4 bushels of ots, 25 pound of tallow, about 20 pound of pork . . . 3 pecks of salt."

456. **George Dunbar** of Newport, merchant, vs. **George Fitch** of Newport, baker, in the custody of the sheriff, for £134:6:8 due by bond dated 31 August 1728, witnessed by **Abraham Taylor** and **Nehemiah Lambert**. Writ dated 9 January 1728[/9]; **Daniel Updike** attorney.

457. **Jabez Howland** of Bristol, blacksmith, vs. **Stephen Mumford** of Newport, for £7:15:0 due by note dated 23 June 1710. Writ dated 17 January 1728[/9]; **Henry Bull** attorney.

458. **John Folkner** of Newport, weaver, vs. **Robt Babcocke** of Westerly, yeoman, for £2:7:0 due for goods sold and delivered in 1728. Writ dated 22 January 1728[/9]; **Daniel Updike** attorney.

459. **Samuel Boon** of North Kingstown, merchant, vs. **Robert Rogers** of Westerly, husbandman, for £19:8:0 due by book for goods sold and delivered from 6 March 1726/7 to 9 July 1728. Writ dated 27 January 1728[/9]. Account for broadcloath, shallone, Irish linnen, sewing silk, coat buttons, brimstone, garters, comb, checkered handkerchief, &c.

460. **Moses Lippett** of Warwick, merchant, vs. **Edward Potter** of Providence, yeoman, for £58:4:6 due for goods sold and delivered in the years 1727 and 1728. Writ dated 29 January 1728/9; **Daniel Updike** attorney.

461. **Robert Carter** of Newport, labourer, vs. **Ebenezer Goddard** of Newport, shipwright, for debt due for labour and money lent beginning in 1726 and ending in 1729.

462. **Thomas Spencer** of East Greenwich, boatman, vs. **Thomas Peckham** of Newport, house carpenter, for debt due by note dated 6 February 1728/9.

463. **Samuel Swan** of Newport, glover, vs. **Robert Wilcox** of South Kingstown, yeoman, for £28:3:5 debt due for sundry expenses in going after the defendant's Negro man named **Jethro** in 1728. **Samuel Bissell** of North Kingstown deposed on 24 March 1728/9 that on 20 July last he had a canew stolen from him . . . a short time after he heard it was at Martins Vinnard or threabouts . . . Samuel Swan of Newport offered to fetch it . . . he did . . . brought [Bissell] some iron ore. **Thomas Hassard** and **Richard Herrington** of North Kingstown deposed on the same date that about 25 August last, with several other people in company, they took a Negro man named Jethro at a celler in **Thomas Place's** land in North Kingstown, not far from **Samuel Slocum's** mill. **Stephen Wilcox Junr** of Westerly, deposed at South Kingstown at the house of **Robert Hannah** 25 March 1729, that "in last summer I met with **Sam^{ll} Swan** of Newport who asked me where my brother **Robert** lived . . . heard he had a Negro y^{t} was run away . . . lately bin to the Vinyard & there heard of such a Negro & I went with sd Swan to my sd Brother . . . Brother told him he would give him £5." Depositions also of **John Bennet** and of **Jeffery Haszard** of North Kingstown, who said he was in company with the abovesaid Stephen Wilcox Junr.

A neatly written bill dated 6 August 1728, signed by Samuel Swan, itemizes costs of the search "for going after y^{r} Negro Man called Jethro going to y^{r} House & my hors hire & ferridg," including "passage to ye Vinard, hiring of people at Sundry times both Day and Night after s^{d} Negro, hors hire to Agertown [Edgartown], to Mr. **Sam^{ll} Bassett** & his Indians to waylay ye Negro at Roaring Brook, to **Saml Norton** and sundry others for searching . . . Having Intiligence by Indians he had stole a Canoo & a Kittle & was gone to the main; my passage in going to ye Main after him to ye place called Fall river; being informed at fall river he was at Worwick I got my passage to Prudence & there I heard he was at an Indian House at Worwick & had a design to go to see his wife, then I hired a boat of **Mr Smith** and two Indians to carry me to **Sam^{ll} Slocums** . . . Then I got a squa to Inform me which he was & Mustred a parcel of hands and by ye squas Treachery catched him and brought him to Sam^{ll} Bissells; to **Jabish Keep**; to **Tho: Place**; to **Jno Bissell**; to **Tho Hazzard**; to **Jno Herington; to Sam^{ll} Slocum juner**; to hapence for ye Negro while at Bissells; to one Bottle of Rum; to ye Squa and her daughter that betrayed him; to Northrups ferry; to Franklins . . . Took him ye 25 day of August & put him in prison by a Mittinuss [?mandamus] from Justis Lawton 27th day of August y^{e} . . . mittinus cost . . . to hors hire August ye 31st of Wm Gardner & ferrige 11/4 to give his master Robert Willcox notice . . . Willcox promissed to pay [£5] in money & all nessescary Charges allowed. . .." Swan added £10 for his own time; the total came to £28:3:5.

A bill dated August ye 26th 1728 shows receipted payments to **John Bissell, Jabish Keep, Thomas Place, John Panin**, and "ye Ingon that told whear hee was," and is followed by a statement: "I **Samuel Bissell** have payd for Sam^{ll} Swan to the a bove menchin porsons the som of [£2:2:0] and have now this 7 day of november rec'd it of him againe . . . the reason of his hiring so many to tack in Robr Willcox negro was becase it was reported hee had a gon and a cotlis and hee toold my man **Danil Gill** that hee would kill or be killed before hee would be tacken."

464. Appeal from execution at October 1728 court whereby **Ezekiel Burroughs**, house carpenter, had obtained a judgment against **James Codden** of Newport, mariner, of £6:3:6 debt and costs. Suit: **Ezekiel Burroughs** of Newport, house carpenter, vs. **James Codden** resident in Newport, mariner, for £6:3:6 due by note dated 4 June 1728 [no witnesses]. Writ dated 15 July 1728; **Daniel Updike** attorney.

465. **Robert Wilcox** (son of **Thos**) of North Kingstown mason, vs. **Joseph Phillips** of South Kingstown, weaver, in the custody of the sheriff, for £12:4:7 due for two cows and a calf sold and delivered in 1728. Writ dated 5 February 1728[/9]; **Daniel Updike** attorney.

466. **Thomas Huxham** of Newport, butcher, vs. **James Brown** of Newport, taylor in custody of the sheriff, for £76:3:0 for meat sold and delivered in 1727 and 1728. Writ dated 7 February 1728[/9]; **Daniel Updike** attorney. Account includes many deliveries of beef, lamb, mutton, and some veal.

467. Wm **Dyre** of Newport, merchant, vs. **John Osband** of Newport, cooper for £5:5:0 due for goods sold and delivered in November 1727. Writ dated 9 February 1728; **Daniel Updike** attorney. Account is for 2 bushels of "flower."

468. **Christopher Champlin Jn^{r}** of Westerly, Esq. vs. **Christopher Perks** of Newport, butcher in custody of the sheriff, for £14 due for 14 swine sold and delivered 16 November 1728. Writ dated 11 February 1728[/9]; **Henry Bull** attorney. Defendant was arrested in Jamestown.

469. **Samuel Holmes** of Newport, merchant, otherwise called of Newport, mariner, vs. **James Cary** of Newport, cordwainer, in the custody of the sheriff, for £40 due by note dated 29 November 1721. In September 1719 the defendant had been Deputy Sheriff to **William Coddington**, Esq., Sheriff of the Colony, and by writ under the hand of **Richard Ward**, Recorder, dated 15 September 1719 had arrested one **Adolph Degrove**, resident in Newport, mariner, at the suit of the present plaintiff [Holmes] and by mischance let Degrove escape out of his custody; his note bore the condition that he bring Degrove to court to answer the plaintiff's charges. Writ dated 12 February 1728[/9].

470. **Rebecca May** of Newport, widow, vs. **Peter Treby** of Newport, sail=maker in custody of the sheriff, for £36 due by note dated 20 February 1723, witnessed by **Thomas Jones** and **William Fanning**. Writ dated 12 February 1728[/9]. The defendant showed an account attested by **Mehetabel Treby** 29 March 1729, for one pipe of wine, a box of pipes, both loaf and powdered sugar, twine and line, a bushel of salt, "making [two] Bed Bottom[s]" and the duck and bed sacking for them. A committee of Joseph Whipple, George Goulding, and Gideon Wanton was appointed to inspect accountings of the plaintiff and defendant, but Rebecca May stated that she had made hers on small pieces of loose paper and had burnt them as she was paid; she evidently found some, which are pinned together in the file, for dinners, wine, etc., and the inspectors set a value due her of £12:15:5½.

471. **Mary Mott** of Newport, widow, administratrix of the goods of **Samuel Mott** of Newport, butcher, deceased, vs. **Giles Slocum** of Portsmouth, Esq., surviving executor of the will of **Jacob Mott** late of Portsmouth, yeoman, deceased, for not selling so much of [Jacob's] lands as should pay the plaintiff £40, her husband's legacy under the will. Writ dated 12 February 1728[/9]; **Nathaniel Newdigate** attorney. Copy of Jacob

Mott's will dated 31 January 1710/11 devising half the furniture, etc., to son Samuel Mott. Depositions were made by **John Mumford Jn^r^**, late of Newport, and **Samuel Collins, John Shreive Junner** and **John Freeborn** 4 March 1728/9 before Job Lawton, J.P. Verdict for the plaintiff.

472. Bond signed by **Benjamin Willson** of Newport, hatter, to Richard Ward, General Recorder, that **Clement Elsworth** of Newport, barber, and **Freelove** his wife prosecute with effect an action against **William Toppin** of Newport, weaver, pursuant to a writ dated 12 February 1729. Witnesses were **John Brown Jn^r^** and **Mary Ward**.

473. **Arnold Collins Junr** of Newport, merchant, vs. **Mary Clarke** of Newport, widow and administratrix of the estate of **Samuel Clarke** late of Newport, pewterer, deceased, for £36:16:8 due for goods sold and delivered and money paid and advanced to and for said Samuel in his lifetime in the years 1726 and 1727. Writ dated 13 February 1728; **Daniel Updike** attorney. Account includes "old pewter, stript dimety, buttons, tabby, fustien, fine pewter," etc.

474. **William Nichols** of Newport, merchant, vs. **Mayes Nichols** of Newport, vintner, for debt of £25 due by note dated 7 April 1729.

— September 1729 —

475. **Major Fairchild** of Newport, butcher, vs. **Benjamin Sawdey** of Newport for debt of £8:5:4 due for beef, lamb, and mutton sold and delivered from 16 August to 4 December 1728; defendant's name spelled Sadey on account.

476. **Joshua Winnock** of Boston, jeweler, vs. **Mary Clark** of Newport, widow and administratrix of the estate of **Samuel Clark**, late of sd Newport, pewterer, deceased, for £80:10:0 of money of the Massachusetts Bay, due by bill under the hand of sd Samuel Clark in his lifetime on 27 October 1726. Writ dated 13 March 1728[/9]; **Nathaniel Newdigate** attorney. Samuel Clark had "received one sett of bills of exchange payable to him . . . on order on Messrs **Edward Winnock** and **Channing** of London for £23 . . . for which [he] promised to pay in June next £80:10:0 to [the plaintiff]." The plea of the defendant by her

attorney **Daniel Updike** was that she had not assets in her hands sufficient to satisfy a judgment of court against her (in her capacity as adminstratrix) received by **Charles Apthorp** of Boston, merchant, at the General Court of Trials in March last.

477. **Samuel Fitch** of Newport, merchant, vs. **George Fitch** of Newport, baker, in custody in the sheriff, for £100 due by note dated 6 December 1723. Writ dated 25 March 1729; Daniel Updike attorney. Bond from George "to my honrd ffather," witnessed by **Jno Odlin** and **Robert Odlin**; condition was that he pay £51 on or before 6 March next.

478. **Joshua Easton** of Newport, cordwainer, vs. **John Cahoone** of Newport, mariner, for defamation. Writ dated 1 May 1729; **Jon^{a} Wilson** attorney. Plaintiff claimed that he had been a good and faithful subject of our Lord the King and his Progenitors Kings and Queens of Great Britain from the time of his Nativity . . . the defendant out of his wicked and forethought mallice designing and malliciously intending the Name, Fame, Reputation, and Creditt of sd Joshua to hurt make worse and Destroy on 28 April 1729 at Newport pretended to have taken or stolen out of his House a Book of accompts and about £12 in Bills of Credit and pretending just Grounds to Suspect sd Joshua to be Guilty . . . following false and scandalous words did publickly pronounce and say . . . directly spoken unto **William Wanton J^{r}** of Newport, Esquire . . . and procure a warrant for his arrest.

479. **Thomas Philips** of North Kingstown, shop-keeper, vs. **Jonathan Baker** of Warwick, boatman, for £4:5:4 due for goods sold and delivered the defendant's wife whilst sole in August 1728. Writ dated 23 June 1729; **Daniel Updike** attorney. Account dated 6 August 1728 to **Elizabeth Joyce**, for 10 yds Chinee, skain of thread, etc.

480. **William Brightman** of Portsmouth, yeoman, vs. **Nathaniel Dunn** of New Shoreham, husbandman, in an action of promise. Writ dated 2 July 1729; **Daniel Updike** attorney. On 29 May 1723 the plaintiff was bound by bond with the defendant and **Richard Dunn** of Newport, yeoman, unto **John Rodman** of Flushing in Queens County, Nassaw Island [New York], phisician, in the amount of £300; at the General Court of Tryals in September 1728, Rodman brought action of debt against William Brightman and recovered £292:10:0 and costs of court, which Nathaniel Dunn refused to reimburse. Receipt from **Samuel**

Holmes to Nathaniel Dunn, 7 June 1729, for £74:5:0 in part of the bond. Verdict for plaintiff.

481. **Mary Joslin** of South Kingstown, widow, vs. **Jeremiah Fish** of South Kingstown, yeoman, for £31 due by bond dated 25 March 1728, witnessed by **John Lillibridge** and **Nickoals** [mark +] **Gardner**. Writ dated 15 July 1729; **Nathaniel Newdigate** attorney.

482. **Zechariah Edey** of Providence, yeoman, vs. **John Marsh** of Providence, husbandman, in action of trespass. Writ dated 16 July 1729; **Daniel Updike** attorney. Land sued for was in Providence, partly orchard, meadow and arable with a dwelling house, described as 36 acres, Lot #35, bounded north on Lot #34 in right of Arthur Fenner, east on land of Abraham Clarke, south on lot #36 belonging to Stephen Northup, and west on the Colony line; it had belonged to **John Scott** late of Newport, merchant, grandson and heir to **Richard Scott**, an original proprietor; John Scott had conveyed his right to **Nathanel Brown** of Rehoboth, shipwright, who conveyed his right to **William Gulley** of Providence, glasier, who conveyed it to Zechariah the plaintiff.

483. **Charles Dickinson Sr.** of South Kingstown, yeoman, vs. **Joseph Rogers** of Westerly, house carpenter, for £40 due by bond dated 22 April 1728 witnessed by **John Shelden** and **Ichabod [mark I] Potter**. Writ dated 21 July 1729; **Jon[a] Wilson** attorney.

484. **Norbert Wigneron** [*sic*] of Newport, physician, vs. **Mary Degrove** of Newport, widow and executrix in her own wrong to **Deric Adolph Degrove** late of Newport, mariner deceased, in the custody of the sheriff, for £3:18:0 due for sundry Remedies administered to the sd Deric Adolph Degrove's son and Attendance on him in the Life Time of the sd Deric Adolph Degrove and at his Instance and request in the month of November 1725. Writ dated 21 July 1729; **D. Updike** attorney. Defendant answered by her attorney **Jon[a] Wilson** that Deric Adolph Degrove left no estate to be administered.

The file contains an Indenture made 27 June 1727, between **Deric Degrave** of the City of New York, mariner, and **Mary Elsworth** of the same place, widow, "Whereas there is a Marriage by God's Grace shortly to be had and solemnized between the said Deric and Mary and the said Mary having three children by her former husband **Jacob Colliar** dec'd and being willing before the solemnizing of the said

Marriage to settle all what she hath now upon her said Children **Urion Colliar, Elinor** the wife of **James Fourd & John Colliar** And hath taken an Inventory of her Goods house and Lot of Ground fronting to the broad Way joining next to the house of **Abraham Astines** which she now maketh over to her said Children to enjoy after her Decease. . . ." Signed by Dirick De Groof, in presence of Thomas Huddleston, Hugh Higgins, and John Buk. In the file is the Inventory of sundry household Goods belonging to **Mary Elsworth** the late Widow of **Clement Elsworth** taken 27 June 1727: a bed and all the Furniture belonging to it, 6 Great Pictures and one doz small wth guilded Frames, 3 Iron pots, 1 Iron dripping pan, 2 dripping Ladles, 2 flesh Forks, 2 Tables, a Trunk and chest, 1 pewter Dish, 1 doz Pewter Platters, 1 looking Glass, a Gradiron, a parcel of Earthen Ware and Glasses, 4 Suits of Cloths, 4 pair of Sheets, 4 pair of Pillow Cases, 8 Chairs, a House and Lott of Ground fronting to the broadway, 4 pot hooks, 1 frying pan, 1 pr of Hand Irons, 2 pr of Tongs and fire Shovel, 1 pair bellows, 3 brass Candlesticks. At the bottom of the page, dated New York June 28th, 1727, "I promise to deliver the aboves[d] Goods to the Children of Mary Elsworth my now intended Wife immediately after her Decease . . . Dirck De Groof . . . Signed in the presence of us **John Buk, Hugh Higgins, Thomas Huddleston**." A memorandum dated 14 February 1729/30 signed by Rip Van Dam, Esq., one of his Majesty's Council for the Province of New York and one of the Masters of the Court of Chancery, states that Mr. Thomas Huddlestone made oath that he saw Dirck Degrof sign and deliver the above instrument and Hugh Higgens and John Buk were present.

485. **Peleg Wilbour** of Newport, house carpenter, vs. **Nathaniel Kay** of Newport, Esq., for £7:10:0 due for keeping and pasturing sundry horses and mares for the defendant, money paid, taking his horse out of the pound, and a bottle of rum, from July to November 1728. Writ dated 22 July 1729; **Nathaniel Newdigate** attorney.

486. **John Trobridge** of Newport, mariner, vs. **William Gardner** late of Newport, merchant, for non-performance of a promise. Writ dated 23 July 1729; **Jon[a] Wilson** attorney. In October 1728 said John being master of a sloop called the *Swanzey* riding at anchor in the Harbour of Newport (**Samuel Holmes** of Newport, merchant, owner) was possessed of goods valued at £60, when Capt. William Gardner was hired

by Holmes to take the sloop to places unknown to the plaintiff and came to take possession. The goods included "a barrel of pork, a case of botels, a bed filled with gees fethers, coverleds, my gun, feather pillers, my under bed, my boyes bed, my chest, a bought stuff jacket, my watch coat, a straight boded Coat and Jacket of Spanish Druget, my Quddern [quadrant], axe, 3 pears of yarn stockens, 3 hankerchif, a good Bible, cod line and hooks, a hat, a pair of cloth britches, drawknif, puter basen, poringer, lookinglas, drinking glass, 2 stoon muges, a spice morter, 6 wooden plates, 3 knives, 3 spoons." **Samuel Holmes** deposed 26 July 1729 before Job Lawton, J.P., that William Gardner had hired the sloop *Swanzey* and told John Trobridge that he would take care of the clothes and bedding he had on board. **Mary Trobridg** testified on the same day that some time in October 1727 Capt. William Gardner "came to our house with Capt holmes and my father . . . they talked about the sloop and they asked my father what ballace was in the sloop . . . my father told them there was all in as he run with all summer . . . [he] asked them what he should do about his things he had on board . . . Capt Gardner said he would take care of them . . . my father asked him if he should send his boy to put the small tings in his chest . . . Capt Gardner said there was no occasion for that." **Ephraim Andrus** deposed that the "sloop was a comeing to Sail I went on Board said Vessel with some others for my Chest and Cloths and they that was on board Desire of them to Lett me have my things and one of them spoke to me who some of them Called him by the name of Mr Gardner . . . he saith that I had gouds Left . . . my things be on board as well as Trobridgs . . . delivered me my things. . . ." Verdict for the plaintiff, £36:17:6 damages and costs of court, reversed upon a rehearing.

487. **Daniel Ayrault** of Newport, merchant, vs. **John Trobridg** of Newport, mariner, for £24:4:9 due for goods sold and delivered from 18 November 1728 and 3 May 1729. Writ dated 24 July 1729; **Daniel Updike**, attorney. Account included "pr fine cotton cards delivered yr wife, cotton wool, various fabrics, sugar, and rum.

488. **Amy Buffom** of Newport, widow, vs. **John Tunly** of Newport, cordwainer, in action of trespass, that on or about 19 March 1728 he "one certain pied cow about five years old . . . the proper cow of sd Almy . . . with an ax did cutt, greviously wound and maim and utterly spoil . . . by means whereof . . . the cow died." Writ dated 24 July 1729; **Jn^a Wilson** attorney. Defendant claimed not guilty. **John Carr** (son to **Daniel Carr** testified before Samuel Vernon, Justice, 10 July 1729 that in the winter last past he saw John Tunley beat the sd cow with a bean pole in his own yard . . . "sd Cow run into my Father's Garden and Tunley said drive her in again but wee turned her through our Stable into the Street . . . Tunley said if she came there again he would kill her." **Hannah Jackwise** deposed [her statement signed by mark X] on 17 August 1729 that the week before the widow Buffum's cow was maimed she heard John Tunley "in Driving sd Cow out of his yard say that if they did not keep the Bitch of a Cow away he would be the Death of her." **Georg Williams** deposed 19 August 1729 before John Coddington, Justice, and said that he lived in the house with John Tunley and saw him take an ax from behind a door at his house and split a calf's head; his wife **Jane Williams** swore to the truth of the statement. **Amy Wood** deposed 2 September before Samuel Vernon, Assistant, that "a little time before Amey Buffums Cow received the Wound which Ocationed her Death John Tunleys wife came to Our House & asked if wee had not a Cow. I told her yes, she said that the Cow was very troublesom that my Husband says he will kill her & he is a very hasty Man & I believe he will be as good as his word . . . she repeated it several times . . . also said her Husband had beat her so today that she was affraid he would have killed her . . . and said her Husband sent her." Verdict for the plaintiff, cost of the cow.

489. **Joseph Borden**, General Treasurer of the Colony, vs. **Edward Larkin** of Westerly, yeoman, for debt of £18 due by note dated 22 November 1721, signed with mark E of Edward Larking [*sic*], witnessed by **Henry Bull** and **Jer. Clarke**.

490. **Elizabeth Carpenter** of Providence, widow and administratrix of the estate of **William Carpenter** of Providence, yeoman, deceased, vs. **William Benchley** of Providence, labourer, for £10 debt, for 2 years rent of a house at £5 per year. Writ dated 21 July 1729.

491. **Ichabod Potter** of South Kingstown, yeoman, eldest son and heir of **Thomas Potter** late of South Kingstown, yeoman, deceased, vs. **Robert Wilcox** of South Kingstown, yeoman, in action of trespass, to recover 100 acres in South Kingstown, bounded east by land of Robert Wilcox and **Stephen Wilcox**, south by **Thomas Sherman** deceased, west on

the Pettequamscutt line, and North on land of the **Barbers**, of which half Thomas Potter was in his lifetime seized in common with the other proprietors . . . he died in the year 1728 or thereabouts intestate . . . leaving the plaintiff his oldest son and heir. The defendant's answer was that Thomas Potter had left several sons and daughters besides the plaintiff, and a distribution had not been made.

492. **Alexander McLester** of Boston, county Suffolk, Massachusetts Bay, marriner, vs. **John Coldwell** late of Cloughon [Cloughorr?] in the Kingdom of Ireland but now resident in Newport, marriner, to recover £31:18:01 due for his passage from Ireland to Newport and sundry goods sold and delivered and money advanced by the plaintiff at sundry times in the year 1728. Defendant claims he owes nothing. Account presented, beginning in June 1728, includes "cash in Irland Belfast . . . shoes . . . handkerchief, black jaccot and britches amaking . . . [July] passedge from Belfast Lough in Irland to Rhod Island in America £15 . . . 3 dozen glass bottles heft with you . . . **Mr James Brown** of Newport for [? ten] weeks lodging for you . . . one broadcloath coat duble breasted . . . one pr wistel stockings you had of mee . . . one silver buckle to the chape of my swoord . . . one pr brass stilyards you took of myn . . . one hat of myn you gave [? George] at Island . . . my Dog you stoole away which you oftimes heared me say I would not give e for a guinea." Sworn to at Boston 6 August 1729. Writ dated 8 September 1729.

Evidence taken 9 December 1729 from **David Harpers** and **John Cochran** both resident in Newport, mariners [both of whom signed their statements], who came in the brigantine *Braintree,* Alexander Mc Lester commander, from Ireland to Newport which arrived in the month of November 1728 . . . one **J. Caldwell** (who is the sd Mc-Lester's sisters son) came the voyage with them and was a hand on board the sd brigantine . . . performed his watch & did his part of all the other service on board . . . during the whole voyage . . . deponents heard sd J. Caldwell say his mother was very much against his coming away, but that she was overperswaded by his sd Uncle McLester to let him come. Upon the sd McLester's promises to do for him something towards his prefement . . . during the passage nor since, they never knew the sd John Caldwell to buy any manner of thing of the sd

Alexander McLester . . . after arrived at Newport . . . sd John Caldwell had the care of sd brigantine *Braintree* for sometime while the sd McLester went to Boston & other places about his affaires."

The Jury's verdict was for the defendant, costs of court.

493. **Thomas Boucher** of Boston, shopkeeper, vs. **John Whitehorn** of Newport, distiller, for £21:09 due for 49½ pounds of [? Bever], sold and delivered 18 August 1727. On account, Whitehorn is called late of Boston, distiller; included is a "bevar hatt, a hatt turn'd, etc."

1730 - General Sessions of the Peace

494. **Samuel Aspin** of Newport, coachmaker, indicted 28 March 1730, charged with stealing a "Lute-string, Hood, one Sarsanet Handkershief, one yard of Ribband, one Hatt and one pr Gloves . . . out of the dwelling house of **Thomas Brown** of Newport, felmonger . . . on oath of Thomas' wife **Elizabeth Brown**." **Daniel Updike**, attorney.

495. **Emanuel Clarke** of South Kingstown, husbandman, indicted last Tuesday of March 1730 "for that with malice aforethought and Evil intending he did on the fourth day of October AD 1729 wickedly and feloniously burn and consume with Fire . . . a certain Out House standing on the Farm of **William Gardner** of sd Kingstown, yeoman . . . value £300. **Daniel Updike**, attorney.

496. **Mercy Chadwick** of Newport, widow, indicted in November; it was charged that on or about the month of May 1730 she "did wickedly and feloniously receive and take of and conceal for **Elizabeth Chadwick** of sd Newport her Daughter one piece of striped cotton cloth" of the value of £2:10.

497. **Negro Scipio** of Newport was indicted; it was charged that on 4 November 1730 at Newport, he with force and arms did take from **Benjamin Belcher** of sd Newport, shipwright, 30 lbs. of cotton to the value of £4:10.
[*Note: A fire in Newport 4 November 1730 resulted in many charges of looting, of which this is only one.*]

March 1730 - Court of Common Pleas

498. **Vertue Jeffery** [signed Jaffery] of Newport, widow, vs. **John Bennet** of Newport, boatman, for £4:12:6 due for one suit of clothes sold and delivered and cash lent in 1729. Writ dated 17 December 1729; **Daniel Updike** attorney. Plaintiff's account shows credit to defendant for house rent, £1:12:2.

499. **Clement Elsworth** of Newport, barber, vs. **Nicholas Spink** now resident in Newport, mariner, for £3:03 due for one wigg sold and delivered 2 April 1726. Defendant answered by Nicholas Spink of

North Kingstown, yeoman, his guardian, that he was a minor [and therefore not liable]. **Elizabeth Corey** of Newport testified that "about nineteen years ago she . . . was midwife to **Sarah Spink** wife to Nicholas Spink then of Kingstown and that she delivered sd Spink of a son and he was then called Nicholas . . . to the deponent[s] certain knowledge [he] is not one & twenty years old. . .." "Clement Alsworth [*sic*] present at the taking this evidence."

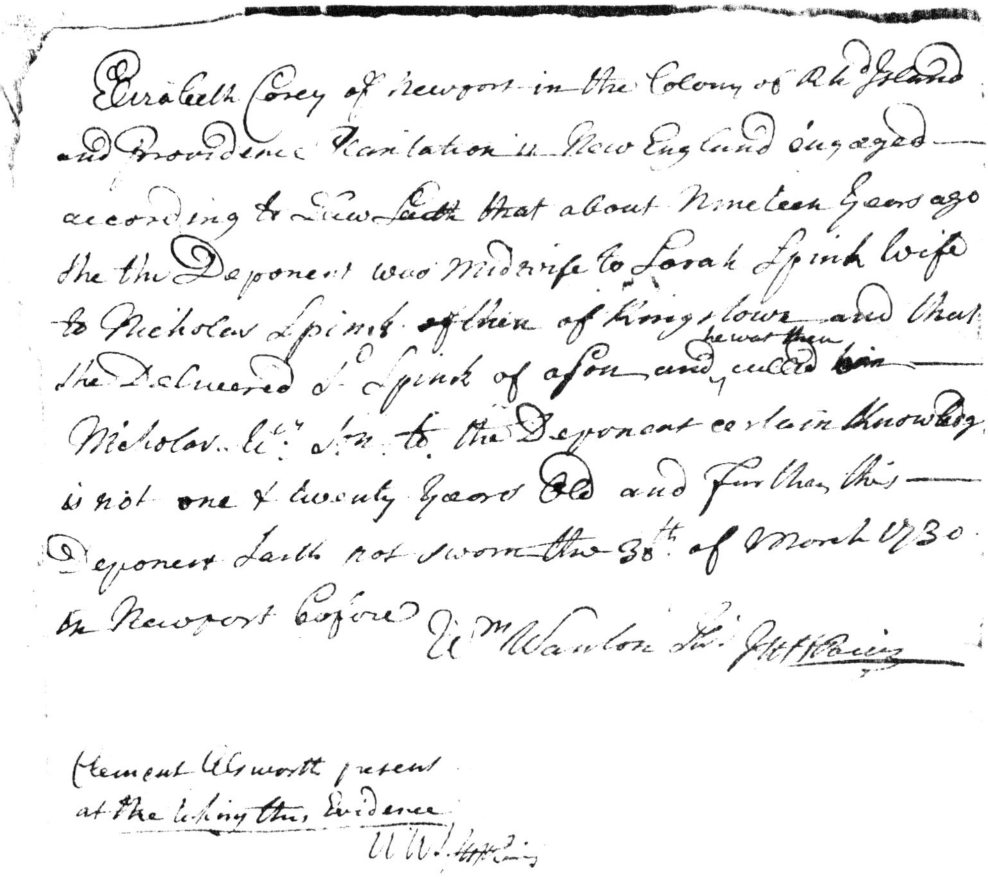
Elizabeth Corey of Newport in the Colony of Rh Island
and Providence Plantation in New England ingaged
according to Law Saith that about Nineteen Years ago
she the Deponent was Midwife to Sarah Spink wife
to Nicholas Spink of then of Kingstown and that
she Delivered sd Spink of a son and he was then called him
Nicholas &c: &c to the Deponent certain knowledg
is not one & twenty years old and further this
Deponent saith not sworn the 30th of March 1730
in Newport before Wm Wanton Jus: [illegible]

Clement Alsworth present
at the taking this Evidence
[illegible]

Elizabeth Corey's deposition about birth of Nicholas Spink [*No. 499*]

500. **Augustus Lucas** of Newport, merchant, vs. **William Hawkins** of Newport, plaisterer, for £15 due for rent. On 4 September 1728 he had let to the defendant a dwelling house with garden and other appurtenances in Newport, last occupied by **Abraham Redwood**, at £30 per year to be paid quarterly. Writ dated 20 December 1729; **Rowland Robinson** attorney.

501. **William Dodge Jun**[r] of New Shoreham vs. **Joseph Case the second** of South Kingstown, yeoman, for £22:10:0 due by note dated 29 May 1728. Writ dated 6 January 1729/30; **Rowland Robinson** attorney.

502. **Daniel Shrieve** of Newport, cordwainer and wife **Sarah** vs. **Philip Shearman** of Portsmouth, weaver, in action of trespass concerning a dwelling and garden in Newport lying in a gore, bounded west 49 feet by land of **Daniel Thurston** and north by the highway 84 feet. **Thomas Starr,** grandfather of **Sarah [Shrieve]** was possessed of the land in 1703 and died in 1704 leaving issue: **Thomas,** the oldest son and heir, died in 1709 leaving **Sarah,** his only daughter. Writ dated 3 Feb. 1730. Defendant said he was an inhabitant of Portsmouth, therefore could not be in possession of the Newport property, "for a Man can't live in two places at one and ye same Time." **Sarah Rogers** of Newport, widow, and **Edith Higgens,** wife of **Richard,** made depositions stating that they were present when Sarah was born of Elizabeth Staire [*sic*] then wife of Thomas, and **Mary Fry** was the midwife. Marriage record: "Daniel Shreave of Portsmouth and Sarah Stare of Newport lawfully Published and accordingly maried the 8th day of October A.D. 1725 by Job Lawton Justice Peace." **Mary Brodick** of Newport, widow, deposed and said that she was at the wedding of **Thomas Stair** and **Elizabeth Marshall,** late of Newport, deceased; they were married by Major **Nath**[ll] **Coddington** and she saw them in bed together the same evening they were married; Thomas was the reputed son of **Thomas Starr** late of Newport, house carpenter, deceased. **William James** of Westerly gave similar testimony. **Richard Clark** deposed and said that some time in 1704, he with **Samuell Warkman** was desired by **Ruth Starr,** widow of **Thomas** of Newport, carpenter, deceased, to take an inventory, "including the fraime of a house that Thomas Starr had set up . . . not underpinned nor anything done to the inside, and the west end all open . . . neither door nor casement. **Samuel Warkman** also testified. Inventory of Thomas Starr, deceased, taken November 1704 in Newport was shown [*see No. 19*].

503. Ebenezer Cook of East Greenwich, mariner, vs. **Wm Cadey** of Warwick, house carpenter in custody of the sheriff, for £5 due by note dated 10 July 1729 [no witnesses]. Writ dated 15 January 1729. **Daniel Updike**, attorney.

504. John Bayley Jr. of Newport, weavour, vs. **Ralph Allen** of Portsmouth, weavour, for money due by bond dated 21 February 1728[/9].

505. Thomas Shearman of Portsmouth, yeoman, vs. **Robert Olds** of Springfield in county of Hampshire, province of Massachusetts Bay, trader, for £18 due by note dated 16 April 1729. Writ dated 23 January 1729[/30]; **Henry Bull** attorney.

506. Christopher Almy of Newport, merchant, vs. **John Trobridge** of Newport, mariner, for £58:6:0 due for rum sold and delivered 26 July 1729. Writ dated 29 January 1729[/30]; **Daniel Updike** attorney. Account is for 211 gallons of rum @ 5/6.

507. Hezekiah Gorton of Warwick, yeoman, vs. **Thankfull Collins** of Warwick, boatman, executor of the will of **Thomas Collins** late of Warwick, husbandman, deceased, for £10:2:8½ due for goods sold and delivered to Thomas Collins in his lifetime, from July 1708 to March 1725/6. Writ dated 12 February 1729; **Nathaniel Newdigate**, attorney. Account begins in July 1716 and includes charges for "tobacco, rackoon skin, Indian corn, chees, mutton, goat mutton, suger, cloth, 10s damage done by his cattle, beef, veal, honey, beeswax, and hay to keep ye docters horse.'

508. Edward Larkin of Westerly, yeoman, vs. **David Nichols** of North Kingstown, yeoman, for £25 due by note dated 20 March 1729, for oxen, to be paid by the following 15 June; no witnesses. Writ dated 5 February 1729[/30]; **Daniel Updike**, attorney.

509. William Toppan of Newport, shop-keeper, vs. **Clement Elsworth** of Newport, barber, and **Freelove** his wife lately when sole named **Freelove Burroughs** for £43:19:7 due by book for sundry clothes the said Freelove had of the plaintiff and for extraordinary charges arising by the sickness of the said Freelove, all before the said Clement was married [to her] . . . beginning 1 November 1727 and ending 18 May 1729. Writ dated 12 February 1729[/30]. Toppan's bill included several yardages of camblett, persian, silk, and callimanco, ribbons, silk gloves, and needles, as well as shoes, attendance in sickness, including 3 weeks when she had ye measles in May 1729, and cash paid ye German Doctor. **Elizabeth Carr** of Newport testified on 30 March 1730 before **Wm. Wanton**, Justice, that she "heard Freelove Burriss now Alsworth often say that while she was at her Fathers in Law he gave her Victualls and the deponent asked [her] why her Father did not imploy her . . . [she] answerd that they had help and further saith that Mr. Toppin bid her go out to work." On the same day, **John Fryers** of Newport testified that "in December 1728 he lived in Wm. Toppan's house and understood that Freelove Burruss now Ailsworth lived with sd Toppin her father in Law to go and come as she pleas'd and that she did some small pieces of work . . . for herself but what they were he cannot tell . . . Mr. Toppin bid her sd Freelove go out of the house if she did not do better. . . ." **Elizabeth Roggers** of Newport testified at the same time that she "often heard Mr. Toppin bid Freelove to minde her business better, and not to run up & down & that he could not maintain her in Victualls after this manner . . . heard her say she lived at her fathers in law contrary to his inclination . . . heard Freelove say that when she had any thing to do she went & did it and other times did work in the house and that she made one shirt & received the money for it. . . ." **Mary Arnold**, wife of **Benedict Arnold** of Newport testified that "about three years past Freelove Burruss now Alsworth made a pair of stays for [my] daughter Patience about two years old and [I] payd [her]. . . ." **John Dennis** of Newport testified that he "lived in the chamber of Mr. Toppin and understood that Freelove Burruss . . . made a gound [gown] for her self . . . heard Gould [and] **John Lillick**, Deceas'd say that Freelove lived with sd Toppin on sufferance. . . ." Verdict for the plaintiff, money sued for and costs of court.

510. **Mial Phillips** of Newport, butcher, vs. **Martin Howard** of Newport, clothier, for £8:1:8 due for provisions sold and delivered in the years 1727 and 1728. Writ dated 14 February 1729[/30]; **Henry Bull** attorney. Bill includes charges for meat (veal, beef), and horse hire, and records an amount received at **Thomas Bayly**'s. Verdict for the plaintiff, money sewed [*sic*] for and costs of court.

511. **Alice Wilson** of Newport, widow, vs. **Content Bull** of Newport, widow, executrix of the will of **Benjamin Bull** late of Newport, gen-

tleman, for £101:10:0 due by note dated 20 November 1728 in the lifetime of sd Benjamin, witnessed by **John Wattsworth** and **Stephen Mott**. Writ dated 18 February 1729; **Nathaniel Newdigate** attorney.

512. **George Dunbar** of Newport, merchant, vs. **John Larrance** of Newport, shopkeeper, and **Joshua Coggeshall** of Newport, sadler, in action of trespass, charging that on 25 March 1730 they abused a servant of Dunbar's, broke his lantern and committed other enormities. Deposition of **John Proctor** that he with Larrance and Coggeshall went from **John Channing's** the last night: "I heard some glass gingle on ye Pavements and see one Foard who was one of the Company have a cain in his hand standing by the Lanthorn. . .but which of the company broke sd Lanthorn I know not it being Dark". Defendants ordered to pay 5 shillings each for breach of His Majesty's Peace.

513. **Benedict Arnold** of Jamestown, yeoman vs. **Tedeman Hull, Richard Tew, James Carr, John Hull, David Green,** and **Gershom Remington,** all yeomen of Jamestown, in action of partition of Dutch Island whereof the plaintiff holds 20 acres in common and undivided with the defendants – sd island lyeth in the Bay between Conanicut Island and the North East part of South Kingstown. Writ dated 16 February 1729.

The plaintiff states that by virtue of the last will and testament of **Josiah Arnold,** late of Jamestown, gentleman, probated 23 September 1721, he is seized of about 5 acres; by virtue of a deed of sale under the hand of **Sion Arnold** of Newport and **Mary** his wife dated 17 June 1728, he is seized of about 9½ acres; by virtue of a deed under the hand of **Benjamin Belcher** of Newport, shipwright, and **Abigail** his wife dated 30 October 1728, he [has] about 2¼ acres; by virtue of a deed under the hand of **John Beere** of Newport, shipwright, and **Sarah** his wife dated 24 July 1729 he [has] about 2¼ acres; and by virtue of a deed from **John Cranston** of Jamestown, yeoman, and **Penelope** his wife dated 6 February 1729 he [has] about one acre, all amounting to 20 acres, it being one fourth part of Dutch Island.

Deeds in file: from Sion Arnold, witnessed by **Rich^{d}** and **Mary Ward**; from John Beere, witnessed by **John Cary** and **Patience Taylor**; from Benjamin Belcher, witnessed by **James Collins** and **Freelove Lillingston**; from John Cranston, witnessed by **Nicholas Carr** and **Nicholas Carr, Juner**. Paragraphs from wills of **Benedict Arnold** dated

8 July 1678 (copied 4 April 1730 by Wm. Coddington, Council Clerk, from Newport Town Council and Probate 2:2-13) and Benedict Arnold [Jr.] dated 10 August 1727 (copied 4 April 1730 from Newport Town Council and Probate 6:233-234) devising all his right in Dutch Island to his son Sion and the latter's heirs. Copies from records of the Proprietors of Quononicut (alias Jamestown), stating that the Jamestown purchasers were to have rights in Dutch Island equally proportionate to their shares in Jamestown. Copy of the will of **Caleb Carr** [*for full transcription of will, see No. 9*].

The defendant's answer was that Dutch Island was to "remain in common for publick use as to putt on rambs, calves, and other cattle to each ones proportion," and could not therefore be divided.

514. **Abraham Borden** of Newport, Esq., gentleman, treasurer of the Colony, vs. **Nathaniel Hall** of Portsmouth, yeoman, administrator of the estate of **Benjamin Hall** late of Portsmouth, yeoman, deceased, for debt due by note dated 18 Aug. 1721 from Benjamin Hall to **Joseph Borden,** late treasurer of the Colony, witnessed by **Mary Corry** (mark O) and **William Anthony**.

515. **Timothy Whiting** of Newport, vintner, vs. **William Jones Jr.** now resident in Newport, merchant, in action of trespass, charging that sd William on last day of December and first of January 1730 at Newport made an assault on the body of **Sarah Witherill** and **Mary Jacobs,** two servant maids to the plaintiff belonging. . .did bruise, wound and evilly Intread . . . plaintiff lost service of two servants and put to charge and expense for curing and healing. Writ dated May 1730. Deposition of **William Wanton Jun**r Esq., who examined a bruise of Sarah Witherill's and said it was an "old soar". Depositions of **John Chace, Priscilla Lyndon,** wife of **Samuel, Edith Higgins**, wife of **Richard**, and **Johanna Lusom**. Verdict for defendant.

516. **Job Casswell** of Newport, house carpenter, vs. **John Partelow** of Newport, carter, for £100. Caswell had done work for Partelow and they had agreed on 10 February 1729[/30] to arbitration by **Joseph Knowlton, Mr. Esbon Sanford**, and **Capt. Richard Coggeshall**, who were to view the work and set a value on it; on 16 February 1729[/30] they judged it worth £65, but defendant refused to pay. Agreement was witnessed by **James** and **Bridget Cary**. Writ dated 18 February 1729/30. Verdict for plaintiff, £65 and costs of court.

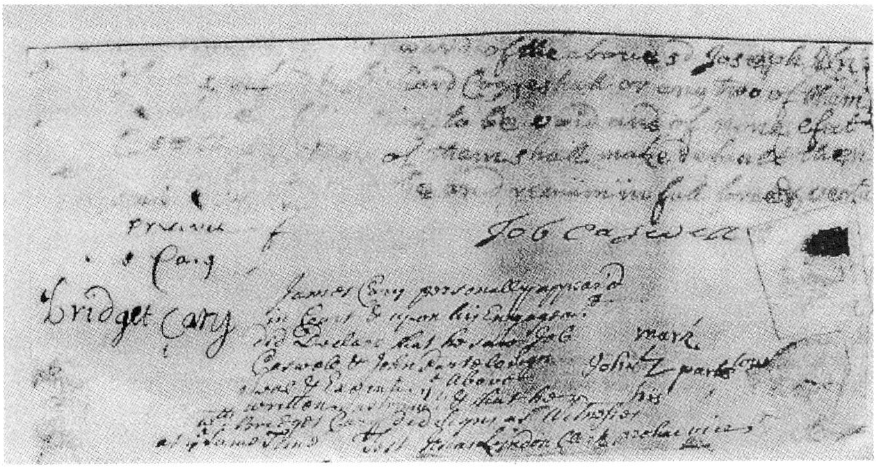

Detail from agreement of Job Caswell and John Partelow [No. 516]

517. **Arthur Fenner** of Providence (son of **Major Fenner**, deceased) vs. **Daniel Abbott** of Providence, merchant alias yeoman, for £100 due by bond dated 2 January 1721/2 witnessed by **Silvanus Scott** and **Joseph Hopkins**. Writ dated 18 February 1729[/30]; **Henry Bull**, attorney. **Mary Mitchel** testified 31 March 1730 before **Richard Waterman**, assistant, that "when she lived at Arthur Fenner's house in Providence about two years ago . . . shee perceived that there was sum Contrivercy betwixt Capt. Daniel Abbott and Arthur Fenner about sum money that Fenner had that came from Abbott's wife . . . heard Arthur Fenner's wife say that Abbott durst not arrest her husband for he had a bond against Abbott: that though Abbott had payed it he had not taken it up. . . ."

518. **Major Fairchild** of Newport, butcher, vs. **Francis Conner** of Newport, house carpenter, for £11:4:10 due for provisions sold and delivered from 5 July 1729 to 26 December 1729. Writ dated 18 February 1729; **Henry Bull** attorney. Bill is mostly for beef, mutton, and lamb.

519. Note, Newport, 30 8[ber] 1730, **James Sheffield** to **Samuel Sheffield,** for £30:10:6 due on last day of June next. Witnesses **John Cook, John Holmes, Tho. Larkin.**

520. Bond [*separated from case*] from **Peleg Tripp** of Newport, butcher, for £20 dated 6 February 1729[/30?] in case **Major Fairchild** of Newport, butcher, prosecuted **Peter Phillips** of Newport, house carpenter, upon a writ; witnesses were **William Bennett** and **Mary Ward.**

521. Depositions [*separated from case*]: **Peter Phillips** of Newport deposed 30 March 1730 before Job Lawton, J. P., and said that he "mett **Jacob Anory** att the Point In the street and he loked like a person Indisposed . . . and so poorly that at first I hardly knew him. He up and Tells me that he was aGoing to the Docter and that his Illness was ocationed by **Rich[d] Wilson** b[eating] of him." **John Partelow** of Newport, carter, deposed 31 March 1730 that he "went to the Dweling house of Jacob Anory on purpose to see him and when I came into the House I saw some Blood on the Hearth and I ask him what was the matter . . . he told me Rich[d] Wilson was the ocation of it by his Beating and Abuse-ing of him . . . spate Blood sev'll times and look[d] very poorly. **Lawrance Bently** deposed at the same time that "on a First Day Morn-ing . . . I Walk through the Burying Place where I see Rich[d] Wilson and **Jeremiah Exsenor Jn[r]** Diging of a Grave and In Discourse the sd Rich[d] Wilson acquainted me where Jacob Anory Lived and [I] gos to See him and when I Come In to the house I saw sd Anory abed and his wife and I askt him how he Did and he Tells me Very Poorly and to appearance he did Look so."

522. **James Nickolls** of East Greenwich, yeoman, vs. **Ezekiell Long** of the same place, yeoman, for debt of £80 due by note dated 22 July 1729, witnessed by **John** and **Lydia Jenkins.** Writ dated March 1730.

523. **Samuel Snell** of Newport, vintner, vs. **David Lake,** labourer, of Tivertown in the Colony of Bristol, Province of Massachusetts Bay, now of Portsmoth [*sic*], yeoman, for debt of £59:01:11 due for goods delivered from May 1719 to 1729. Writ dated 17 February 1730. This was evidently a continuation of an earlier case, when on 12 July 1726 Snell and Lake chose referees: Snell chose **Capt. John Palmer,** Lake chose **Thomas Manchester,** and the Court appointed **Capt. Robert Dennis.** There are two verdicts in the file, both "wee find a Reversion of former Judgement with costs of court."

524. **Sylvester Sweett** of Newport, vintner, vs. **Samuel Pike** of the same place, taylor for debt of £6:13:02 due for Sundry Liquors sold and delivered 22 November 1726 to 10 January 1729.

525. **Abraham Borden** of Newport, Esq. vs. **James Brown Junr** of same place, mariner, for debt of £29:17:00 due by book for wharfedge and for use of a winding tackle fall and for Lumber . . . in the yr 1729, at which time Brown was master of the brig *Dolphin*.

526. **Edward Morse** of Newport, mariner, vs. **John Trobridge** of the same place, mariner, for debt of £34 due by note dated 29 July 1729, signed "John Trobridg" and witnessed by **Nath^{ll} Hatch** and **James Martin**.

527. **Lott Strange** of Freetown, County of Bristol, cooper, vs. **Jonathan Barney** of Newport, mariner, for causing one thousand of Hogshead hoops to be taken from the Plaintiff in Newport afores^{d} on or about the 15th day of December AD 1729 without leave or license of the Plaintiff; requesting payment and £36 damages. Whereas the Pltf. having a considerable quantity of Hoops lying in Newport, the Defendant att ye time afores^{d} did ord^{r} his People belonging to a certain Sloop he then was master of to take away and carry from ye said quantity one thousand of said hoops which consisted of bilge or the longest hoops being in sd quantity . . . proportionable part for each part of a hogshead (viz) bilge and China hoops, by means whereof the Plaint^{f} lost . . . Defendant pleaded not guilty. Evidence given 31 December 1729 in Newport by **John Mitchel** of lawful age, that he being Mate on board the sloop *Sarah* of which **Capt. Joseph Whipple** was chief owner, was "ordered by sd Whipple to take one thousand of Hoops from off Mr. Goulding's Wharfe and carry them on bord sd sloop which accordingly I did, and while I was taking off sd hoops there came a man and forwarned me taking any more and also bid me land them I had gott, but sd owner told me to go off with them I had gott." Verdict for the plaintiff £5:10:00 damages and court costs.

528. **Joseph Belcher** late of Boston, now of Newport, cordwainer, vs. **Charles Marreno** of Newport, cordwainer, for £3:15:00 due by book for shoes made for the defendant sundry times in the year 1729. Depositions given: **James Burges** on 5 February 1729/30 at Newport signed a statement that "sometime in January last past **Charles Morrena** and **Joseph Belcher** being att the house of **Hezekiah Dodg** in Newport, I heard sd [parties] agree for the making a quantitie of shoes

and sd Belcher agreed to make y^m for sd Morrena att three shillings a pair, and said Belcher to find himselfe vicktuals and lodgin." Hezzekiah Dodg "swair to the truthe of the above Evidence he being Present." **Robt Audlin** (signed Odlin) stated that on 14 February 1729/30 he did see Belcher sign a note for £2:13:00 to Morrena, etc. **Nathl Allcock** stated on 9 March 1729/30 that he had been witness to the note.

529. **William Fanning** of Newport, mariner, received judgement in May 1730 against **Martha Russel** of Newport, widow, administratrix of the goods of **Joseph Russel** late of Newport, mariner, deceased. Martha appealed, and bond for her was posted by **John Rogers** of Newport, house carpenter, dated 3 June 1730, witnessed by **Job Bennet** and **Peter Easton**. Martha failed to prosecute.

530. **Job Green** of Warwick, Esq., vs. **George Pigot** of Marblehead, Co. Essex, yeoman, for debt due by note dated 18 October 1728, witnessed by **Catherine Green, Barlo Green**, and **Edward Pigot**. Writ dated February 1729[/30].

– 1731 –

531. **John Dixson** and **John Smith**, of lawful age, signed their names to written testimony in Plainfield [Connecticut] on 26 March 1731 before **Timo: Peirce**, Assistant, that they "ware in company with the comitees of the two goverments namly coniticut and Roadisland at their meting in the year 1728 sum time in May or the bening of June in sd year: they meet at a heap of stons comenly called the south west corner of Warrick town ship in order to run the line betwen the sd goverments as it was stated in england and we heard the two comites dicors conserning that afaier: and did not agree in their discors: Roadisland comitee did say that heap of stones was in the green line and said they would not be moved from it: becaus the crown of england have stated the line at this plase: we allso did hear corronall wanton who was one of Rodisland comitee say that we disclaim the land west and we will not be driven east: he all so said to coniticut comitee if you will not joyn with us to run the line from this heap of stones we will run it our selves and we did see them take their departier from sd heap of stones."

532. **Sarah Mory** of Westerly, widow, deposed 26 March 1731 and said that in the year 1728 by request of **Joseph Sheffield** of South Kingstown, yeoman, and more especially for that [i.e. because] **Benjamin Mory** late of North Kingstown had before 1728 mortgaged some land in North Kingstown, a part whereof is land where **William Eldred** now liveth, unto **Thomas Potter** late of South Kingstown, deceased . . . sd **Sarah Mory** gave a quitclaim deed unto **Thomas Potter** of Westerly executor of his father's will delivered a quitclaim to Joseph Sheffield and she never saw Thomas Potter of Westerly after the time **Benjamin Mory** went or run away in the year of our Lord 1727/8 until [Mory] returned in 1729.

Deed from **Thomas Potter** of Westerly, cordwainer, for £570, to **William Eldred** of North Kingstown, yeoman, dated 16 July 1728, for 66 acres in North Kingstown bounded north by the highway, west by land of **Francis West**, south by land of **John Crowder** and **Daniel Bly**, east by land of **Charles Browne**; witnesses **Thomas Phillips** and **Benjamin Weight**; copy of North Kingstown Deeds, 5:909-910.

William Eldred of North Kingstown deposed there 10 March 1729/30 before **William Spencer**, Justice, and said that he paid £25 to **Joseph**

Sheffield of South Kingstown some time in the year 1728, he having a power of attorney "from **Sarah Morey** widdo of **Joseph Morey** to receive money due **Benjamin Morey** Jr. for rent for ye farm whereon ye sd Eldred now dwelleth sd **Benjamin Morey** having a bond for ye same sined over to ye abovesaid **Sarah Morey**." It was noted that Morey and Sheffield did not live within ten miles [of the court].

533. Signed deposition of **Clement Elsworth** of Newport, barber, dated 7ber 6th A.D. 1731 [6 September 1731] before **Job Lawton**, J.P., that "some time last faul he hapen'd to be at the shoop of **John Burt**, and there came **Capt. Potter** and askt whether there was any hogshead there . . . Burt answered yes and the s^d^ Potter askt the prise and s^d^ Burt made answer & said twelve shillings . . . Potter tells him that he could have them for ten shillings at Bristoll and the s^d^ Burt told him that he would not lett his go lo and upon which the s^d^ Capt. Potter order'd **Capt. Rouse Potter** to send his men to fill them with water and take them on board . . . ."

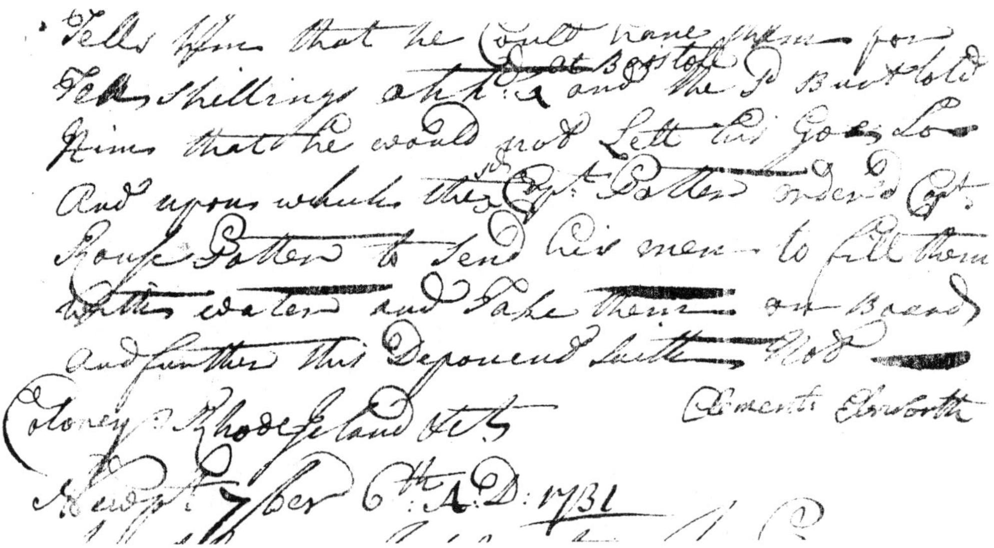
Tells him that he Could have them for
Ten Shillings at Bristoll and the sd Burt told
him that he would not Lett his Go lo
And upon which the sd Capt. Potter order'd Capt.
Rouse Potter to send his men to fill them
with water and Take them on Board
and further this Deponent saith not
Clement Elsworth
Colony of Rhode Island &c
Newport 7ber 6th A:D: 1731

Detail of Clement Elsworth's deposition, 1731 [No. 533]

534. **John Lillibridge** of South Kingstown, husbandman, received judgement at the Inferior Court of Common Pleas at South Kingstown in January last against **Henry Davison** of Jamestown, schoolmaster, for £5:19:6 debt; Henry appealed but failed to prosecute. Bond of **James Honeyman Junr**, dated 12 January 1730, witnessed by **Cuthbert Campbell** and **Isaac Fowler** (mark +), for **Henry Davison**, late of South Kingstown but now resident in Jamestown.

535. **Benjamin Perry**, yeoman of South Kingstown vs. **Hannah Osborn** of South Kingstown, widow, for £37:11:01 owed him for labor and boarding her daughter and burying her, from June 1724 to 1726. Writ dated 20 May 1731. Account included medical charges for mother and daughter . . . "board and schooling y^r^ daughter **Anne** for month July 1724 - June 1727". Deposition of **Margaret Condon** of South Kingstown that she heard **Mary Perry** late wife of **Benjamin Perry** of South Kingstown, now deceased, say she took Ann Osborn of her mother as a gift in the 13th year of said Ann's age and that said Ann died in the 15th year of her age . . . as own child . . . when Ann was dead and laid out in sd Perry's house, Mary lamented much. Deposition of **Abraham Perkins** of South Kingstown that he heard **Benjamin Perry** commend **Ann Osborn** and speak much in praise of her; a little before Benjamin Perry was married to **Susannah Barber** which was in the year 1727 he brought a 5 shilling bill to my house and said he was indebted to widow **Hannah Osborn** . . . left it with the deponent for her . . . she did receive it and said Benjamin was indebted to her £3.

536. **Emmanuel Clark** of South Kingstown vs. **Mary Smith** of South Kingstown for rent of farm. Receipts in file: **Jeremiah Smith,** 14th day [?December] 1727 - paid to **Emmanuel Clark** £8:6:8, one third part of £25 for the building the addition to the house that **Joseph Whitford** now liveth in according to my Honor'd grandfather **Jeremiah Smith's** last Will & Testament." **John Smith** (mark X) of Kingstown, December 1727, "to **Emmanuel Clark** of South Kingstown £8:6:8 [*as above*] . . . Honor'd Father **Jeremiah Smith's** last Will & Testament." 28 December 1728 Prudence Island, "£2 on behalf my son **John Smith** for his Legasie in full for this year which is due the 25 daye of next March," signed Mary Smith.

Agreement between **Emmanuel Clark** of South Kingstown and **Ebenezer Smith** of Prudence Island: Smith to let his farm in South

Kingstown to Clark for £60 for one year, 1729, for four years . . . Smith promised to deliver 1000 good oak rails to Clark at the ferry wharf for use of said farm.

Receipts: 12 February 1729/30 "to **Ebenezer Smith** from **Emmanuel Clark,** £5 in payment of rent due to my mother." Prudence Island 27 April 1730: Mary Smith to Emmanuel Clark: "send by Barrer **Josiah Remmington** 40 shillings which is due for John's Leagesy. . .should be paid in March and I am now in want of it. . ." Received on book 11 May. Deposition of **Marcy Smith** of South Kingstown and **John Smith** of South Kingstown, that when **Margaret Clarke** was widowed, she paid rent to **Mary Smith** of South Kingstown, widow of Jeremiah, late of Portsmouth, deceased, for the farm where her husband **Immanuel Clarke** now lives in South Kingstown, in Boston Neck.

Verdict for plaintiff, to recover £226 and costs.

537. Deposition 7 September 1731 by **Mary Hassard** of South Kingstown, widow, being 90 years of age or thereabout, . . . before **Robt Hannah,** Justice of the Peace, "that her grandson **Robert Willcox** of sd South Kingstown was born at her house and his mother did die when he was about a fortnight old and he was brought up at y[e] charge of this deponant until he was twenty one years of age."

538. September term: **Francis Borland** of Boston, merchant, and wife **Jane** vs. **Jahleel Brenton** of Newport, Esq., in an appeal from judgement of court in May 1731 for defendant.

Plaintiffs sued to recover a third part of the rents of a messuage which had been part of the estate of **William Brenton** on 9 February 1673 when he made his will devising the sd land in fee with diverse other lands and tenements to be equally divided by his overseers among all his children. He died 18 November 1676 and the overseers made a division to **John Pool**, who married **Elizabeth,** one of the daughters of the testator, and **Joseph Eliot** and **Joseph Brown,** who married two other daughters, to hold in common, the children of the testator by their joint deed satisfying and confirming that division and particularly the sd Jahleel Brenton, and on the same day Jahleel Brenton purchased of Joseph Brown part of his share and covenanted that the sd Brown would possess all the rest of his share besides what he had purchased of him, whereby it plainly appeared that the sd John Pool was then heir of the one third part of y[e] messuage aforesaid, in right of his wife Elizabeth, and afterwards the sd John Pool and his wife Elizabeth deceased, and the same descended to Jane, the plaintiff, only daughter and heir of Jane the wife of Timothy Lindol, Esq., only daughter and heir of Elisabeth the wife of John Pool aforesaid.

Deposition of **Richard Clark**: for near 20 years I followed trade of carpenter and joyner in this town . . . did chief part of framing house [*for* **Jahleel Brenton**] . . . had expect of doing more, but Esq. Brenton stopped work . . . told me that truly the land was not all his own . . . part belonged to kinswoman in Boston . . . Col. Pool's daughter or granddaughter . . . **Col. Pool** married his sister . . . I told him best to buy her out rather than let so much money lye Dead . . . his answer was that she was an infant under age. Deposition of **John Cranston** of Newport, merchant. Evidence: "**Mrs. Elizabeth Pool** wife of **Mr. John Pool**, daughter of Governour Brenton Esq. aged 44 years, d Oct. 17 1694," from tombstone, attested by **James Williams**. "**Jane** wife of **Timothy Lyndall** dyed 15 December 1710," from registry of deaths in the town of Boston attested by Samuel Checkley, Town Clerke. Verdict for plaintiff, reversing former judgement.

539. September. **Timothy Whiteing** vintner, and wife **Frances**, of Newport, vs. **William Jones Junr** of Newport, concerning a judgement in May 1731 in an action of trespass. "William Jones was guilty of breach of peace and Frances did break the peace, yet that must be tried in another action brought against her appeal by other evidence that ye head of Frances was cut and blood draw'd from her by Jones who also assaulted said Timothy by takeing him by ye throat in a violent manner . . . ." **Henry Bull** attorney. Earlier judgement reversed.

— 1732 —

540. **Benjamin Stanton** of Newport, yeoman, vs. **Isaac**, a molatto man of Newport, labourer, in custody of sheriff, in action of trespass, for maliciously and wickedly instigating and enticing the plaintiff's servant or slave called **Jupiter** and causing him to run away. Writ dated 20 April 1732. About the last of June Jupiter was in the possession of the plaintiff, who employed him in husbandry labour and other like service for several years before . . . on or about 1 July 1731 Isaac delivered a fictitious certificate purporting Jupiter to be a person free and at liberty . . . on or about 3 July Jupiter absented himself from the service of his master. The certificate enabled him to pass the road among strangers as far as New London in the colony of Connecticut, where he had been apprehended. At New London 13 July 1731 in court before **J. Plumber**, Justice of the Peace, **Tomas alias Tom** a Black man supposed to be a mustee or molatto or negro was brought before the court by **Mr. Daniell Shepley** ferryman at New London . . . supposed a runaway servant . . . confessed he was servant to one **John Bryant** of Newport . . . to be returned. Jupiter was brought in at the same time, and ordered transported back to Newport. Plaintiff sued for damages to cover costs of bringing him back: having notices printed, ferrying, liquor at the ferries, horse hire for **Shelly** and for himself, paying Shelly for his time, paying **Peleg Rogers** for a warrant, etc., and bounty for sd Negroes, £6.

The defendant, called **Isaac Anthony**, a molatto man, was examined in court 16 July 1731, and asked what justification he had of himself for giving passes to Tom and Jupiter, replied "I gave them each one and they gave me a pair of striped satin britches and a Bible for it, which I was very sorry for and I hope God will forgive me and I hope never to be guilty of y[e] like again." Judgement was for the plaintiff, £18:16:2 and costs of court; the defendant appealed, saying that his pleas for abatement should have prevailed, and the court reversed the earlier decision.

541. Deposition of **Paul Richard** of New York, 22 August 1732 at Newport, that **Samuel Sheffield** late of Newport, mariner, told him at New York some time ago that he had sold to his brother **James Sheffield** of Roade Island the part of the land his father **Nathaniel** had bequeathed him in order and on condition to discharge the debt due from his father . . . £500 bond . . . in hands of **Mr. Collens** of Newport.

542. **David Ripley** of Windham, Connecticut, yeoman, vs. **David Ingersoll** of Springfield, Massachusetts, and **Stephen Kellogg** of Westfield, County of Hampshire, province of Massachusetts Bay, in case of trover. Writ dated 29 February 1731[/2]. Appeal at September term from Inferior Court of Common Pleas at Newport in May 1732, when the present appellant, Ripley, had been the defendant. Ingersoll and Kellogg at Gunderwhook in the county of Albany, government of New York, in the month of January 1731 was possessed of a horse which afterwards on or about February 1731 at Springfield they lost . . . about the middle of February it came into the hands and possession of [Ripley] who converted it to his own use. Ripley pleaded not guilty.

Henry Burgother testified at Newport 5 April 1732 before **John Coddington**, Justice, that the horse David Ripley brought down to Newport was the horse in controversy [and] is now in the possession of **David Wyatt** of Newport . . . "the very horse which I sold to said Ingersoll and Kellogg and delivered to them by me at Gunderwhook . . . black stallion with a starr in his forehead and a Brand on ye near thygh . . . ." **Ezra Kingsley** deposed at Windham 27 May 1732 before **John Fitch**, Justice of the peace, that about 8 February last, he was at the house of David Ripley in Windham [and] **David Smith** of Hartford came and enquired of Ripley about the horse, whether he was well of his lameness or no . . . Ripley said better than he was but lame yet . . . Smith said "if he is able to go I would have you take him down to Newport and leave him at Wyatt's stable." **Joshua Wright Junr** testified to the same.

At Inferior Court of Common Pleas 30 May 1732, judgement was for the plaintiffs [Ingersoll and Kellogg], money sued for and costs of court.

Ripley appealed. **Edward Thurston** testified that he had been "desired by Mr. David Ingersoll and Stephen Kellogg who had a writ to go with them in February last past to the house of David Wiatt to see a horse . . . mett him setting by the fire and went to the stable together . . . Ripley signified the horse belonged to Mr. Wyate [and] he only brought him to him . . . but led him to the Dore and then delivered him to **Fortune**, Mr. Wyate's Negro man who led him out of dores. Mr. Ingersoll took the halter and turned him around several times then put the halter in Ripley's hands [and] told me to do my office [*i.e., deliver the writ*]."

Ebenezer Day Jr. of Springfield deposed 29 May 1732 before **Wm Pynchon,** Justice of the Peace, that towards the latter end of January last, he was at the house of **Mr. Benjamin Smith** at a place called Paucatuck in Springfield . . . "when a young lad, sonne of Mr. Thomas Ingersoll of Westfield, brought some horses there for **John Bodurtha** of Springfield (who is since deceased). Bordurtha was then present and had been waiting . . . said to the lad, here is one horse is not mine, a black horse . . . the lad replyed, it is the horse you left at my father's. Bodurtha continued saying it is not mine but it is one of the coach horses belonging to Kellogg and Ingersoll . . . the lad said well if not yours it is mine [and] John Bodurtha took the halter off from another horse and put it on the aforementioned horse and delivered it to the lad who immediately led the black horse away toward Westfield . . . it was about the middle of the day."

David Smith of Harford [*sic*], yeoman, deposed 4 September 1732 before **Job Lawton,** justice of the peace, that he was "employed by **John Anderson** of Windsor to bring down seventeen horses to Newport in and for a market . . . on the way at Windham at the dwelling house of David Ripley one of the horses fell lame . . . horse about 13½ hands or 3 feet high. Ingersoll saw him and asked how I came by him and said it was his horse. I told him John Anderson delivered said horse to me, who said he had all those horses of one **Darby** of Springfield. Ingersoll replied he intended to have bought another black horse to match him which was a horse I had in company . . . also said he beleaved that Darby had bought the lame horse of **Callocke** . . . I left him behind with David Ripley to bring down to Newport and leave with David Wyate to sell with his mate which was another black horse brought down before."

David Wiatt of Newport testified 5 September 1732 before **Jno Coddington Junr,** that some time in January last **David Smith** brought a parcell of horses to his stable for **John Anderson** of Winzer . . . to dispose of for Anderson.

Verdict for the appellant (Ripley), reversion of former judgement, and costs of court.

543. **Thomas Watson** of Newport, mariner, vs. **Mary Harwood** of Newport, widdow, gentlewoman, for £12:09:00 due by book for schooling and learning the defendant's daughters **Mary, Elizabeth, and Judith** to Dance by the plaintiff's wife **Sarah Watson,** beginning the 3rd day of August AD 1730 and ending 3 November 1730 and the rest on former reckoning 7 August 1732.

Eunice Greenman testified at Newport, 17 September 1732, that "**Elizabeth Harwood** came to school to me the 27 of September in the year 1731." **James Gould** testified that **Mary Harwood Jr.** came to school to [Greenman] May ye 31st 1731. **Freelove Stevens** testified that "**Judith Harrard,** daughter of M^{rs}. **Mary Harrard,** came to school to me the 27: day of September AD 1731." **Mary Harwood Junour** on 21 November 1732 stated that "I being bid by my Mother **Mary Harwood** when I went to **Mr. Watsons School,** to bid said **Mrs. Watson** not to Learn my Two Sisters – Elizabeth & Judith Harwood to Dance for Mother would not have them to Dance nor never would pay for their Learning to Dance." **Abigail Pinniger** tetified that, being at M^{rs}. Watson's school in company with Mary Harrod, she heard sd Harrod say that her Mother said she would not pay for her children learning to Dance, and M^{rs}. Watson made Answer that She would Learn them if she never had a Farthing. Verdict was for the plaintiff.

544. **William Almy** of Newport, merchant, vs. **William Heffernan** of Newport, vintner, for £8, claiming that sometime in May 1732 the plaintiff and one **Moses Parnels** of Newport after some Talk [they] had concerning the swiftness of Horses . . . came to an Agreement to run a Race with two Horses at Newport Beach for £8 . . . in a Fortnight from sd Time. Plaintiff was to produce a Small Black Horse of **Capt Godfrey Malbones** & the sd Moses Parnels a large Black Stone-Horse of his own & each to go £8 on the Horse produced . . . lodged in Hands of sd William Heffernan the defendant £8 each in Bills of Public Credit which was to be delivered to the Person whose Horse produced was the swiftest in the Race. Now the plaintiff saith that he produced the Horse pitched upon & had him ready at all consonent Times during said Fortnight & after & was ready & willing that a fair trial should be made at sd Newport Beach . . . But the sd Moses Parnels was fearful & declined the leting his Horse run after he perceived the swiftness of the Horse produced by the plaintiff . . . therefore the money ought to be returned. Writ dated 26 July 1732. Verdict for defendant. (Docket No. 136)

545. Appeal of **Henry Sweeting Jr.** of Providence, mariner, vs. **Robert Barker** of Newport, merchant, for detaining one foarth part of a barill of Sparmacitey belonging to the plaintiff, who stated that he was taken in a sloop belonging to Barker on a whale fishing voyage . . . sd sloop went on Shares of what was taken in the voyage & y[t] he bought sd sparmacitey of **Eleazer Hamblin.** Writ dated July 27. Earlier judgment had been for Barker.

546. **George Webb** of the City of Perth Amboy in the Province of East New Jersey, mariner, vs. **John Jackson** of Newport, labourer, Free Negro, for £11:13:10 due by note dated 15 December 1729 and signed by the defendant. (Docket No. 28)

547. **John Jeffrey** of Groton in y[e] County of New London, Colony of Connecticut, shipwright, vs. **John MacDaniel alias John Erwin** now resident in Newport, mariner alias ship carpenter, for £22 due for goods sold and delivered. Defendant answered that the plaintiff didn't specify when. (Docket No. 43)

548. **Thomas Staples** of Newport, bricklayer, vs. **Caleb Coggeshall**, house carpenter, **James Langworthy**, joyner, **Benjamin Wyatt**, house carpenter, **Reuben Peckham**, joyner, and **Hopestill Potter**, carter, all of Newport, for non-performance . . . whereas [they] purchased of the plaintiff several Lottery Tickets of a Lottery settep by the plaintiff in Newport [and it was] drawn according to the usuall way of Lotteryes at sd Newport the 7th day of September AD 1732, in Drawing of which a small house in Newport, valued at £91 fell to the rightfull owner . . . number 64. [They] came to the plaintiff's house 9 September and did aver that they were owners of the sd tickett number 64 and therefore requested the plaintiff to make them a Deed of Sale . . . they claimed to have misplaced the ticket . . . they were not the rightful owners. **Gershom Keyes** of Boston, having taken out several tickets for himself and partners, laid claim and produced the ticket to the plaintiff. [*At this point the defendants fell back on moral arguments about lotteries: "get money no ways laudable . . ."*]

Gershom Keyes deposed at Boston 16 October 1732. **Samuel Wickham** of Newport made a deposition 7 November 1732 and said that he was at the house of **Thomas Staples** in Newport on 9 September, and sd men came to see what fortune they may have had in the Lottery. "I took the book up and bid them read over numbers of their Tickets and amongst other numbers which they read over they read number 64 ... I told them that number draw'd the small house valued at £91 ... gave it into Staples's hands and I think he wrote something upon it and returned it into one of their hands ... told they must keep it untill the deed was made and be sure they did not lose it ... aye to be sure or words to that purpose." Verdict for the defendants. (Docket No. 61)

549. **Robert Little** Junr of Newport, mariner, vs. **Jacob Long** of Newport, mariner, for £20 due by book for his Passage from London to Newport in the year 1730 ... on board the ship *Greyhound* whereof the sd Robert Little was master. Verdict for defendant. (Docket No. 71)

550. **Edward Pelham** of Newport, gentleman, vs. **Peter Coggeshall**, yeoman, **Eleazer Arnold**, blacksmith, **William Lassells**, barber, **Caleb Arnold**, tailer, **James England**, black-smith and **Christian Clarke**, widow, all of Newport, in an action of trespass. Writ dated 13 September 1732; **D. Updike** attorney. The property sued for was a piece of land with five shops thereon standing, in Newport, in Width about Eighty Feet and in Depth about 110 feet ... bounded northerly upon land of the plaintiff, easterly upon Thames Street, southerly upon land of the plaintiff, and westerly upon the salt water or harbour of Newport ... of which land **Benedict Arnold** late of said Newport, Esqr on or about 20 June 1678 died seised in fee, and by his will dated 24 December 1677 bequeathed to his daughter **Freelove Arnold** (mother to the plaintiff) and to her heirs and assigns for ever by the name of the Lesser Parcel of Land in Newport ... Freelove without alienating or disposing thereof on or about the 18th day of April 1682 intermarried with Capt. **Edward Pelham** late of Newport Gentleman deceased Father to the Plaintiff, and continued so seised under Covert until the 8th of September 1711 when [she] died seised of the premises sued for ... Whereupon the said Capt. Edward Pelham as Tennant by the Courtesie of England possessed and enjoyed the land from 8 September 1711 until 20 September 1730 which was during his natural life, and when [he] died the premises descended to the plaintiff who is the Eldest Son and Heir of the said Freelove as an Estate in Fee Simple. Plaintiff claims damages of £4000.

The defendants by their attorney **Henry Bull** made answer to the declaration and complaint of **Edward Pelham** of Newport, yeoman, plaintiff, called in his declaration gentleman . . . that the plaintiff calls himself gentleman whereas the Law looks upon noe man to such unless he hath it by birth, office, or education, which the Plaintiff has not. Verdict for defendants. (Docket No. 82)

551. **Edward Pelham** of Newport, Gentleman, vs. **Peter Coggeshall** of Newport, yeoman, in an action of trespass. Writ dated 16 October 1732; **Daniel Updike** attorney. The property sued for was two lots or parcels of land in Newport, one of which contains about 3 acres of pasture land and garden land called by the name of the Lower-Field, the other lot contains about 8 acres of meadow land with an old Stone-Windmill thereon standing and being and known by the name of the Mill-Field. The Lower-Field is bounded northerly partly upon a High-Way or Lane commonly called **Caleb Carrs** Lane, partly upon a small Inclosure or Garden in ye Improvement of **Richard Ward** Esqr, partly upon a yard and garden in the possession of the plantiff, and partly upon a house lott or yard and garden in the possession of **James Allen**, easterly upon a Street or High Way leading into the Neck, Southerly upon Land and Buildings in the possession of the defendant and westerly partly upon Thames Street, partly upon said house lott or yard and garden in the possession of James Allen, partly upon two gardens in the possession of the plaintiff, one to the southward and the other to the eastward of the plaintiff's dwelling house, and partly upon the East end of said Inclosure or garden in the possession of Richard Ward. The Mill-Field is bounded northerly partly upon Caleb Carrs Lane, partly upon a Work-House standing in said lane and partly upon a Burying Place to the northward whereof stands a Meeting House, Easterly upon land in the possession of **Josias Coggeshall** and **Jacob Barney**, southerly partly upon land in the possession of **Jonathan Bennett** and partly upon land in the possession of the defendant and partly upon the street or highway leading into the Neck. The lots in question had belonged to Benedict Arnold who devised them by will to his daughter Freelove [*see case 550 above*]. At the time of devising the two parcels were contained in one piece but since separated into two by a highway running through them. Plaintiff claims £10,000 damages.

552. **James Franklin** of Newport, printer, vs. **John Walton** of Providence, gentleman, for £39:3:0 due for Printing & Paper found [*i.e., provided*] all

in the year 1731. Writ dated 23 October 1732. Bill includes printing 7 sheets of [Walton's] remarks and stitching 450 @ 18. pr 100, 9 reams of paper @ 28/ pr ream. (Docket No. 90)

553. **John Harrys** of Newport, chirurgion, vs. **John Wells** and **Benjamin Wells** of North Kingstown, yeomen, executors of the will of **John Wells** late of North Kingstown, yeoman, deceased, for £40 for attending on sd John Wells in sickness and lameness of a mortification in his foot and for medicines administered to him in the months of May, June and July AD 1732. Defendant asked for an abatement because Benjamin Wells was never executor. Verdict for defendant. (Docket No. 106)

– 1733 –

554. **Orders to be Observed by the Watch set by the Cunstables** [*sic*] **in the Town of Newport**:

1. that they appear at the Watch house and begin the Watch at Nine a Clock at Night.

2ly that Two of the persons watching walk through the Streets of the Town and that the Other two Continue in the Watch house til those Return who have first Taken their Rounds, and then those who have been the Rounds to Continue at the Watch house and the Other two to take their Rounds through the Streets of the Town.

3ly that where they See lights in houses after Reasonable bed time to Call on them to take Care of their Lights & to Continue to watch till brode day light.

4ly To take up all Negros, Servants & Disorderly persons and Inform the Authority or Commit them to Gaol as the Circumstances may Require.

Signed by Order of Council August 6th 1733 **Wm Coddington** C[lerk]

555. **Joseph Wilson Junr** of Newport, tayler, vs. **John White** of Newport, tayler, in an action of trespass. Writ dated 29 December 1732. About 27 December 1732 the defendant made an assault on the body of the plaintiff and his "right ear did then and there maliciously bite off and other enormities did do . . . ;" request £200 damages. Depositions were made 20 January 1732/3 by **Joseph Wilson Junr**, with notation "not to go in case," stating that he "in company with severall . . . namely **John White, Joseph Sabins,** and **James Miller** . . . agrees to go into the fields to fight and we also desire tha **Joseph Sabins** woud go with us and se fair play and we engaged each other and in striving the said John White having an opportunity with his teeth laid fast hold of one of my Ears being the Right Ear and took a piece clean off . . . ." **Joseph Sabin** of Newport, cordwainer, testified that "in striving they were up and down several tims and the third time they fell with their heads close together having hold of each other . . . I heard Joseph Wilson call out and said the said John White bit his ear upon what I steps unto the sd Joseph Wilson and saw that his right ear bled very freely and they two fought after that some time . . . ." **James Miller** also testified. Bill from **John Harriss** of Newport, Chirurgeon, "to curing a

large wound in his ear which was occasioned by a Bite with loss of substance, £1:10:0. Verdict at the Inferior Court of Common Pleas in May 1733 for the plaintiff was later reversed, it being judged that the two "went out to fight by consent . . . wound [was] magnified to the jury."

556. **Joseph Jennings** of Brookfield in county of Worcester, province of Massachusetts Bay, yeoman, vs. **Richard Jerson**, labourer, **Aaron Sutton**, mariner, and **Richard Chapman**, mariner, and **Nicholas Otes**, tayler, all of Newport, in custody of sheriff, for trespass. Writ dated 1 March 1732/3. Premises sued for were two certain dwelling houses and one lot of land in Newport whereon they stood, about 50 feet north to south and 40 feet east to west, with a yard, bounded northerly on the street, easterly partly on land of **John Cook** and partly on land of **Nathaniel Newdigate**, southerly on land of **David Pinder**, westerly on the street leading from Kings Street to a Brook running on the backside of the Prison yard . . . of which **Gabriel Jennings** late of Newport, husbandman, was in his lifetime seized on or about the month of June 1715 when he died intestate. The property descended to the plaintiff as nearest of blood surviving, he being the eldest son of **Stephen Jennings** who died on or about 7 February 1710 who was the eldest son of the said Gabriel Jennings that had issue surviving at the time of the death of said Gabriel. The defendants claimed that they and those they hold under had been in quiet and peaceable possession upwards of 20 years.

Capt. Richard Dun of Newport, yeoman, aged about 70 years, deposed on 28 May 1733 and said that about 28 years ago and upwards he was well acquainted with Gabriel Jennings of Newport, labourer, who then went to sea along with **Capt. Halsey** a Privateering and never was heard of since. **Mary Bun**, wife of **Nathaniel Bun** of Newport, aged about 65, said much the same thing. Capt. Richard Dun in a second deposition in court said that he knew one **Thomas Jennings Jr.** of Portsmouth, son of Thomas Jennings and brother to Gabriel Jennings of Newport the eldest brother of Gabriel Jennings and son of sd Thomas Jennings Sr., deceased upwards of 50 years ago. **Daniel Pearce** of Prudence Island in the township of Portsmouth, aged about 66, deposed and said that he knew Thomas Jennings Jr. of Portsmouth, son of Thomas Gennings [*sic*] of Portsmouth, his eldest son and brother of Gabriel Gennings.

Deeds shown: **John Bayley** of Newport, yeoman, for £52:09:00 paid by Gabriel Jennings of Newport, husbandman, sold to him one house and town lot in Newport, on 6 May 1704, bounded easterly by a house and lot in possession of **Deborah Sabear**, southerly by the house and lot of **Benjamin Newberry**, westerly by a lane or street, and northerly by the way or lane next the brook which runs below the prison. John Bayley and his wife **Sutton Bayley** both signed by marks. Witnesses were **John Rogers** and **Thomas Fox** to John's signature, and **Samuel Down** and **Joseph Weatherhead** to Sutton's. Sutton did not acknowledge until 20 June 1704, and the deed was recorded that day in Newport Land Evidence 5:145-6.

Adam Mott of Newport, blacksmith, and wife **Sarah** on 27 February 1716/17 for £10 quitclaimed to **William Blades** of Newport, cordwainer, their right in a lot of 40 feet square with buildings and improvements in Newport, bounded east on **Daniel Sabeere's** land, south on the **widow Vaughan**'s land, north and west on streets or highways, it being formerly the estate of Gabriel Jennings deceased Unkle to said Sarah Mott late **Sarah Gennings** the daughter of Thomas Gennings and heirs at law to sd Gabriel. Both signed by marks. Witnesses were **Leonard Cozzens** and **Charles Bardin**. The deed was acknowledged 28 February and recorded 1 March 1716/17 in Newport Land Evidence 5:334-335. **William Blades** of Newport, cordwainer, on the same day sold the land and house to Leonard Cozzens of Newport, tayler, witnessed by **Charles Lowther** and **Charles Bardin**; acknowledged same and recorded 2 March 1716/17 in Newport Land Evidence 5:338-339. Cozzens mortgaged the property to **John Tayler** of Newport, yeoman, 7 March 1716/17 for £60, describing it as a lot 40 feet square, etc., witnessed by **Frankland Morton** and **John Hammet**; recorded Land Evidence 6:20. Tayler quitclaimed it back to Cozzens on 31 December 1723, witnessed by **Job Lawton** and **Samuel Rodman**. **Leonard Cozzens** sold it 16 January 1723/4 to **Richard Jerson** of Newport, carter, for £66; at that time it was bounded easterly on Daniel Sabeere and **Samuel Mott**, and south on **Daniel Pinder**. Witnesses were **John Holmes** and **Samuel Rodman**. **Margaret Cozzens**, wife of Leonard, also signed, witnessed by **Job Lawton** and **Joseph Fry**. She acknowledged 27 April 1724 and the deed was recorded 8 May in Newport Land Evidence 7:56-57.

The defendants argued that the statute of limitations passed ten years ago under Queen Ann should apply, and that action should be barred, which the court ruled, with the defendants to receive costs. The plaintiff appealed to the Superior Court.

557. **George Lawton** of Portsmouth, Esq., vs. **Jacob Anthony** of Portsmouth, glasier alias yeoman, for £224 due by note dated 9 November 1730 witnessed by **William** and **Mary Sandford.** Writ dated 3 April 1733. Decision for plaintiff; defendant appealed.

558. May: **Benoni Gardner** of Newport, mariner, vs. **Edward Boss** of Newport, merchant, to render an account for time [when] he was receiver of money of the plaintiff at Warwick in April 1733. Plaintiff had procured a Lottery Ticket to be drawn by **John Dickinson** at Warwick . . . No. 448 whereon was written the name of Benoni Gardner; on or about 26 April 1733 lot was drawn and 448 fairly and regularly drew a prize of £50 which the defendant received. **John Case** of South Kingstown deposed on 14 May 1733 that he had been with Capt. Edward Boss after some time, being in the house of Capt. **William Havens** of North Kingstown . . . he took out three tickets. Capt. **John Dickinson** of Warwick deposed that he had a few tickets left so let Boss have a number of tickets for said Gardner - Boss had only one that drew above 55 shillings. **Ebenezer Richardson** of Newport deposed 14 May 1733 that he heard Capt. Boss say that Gardner had drawn £50 prize. **Henry Sabin** of Newport, gunsmith, deposed . . . had been at Warwick . . . Verdict for defendant, costs. (Docket No. 10)

559. September: **Joseph Whipple** of Newport, merchant, executor of the will of **James Green** late of Newport, millwright, deceased, appealed a judgement given May 1733 at Inferior Court of Common Pleas in favor of **Benjamin Church** of Newport, gentleman, when **James Green** had commenced action for money due by book.

560. **Robert Robinson** of Newport Esq. vs. **Benjamin Church** of Newport, merchant, in action of covenant; writ dated 17 October 1733. Church had leased to the plaintiff on 30 May 1730 for a term of three years a messuage and tenement with dwelling house, yard, garden, and outhouse thereunto belonging and all shops, cellars, rooms, etc., and commodities and appurtenances belonging in Newport, at £35 per year payable quarterly. Yet, the defendant let to one **Thomas Davis** of Newport, mariner, the westerly part of the front cellar; plaintiff seeks damages of £60. The property was in a Street called Thames Street,

bounded west by the Main Street, north by land of Mr **Augustus Lucas**, east by land of **Jahleel Brenton**, Esq., and south on a house belonging to the Rev. Mr. **James Honyman. Martha Osborn** and **Matthew Robinson** witnessed the indenture of lease.

Kathrine [*signed* **Catherine**] **Davis** wife of **Thomas Davis**, mariner, deposed at Newport 9 March 1733 and said that she "hired a house of **Mr. Benjamin Church** standing in the fore street . . . to give the sd Church £18 per annum and for want of room Mr Church gave me a peice of the cellar for pertitioning it . . . Mr Church letting the house to Mr Roberson forgot to mention the cellar and when Mr Church came to give Mr Roberson possession of house and cellars Mr Roberson refusing me the cellar Mr Church told him that he hoped he whould not take it from me because he forgot to mention it . . . Mr Roberson answered I have cellar room enough and if the woman will run a pertition betwixt hers making a sufficient door for a hogshead to go in she shall possess the cellar which accordingly I did."

Wm Wanton Jr deposed, saying he very well knew of Mr. Robinson coming to live where Mr Benjamin Church now lives and that Thomas Davis made use of part of the cellar . . . all the time sd Robinson lived in the house . . . carring in molasses, limes, butter, pork, and sundry other things and bringing them out again.

Matthew Robinson of Newport testified in court that at the later end of May or beginning of June 1730 he went with his father **Mr Robinson**, and Mr **Benjamin Church** to the house; he described the situation and said that **Mrs Davis** was "very much inrag'd against Mr Church for letting said cellar to the said Mr Robinson . . . that she had partitioned it for her own use, with much more that she passionately spoke."

Bill from Robinson to Church, 1732, included "advice about title of your wife's estate, £1; cash pd you at your own house by my son; my son's journey to Bristoll Connecticut to transact for you against **Mr Bannister**; cash paid **Mr Peck** at Bristol for my son's horsekeeping when there about your business," totaling £13:09:10. Counter bill from defendant for a year's rent, £35, and 2 months from March to May, £5:16:06.

Verdict: for plaintiff, £16 and costs of court.

561. **Thomas Borden** of Portsmouth, yeoman, vs. **George Cornel**, Jr. of Portsmouth, husbandman, in an action of trespass. Writ dated 20 Sep-

tember 1733. Plaintiff charged that the defendant on or about 18 September 1733 into the close of the plaintiff entered and did pull up and throw down sixteen rod and a half of stone wall and post and rail fence to the plaintiff belonging; damages of £100 claimed. List of Roads Ways and Lands in Portsmouth, etc., in file. **Thomas Hicks** of Portsmouth, aged 57 years and upwards [*in November 1733*], testified that he had seen a list of the highways in Portsmouth dated 10 June 1717 . . . [it contained] several great mistakes. Depositions were made 19 November 1733 by **George Lawton**, who said he was one of the committee to lay out the roads; **Nathl Hall**, yeoman, who said he was commanded to assist George Cornell in pulling down the stone wall; **John Wing**, who said he saw the above event; **Roger Burrington**, yeoman, who swore to the truth of the above and mentioned a £6 cost for repairing the fence and the fence standing so near where the Old Virginia Fence stood. **William Anthony**, 56 years and up, and **Abial Tripp** also made depositions. The file contains a complaint made in September 1732 by **William Anthony Jr.** of Portsmouth that **Morgan Jones** of Bristol, ditcher "is this present day Committing of a Nuisance by digging of a ditch in the highway between two pieces of land now in the Improvement of **Thomas Borden** which highway leadeth from the east end of a Stonny Lane towards William Anthonys now dwelling house."

562. **Solomon Hews** of Wrentham in Co. Suffolk, Province of Massachusetts Bay, vs. **Robert Currie** of Providence, glazier, charging deceit. Defendant had published a scheme for a lottery to be drawn at Providence on 1st of March 1732 provided the tickets were all sold and did leave tickets in divers places to be sold for the use of the sd Robert Currie dated 14 December 1732 . . . plaintiff did purchase nine tickets at the prise of £4 each. The lottery had not been drawn and Currie refused to refund Hews' money. Writ dated 7 December 1733.

In file: "A Scheme for a Lottery of 3000 £ set up by Robert Currie of the Town and County of Providence to be drawn . . . the first of March next provided the tickets are all sold there being 750 tickets in all whereof there will be 150 prizes. . . . " Prizes consisted of: a lot of land in the center of the town of Glocester on the country road leading to Killingly, 197 acres, well watered &c.; a lot in Smithfield at Wansoket Hill, adjoining land of **Woodward Arnold** and **John Comstock**, 120 acres; a lot in Glocester with the Killingly Road going through it with a

A plat of Providence Neck made in 1736 by James Olney and Joseph Brown. It is not directly relevant to No. 562, but shows land owned by Robert Currie.

very good stream running through "where nature hath furnished a place at the falls called Pascogue wherein two days time one man may make a dam suitable for any sort of mill, 98 acres"; a small sloop burthen about 20 tons, 2 years old, with good cables, anchors, sails, and rigging, and other appurtenances fit to go to sea; a lot in Scituate "near to a place called George's Brook, exceeding well wooded and watered, containing 80 acres with a very good brook in the same"; a convenient dwelling house and lot, with a good cellar, in Providence near the dwelling house of **Robert Currie**, fronting the country road that leads to Boston, having three convenient rooms on a floor besides a good chamber; a lot of good wood land in Glocester, 70 acres adjoing the road to Killingly; a lot near the town of Providence, 5 3/4 acres with 800 good cedar and chestnut rails which partly fence the same; half a right of all the undivided lands on the west side of the 7 mile line in the propriety of Providence; and a town lot containing 55 feet fronting the main street and so back towards toward the mill dam or highway opposite the house of **Thomas Olney**, Esq. All the prizes amounting to £1620 were valued and apprized by Col. **Daniel Abbott** and **Capt. John Whipple** of Providence and **Elisha Knowlton** Esq. of Glocester, "all gentlemen of approved judgment and known integrity." Tickets at £4 each may be had of Robert Currie in Providence, Mr. **Daniel Jencks** and Mr. **Benjamin Paine** in Smithfield, **Elisha Knowlton** Esq. in Glocester, **Stephen Hopkins** Esq. in Scituate, and Mr. **Daniel Go[sse?]** of Boston. Four tickets in file, bearing date 14 December 1732. Verdict for plaintiff, £36 and costs.

563. **Content Bull** of Newport, widow and executrix of the will of **Benjamin Bull** late of sd Newport, gentleman, deceased vs. **Daniel Sabeere** of Newport, brewer, for £30 due by note dated 29 August 1726 to Benjamin Bull and damages of £60. Writ 18 May 1730, Inferior Court of Common Pleas at South Kingstown. Defendant answered that the action was "purely vexatious," and that since both parties were settled inhabitants of the town and county of Newport, the action ought to have been brought there. Verdict for plaintiff; appealed.

564. **Elizabeth Borden** of Newport, widow, executrix of the will of **Joseph Borden** late of Newport, Esq., deceased vs. **Shubael Goreham** of Barnstable in the Province of Massachusetts Bay, yeoman, for £490:14:0 due for one Negro boy sold and delivered by Joseph Borden and cash advanced to the defendant in June 1725. Heard at Inferior Court of Common Pleas in November 1733. Bill dated 1725 to **John Davis** and Shuball Goreham: To John Davis a Negro Boy of Jn° Borden, £65 . . . pd Cooper for packing the fish at 2/6 barrel . . . salt at 4/ bushel. To **Joseph Atwood** cooper for hoops, 10s, to **Edward Thurston**, cooper for hoops, 4/ . . . Credit: 300 lb. herrings at 30/ per barrell. The file includes a deposition by **John Gardner** of Newport, cooper, taken at Newport 9 October 1727, his father **Joseph Gardner** then being present, that he was employed in January 1725/6 to pack herring with Mr. **Mark Maylem** and Joseph Atwood, coopers . . . herring was not merchantable or fit for shipping . . . wanting salt being foul and nasty and not being stowed in cask according to custom. **Edward Thurston** of Newport, cooper, testified that he was employed by Capt. John Borden and Mr. Godfrey Malbone to pack some herring which he understood were brought from the Cape . . . fish very foul having sand and seaweed mixt with them and the barrells not full. [*The file contains numerous other documents not abstracted here.*]

565. **Henry Hooper** of Newport, practitioner in physick and surgery vs. **Thomas Green** of Newport, glazier, for trespass, for heavily loading and swiftly harmfully and inordinately driving and ill using a horse and calash belonging to the plaintiff, whereby the horse died. On or about 15 May 1733 at Newport he had delivered to the defendant a horse and calash of his to ride with himself and his wife from Newport to the house of **Thomas Borden** in Portsmouth . . . Writ dated 26 October 1733.

Job Bissell of Newport, blacksmith, deposed and said that he had been "desired by Doctor Hooper to go and see his horse that was very bad . . . when we came there he was dead." **Jere Exsenior** of Newport testified that "I . . . was agoing to the Burying Place and **Martin Howards** wife calls to me and askt me what aled the horse which was then lying on the ground I told her I believed he could not continue long . . . some little time after the horse died and I help **John Platts** to set sd horse up to skin him." **James England** of Newport, blacksmith, deposed on 14 9ber 1733 that he had "viewed the horse and found his kidneys very much swelled and caul melted . . . judge that sd horse died by having his greese melted." **John Platts** of Newport, butcher, stated that Dr. Hooper had come for him to skin the horse, etc. **Ann Howard**, wife of **Martin Howard**, stated that Dr. Hooper had "put his horse to pasture in the Burying Place the beginning of May 1733 at which time it was fat and brisk till on or about the 15th of sd month some of our people went out into the field and comes and acquaintes me that Dr. Hooper's horse was adying upon which I goes out to the sd horse and found him very bad and instantly sends for Doctor Hooper and he and **Major Brown** came up and the Doctor blead him in the mouth and the next moring he died and was opened by John Platt and some others and I apprehended by their discourse amongst them that the sd horse's caul was melted by hard riding." **Perkins Chase** "of the age of fifteen or sixteen years" deposed on 19 November 1733 that he had been hired by Thomas Green to drive the chaise to Bristol Ferry "and when we came there they had no oats and we gave the horse one quart of Indian corn and one of barley and the horse seemed to be very brisk when I came from the ferry and came home very well and it was only **Thomas Green** and his wife and a little child and my self that went to the Ferry and I came home alone." **Jonathan Chase** of lawful age testified on 26 March 1734 that his son Perkins went with Mr **Thomas Green** to Bristol Ferry with Dr. Hooper's horse and shay and "at his return he came to his door with sd horse and shay which he saw and to the best of his judgment the horse seemed to be as well as a horse could be."

At Inferior Court of Common Pleas 20 November 1733; verdict for plaintiff, £15 and costs. Defendant appealed; verdict reversed.

566. **Christopher Champlin** of Westerly, gentleman, vs. **Betty Thompson** (Indian woman) of Westerly, spinster, at Inferior Court of Common Pleas at South Kingstown in June 1733, for debt due by book for goods sold and delivered beginning in 1727 and ending in November 1730. Bill presented: "Betty Peter otherways called Betty Tomson, boards and nails for a coffin (19 September 1727); rum; sundrys taken from Chalk Schore; plowing a day; shirts, jackit . . . " A counter claim credited Betty with work, £16:7:0. Betty presented a copy of bill showing more credit than the debt demanded, and action was barred; plaintiff appealed.

567. **David Cheesbrough** of Newport, merchant vs. **William Coffin** of Boston in Co. Suffolk, Province of Massachusetts Bay, distiller, for non-fulfillment of promise, appealing verdict given in court at Boston for the defendant. On or about October 1731 the plaintiff committed

to the care and custody of the defendant's wife at the defendant's house in Boston a large sum of money out of which was missing and lost the sum of £100; defendant had promised to make satisfaction. Writ dated 23 June 1733; heard in court in Boston, November 1733, with verdict for defendant on grounds that plaintiff could not prove the loss.

New evidence: **Thomas Chesebrough** of Stoningtown in Connecticut Colony deposed there on 24 September 1733 that he had been at the house of **David Chesebrough** in Newport 10 September 1731 in company with William Coffin of Boston, innholder . . . also present were the wife of sd Chesebrough and Mary Chesebrough . . . sd Chesebrough told him that when he was in Boston at the beginning of September he delivered to sd Coffin's wife [**Ann**] six bundles of money containing £900 and the next day he received from her but five bundles containing £800 . . . **Mary Chesebrough** deposed at Stonington the same day to the same effect. **Benjamin Norton** of Newport deposed there 23 November 1733, and **Joseph Wanton** of Newport on 24 November 1733. Verdict for plaintiff, money sued for and costs.

568. **Henry Whitton** of Boston, wine cooper, vs. **Hugh Beatty** of Providence, vintner, to recover £40 due for one pipe of madeira wine sold by the plaintiff and delivered to the defendant by **James Franklin** of Newport in July 1731. Defendant answered that he was no vintner, never was more than an innholder. **David Jackson**, late servant to Mr. James Franklin of Newport, bookbinder, testified on 4 April 1733 at Newport that on or about April 1731 he saw a pipe of madeira wine hauled out of Mr. Franklin's cellar under the school house and delivered by sd Franklin to **Mr Mitchell**, boatman of Providence for Mr. Hugh Beatty . . . all the wine in the cellar belonged to Mr Henry Whitton. **William Thompson** of Brantry in Co. Suffolk, cardmaker, deposed at Boston 1 May 1733 that he was at the dwelling house of **Henry Beatty** in the latter end of June 1732, when and where Mr. Hugh Beatty was settling accounts . . . had some disputes . . . Whitton said there were two pipes of wine delivered, Beatty said one but then owned there was one in April and that he had paid for it. Note in file signed by **Margaret Beatty** of Providence, dated 8 July 1731 to Mr. Whitton: "I shld be glad to have the oppertunity to see you & I have some money for you I'm so tired Sr that I'm not able to come & see you Sr I hope you will pardon my boldness in this yet I want to know

where & when to see you - This is all from your friend." Receipt signed, same day, by **John Caswall** for "£20 from M[rs]. Beatty for use of Henry Whitton." **Robert Currie** of Providence testified 29 May 1733 at Newport that in June 1732 he had made up accounts for Whitton and Beatty, referring to a pipe of wine which Mr. Whitton had from Mr. Franklin the printer at Newport. Verdict for defendant; appealed. **James Mitchell** [*signed Micthall*] of Providence testified at Newport that he very well remembered receiving the pipe of wine from James Franklin in the summer season in the year 1731 . . . "do not remember that ever I carried any other type of wine for the said Betey before or sence . . . " Judgment confirmed.

569. **Giles Goddard** of Groton, Co. New London, Connecticut, vs. **William King** of Westerly, labourer, otherwise a transient person, for debt of £14:04:00. Appeal from a judgement at New London 28 November 1732 for the defendant. At Newport 3 December 1733 William King of Westerly, yeoman, petitioned, on grounds that his attorney had not presented his case; granted.

570. **Henry Laughton** of Boston, administrator of the goods and chattles of **Adam Tuck**, late of Boston, farrier, deceased, vs. **John Forrister** of Newport, glasier, to recover a debt of £20 which Tuck had lent Forrister 9 September 1729 at Newport. (Appeal from judgement of Inferior Court of Common Pleas May 1730.)

571. **John Clark** of Newport, mason, vs. **Joseph Tillinghast** of Newport, shopkeeper, for non-fulfillment of promise. (Appeal from judgement of Inferior Court of Common Pleas May 1733.) One **Bethia Hedges** of Newport, widow, on 18 January 1732/3 had set forth a lottery consisting of lands, several sorts of goods, and bills of publick credit, to the amount of £1002, including a lot at Palmers River. The plaintiff became an adventurer in the lottery, and bought ticket no. 597, which fortunately and fairly drew a prize of the fourteen acre lot at Palmers River, which the defendant failed to convey [to him].

Note signed by Joseph Tillinghast: "The House that Bethia Hedges now lives in at the Point is made over to me for a certain sum . . . 28 February 1732/2 . . . house now set forth in the lottery . . . also a lot of land in Palmers River . . . ."

Copy of the Lottery terms, dated at Newport 18 January 1732/3: Tickets from 1 to 1002 @ 20s per ticket. Prizes: 334. Blanks, 668.

1. House and lot at Eastons Point, 50 ft. in front, 100 ft. deep; house is 20 ft. in front, 16 ft. wide, two story with an additional room 14 ft. one way, 3 fireplaces, valued at £235.
2. Fourteen acres on east side of Palmer River in Rehoboth near land of **Mr. James Lewis** and **Mr. Jonathan Kingsley**, good for planting, sowing, mowing, and pasturing, most already improved.
3. Lot No. 90 in Second Division [*? Eastons Point*], 108 by 100 ft.
4. Lot No. 74, ditto, 65 by 100 ft.
5. Shop of 10 ft. square on **Mr. Pelhams** land near **Mr. Davis**, fronting the main street with good chimney and oven, valued at £32.
6. Very good new desk valued at £9.

2 prizes of £5, 6 of £4, 2 of £3, 38 of 40 shillings, 280 of 30 shillings.

Prizes may be seen three days before the drawing . . . those who think they are overvalued may receive their Money advanced on return of the tickets. Drawing on 25 March next. Tickets may be delivered by **Mr. Edward Thurber** of Rehoboth, **Mr. Nathaniel Blackwel** of Dartmouth, and the said Hedges in Newport.

Deed, Bethiah Hedges of Newport, wife of John Hedges late of Newport, housecarpenter, to **Joseph Tillinghast** of Newport, merchant, for 14 acres in Rehoboth [*see Item 656*]. Mortgage deed from **Benjamin Hagger** of Newport, tanner, for £218 to **Henry Sabin** of Newport, gunsmith, dated 9 February 1731, for two adjoining lots, nos. 69 and 85, in the Second Division in Easton's Point, 50 ft. in front or breadth, 200 ft. in back or in length, bounded west on a street, north on the 70th and 86th lots, east on the street, south on the 84th lot, with houses. **Susannah Hagger** also signed; witnesses were **Henry Hooper** and **Josias Lyndon**. Recorded Newport Land Evidence 8:560-562 on 26 March 1732.

Deed, 4 September 1733, **Joseph Tillinghast** and wife **Mary** for £100 paid by Joseph Clark of Newport, deeded the property in controversy, witnessed by **Peter Bours** and **Henry Bull**.

572. **Thomas Staples** of Newport, bricklayer, vs. **Benedict Arnold** of Newport, merchant, for £2:19:7 for soap sold and work done by the plaintiff for the defendant in 1728. Writ dated 7 May 1733. Counter claim included ashes, turneps, etc. **Elizabeth Hewit** of Newport, spinster, deposed 4 August 1733 before **Job Lawton**, Justice of the peace, signing by mark, that she had lived in Benedict Arnold's house in Newport some years ago and knew he had a barrel of soft soap of Thomas Staples which "proved to be very stinking . . . don't know if all used or what became of it . . . not fit for use." **Hannah Curtis** of Newport, signing by her initials, deposed the same day that she "whent into Mr. Benedict Arnold's house . . . smelt a stinking smell . . . told was a barrell of soape that lay in a dish which looked like lime and watter . . . as to say it was sope I canot call it so . . . so exstordenary bad . . . heard M^{rs}. Arnold say they never had no sope of sd Staples besides that barell . . . nor never desired to have another such." Case heard at Inferior Court of Common Pleas at Newport 29 May 1733; defendant defaulted; continued to Superior Court in September.

573. **Samuel Holmes** of Newport, merchant, vs. **Roger Elderton** of Westerly, yeoman, in custody of the sheriff, for £90:5:1 due for goods sold and delivered from June 1723 to September 1727. Writ dated 15 October 1733. Bill includes plush britches, cordage, twine, powder, **Ephraim Hicks** pr order, salt, drink, red oak staves, white oak staves. Note to "Cousen **Martin** & frind **Lindon**" from **John Richmond** at Westerly 24 June 1734, concerning delivery of planks bought by Samuel Holmes; writer agreed with Roger Elderton to "Bott [?boat] them down to the Island." Decision for plaintiff; appealed.

574. **John Mumford Jr.** of North Kingstown, yeoman, vs. **John Morse** of North Kingstown, yeoman, for £9:8:9 due for planks in May 1730. Writ dated 7 December 1733. Countersuit by the defendant against the plaintiff entered. **Thomas Rathbone** and **Richard Robins** both of North Kingstown, yeomen, testified 20 March 1733 before **George Hazard**, J.P., that they saw Morse deliver to Mumford 63 parcels of oak planks, some an inch and a quarter, some better and some but little more than an inch thick, and Mumford desired Morse to measure them but he replied he had no ruler . . . desired Mumford to carry them home and measure them himself . . . heard Morse say he had sold them for 6*s*. per hundred; the deponents assisted Mumford both in carting them home and also in working of them up in a mill dam . . . Mumford hath lived near them about 5 years. **William Enos** of South Kingstown deposed there 25 March 1733 before Rowse Helme, Assistant, and said that "3 years agoe he lived in East Greenwich and tended a saw mill belonging to John Morse of Greenwich and I then sawed in sd mill 2250 feet of oake plank an Inch and a halfe thick for the sd John Morse to use . . . were for John Mumford and in the beginning of the summer 1730 I see John Mumfords teame carry away one

loade of said Planks." Bill shown, Mumford to Morse, dated 1729/30, for molasses, beens, nails, shoes, sugar, rum, "thy oxen came to winter for 4*s* a week and was heer 3 weeks . . . 12 pounds of sugar by **James Hyames** wife, 8*s*. . . . indico, pipes, alspice." Credit: 1200 foott of plank, £3:12:0. Decision for plaintiff, £10:6:1 deducting £3:12:0 by credit in court; appealed but verdict affirmed.

– March 1733[/4] – Superior Court –

575. **Wharton vs. Northup** *et al.* Citation to **Stephen Cooper** or either of the Constables of North Kingstown, upon petition of **Eunice Wharton,** widdow and devisee of **William Wharton** late of the Parish of St. Bartholomew Exchange, London; she had brought a case of ejectment at the General Court of Trials at Newport in September 1727 against **Stephen Northup,** yeoman, **Thomas Northup,** ferryman, **Benjamin Northup,** yeoman, **Henry Northup, jun^{r},** husbandman, **Nicholas Northup,** husbandman, and **Lawrence Whaley,** weaver, lately all of North Kingstown. Writ dated 7 March 1734. Earlier verdict had been for the defendants, upheld at a rehearing in Newport in March 1728. On 23 December 1730 His Majesty, by and with the advice of his Privy Council at the Court of St. James, was pleased to order and direct that both the sd verdict or Judgements should be set aside and reversed, and that there should be a new Trial of sd Cause.

576. **William Potter** of Newport, mariner, vs. **Philip Wanton** of Newport, shopkeeper, in custody of the sheriff, for £8:5:5 due for work done, leather sold, and money advanced sundry times from March 1730 to August following. Writ dated 30 October 1733. Bill included 2 days work aboard the schooner *Speedwell* at 6s, 9½ lb. Pump leather, sum paid for entering and clearing the schooner, £8:2:6 paid to Indian **Joseph Greenwell** for 2½ months wages on board the schooner, and "half the horse hire to go to Barnstable for your money, half my expense going to Barnstable, " etc. Defendant's plea was that the account sued was pending at the Court of Admiralty, and the court considered that the action should abate. At Inferior Court of Common Pleas in November 1733 decision was for defendant, costs of suit; plaintiff appealed and case went to the Superior Court in March 1734.

577. **Henry Hooper** of Newport, practitioner in physick vs. **Charles Jarrat** of Newport, wheelwright, in custody of the sheriff, for £6:2:3 due by book for sundry medicines for his wife in her last illness and attendance from 5 January 1731/2 to 18 March 1731/2, together with cerecloths, emplasters and bleeding her during said time. Writ dated 19 April 1733. Defendant's answer was that he had publickly declared and forbid all persons from Entertaining his said wife or Trusting her upon any account without his leave or approbation . . . operations performed by the plaintiff upon [her] was without orders or Privity of the defendant. Verdict for plaintiff at Inferior Court of Common Pleas in May 1733 was confirmed in an appeal heard in Superior Court in March 1734.

– November 1734 – Inferior Court of Common Pleas –

578. **John Chapman** of Newport, schoolmaster, otherwise called John Chapman late of Newport, schoolmaster, vs. **Job Lawton** of Newport, Esq., administrator of the goods of **George Lawton** late of Newport, yeoman alias gentleman, deceased, for £233:6:9½ due for labour and service done by the plaintiff's wife for said George in his lifetime and for goods sold and delivered and cash advanced by the plaintiff's wife and for service done by the plaintiff's Indian girl, beginning in October 1726 and ending 28 May 1732. Writ dated 29 October 1733.

Account signed by **Joanna Chapman** with her mark, 21 9ber 173[2?], for chocalet, raisons, nutmegs, sheets, 2½ oz. gold, attendance and service, shoes, osnaburgs & kersey, goods at Mrs. Cranston's, 15 yds. calaminco, silk, indigo, muslin & galoon, starch & alspice, silk fan and thread. **Joseph Ward** of Portsmouth deposed 22 May 1733 that he had gone to the dwelling of Joanna Chapman where **George Lawton** lay very ill, for money owed him, and he "ordered Joanna Chapman to fetch money and pay me and accordingly she did several times . . .", and he saw a leather trunk there that looked like a trunk he had seen of sd Lawton's before his removal. **Joseph Holmes** of Newport, yeoman, stated that "last March was 4 years It being 1729" he purchased a farm of George Lawton late of Newport, yeoman, deceased, for which he was to pay him £3200. On the same day, **Capt. Adam Lawton** of Portsmouth, of lawful age, deposed about things in the gilded leather trunk, including pieces of eight, and speckled calico that Lawton "intended to make a sett of curtains thereof."

On 5 September 1734, **Mary Peckham** [*signed by mark*], testified that she knew **George Lawton** brother to **Job Lawton** Esq., when he was at the house of **Johannah Chapman** "which I being a neighbour was often at . . . saw George Lawton in great distress being in a very weak and sick condition . . . not being sencible what he did so that the trouble in cleaning and tending him which sd Chapman had was considerable and very nausious to tend"; she would not have tended him all that time for the money the Chapmans charged the estate. **Edward Richmond** signed a statement that he was often at the house of Mistress Chapman in the time of Lawton's sickness, "a long time in a very aufull condition . . . aufull to behould, so bad, that it was as much as thre or four could keep him in his bed."

On 5 November 1733, **Samuel Fowler** of Newport, cordwainer, deposed that he lived near the dwelling house of **Joanna Chapman** in Newport and was called over to her house to be witness to a bond which Lawton was to give to Holmes, and saw that Lawton lay very ill and sick and he never did see him abroad after that.

Upon a rehearing, the verdict was for the appellee.

— May 1734 — Superior Court —

579. **Daniel Fish** of Portsmouth, yeoman, vs. **Daniel Vaughan** of Newport, husbandman, for £220 due by note dated 9 May 1732 for £120, signed by the defendant with mark and witnessed by **Job Lawton** and **James Strange.** Writ dated 26 April 1734. A note signed at Boston 8 February 1732 signed by the defendant with mark, witnessed by **Zachariah Trescott** and **George Lamott** states, "I promsise to pay to Col^{o} Daniel Abbot on order . . . £53:18:0 for vallue Rec'd." A bond dated 26 February 1732/3, witnessed by **Thomas Fleet** and **Zachariah Trescott,** describes Danl Vaighn [*sic*] as late of Newport, tanner alias husbandman, who is being arrested for a debt belonging to **John Hennery** of Providence to satisfy a judgement of £53:18:0 paid by Co^{l} **Daniel Abbot** of Providence, and **John Bennett** and **Isaac Peckham** both of Newport become bound to Abbot for £20 of the debt; Vaughan agrees "I do bind myselfe a servant to said Daniel Abbot, John Bennett, and

Isaac Peckham for two years time from this date . . . proportionable time to each according to ye times and season of ye yeare so as to work and pay Daniel Abbot £32:18:0 and [the other two] £20 . . . [they] to find suitable vittles and loging for such a servant."

580. **Thomas Sherman** of Swansey, husbandman, vs. **Samuel Rogers** of Newport, vintner alias yeoman, in action of covenant. Writ dated 30 April 1734. By deed dated 24 April 1734 the defendant had sold Sherman for £46:12 a Negro boy named **Cesar** near the age of eight years . . . boy was distempered by reason of a rupture in the groin which he had had from birth or a little after, and was unfit for service. Deed shown from **John Lawton Junr** son of **Isaac Lawton Junr** deceased of Portsmouth, dated 10 March 1731/2 to Samuel Rogers grandson of **Thomas Rogers** deceased of Newport, husbandman, for the same boy, aged five years, sound in wind and limb; witnesses were **John Lawton** and **George Lawton**. Sherman took the boy off to Swanzey, where he discovered that he was "burst" and unfit for work. Depositions were made 27 May 1734 by **Richard Sherman, John Forrester**, and **Sarah Kelles** of Newport, who said that two years ago in August, John Lawton Jr. of Portsmouth sold [Cesar] to "my brother Samuel Rogers." **Neomy Lawton** of Portsmouth testified 29 May 1734 that "my husband" sold the boy and he was burst when he sold him. Judgement for plaintiff, £10 damage and costs.

581. **Pasko Whitford** of North Kingstown, yeoman, vs. **Jonathan Nickols** of South Kingstown, ferryman, for £3:3:7 due for cheese sold and delivered to his wife 28 November 1732. Heard in June 1734 at Inferior Court of Common Pleas in South Kingstown, where decision was for the plaintiff; defendant appealed to Superior Court in September. Bill was for 109 lbs. of cheese at 7*d.* lb. **Christopher Curtis** of South Kingstown testified 2 September 1734 that he was at Jonathan Nickols's and asked if Pasko Whitford had delivered any cheese for sd Curtis and Nickols said he had not. **Sam^{ll} Hazzard** of South Kingstown testified that in June 1734 he was "at the Court House in South Kingstown and heard **James Honeyman Jr.** interrogate Whitfourd concerning the cheese. . . ." **Jeremiah Sheffield** of South Kingstown testified that he didn't sell any cheese . . . only delivered it. Earlier verdict for plaintiff confirmed.

582. **Mary Hart**, widow, **George Gibbs**, baker, and **Ruth** his wife who when sole was named **Ruth Hart**, all of Newport, vs. **John George** of Newport, rug weaver, in an action of review of an action of trespass and ejectment first prosecuted at the Inferior Court of Common Pleas in November 1733. Defendant was accused of witholding from the plaintiff a piece of land in Newport containing about 20 acres, with two dwelling houses and a stable thereon, part orchard, part meadow, and part pasture land, bounded northerly partly upon land of **Daniel Gould**, southerly partly upon land of **Joseph Whipple** and partly on **Job Almy**, westerly upon a highway, of which land and premises **Isaac George** late of Newport, yeoman, deceased, was in his life time seized, to wit, on or about 23 June 1731, when he made his will; he died on or about 22 April 1732. In his will he devised the property to his daughter Mary Hart one of the plaintiffs and to his granddaughter Ruth Hart (now wife to plaintiff George [Gibbs]); original writ dated 25 October 1733. Judgment had been rendered for plaintiffs to recover, but the defendant appealed to the Superior Court in March last past, and judgment was reversed. Warrant served on John George 3 June 1734 by Peleg Rogers, town sergeant. Note on outside of case: "agreed."

— May 1735 — Superior Court —

583. **Mary Sanderson** of Boston, widow and administratrix of **Fexley Sanderson** late of Boston, taylor, deceased, obtained a judgement in November 1734 against **Benjamin Mitchel** of Newport, hatter, for £17:13 and costs. She filed a prosecution in March 1735.

584. **Darias Tallman** of Little Compton, yeoman alias Dictus Darias Tallman of Dartmouth, yeoman, vs. **Edward Burges** now resident in Warwick, husbandman, late of Little Compton, in custody of the sheriff, for debt of £15:19:6. First heard at Inferior Court of Common Pleas, Providence, in December 1734; appealed to Superior Court at Newport, March 1735.

585. **John Anderson** of Windsor, Connecticut, appealed from a judgement of the Inferior Court of Common Pleas at South Kingstown in January

1734 in an action of debt against him by **Jeremiah Hazard** of South Kingstown.

– May 1735 – Inferior Court of Common Pleas –

586. **Henry Collins** of Newport, merchant, administrator of the goods of **Arnold Collins Junr** late of Newport, merchant, vs. **Ichabod Potter** (son of **Ichabod Potter** deceased) of South Kingstown, inn-holder alias gentleman, in custody of the sheriff, for £60:13:3 for goods sold and delivered 21 August 1723 to 14 February 1726 by the books of Arnold Collins. Writ dated 27 March 1735. Defendant did not appear; plaintiff received judgement of the amount sued for, by default; defendant appealed. **Samuel Wickham** testified at Newport 19 March 1735/6 before **Peter Bours**, Justice of the Peace, that he had been at South Kingstown at the house of Mr. Ichabod Potter in March 1731/2 . . . Potter called him aside and owned he was indebted to Mr. Arnold Collins, deceased, about £12 . . . desired me to tell Henry Collins to have a little patience. . . ."

587. **Thomas Potter** of Westerly, yeoman, vs. **John Shelden Junr**, husbandman, and **Benjamin Shearman**, yeoman, both of South Kingstown, in custody of the sheriff, for trespass; on 28 January 1734 at Westerly with force and arms they did enter his dwelling house and carry away two Negro boys named **Pero** and **Scipio** of the price of £240 together with other goods valued at £20: two brass kittles, one coverlid, six pewter plates, one cane and one candle box. Writ dated 30 January 1734/5. Defendants' plea was that the goods were taken by virtue of an execution against the estate of Thomas Potter late of South Kingstown, deceased, and they had a right to do it. Will and inventory of Thomas Potter shown. Depositions were made at Westerly 3 February 1734/5 by **Rebecca Warden** of Westerly and **Anne Tanner** of South Kingstown, both of whom said they had been at the house of Lt. Thomas Potter in Westerly on 8 January last past when Sheldon and Shearman came . . . **Mary Potter** demanded their order ". . . we did not see them shew any . . . ." Earlier court papers from Inferior Court of Common Pleas held at South Kingstown in June 1733 shown, when in two separate cases **Lydia Potter** of South Kingstown, widow, and **Martha Potter** of South Kingstown, infant, by Lydia Potter, her mother

and guardian, received judgements against Thomas Potter of Westerly at Superior Court at Newport in September 1733 after the cases had been previously heard at the Inferior Court of Common Pleas at South Kingstown in June 1733. **Parsavel Allen** of Westerly deposed on 26 June 1735 that on 9 June instant he was desired to go with John Shelden to see him return some goods to Thomas Potter of Westerly which he had taken by virtue of an execution as he understood it. . . . Verdict for defendant, costs of court.

By writ dated 27 May 1735, **Henry Bull** attorney, **Lydia Potter** of South Kingstown, widow of Thomas Potter, sued **Joseph Potter** of South Kingstown, yeoman, for her dower, a third part of about 45 acres of land with appurtenances in South Kingstown, bounded north on land of **Moses Barber**, east on land of **John Reynolds**, south on land of **Mary Shearman**, an infant, and west partly on land of **Isaac Shelden** and partly on land of **Isaac Fowler**.

588. **Henry Collins** and **Samuel Wickham** of Newport, merchants, vs. **John George** of Newport, rugweaver, for £5.18.4 due for goods sold and delivered in the month of April 1734. Constable **James Bull** attached one pewter spoon as the proper goods of the defendant for want of his body, 7 May 1735. (Docket No. 4)

589. **Henry Collins** and **Samuel Wickham**, of Newport, merchants, vs. **Thomas Wrightington** of Newport, hatter, for £62:15:11 and 3 farthings, due for sundry goods and merchandise sold between 25 April 1732 and 20 September 1734. (Docket No. 5)

590. **Daniel Gould Esq.** and **Samuel Collins**, blacksmith, of Newport, administrators of the goods of **Major Fairchild**, butcher, deceased, vs. **Joshua Easton** of Newport, cordwainer, for £2:12:6 due by note dated 4 February 1734. (Docket No. 6)

591. **Jonathan Weeden** of Newport, shopkeeper, vs. **Jos. Babcock Junr** of Westerly, yeoman, for £78:14 due by bond dated 26 March 1734 witnessed by **Jonathan Maxson** and **G. Gould**. (Docket No. 9)

592. **Richard Ward** of Newport Esq. vs. **Edward Hunt** of Newport, painter, for £3:12:9 due for goods sold 26 July 1732. (Docket No. 15)

593. **Samuel Clark** of Newport, hatter, vs. **Jos. Babcock Jr.** of Westerly, yeoman alias husbandman, for £3:5 due for one beaver hat sold and delivered 2 May 1734. (Docket No. 14)

594. **Noah Clark** of Colchester, Conn., whitesmith, vs. **Samuel Taylor** of Newport, cooper, for £5:10 due by note dated 5 April 1734, witnessed by **Charles Boulkley** and **Jabez Dean. Thomas Wrightington** taken as surety 31 December 1734 by **Martin Howard,** constable. (Docket No. 15)

595. **Samuel Pike** of Newport, tayler, vs. **John Reed** of Warwick, husbandman alias yeoman, for £10:10 due by note dated 7 July 1733, **Joseph Sabin** witness. (Docket No. 16)

596. **Daniel Amory** of Newport, mariner, vs. **William Tilley** of Newport, ropemaker, for £6 due by note dated 5 June 1734 (Docket No. 21)

597. **Lawrence Clarke** of Newport, gentleman, vs. **William Dyre** of Newport, Esq., claiming that William had received moneys due to sd Lawrence. (Docket No. 45)

598. **James Blackstock** of Newport, merchant, vs. **John Fletcher** of Newport, painter, for non-performance of promise: a note dated 10 March 1730/1 for consideration of £21:10*s*, defendant had agreed to "filly paint and finish the Houses" wherein the plaintiff and the now defendant then lived in Newport, on or before the first day of May . . . work not finished. Writ "executed on the body of John Fletcher and have taken **Charles Smith** as surety . . . **Martin Howard,** constable." (Docket No. 73)

599. **Thomas Hicks** of Bluefields in Co. Bluefields in North Carolina, yeoman, now resident in Newport, vs. **Bethia Hedges** now resident in Newport, widow lately named **Bethia Thurber,** for £13:4:7 due for rent of plaintiff's house, hired by the defendant beginning in month of January 1729 and ending month of December 1730. Hicks' accounting included rent, apples, flour, veal, wood, glass windows, and 10 weeks lodging of **Thomas Creese,** defendant's Journeyman. Certificate dated 2 March 1727/8, Newport: banns between John Hedges and Bethia Thurber published according to the Church of England by **James Honeyman;** joined in marriage in Newport February ye 29, 1728 by **John Coddington,** Justice of the Peace. **James Sheffield, Peter Easton** and **James Gould** testified that Bethia Hedges has since proved her husband to be alive so she cannot be sued, and also that the account sued for appears to be one that had been accounted for heretofore. At court 27 May 1735 plaintiff and defendant agree to arbitration; plaintiff

chose **Mr. Peter Easton,** glasier; defendant chose **James Sheffield, Esq.**; Court chose **James Gould**; decision reached 10 November 1735, plaintiff to pay costs. (Docket No. 91)

600. **James Allen Jr.** of Newport, butcher, vs. **Thomas Creese** of Newport, apothecary, for £29:9:7 due for butcher meat sold and delivered from 1 March 1733 to 5 April 1735. (Docket No. 117)

601. **Thomas Stevens** of Newport, late keeper of the Gaol in Newport, victualer, vs. **Charles Dickinson** of Warwick, yeoman, for £5:13:8 due by note dated 15 May 1734. (Docket No. 120)

602. **Simeon Davis Esq.** and **Bethiah** his wife of Bristol in Colony of Massachusetts Bay and **Oatis Little**, gentleman and **Elizabeth** his wife, of Marshfield, Colony of Plimouth, Bethiah and Elizabeth being administrators of the estate of **Jabez Howland** of Bristol, who deceased intestate, vs. **Tideman Hull** of Jamestown, Esq. alias yeoman, for £3:18:7 due by note dated 14 June 1733 at Newport, to **Bethiah Bragg** [*sic*] and **Elizabeth Howland,** administrators of the estate of Jabez Howland . . . (Docket No. 121)

603. **Ebenezer Shepherd** of Newport, taylor, vs. **Joseph Johnson** of Newport, carpenter, for £17:1:6 due by book for a suit of clothes delivered in 1734. (Docket No. 122)

604. **James Gardner** of Newport, shopkeeper, vs. **Benjamin Mitchel** of Newport, hatter, for £18:1:9 due by note dated 1 June 1734, witnessed by **Daniel Fourtane** and **Daniel Carr.** (Docket No. 125)

605. **Nathan Townsend** of Newport, currier, vs. **John Moore** of Newport, upholsterer, for £21:4:6 due by book for dressing and colouring leather, including horsehides and calfskins, and leather sold and delivered from July 1733 to August 1734. (Docket No. 126).

606. **Peter Roe** of Boston, butcher, vs. **Tobias Reynhart** now residing in Newport, blacksmith, for £6:14:6 due for butcher's meat sold and delivered from 23 March 1733 to 1 November 1734. (Docket No. 132)

607. **James Allen Junr** of Newport, butcher, vs. **William Robinson** of Newport, joyner, for £60:12:4 due for beef, mutton, veal and lamb sold and delivered. (Docket No. 134)

608. **Robert Little** of Newport, mariner, vs. **Sylvester Sweet** of Newport, innholder, for £8:15 due, claiming that on 20 September 1734 he let to the defendant a dwelling house, stable, and garden in Newport, adjoining land now in possession of **Richard Mumford** and upon three streets, from 20 September for a quarter year at £8:15 per quarter. (Docket No. 135)

609. **James Allen Junr** of Newport, butcher, vs. **Joseph Sabin** of Newport, cordwainer, for £20:11:7 due for meat delivered. (Docket No. 138)

610. **Robert Little** of Newport, mariner, vs. **Sylvester Sweet**, vintner, for £26:5 rent due [see No. 525 above]; for want of the defendant's body, **Nathan^l^ Townsend Jn^r^** attached his household goods. (Docket No. 139)

611. **Jeremiah Weeden Jn^r^** of Newport, cordwainer, vs. **Jeremiah Staniford** of Newport, Fellmonger, for £118 due by note dated 7 March 1731, witnessed by **Caleb Gardner** and **Benj. Haggar**. (Docket No. 140)

612. **James Allen Jr.** of Newport, butcher, vs. **Henry Shepherd** of Newport, mariner, for £16:4:2½ due for meat. (Docket No. 141)

613. **James Hastings** of Newport, mariner, vs. **Peter Will**, an Indian man residing Newport, labourer, for £4:7:2 due by note dated 26 February 1734, signed **P**. (Docket No. 143)

614. **Robert Little** of Newport, mariner, vs. **Sylvester Sweet**, inn-holder, for £18:10 due for one hogshead, two pipes and four barrels of cyder and use of a Biliard Table and sticks and balls in the year 1734. (Docket No. 145).

615. **Abraham Chace** of Newport, mariner, vs. **William Lassells** of Newport, barber, for £6:13 due by book for washing done by plaintiff's wife and lodging the defendant's servant in the year 1734; bill includes a Lamskin wigg; signed by **Bothier [?Bethiah] Chace**. (Docket No. 155)

616. **Samuel Willes** of Dartmouth, co. Bristol, Province of Mass. Bay, Esq., vs. **Phillip Underwood** of Newport, boatman, for £8:5 due by note dated 16 August 1734, witnessed by **Alexand^r^ Forrance**. (Docket No. 160)

617. **Jeffery Davis** of East Greenwich, co. Providence [*sic*], miller, vs. **Samuel Tailor** of Newport, cooper, for £26. due by note dated 3 May 1733. (Docket No. 161)

618. **Peleg Carr**, merchant, and **John Gould**, yeoman, of Newport, administrators of the estate of **William Swan** late of sd Newport, mason, deceased, vs. **William Lasells** of Newport, barber, for £10 due by note dated 5 April 1733, witnessed by **James Bull** and **Thos Staples**. (Docket No. 162)

619. **Hezakiah Carpenter** of Newport, gentleman, vs. **Nathaniel Rutter** of South Kingstown, schoolmaster, for £5:18:6 due on note dated 11 March 1733/4. (Docket No. 163)

620. **Daniel Updike** of Newport, gentleman, vs. **Samuel Pike** of Newport, taylor, for £6:18:4 due by book in 1734, including cost of bills [*i.e. legal fees*] for [*cases against*] **Herbert Nichols, Thomas Marchall,** and others. (Docket No. 165)

621. **George Cornell** of Portsmouth, Esq., vs. **Nathanael Hall** of Portsmouth, yeoman, for non-performance of promise made 11 January 1734; Cornell paid to **John Coddington** of Newport £29:18 to discharge a debt due from the defendant to sd Coddington who [defendant Hall] promised to repay and did not. (Docket No. 166)

622. **Daniel Ayrault** of Newport, merchant, vs. **Thomas Hazard** of North Kingstown, yeoman, son of **Stephen,** deceased, for £10:12:6 for goods sold and delivered in the year 1730. (Docket No. 168)

623. **Abigail Pinnegar** of Newport, widow, vs. **Peter Wills,** an Indian man, resident in sd Newport, marriner in the custody of ye sheriff, for £3:17:6 for one hat sold and delivered by the plaintiff, cash advanced in the year 1735, and "my charge of bringing him back when he run away," £1:2:6. (Docket No. 173)

624. **John Freeborn** of Portsmouth, yeoman, vs. **Daniel Gould**, Esq. and **Samuel Collins**, blacksmith, both of Newport, administrators of the estate of **Major Fairchild** late of sd Newport, butcher, deceased, for £75:13 due for cattle and sheep sold and delivered by the plaintiff to sd Major in his lifetime in the year 1733. Bill signed by **Mager Fairchild,** dated 21 July 1733. (Docket No. 179)

625. **George Lawton** of Portsmouth, Esq., vs. **Nathaniel Hall** of Portsmouth, yeoman for £425:12 due on bond signed 15 August 1730 by defendant for payment on or before 26 May 1731, witnessed by **Wm.** and **Hope Sanford**. (Docket No. 181)

626. **Peter Shaw** of Little Compton in Co. Bristol, Province of Massachusetts Bay, yeoman, vs. **Samuel Taylor** of Newport, cooper, for £8 due for one Heiffer sold and delivered in the year 1733. Writ dated 8 January 1734[/5]. (Docket No. 184)

627. **Henry Collins** and **Samuel Wickham**, both of Newport, merchants, vs. **Roger Elderton** of Westerly, Co. Kent [*sic*], husbandman, for £10:15 which to them he oweth and unjustly detaineth for one piece of fine 7/8 Garlic sold and delivered 3 July 1734. Writ dated 13 March 1734/5. "Westerly, 24 March 1734/5, then for want of the within Roger Elderton's body I attached a two mast Boat and several goods . . . One Bed One Bolster One Coverlid Two Blankits One Sheet One Iron Pot One Great Iron Kettle Three Pair of Breeches One Jacket One Canoo One Chair One Dish One Bason Two Spoons Two Small Baskets Three Lb. Candles One Mariner's Compass One Broad Hatchet One Hammer One Caulking Mallet One Caulking Iron One Quart Pot One Firkin of Meat Two Coils of Rope Halfa Barrell of Tar Ten Gal^{n} Rum and Two Pine [*illegible*]," signed by **Samuel Babcock**, Sheriff. (Docket No. 185)

628. **David Nickerson** of Chatham in Co. Barnstable, mariner, vs. **Manassah Kempton** late of Raynham, Co. Bristol, mariner, for £7:13:7 due by book for goods sold and delivered in the year 1734. Writ dated 12 April 1735; **D. Updike**, attorney. **James Bull**, constable, ordered to arrest body of Kempton. (Docket No. 186)

629. **John Freebody** of Newport, merchant, vs. **Roger Elderton** of Westerly, yeoman, for £84 due by note of 4 November 1731 witnessed by **John Cook** and **Christopher Townsend**. (Docket No. 187)

630. **John Anderson** of Windsor, Co. Hartford, Colony of Connecticut, yeoman, vs. **Samuel Pike** of Newport, tailor, for £7:6*d* due by note dated 20 February 1734/5, witnessed by **Martin Howard** at Newport. (Docket No. 189)

631. **John Lawrance** of Newport, shopkeeper, vs. **William Parry** of Newport, cutter, for £11 due for rent. The plaintiff did on 25 July 1732 devise and let unto the defendant a dwelling house in Newport . . . fronting to Thames Street and near the upper Market House with the yard and appurtenances, for one quarter of a year and so thence for-

ward from Quarter to Quarter as long as both Parties should agree. Writ dated 21 April 1735. (Docket No. 190)

632. **Samuel Rhodes** of Newport, merchant, vs. **Jos. Fox** of Newport, scrivener, for £7:15:8 due for work done and goods delivered in the year 1735. Bill included "work & stuf, 8 yds hollon at 10s., 2 scains fine thread, a stone mustard pot, nails, 3 pr white glovs, milk at 2. per pint." Writ dated 4 April 1735. Defendant arrested by constable **James Bull,** 2 May. (Docket No. 191)

633. **Thomas Rogers** of Newport, marriner, vs. Mr. **John Baptist Vale** now residing in Newport, merchant, for £115:5 due for goods sold and delivered and services done by the plaintiff on board the defendant's sloop and for cash advances, all at sundry times in the latter part of the year 1734 and the beginning of the year 1735; bill included "flower at 30*s* pr barrell, beef at 40*s* per barrell, 14 gammons at 6/3 each, 10 pr shoes at 5*s* each, a pr gould buttons at £1:10, pr silver buckles, 2 tun logwood on **Clements** acc't pr agreement, Jamaica currency, New England currency, 8 days serving on board ye sloop *Fox* at 10*s* per day." Writ executed by **Job Howland,** Constable, 26 April 1735, Jamestown: "I have attached one Negro man called **Pero** for want of the body of the defendant . . . as [his] proper goods." (Docket No. 193)

634. **James Collins** of Newport, mariner, vs. **Silvester Sweet** of Newport, vintner, in action of trespass, claiming that on 8 March 1734 the defendant with force of arms entered the stable then in possession of the plaintiff . . . and did improve contrary to the will of ye plaintiff by putting in of Horses and eating the plaintiff's hay. Plaintiff awarded £6. (Docket No. 194)

635. **John Partelo** of Newport, carter, vs. **Thomas Creese** of Newport, apothecary, for £22:11:8 due by book on balance of accounts 6 May 1735. Bill refers to **Doct^r Thomas Creese**; settled same day. (Docket No. 195)

636. **John Cranston** of Newport, merchant, vs. **Samuel Pike** of Newport, tailor, for £180 debt, claiming the plaintiff on 1 April 1720 did demise and let unto the defendant a shop near adjoyning the plaintiff's present merchant shop in Newport . . . continued 15 years and is now in arrears. Defendant answered that he held the land in the right of heirs of **William Sandford** late of Newport, gentleman, deceased, and the plaintiff did not rent it. (Docket No. 196)

637. **William Lawton** of Portsmouth, husbandman, vs. **Samuel Collins,** blacksmith, and **Daniel Gould** of Newport, administrators of the estate of **Major Fairchild,** for £25:18:7 due by note dated 8 January 1733/4. (Docket No. 198)

638. **Christopher Almy** of Newport, merchant, vs. **Robert Case** of South Kingstown, sadler, for £52:11:3 due for West Indian goods sold and delivered in 1730 and 1731. Includes bill from **Robert Casey** [*sic*] to **Mary Almy,** for "shuger [and] rom." (Docket No. 199)

639. **Daniel Updike** of Newport, gentleman, vs. **John Morse** of North Kingstown, labourer, for debt due for sundry costs, including **John Mumford's** bill [*probably court costs*]. (Docket No. 205)

640. **Samuel Dyre** of Newport, yeoman, executor of the will of **Mary Slocum** late of Jamestown, widow, deceased, vs. **Benjamin Nichols** of North Kingstown, for debt due for witholding a Negro man slave named **Fortune** to the plaintiff belonging as executor, valued at £120. By her will dated 5 November 1729 with codicil added 7 November 1732, Mary Slocum appointed the plaintiff her sole executor; she made disposal of sd slave in her lifetime but on or about 15 November 1732 she died, the true and proper owner of sd slave. Defendant answered and claimed bill of sale dated 22 May 1733. Parties agreed to arbitration; chose **Maj. Tho. Fry, Mr. Jeremiah Gold,** and **Mr. John Rice, Jnr;** at Superior Court, Newport, September 1734, verdict for defendant.

The case was appealed. **Sarah Rowse** of East Greenwich deposed in January 1734/5 and said that "some time before **Joseph Slocum** late of East Greenwich, deceased, was married I lodged at his mother's Mary Slocum's dwelling house upon Conanicaut in Jamestown . . . saw Negro man called Fortune lying ill . . . asked [her] whose Negro he was, She then answered and said . . . bought equally between her and her son Joseph Slocum . . . and her sd son as she said was then agoing to be married and to settle himself and he could not tell how to keep Howse without sd Negro and he must take him . . . some time before sd Joseph Slocum died he was at my son-in-law **Thomas Nicholls'** house in East Greenwich . . . [I] heard him say . . . his mother had made an agreement concerning said Negro that he was to give his mother £35 for her part if she called for it in her life time." **Hannah Weaver** of East Greenwich made a deposition with the same information. **Mary Slocum** of East Greenwich, widow, testified 6 January

1734/5 that about "five years ago when she lived at her mother in law Mary Slocum's upon Cononicut, in Jamestown, she saw **Giles Slocum** now of Warwick in the County of Providence [*sic*] draw a writing concerning a Negro Man named Fortune [who] belonged in partnership between her said Mother Slocum and her said Husband Joseph Slocum . . . as I then understood for £35 in Money from said Joseph Slocum to his mother Mary Slocum . . . and in Case her said Mother did not call for said Money in her life time then after her Death her heirs should be for ever after excluded from having anything to do with said Negro man . . . Joseph Slocum signed . . . my said Mother then said that the writing should be laid up among her other papers that it might decide all Controversies about said Negro after her Death. . . ."

Caleb Carr of East Greenwich testified upon interrogation 15 March 1734/5 before **John Spencer**, J.P., that he had given evidence 1 March that Joseph Slocum of East Greenwich had told him that "ye Longest Liver of he & his mother Mary Slocumb of Jamestowne . . . was to have all sd negro man . . . this same negro was in ye posesion of Mary Slocumb of Jamestowne . . . for several years & afterwards I do sertainly know that ye same negro man Called fortin was In ye posesion of Joseph Slocum of East Grinwich [and] . . . in the possesion of the widder of Joseph Slocum after sd Josephs death . . . saw ye same negro man Called fortin in the possesion of benjaminne Nickeles of North Kingstonne . . . that was in controversy betwixt ye above sd Giles Slocum & benjamine nickoles." **Capt. Thomas Nickols** of East Greenwich deposed 18 March 1735 and said he was with **Giles Slocom** and heard sd Slocom refer to half of the sd Negro his mother purchased, etc. **Abigail Thomas** deposed 20 May 1735 in North Kingstown that she knew Mary Slocum bought and paid for all that Negro man called Fortune now in controversy, of **Samuel Dyre** of Newport. **Susannah Carr** of East Greenwich testified that Mary Slocum bought the Negro and had for several years lent him to her son Joseph; **Joseph Carr** of East Greenwich swore to the same. **Merriam Capron** of Warwick deposed 21 May 1735, stating that she was in company with Joseph Slocum's wife Mary at the deponent's grandmother, Mary Slocum's, house on Jamestown, and sat by the fireside with her grandmother, and asked whether Joseph Slocum was to live with her or move off, and she answered he was to go away and carry his Negro man Fortune away with him, but she intended to have a note. **George Thomas** deposed that since Mary Slocum's death he saw somebody the which he thinks was Giles Slocum burn a paper that might be [the note]. **Samuel Slocum** deposed, referring to his mother Mary Slocum.

Daniel Weeden testified 27 August 1735 before **Samuel Clarke**, Warden, saying that he "was one of the Inventoriors" of the estate of Mary Slocum and he saw "amongst her papers a writing som ways like a note signed with the name of **Joseph Slocum** And according to the best of his rememberance the writing was for £35 to be paid on demand to ye said mary slocum for the one half of a negro boay cald **fortin** . . . there was an Article in the said writing to exclude or forbid her heirs from Demanding the £35 after her deseas . . . **Samuel Dyre** asked If we wold prize the note and we told him no . . . herd the above sd negro was purchised between mary Slocum and her son Joseph. **John Weeden** of Jamestown testified at the same time, that he was at the house of Mary Slocum some time before her decease, asking her to "send sum body to work on the highway she Replyed that she and her son Joseph had onely one Negro Man between them and that she Intended upon her sons Remooving to give him her half." **Samuel Dyre** was present at this testimony "but would not tarry untel the Evidence was writ."

On 28 August 1735, **Jeremiah Gould** of North Kingstown testified before **George Tibbits**, Justice, that at "sum time past [he had been] appoynted with Major and **John Rice** Junr to Determen a Differeanc between Samuell Dyre of Newport as Executor to the Estate of Mary Slocum late of Jamestown Deceased and Mary Slocum Widdow to Joseph Slocum of East Greenwich Deceased Relateing to a man Caulled **forten** . . . as I did then Understand be purchased between the sd Mary Slocum of Jamestown and her Deceased son **Josep Slocum**"; it was noted that the "advers party [was] not within teen miles." On 29 August 1735 **John Rice Jun**^r^ of Warwick testified that he had been an arbitrator with Major **Thomas Fry** and **Jeremiah Gould** in order to end a controversy between **Samuel Dyre** of Newport, executor to the estate of the widow **Mary Slocum** late of Jamestown and **Mary Slocum** widow to **Joseph Slocum** late of East Greenwich, deceased; the aforesaid parties "appeared and agitated ye Premises Concerning sd Negro before us; **Samll Dyer** in all ye Dispute then before us Never challenged but one half of sd Negro; and Submitted ye other half to belong to sd **Mary Slocum** widow to sd **Joseph Slocum** . . . he said that sd Negro was Equally Purchased between;" but Mary Slocum, widow of Joseph, "pleaded ye whole Negro belonged to her" because her husband had purchased his half from his mother.

Bill of sale shown, from **Joseph Whipple** of Newport, merchant, for £70, to **Samuel Dyre**, yeoman, "sometime in September 1724," for Negro man named **Fortune**, signed 29 June 1733 [*sic*], witnessed by **David Chesebrough** and **Alexander Taylor.** Jury verdict for plaintiff, that the slave had belonged to **Mary Slocum**, widow; signed by **Peleg Wood Jr., Saml Buffum, Robert Little, Edwd Easton, Samuel Vernon Jr., James Fenr, Henry Clark, Henry Wright, Ebenezer Rumreill, George Cornell Jr., Peter Easton, and John Tillinghast**. (Docket No. 207)

641. **John Lawrence** of Newport, shopkeeper, vs. **William Parry** of Newport, cutter, for £9:8:2 for goods delivered in July 1732. Account includes 2 yds garlick, silk, moheare, coat buttons, bucharaum, oxumbrigs, thred. (Docket No. 208)

– June 1735 – Superior Court –

642. **Edward Dyre** of North Kingstown, yeoman, (one of the constables of North Kingstown), vs. **Joshua Morse**, blacksmith, in action of trespass, claiming that on 15 March 1734/5 the defendant had taken a cow valued at £12 and carried her away.

Susana Hyams of East Greenwich, widow, deposed there 25 June 1735 before John Spencer Jr., Justice: ". . . sometime in March 1734 **Benjamin Mors** of North Kingstown came to me to buy a brindle cow with a white star in the forehead for his brother **Joshua Mors**; I said I would not go after his brother for the money and Benjamin gave me a bond . . . never paid . . . sometime after I went to Joshua for the money and he gave a bond to **John Reynolds** for the money by my order sometime in June 1734." At the Inferior Court of Common Pleas at South Kingstown in June 1735 verdict was for the defendant, cost of court; plaintiff appealed.

William Spencer of North Kingstown, Esq., deposed there 1 August 1735 before **Christo^{r} Phillips**, Justice of the Peace: "at a Justices

Court held at Capt. **George Thomas**'s dwelling 15 March 1734/5 we brought Joshua Morse to answer the complaint of **Edward Dyer** for refusing to obey sd Dyer in the execution of his office in driving a cow of[f] the land which sd Morse lived on in sd town . . . Dyer said he had attached it as part of the estate of **Benjamin Morse** then of North Kingstown which **Joshua Morse** shewed to [him] to be the sd Benjamin Morse's." **Maj. George Thomas** of North Kingstown attested to the truth of Spencer's testimony. On 1 August 1735 at North Kingstown, **Jonathan Chase** deposed saying that he had gone along with Edward Dyer, constable, when he went to attach the cow as the estate of Benjamin Morse. They left her with Joshua Morse who said he would see her forthcoming whenever Dyer call'd for her . . . when demanded utterly refused to deliver . . . sd Joshua Morse and his brother **John Morse** withstood and molested them so they hindered them. Later, on 21 August 1735, in order to explain further, Chase deposed before **Thomas Stafford,** Justice, at Warwick, he living above ten miles away, and said that Dyer had the cow in custody, seized as part of the estate of Benjamin Morse by virtue of a writ to him directed . . . left cow on sd farm and some time after [when they went] again to serve an execution and drag her away [she] was rescued in a violent manner from sd Dyer by Joshua Morse and John Morse brothers to sd Benjamin Morse.

Benjamin Wells of South Kingstown deposed 6 September 1735 at East Greenwich that he had been at the dwelling house of Cap^{n} **George Thomas** in sd town 15 March 1734/5 and heard Dyer and Joshua Mors discourse [about the cow]. **Thomas Jackways** of South Kingstown swore to the truth of Thomas's testimony.

— September 1735 — Superior Court —

643. **Roger Morey** of North Kingstown, yeoman, vs. **Joshua Champlin** of Westerly, yeoman, for £100 due by note dated 13 August 1734. Constable **Edward Dyre** attached a bridle belonging to the defendant. **William Champlin Jr.** of Westerly on oath declared on 25 June 1735 that the bridle attached belonged to him. Case heard at Inferior Court of Common Pleas South Kingstown, June 1735; judgment for defendant to receive costs of the plaintiff; appealed.

644. **William Nichols** of Dighton, Co. of Bristol . . . Massachusetts Bay, yeoman, Esq., vs. **William Brown** of Portsmouth, Esq., for an accounting of when he was bailiff at Newport of one yoke of oxen committed to his care to sell and dispose of to the plaintiff's advantage, on or about November 1732. Defendant, arrested by constable **James Bull** at Newport 4 June 1735, answered that he had rendered an account.

Samuel Boyes deposed in Boston 13 August 1735 before **Habijah Savage**, Justice of the Peace, he living more than 30 miles distant from place of tryall: in November 1732, as a deputy sheriff in the County of Suffolk, he had served a writ on **Capt. William Brown** for £29, **Mr. William Nichols** being plaintiff . . . he waited on sd Brown to Mr. **Stephen Boutineau** who was attorney to Nichols . . . in talk sd Boutineau told him Brown had sold the cattle and had then tendered to Boutineau all the money, who refused, saying he could not take less than £29, whereupon Brown gave [Boyes] his bond. Bill shown, "ye Drift one pr Oxen to Boston £2:0:0 . . . [*Credit*] sold [to] **Bena[a] Bodge** £28 . . . 2 November 1732." Case was heard at Inferior Court of Common Pleas at South Kingstown in June 1735; judgement for plaintiff to recover money sued for; defendant appealed.

645. **Job Almy** of Newport, merchant, vs. **Thomas Gardner** and **James Gardner** of Newport, shopkeepers, to recover debt of £131:5:3 due by bond dated 11 December 1728 witnessed by **Rich[d] Smith** and **W[m] Rock**. Appealed from Inferior Court of Common Pleas at Newport in May 1735.

646. **Michael Cary**, now resident in Newport, petitioned the Superior Court 10 September 1735: he has a watch in his hands [*which was*] attached at the suit of Capt. **John Beard** under pretence of its being the estate of **John Davis** lately in Newport, mariner . . . is a hardship on him and he requests the court to relieve him.

647. **Peter Coggeshall**, yeoman, vs. **Edward Pelham**, gentleman, in custody of the sheriff, for £210 due for one negro or molatto man (called **Lawrence**), broadcloth, coco nuts, rum, sugar, molasses, money lent and advanced, and sundry other goods sold and delivered between AD 1720 and 1730. Account shown included items for Lawrence, £50, 3/6 for a child's coffin in August 1721, a candlebox, a lot of rum, Indian corn at 4s per bushel, cash paid **Ned Almy** in January 1724/5 for carting, Indian corn out of **Capt. Nott**'s sloop in June 1727, chocolate at 7s

a pound, and in December 1730 "his part of **Judge Dudley**'s debt." Defendant requested that action be abated because the account sued for ended in 1730 and the one produced in court extended to the year 1735. Defendant received costs of court. Plaintiff appealed.

– November 1735 – Superior Court –

648. **Daniel Coggeshall** of North Kingstown, Esq., vs. **Mary Coggeshall** of Portsmouth, widow, for possession of 140 acres in Portsmouth of which **Joshua Coggeshall** late of Portsmouth, Esq., was on or about 31 March 1735 seized until 25 April next when he died, leaving surviving the present plaintiff, his only brother and heir-at-law. Birth record: **Peleg Coggeshall,** son of **Daniel and Mary** of Portsmouth, was born 20, 2m 1712, first day of the week. File contains the declaration of an earlier case, **Henry Bull** and wife vs. **Joshua Coggeshall,** claiming that Peleg Coggeshall, brother of sd Joshua, died on or about [*blank*] August 1730. Portions of the will of Joshua Coggeshall, which was entailed. Inventory of **Daniel Coggeshall** late of Portsmouth, deceased, dated 17, 3m 1717. Inventory of personal estate of Peleg Coggeshall, infant, dated 10, 2m 1731. (Docket No. 61)

– December 1735 – Superior Court –

649. **Solomon Pane** of Providence, shopkeeper, vs. **Joseph Snow** of Providence, blacksmith, for £6:18:0 due for 3 loads of charcoal sold and delivered 3 June 1735. Writ dated 18 November 1735. **John Thornton** deposed on 7 November 1735 that he had at sundry times in the past borrowed Solomon Pane's coal cart and it held 92 bushels each load when heaped up. On 11 December 1735 **Eleaner Crosman** and **William Bossey** testified in court that they had been in Providence in company with **Timothy Blansher** and others at the measuring of three loads of charcoal which the defendant had of the plaintiff . . . they stopped in Snow's shop with Paine, who asked him to buy coal . . . Snow "seemed to be sum thing bacward but Paine insisted saying he wod take ye pay in sd Snow's way . . . Snow asked what will sute him

. . . he answered rum . . . agreed . . . Snow to allow 6*d* per bushel and gave sd Paine an order to **Capt. James Brown** for rum for y[e] pay." **John Snow** of Providence testified that he also had been present. **Timothy Blanchard** of Providence testified that he heard Solomon Paine and his wife **Abigail** have considerable discourse with Joseph Snow about some coals. **Joseph Tucker** of Providence testified that in the spring last past he had carted three loads of coal and delivered two at sd Snow's shop and the other at Timothy Blanchard's shop by order of the sd Snow. Judgement for plaintiff to recover £6:18 and costs.

— March 1735/6 — Superior Court —

650. **Samuel Pike** of Newport, tayler, vs. **John Cranston** of Newport, cooper alias mariner, for 19*s* 4*d* due by note dated 15 February 1728/9. One **Stephen Davies** stood indebted to the plaintiff for sundry goods sold and delivered at sundry times and work done. Plaintiff had been drawing out [*drawing up*] the account and intending to sue sd Davies, when Cranston, to prevent a suit and in discharge of a debt, endorsed the backside of the account with his note and promised to pay on demand . . . hath not yet done so. Writ dated 30 April 1735. Heard at Inferior Court of Common Pleas at Newport, May 1735, where judgement was for the plaintiff; appeal filed 15 March 1735/6. Bill, from October 1721 to February 1725, included items, "making you a coat, 18*s*; making a jacket & britches, £1 5*s*; holland jacket & britches, 16*s*; suit, £1 5*s*., another [suit] £1 10*s*; 4 dozen coat buttons @ 2/6; 2 linnen jackets & britches, 1/4; great coat, 12*s*; 5 yds of ferreting @ 10*s* . . ."

651. **Judith Cranston** of Newport, widow, vs. **Samuel Pike** of Newport, tailor, for £65:10:7 awarded at the Inferior Court of Common Pleas in November 1735. Samuel had appealed, but failed to prosecute; attorney **Daniel Updike**. File includes a bill to Capt **Simon Peaise** from March 1727 to November 1730, for "making grate coate . . . making yr son a Coate . . . mohair . . . making yr Neager Jacket and briches . . . making yr son a flag . . . ."

652. **Augustus Lucas** of Newport, merchant, vs. **Jahleel Brenton** of Newport, Esq., executor of the will of **Jahleel Brenton** late of Newport, Esq., deceased, to render account of the time the testator was bailiff of

the plaintiff in South Kingstown of one fourth of one-seventh part of three messuages and 2460 acres of land there of which they were tenants-in-common from 24 June 1714 to 8 November 1732. Writ dated 28 November 1735. Defendants answered that the testator never was bailiff in the manner and form declared. Case was heard first at Inferior Court of Common Pleas in South Kingstown in January 1735/6 where judgment was for the defendant, costs of court; plaintiff appealed.

653. **Abraham Redwood** of Newport, merchant, vs. **John Hill Jr.** of Westerly, in custody of the sheriff, gentleman. The defendant on 18 March 1733 received of **Harrison Gray** £58:10 of the plaintiff's money and had not yet delivered it. Writ dated 8 November 1734. Case was heard first at Inferior Court of Common Pleas in South Kingstown, January 1734, where judgement was for the plaintiff to recover money sued for and costs. Defendant appealed.

654. **John Clarke** of Providence, yeoman, vs. **Robert Currie** of Providence, glazier, in custody of the sheriff, for £44 due by note dated 13 [*?Sept*]ember 1735, witnessed by **John Henry** and **Watt. Currie**. Writ dated 14 November 1735. Case heard at Inferior Court of Common Pleas at Providence in December 1735; judgement for plaintiff to recover money sued for and costs; appealed. **Samuel Currie** and **John Currie** both of Providence deposed there 27 March 1736 before **Wm Hopkins**, Justice of the Peace: they were at their father's Mr. Robert Currie's house on 23 September last past in the evening and there came Mr. John Clarke and asked for money whereupon their father went to his desk and fetched a considerable quantity of paper money and asked Clarke what it was he owed him and Clarke said £22, whereupon their father desired him to shew the bond which should speak for itself . . . Clarke refused . . . father would not pay. **Mary Little** of Providence testified to the truth of their deposition.

655. **Charles Campbell** of Vollingtown [*Voluntown*], County of Windham . . . Connecticut, gent., vs. **James Reynolds** of East Greenwich, yeoman, in custody of sheriff, in action of trespass. On 1 June 1735 defendant did enter the lands of the plaintiff [which were] in his actual possession and destroy one small outhouse to the value of £24 . . . did continue his trespass till the date of the writ [30 October 1735] in which time he did cut down and destroy about 100 of the plaintiff's

white oak trees to the value of £20. The property was the eastern part of a larger tract of land which the plaintiff on 27 November 1725 had purchased of **Henry Champian** and **Sarah Champian**, laid out in Voluntown to **Henry Peterson** and entered in July 1706, about 120 acres. The defendant answered that the declaration says Campbell was of Voluntown, not in fact of East Greenwich where his dwelling house stands . . . impossible to be in both places at once . . . therefore not guilty. Case remitted to Inferior Court of Common Pleas at Providence, June next.

Case contains copy of the document in Secretary [*of State*]'s Office re the settlement of the boundary between Rhode Island and Connecticut. Also, a copy of the deed dated 27 November 1725 whereby **Henry Champian** and **Sarah Champian** of Lyme in County of New London . . . Connecticut, for £17 sold to **Charles Campbell** of Voluntown half a lot and rights of land in Voluntown which did belong to our Honoured Father **Henry Peterson** of Lyme, deceased; witnesses **Moses Noyes Jr., Mary Noyes.**

On 4 December 1735, at East Greenwich, before **John Jenkens**, Justice of the Peace, **Christopher Carpenter** of East Greenwich testified that some time in November last he was in company with **William Green**, surveyor, Capt. **Ishmaiel Spink** and several others at or near the dividing line between the colonies . . . some distance to northward of ye dwelling house of Mr. Charles Campbell called Charles Campbell of Voluntown . . . sd Spink showed a heap of stones which they declared was the Boundary . . . set his compass and run the line . . . to southwest of sd dwelling house . . . dwelling of Charles Campbell stands about a rod and a half or more to the eastward of sd line and Charles Campbell hath lived in sd dwelling house for some years past. **Joseph Nichols** son of **Benjamin Nichols**, of East Greenwich testified to the truth of Carpenter's deposition.

Joshua Greene of North Kingstown testified that in the summer last past he went to work with James Reynolds of East Greenwich and on sd Reynolds' new place near **Charles Campbell**'s dwelling house . . . cleared ground and such like work . . . saw no fence nor enclosier . . . saw a small shelter where he supposed people had made shingles or other ceder weare by ye shavings that lay about . . . Reynolds showed him a ceder stake or pole which he said stood in ye dividing line [and] their work was to the eastward. The night that he lodged in the aforesaid shelter sd **James Reynolds, Elisha Hambleton, William Sweet** son of **Richard Sweet Jr. & John Reynolds** son of sd James lodged there likewise and they made a fire against a flat stone that stood up against the logs of sd shelter and cleared land within a rod or two of Campbell's fence. **William Sweet** son of Richard testified to the truth of Greene's statements.

Seth Jones of East Greenwich, son of **Jeremiah** testified that he held the plow for James Reynolds . . . saw the small shelter built four square with logg sides and covered with Barke which we plowed round in land for two or three days . . . before we had gott very near . . . one morning or forenoon we saw sd shelter on fire but know not how it came on fire . . . when we saw it we stopt in order to put it out but soon found it was to late . . . burnt oxon's feet . . . never plowed in ye place where it stood. **John Reynolds**, son of James, 18 years of age and upwards, testified to the truth of Jones's deposition.

At Plainfield on 8 December 1735, before **Timothy Pierce**, assistant: **John Mungummery** of Plainfield deposed that some time about the last of August last past he was on the land in controversy . . . saw James Reynolds cuting of timber . . . saw one **Elisha Hambleton** (servant to sd Reynolds) cuting timber with [him] and a young man which I understood to be Reynolds' son with a teem a halling of timber on sd land. **James Gallup** and **Samuel Gordon** deposed that in July last past they saw Elisha Hambleton, servant of James Reynolds, cutting timber . . . lott known by ye name of **Henry Petersons** Lott. **Robert Campbell Jr.** deposed that "in June last I saw the house on the lot known as Henry Peterson's on fire and two teems aplowing round sd house and in about half an hour afterward I saw James Reynolds of East Greenwich a casting of ye brands and ye remainder of sd house together in a heep and in a short time afterward I saw sd Reynolds acasting turf and earth on the place where [it] stood . . . least ye oxen should burn their feet as they passed over same as I suppose." **John Campbell Jr.** testified to the truth of his statements. **Alexander Gordon** and **Samuel Gordon** testified that to their certain knowledge Charles Campbell was in actual possession of the land above this eight years last past. **John Gordon** tesified to the truth of their statement.

On 8 December 1735 at Newport, before **Wm Dyre**, Justice of the Peace, **John Mumford** of North Kingstown, yeoman, stated that about nine or ten years ago he "was surveyor for ye Colony . . . Draw'd a

Draught of ye Colony . . . which was sent to England. I Draw^{d} two lines on ye westward part of sd Governement betweixt Conecticut and Rhoad Island . . . a Red Line and a green line . . . ye Green Line was drawn twenty miles from Warwick Neck to a heap of stones, which now I call ye Middle Line . . . ."

On 27 May 1736 at East Greenwich before Benjamin Sweet, Justice, **John Gallup** of Voluntown deposed that he "was well acquainted with the land in controversy for more than 20 years last past . . . land then Henry Peterson's . . . I did work for sd Peterson on ye sd land above fourteen years last past by fenceing and soeing of Inglish Grass Ceed." To questions, he responded that it was eight or ten years since he had seen a fence on the land, and he saw more than 100 stumps. **Robert Campbell Jr.** and **John Campbell Jr.** deposed at the same time that they had known the land in controversey for more than nine years . . . Campbell had been in improving of the land ever since by feeding of cattle there and by cutting of timber and wood without any interruption till some time since ye first of June last. **James Campbell** of Voluntown testified to the truth of their statements. **John Dickson** of Voluntown testified that in May 1728 he had been in company with two committees . . . heard them debate . . . Mumford was there. . . . **Alexander Gordon** of Voluntown attested his statement.

656. **Bethyah Hedges** of Rehoboth, perukemaker, vs. **John Hunt**, now resident in Providence, tayler, in custody of the sheriff, for £95 for cash laid out and work done, boarding and washing and 84 tickits sold and delivered and goods sold and delivered sundry times beginning in the month of October 1732 and ending in January following. Case was heard first in Inferior Court of Common Pleas at Providence in June 1735, when defendant requested an abatement because the plaintiff's husband was living and she could not therefore bring the suit in her own name. Plaintiff appealed by writ dated 7 January 1735/6.

The plaintiff produced a deed dated at Newport 1 January 1732/3 whereby **Bethiah Hedges** of Newport, wife of **John Hedges** late of sd Newport house carpenter, by virtue of a power of attorney dated 5 October 1728, sold to **Joseph Tillinghast** about 14 acres in Rehoboth, bounded easterly on Palmers River near adjoining to Rocky River, at the northwest corner of **James Lewis**'s ten-acre lot; witnesses were **Mary Ingraham** and **Ann Ingraham**. The deed and the power of attorney, from **John Hedges** of Newport, house carpenter, to his loving wife Bethiah Hedges, witnessed by **Josias Lyndon** and **Mary Lyndon**, were acknowledged 3 February 1732/3 by **Sam^{ll} Vernon**, J.P.

John Osbon Jr. of Newport, cooper, deposed there 8 September 1735 that in 1731 he had been "at the house of J. Hegges in Newport when one **Dunkin Kelly** came in and brought a letter which gave an account of the deth of sd John Hegges and several other papers and delivered same to Bethiah Higges who was the wife of John Higges . . . I being in Jemaca in the December following he saw a man there that told me he was one that lade sd higges out after he was dead and also showed me his grave." **Mary Osbon**, wife of John, testified to the truth of his statement.

Letter in file: "John Hodges the carpenter you brought from New England died in about a Fortnight's time after he came to me. There were found in his Pocketts some Writings that will be of service to the widow viz. a Bill of sale of some lands that belong to her, a certificate of the marriage, one receipt, an Acquittance from **Peter Puor** and an order upon **Wm Cox** Esqr for the payment of £6 - all enclosed - desire you 'd send on as soon as possible to the poor widow - (wishing you a safe return to Jamaica . . . Yr most humble Servt [*signature torn off*]."

— May 1736 —

657. **Mary Wing** now resident in North Kingstown, widow, by **Henry Bull**, attorney, vs. **Mary Coggeshall** of Portsmouth, widow and executrix of **Joshua Coggeshall** who was administrator of his deceased brother **Peleg Coggeshall**, re one-sixth part of £600 left by Peleg Coggeshall, who died intestate on or about August 1730 without issue, leaving surviving the plaintiff [who is] his mother, two brothers: **Joshua** and **Daniel Coggeshall**, and three sisters: **Mary**, wife of **Samuel Clarke**, **Anne**, wife of **Clarke Rodman**, and **Phebe**, wife of **Henry Bull**. (Docket No. 22)

658. **Mary Wing** of North Kingstown, widow, vs. **Mary Coggeshall** of Portsmouth, widow, for her dower, one third of about 150 acres in Portsmouth, of the endowment of **Daniel Coggeshall**, her former husband, deceased, bounded north on **George Cornel**, east on the highway, south on **John Coggeshall**, west on the bay or salt water. Writ

dated 30 April 1736. Inventory of **Daniel Coggeshall,** deceased, 17, 3rd month 1717, sworn to by widow **Mary** and **Joshua,** son and executor.

Will of **Daniel Coggeshall** shown:

In the fear of God Amen I Daniel Coggeshall of Portsmouth in the Colony of Rhode Island and Providence Plantations in New England yeoman, being at the time of the writing hereof very sick and weak of body, but of perfect memory and in right understanding thanks be given unto God therefore calling unto mind the many inconveniences troubles and discords that doth often arise amongst Relations for want of setling, setting in order and disposing of these outward Temporal and worldly Estates.

Therefore to prevent all future differences that might arise for want thereof. I do make this my last Will and Testament Renouncing and Reclaiming, and by these Presents making Null and Void all other former Will and Wills, Testament and Testaments either by word or writing, declaring this to be my absolute last Will and Testament in the following manner and form (that is to say) First and Principally I Recommend my soul into the hands of Almighty God from whence I had my first being And my body to the Earth decently to be Interred at the discretion of my Executrix and Executor hereafter named.

I do by these Presents also order and ordain, nominate and appoint my Executrix and Executor to pay all my Just and lawful debts, and also to receive all debts as are lawfully due unto me.

And I do by these presents, Nominate appoint Constitute make and ordain my well beloved wife **Mary Coggeshall** and my loving son **Joshua Coggeshall** my whole and sole Executrix and Executor to see that this my last Will and Testament be truly Executed fulfilled and performed in every respect according to the true Intent & meaning thereof.

Item I give and bequeath unto my son **Peleg Coggeshall** the sum of six hundred pounds in Bills of publick Credit or current money of New England to be paid unto him the s^{d} **Peleg Coggeshall** the sum of one hundred pounds when he attains to the age of fifteen years, and so to be paid the sum of one hundred pounds a year and every year until he the said Peleg attains to the age of one and twenty years to receive the whole sum of six hundred pounds. And my Mind and Will is that the said money be put to lawful Interest by his Guardian as it comes due to be paid, for the best Use and Advantage of him the said **Peleg Coggeshall** that he may receive the said sum of six hundred pounds with the Interest accrewing thereon when he attains to the age of one and twenty years as abovesaid.

Item I give and bequeath unto my daughter **Anne Coggeshall** her heirs and assigns for ever my two twelve acre lotts of land scituate lying and being in the Township of Portsmouth aforesaid, the one lately granted and laid out unto me by a Comt[ee] Chosen and fully Impowered to lay out all the Commons or undivided land in s[d] Township as may appear by a Return thereof under their hands, and is bounded as by a Plat of the same may more at large appear, and the other lott which I Purchased of **Daniel Lawton Jun[r]**, and is bounded as by a deed thereof under his hand and seal may more at large appear bearing date the eighth day of the Eleventh month 1714 and also my Indian girl **Phillis** during the term of her natural life.

Item I give and bequeath unto my son **Joshua Coggeshall** the sum of twenty pounds in or as money out of my moveable Estate.

Item I give and bequeath unto my son **Joshua Coggeshall** so many bills and Bonds for money due to me as amounts to the sum of five hundred pounds, he paying the money due from me to the Colony abovesaid and clearing up the Mortgage.

Item My mind and Will is, that all the rest of my money due to me upon bonds be by my Executrix and Executor Improprited for the building of a house at the head of my homestead farm next to the highway at the place appointed for the setting of the same according to the demensions already prescribed.

Item I give and bequeath unto my son **Joshua Coggeshall** and his heirs male lawfully begotten of his body, so to remain in that line or lineage for ever all the rest of my housings and land in Portsmouth whereon I now dwell, and also all my lands in the Township of Newport which I purchased of **Bartholomew Hunt** as by a deed thereof under his hand and seal may more at large appear, he the said **Joshua Coggeshall** paying therefore the abovesaid sum of six hundred pounds unto his brother **Peleg Coggeshall** at the times and limits above exprest. But in case my son Joshua Coggesnall will not conform to my manner of disposition of the aforesaid land and housing to him the said **Joshua Coggeshall**, and shall neglect or refuse to pay the abovesaid sum of six hundred pounds unto his brother **Peleg Coggeshall** at the times above expresst and limited, that then my mind and Will is that my said son **Peleg Coggeshall** shall enjoy the aforementioned bequest unto him his heirs and assigns for ever.

Item My mind and Will is that if my son **Joshua Coggeshall** will conform to my manner of disposition as abovesaid, that then he shall enter into the possession of all my Estate herein given to him my s[d] son **Joshua Coggeshall** with all my living stock immediately after my decease.

Item Whereas my honoured father **Joseph Morey** well considered in and by his last Will and Tstament in bequests to my Children hereafter named. In Consideration whereof I have according to the best of my understanding made each legatee equal.

Item I give to my daughter **Mary** the wife of **Samuel Clarke** the sum of ten pounds in or equivalent to money.

Item I give to my son **Daniel Coggeshall** the sum of ten pounds in or equivalent to money.

Item I give unto my daughter **Phebe Coggeshall** the sum of ten pounds as aboves[d].

Item I give to my son **Joseph Coggeshall** the sum of ten pounds in or as money and also my Indian boy **Peter** during the term of his natural life.

Item I give and bequeath unto **Mary Coggeshall** my well beloved wife as a free gift my best feather bed and furniture thereunto belonging, and also my riding horse, and my Indian woman and her sucking child **Jeffery**, but in case my wife shall decease and not sell the said woman and child, then my mind and will is, that either or any of my children enjoy the said woman and child during the term of their natural lives which or to whom of them my wife shall please to bestow them on. Also I give unto my well beloved wife to be at her command all the rest of my houshold goods, whatsoever and wheresoever, and the one half of all my housing so long as she remains my widow, also I give unto my wife one good milch cow out of my Stock such an one as she shall be pleased to chuse, and my mind and Will is that my Executor take care to provide and maintain for one horse and Cow with good winter meat and summer pasture sufficiently for them for the Use and benefit of my wife, and also to provide and allow unto my s[d] wife sufficient firewood during her widowhood, and also provide and keep one [*"good" interlined*] gentle Riding horse for my three younger sons to ride to meeting or other necessary occasions until each of them shall attain to the age of one and twenty years. Also I give unto my wife the sum of eighteen pounds to be paid unto her by my Executor yearly and every year which is in lieu of her thirds during her widowhood.

Item: My mind and Will is that my Executrix and Executor be at equal charge in the bringing up of my younger children until they attain to lawful age according to the discretion of my overseers hereafter named, And further my mind and will is that if my wife sees cause to alter her condition by marriage, then she shall Resign and deliver unto my s[d] Executor all her priviledge in my housing, houshold goods, firewood and keeping for the said horse and Cow (Excepting what is above mentioned given and bequeathed unto her (viz) one horse, one Cow, my Indian woman and child feather bed and furniture thereunto belonging to dispose of as she pleases) and to be paid by my Executor the sum of one hundred pounds which shall then be in lieu of all her thirds of all my Estate whatsoever.

And I do hereby nominate appoint and Request my loving brother

Joshua Coggeshall and my loving son in law **Samuel Clarke** to be my overseers of this my last Will and Testament, desiring them to Counsel and assist my s^{d} Executrix and Executor in the due performance of this my s^{d} Will according to the true purport and meaning thereof, and for their trouble and pains I give unto each of them the sum of five pounds to be paid by my Executor.

In Witness whereof I the said **Daniel Coggeshall** have hereunto set my hand and seal this thirteenth day of (the 3^{d} m^{o}) May 1717

. . . in the presence off
Jonathan Nickolls
Thomas Coggeshall
Wm Sanford

The witnesses were sworn 10 June 1717 and the will recorded by **Wm Sanford**, Council Clerk, who still held that office 3 November 1735 when he made a copy from "the 194th 195th & 196th pages in the Council book or Reg^{r} of Wills $^{\&c}$ N° 2 belonging to the Town of Portsmouth and compared therewith . . ."

Plea of the defendant, **Mary Coggeshall**, widow of **Joshua Coggeshall**, deceased, that she holds the premises by virtue of her husband's will. She had been sued in November 1735 by **Daniel Coggeshall Esq.** of North Kingstown to recover 140 acres. **Josiah Coggeshall** of Newport, cordwainer, on 26 May 1736 testified that he knew Mary, widow of Daniel Coggeshall, kept possession of the houses and land of her sd husband from his death and that she kept her family of children and servant with her until she married **John Wing** of Sandwich; sd Mary Coggeshall was left in possession of sd house and land when **Joshua Coggeshall** went away to Philadelphia for some time. Verdict for plaintiff: £342 damages and costs. (Docket No. 23)

659. **Nathaniel Newdigate**, gentleman, vs. **Capt. Peleg Carr,** shopkeeper, in action of assumpsit re Negro man named **Will**, "sold him by Inch of Candle att **Cap. Gardner**'s Tavern . . . the money to be paid down or bond to me to pay in two months from the day of sale £34:0:0," dated 5 December 1735. Bill of sale in file. (Docket No. 32)

660. **Job Lawton** of Newport, Esq. vs. **Ezekiel Dennis** of Newport, cordwainer, for debt due by note dated 16 May 1735. (Docket No. 126)

661. **Thomas Jeffries** of Newport, cordwainer, vs. **John Talman** of Tivertown, colony of Massachusetts Bay, physician, for debt due by

note dated 12 February 1734. **Stephen Cook** signed as bondsman for Talman, £600. (Docket No. 140)

662. **John Cook** of Newport, shopkeeper, vs. **Reuben Peckcom** of East Greenwich, joyner, for £3:15 due by note dated 1 March 1735. (Docket No. 151)

663. **Mary Coggeshall** of Portsmouth, widow, vs. **Richard Rose** late of Portsmouth, worsted comer, in custody of sheriff, for £7 due for keeping his horse in 1735. (Docket No. 155)

664. **Hopestill Potter** of Newport, shopkeeper, vs. **Joseph Pierce** an Indian man so-called, now resident in Newport, labourer alias mariner, for £6:19:6 due by book for 2 caps, 3 handkerchiefs, one great coat. (Docket No. 162)

665. **Hope Moon** of Newport, spinster, vs. **Walter Cranston** of Newport, merchant, charging that Cranston was the father of the child she was then pregnant with. This is an appeal of a judgement against her received in December 1735 dismissing the defendant. Under examination, Hope stated that "it happened in June" when she had lodged at **Capt. Daniel Amory's** house, where she watched with **Mrs. Lydia Amory** and her child. **Ann Staples** testified that she had been in company with **William Taylor** and Hope Moon in Portsmouth at the house of Taylor's mother, and said Hope told her he had been the ruin of her and the child was his. Hope's mother told her she was going to forswear herself in alleging the child was Cranston's; Ann went to the room of William Taylor at 11 or 12 o'clock at night and asked if Hope Moon was there and sd Taylor said not — upon which she went to the bed and looked under it and sd Hope came out from thence and went and lighted a candle.

666. **John Lawton** of Portsmouth, yeoman, vs. **Lawrence Langworthy** of Newport, pewterer, and wife **Mary,** administratrix of the estate of **Isaac Lawton Jr.**, late of Portsmouth, yeoman, deceased, who died intestate 6 December 1728 leaving personal estate of £2470. The plaintiff being the only son, claimed to be equally entitled to share of estate with the other children of said Isaac Lawton Jr. On back of one document is written: "Mary an infant." **Mary Lawton, John Lawton, Elizabeth Lawton** and **Rebeckah Lawton**, "widow and three of the children of **Isaac Lawton Jr.** of Portsmouth, deceased." Reference to

Town Council meeting 2 March 1729/30 [*? when Mary given administration*]. Judgment for plaintiff. (Docket No. 108)

667. **Robert Taylor**, merchant, and **Patience** his wife, **John Beer**, shipwright, and **Sarah** his wife, all of Newport, vs. **Benjamin Sheffield**, yeoman, and **Ezekiel Johnson**, ferrymen, both of Jamestown, in action of trespass concerning one half part of about four acres of land with houses and buildings in Jamestown. Writ dated 30 April 1736. Many miscellaneous papers, some from an earlier case tried in General Court of Trials in March 1716. Meeting [*? of Jamestown Proprietors*] at **Robert Nichols's** in Newport, 5 March 1708, to discuss "laying out of a highway four rods wide on the south line of township land from sea to sea for use of the countrey for ever . . . have prevailed with Mr. **John Mumford** a noted Surveyor to go with us for to do the work and proceeding on the Premises were forewarned by **Robert Barker** and his wife which stood on the Chain which caused us to desist and which now forces us to lay our Agrievances before this Assembly." **Josiah Arnold** sued **Robert Barker** in March 1710 for possession of four acres of pasture land in Jamestown; Barker claimed he held it as guardian to **Oliver Arnold Jr.** Deposition of **Thomas Parker**, aged 36, dated 24 March 1710/11. Deposition of **Samson Battey.** Copy of Proprietors Meeting at house of **Col. Samuel Cranston, Esq.**, Governor, 17 March 1711/12: order 5 acres be allowed to **Mr. William Sanford.** Meeting of Proprietors 8 April 1712 at house of **Joseph Morey** in Jamestown, at which those present included **Mrs. Phebe Barker** (the only woman); at a meeting 19 May 1712 Phebe Barker drew in right of her son **Oliver Arnold** 20 lots. Deposition 5 September 1715 at Westerly by **Thomas Noyce** of Stonington, about being on Jamestown in June 1712. Thomas Parker made a second deposition on that date, and Mr. **Peter Parker** of Jamestown testified to the truth of Thomas's statement. **Robert Taylor,** shipwright of Newport, and wife **Patience,** sold land on Jamestown to **Teddeman Hull** of Jamestown, yeoman, 16 June 1727, entered in Jamestown Land Evidence 1:35.

– September 1736 – Superior Court –

668. **Daniel Smith** of Warwick, yeoman, vs. **Richard Ireson** of Newport, butcher, for £16:3:11 due for goods sold and delivered from September 1732 to October 1733. Writ dated 8 November 1735. **John Smith** of South Kingstown, yeoman, deposed at Newport 10 September 1736 before **Wm Dyre**, Justice of the Peace, that to his certain knowledge, Daniel Smith of Warwick "has for these twenteyears past ales taken and killed what sheep he had a mine to and carred them out of my flock." Case appealed from Inferior Court of Common Pleas at Providence in December 1735 when plaintiff had received a judgement of £15:6:10. Judgement confirmed.

– 1737 –

669. Appeal of **Thomas Northup** of North Kingstown, yeoman, administrator of the estate of **Stephen Northup** late of sd North Kingstown, deceased, from a judgement of the Town Council of North Kingstown held 8 February last, in favor of **John Rose** of Preston in the Colony of New London, Connecticut, and **Elizabeth** his wife, creditors to the estate of sd Stephen Northup. Writ dated March 31. Judgment affirmed.

670. **Gideon Wanton, Esq.**, General Treasurer of the Colony, vs. **James Austin** of South Kingstown in County Kings, husbandman, and **Margaret** his wife who is executor of the will of **William Gardner** (son of **Henry**) of South Kingstown, yeoman, deceased, for debt of £9:15 due by note dated 17 September 1731 and signed by "William Gardner Son to henery," witnessed by **George Hazard J^{nr}** and **Ichabod Potter.** The writ was endorsed by **James** and **Margret Austen,** witnessed by **Margaret Eldred** (her mark O). Defendant pleaded that the estate had been fully administered.

– May 1738 –

671. **John Taber** now resident in Newport, chairmaker, indicted, charged with stealing one silver spoon valued at 50s from Hon. **John Wanton, Esq.**, of Newport, about 4 May 1738.

672. A warrant was issued for **Thomas Woodman** as father of a bastard child likely to become chargeable to the town . . . sureties required, 28 March 1738. **Ann Cratty,** singlewoman, testified 28 March 1738 that she was a servant to **Benjn Chander** of Newport, cooper, and continued so for seven months, and one **Thos Woodman** was apprenticed to sd Chander. One Sabbath morning in ye month of October 1737, she delivered a child. **John Easton** deposed and said that he was an apprentice to Benjamin Chander, and that sd Ann Cratty had said it was his [but] she would swear it on her master if he asked. **Benjamin Peckham** and **John Dennis,** apprentices, made depositions. **Robert Woodman** of Little Compton, yeoman, and **Benjamin Chanders** of Newport, cooper, gave bond for the appearance of Thomas Woodman.

673. **John Forrester**, glazier, of Newport, vs. **Caleb Carr**, yeoman, of Co. Providence, surviving executor of the last Will and Testament of **Peleg Carr,** late of Newport, merchant, deceased, for £27 due by book for glass, lead and glazier work and liquor at sundry times for **Peleg Carr** from 1 August 1731 to 19 August 1736. (Docket No. 29)

674. **John Forrester**, glazier, of Newport, vs. **Caleb Carr** and **Daniel Carr**, co-executors of the will of **Peleg Carr** [*see case above*]. **Peleg Carr** was bailiff of John Forrester in Newport from 11 May 1732 until he died. Account included silk stockings, 12 pr gloves, chocolate, a suit of silk damask, silver spoons, salt cellars, pepper box, silver spoons, 4 gold rings, etc. A document in the file dated 25 April 1738 at Newport: "I the subscriber do acknowledge that I bought one Suit of Woman's Clothes of Damask of Peleg Carr which did belong to John Forister[s] former wife and paid sd Peleg Carr £12 for the same, signed in Behalf of **Timothy Whiting** pr **James Bull** [constable]." (Docket No. 30)

675. **James Bowdoin** of Boston, merchant, vs. **John Forrester** of Newport, glazier, for £49:14:9 due by note dated 18 November 1736 at Boston. (Docket No. 37)

676. **John Rhodes** of Newport, shopkeeper, vs. **Daniel Underwood** of Newport, hatter, for debt. (Docket No. 38)

677. **James Peckham** of Newport, house carpenter, vs. **John Coddington** of Newport, Esq., for £115:10 owed for labour, work done and material found in building and working on house wherein the defendant now

dwells in Newport, beginning in March 1734 and ending in the year 1735. Included was a receipt from **Robert Sisson** for 5 days and a half at 12*s*/3*d* per day, and a receipt from **Jeremiah Peckham**. (Docket No. 47)

678. **James Gould** of Newport, schoolmaster, vs. **William Ross** of Newport, boat builder, for money due for schooling his son-in-law **Thomas Standley** from 1 March 1736 to September 1737, "to his winters fireing, 5*s*," schooling his son **William** from November 1736 to September 1737, and for writing sundry letters for his wife, 10*s*. (Docket No. 84)

679. **Jared Caswell** of Newport, carter, vs. **Samuel Crandal** of Newport, carter, for debt due by note dated 31 January 1736/7. (Docket No. 87)

680. **William Mumford** of Newport, merchant, vs. **William Brand** of Westerly, husbandman, for debt due by book for a scythe and a gimblett in 1737. (Docket No. 116)

681. **Gideon Freeborn Jr.** of Portsmouth, yeoman, vs. **John Cook** of Portsmouth, husbandman, in custody of sheriff, for trespass. On 32 January 1736/7 Cook struck the plaintiff and broke the little finger of his right hand; the affray took place at the house of **John Freeborn** in Portsmouth. Verdict for the defendant; both guilty of an affray. (Docket No. 134)

682. **Coggeshall vs. Hooper**. Lease from **Job Almy** of Tiverton, Esq., to **William Coggeshall** of Portsmouth, Esq., for land in Newport, dated 21 November 1735. **Dr. Henry Hooper** bailiff. (Docket No. 169)

683. **Simon Peas, Jonathan Tillinghast,** and **Pardon Tillinghast** of Newport, merchants, late owners of sloop *Prudence*, vs. **Resolved Waterman** of Warwick, mariner (late master of sd sloop), for an accounting of the cargo of which he was bailiff. On 19 June 1736 the sloop shipped for the Leeward Islands in the West Indies, carrying 12,500 feet of boards, 7,000 staves, 2,000 shingles, 2,300 hoops, 1,500 heading, 10 barrels of flour, 16 barrels of fishes, 6 barrels of tar, 5 barrels of pork, 5 barrels of beef, 9 boxes of candles, 25 horses, and 50 hogsheads of water. Receipt in file signed by **James Carder** at St. Eustatius, September 1736. (Docket No. 173)

684. **John Cook** of Portsmouth, husbandman, vs. **Gideon Freeborn Jr.** of Portsmouth, yeoman [*cf. No. 681*]. Depositions were made by **Barnet Sisson** and **William Coggeshall, Jr.**, that Cook said to Freeborn, "you

have bit my thumb and finger and tore my lip," and the landlady with her Negro separated them. **John Albro** deposed and said that Cook said he "would not strip to fight with no such sorry Rascal." **John Coggeshall** and **William Cornell** made depositions, and **George Cornell** stated that "Freeborn first threw Cook but Cook soon got uppermost . . . [he said] 'Don't care if yr Neck is Brock I should not be y[e] means of setting of it.'" Verdict was for the plaintiff. Freeborn filed an appeal but withdrew it and paid court costs. (Docket No. 211)

685. **Joseph Dennis** of Portsmouth, yeoman, vs. **Thomas Durfey** of Portsmouth, ferryman alias yeoman, charging that on 15 May 1736 the plaintiff and defendant with other owners of the sloop *Sarah and Mary* made up accounts and the defendant had received £52:16:11 more than his due proportion. Verdict for plaintiff. (Docket No. 216)

686. **John Hoag**, late resident in Newport, cooper, vs. **Richard Babcock** of Newport, mariner, for £21:8 due by book for making and trimming of casks and helping to load the *Charming Betty* from 28 December 1736 to 19 March 1736/7. (Docket No. 260)

687. **James Hawden** of Boston, shopkeeper, vs. **Daniel Greene** of Newport, practitioner in physick alias shopkeeper, for £494:19:5 due for sundry goods . . . nutmigs, stockens, knives, handkerchief, brown holland. . . . (Docket No. 265)

– November 1738 –

688. **Theophilus Bradford** of Newport, mariner, vs. **Josias Jennings** of Newport, mariner, in action of trespass. On 15 August 1735, the defendant entered the dwelling house of the plaintiff and threw down y[e] tea table of y[e] plaintiff and broke diverse china vessels thereon to y[e] value of £20. **John Trobridge** of Newport, mariner, made a deposition and said that sometime in June 1737 he agreed with **Ruth Bradford** the wife of Theophilus Bradford for about £3 for the damage that Josias Jennings did in "Braking of Her Channey Ware." **Ruth Trowbridge**, wife of John, agreed. **Bathsheba Baker**, wife of **Benj[a] Baker** of Newport, mariner, testified that she saw Josias Jennings "a Playing with **Moriah Chace** ye wife of **Ezekiah Chace** of sd Newport, mariner . . . Chace took up a mugg of Beer and made an attempt to through it at sd Josias and the wench to hinder her and he stepping Backwards

Run against ye Tee Table and over set." **Samuel Perry** of Swansey, Co. Bristol, ship carpenter, deposed and said that he was at the house of Theophilus Bradford and saw Josiah Jennings and Moriah Chace, etc. (Docket No. 237)

689. **Christopher Palmer** of Westerly, innholder, vs. **Thomas Havens** now resident in New Shoreham, mason, for money due by note. (Docket No. 26)

690. **Anna Dennis** of Newport, widow and executrix of **John Dennis** late of Newport, yeoman, deceased, vs. **Kendal Nichols** of Newport, Esq., for £11:17:6 due for work John had done from June 1728 to June 1729, "carting loads . . . 2 days with my team and 2 hands . . . ." (Docket No. 58)

691. **John Brown** of Newport, distiller, vs. **John Anderson** of Windsor, Co. Hartford, Connecticut, yeoman, for debt of £330. (Docket No. 82)

692. **Benjamin Sheffield** of Jamestown, gentleman, vs. **Parker Hall** of Newport, cordwainer, for £90 due for leather sold to him from 1736 to 1738. (Docket No. 84)

693. **James Hill** of Newport, taylor, vs. **Daniel Underwood** of Newport, hatter, for £3:16:6 due for making cloaths, etc. (Docket No. 85)

694. **Thomas Durfey** [*sic*] of Portsmouth, yeoman, vs. **Job Durfee** [*sic*] of Portsmouth, mariner, for £212:14:4 lent in cash and for wool, sugar, liquor, port and beef sold and delivered in 1735. (Docket No. 95)

695. **Gideon Wanton Esq.**, General Treasurer of the Colony, vs. **Nathaniel Hatch** of Newport, sailmaker, for money due by notes dated 24 August 1728.

696. **William French** of Stonington in Co. New London, merchant, vs. **John Cahoone** of Newport, mariner, for refusing to render an account; defendant had been mate of the sloop *Neptune* which carried wheat to Boston to **Thomas Green** of Boston. (Docket No. 188)

– March 1739 – Superior Court –

697. **Daniel Howland** of Portsmouth, merchant, vs. **Jeremiah Finney** of Bristol, province of Massachusetts Bay, mariner, for debt due by note dated 29 April 1738, witnessed by **Josiah Haynes** and **Jos: Fox**. Case

was heard at Providence County Inferior Court of Common Pleas, December 1738. The defendant defaulted; verdict for plaintiff to recover £147:06:10; defendant appealed but did not prosecute. Earlier judgment affirmed with double costs and interest.

– May 1739 –

698. **Ephraim Bull** of South Kingstown, yeoman, vs. **Phillip Underwood** of Newport, boatman, for £12:16 due for steers sold and delivered in June 1733. Writ dated April 1739.

699. **Return Humery** of Newport, cordwainer, otherwise Return Humery of Portsmouth, vs. **Robert Gardner** of Newport, mariner, and wife **Ann**. By an Indenture dated 15 February 1737, Return Humery had put and bound his daughter **Ruth Humery** unto the defendants as an apprentice from 8 February 1737 for 10 years and 8 months . . . Ruth serves but they refuse to provide her with two suits of apparel. . . . Writ dated 8 May 1739. (Docket No. 30)

700. **Jonathan Wood** of Dartmouth vs. **Stephen Manchester** of Tiverton, blacksmith, for £23 due from a pair of oxen sold and delivered in November 1732. (Docket No. 230)

– November 1739 –

701. **Daniel Shapley** [**Staples** on outside of file] of New London, cooper, vs. **Clement Nichols** of the Island of St. Christopher in the West Indies, merchant, now resident in Newport, in an action of assumpsit. Writ dated 22 June 1739; **James Honyman**, attorney. Nichols had promised to remit and send to the plaintiff or his assigns £28:7:0 in St. Kitts money in rum at 1*s*/6*d* per gallon, in return for value received. Bond signed, witnessed by **Joseph Truman** and **Denis Hogan** at New London.

702. **Deborah Knowlton** of Newport, widow and administratrix of **Joseph Knowlton** of Newport, house carpenter, deceased, vs. **John Coddington** of Newport, Esquire, for £280:3:0 due by bond dated 21 March 1736, witnessed by **Samuel Haydon** and **James England**. Writ dated 30 October 1739; **M[atthe]w Robinson** attorney.

703. **Samuel Hull** of Newport, gentleman, vs. **John Lance** of Newport, brewer, in action of trespass, charging that the defendant made illegal entry into a lot with stable and mansion house thereon, which **Henry Hedley** of Dartmouth on 17 January 1738 sold to the plaintiff. Depositions by **Robert Odlin** and **John Bazin**, both blacksmiths of Newport. (Docket No. 230)

704. **Thomas Stodder** of Newport, mariner, vs. **Christopher Almy** of Newport, merchant, for £27 due for 14 days service done on the defendant's sloop, of which **Charles Whitfield** was master, and 8 days service by the plaintiff's Indian man, and 3 months lost time and disappointment "before I had another employ." Writ dated 23 October 1739; **Henry Bull** attorney. Bill, "Christopher Almy sloop that Charles Whitfield is Gone to Sea in from 16 April - 30 April, 10*s* pr day." Verdict for plaintiff, £9:8 and cost of court, reversed upon a rehearing.

705. **Jonah Baley** of Newport, executor of the will of **John Clarke** late resident in Newport, chirurgion, deceased, vs. **Nicholas White** of Newport, mariner, in custody of the sheriff, for not delivering to the plaintiff as executor 5 baggs of cotton wool containing 863 lbs weight to the value of £172:12:0 which the defendant received of sd John Clarke at the Island of Nevis in the West Indies in August 1738 to transport to Newport in the sloop *Phenix* whereof he was master and there redeliver . . . [he] did transport it and convert it to his own use. Writ dated 31 October 1739. Verdict for the defendant, costs of court; reversed upon a rehearing, for the plaintiff, goods sued for and costs of court.

– Miscellaneous –

706. **Dispute about church land in Kingstown.** [*Found in a box with cases dated in 1739, evidently a copy of an earlier case. This well-known controversy dragged on for some years.*]

In September 1723 **James M^c^Sparran** of South Kingstown, clerk, present incumbent of the Church of England called St. Paul's in Narrangansett in North Kingstown, vs. **George Mumford** of South Kingstown, yeoman alias gentleman, in an action of trespass, concerning 280 acres in North Kingstown, bounded south on land of **Jahleel Brenton**, west on Wordens Pond and Pine Swamp, north on the

Swamp and on land of the plaintiff now in possession of **William Gardner** son of **Henry** of South Kingstown, yeoman, and part on the highway, and east on land of **Henry Gardner**.

At Superior Court in September 1735 **Joseph Torrey** vs. **Ephraim Gardner**. On 21 January 1734[?5], **Thomas Harvey**, aged 94, and **Robert Crosman**, aged upwards of 77, both of Taunton, Massachusetts, members of the Church of Christ in Taunton, testified that Crosman had been minister there, and Harvey since . . . "in the time of the ministry of the Rev. **George Shove**, the Honble **William Brenton** and his wife and family came from Rhode Island to sd Taunton and bought considerable lands and built upon it near the Meeting House which was also Mr. Shoves and were very liberal and free hearted to Mr. Shove and his family and also attended the publick worship of God on Sabbath Days under his ministry and also manifested such a love for the minister and our Church way which was Congregational that they gave a velvet cushion of considerable value for the pulpit and was at great charge in building a new meeting house, and had a particular seat or pew in it at their own charge and continued beloved both by church and town and she died in Taunton aforesaid much missed . . . we would farther say that the church way of England was very dissagreeable with us in Taunton in that day and we believe that Mrs. Brenton joined to our Church. Neither did his Honour Mr. Brenton nor any others profess and practice the Church way, but the Congregational."

On 17 May 1735, **Mrs. Mary Webb** of South Kingstown, widow, aged 72 or thereabouts, stated that her honored father **Samuel Wilson** late of Kingstown, deceased, was one of the original proprietors of the Pettaquamscutt Purchase and was always of the Presbyterian Perswasion. On 23 March 1738[/9], **Jeremiah Hazard** of North Kingstown, aged 63 or thereabouts, deposed before **Rowse Helme**, assistant, and **Abiel Shearman** of South Kingstown also, who stated that he had lived in the town 30 years or upwards and had heard it reported by the ancient people that the land called the Minister's Land was laid out and intended for the Presbiterian Society. **Mr. Thomas Hazard** of South Kingstown, aged 78 years and upwards, stated that his father was formerly a surveyor and "imployed by the Purchasers of the Pettaquamscutt Purchase to survey a great part of sd Purchase . . . often heard father say the Purchasers had ordered a tract laid out for the

Presbiterian Society." The same day, **Joseph Case ye 2d** of South Kingstown, aged 63 and upwards, stated that he often heard **Henry Gardner** say the land was given to the Presbyterian ministry. He had seen **James Bundy** at work on sd Minister's Farm who told him he worked there under Mr **Samuel Niles** who was a Presbyterian. The same day, **Michael Gardner** of South Kingstown stated that "when Mr Samuel Niles lived in Kingstown and presented the land to the inhabitants of sd town, the deponent cut some firewood on the farm called the Minister's Farm . . . when he went to cart it away **James Bundy** opposed him . . . he [was] settled there by Niles to take care and preserve the wood on sd Farm . . . deponent went to Niles and [was given] liberty to take off what wood he had already cutt . . . the Farm was laid out for the Presbyterians . . . often heard his father and unkles declare the same who were assignes to **John Porter** one of the Proprietors of the Pettaquamscutt Purchase." The same day, **Jeremiah Willson** of South Kingstown, aged 64 or thereabouts, professed himself "a Prisbiterian and generally attends Mr Torry's meeting," stating that he was "the only surviving son and heir to Mr **Samuel Wilson** deceased who was one of the grantors of land called the Minister's Farm in South Kingstown; he never heard his father was a churchman untill he heard Henry Gardner's evidence . . . never knew that any of his father's posterity were ever churchmen or ever pretended to it." On 26 March 1739 **Sarah Potter** of South Kingstown, widow, aged 73 or thereabouts, gave evidence concerning her father **Samuel Wilson**. On 28 March 1739 Major **Job Green** of Warwick, aged 83 or thereabouts, stated that Gov. **William Brenton** and Mr. **John Hull** were of the Presbyterian Perswaysion, and that Mr. **Sam^{ll} Wilbore** was inclined to the same religion, before any church of England or Presbyterian ministry was settled in Rhode Island Colony.

— February 1739/40 —

707. **Jonathan Metcalf** of Dedham [Massachusetts], merchant, vs. **Nathaniel Sweeting** of Providence, mariner, in custody of the sheriff, for an accounting of the time he was the plaintiff's bailiff and receiver at the Island of New Providence in the West Indies, of about 2300 feet of mahogany planks. Writ dated 7 January 1739[/40]; **Matthew Robinson** attorney. On 29 May 1739 at New Providence the defendant

was in the capacity of Super Cargo on board the sloop *Mary-gold* of which he was master; he did ship mahogany valued at £200 which he was to trade for the plaintiff's profit and advantage. The defendant proceeded to Jamaica where he disposed of sd planks and received the proceeds thereof, but refuses to render an accounting. The defendant by his attorney **Daniel Updike** answered that he was an infant under 21 both at the time of the charge and the writ. Record in file: **Nathaniel Sweeting** son of **Henry Sweeting** and his wife **Esther** was born in Rehoboth November 8, 1720.

The portage bill for the sloop lists the crew: **Nathaniel Sweeting**, master, **William Blyth**, mate; and sailors: **James Sheld** (run away), **Samuel Robbin, Joseph Day, Samuel Frank, James Perse**, and **Uriah [--]deson**, and specified a voyage to South Carolina "or else where and so home to Rhode Island," the men agreeing to "obey orders and do our duty as seamen according to the Quality we are shipt in, in consideration of wages. . . ."

Charles Tillinghast of Providence, merchant, deposed 29 January that in December last past he received on order of Mr. **Henry Sweeting** of Providence, inn-holder, one hogshead of sugar from **Capt. Crook** at Newport, delivered to a Negro man belonging to **John Brown** of Newport, mariner. **James Pearce** of Providence, sailor, testified that **Daniel Belon**, a Linguister, was on board the sloop . . . from New Providence they sailed for the Coast of Hispaniola where Metcalf and Belon went ashore and ordered Sweeting to bring the sloop ashore into a certain place or port on a certain day . . . Sweeting did not do nor attempt to do it . . . Some time after [he] sailed away from the Coast of Hispaniola without taking on board Metcalf and Belon and arrived at the Port of Kingston in Jamaica where he sold the mahogany planks . . . part belonged to Belon, for which Sweeting took sugar. Depositions were made 14 February before **Richard Waterman**, J.P., by Mr. **Joseph Snow** of Providence, who said he was present when Nathaniel Sweeting signed the portage bill and Nathaniel's father Mr. **Henry Sweeting** was present also; by **William Blyth** [Bly in summons] of Newport, mariner, who said he had been mate on the sloop and saw a hogshead of sugar marked *HS* on board the Brigantine *Tyger*, **Thomas Crook** commander, and thought it was the plaintiff's; and by **Joseph Day** of Attleborough who said he had been on board in Quality of a mariner and said it was "publickly reputed that Sweeting did follow Gaming and fooled away the cargo." **Nicholas Cook** of Providence testified 14 February before **William Hopkins**, J.P., that at the end of August last he was at Kingstown on the Island of Jamaica and there Nathaniel Sweeting told him that he had sold a certain quantity of mahogany planks at 20*s* pr 100 and was about to ship a hogshead of sugar to his father . . . he was afraid that one Belon a Linguist on Board would sue him for some planks he took on board of his.

Depositions were made 20 February before **Charles Bardin**, J.P.: **Samuel Rodman** of Newport testified that he saw the sugar on the arrival of his Brigantine, Capt. **Thomas Crook** master, in December last, and saw the Captain deliver it to **Charles Tillinghast** of Providence; **Thomas Rodman** testified that he was a mariner on board the Brigantine *Tyger* and saw the sugar, etc.; **Samuel Sanford** testified that in December a hogshead of sugar was trucked from **Capt. Whipple's** wharf by Capt. John Brown's trucks and put in store on Capt. Brown's wharf . . . he was desired by M^{rs}. Sweeting, wife of Henry of Providence, to put it into barrells . . . filled three large full gaged barrels and two flower barrels [and] about half of another.

Judgement was for Henry Sweeting to receive the sugar, the defendant to render an accounting, and the plaintiff to recover costs of court.

– 1740 –

708. **Simon Pease** and **Benjamin Norton**, both of Newport, merchants, late owners of the sloop *Sea Flower*, vs. **John Bristow** of Newport, mariner, late master of said sloop, for an account of when he was bailiff in 1737 of goods shipt on a voyage to the Island of Jamaica: 6 horses, 21 barrels of mackril, 20 barrels of munhaden, 6 hogheads of dry fish, 4 barrels of oyls, 11000 staves, 2000 hoops, 2000 heading, 13 barrels onions, 20 barrels flour, 15 barrels beef, 25 barrels pork, 4 half-barrels hogsfat, 127 cheeses, 12 boxes candles, 7000 shingles, 52 sheep, 54 hogs and 26 water casks, on the account of the plaintiffs. Writ dated 15 April 1740; heard at May term. The defendant's accounting of disbursements included sums "to Spanish Town for a chariot, my dinner and Bondsman, for a wherry to find our Boat, Gunner at Fort, twine for mending sailes, wherry hire, dining and chariot at Spanish Town, pilotage and storage, rum for vessel and cooper, fresh meat, horse hire, paying for Doctor for **Edward Williams** and carpenter for making a coffin for [him]." The cargo brought £495:2:4½, and after expenses amounted to £426:16:10½ which was spent for molasses, purchased from **Curn^{ll} Herning, John Stout, John Ferris, Thomas Williams, Paul Stevens, John Lawrence, Capt. Partick, Corn^{l} Guttery, Henry Shorklewood, Hugh Hynes, Lewis Williams, John Graves, William Rickits, Jno Woolery, Capt. George Goodin, Madam Hynes, Robert Ruddyford,** and **Samuel Records**. He had given one cheese to the pilot, one barrel of onions rotted, 3 hogs were lost in the voyage, one small cheese was given to "my Bondsman," and 29 sheep were lost in the Passage. John Bristow attested the accounting 20 May 1740. The file contains an extremely carefully detailed accounting of molasses taken on board in Jamaica for the owners, attested by **Hen: Terrell**, now resident in Newport, "attsettory mariner," as being true and just.

Jno Beard of Newport, mariner, deposed in Newport 19 May 1740 before **William Dyre**, J.P., and said that on or about 26 March 1738 he was at the house of **Mr. Paul Stevens** in Jamaica . . . "heard a great dispute about 2 hogsheads of molasses which the wharfinger had charg'd him with . . . Capt. John Bristow told him he never received them aboard . . . which sd deponent verily due believe fort its yousually for one Boat to bring for and other Vesle if there is none ready for themselves . . . did hear sd Paul Stevens in March 1740 say that he did believe it was owing to the Wharfinger being a drunken Fellow and is since run away . . . if Capt. Bristow's owners did insist upon Bristow to pay it that he would pay it to Capt. Bristow. . . ." The case went to referees; Bristow chose Capt. **Richard Mumford**, the plaintiffs chose **Capt. Elnathan Hammond**, the court appointed **Charles Bardin**, Esq. On 12 March 1741 they found Bristow justly indebted £62:19:4, and any balance in Jamaica, debt or credit, was to be his.

709. **Jeremiah Sheffield** of South Kingstown, yeoman, and wife **Mary** vs. **Abraham Briant** of South Kingstown, blacksmith, in custody of the sheriff, in an action of trespass. Writ dated 25 August 1740; **Daniel Updike** attorney. The plaintiffs charged that the defendant on 21 August 1740 struck Mary with a large cane having an iron spike therein and hurt her left arm so that she lost the use of it; claimed damages of £1000.

On 9 September 1740 before **Isaac Sheldon**, Justice: **Jedediah Collins** testified that on or about the 21 August last past he went to the House of **Capt. Jeremiah Sheffield** in South Kingstown in order to talk with **Abigail Sabins** who was then there & to tell her how the case went on & how Mr Briant had pleaded against her and **Mary Sheffield** the Wife of the afores^d^ Capt Sheffield standing by as this Deponent was talking with the said Abigail, said to [her] 'if you & Aunt Hannah will stand by me We will lick him' then **Hannah Brooks** spoke & said 'how shall We come at him?' whereupon Abigail Sabins replied that She would call to him & tell him that She wanted to speak wth him & so get him into the Bedroom, and then they should come in & lick him . . . heard Mary Sheffield say 'if he has got his Ruffles on I'll tear them off' . . . saw one of the women have a stick in her Hand but which of them he cannot tell. . . .

Nicholas Lee testified that he was at the house of Capt Jeremiah Sheffield, etc. ". . . saw Abigail Sabins go out and return with a stick in her hand & then Mary Sheffield went directly out and brought in two Sticks & then Jedediah Collins being in sd House & sitting at the Window got up & looked out of the window & said 'Mr Briant is coming & when he does come along I Question if he will come in.' Then Abigail Sabins made Answer & said 'I will contrive a way to get him in then' . . . would step out & call him & tell him that she wanted to speak with him and she knew that he would come in . . . asked Mary

Sheffield if he had got his Ruffles on and [she] said he had, then said Abigail 'if I can get hold on them I will pull them off.' Then this deponent began to laugh whereupon [Mary & Abigail] desired him to hold his Tongue & tell Briant nothing when he came & then [Mary] said to [Abigail] 'I am afraid Aunt Hannah won't be of good Courage as she pretends to now' and then Capt **Job Babcock** coming in they held their Tongues And [I] heard no more & went of[f]."

Warrant for Mary, Hannah, and Abigail to appear before some of his Majesty's Justices to answer complaint of **Abraham Briant** of South Kingstown, blacksmith, against **Mary Sheffield** wife of Capt Jeremiah Sheffield, yeoman, and **Hannah Brooks** wife to **John Brooks**, blacksmith, all of South Kingstown, and **Abigail Sabins**, wife to **Elizer Sabins** late of Jamestown in the county of Newport, mariner, For that the said Mary, Hannah, and Abigail in South Kingstown on or about 21 August last past with Force & Arms upon the Body of the said Abraham an Assault did make and in a violent & hostilent Manner did tear his Cloaths with a Design of maiming his Body all which is against the Peace of our Sovereign Lord the King –

In Court on 12 September 1740: **Ichabod Sheffield** testified that on 11 September 1740 "**John Brookes** of South Kingstown blacksmith came to my House in the Evening . . . told me he was summoned to appear at Court the Tuesday following to give an Evidence Between Abraham Briant & Mary Sheffield, Nab & his Wife which Nab I understood to be Abigail Sabins concerning an Affray which happened between the sd Briant & the aboves^{d} Women . . . I asked him . . . how the Fray was or what he could say in the Affair or something to that Effect whereupon he answered he would tell me how it was & then he began as followeth. 'They are related to me' . . . by which I understood he meant the aboves^{d} Women. But said he I must or will say what I now for I will not wrong my Conscience for any of them. . . . Then he said he heard the Women talking about Briant and one of them said that Briant was coming or that they expected him there or along by there – And so they begun to contrive how to get him into the House . . . one of them said she would call him in and **Mary Sheffield** swore that she would geld him for getting her Sister with Child. And Nab as he called her swore that she would ackx him or beat him & then they bean to provide sticks or clubs and Brooks said there was handy sticks or clubs in the oven or corner so that they need not seek far for them . . . it was concluded upon by s^{d} women to call or intice Briant into the House and then to fall on him with the clubs or sticks . . . **Jedediah Collins** the Constable was there and he was to [go] out far away from said House if they could perswade Briant in. And he said more by which I understood that he & Collins went from the House and that Briant went towards the House & presently after he said that he see Briant have hold of Mary Sheffield by the Hand & Beating of her with his Cane." **Abigail Sabins** stated that she was at the house of **Jeremiah Sheffield** on 21 August and seeing **Abraham Briant** riding by, called to him to speak with him . . . he made answer that as soon as he had left his work at the Smiths Shop he would come.

Arthur Gates Auchmuty testified that on or about the 7th of September, **John Brooks** came to his house and told him that he was summoned by **Abraham Briant** to swear against his wife his Daughter in Law & **Mary Sheffield**, And that he could swear nothing against his Wife but that he should make the Court laugh when he gave his Evidence . . . because he heard Mary Sheffield say to the Women I will geld the Dog. . . . Brooks told him he was almost all the Day at the House of **Jonathan Nash** & had sent to **Esq. Potters** for Rum but could get none & so was forced to drink Nothing but Water.

Ebenezer Brenton testified in court 17 February 1740[/1] that he was at the house of **Capt. Jeremiah Sheffield** in August last "& seeing the wife of sd Sheffield sit in a Disconsolate Posture asked her what ailed her she answered she had been much beat & abused by **Abraham Briant** And in a few Minutes **Doct^{r} Rodman** & some others came in And she shewed the Doct^{r} her Head, Back, Armes, Wrist, and Fingers which were much hurt especially her Back & Wrist. **Thomas Rodman** testified to the truth of that, adding that the upper bone of her wrist was cracked.

— November 1740 — Court of General Sessions —

710. **Mary Maddin**, an apprentice girl, vs. **William Brown**, barbour, and wife **Mary**, of Newport, charging them with abuse and hard usage. Mary Maddin, a minor of her own free will and with the consent of her father **Thomas Maddin** of Boston, currier, on 4 May 1734 bound herself apprentice to **Michael Wood** of Boston, shopkeeper, and his

wife **Mary** for 11 years to begin 29 May 1734. Michael and Mary agreed to teach her to read, etc., and at expiration of the time to deliver to her a feather bed and bedcloaths, 6 chairs and one oval table, a brass kettle, a trammel and gridiron, all compted to be worth £15:2:0. Thomas signed his name, Mary her mark. Witnesses: **Thomas (*mark X*) Power, Allen Drummond, Arth^r Weals.** **Mary**, wife of **William Brown** and late wife of Michael Wood late of Newport, deceased, was ordered to appear at the house of **Samuel Webb** of Newport, vintner, 3 December 1740. M^rs. **Lance**, wife of **Jno Lance** deposed and said that she saw Mary sundry times without a shift and with marks of a whip upon her back. **Mary**, wife of **William Claggett** testified that she saw her barefoot in snowy weather, and **Henry Osborn** said that she came to borrow in her mistress's name and afterwards her mistress swore that she did not send her. **Bathsheba Gallagher** testified that the apprentice had two new gowns and two shifts since the death of her former master Mr. Woods [*sic*]. **William Waters** testified that he had seen William Brown's wife with several things in her apron that she said her apprentice had stolen from her. **Nathl Langly** said that the apprentice came to his house and was there four days, her cloathes ready to drop off her back . . . his wife put a shift upon her . . . **William Brown** came to get her and sd she was guilty of no crime but running away. The court decided that **Mary Madin** was greatly abused and ill-used and discharged her from her apprenticeship with orders to the Browns to deliver to her all that was due her.

— November 1740 — Inferior Court of Common Pleas —

711. **Thomas Huxham** of Newport, butcher, vs. **Abraham Brown** of Tiverton, county of Bristol, yeoman, in custody of the sheriff, for driving into the water at Tiverton four oxen valued at £240 belonging to the plaintiff; one drowned and the others were much hurt. Writ dated 23 September 1740; **J. Honyman** attorney. **Peleg Sherman** of Portsmouth, yeoman, deposed on 18 November 1740 before **Wm. Dyre**, J.P., that he "saw four oxen feeding in the Marsh and some English Hay which I thought was not sufficient for Cattle by reason they were fattining Cattle." **Daniel Howland** of Portsmouth, Esq., testified that some time in the year 1738 **Abraham Brown** brought four oxen he said

were **Thomas Huxham**'s and desired Howland to carry them over the Ferry . . . they were tied to the boat but were so large they could not be carried so they towed them over. Four or five weeks afterwards the deponent was at the other end of the Ferry and Huxham's man and Brown brought back the said Oxen to John Howland's Ferry and asked him to bring them over . . . "after they came to shore several of the People stept on Shore in order to save sd Oxes life & endeavoured all they could by Turning his Head down Hill but all to no Purpose whereupon one of the company cut [his] throat . . . deponent together with some of the others helped Huxham's Boy get sd Ox up to the Gallows and dress him . . . Huxham came himself and acknowledged the kindness . . . and sent sd Beef to Newport." **Baze Manchester** of Portsmouth, cordwainer, testified that he helped put the ox on board **Byal Tripp**'s boat and deliver him. On 20 November **Edward Perry** of Portsmouth testified before William Anthony, Justice, that he had received by Huxham's order the beef of an ox dressed at Daniel Howland's Ferry and carried it and delivered it at Newport to Huxham's people in his Slaughter House. **Edward Kerby** of Newport, butcher, deposed 24 November 1740 before William Dyre, J.P.,that he was going with his master Thomas Huxham to Dartmouth in the year 1738 when his horse tired and his master left him at Abraham Brown's. Brown was not home but came that night, and the next morning he and Brown drove the four oxen down to John Howland's Ferry where they were "Roped or drove into the Water and toed over the Ferry . . . Brown had hold of the rope to one [which] was drowned . . . Brown went and got four oxen to draw [it] up to the Gallows and there said ox was drest and sent in a boat to Newport. [I] came home that night afterwards, to Newport on horse back to meet the Boat with the Ox . . . [it] did not come . . . [I] told **Henry West** to take care of ye Beef when it did come . . . afterwards met Mr. Thomas Huxham on sd Island and when we came home we found sd Beef so damnified it was not merchantable. In the afternoon when [I] was at Browns house [I] went down into the Meadow to see the Cattle belonging to Huxham and there was nothing but Ledge Hay and salt marsh [for them] to feed on. Huxham gave orders not to take ye Cattle away without sd Brown coud deliver them safe over the Ferry." Verdict for the defendant, costs of court; appealed.

712. **Thomas Toman** late of Newport, mariner, vs. **Isaac Beauchamp** late of Newport, mariner, in custody of the sheriff, for £4 in Virginia currency due by note dated 2 January 1737[/8]. Writ dated 13 October 1740. Bond made out to Thomas Towman . . . it being his proper right of a note from **John Scarbrugh** to Isaac Beauchamp dated 8 July 1737.

713. **John Benson** of Newport, cordwainer, vs. **Daniel Dunham** of Newport, house carpenter, in custody of the sheriff, for £12 due for the plaintiff's extraordinary trouble and attendance night and day in nursing the defendant in small pox, finding rich cordials, victuals, and also victuals for his wife in the year 1739. Writ dated 14 October 1740; **Henry Bull** attorney. The bill showed credit for "my wife tending sick fore weeks at Costrs harbor [at £3 per week], making a well pole, a cobbing for West, 2 Behives, 2 days making of hay, 2 mobs, 1 holon hankacur, 1 flannel wescot al thees never returned to the vallew of. . . ." **Sarah Dunham** swore in court to the truth and justice of the first and last articles, and **Daniel Dunham** to the rest. **James Bull** of Newport, shipwright, deposed 19 November 1740 before **William Dyre**, Justice, that he was "in the months of June and July 1739 at Coasters Harbour sick with ye small pox and at the same time among others **Daniel Dunham** was there also sick of the same Distemper in the same room with [me] . . . the Defendant's wife was there to assist her husband . . . at sundry times brought [me] Drink & Victuals & Watched in the same room with others." **Gershom Jennings** of Newport, tailer, testified to the truth of the above. Verdict for the plaintiff, £8:19:0 and costs of court; reversed upon a rehearing for the defendant.

714. **Nathaniel Newdigate** of Newport, gentleman, vs. **Benjamin Pitman** of Newport, mariner, in custody of the sheriff, in an action of Wast[e]: whereas it is unlawful for anyone to make Wast or Distruction in Houses Lands or Gardens to him demised for term of life or years . . . sd Benjamin had made wast and Distruction of a House and Garden to him demised for a term of years, to the Disinheriting of the Plaintiff. Writ dated 16 October 1740; plaintiff his own attorney. On 6 September 1735 Nathaniel was seized in fee simple of one dwelling and garden in Newport which he did demise and let to said Benjamin one large roome with two bed Roomes in the Ground Floor with the Cellar underneath and garden thereto adjoyning fenced in by a post and

board fence with a Little house, commonly called a House of office in sd Garden built and erected, and the defendant from then to 12 September 1740 enjoyed [it] during which time he made wast . . . suffering the Little House of the price of £5 to be pulled down and destroyed and the Vault under it to be filled up and by suffering the fence of the price of 40 shillings between ye street and sd garden to be broken down and ye garden spoyled by laying a great Quantity of Bricks and Rubbish on same . . . suffering ye Cellar Door of sd dwelling of ye price of £3 to be broke to pieces and destroyed . . . damages £40.

Thomas Dunham of Newport, house carpenter, deposed 5 March 1740 before William Dyre, J.P., and said that he had been ordered by the plaintiff some time in the month of July or August last past to make cellar doors . . . "seller was over shoes in mudd and was ussless." **Thomas Chadwick** of Newport, fisherman, deposed that some time in May 1739 "I took down ye Boards on ye street side of house and ye Gate . . . Laied them Down by South part of sd House . . . to Best of my Knowledg Every one of them Boards was nailed up on ye Eastermost side of sd House . . . ye Little House stood a foot and a Half on my Land . . . Tooke [it] and Laid it Down on His Land . . . some time after I saw [the plaintiff] and Told him I would be at one Half ye Cost to set it on His Land because I had not Room of my own and all ye answer sd Nathaniel made me that he would sue me for moving his Little House."

715. **Charles Smith** of Newport, bricklayer, vs. **John Cole** (son of **Elisha**) of North Kingstown, gentleman, for £11:10:0 for work done and 12 bushels of lime sold and delivered in April 1740. Writ dated 27 October 1740; **Thomas Ward** attorney. The account was for "building a stack of Cimnys wth Stone wth 2 funnils and an oven wth bricks £10, and 12 bushels of lime at £1:10:0." The defendant charged that the plaintiff had not built sd chimneys workmanlike.

— May Term 1741 —

716. **Robert Spencer** of North Kingstown, yeoman, vs. **John Reynolds Junr** (son of **Joseph Reynolds** dec'd) of North Kingstown, yeoman, in an action of account, for the time he was receiver at North Kingstown of £50, by the hand of the plaintiff and to the plaintiff belonging, on or

about 25 December 1737. Writ dated 17 January 1740[/1]; **Thomas Ward** attorney. At Inferior Court of Common Pleas in South Kingstown in February 1740[/1] the judgement was for the defendant, cost of suit; plaintiff appealed.

Henry Tibbits of East Greenwich deposed 12 February 1740/1 before **Benoni Hall**, J.P., that "in the first of January 1738 I was at the House of **John Reynolds Jr** of North Kingstown to hire some money of sd Reynolds which I understood Reynolds was to receive of **Robert Spencer** . . . I being at the dwelling house of my Father Reynolds some time in Husking Time last, Capt. Spencer asked me whether I see any Bond delivered [to Reynolds] . . . I told him no I could not see for they went into Another Room . . . Capt. Spencer said he remembered it very well for he took the candle and went into the other Room and gave him the money . . . I told him it was not Night nor they had no candle . . . Spencer replied then it was first Day . . . I told him it was not first Day. . . ." On 13 February depositions were made by **James Reynolds** of North Kingstown, son of **Francis**, and **Samuel Weight Junr** of North Kingstown, who said that "last September it was a twelve month or last August two year agoe . . . I wanted to borrow some money of John Reynolds Jr and sd Reynolds answered and said I have money due to me by Several Men . . . I asked by who . . . He makes Answer and said Father Spencer owes me money and several others . . . sd Father Spencer had paid him part of a Bond and it never was indorsed . . . no Flesh knew of it but they two . . . if either of them should dy it would Creed a Confusion . . . I made answer and said that you 'ont be so wicket a man surely will you . . . sd Reynolds ansrs No Lord 'a' Mercy Samuel Weight not for the World." Weight was asked what he was doing at Reynolds' when he heard this discourse and he answered that he was either stoning a well or making a pigeon net, and when asked whether he had helped Reynolds to do either of these more than once, he replied no.

On 16 February **Job Lawton** of North Kingstown testified that he had been "in partnership with **Capt. Robert Spencer, John Reynolds, Jr.**, and **Samuel Weight Jr.** in a Pigeon Nett which nett was made by **William Bly** . . . some time last June or July was a twelvemonth ago and sd partners did catch pigeons in sd Nett in that Summer following." **Benoni Hall** of North Kingstown testified 17 February before **Christopher Phillips**, Assistant, that he had been desired to take depositions at **Job Lawton**'s, and he started taking that of **Samuel Weight** and sd Samuel "made a stop and desired he might be excused of saying any more till tomorrow for he had forgot some things . . . thought he could remember better tomorrow. [Next day] Weight desired I would go into another Room to write his Evidence for he said he could tell his Story best if only he and I went together."

On 16 May 1741, **Sylvanus Whitford** late of North Kingstown deposed at Dighton [Mass.] before **Sylvester Richmond, Jr.**, J.P., that he saw **Robert Spencer** deliver money to **John Reynolds** and **Henry Tibbits** and there was no bond delivered.

717. **Thomas Phillips** of North Kingstown, shopkeeper, vs. **Samuel Thomas** of North Kingstown, yeoman, executor of the will of **George Thomas** late of North Kingstown, gentleman, for £12:5:7 due for goods sold and delivered to George in his lifetime. Writ dated 23 January 1740; **Daniel Updike** attorney. Bill is addressed to Coll. George Thomas, and includes callico, silk handkerchief, powder, pair of briches, pound of shot, 2 sticks of mohair, etc.

Thomas Justin of North Kingstown deposed 12 February 1740/41 before **Christopher Phillips**, Assistant, that he had been living with **George Thomas** and "Col. Thomas ordered [me] to go to **Thomas Phillips** and take up some goods upon his account to Cloathe him therewith . . . Jacket & Britches [I have] on at this present time was part of the Goods Col. Thomas ordered [me] to take up." **Samuel Bentley** of North Kingstown deposed that he had made a jacket and britches for **Thomas Justin** which he supposed to be the same he had on . . . Col. George Thomas paid him for making the same. . . ."

718. **George Gardner** of Newport, tallow chandler, vs. **John Niles** of West Greenwich, for £135:19:3 due by book for rum, flower and molasses delivered from May 1739 to May 1741. (Docket No. 73)

719. **John Potter** of South Kingstown, yeoman, vs. **Richard Thomas Junr.** of Newport, house carpenter, for £47:5:4 due by note dated 26 January 1739/40, **Anne King** and **William Potter** witnesses. (Docket No. 241)

720. **Samson Shearman** of Portsmouth, weaver, vs. **John Butts** of Portsmouth, miller, for vending strong liquor by retail and in less quantities than by gallon, contrary to law. **Barnet Sisson** of Portsmouth, **James Griffeth** now sojourning in Portsmouth, **Thomas Durfee** of Bristol, **David Anthony**, and **Thomas Slocomb** testified in the case 9 March

1740/1. **Silas Tallman** accused Butts of suffering card playing in his dwelling house.

May 26: Portsmouth Town Council vs. **John Butts**, for allowing card playing, etc. at his inn. Summons were issued to **David Anthony**, mariner, **David Fish**, blacksmith, **John Egland**, schoolmaster, and **John Butts**, miller, otherwise innholder. A deposition was made 26 May 1741 by **David Anthony** of Portsmouth, who said he saw **John Egland** and **William Fish** playing cards and John Butts forewarned them. "Last fall past . . . saw **John Egland** and **Pelick Shearman** . . . Butts not home . . . **Philip Shearman** and **Joseph Wilcocks** . . . but **John Butts** knew nothing of their playing . . . play'd for liquor not money." Dated 26 May 1741.

721. August 5: **Elisha Card** of Newport, innkeeper, and **Robert Benitt** of Newport, joyner, were bound on recognizance: **Margrit Springer** dotter of **Beniamen Springer** of Newport, singlewoman, is with child by **Sam**^{ll} **Card** son of sd Elisha. A copy of the record calls her *Martha* **Springer**, daughter of **Benjamin** of Newport, labourer.

722. **David Green, Josiah Arnold**, and **Edward Carr**, all of Jamestown, yeomen, commenced an action of partition against **Clark Rodman**, physician, and **John Martindale**, shipwright, both of Newport, and **Nicholas Carr** of Jamestown, yeoman, Proprietors of the undivided lands in Jamestown, to an Inferior Court of Common Pleas held at Newport in November last, for partition and division of one piece of beach land lying in Jamestown, two rods by fourteen rods; defendants recovered judgment for their costs, and plaintiffs appealed to Superior Court at Newport in May last. Order dated 12 August 1741 for partition in two & twentieth parts, six to **David Green**, three to **Josiah Arnold**, and one four & fortieth part to **Edward Carr**. Property of the defendants to satisfy judgement of £23:4 was to be taken or they were to be taken to Gaol in Newport until they paid it.

– May Term 1742 –
Superior Court of Judicature, Court of Assizes & Gaol Delivery

723. May 19: **Nicholas Fowler** of Jamestown, cordwainer, and **Thomas Fowler** bound on recognizance: Nicholas was the putative father of a female bastard child lately born of **Abigail Lowrea** of Jamestown, widow.

724. May 26: **Thomas Davenport** vs. **Sarah Peters** of Newport: in May 1742 two ditches were dug in the street to the southward of his dwelling house by M^{rs}. **Sarah Peters** and a Negro man she employed to do it . . . "of very dangerous consequence, in particular of children's falling into the same."

725. **Caleb Carr** of Newport, blockmaker, presented as above, for having the pavements dug up . . . "a drean dug for the house that **Sam^{ll} Webb** now dwells in."

– May Term 1742 – Inferior Court of Common Pleas –

726. **Gideon Worden** of Portsmouth, yeoman, and **Rebecca** his wife who when sole was named **Rebecca Brown** of Portsmouth, widow, vs. **Margaret Woodman**, widow, and **Richard Billings**, innholder, both of Newport, administrators of the goods of **Edward Woodman** of Newport, yeoman, deceased. (Docket No. 24)

727. **Samuel Holmes** of Newport, merchant, vs. **Southcote Langworthy** of Newport, pewterer alias brazier, for £173:18 due for Brass Kittles sold and delivered in July 1741. (Docket No. 33)

At the same court, **Samuel Holmes** of Newport, merchant, sued **Samuel Baley** of Newport, yeoman, in matter concerning the dividing line fence between the farms of plaintiff and defendant, which was part stone wall and part rail fence, about 60 rods long and valued at £30; the law of Rhoad Island required each to make half, and the defendant had failed to make his half. (Docket No. 38)

728. **Jane Peckham** of Newport, widow, vs. **Ruth Peckham** of Newport, widow, in action of trespass, to recover 20 acres of land in Newport, of which 13 were meadow and one arable, five pasture, and the remainder consisting of orchard and garden, dwelling and cowhouse,

bounded north on **Edward Tew**, east on highway, south partly on land of **Jonathan Easton** and partly on land of **Peter Easton**, west on the tract called Charity Farm in occupation of **Isaac Peckham**, whereof **Phillip Peckham**, yeoman, deceased, husband of the plaintiff, was seised on 1 November 1722; he died 20 December 1722 and in his will, probated 7 January 1722[/3], left to his beloved wife **Jane** the use of the land called Slades Land. (Docket No. 49)

729. **Mercy Weeden** (signed *Marcy*), of Jamestown, widow, vs. **Thomas Huxham** of Newport, butcher, for money due from one score of sheep and one pair of oxen. (Docket No. 58)

730. **Robert Taylor** and **Edward Scott** of Newport, merchants and administrators of the goods of **Elisabeth Cupid** late of Newport, widow, deceased, who was administratrix of the goods of **John Cupid** late of Newport, mariner, vs. **John Gidley** and **Sueton Grant** of Newport, merchants. Bills drawn by **John Hilegar** payable to owner of the Brigantine *Defiance*; **Nathan Bull** for £206:3:6. One fourth part of total (£1300:6:6) due to Mrs Cupitt = £325:1:7½. (Docket No. 91)

731. **Henry West** of Newport, butcher, vs. **William Brown Junr** of Newport, mariner, for £14:10 which he in the month of September 1741 promised to pay for his father **William Brown**. (Docket No. 96)

732. **George Owins** of Newport, innholder vs. **Thomas Chadwick** of Newport, fisherman, who had promised to pay £10 in good white merchantable sugar if plaintiff would forebear to sue one **George Mitchel** of Newport, mariner, who was indebted to plaintiff. (Docket No. 106)

733. **Job Caswell** of Newport, gentleman, vs. **Hannah Forrester** of Newport, widow and devisee of John Forrester, for money due from 1737/8 to April 1739 for shingles, work, window frames, casements, boards, etc. (Shingles at 50s per thousand), £369:17:0. (Docket No. 123)

734. **Caleb Philips** of Boston, merchant, vs. **Solomon Von Heinem** of Bristol, mariner alias shopkeeper, now resident in Newport, for debt of £359 for laces (priced by box), cloth, buttons, & pins. (Docket No. 143)

735. **David Melvil** of Newport, peruke-maker, vs. **Benjamin Brenton** of Newport, mariner alias goldsmith, for £33 due for wigs and a black ribbon in the year 1739. Account includes a Grey Bob Wigg, £12; Wig Box; Wigg for his son, £5; a years shaving, £6; a Dark Bob Wigg, £5. (Docket No. 150)

736. **Jonathan Easton** of Newport, yeoman, vs. **Isaac Rogers** of Newport, yeoman alias labourer, in action of trespass, charging that on 1 April 1742 he killed a brindled ox belonging to the plaintiff. (Docket No. 208)

737. **John Mitchell** of the Island of New Providence in the West Indies, mariner, vs. **John Hammatt** of Newport, schoolmaster, in an action of trespass involving a lot of land in Newport 60 feet square with house thereon, bounded north by land of **Jonathan Clark**, east on land of **Jonathan Thurston**, south on land of **Elisha Johnson**, and west on the street or lane. It was land whereof **Sarah Mitchell** late of Newport, widow, deceased, who was the mother of the plaintiff, was seized on 15 May 1714 until 6 April 1718 when she died intestate, leaving the plaintiff her only son and heir. Deed shown, dated 20 December 1701 [*copied from Newport Land Evidence 3:363-365*], **John Rhodes** of Newport, cordwainer, and wife **Susanna**, for £16 to Sarah Mitchell of Newport, spinster, the land described as "coming from the orchard of the late Col. **Peleg Sanford** of Newport, deceased, southerly and extending northerly to the main street, next to **John Hedleys**, being the 6th Lott from ye sd Orchard . . . 50 feet in breadth, 60 feet in depth, bounded east by land of **Jonathan Clarke**, north by land of **Simon Parrott**, west by Clarkes Street of two rod wide, and south on a small lot in the possession of **Walter Clarke** when Rhodes bought the land but now in possession of **Sarah Carr**, widow." Witnesses were **Thomas Lillibridge** and **Thomas Fox**.

Capt. Jeremiah Clark of Newport deposed that he was well acquainted with John Mitchell, reputed son of Sarah Mitchell, late of Newport, school mistress, and saw him in the year 1734 in New Providence where he was then a settled inhabitant. **Capt. Samuel Dyre** of Newport deposed that he saw John Mitchell in New Providence in October 1741 and told him about the land — he had given power of attorney to Capt. **Benjamin Pittman** . . . "goods were left with Sarah Mitchell who sold some and left some in the hands of one **Robinson** who ran away to the West Indies . . . the rest she carried to Boston. She is dead in Boston for George informed me he saw her grave."

Letter from Hammatt to John Mitchell, dated at Newport 10 January 1739: ". . . at the beginning of September last your son **George** came to me . . . came into New London from a Voyage in a very sick condition . . . news came here that he was dead but it pleased God to recover him . . . obliged to run in Debt. [He was] very sober and industrious . . . neat . . . very handsom likely young man . . . honest . . . he intreated me to buy the house and land . . . I ran the Venture of it and the deed . . . he went to South Carolina intending to [inform] you in letters . . . but there were there four men of warr and the Press was very hot which so terrified him that he immediately shipt himself on board one Capt. **Dunbar** bound down to Newport in a dull Sailor deep loaded and bad sailors and it is three months since and no news . . . general conclusion is that they are foundered, especially having a dreadful storm just after sailing. . . ."

The will of Sarah Mitchell, dated 25 July 1716, was entered into evidence:

In the Name of God Amen the twenty fifth Day of July in the Year 1716 I Sarah Mitchell of Newport on Rhode Island Widow being weak in body but of Perfect Mind & Understanding Thanks be given unto God & calling to Mind the Mortality of my Body knowing that it is appointed for all Mankind once to die do make and ordain this my last Will & Testament that is to say Principally & first of all I Give & Recommend my spirit into the Hands of God that gave it and my Body I recommend to the Earth to be buried in decent burial at the Discretion of my Executors and as touching Such Worldly Estate wherewith it hath pleased God to bless me in this Life I Give Devise & Dispose of the same in the manner & form following: –

Imprimis: That all my Just Debts which I owe to any Person together with my Funeral Charges be first answered & paid by my Executors –

Item, I give & Bequeath unto my well beloved sister **Mehetabel Fish** my now dwelling house wth the Land or Garden thereunto belonging during her Natural Life –

Item, I Give and Bequeath unto my beloved Son **John Mitchell** my house and Land to be possessed by him after the Decease of my said Sister from thence to be possessed & enjoyed by him during his Natural Life and at & after his decease to be possessed & enjoyed by the first Child of my said Son Lawfully begotten of his Body & his or her assigns as a free Estate of Inheritance for ever –

Item, I Give and bequeath unto my said Son a Certain Lott of Land which I bought of **Walter Clarke** Esqr mentioned in a certain Deed bearing date April 28th 1708 to be possessed & enjoyed by my said Son during his Natural Life and at his decease to be possessed & enjoyed by the Second Child of my said son lawfully begotten of his Body and his or her assigns as a free Estate of Inheritance for ever. –

Item, I Give & Bequeath unto my said Son ye Sum of £52 in Money to be laid out & Improved in Building of a Dwelling House on the lot of Land above & last mentioned and whereas the said £50 [*sic*] is not Sufficient to build a Dwelling House as abovesaid my Will is that my Executors shall retain the money at Interest untill such Time as my said Son shall be able to add so much thereunto as will erect and build a Dwelling House thereon and they to receive good Security before the Delivery of said £50 that the same shall be laid out & improv'd as afores[d]. Also I Give and Bequeath unto my said Son one Dozen of Pewter Plates three Platters four Silver Spoons one bed & Furniture two Cedar Chests & two Gold Rings.

Finally I do hereby nominate Constitute & Ordain my trusty and beloved Friends **John Odlin** & **John Hammet** to be my Executors to this my last Will & Testament desiring that the same may be performed & executed according to the true intent & meaning thereof ratifying allowing and confirming this & no other to be my last Will & Testament hereby disannulling & making void all former & other Wills or Testaments by me made whatsoever. In witness whereof I have hereunto set my Hand & seal the day & Year abovewritten.— [signed] *Sarah Mitchell.*

Witnesses were **Daniel Pearce, John Hammet**, and **John Wright**. The will was proved 22 April 1718 and recorded in Newport Town Council and Probate, 5:253-254, from which it was copied 3 September 1739. (Docket No. 223)

In a second trespass case, **John Mitchell** sued **Samuel Holmes** of Newport, merchant, to recover possession of a lot of land with a coach house and stable, bounded south on land of **Simon Pease**, west on land on which there was a school house called the Presbiterian School house, and north on land of **Ebenezer Davenport**. The file includes a copy of the deed from **Walter Clarke** to **Sarah Mitchell**, mentioned in her will. Verdict in both cases was for the plaintiff. (Docket No. 224)

738. **William Dyre** of Newport, shopkeeper, vs. **James Austin** of North Kingstown, labourer, and wife **Margaret**, who when sole was called **Margaret Gardner** of South Kingstown, widow, for money due by note of 9 June 1732. (Docket No. 234)

739. **John Rouse** of Newport, mariner, vs. **Edward Barker** late of Newport, mariner, in action of trespass, charging that on 17 September 1741 the defendant beat him with a cane. Deposition of **Henry Jones** of Newport, mariner, that he was at house of **Jonathan Nichols**, innholder, "in company with Capt. **John Rous** and divers other persons . . . Capt. **Edward Barker** came . . . sd Rouse gave sd Barker a great deal of provoking language . . . as calling him Bully and other opprobrious names upon which sd Barker struck him one blow with a walking staff or stick in his hand which broke sd Rouse's head so much . . . blood ran down his forehead." Deposition of **Silas Cook**, mariner, of Newport, who had been present also and swore that the above was true. Judgment for defendant, £5:16:4 and costs. (Docket No. 254)

740. **Robert Lawton** of Portsmouth, yeoman, administrator of estate of **George Lawton**, late of Portsmouth, gentleman, deceased, vs. **Daniel Fish** of Dighton, cordwainer, otherwise called Daniel Fish of Portsmouth, yeoman, for money due by bond signed with **Robert Fish** of East Greenwich, blacksmith, dated 22 September 1737. (Docket No. 273)

741. **John Brett** of Newport, physician, vs. **Elizabeth Bryer** of Newport, widow, for money due for medicines from 16 August 1737 to 10 January 1741. Elizabeth countered by presenting an account due from Brett for washing and ironing, patching and mending, and cutting out Ruffels. (Docket No. 278)

742. **Joseph Healy** of Newport, weaver, vs. **Joseph Cundal** of Portsmouth, clothier and **William Taylor** of South Kingstown, clothier, to collect £176:17:8 due for weaving, warping and sizeing of cloth and doubling and twisting said yarn, from 31 January 1737/8 until April 1740.

Deposition of **Benjamin Shearman** of Portsmouth, weaver, about "prizes" [prices] for weaving in the year 1737; he wove for **Joseph Cundall** or **William Tiler**. Deposition of **William Shearman** of Portsmouth, weaver, that he "has not wove any ell wide cloth under 18*d* a yard for 3 years past. Deposition of **Clark Cornell** of Portsmouth, weaver, dated 28 May 1742 at Newport, that "he hath had for weaving eal wide cloath from 18*d* per yeard to half a crown a yeard from the year 1738 to present . . . has wove for Cundall." Deposition of **Ebenezer Shearman** of Portsmouth, that on 10 February 1740 Cundall and Taylor came to his house and did tender unto Healy the sum of £34:13:3 for the balance of their account. Deposition of **Samuel Southall** of Newport that in the year 1736 he did work at the weaving trade for **Joseph Condell** and **William Taylor** and **Mary Earl** and the customary price was 12*d* the first sort and 19*d* for the third sort. Deposition of **Thomas Brayton** of Portsmouth that in February 1740 he went to the house of **Ebenezer Shearman** with Cundall and Taylor and did tender to Healy £34:10. Deposition of **Caleb Earl** of Newport that in the year 1737 the price for weaving "first sort cloth or coating was 12*d* per yard and for second sort 16*d* and for third sort 18*d*; what was wove in the House and the Weaver had his Diet and Loom found him, each of the above sorts was wove at half price." Deposition of **Sandyfor Lindy** of Newport that in the year 1738 he had been at the house of Capt. **Jeremiah Sheffield** of Narrangansett in South Kingstown in company with **Joseph Right**, and Right said Haley had left Cundall and Taylor in order to raise his prices. Terms used re weaving (types of cloth): searge, drugget, durvy. Judgment for plaintiff, £36:12:3 and costs. (Docket No. 293)

– May Term 1743 –

743. **Richard Whitehorn**, feltmaker, vs. **William James** of Newport, feltmaker, for debt of £25 for one and a quarter year's rent of three chambers in the plaintiff's house in Newport and yard room for his wood and privilege of the cellar, leased to him 18 December 1741. Writ dated 16 April 1743. Verdict for plaintiff to recover.

744. **Nathan Bull**, mariner, and **Joseph Scott**, merchant, both of Newport, vs. **Joseph Power** of Newport, mariner, for £200 damages for unlawfully enticing away a molatto man servant named **James Dunbar** belonging to the plaintiffs. Indenture dated 4 June 1741: James Dunbar a mulatto man now residing in Newport, for £70 paid by Nathan Bull, mariner, and Joseph Scott, merchant, bound himself for 5 years; signed *J*, witnessed by **Walt^r Chapman** and **James Davis**. Deposition of **William Tosh** of Newport, that he being Capt. Quartermaster on the brig *Victory* whereof **Joseph Power** was commander, "did on 18th day of May see the molatto fellow named **James Dunbar** on bord . . . heard Capt. Power say he knew sd molatto at Suranam . . . knew him to be a servant . . . next day when we came to sail sd Dunbar was upon deck and was active in getting under sail . . . acted as hand on board . . . till arrival at Isle of Blanes [*Blanco?*] and then he ran away from sd brig . . . going ashore in boat to get wood for vessell's use." Deposition of **William Allen** of Newport, Lieut. of brig *Victory*, that at the Island Blanco he heard Capt. Power "desire some people that were at sd Island Turtling to catch sd Fellow for him & the Brig went under sail & stood to sea & in the night we tacked & stood in again for the Island with a Design as the Capt. told me to go to the same Place & see if those Turtlers had not caught sd Fellow . . . but we could not fetch the Island again then by a strong Leward current." **John Mawdsly** of Newport, mariner, deposed that he was at Suranam [*sic*] in November 1741 and came from thence with **Capt. Joseph Power** as a mariner to this place . . . while at Suranam saw mulatto fellow on board. Other depositions made by **Peter Marshall** of Newport, mariner, **William Edmunds** (signed X), **Stephen Tripp** of Newport, and **Samuel Scranton** of Newport. Plaintiff awarded £100; verdict appealed.

745. **Edmund Pendleton** of Westerly, yeoman alias boatman, vs. **William Riggers** of Newport, Negro, labourer, for freight of rum, etc., 29 lbs. mutten at 9*d*, 20 cabbidges at 8*d* per head, 9 cord of walnots, etc. (Docket No. 4)

746. **Thomas Weaver** late of Westerly now of Bristol, cordwainer, vs. **William French** of Westerly, shopkeeper, for money due by note dated 27 March 1741. (Docket No. 17)

747. **Sueton Grant** of Newport, merchant, vs. **Mary Smith** of Newport, widow and administratrix of estate of her deceased husband **Charles Smith**, late of said Newport, mason, for money due from debt of 23 March 1742/3; Charles Smith had been very sick and indisposed and requested Capt. **Godfrey Malbon** to pay Grant. (Docket No. 35)

748. **William Wickes** of Warwick, yeoman, vs. **Meribah Jones** of Newport, widow, for money due by note. (Docket No. 38)

749. **Stephen Tallman** of Portsmouth, physician, vs. **John Potter** of South Kingstown, yeoman, executor of the will of **Sarah Potter** late of South Kingstown, widow, for £12,000 debt.

Testimony of **Daniel Thomas** of Portsmouth, who in reponse to questions, said that the bond was executed in September last at Doctor Tallman's house in the bedroom where he usually lodged; that only the aforesaid Sarah Potter, Stephen Tallman, and a witness were present. Dr. Tallman said to his mother, "is it not a good time to sign ye bond there being several neighbours here," and she answered "yes"; Dr. Tallman went and fetched it out of his desk; the upper one half or two thirds were covered over with paper. "She desired us not to say anything about it . . . for fear it should get home and she should have no rest . . . " Evidence of **Thomas Slocum** of Portsmouth that "the Doctor, his mother Potter and Daniel Thomas and myself were present . . . would make Disturbance between them . . . if it got to her grandson . . . at Narragansett at her dwelling." Bond dated 11 September 1742, for £12,000; condition that £6000 be paid on or before 11 November 1742. Signed by **Sarah Potter** with her mark. Judgment for plaintiff: bond sued for and cost. (Docket No. 39)

750. **Sueton Grant** of Newport, merchant, vs. **Hannah Forrester** of Newport, widow, for £100 due on her note of 24 January 1740/1 for value received. (Docket No. 45)

751. **Peter Cornish** now resident in Newport, Negro man, mariner, and late one of the company on board the *Boneta* Privateer whereof **Robert Flower** is present commander, and lying in harbour of said Newport, vs. **John Lusk** now resident in Newport, mariner, and quarter-master of the *Boneta*, and **John Freebody** of Newport, shopkeeper, for accounting of goods, being the whole share of Prize goods of several vessels and Cargoes taken by said Privateer and legally condemned as Spanish prizes. (Docket No. 51)

752. **Mary Carr** of Newport, widow and relict of **Samuel Carr** late of Newport, gunsmith, deceased, vs. **Samuel Webb** of Newport, vintner, and **John Alison** of Newport, barber, to recover her right of Dower in one-third of a large dwelling house and land in Newport, belonging to her late husband, "whereof the plaintiff hath nothing," bounded north on land of **Thomas Huxham**, east on land late in the estate of Samuel Carr, south on a street sometimes called **Caleb Carr's** Lane, west on Thames Street, whereof Samuel Carr was at his death on or about 16 June 1739 seised. Copy of **Samuel Carr's will** attached. (Docket No. 56)

Will of Samuel Carr: In the Name of God Amen, the Second Day of June in the twelfth year of the Reign of our Sovereign Lord George the Second King of Great Britain &c Annoq. Dom: One Thousand Seven Hundred and Thirty Nine, I Samuel Carr of Newport in the County of Newport in the Colony of Rhode Island & Providence Plantations in New England Gunsmith being in good Health of Body and of Sound and Perfect Mind & Memory blessed be God for the same and knowing that it is appointed for all Men once to die and the Time thereof being Uncertain Do make and Declare this to be my Last Will & Testament in Manner following (that is to say) —

First I Recommend my Soul into the Hands of almighty God that gave it hoping through the Merits Death and Passion of my blessed Lord and Savior Jesus Christ to have full and free Pardon & Remission of all my Sins and to Inherit Eternal Life and my Body I recommend to the Earth to be decently Interred And as touching & Concerning such Worldly Estate wheretowith it hath pleased almighty God to bless me after my Just Debts & Funeral Expences are fully satisfied & paid I Give and Devise the same in the following manner –

Imprimis I Give Devise and Bequeath unto my dear & loving wife **Mary Carr** all my Personal Estate (except such part as is herein after given & devised) To hold to my said Wife Mary Carr her heirs & assigns for ever ----

Item I Give Devise and Bequeath unto my loving son **Caleb Carr** the one full Moiety or equal half part of a Certain Lott or Piece of Land situate lying and being in Newport aforesd (which said half part of sd Lott or Piece of Land is where my Grandfather &c. was buried and is bounded Easterly on the other half part (given to Samuel) Southerly on a Street Westerly on **James Greens** Land & Northerly on Land of **Polipus Hammond** In Trust to and for to be kept and maintained for a Burying Place for my Family and their Heirs for ever –

Item I Further Give and Bequeath unto my said son **Caleb Carr** the Messuage or Tenement and piece of Land whereon ye same stands Situated lying & being on the East side of Thames Street in Newport aforesd now in the Possession of **Mary Channing** widow Together with a Slice of Land extending in Length from a street the whole Length or breadth of said Messuage & also extending from the East Side of the said Messuage to a Board Fence the length aforesaid (according as is mentioned & expressed in the Original Lease to **John Channing** of Newport aforesd dec'd) And also a Certain Piece of the Wharf called the Ferry Wharf which is to begin five feet below the West End of the Ferry house and to extend twenty five feet westward – Ranging back northerly to Capt **John Browns** Line Together with their appurtenances To hold to him my said Son Caleb Carr his heirs and assigns for ever. –

Item, I Give Devise and Bequeath unto my loving son **Samuel Carr** the other one full Moiety or equal half part of the said Lott or Piece of Land (herein first mentioned & described for a Burying Place) Being bounded as follows --- Vizt Northerly on a Highway Westerly on the Land for the Burying Place aforesd Northerly on Land of **Elizabeth Godfrey** & Easterly on the said **John Browns** Land Together with the appurtenances To hold to him my said son Samuel Carr his Heirs and Assigns for ever.

Item I Give Devise & Bequeath further unto my sd son **Samuel Carr** & loving son **Ebenezer Carr** the Ferry House and all & Singular the Remaining Part of the said Ferry Wharf (not herein before given to my said son

Caleb Carr) Together with the appurtenances to be equally divided between my s^d Two Sons Samuel Carr & Ebenezer Carr To hold to them their Heirs & Assigns for ever (excepting & reserving unto all my Children herein mentioned the Liberty & Priviledge of Landing of Wood upon the said Wharf for their own use only.

Item, I Give Devise and Bequeath unto my Loving Son **John Carr** the Messuage or Tenement where I now dwell situate lying & being in Newport aforesaid together with the Lot or Piece of Land therunto belonging being bounded as followeth Vix^t Southerly on the Street Westerly on the s^d Lott of Land in the possession of the said **Mary Channing** (herein before given to my said Son Caleb Carr) Northerly partly on Land of **Edward Thurston** and partly on Land of **Caleb Barker** & Easterly on s^d Caleb Barker Together with ye appurtenances to hold to him the said John Carr his Heirs and Assigns for ever –

Item, I Give Devise & Bequeath unto my loving Daughter **Wait Carr** the two Shops in the Possession of **Thomas Huxham** & **Paul Tew**, & Little old Kitchen also in the Possession of the said **Mary Channing** Situate lying and being in Newport aforesaid together with the Land thereto belonging (whereon they stand) Together with a Slip or Piece of Land adjoyning to the said Kitchen and two Shops extending in Length from the s^d Kitchen to the north side of the said Shop in the Possession of the said **Paul Tew** & Extending in Width from the East Side of the said Shops and Kitchen as far as the said Board Fence & Lott of Land herein before given to the s^d John Carr (which said Kitchen joyns to the said Messuages herein given to my said son Caleb) together with their appurtenances And also a Negro Boy named **Bristow** To hold to her my said Daughter Wait her Heirs & Assigns for ever –

Item, my Will is and I do hereby Order that my said Wife **Mary Carr** have and keep all and singular my Estate both Real & Personal in her possession untill my said Son **Caleb** arrives to the age of twenty one years and receives the Rents and Profits of the same and so to keep in her possession the Remainder of my said Estate untill each & every of my said Sons and Daughter shall arrive to their respective ages of Twenty one years & receive the Rents & Profits thereof for the bringing up of my s^d Children.

Item, my further Will is and I do hereby Order that my Debts be paid out of the Rents and Profits of my said Real Estate –

Item, my further Will is [and I do hereby Order, *crossed out*] that my said Wife **Mary Carr** have Use, Occupy Possess and Enjoy the one half of the Messuage or Tenement where I now dwell and herein before given to my said Son John (which half she shall choose) for & during the Term of her Natural Life –

And Lastly I Do hereby make Ordain Constitute Nominate & appoint my said Wife Mary Carr Executrix & my said son Caleb Carr Executor of this my Last Will & Testament, And Do hereby Revoke and make Null and Void all former Wills & Testaments by me, at any Time heretofore made and declare this only to be my last Will & Testament In Witness whereof I the said Samuel Carr have hereunto set my hand and Seal the Day and Year first within Written. –

And my further Will & Mind is and I Do hereby Order that my son Caleb after he shall receive his part of my said Estate herein given to him into his Hands to pay to his Mother my said Wife Mary Carr the sum of Twenty Pounds a Year – during her Natural Life also my said Son Saml Carr after he hath received his Part to pay to his Mother the sum of Ten Pounds a Year during her Natural Life and my said Sons Ebenezer & John & Daughter Wait after they have received their parts respectively to pay each of them to their said Mother the sum of five pounds a year during her Natural Life –

[*signed*] *Samuel Carr*

Signed sealed published Pronounced & declared by the within named Samuel Carr for & as his last Will and testament in the Presence of us the Subscribers – Mordecai Dunbar Peleg Wood Junr Jos: Fox

Newport August 6th 1739

In Council appeared **Mordecai Dunbar Peleg Wood Junr** & **Joseph Fox** & on Oath declared that they saw Samuel Carr Sign Seal and declare the above & foregoing Instrument. . . .

753. **Daniel Howland** of Portsmouth, Esq. vs. **Stephen Tallman** of Portsmouth, physician, otherwise called Stephen Tallman of Portsmouth, yeoman, for £1400; writ dated 26 August 1742. Deed dated 21 February 1742 for 400 acres in Tiverton purchased of **Robert Lawton**, from Stephen Tallman to **Jonathan Nicholls** of Newport, merchant, **John Coggeshall**, yeoman, **David Fish**, blacksmith, and **Jeremiah Tallman**, mariner, all of Portsmouth. Bond: Stephen Tallman to Daniel Howland of Portsmouth, Esq.; witnesses **William Anthony Junr**, and **Caleb Bennet**.

John Dexter Esq. of Portsmouth deposed 30 May 1743, saying that he was at Newport near the house of **Jonathan Nichols**, tavern keeper, and "heard **Daniel Howland Esq.** and **Jonathan Nichols Esq.** atalking about the sd Howland's attaching of **Docter Tallman**'s Estate and sd Howland said to sd Nichols I hope thee will not hurt me but Lett the Court know what the deed is for: for I do not intend to hurt you, and the sd Nichols Replied and said that he had told **John Potter** If he would Levy the Execution upon the Land he would burn the deed." **Thomas Shearman** of Portsmouth deposed and said that he was at Newport the day **Stephen Tallman** came out of gaol and heard **Jonathan Nichols** say he would have said Tallman's land at the Main for security as well as his land upon the Island. **John Eglin** of Portsmouth testified that he "was at the house and 23 April in ye night that **Stephen Tallman** whent away from home . . . he left two powers of attorney one for his wife the other for **Mathew Robinson** the Lawer; writ a bill of sail for **Stephen Tallman** to **Silas Tallman** of all ye said Stephen's stock . . . **John Coggeshall** and myself witnessed . . . signed blank paper because in hast to go away . . . for a lease . . . ." **Jonathan Peck** of Bristol deposed and said that on 3 May at **Mr. Samuel Howland's** house in Bristol, with Silas Tallman brother of **Stephen Tallman** ". . . he asked me if I was willing to give bond to him for what I owed his brother which I was content to do." Deposition of **Jeremiah Phiney** of Bristol, who agreed with Peck. (Docket No. 68)

754. **John Topham** of Newport, butcher, vs. **Francis Fletcher**, taylor, for money due for this last year's meat, £82:19:8. (Docket No. 73)

755. **Benjamin Haszard, Robert Carr** and **John Easton** of Newport, merchants, and **Jonathan Haszard** of South Kingstown, yeomen, vs. **John Rous** of Charlestown, County of Middlesex, Province of Massachusetts Bay, mariner, late captain of the Bilander Privateer *The Young Eagle*, claiming that on 18 March 1741 in the aforesaid Bilander, he being commander thereof, furnished with a great number of men and fitted for War, did unlawfully take one sloop called the *South Kingstown* of a burthen of 100 tons and cargo of 50 gallons of rum, 14,000 gallons of molasses, sugar and indigo. Depositions of **William Foye** and **Jonathan Armitage** of Boston, merchants, that **John Rouse**, commander of the Billender *Young Eagle*, was an inhabitant of Boston. . . . his wife and family had dwelt in a House in Hanover Street from 2 March 1741 till this 23 May 1743 and he with them. Power of attorney given by **John Rous** to **Thomas Ward**. Capt. Rous's bond, dated 19 December 1741, of Charlestown, £15,000, license to privateer. Copy of instructions from the Crown concerning privateering. Judgment for plaintiff, £8000 damages and costs. (Docket No. 106)

756. **Eleazer Arnold** of Newport, blacksmith, vs. **John Jones** of Boston, merchant, executor of the will of **William Jones** late of Newport, merchant, in action of debt due for Iron, Ironwork, etc., from May 1736 to December 1738 for various ships: Brig *Dove,* Davison commander, Sloop *Collingwood,* **Davison** commander, Sloop *Perkins,* Davison commander, a Brig, **John Waterman** commander, and a Schooner, **Robinson** master. Stillhouse account: Mr. **William Jones, Daniel Arault** [*sic*], the Brig *Samuel Serson.* (Docket No. 199)

757. **John Clark** of Newport, mariner alias boatman, vs. **Samuel Robins** of Newport, mariner, in action of debt due by bond dated 29 April 1742 for £20:5:9. (Docket No. 263)

758. **Joseph Thurston** of Newport, mariner, vs. **John Jones** of Boston, merchant, for £60 due by note of 27 July 1741, it being Jones's half of the plaintiff's commission on the sloop *Prudent Abigail* on a voyage to Guinea. (Docket No. 264)

759. **Nicholas Easton** of Newport, yeoman alias Esquire, vs. **Hannah Forrester** of Newport, widow and executrix of the will of **John Forrester** late of Newport, glazier, for money due by note dated 25 September 1742. (Docket No. 325)

760. **Nicholas Easton** of Newport, yeoman alias Esquire, vs. **Hannah Forrester** of Newport, widow and executrix of the will of John Forrester late of Newport, glazier, in action of trespass, to recover a house and land in Newport, bounded northwest 50 ft. on **John Partelow**, southwest ca. 97 ft. on **Edward Tew**, southeast 54 ft. 9 in. on Main Street, northeast 97 ft. 8 in. on **James Tew** – the dividing line between said premises and **James Tew** makes an elbow; plaintiff seised of land 7 June 1739 when dispossessed by defendant. Deed from **John Forrester** of Newport, glazier to **Nicholas Easton**, Esq., dated 7 June 1739, for £125, acknowledged same day. (Docket No. 326)

761. **John Davis** of Newport, baker, vs. **John Tennant** of Newport, gardner, for money due by note dated 19 October 1742. (Docket No. 381)

762. **Gideon Cornel** of Newport, Esq., vs. **Francis Fletcher** of Newport, taylor, for £358.11.8 for keeping a horse hired of the plaintiff for one hunt. Account: July 1741, "one hunt to go 50 miles beyond boston, gone a day £10," coffee, many other things. (Docket No. 389)

– 1743 – Miscellaneous –

763. Deposition of **Thomas Paine** of New Shoreham, taken 22 April 1743, that about 20 April he "was in the woods which Capt. **Simon Ray** leased to **Samuel Champlin** at New Shoreham and saw 109 trees cut down on sd Ray's farm now in the possession of Samuel Champlin and two thirds of sd trees was Green Oak before Champlin cut them down . . . a grate quantity of stumps."

764. **Rebecca Lawton** of Newport, widow, vs. **George Lawton** of Newport, Esq., concerning an annuity dating from November 1740 and debt of £30. Writ dated 9 September 1743. Plaintiff recovered. (Box 1110)

765. Deposition signed by **George Cook** of Newport, caulker, dated 17 January 1743 before **John Freebody**, J.P., that "he was at work on board a new snow whereof **Samuel Forst** was Master at the same time with **William James** Junr, a caulking the said vessels deck &c, when **Joseph Kettle** & **William Man** and **William Hood** shipwrights was at work on the s^{d} vessles in laying a deck &c, and when they had found some holes & places in the s^{d} vessle that wanted to be stopt, asked sometimes one of the above named shipwrights & sometimes another of them, to stop the holes & places they found open the s^{d} persons when asked to come & stop them replied they was at work for ___ **Marshal** who he supposes was the man that built the s^{d} vessle . . . could not tell whether [they] were in earnest or in jest when they made the aforesaid reply when they wre asked to come & stop the holes & places found open which places & holes [they] always stoped after they was asked."

766. **William Cranston** Jr. of Newport, **Peter Porter** of Newport, **James Edmondson** of Poulton in Lancashire in the Kingdom of Great Britain, and **Zebulon Spinney** of Portsmouth in the Province of New Hampshire, all mariners, vs. **Benja[min] Dorby** now resident in Newport, for non fulfillment of promise. On 11 August 1742 at Oratavia Harbour in the Port of Teneriffe the plaintiffs were mariners aboard the snow *St. Andrew* of which Dorby was then master, lying in sd Harbour . . . if they would agree to go to the Cape de Verd Islands and return again and proceed to Suranam [he] would put on board sd snow a hogshead of good wine for [them] to drink on sd passage . . . and on the

return to Oratavia or the arrival at Suranam to deliver to each of them one quarter cask of good wine as a reward over and above their wages . . . the same being a deviation from the voyage [*for which*] they were shipped on board. Defendant provided wine for the voyage but after the arrival at Suranam or at any time since never had. Writ dated 12 December 1743.

— 1744 —

767. **John Staniford** of Boston, Gentleman, vs. **Rachel Dunaum**, widow, **William Stevens**, stonecutter, **James Hawkins**, fellmonger, **Joseph Brown**, tanner, and **David Mathews**, glover, all of Newport, in an action of trespass for withholding possession of one lot of land in Newport about 70 feet in width and about 180 feet in depth, with two dwelling houses, one work house and one stable, and the appurtenances thereon standing, butted northerly upon land in possession of **Joseph Scott**, easterly, southerly & westerly upon **Timothy Newell**; damages £3000 demanded of **Timothy Newell**, tinman and **Margaret** his wife, under whom the defendants hold the premises. [*Case heard originally in November 1743*]

Letter dated "Newport April 29th 1743," addressed to "Honoured Uncle," signed by Timothy Newell: "These with our dutifull respects to you & Aunt hopeing you are in good health as through Gods Goodness we enjoy, it is with much trouble of mind and sorrow of heart that I now write unto you of so melancholly a subject, our Beloved Uncle **Jer^{h} Staniford** is thought by the Doctor & others to be in a deep Consumption, and very far gone, he has been several times deprived of his senses, at times this Week, the Lord only knows what the event will be I fear he is not long for this life . . . I am much concerned least you should never see him any more in this world . . . Please to let us hear from you the next post, I should be heartily glad to see you here."

Copy of **Jeremiah Staniford's will** entered in evidence:

In the Name of God Amen the twenty ninth day of April in the sixteenth year of his Majesty's Reign George the Second King of Great Britain & Annoque Domini One Thousand Seven hundred and forty three I **Jeremiah Staniford** of Newport in the County of Newport in the Colony of Rhode Island & Providence Plantations in New England Leather Dresser being sick & weak in Body but of Perfect Mind and Memory Thanks be given unto God Therefore calling to Mind the Mortality of my Body & knowing that it is appointed for all Men once to die do make & Ordain this my last Will and Testament that is to say Principally and first of all I give & recommend my Soul into the Hands of God that gave it & my Body I Commit to the Earth to be Decently buried at the Discretion of my Executor hereinafter named and as touching such Worldly Estate wherewith It hath Pleased God to bless me in this Life I Give and dispose of the same in the following Manner & form.

Imprimis I Will that all my just Debts & Funeral Charges be well and truly paid in some Convenient Time after my Decease.

Item, I Give and Bequeath unto my three Cousens **Thomas Staniford** of Ipswich, **Daniel Staniford** of Ipswich & **Jeremiah Staniford** of Boston the sum of One Hundred Pounds in good and passable Bills of Publick Credit of sd Colony old Tenor to be equally divided between them.

Item, I Give and Bequeath unto my Brother **William Staniford** of Hampton the sum of fifty pounds in like Bills of Credit as abovesaid.

Item, I Give and Bequeath unto my Cousen **Love Rendels** of Gosport the sum of Fifty Pounds in like Bills of Credit as abovesaid.

Item, I Give and Bequeath unto my Brother **Samuel Staniford** of Ipswich and my Cousen **Mary Sweet** of Ipswich the sum of Sixty Pounds in like Bills of Credit as abovesaid to be equally divided between them.

Item, I Give and Bequeath unto my Cousin **Samuel Lord** of Newport the sum of One Hundred Pounds in like Bills of Credit as abovesaid.

Item, I Give and Bequeath unto my Cousen **John Calfe** of Ipswich the sum of Thirty Pounds in like Bills of Credit as abovesaid.

And my Mind and Will is that my Executor herein after named shall pay & discharge all the abovementioned Legacies after he has paid & discharged all my just Debts & Funeral Charges & shall have Collected in a sufficient sum of my outstanding Debts to pay said Legacies.

Item, I Give and Bequeath unto ye Poor of the Church and Congregation in Newport afores^d^ under the Pastoral Care of the Revd Mr **James Searing** & to their Successors the Interest of One Hundred Pounds for ever of like Bills of Credit as abovesaid.

Item, I Give and bequeath unto **David Mathews** of Newport aforesaid Leather Dresser the sum of five pounds in like Bills of Credit as abovesaid Yearly and every Year during his Natural Life.

Item, All the Rest Residue & Remainder of my Estate whatsoever both Real & Personal of what Nature or kind soever & wheresoever the same may be found I Give Bequeath and Devise unto my Cousens **Timothy Newell** of Newport afores^d^ Tinman and **Margaret Newell** his Wife and to their Heirs and Assigns for ever.

Lastly I Nominate Constitute & appoint my s^d Cousen **Timothy Newell** my sole $Exec^r$ of this my last Will & Testament And I do hereby utterly disallow Revoke & disannul all & every other Wills Legacies Bequests & $Exec^{rs}$ by me at any Time heretofore made named willed or bequeathed Ratifying allowing & confirming this & no other to be my last will and Testament In Witness whereof I have hereunto Set my hand & seal y^e Day & Year first abovewritten.

Signed *Jer*^{h} *Staniford.*

Witnesses: **William Dyer**, Job Bissell, James Robinson.

Proved 16 May 1743 on oaths of Job Bissell and James Robinson; recorded in Newport Town Council Book 10: 1-2, 20 May 1743 by Wm Coddington Junr, council clerk.

Quitclaim, or release, dated 19 November 1743, from **Job Bissell**, blacksmith, and **James Robinson**, physician, both of Newport, as members of the church mentioned in Jeremiah Staniford's will, for 5s, to **Timothy Newell**, executor; witnesses **Jonathan Nichols** and **Samuel Baley.**

Walter Rodman of Newport, Practitioner in Physick, testified before **Benja. Brenton**, J.P., 21 March 1744 that he had attended the testator the same day he signed the will, and believed him to have been in his right mind.

On 2 April 1744 depositions were made in court: **William Dyre junr** of Newport, yeoman, said that some time in the month of April 1743 he was called by Timothy Newell to go with him to be a witness to Jeremiah Staniford's will . . . went to Staniford's house and the will was brought "and handed to sd Staniford upon which he asked what that was, & they told him it was his Will, whereupon he seemed to be some what surprized and asked who made said Will and when it was made and they told him Mr Lyndon wrote it, then said Bissell told him he must sign it, Upon which [I] desired sd Will might be read and after sd Staniford heard it Read he sayd it was his Will but he was very ill and just going, and then signed it . . . Newell told [me] Mr Lyndon took ye Minutes of said Will. . . ." **Oliver White** of Newport, blacksmith, gave similar testimony, adding that the testator "arose up in his Bed & took [the will] & tried to read it . . . could not & desired **William Dyre** to read it, & sd Dyre called **Edward Smith** to read it. . . ." **James Robinson** of Newport testified that for many years last past he had been intimately acquainted with Jeremy Staniford "& hath (when in

Town) constantly attended him as a Physician when he was sick . . . frequently heard him talk about his estate & the disposition thereof at which Times he told me he desired to give his estate among the Children of his Brothers & Sisters. . . ." Dr. Robinson continued that Staniford has asked him to write a will for him, but he refused to undertake it and recommended that he have Josias Lyndon do it, and spoke to Lyndon for him. **Josias Lyndon** gave lengthy testimony about the circumstances of writing the will. **James Hawkings** of Newport, fellmonger, stated that he had been living at Jeremiah Staniford's when he fell sick, and the day the will was signed he was "not in a capacity to order his affaires but the day before . . . I saw him & he semed to be ratinall . . . did not see him till Next day aboute two a Clock in the afterpart: day & he was then much oute of his senses . . . Newel told [me] that had it not been for him & wife **Sam^ll^ Lord** had not so much and further that he had Got Better men to advise aboute his will and some time before he sd Staniford was sick Newell asked him to make him ye sd Newel a free man and he would not." **William Stevens** of Newport testified that Newel had come to his shop and asked him to go with him to witness his uncle's will; he went and when "I went in to the Bedroome where he lay . . . he ask'd me whether my Negro Boy was gon to or cum from Boston which caused me to think he was not sensible there being no such talk before & I came out & told Mr Newel that it would not do for me to sine as a witness for I did not think he was sensible . . . we went into my Roome I living under ye same Roof & there was Docter **Walter Rodman** we told him the affair and desir'd him to go in which he did & when he Return'd he said he thought he was sensible then Mr Newel desir'd him to be a witness but he Refus'd saying he did not Love to have any thing to do with things of that Nature & we advis'd Mr Newel to call Docter Robinson & while he was gone Mr Rodman & I came from the House & wee meet Mr Newel & Docter Robinson going to it." Stevens answered "yes" when asked whether he had any Negro boy at the time, "no" to whether he had ever sent the boy to Boston. **Edward Smith** of Newport, joyner, testified that the night before the will was signed, he had "watched with Jeremiah Staniford, who slept very little that Night & not in his senses all Night, and on friday morning following [I] went to [his] house to enquire how he did & **David Matthews** (who then lived with him) told [me] that he was worse" . . . he went into the house and talked with **Job Bissell** in the Great Room and Newell and his wife in the bedroom . . . William Stevens's house was under the same roof as Staniford's. He reiterated some of what Dr. Rodman and Stevens testified, and said that after the signing Newell told him he was "glad it was over for he had been much fatigued & did not know but he had lost several pounds of Flesh."

Verdict was for the defendants Timothy and Margaret Newell, to recover costs of court from the plaintiff.

768. 1744, May 30: **Mary Tripp** power of attorney to **Matthew Robinson**, gentleman, of Newport, to act in suit between "my son **Benjamin Tripp** [a mariner] and me and my daughter-in-law **Wait Tripp**." Signed by mark: *O* ; witnessed by **Abraham Coggeshall** and **John How**. Receipt dated Dartmouth, 1 March 1743 from **Jedediah Allen** for a silver spoon bequeathed to **Othniel Allen**, witnessed by **Mehitabel** and **Susannah Allen.**

Will of Othniel Tripp of Newport, dated 12 April 1740.

The last will and Testament of Othniel Tripp of Newport in the County of Newport in the Colony of Rhode Island and Providence Plantations in New England who being in good Health of Body and also of Sound & Disposing Mind Memory and Understanding thanks be given to God for it, But calling to Mind the Mortality of My Body knowing it to be appointed of God for Mankind once to dye do make & ordain this my last Will and testament that is to say principally & first of all I recommend my Soul to God who gave it and my Body to ye Earth to be buried in decent manner and as to Such Worldly Estat as it hath pleased God to bless me with in this Life I Give Devise bequeath and Dispose of this same in the manner and form herein after mentioned. Imprim^{s} that all such Just and Lawful Debts which I owe to any Person or persons together with my funeral charges and Disbursements be answred paid and fully discharged by my Executor herein after named. Item I give & bequeath to my beloved wife in lieu of her Thirds of my Estate all my household Goods during her Natural Life or day of her Marriage which shall first Come to pass and also the whole Profit Benefit and Improvement of my Mansion House and the Land belonging to it and also the Lott of Land of Seven Acres herein after mentioned for and during the term & space of Two Years next after my Decease Upon Condition that she do pay the money that shall be due to ye Colony from me or my said Estate during the said Term of Two Years and also the one half of the Yearly Rent of the whole from thenceforward for and during her Natural Life or day of her marriage which shall first come to pass upon

Condition that She do pay the one half of the money that shall be due from me or my said estate to ye Colony aforesaid during the said Time. Item I give & bequeath to my beloved *son* **Othniel Tripp** and to his heirs and assigns forever my Piece of Land in Newport aforesaid measuring and containing about seven acres be the same more or less being bounded and described as in the deed of the same and the same to be possessed and enjoyed at the End of Two Years next after my decease on condition and in consideration of his paying to his four sisters the sum of £30 to each of them two years after my decease and also he or they paying to my wife the full half of ye yearly rent of ye same for & during her natural life or day of her marriage which shall first come to pass also I give and bequeath my shoe buckels to my *grandson* **Othniel Tripp**. I give and bequeath to my beloved *son* **Benjamin Tripp** and to his Heirs and assigns for ever my Mansion House and the Land or Garden thereunto belonging and the same to be possessed and enjoyed at the end of two years after my decease upon condition and in consideration of his or their giving to **Othniel Allen** a Silver Spoon and also to pay to my wife the full half of the yearly rent of the said house and land for and during her natural life or day of her marriage which shall first come to pass also I give to my son Benjamin my sword & cane.

Item I give and bequeath to my *four beloved daughters* the sum of £30 apeice and the same to be paid by my son Othniel Tripp his heirs or assigns two years next after my decease in the same as before herein mentioned.

Item I give and bequeath a Featherbed and furniture to each of my four daughters.

Item I give and bequeath to **Othniel Allen** a silver Spoon to be delivered him by my son Benjamin or his heirs two years after my Decease in the Same as before herein mentioned.

Item My will is & I do hereby order and determine that all my household goods that shall be left at ye decease of my wife or day of her marriage which shall first come to pass shall be equally divided among & between my afore mentioned children both sons and daughters.

Item I give and bequeath my Great Bible to my *Daughter* **Mary Atwood** after my wife's decease or day of her marriage which shall first come to pass. Finally and lastly I do hereby nominate appoint and ordain my beloved son Othniel Tripp to be the sole and only executor of this my last will and testament desiring him to see the same and every part thereof performed fulfilled and accomplished according to the true and real intnt and meaning hereof. But if it should please God that my said son Othniel should die before he shall have executed and performed this said office of executor then my will is and I do hereby nominate [---] appoint and ordain my beloved son Benjamin to be the executor of this my will in all respects as I before mentioned and in testimony that this is my Last Will and Testament I have here unto subscribed my hand and affixed my seal this twelfth day of April in the year of our Lord one thousand Seven hundred and fourty. Witnesses: **Jonathan Easton, George Wanton Junr, John Hammett.** John Hammett, schoolmaster, wrote the will.

769. **Lydia Potter**, widow of **Thomas Potter** late of South Kingstown, vs. **Isaac Fowler**. Writ dated September 1744. In 1729 she had requested the South Kingstown Town Council to order her third of her former husband **Thomas Shearman**'s land, and **Nathaniel Niles, Jeremiah Fish, Christopher Helme** and **Job Babcock** were appointed to set it off for her. In September 1744 **Nathaniel Nyles** was of Groton, Connecticut.

— 1745 —

770. **Banister Case,** Murder of James Osborn. [Large bundle: Samuel Banister's Papers, March 1745.] File includes: Letters of administration to M^rs^. **Elizabeth Gidley**, widow of Mr. **John Gidley**, late of Newport, merchant deceased intestate, and to Mr. **Peleg Brown** of Newport, gentleman, 17 October 1744. On 21 January 1744/5, it was reported that **Peleg Brown** of Newport, sheriff of sd County of Newport, last May attached real estate of **John Cane** late of Newport, mariner (not in the colony), at the suit of **John Gidley**, late of Newport, distiller. **Thomas Potter,** Esq., late sheriff, had died 29 November 1744, after the real estate was sold and before the deed was made. Capt. **Jonathan Nichols** and Capt. **John Tillinghast** were named a committee to receive all writs, executions, and other papers belonging to the office of sheriff that had been in his hands at the time of his death.

Present deed for £240 to **Walter Cranston**, merchant, highest bidder; property described as 80 sq. ft. in Newport, bounded north on the lane from the Neck to Thames Street, east on **Simon Newton**, south on **Nathaniel Kay**, deceased, west on **John Bryer**, with dwelling house. Summons were issued 22 January 1744[/45] to **William Dyre**, gentleman, **Job Bennet** Jr., joiner, **John Griffith, John Brown Junr**, merchant, **George Wanton**, merchant, **Daniel Lambert**, shipwright, **Brice Eccles**, distiller, **Edward Church, Martin Howard**, gentleman, **Edward Wanton, Peleg Wood, Junr, John Gibbs, John Belitho**, distiller, and **David Fairbanks**, all of Newport, and also **Henry Hooper, Robert Keith** and **Samuel Nixon**, surgeons, and **John Brett**, physician, all of Newport, to appear 23rd January at 10 a.m. concerning the murther suspected to have been committed by **Samuel Banister** of Newport, book keeper, upon the body of **John Osborn** of Newport. Signed by Joseph Whipple, Dep. Gov., Benj. Haszard, Ass't and Samuel Wickham, Justice.

William Dyre of Newport, gentleman, deputy sheriff, testified that on 21 inst. January, about 4 o'clock, he had gone to take possession of the house that was late the estate of **John Cain** of sd Newport, mariner, against which house and land **John Gidley** of Newport had obtained judgement of court, which **Walter Cranston** bought at public vendue. ". . . got a rail and the sheriff (**Peleg Brown** Esq.) and I forced the door open . . . Banister appeared in the gangway gun in hand." **Martin Howard**, gentleman, testified that Banister swore he had a gun charged and would shoot the first man that offered to break into the house upon him . . . tried to persuade him to quit the possession peaceably. **Job Bennet Jr.** testified that he was desired by **Peleg Brown** Esq. to go with him and **William Dyre** to take possession of [the] house "and when we came . . . found the door fast . . . **William Dyre** knocked . . . upon which **Samuel Banister** came to a closet window at the west end of the house . . . replyed he would shoot . . . while **John Brown** was speaking to him, **Capt. Griffiths** took hold of the barrel of the gun and pushed the muzle from him and slipped into the house . . . **John Brown** followed and William Dyre and directly I heard the gun go off and saw **James Osborn** fall upon the steps and saw the blood run from him." Deposition of **Dr. Henry Hooper** that on Monday 21 January 1744/5 "about 3 of the clock **Mary Gage** came to call me to go see a man that her father-in-law Mr. **Samuel Banister** had shott as the officers was coming into the house . . . the wounded man was carried to **Capt. Thompsons** . . . was told they had brought him home to **Capt. Griffiths** house for he was his servant . . . [*description of thigh wound*] . . . blood exhausted before Dr. Nixon got to him . . ." Statement of **Samuel Nixon,** surgeon in Newport, 23 January 1744, re wound of **James Osborn,** servant to Capt. **John Griffiths** of sd Newport in presence of **John Brett**, physician, and **Robert Keith,** surgeon [*who also testified*] . . . wound in upper part of thigh was cause of death.

Brice Eccles, distiller, testified that about 15 January last **Mr. Samuel Banister** came "to my house in order to have my evidence concerning an affair between **Mr. Langley** and he – I told him I would due him all ye service I could – he then began to talk of ye ill treatment that he had received of **Mr. Dyer** and further said that his gun was then loaded with a brace of balls in order to blow his brains out – I expostulated with him about ye haineousness of ye crime and what a barbrous thing it was in its nature and at the same time mentioned ye strictnes of Boston in such cases for a man to offer to present a gun tho perhaps he never intended to fire it – he semeingly was well satisfied with my discourse and so we parted." On examination, **Samuel Banister** stated that the gun went off by accident when **Capt. Griffiths** laid hold of him. Eighteen good and lawful men were summoned to view the body of **James Osborn** "lying dead at the house of the **widow Arnold.**" **Elisha Gibbs, William Pinnegar, Nathan Carpenter, John Potter, Samuel Pitman**, [*Ezekiel Burroughs crossed out*], **Arnold Belcher, Simon Rhodes, William White, Walter Cranston, Thomas Thompson, Handley Chipman, John Cahoone, John Whitehorn, John Lyon, William Weeden, William Gardner**, all signed; they decided that they "cannot tell who fired the gun off."

– May Term 1745 –

771. **Daniel Weeden, Joseph Clark,** Warden, and **Richard Tew**, yeoman, **Thomas Carr**, yeoman, **John Paine**, yeoman, and **Abel Franklin**, yeoman, all of Jamestown, [comprising] the Town Council of sd Jamestown vs. **Edward Carr** of Jamestown, yeoman, in custody of the sheriff, for debt of £1182:10; on 17 September 1744 he had acknowledged himself jointly endebted with **Thomas Eldred** of Jamestown, ferryman, and **Benjamin Sheffield** of Jamestown, yeoman, concerning his administration of the estate of **Ebenezer Slocum** of Jamestown, deceased.

Edward Carr had not made rightfull and due administration of the estate as the will ordered. By his will dated 28 September 1715, Ebenezer Slocum had directed that if the child with which his wife was pregnant was a female, she was to have £100 paid at 18 or day of marriage. The child, named **Ruth**, was now the wife of **Peter Wells** of Warwick; the defendant had refused to pay her legacy. The defendant's plea included the statement that the widow of Ebenezer Slocum died in January 1726. At a Jamestown Town Council meeting in October 1744 Edward Carr had appeared and exhibited an account of the administration of **Naomi Slocum**, executrix of the estate of Ebenezer Slocum, yeoman, deceased, and *late wife of the said Edward.*

The will of Ebenezer Slocum, dated 28 September 1715 and proved at Jamestown 4 8m (Oct.) 1715, from Jamestown's First Book of Land Evidence, 186 and 187, was shown. He called himself sick and weak of body, and directed that "the child my wife now goes with if a male child I give and bequeath him five pounds . . . at twenty-one years . . . if a female one hundred pounds. . . ." He left to his brother **Samuel Slocum** "my Brand Cloth Suit," to brother **Giles Slocum** "my next best Suit of Aparrell," and to brother **Joseph Slocum** "the Cloake that was my fathers." He left all his estate "unto my Loveing Wife **Neomy Slocum**"; if the child was a son, he was to have the house and land in Jamestown at age 21, the widow to have it until then. He named his wife executrix and his father-in-law **Benjamin Barton** of Warwick to be executor with her. Witnesses were David Green, John Underwood, and Nicholas Carr.

772. **Richard Gill** of the City of New York, merchant, vs. **Edward Fogg** of Newport, merchant. Writ dated 12 April 1745.

773. **Job Almy** of Newport, merchant vs. **William Coggeshall**, yeoman, and **Newby Coggeshall**, husbandman, both of Portsmouth, in an action of trespass, charging that they did break and carry away two black oak trees lately growing on his property, valued at £10. Writ dated 1 May 1745. Deed from **John** and **Elizabeth Coggeshall** to Job Almy, dated 2 April 1744. Will of John Coggeshall, dated 20 March 1701/2, bequeathing the right to cut wood, etc. Verdict for the plaintiff.

774. **Richard Gill** of the City of New York, merchant, otherwise called Capt. Richard Gill, vs. **Daniel Russell** of Newport, goldsmith alias shopkeeper. Writ dated 2 May 1745.

775. **Christopher Phillips** of North Kingstown, Esq., and his wife **Sarah** vs. **Southcott Langworthy** of Newport, brasier alias pewterer, in an action of trespass to recover a dwelling house, two shops, one warehouse, and a lot of land containing a yard and garden in Newport, 26 feet in front and 164 feet deep. Writ dated 3 May 1745. The land sued for had been possessed on 7 November 1707 by **Peter Brock**, late of Newport,

mariner, who in his will of that date devised it [to his children, of whom the plaintiff Sarah was sole surviving] . . . until on or about 15 November 1707, when he died. Copy of the will of Peter Brock attached [*for full transcript of will, see No. 25*].

776. **Joseph Cundall** of Portsmouth, clothier vs. **Simeon Tilley** of Newport, house carpenter alias wheelwright, in action of debt to recover £12:2. Writ dated 6 May 1745. Defendant countered by stating his Christian name was Simon, not Simeon.

777. **David Seaver** of Newport, house carpenter, vs. **Thomas Coggeshall** of Middletown, yeoman, for £18 for non performance of a promise. Writ dated 7 May 1745. Summons issued to **James Tew** of Newport, house carpenter, **Leonard Lockman,** Esq., **William Lawton**, house carpenter, and **Nicholas Brown**, yeoman, all of Middletown, and **Wing Spooner** of Newport, house carpenter. (Docket No. 6)

778. **Phillip Tillinghast** of Newport, merchant, vs. **Thomas Chadwick** of Newport, fisherman, for £10 due and damages. Writ dated 30 April 1745. (Docket No. 7)

– Indictments – November 1745 –

779. **Samuel Havens** of North Kingstown, labourer, indicted for having stolen rigging from the Brig *Sea Horse* on 4 November 1747 with **Stephen Shearman** of North Kingstown, labourer. He pleaded guilty and was sentenced to pay **Henry Collins** £30 and a fine of £5 to the General Treasury or be whipped 20 lashes on his naked back.

780. **Stephen Sherman** of North Kingstown, labourer, indicted as above; found guilty.

– 1745 – Miscellaneous –

781. **William Smith** of Providence, administrator of the goods of **Prince Smith** late of sd Providence, yeoman, absent for more than 3 years, vs. **Jno Hopkins**. Writ dated 27 May 1745.

782. **John Tillinghast** of West Greenwich, yeoman, vs. **William Weaver Jr.** of East Greenwich, husbandman, for £28 due for wood. Writ dated 18 June 1745. Depositions from **Thomas Matteson** and **John Godfrey** both of East Greenwich.

783. **William Warner** of Newport, ferryman, vs. **William Anthony Gavett** now resident in Newport, mariner, for £101:10:06 debt. Writ dated 4 November 1743.

784. **Isaac Beauchamp** of Newport, mariner, vs. **Joshua Bill** of South Kingstown, ferryman, in action of trouver for a certain bay horse prized at £42:10 and damages. The plaintiff charged that he lost the horse and the defendant disposed of it to his own use at Jamestown in December 1742. Writ dated 22 August 1743. Deposition of **James Venable** of Newport, book keeper, of lawful age, that **John Beauchamp**, son of Isaac, late of Newport, mariner, went out with Capt. **Benjamin Cranston**, "on their cruise," and John told sd Bill that his father went with the horse either to Hartford or Boston. On 3 September 1744 Isaac Beauchamp "lived without this Colony" so was not present in court. Summons issued to **Josiah Arnold** and **John Martin**, both of Jamestown.

785. **Henry West** of Newport, butcher, vs. **Joshua Bill**, ferryman, for non performance of promise to discharge the plaintiff from demands of **Peter Bulkley**. Note from Peter Bulkley dated 16 December 1741 at Colchester to Mr. **Samuel Rhodes** &c. Writ dated 7 May 1745.

786. **Elizabeth King** of Newport, widow and administratrix of **William King** late of sd Newport, cordwainer, deceased, vs. **Robert Duncan** of Newport, taylor; writ dated 30 October 1745. Receipt dated 26 January 1743/4 at Newport, to Mr. **David Melvil**, £23 in full payment of account of **Thos Richardson**['s] bastard child which he had by **Sarah Arnold** . . . signed Wm King. Deposition of **Lydia Ross** of lawful age, that "sometime in the later end of last summer I helped . . . my uncil **Robert Dunkin** . . . to make a Brode Cloth coat for **William King's** son on account of the bastard **child Sarah Arnold** had by **Thomas Richardson**."

787. Deposition of **Capt. Elisha Reynolds** of South Kingstown, yeoman, taken 24 March 1745 at South Kingstown . . . question asked by **Latham Clark** of Jamestown, power of attorney for **Matthew**

Robinson of Newport, empowered by **Stephen Tallman** late of Portsmouth, physician, whether Capt. **Ichabod Potter** late of South Kingstown, deceased, was indebted to the estate of **Sarah Potter**, late of South Kingstown, deceased . . . replied, to the best of his knowledge, about £120 or £130. When asked who discharged the debt, he replied that it was **John Potter** of South Kingstown, yeoman. **John Seagar** and **Rowse Helme** and **John Shelden** of South Kingstown, yeomen, also testified. *(cf. Nos. 749 and 753)*

788. **Amos Kinne** and **Jonathan Gibbens** of lawful age, testified on 30 December 1741 before John Cook, Justice of the Peace at Preston, Connecticut, that on 3 December they were both at the dwelling of Mr. **Roger Billings** in Preston. Kinne signed a statement that they did see there two "young men who ware straingers to us and thay did not tell thare names thay had thare hair cut and white capes [*sic*] on y^{r} heads one of them had on a blue Coulared Cloth grate Coat on ye othere had on a donish grate coat on and we herd y^{m} say thay ware travelers and being asked from whence thay answared from Newwark in ye Gersies and we herd y^{m} furthere say that thay ware a going to Naraganssit to buy passing [*i.e. pacing*] Mairs and that thay should go back to ye Garsies as soon as they had bought what Mairs they wanted and . . . sd blue Coated man moved [*for?*] a swap of horses, with sd Kinnie and when we came to look on his Horse we knew it and told him that was **John Burlison's** Mair and he answared he did not care whose it was he [*met?*] an old Converted [*sic*] woman about a mile of[f] and swapt to her and gave her three pounds of money to boot." Gibbens added to the above that "in ye morning of ye 4th day sd December ye wife of sd Burlison shewed ye Money y^{t} she said shee had of ye sd blue Coated man ye day before in ye abovesd swap and looked on it and I told her it was Counterfitt."

789. **John Tweedy** of Newport, apothecary, vs. **Robert Keith** of Newport, surgeon and practitioner of physick, for £154:0:5 due by book, giving detailed account of apothecary items. Writ dated 24 October 1744.

790. **Ephraim Smith** of South Kingstown, cordwainer, vs. **Michael Dawley** of Exeter, yeoman, for non performance. Writ dated 15 July 1745. Bill of sale dated 17 May 1743, from Dawley to **John Smith**, yeoman, both of South Kingstown, £140, for one Negro man called **Will**, being now about 18 years of age. Witnesses: **Ebenezer Smith, Jeffrey Watson,**

and **Mickel Dally**. **Sarah Smith**, daughter of Ebenezer, and **John Honyman Jr.** of Newport testified that John Smith sold Will to Michael Dawley 7 June 1743. Defendant claimed that the plaintiff was not a freeholder in the Colony. Case went to the Superior Court and was committed to Jury; verdict for defendant.

791. **Job Tripp** and wife **Elizabeth** of North Kingstown vs. **John Gardner** of Exeter, cordwainer, and **John Toms** of Exeter, labourer, for Elizabeth's dower right in estate of her late husband, **John Sweet**, deceased, of Kingstown, yeoman. Writ dated August 1745.

792. **Ann Macomber** of Newport, widow, **John Easton** of Newport, cooper, and wife **Elizabeth** lately named **Elizabeth Wallen**, and **Mary Dyre** of Newport, spinster, vs. **Richard Whitehorn** of Newport, hatter, for money due for rent November last. Verdict for plaintiffs to recover. Writ dated 27 August 1745.

793. **Freelove Westcot** of Providence, spinster, vs. **Basil Dixwell** of Providence, goldsmith alias shopkeeper, in custody of the sheriff, for fraud and deceit. Case first heard in December 1745, Inferior Court of Common Pleas, Providence County. "The defendant at Providence did by marriage courtship, fair promises & delusive arguments persuade the plaintiff to consent to be married to ye defendant and gained her consent and thereupon had carnal knowledge of her body whereby she became pregnant of a bastard child and after that perfideously forsook [her] & refused to marry her . . . on 15 November 1743 [he] visited [her] . . . on or about 25 December [she] consented and mutual promises of marriage were made & [he] then being desirous to ruin & deceive [her] . . . with her committed fornication on the first day of January 1744 . . . on 1 September 1744 [he] wholly refused her." Defendant pleaded technicalities: no signed memorandum existed. Case remitted to next Inferior Court in June.

– May Term 1747 –

794. **Benjamin Norton** of Newport, merchant, vs. **Job Bennet Jr.** of Newport, house carpenter, claiming that he did on 23 June 1746 carry away a certain captive (named **Ralph**) of the price of £250 Old Tenor. Bill of Sale: to Capt. Benjamin Norton, £126 for Negro man named **Ralph**

Barker sold at publick vendue, brought in by Capt. **Robert Morris** in ye Snow *Duke of Marlbrough* . . . condemned as lawful Prize at Newport 6 June 1745. Receipt: "received for my father **William Coddington,** Vendue Master," signed by **William Coddington Jr.**

– November Term 1747 –

795. **James Coggeshall** of Newport, yeoman, for **Thomas Brooks,** late of Newport, mariner, deceased, who in his lifetime was mate and one of the company of the sloop *St. Andrew,* a private Man of Warr whereof **Charles Davison** was late commander, vs. **Walter Cranston,** merchant, and **John Smith,** mariner, of Newport, and **Temperance Grant,** shop-keeper, of Newport, administrator of **John Calder** late of Newport, deceased.

796. **Peter Coggeshall** of Newport, yeoman, vs. **Susanna Anthony** of Middletown, widow, for trespass: she withheld a dwelling house, stable, and 40 acres in Middletown, described as bounded east partly on highway, partly on widow **Hannah Rider's** small tenement, west on land of **William Turner,** north partly on school land, partly on **James Barker,** of which land **Jared Eliot** of Kilingworth in County of New London, clerke, was seized on 25 March 1747 as attorney for Yale College.

797. **Thomas Durfy** of Bristol, ferryman, vs. **John Grinel** of Portsmouth, an Indian man, labourer, for £100 for goods delivered.

– November Term 1748 –

798. **Elizabeth Davenport** had female child lately born; **James Bell** of Newport, carter, was the putative father. The child was born 22 September 1748. Elizabeth was questioned 29 September 1748.

799. **John Corey,** bound apprentice to **Caleb Bennet** late of Portsmouth, weaver, deceased, and his heirs, hath departed from the service of **Mary Bennet** of said Portsmouth, widow and administratrix of the estate and guardian to the heir of said Caleb Bennet; warrant to apprehend him. Deposition of **Sarah Earl,** wife of **William,** dated 24

November 1748, that she signed a paper Caleb Bennet told her was an Indenture but she "never read a word of it but . . . see **Deliverance Corey** sign the sd paper but don't remember that the Boy named John Corey signed the same."

– May Term 1749 –

800. **Gideon Worden** of Portsmouth, yeoman, and **Rebecca** his wife who when sole was named **Rebecca Brown** of Portsmouth, widow, vs. **Margaret Woodman**, widow, and **Richard Billings**, innholder, both of Newport, administrators of the goods of **Edward Woodman** of Newport, yeoman, deceased. (Docket No. 24)

801. **Seth Harvey** of Newport, mariner, deposed that in October last he saw a man named **Wilcox** who informed him he was taken by a Spanish privateer with **Capt. Gideon Wanton Jn^r^** of Rhode Island some time before and brought into St. Iago De Cuba where sd Harvey saw him and Wilcox informed him that Capt. Wanton and the rest had put ashore at Hispanola and he was brought to Cuba . . . he informed Harvey that he had saved some quantity of gold that Capt. Wanton had put between the sloop's stem and bowsprit and that he lost either a single pistole or a half pistole which dropt overboard whilst he was agitting the money out; deposition taken by **Peter Easton** J.P., 15 May 1749 at Newport. **Josiah Willcocks** was notified but was not present. **Joseph Graham** now resident in Newport, mariner, made the same deposition but said the amount was 35 or 36 pistoles; **William James Junr**, who signed by mark, stated the same. **Daniel Willcock** of Newport, mariner, stated that Josiah Willcock had a parcel of gold.

802. **Samuel Durfee** of Tiverton, Esq., on behalf of the Tiverton Town Council, vs. **Alice Fish** of Tiverton, singlewoman, who on 20 January 1748/9 at night had a female bastard child by **Benjamin Manchester** of Tiverton, single man and apprentice to **John Howland** of sd town, Esq. Writ dated 27 April 1749. **William Fish** and **Stephen Cook**, yeomen, were sureties for Alice to appear. **Elisabeth Shrive** and **Mary Cook** deposed on 27 March 1749 that they were present at the birth of the child, and Alice said that Benjamin Manchester was the father. Benjamin was ordered to pay to the town council or overseers of the poor 12*s* per week and to Alice £10.

803. **Elizabeth Langford** of Newport, spinster, vs. **David Jones** of Newport, shipwright, for debt of £23 for nursing the defendant's wife in 1748. (Docket No. 13)

804. **Job Tripp** of North Kingstown, yeoman, vs. **James Easton** of Newport, shipwright and **Samuel Borden** of Tiverton, yeoman alias tanner, executors of the will of **John Mumford Jr.** late of Exeter, yeoman deceased, re note. (Docket No. 48)

805. **James Linscom** of Newport, clothier, vs. **Bethiah Clark** of Newport, widow, executrix of the will of **Aaron Clark** late of Newport, yeoman, deceased, re debt due for goods: "several pair of ox feett . . . making yr daughter's gound . . . cash by yr daughter **Huldah**, lock and key, mugg of salt, bushel of chestnuts."

806. **Henry West** of Newport, butcher, vs. **William Dunbar** of Newport, mariner now resident in Providence, re £110:11:00 for meat sold and delivered in 1747. (Docket No. 116)

807. **Charles Whitfield** and **Matthew King** of Newport, merchants, vs. **Abigail Stoddard** of Newport, widow and administratrix of **Thomas Stoddard** late of Newport, mariner, re debt due for cheese, potatoes, cyder, sugar, apples, rum. . . . (Docket No. 201)

808. **Richard Rennols** of Newport, mariner, and late master of the Snow *Duke of Cumberland* vs. **John Brown** and **William Mumford** and **John Bannister** of Newport, and **Christopher Scott** of Kingston upon Hull in County of Kingston [*sic*] in Great Britain, merchants and late owners of sd Snow, for debt due by book: £1294:4:9 money of the Province of North Carolina, from a voyage to New Bern in 1746. (Docket No. 220)

809. **Israel Abrahams** of Newport, merchant, vs. **Phebe Strengthfield** of Newport, widow and administratrix of the estate of **William Strengthfield** late of Newport, Esq., deceased. William had delivered to the plaintiff £2250 and desired him to lay out sd sum in molasses to best advantage . . . they to split the profits . . . molasses was distilled by the plaintiff into rum and in October 1747 he pd to **William Stevens** by order of sd William Strengthfield. Defendant had asked for part of payment in loaf sugar, and plaintiff had it in Boston; mentioned [?*Samuel or Stephen*] **Greenleaf** in Boston as defendant's brother. (Docket No. 222)

810. **William Caswell** of South Kingstown, perriwigmaker, and his wife **Susannah**, executrix of the will of **Ben^{n} Hagger** late of Newport, tanner, deceased, vs. **William Almy**, merchant, and **Walter Chaloner** Esq. alias merchant, both of Newport, executors of the will of **Christopher Almy** late of Newport, merchant, deceased. Christopher had been bailiff of sd Benjamin in Newport . . . Christopher in his lifetime was assignee of **Henry Sabin** of Newport, gunsmith, who was mortgagee of sd Benjamin Hagger of a messuage or dwelling house and land at Easton's Point in Newport in 1733; he never rendered an account. Plaintiff was awarded £100. (Docket No. 237)

811. **Samuel Brownel**, a Negro man (so called) of Portsmouth, butcher, vs. **Joseph Brown** of Newport, mariner, re debt of £37 due for meat. (Docket No. 239)

812. **Deborah Carr** of Little Compton, widow, vs. **William Jameson** of Little Compton, taylor, re debt of £20:5 due her for keeping his cows and hog in 1748. (Docket No. 251)

813. **Charles Ninegret** of Charlestown, gentleman, an infant, by **Catharine Ninegret** of sd Charlestown, widow, mother and guardian, vs. **Thomas Ward** of Newport, Esq. and clerk of the Superior Court, referring to action of trespass brought by one **Thomas Ninegret** of sd Charlestown, gentleman and infant, against **Samuel Clark** of Charlestown, yeoman, for one dwelling house and 300 acres of land.

814. **Dorcas Freeborn** of Newport, widow, administratrix of **Joseph Freeborn** of Newport, tanner, deceased, vs. **William Keas** of North Kingstown, schoolmaster, re £7:10 due for leather breeches sold and delivered to him 14 February 1746. (Docket No. 304)

815. **Joseph Irish** of Little Compton, yeoman, overseer of the poor for Little Compton: on 2 May 1749 the town sergeant of Middletown carried **Edward Burgess** and his family out of Middletown into Little Compton, by virtue of an order of Middletown saying Little Compton was their legal residence . . . claims this an error and sd Burgess was legally settled in Middletown above one year before the warrant. File includes an indenture between **Henry Tew** of Middletown, yeoman, and **Edward Burgess** of Little Compton, husbandman, dated 4 April 1748 for lease of a 73-acre farm in Middletown, witnesses **John (X) Corlein** and **Henry Palmer**. (Docket No. 313)

816. **Joseph Tripp** of Dartmouth, yeoman, vs. **Josiah Willcox** of Tiverton, yeoman, re debt.

817. **Joseph Fox** of Newport, scrivener, deposed and said that some years ago **John Gidley** Esq. deceased was Judge of the Court of Vice Admiralty in sd Colony and . . . the snow *Caulker* and her cargo taken as a Spanish prize . . . retaken by **Capt. John Griffith** in a Rhode Island privateer.

We find for the Plantif The Money Sude for & Cost of Cort
Benjn Norton
Larance Clark
Thomas Olney
Nathaniel Potter
Willm Havens
Nath^{nl} Jenks
Robard Nikols
Ammos Staford
Jer^{h} Niles
John Hill
Joseph ffry
Edward Boss

Left:
A typical court verdict: *We find for the Plantif The Money Sude for & Cost of Cort*, with names of the jurors:

Benjn Norton
Larance Clark
Thomas Olney
Nathaniel Potter
Willm Havens
Nath^{nl} Jenks
Robard Nickols
Ammos Staford
Jer^{h} Niles
John Hill
Joseph ffry
Edward Boss

The slip of paper is just large enough to hold the writing on it. This, like most of the verdict slips, is separated from its case, bundled with many others.

– November Term 1754 –

818. **Gideon Borden** of Portsmouth, yeoman, vs. **Gideon Cornell** of Portsmouth, Esq., in action of trespass, charging that he entered the plaintiff's land in Portsmouth in 1752 and took away one large Bay Stone Horse valued at £215. Verdict for defendant. (Docket No. 1)

819. **John Hadwen** and **Edward Thurston Junr** of Newport, shopkeepers, vs. **Walter Chaloner** of Newport, merchant, for £101:10:4 due for sundry goods, including [mostly] loaf sugar at 12*s* per pound, tea, trousers, starch. (Docket No. 13)

820. **Henry Bliss** of Newport, yeoman, vs. **Joseph Weeden** of Newport, house carpenter, for trespass, concerning three-quarters of an acre in Newport with house, etc., of which said Joseph Weeden was seised 10 May 1753 and did with **Hannah Weeden** convey to Henry Bliss. Deed in file: Joseph Weeden of Newport, house carpenter, and Hannah Weeden [who signed by mark X], widow and devisee of Joseph Weeden Senr. late of Newport, yeoman, deceased, to Henry Bliss, etc., stating that **Joseph Weeden Senr.** in his will dated 17 March 1744 gave to his wife the use and improvement of the house and to his son Joseph and his heirs a half lot of land after the decease of his wife, recorded Newport Land Evidence 10:165-6. The deed was witnessed by **Will. Clark** and **Phebe Philips**, and was acknowledged 21 May 1753; the land was described as bounded east on land of **Edward Scott**, south on a highway, west on land of **Job Wilkins**, and north on land of **Jonathan Wilkins**. (Docket No. 14)

821. **John Martin** of Jamestown, yeoman, vs. **George Foster** of Coventry, schoolmaster, for non-performance of promise. Document in file bearing Spanish seal of Philip *Rex*. (Docket No. 16)

822. **Mahitabel Treby** of Newport, widow, vs. **Abraham All** of Newport, taylor, in action of trespass concerning part of a dwelling house in Newport and the lot on which it stood, bounded north on land of the plaintiff, east on the street, south on Queen Street, west on land of **Thomas Rogers**, of which she claimed to have been dispossessed by the defendant 28 June 1754. (Docket No. 18)

823. **Joseph Gifford** of Tivertown, blacksmith, alias Joseph Gifford of Warwick, yeoman, vs. **Benjamin Cundall** of Newport, clothier, alias Ben-

jamin Cundall of Coventry, for £225 due by note dated 16 November 1752, witnessed by **John Langford** and **Thomas Brayton**. (Docket No. 21)

824. **Temperance Grant** of Newport, shopkeeper, vs. **Joseph Wilson** of Newport, mariner, administrator of the estate of **Alexander McDaniel** late of said Newport, mariner, deceased, to render unto the plaintiff two tons of Merchantable Logwood for which he had earlier received judgement. Testimony taken from **Anne McDonald**, widow of Alexander. (Docket No. 32)

825. **Archibald Campbell** of Newport, schoolmaster, vs. **Jonathan Easton** of Middletown for £18:2 due for cash paid and goods delivered, loaf sugar and tea at £3 per pound. (Docket No. 37)

826. **Nicholas Carr** of Newport and **Mary** his wife vs. **Joseph Scott** of Newport. File includes Articles of Agreement between **Mary Gould** of Newport, relict of **Daniell Gould Sr.**, late of Newport, deceased, and **Joseph Scott** of Newport, mariner. Mary received judgement at Court of Common Pleas in Newport May 1731 by her [right] of Dower for one third part of a lot in Newport with dwelling house and buildings, bounded north by land of **George Cornell**, east on Thames Street, south on land of **Jonathan Marsh**, west on the harbour or salt water, and also one third of three acres bounded west on land of **Ezbon Sandford**, north on land of **Samuel Holmes** and **Simon Peas**, east on land of **Job Peckham**, and south on land of **Thomas Richardson**. Agreement dated 1 October 1731 shown: "to prevent the Difference & Mischief of setting of the third part by moots and bonds [*sic*] . . . [parties] agree that **Joseph Scott** should pay to **Mary Gould** £12 per annum during his natural life unless the house should casually be burnt down or otherways destroyed." Defendant, Scott, answers that **Mary Carr** was then **Mary Gould**, and therefore the suit is not valid. (Docket No. 25)

827. **Abigail Cornell** of Portsmouth, widow, vs. **Thomas Ayres** of Newport, ropemaker, for £347 due by note. (Docket No. 56)

828. **Content Baggs** of Tiverton, spinster, vs. **Jacob Strange** of Newport, for breach of promise, claiming damages of £6000 current money of New England, stating that at Newport on 29 March 1753/4, the said plaintiff and defendant had discourse together concerning wedlock, and said

Jacob for and in consideration that she the plaintiff would consent to be married to him did faithfully promise & upon himself assume & take that he . . . would be married . . . & now hath hitherto refused. Writ dated 4 July 1754. (Docket No. 58)

829. **Jeremiah Tallman** of Shrewsbury, County of Monmouth, Province of New Jersey, mariner, otherwise Jeremiah Tallman of Newport, mariner, vs. **John Coggshall** of Portsmouth, yeoman, for £149 due by note dated 16 April 1744 at Newport. (Docket No. 107)

830. **Thomas Durfee** of Middletown, innholder, vs. **Nicholas Brown** of Portsmouth, yeoman, for £130 due by note dated 1 June 1754. (Docket No. 115)

831. **Dudley Woodbridge** of Groton, Co. New London, Colony of Connecticut, merchant, vs. **Michael Phillips** of Bristol, Co. Bristol, mariner, and **Elizabeth** his wife lately when sole called **Elizabeth Duffils**, for £42:6:9 due for goods delivered to Wid^{w} Elizabeth Duffils, including whalebones, lace, chince, paper pinns, needles and thread. (Docket No. 136)

832. **Henry Bowers** of Swanzey in Co. Bristol, Province of Massachusetts Bay, merchant, vs. **John Bannister** of Newport, merchant, in action of trespass: at Swanzey on 1 April 1748 the defendant did entice away from and out of the service of the plaintiff one **John Smith**, an indentured servant. Damages claimed, £2000. (Docket No. 138)

833. **Gilbert Sisson** of Portsmouth, labourer, vs. **Benjamin Cornell** of Portsmouth, for money due by note dated 5 October 1754. (Docket No. 142)

834. **John Holmes** of Middletown, gentleman, an infant by his guardians **John Rogers and Jonathan Easton** both of Middletown, yeomen, vs. **Margaret Holmes** of Middletown, widow, for trespass, concerning a farm of 170 acres in Middletown, with a house, etc., bounded north on land of **John Taylor**, partly on land of **John Wood** and partly on land of **Jonathan Luther**, east on the sea, south on land of **Elisabeth Smith** and **Isaac Smith**, and west on land of **Peleg Smith**, of which his brother, **Joseph Holmes**, late of Middletown, gentleman, on 26 April 1753 was seized . . . till on or about 27 April 1753 when he died intestate, leaving the present plaintiff, his only brother and heir, who on 25 October 1754 was dispossessed by the defendant. (Docket No. 185)

835. **John Whiting** of Newport, goldsmith, vs. **William Stirtevant** of Newport, mariner, for failure to keep his promise to deliver 140 barrels of turpentine. (Docket No. 186)

836. **John Lynscomb** of Newport, mariner, vs. **Penelope Lynscomb** of Newport, widow, administratrix of the estate of **James Lynscomb** of Newport, worsted comber, deceased, for recovery of one third part of £1,011:13:3 Old Tenor due as he is one of the children of the said James . . . said sum being the amount of personal estate of the deceased. On or about 10 September 1753 James died, leaving the defendant, the plaintiff, and one daughter. Inventory taken 5 November 1753 by Job Townsend and Matthew Borden shown, from Newport Town Council Book 11, page 190, personal estate £615:3:3, including a large pair of silver shoe buckles, a neck buckle, a Hart & Hind Ring without price, being left as a Pledge, a German-Serge coat, a Camblet Jacket, and a Stript Holland shirt left as a Pledge . . . left by **Laurence Anderson**, a Seafaring Man. Account dated 19 November 1753, Mr. **John Linscomb** debtor to **Wm. Stevens**, for "one pare green stockings you ordered me to cut for your father Mr. James Linscomb, £15, 35 letters at *6d* . . ." Verdict for plaintiff. (Docket No. 231)

837. **John Bennet** of Newport, yeoman, vs. **Thomas Shearman** of Portsmouth, yeoman, for non-performance of promise: on 20 November 1752 **Thomas Pope** drew on order £72; money due also for wood, keeping sheep, etc. (Docket No. 234)

838. **Joseph Baley** of Newport, shop joyner, vs. **John Baley** of Little Compton, yeoman, for one-ninth part of one-sixth part of 250 acres in Little Compton with salt marshes, and a house. Verdict for plaintiff. (Docket No. 238)

839. **Elisabeth Coggeshall** of Newport, widow, who was wife of **Peter Coggeshall** late of Newport, yeoman, deceased, vs. **Daniel Coggeshall** of Newport, merchant, in action of dower, to recover her right in a lot and house measuring 44 by 88 feet, bounded west on Thames Street, partly on land of **Robert Stoddard**, east on Howland land, south on a highway; her husband died on or about 10 April 1748. (Docket No. 239)

840. **John Eldred** of Jamestown, mariner, vs. **Joseph Bull** of Newport, merchant, administrator of the estate of **Francis Ferrari**, late of Newport,

deceased, merchant, and **Jonathan Nichols**, innholder, and **Mary Nichols**, widow, both of Newport, administrators of the personal estate of **Jonathan Nicholas Junr**, late of Newport, mariner, deceased, for debt of £340:18:1. (Docket No. 245)

841. **Philip Mosher** of Newport, setwork cooper, vs. **Jonathan Haszard** of Newport, for £60 due by note dated in June 1754. (Docket No. 251)

842. **William Read** of Newport, merchant, vs. **William Perkins** of Newport, labourer, and **Robert Carr** of Newport, merchant, administrators of the estate of **John Shearman** late of Newport, deceased, mariner, for £1000 due from the time when John Shearman was Bailiff of the plaintiff of 417 gallons of rum and 455 gallons of molasses. (Docket No. 253)

843. **Mary Almy** of Newport, widow, vs. **Isaac Sheffield** of Warwick, yeoman, and **James Sisson** of Newport, innholder, for £803:15 due by note dated 15 June 1752, witnessed by **Aaron Aldrich** and **Sarah Newton**. (Docket No. 254)

844. **Thomas Fletcher** of Boston, merchant, vs. **Thomas Phillips** of North Kingstown, shopkeeper, for debt, £52:2:2 of Province Money and £8:16:8 Old Tenor which he oweth. (Docket No. 271)

845. **John Channing** and **Walter Chaloner** of Newport, merchants, vs. **Henry Livingston** of the Island of Jamaica in the West Indies, merchant, for an accounting of the time he was Bailiff of two-fifths of certain goods and merchandise being the cargo of the snow *Angola* whereof **Robert Stoddard** was master, to be disposed of at the Island of Jamaica . . . in February 1754 defendant was Bailiff of plaintiffs' 80 Negroes, valued at £2,470 current money of Jamaica. Writ dated 24 October 1753. (Docket No. 274)

846. **John Wanton** of Newport, shopkeeper, vs. **Abraham Redwood Esq.** and **Nathaniel Coggeshall** of Newport, executors of the will of **Henry Tisdale** of Newport, gunsmith, deceased, in action of covenant, that they keep the covenant made by said Henry in his lifetime, concerning a deed dated 28 February 1740. Deed: Henry Tisdale of Newport, gunsmith, and **Elizabeth** his wife, for £1500 sold to John Wanton of Newport, land bounded north on the street 21 rods and a half, east on land of the heirs of **Benjamin Bull**, deceased, now in tenancy or occupation of **Peter Coggeshall**, and west on Thames Street 18 rods 6½ feet. (Docket No. 297)

847. **Joseph Bull** of Newport, merchant, vs. **John Hicks** of Newport, boatman, for £17:10:6 due for sundry goods, including sugar, molasses, tea and rum. (Docket No. 298)

848. **John Leopold Gosler** of London, Co. Middlesex [*sic*], Kingdom of Great Britain, ropemaker, vs. **William Richards** and **John Coddington** of Newport, merchants in company, for £103:10:11 sterling due by note signed 21 October 1752 in London. Richards answered that when he signed the note Gosler had agreed to accept tarr, and it had been sent, but they did not agree on the price. **Edmund Jacklin** on oath declared in August 1753 as mate of the ship *London* he had delivered 199 barrells of tarr to a Lighterman on the account of Capt. Wm Richards to be carried to John Leopold Gosler in London. (Docket No. 362)

849. **Caleb Earl** of Newport, clothier, vs. **Peter Tribee** of Newport, sailmaker, for £60, charging that on 20 May 1754 at Newport, a Negro Man Slave named **Pompey** belonging to the defendant had broken the leg of a cow belonging to the plaintiff . . . on 21 May the defendant had taken the cow into his possession and killed her. Plaintiff expected to recover full value. Case went to arbitration: referees chosen, Mr. **Benjamin Stanton** by plaintiff, Mr. **Rowse Potter** by defendant, Mr. **James Coggeshall** by the court. (Docket No. 364)

850. **Caleb Earl** of Newport, clothier, vs. **Newport Wood**, a free Negro Man so-called of Newport, labourer, for £480 due by note dated 17 March 1752, signed by defendant with a mark C. (Docket No. 365)

851. **John Cooke** of Newport, shopkeeper, vs. **Caleb Sisson** of Portsmouth, mariner alias cordwainer, son of **John Sisson**, for £19:17:9 due for sundry goods, including "camblet, everlasting, Roshalinin, silk, thread," etc.

852. **Temperance Gibbs** of Dartmouth, widow, otherwise **Temperance Grant** of Newport, vs. **Joseph Turner** of Newport, mariner, for debt due by note dated 15 August 1749. (Docket No. 368)

853. **Thomas Crossing** of Newport, practitioner of physick & chirurgeon, vs. **Benjamin Greene** of Newport, taylor, administrator of the estate of **James Walchin** late of Newport, deceased, for £83:11 due for sundry medicines sold and delivered in the year 1753 for the deceased's last sickness. (Docket No. 397)

854. **John Fryers** of Newport, shopkeeper, vs. **Henry Sowle** of Newport, taylor, and **Ann Courtney** of North Kingstown, widow, administrator of the estate of **John Courtney**, late of Newport, trader, deceased, for money due for sundry Braziery delivered to said intestate in 1752 and 1753. Account included locks, nails, etc. (Docket No. 420)

855. **David Lake** of Newport, gentleman, infant who sues by his father **William Lake** of Newport, schoolmaster, his natural guardian, vs. **Jandifor Lyndy** of Newport, innholder, for £52:10 Old Tenor, due by note dated 21 June 1754. (Docket No. 476)

856. **Jonathan Sowle** of Portsmouth, yeoman, vs. **Nathaniel Walker** of Newport, blacksmith, for non-performing his promise to deliver rum in return for note dated 1 June 1754 at Newport for £52. (Docket No. 481)

857. **Thomas Rees** of Newport, innholder, and wife **Hannah**, said Hannah being administratrix of the estate of **Thomas Duin** late of Newport, innholder, deceased, vs. **James Duncan** late of Newport, mariner, for £38:17 from a judgement obtained against **Joseph Brooks** at May Court 1754. Plaintiff recovered. (Docket No. 494)

858. **Henry Sowle** of Newport, taylor, vs. **James Baley** of Middletown, yeoman, for money due by note dated 1 May 1754. (Docket No. 496)

859. **David Cummings** of Newport, perukemaker, vs. **Mary Pinniger** of Newport, spinster, who had estate of **Jacob Peterson** in her hands when the plaintiff obtained a judgement. (Docket No. 507)

860. **Francis Borland** of Boston, Esq., vs. **James Perry** of South Kingstown, Esq., concerning a lease of land in South Kingstown called Green Hill Farm. (Docket No. 508)

— 1755 —

861. **Mary Bennet Jr.** of Portsmouth, an infant spinster, by **Mary Bennet** her mother and guardian, vs. **Benjamin Cornell** of Dartmouth, gentleman, charging that he had received £43:6:8 from the hands of **Daniel Lake**, for land in Portsmouth held in common between the

plaintiff and defendant from 25 March 1754 to 25 March 1755; the defendant said he never did. Benjamin was administrator of the estate of **Abigail Cornell**, late of Portsmouth, widow, deceased.

862. **Hope Almy** vs. **Benjamin Cornell** (as above) for debt due from **Abigail Cornell** by note 11 October 1754.

863. **Ozias Pitkin** of Hartford in the County of Hartford & Colony of Connecticut yeoman and **Godsgift** his wife Late when sole called **Godsgift Bull** vs. **James Easton** of Newport, Shipwright, in custody of the sheriff, in an action of trespass for entering and unjustly witholding the possession of a lot in Newport about 70 feet in breadth and 100 feet in length with a blacksmith shop thereon, which lot is commonly used as a Ship Carpenters yard, bounded easterly on the Street, northerly upon land of **Thomas Coggeshall**, westerly by the Sea & southerly on land of **Thomas Cranston, Capt. John Brown** and **William Giles**. Plaintiffs claimed damage of £3000. Writ dated 17 October 1755; **J. Honeyman** attorney.

Henry Bull, Gent., Deceased, was in his lifetime seised of said land on 10 December 1693 and so continued until 11 December 1693 when by his will of that date he gave the land to his grandson "Jireth Bull & to the Heirs of his Body unto the third Generation & from thence to be fee simple all my Farm Lying and being in the Precinct of Newport" . . . he paying to his sister **Mary Coggeshall** the sum of £100. The testator died on or about the first day of February 1693[/4] and the property descended to his grandson Jireth, who paid the £100 legacy to his sister Mary Coggeshall and continued in possession until 15 October 1715 when he died and it descended to Benjamin Bull, late of Newport, gentleman, eldest son and heir of the said Jireth Bull. Benjamin continued as tenant in tail until on or about 10 May 1729 when he died, and Gods Gift Bull, the only child and heir of the said Benjamin, became seized as tenant in tail of the lands and so continued until on or about 16 October 1755 when the defendant refused to surrender the property to her upon being asked to do so.

Entered in evidence: Copy of will of Henry Bull [*for full transcript, see No. 11*]. Marriage record: "Hartford in Connecticut August the 7th 1749 Mr. Ozias Pitkin of Hartford and Mrs. Gift Bull were Joyned in Marrage by me Wm Pitkin Assistant as appears by my entry on Record. Certified pr Wm Pitkin Assis^{t}."

Thankful Hunt, wife of **Edward Hunt** of Newport, painter, testified in court that "she was at the Birth of Godsgift Bull, Daughter of Benjamin Bull late of Newport aforesaid deceased and Content his Wife, which Godsgift is now the Wife of Ozias Pitkin. . . ."

In another case (S.C. 14,015), in 1762, **George Pitkin, Daniel Pitkin,** and **Gift Pitkin**, administrators of the estate of **Ozias Pitkin** late of Hartford, yeoman, deceased, petitioned for liberty to sell real estate in Newport now in the possession of **Isaac Peckham**, stating that the demands against the estate exceed the amount of personal estate by £270.

864. November: **Abial Cook** of Little Compton vs. **Samuel Cook** of Tiverton, claiming that said Samuel had taken more than his half of the residual estate of their father **John Cook**. The case was "agreed."

– November Term 1756 –

Indictments

865. **John Palmer** of Little Compton, husbandman, indicted for [stealing] from **John Briggs** of Little Compton, innholder, on 25 February 1756, two large cheeses, two gammons pork, one barrel of salt pork, one pewter plate, to the value of £50 Old Tenor. **Mary Palmer** and **Phebe Palmer**, both spinsters of Little Compton, named as accomplices . . . [stole] sewing silk from **John Briggs**.

866. **Julian Wolford**, widow, and **Christiana Renshon**, both transient persons, now resident in Newport, indicted for having stolen on 9 October 1756, from the shop of **John Cooke** of Newport, shopkeeper, 16 yeards of camblett, valued at £64 Old Tenor. Julian swore [*signing by mark X*] that she brought it from Virginia where she had paid for it in tobacco, and Christiana swore that "my sister [Julian] swapped tobacco for it in Virginia to make her a cloak." They were also accused of having stolen a handkerchief from **Moses Levy's** shop; Julian said she had brought "China handkerchiefs" from Virginia and sold three in Philadelphia, two in Newport, and one in Bristol. Verdict: not guilty.

– November Term 1756 –

Inferior Court of Common Pleas

867. **Abner Towsley** of Brimfield, Hampshire County, yeoman, vs. **John Taylor** of South Kingstown, clothier, for money due by note dated 15 December 1755. Witnesses to the note were **Kg°** or **Kg^{a} Taylor** [*who signed with an unusually bold signature*] and **Nathan Gardner**. (Docket No. 27)

868. **Levi Irish** vs. **Christopher Borden**, charging assault. Levi was clerk of the second company of Trained Band and required to collect fines or "distrain" [*i.e. take goods and chattels*]. He had a warrant from Capt. **Richard Durfey** of the Train'd Band of Tiverton, and sundry of the enlisted soldiers [including the defendant] neglected to make a personal appearance accoutred according to the law on Training Day, 26 April last. Decision for plaintiff. (Docket No. 38)

869. **John Rodman** of Burlington in the Western Division of the Province of New Jersey, physician, vs. **Jeoffrey Haszard** of South Kingstown, yeoman, for debt of £2000 due by bond dated 10 June 1756 from the defendant to **John Reynolds** of South Kingstown, husbandman. (Docket No. 39)

870. **Elizabeth Briggs**, widow and relict of **William Briggs**, late of Little Compton, now resident in Richmond, King's County, vs. **Abiel Cook** and **George Rowse** of Little Compton, yeomen, for £500 due by bond. (Docket No. 44)

871. **Joseph Cook** of Tiverton, yeoman, vs. **Benjamin Durfy** of Tiverton, yeoman, in action of trespass, charging assault, that on 26 June 1756 the defendant knocked him down, kicked him, etc. (Docket No. 46)

872. **John Wing** of Newport, husbandman, vs. **John Sisson** of Portsmouth, yeoman, in action of assumpsit. In the year 1754 at Newport the plaintiff promised to fit out for sea and furnish the sloop *Elizabeth* whereof the defendant was then owner, and the defendant would pay one third, to the amount of £359:15:2 Old Tenor. A deposition was made by **Thomas Howland** of Tiverton, merchant. (Docket No. 98)

873. **James Easton**, merchant, **Nicholas Easton, Esq.**, both of Newport, **Peter Barker** of Middletown, yeoman, and **Giles Slocum** and **Jacob**

Mott Jr., both of Portsmouth, yeomen, vs. **Constant Cook** of Newport, carter, and **David Newton** of Newport, blacksmith, charging that the defendants dispersed [*sic; dispossessed?*] the plaintiffs of two lotts of land with dwelling and shop, about 100 square feet, on 27 October 1756. The land was on Easton's Point, and the plaintiffs were legally seised of it 25 March 1754, the annual rent being 6 oz 17 dwght and 12 grains of silver payable 25 March annually. **Job Bennet Jr.**, deputy sheriff, on 27 October 1756 "served this writ on ye Body of ye within named **David Newton** but the within named **Constant Cook** I could not find." (Assize Docket No. 100)

874. **Constant Baley** of Newport, joiner, vs. **Abiah Hathaway** of Newport, mariner, in action of assumpsit, charging that on 3 November 1755 he had given to the defendant one mahogany desk which he had promised to carry to sea with him and dispose of in the best manner and lay out half the price it sold for in West Indian goods. (Docket No. 109)

– November Term 1757 –

875. **Peleg Barker** of Tiverton, innholder, vs. **Robin Briggs**, an Indian man so-called of Tiverton, mariner alias labourer, to recover £223:8 due for sundrys. . . vitels and drink . . . from 12 November 1755 until 13 June 1756, allowing credit for 42 days of work at 20*s* per day. Referees chosen: Mr. **David Durfey** by the plaintiff, Mr. **Ebenezer Tabor** by the defendant, Mr. **Giles Brownell** by the court. (Docket No. 219)

– May Term 1758 –

876. **Jonathan Easton** of Newport, yeoman, vs. **Daniel Wilcocks** of same, mariner, in action of assumpsit, that 23 November 1756 he received of the plaintiff on board the Schooner *Nancy* 4 barrells of Fish called Shad . . . promised to take on himself to carry the same to ports beyond the sea and dispose thereof to plaintiff's best Advantage. (Docket No. 7)

877. **Silas Cooke** of Newport, merchant, v. **Jonathan Pearce** of Prudence Island, yeoman, to recover £45:5 due by book. Bill dated 3 June 1757 [for] an old foresail and twine. (Docket No. 9)

878. **Sylvanus Strange** of Freetown, mariner, vs. **John Kilbee** and **Melatiah Strange**, both now residing Newport, traders alias mariners, for £42:10 lawful money of the province of North Carolina and £15:16 old tenor due for goods. In 1757 and 1758 Kilbee and Melatiah Strange were owners of the sloop *Speedwell*. Capt. **Sylvanus Strange** billed for turpentine, Carolina currency received of **Andrew Hunter**, and "7 months Hospitable Money"; this was countered with a credit for "wayges, horsehayer to the Navel Office . . . potatoes." **John Strange** deposed and said that on or about 10 August 1757 he was in company with **Melatiah Strange** and asked him what he gave **Sylvanus Strange** a month and he replied that he shipt him at £6 per month. Deposition of **William Ware** that **Melatiah Strange** was brother of **Sylvanus Strange. Sylvanus Strange** swore to account 17 April 1758 in Onslow County, N.C. Agreed 25 May 1758 at Newport, **Sylvanus Strange** being in North Carolina. (Docket No. 12)

879. **Evert Byvanck, Cornelius Van Rans'l, Stephen Thom** [*or Thorn?*] and **Christopher Codwise**, all of the City of New York, merchants, alias **Evert Byvanck & Co.**, owners of the sloop *Catharine*, **Isaac Sears** master, vs. **Thomas Kinsman** now residing in Bristol, mariner, for money due by note dated 13 June 1757. (Docket No. 30)

880. **John Rogeral** now of the Parish of St. Dorothy in the Island of Jamaica, merchant, vs. **Joseph Stafford** of East Greenwich, mariner, to recover £50:6:9 due for sundries; Rogeral was Factor to **Denis Kelly** Esq., Stafford formerly commander of the Brigantine *Duke of Cumberland* loaden at Old Harbour in the Parish and Island aforesaid and bound from thence to Rhoad Island in North America . . . 850 gallons of molasses. (Docket No. 31)

881. **Thomas Gillet** of Lucia in the parish of Hanover in the Island of Jamaica, innholder, vs. **John Dennis** of Newport, mariner, in case of promise & assumpsit. Defendant on 28 April 1755 at Newport promised, on payment of the usual accustomed price for the passage of a Negro Boy belonging to the plaintiff named **Sharper** which he [Dennis] brought from the Island of Jamaica to Newport with and in a vessell of [his own], to deliver the boy to the plaintiff; the plaintiff avers that he is ready to pay for the passage but the defendant refuses to deliver the said Negro who is of the price of £1000 old tenor. Writ dated 15 December 1757.

882. **John Arthur Johnson** of Newport, mariner and late gunner of the Privateer Brigantine *King Hendrick*, **Samuel Tompkins** late commander, vs. **William Richards** and **John Coddington** of Newport, merchants in Company and agents for the owners and company of said privateer, in action of assumpsit for his share of prizes taken in a cruise in company with a privateer called the *Harlequin* belonging to New York. Memorandum of Shares on board the *King Hendrick* 1757, included **George Cook**, Boy, 1/2. Judgment for plaintiff. (Docket No. 34)

883. **Peter Poheag**, an Indian man of Stonington, County of New London, Connecticut, labourer, vs. **Thomas Attwood** of Newport, joiner, to recover £5 due by note dated 5 Oct. 1757. (Docket No. 49)

884. **James Fanning Jr.** of Southold in County of Suffolk, Province of New York, yeoman, vs. **James Rogers**, shopkeeper and **Thomas Atwood**, cooper, of Newport, claiming that on 16 February 1758 the defendant received of **William Richards** and **John Coddington** of Newport, merchants and agents for the privateer *King Hendrick*, **Samuel Tompkins** commander, one full share amounting to £36, which was the share of 2 prizes coming to **Sampson Paris**, an Indian man late one of the company of said privateer and an apprentice of the plaintiff during the cruise. (Docket No. 53)

885. **Ephraim Macomber** of Newport, cooper, vs. **John Wing** of Newport, yeoman, in action of trover, claiming £75 old tenor; on 10 Oct. 1757 he had been possessed of one cow which on 30 October the defendant had converted to his own uses. Judgment for defendant. (Docket No. 54)

886. **Joseph Proud** of Newport, chairmaker, vs. **Thomas Cornell** of Newport, butcher, to recover debt of £122:5; reference made to judgment obtained against **Jonathan Phillips Jr.** of Newport, joiner, in November 1756. (Docket No. 60)

887. **Philip Tillinghast, Samuel Holmes, Jonathan Tillinghast, Oliver Ring Warner, Benjamin Ellery** and **William Ellery Jr.** all of Newport, merchants and late owners of the brigantine *Dolphin* vs. **Benjamin Ingraham** of Groton, New London, Connecticut, labourer, son and heir at law of **Benjamin Ingraham** late of Newport, mariner, to recover money due by note [of the father] dated 16 July 1756. (Docket No. 66)

888. **Jonathan Sowle** of Portsmouth, yeoman, vs. **Benjamin Nichols** of Newport, Esq., executor of the will of **Jonathan Nichols Esq.**, deceased, appealing judgment of May 1757. (Docket No. 74)

889. **Constant Cooke** of Newport, labourer, vs. **Benjamin Nichols** of Newport, Esq., executor of the will of **Jonathan Nichols Esq.**, deceased, appealing judgment of May 1757, claiming debt of £939:4:4. Defendant pleads not enough assets in his hands to pay claims. (Docket No. 76)

890. **John Wing** of Newport, yeoman, vs. **Phoebe, Deborah,** and **Amy Wing** of Dartmouth, spinsters, infants and daughters of **John Wing Jr.** late of Newport, mariner, deceased, who inherited real estate of said John Wing Jr. at Dartmouth, claiming that on 8 September 1753 the plaintiff had been bail for the defendants in two actions brought by **Joseph Royal** and **Amos Mendel**. (Docket No. 165)

891. **Walter Cranston** of Newport vs. **Mrs. Alice Townsend** for half a year's rent of a dwelling house (Docket No. 170).

892. **William Earl** of Portsmouth vs. **John Butts Jr.** of Portsmouth, weaver alias butcher, claiming that on 10 October 1757 he received £150 and promised to [re]pay in cattle hides at common market price on demand. (Docket No. 174)

893. **Elisabeth Cranston** of Newport, widow, vs. **Leah Hicks** of Newport, spinster, in an action of trespass concerning one lower room, kitchen and shop in a house in Newport, situated east on the street, north on land of **Caleb Gardner**, west and south on land of **Walter Cranston**. (Docket No. 175)

894. **Martha Sheffield** of Newport, widow, vs. **John Shepherd** of Newport, boatbuilder, for rent due, charging that she had on 10 January 1757 let to the defendant one half a stable in Newport standing upon a wharf belonging to **Joseph Slocum** of Middletown, at 20*s* every week. (Docket No. 176)

895. **Benjamin Cornel** of Portsmouth, gentleman, vs. **Thomas Slocum** of Portsmouth, mariner, charging that on 1 August 1757 **Nathaniel Little** late of Tiverton, yeoman, had an execution against the defendant for £180, which the plaintiff had paid to said Little . . . (Docket No. 177)

896. **Thomas Rogers** of Newport, house carpenter, vs. **John Gibbs** of Newport, mariner alias carter. On 10 May 1754 the defendant had put his

son **James Gibbs** to live with the plaintiff, who was to find him meat, drink, washing and lodging, and learn him the trade of house carpentering and he would bind his son to the plaintiff as an apprentice [until] he was 21. Letter from **Jn° Gibbs** dated 6 August 1754 stated that **Thomas Rogers** was out of town, Gibbs was going to sea and hoped to be back the end of October; he asks that Rogers take care that the boy not take too much liberty on the Lords Day and see that he goes to some Publick worship. (Docket No. 183)

897. **Timothy Bacchus** of Canterbury, Co. Windham, Colony of Connecticut, yeoman, vs. **Peleg Tripp** of Exeter, Esq. On 10 June 1756 the plaintiff delivered a pair of oxen and the defendant promised to deliver to the plaintiff's dwelling house 55 gallons of good West Indian rum within one week. Capt. **Ezekiel Peirce, Esq.**, of Plainfield and **Isaac Alarton** of Canterbury testified that **Peleg Tripp** was then [June 1756] of Pomfret. **Timothy Backiyis** gave power of attorney to **Isaac Tripp** of Warwick, 6 December 1757. (Docket No. 184)

898. **Ruth Briggs** of Little Compton, widow, administratrix of the estate of **Job Briggs** late of Little Compton, labourer, deceased, vs. **William Briggs** of Little Compton, yeoman, who on 5 April 1758 had acknowledged to have goods [of hers] in hand but refused to deliver them to her. Information from the town clerk of Little Compton: Ruth was the widow of **Job Briggs** and daughter-in-law of **William Briggs**. William had a wife **Deborah** and son **Enoch**. Job's sister **Judith** was the wife of **Thomas Woodworth** of Little Compton.

William Briggs made a statement at Little Compton 20 May 1758, that his son Job left with him one of his children about 5 years old when he went into the service the latter end of May 1756, and the child has been with him ever since and still remains . . . keeping it costs 30*s* per week.

Enoch Briggs of Little Compton testified that about a year ago **Ruth** had asked him to fetch all her goods at **Thomas Woodworth's** and carry them to his father's, to keep for the children . . . she was afraid her own father would contrive to get the goods away. **Jonathan Records** of Little Compton deposed and said that the night before **Job Briggs** late of Little Compton, deceased, went away into the Expedition to Fort Edward, he heard said Briggs "tell his mother he was agoing away and he would not have her let Ruth have any of his things, but keep them for his children and if he ever lived to come back he would try for the things that was carried away out of his house . . ."

Verdict for the plaintiff. (Docket No. 188)

899. **William Cory** of Tiverton, yeoman, vs. **Thomas Howland**, merchant, and **Job Manchester**, husbandman, of Tiverton, in an action of trespass, for possession of the south half of the 22nd Great Lott in Pocasset Purchase in Tiverton, with a house thereon. The plaintiff was the eldest son and heir of **Roger Cory**, who died 10 May 1755. The property had been left to Roger by the will of **William Cory** who died 20 January 1681, and upon Roger's death it descended to the plaintiff, who was dispossessed of it 7 May 1758 by the defendants. The land was described as 60 acres, part pasture, part meadow, bounded east on the plaintiff, south on the 23rd Great Lott, west on the sea, north on the north half of the same lot. A warrant was issued for **Samuel Corey** of Richmond, yeoman alias cordwainer, devisee of Roger Corey late of Richmond, yeoman, deceased.

Copy of the will of **William Cory**:

In the name of god Amen I William Cory of the Town of Portsmouth on Rhode Island being Sick in Body but of perfect memory, and calling to remembrance the uncertainty of this transitory life and being desirous to settle that estate which God hath been pleased to lend me in order thereunto and for preventing future trouble and differences amongst those to whom it may belong do make & declare this my Last Will & testament revoking & making null all former testaments or wills by me made either by word or writing first and principally I commend my soul to Almighty God my creator, and my body to the earth from whence it was taken to be buried in such decent manner as to my executrix after named shall be thought meet —

My will is that all ye just debts I owe to any person or persons be truly paid & that all debts justly due to me from any may be received by my executrix afternamed Item I give & bequeath unto my loveing wife **Mary Cory**, & to be freely & absolutely at her dispose as she shall see cause, all lands & hereditiments to me belonging, with my Wind=mill in the Town of Portsmouth, and all other my movable or personal estate wheresoever & whatsoever, excepting only what I have in this my will hereafter exprest and bequeathed unto my several children.

And further I give and bequeath unto my loving wife dureing her natural life y^e use benefit and profit of all my dwelling house in which I dwell, at the time of the date of these presents (two rooms thereof only excepted to my son **William** as is hereafter exprest) and ye one half of the orchard, & ye use & benefit of one half of the barn and of all that tract of land both upland & meadow land as the said land is scituate lying & being between the land latly belonging to the deceased **William Hall** on the northwesterly side, and ye lane or highway on the southeasterly side: and after her decease the sd land & premises to return as is hereafter exprest

Item I give & bequeath unto my Eldest son **John** to come into his possession emediately after my decease, all that tract or parcel of land to be belonging, scituate, lying & being between the land of **George Sisson** on ye northerly part & ye land latly belonging to ye deceased **David Vaughan** on ye southerly part & is within ye afores^{d} Township of Portsmouth, together with all ye houseing fenceings rights, previledges & emoluments thereunto belonging & being: The same to be and belong unto my s^{d} son John dureing his natural life, & after his decease to such child or children of his body lawfully begotten, as he my s^{d} son John in his last will, & testament in writing shall see cause to dispose ye same unto And according to his s^{d} will ye same to be to such child or children an estate of inheritance either in fee simple or feetail, & for want of such disposal ye inheritance is to come & to decend to the heirs of ye body of my s^{d} son John lawfully begotten & ye s^{d} inheritance is to be to that lawful heir in fees, But in case my s^{d} son John shall not have such lawful heir or heirs, then ye s^{d} land and inheritance shall be at ye fre disposing of my s^{d} son John provided he bequeath & give ye same amongst his brothers & sisters of ye whole blood or to any one or more of them, And if no such will be made by my son John at his discease, neither any such lawful heir of his body, then my will is that ye s^{d} inheritance shall decend unto ye next lawful heir of me ye s^{d} William Cory

Item I give & bequeath unto my second son **William** to come into his possession emediatly after my decease ye lower great room of ye southerly part of ye dwelling house where now at ye time of the date hereof I do inhabit, with ye leanto room adjoining commonly called Margarets Room, & also ye one half of ye orchard adjoining that is to say the southerly part, ye whole orchard being to be equally divided making quantity equall to quality, & also my s^{d} son William to have ye profit & benefit of ye one half of ye uplands & meadow lands of all that tract of my land lyig scituate and being between ye lands lately belonging to ye deceased **William Hall** northwesterly & ye common highway southeasterly, & ye use of ye one half of ye barn on ye s^{d} land, And after ye decease of my wife his mother, all ye rest of those housings ye other half of ye orchard & that whole tract of land with all the rights & previledges thereunto belonging shall return and belong unto my s^{d} son William during his natural life & after his decease to such child or children of his body lawfully begotten as my s^d son William by his last will & testament shall see cause to give & bequeath ye same unto, & according to his s^d will the s^d inheritance is to be to such child or children an estate of inheritance either in fee simple or feetail, & for want of such disposal ye s^d inheritance is to decend and come to ye heirs lawfully begotten of ye body of my s^d son William And ye said inheritance to be to that lawfull heir in fee But in case my son William shall not have such lawful heir or heirs then ye said inheritance may be disposed of by s^d son William as is exprest concerning my son Johns inheritance or else ye same to decend as is mentioned of Johns

Item I give & bequeath unto my third son **Thomas** to come into his possession at one and twenty years of age the true one half of all that my right it being a whole share or thirtieth part by me purchased in and of ye lands at Pocasset and places adjacent in ye jurisdaiction or Colony of New Plimouth both of that part already divided & that part undivided, my s^d son Thomas to have the northerly part of that already divided and when by division that undivided is certainly known ye same to b equally divided by lot between him and his brother **Roger**. And ye inheritance by me given unto my son Thomas, is to him and the heirs of his body lawfully begotten forever, and if my said son Thomas shall decease this life without such lawful heirs then my will is that the said inheritance shall decend unto my son Roger & to be to him & his lawful heirs lawfully begotten forever

Item I give and bequeath unto my fourth son **Caleb** to come into his possession at one and twenty years of age, all that my right it being one third part of a share or purchasers right off and into all the lands being & belonging to ye Town of Dartmouth in ye Colony of Plymouth afores^d as well as in ye lands undivided as that part already divided with all ye rights profits priviledges and emoluments thereunto belonging & ye s^d inheritance to be and belong to my s^d son Caleb during his natural life and after his decease to such child or children of his body lawfully begotten, as he my said son Caleb in his last will and testament in writing shall see cause to give & bequeath ye sqme unto and according to his said will ye s^d inheritance to be to such s^d child or children an estate either in fee simple or fee tail. and so succesfully ye s^d inheritance is to be inherited disposed and decend in like manner as is expressed in this my will to my son John.

Item I give and bequeath unto my fifth son **Roger** to come into his possession at one and twenty years of age ye true one half of all that my right it being a whole share or thirtieth part (by me purchased) in and of ye lands at Pocasset & places adjacent in ye jurisdiction or Colony of Plimouth both of that part already divided & that part undivided my s^d son Roger to have the southerly part of that already divided & when division of that undivided part is certainly known ye same to be divided by lott between him & his brother Thomas, and the inheritance by me given to my son Roger is to him & ye heirs of his body lawfully begotten forever And if my said son Roger shall decease this lfe without such lawful heir then my will is that ye s^{d} inheritance shall decend unto my aforenamed son Thomas & to be to him and hs heirs lawfully begotten forever And further my will is that if my s^{d} two sons thomas & Roger shall decease this life without such lawful heir or heirs as is afore exprest then ye lands & inheritance by me given & bequeathed to them ye s^{d} Thomas & Roger shall decend and return unto all my children both males & females that shall then be living & every of their heirs in fee, the same to be equally divided amongst them

Item I give & bequeath unto my eldest daughter **Marcy** to be paid unto her Emediately after my decease the full & just sum of Ten Pounds in or as money

Item I give & bequeath unto my second daughter **Ann** to be paid unto her at the age of eighteen years or her marriage if she marry sooner the sum of Ten Pounds in or as money Item I give and bequeath unto my third daughter **Mary** to be paid unto her at ye age of eighteen years or her marriage if she marry sooner the sum of Ten Pounds in or as money

Item I give & bequeath unto my fourth daughter **Joan** to be paid unto her at ye age of eighteen years or her marriage if she marry sooner the sum of ten pounds in or as money – And my will is that if any of my aforenamed daughters shall decease this life before the time of receiving their portions as afores^{d} that then the legusie of ye deceased shall be equally divided amongst and unto the rest of my daughters surviving and truly paid unto them or their lawful heirs: And for ye true and faithful performance and execution of this my last will and testament I do by these presents constitute & apoint my beloved wife **Mary Cory** my true & only executrix, for me & by vertue of this my will where I am indebted to any person or persons to pay them and where any person or persons [are] owing any debts to me to receive them, and at ye times mentioned in this my will to perform and pay all such legusies as I have bequeathed to all my children in this my last will and testament in manner and form as is afore exprest: And in case my wife should see cause to change her condition from widowhood to an estate of marriage, Then my will is that the overseers hereafter named or so many as shall then be living, shall before ye day of her marriage require & take good cawtion & security to insure ye childrens portions with whatsoever my loving wife shall add thereto after my decease –

And I do bequeath my children unto my wife next under God desiring they may be tenderly brought up & educated till they come to the age of one and twenty years the males & ye females at marriage estate & then they are to provide for themselves as ye providence of God shall direct them, And if any of ye aforesaid legusies shall be unpaid at ye day of my wifes death or before sufficiet cawtion & security be given for ye payment of them, Then my will is that such of my children and their portions shall be taken care for by the overseers or those of them then living –

And for as much as my desire is that this my last will and testament may be faithfully & truly executed, I do by these presents constitute and ordain my loving friends **William Wodell, John Sanford & George Brownell** all of ye town of Portsmouth aforesaid to be overseers of ye true execution of this my last will and testament or so many of them as shall be living until ye last legusie be paid, intreating them that if at any time there should be any differance or strife between my executrix & my children, or any one of them, that the overseers would be pleased to hear their grievances and reconcile in a way of peace and love without delays that so peace and love may be continued –

And for confirmation of this my last will and testament I have hereunto set my hand and seal the fourth day of January in ye three and thirtieth year of ye reign of our sovereign lord Charls the Second King of England, Scotland, France & Ireland Annoque Domine Six hundred eighty one.

Witnesses were Thomas Manchester Senr [his mark *T*], Peter Talman, Thomas Havens [mark *H*] and Caleb Cranston. Proved 24 February 1681/2 and recorded 3 1st month [March] 1682. Copy attested by Robt. Dennis, Clerk, Portsmouth, 13 January 1754.

Deed: On 18 January 1752 **Roger Cory** of Tiverton yeoman, for £1500 in good bills of credit old tenner, sold to **Thomas Howland** of the same place, distiller, a parcel of land in Tiverton containing sixty acres, it being the south half of the 22nd Great Lot in Pocasset Purchase, beginning at the sea or salt water and running to within two rods of **William Cory**'s dwelling house, bounded north on the north half of the 22nd Great Lot, on the south by the 23rd Great Lot, and on the east by land of William Cory. Roger signed by mark and his wife **Remembrance Cory** also signed by mark. Witnesses were **George Westgate Juner** and **Benjamin Brown**. Acknowledged 21 January 1752.

Deposition of Restcom Sanford at May Court 1758 that William Cory of Tiverton "hath been a freeman of the sd Town of Tiverton for ten years past And that I never heard nor understood that he had any Land of his own in the time whilst his father Roger Cory Lived in sd

Tiverton which Qullified him to be made a freeman of sd Town but Ever understod that what Qullified him . . . was that he was Called the Eldest son of Roger Cory Late of sd Tiverton Deceased . . .

Thomas Jeffers of Newport, cordwainer, and **Sarah** his wife testified at Newport 2 June 1758 before Martin Howard, J.P., that in the Year 1701 they "were Housekeepers in Portsmouth . . . in the month of June in said Year **Roger Cory** who then lived at Tiverton and **Mary Hubbs** of said Tiverton in company with **Japhet Alderson** and **Deliverance** his Wife came to our House in said Portsmouth where the said Roger Cory and Mary Hubbs said . . . they were going to Captain **Joseph Sheffields** House in said Portsmouth to be married, - Accordingly the said Roger and Mary on the same day came back to our house and Din'd with us . . . Saying they had been at the said Capt. Sheffields House and were married by him, after Dinner the said Roger and Mary went Home to said Tiverton and to [our] knowledge they Lived and Cohabited together as Husband and Wife in said Tiverton for Twenty or Thirty Years . . . had during said Term of Years Nine Children . . . on or about the Year 1703 [we] went several Times to said Tiverton to see the said Roger and wife she being lately delivered of a son her second Child who they called **William** the first Child being a Daughter and that the said Son William [we] have Always Known to this day. . . . (Docket No. 197)

900. **Caleb Gardner** of Newport, shopkeeper, vs. **Cesar Bartholomew**, a Negro man late residing in Newport, mariner, for debt due by book. (Docket No. 227)

901. **John Weight** of Tiverton, yeoman, vs. **Benjamin Macomber** of Tiverton, yeoman, charging him with waste when he was tenant of a farm in Tiverton owned by the plaintiff. (Docket No. 231)

[*In a second case*] **John Weight** of Tiverton, yeoman, administrator of the will of **Thomas Weight**, late of Tiverton, yeoman, deceased, vs. **Benjamin Macomber** of Tiverton, yeoman, for an accounting of the personal estate which the defendant had which belonged to his father-in-law **Thomas Weight** . . . by letter of guardianship he now had possession and care of father-in-law. (Docket No. 232)

902. **Jeremiah Fones Green** and **James Greene** of Newport, infants, gentlemen, by their friends and guardians **Samuel Greene** of Newport, joyner, and **Samuel Tillinghast** of Warwick, merchant, vs. **Benjamin**

Tripp of Newport, in action of trespass to recover possession of a half acre with a house and stable in Newport, bounded north on **Abraham Redwood**, west on the highway, south on land of **Robert Taylor**, of which premises **James Greene** late of Newport, gentleman, was seized and by his will dated 16 February 1758 had devised to the plaintiffs, ". . . to sons **Jeremiah Fones Greene** and **James Greene** all ye rest residue and remainder of my estate," and died 15 April 1758. (Docket No. 233)

903. **Nathaniel Alcock** of Newport, cordwainer, vs. **Daniel Read** of Newport, taylor, in an action of trespass to recover two lower rooms in the northwest part of a dwelling house belonging to the plaintiff, bounded north on land of **Elizabeth Cornell**, widow, and **Isaac Lawton**, south and southwest on streets, east partly on the plaintiff and partly on the street. (Docket No. 304)

904. **Oliver Earl** of Portsmouth, yeoman, town treasurer, vs. **Joseph Shearman** of Portsmouth, yeoman, administrator of the estate of **Mary Shearman** late of Portsmouth, spinster, deceased, in an action of assumpsit concerning a debt of £93 allowed **George Sisson** for his care in nursing and attending said **Mary Shearman** while she was sick with smallpox. File includes a page from the Portsmouth town council records, dated 4 November 1757 re control of smallpox: a fence to be built across the highway near Cooks Corner so-called, against the land of **Benjamin Fish**, and is to be kept up. Verdict for defendant. (Docket No. 307)

905. **Henry Tew** of Middletown, yeoman, vs. **Joshua Coggeshall** of Middletown, town treasurer, claiming that the defendant on 25 February 1757 assured the plaintiff [the town] would take in and keep **Sarah Springer**, a poor woman, and find and provide for her. A bill presented for £276:7:6 included a coffin and digging her grave, and 9 weeks nursing by **Abigail Springer**, 25 February til 27 April 1757. (Docket No. 330)

906. **Mary Bennett** of Tiverton, widow, vs. **Richard Durfee** of Tiverton, gentleman, for debt of £172:10:6 due by book for "Licker & sundries, rhum, hay, corn, and makeing sider in my mill 1752-1757"; writ served by **William Cook**, sheriff. (Docket No. 355)

– November Term 1758 –

Court of General Sessions

907. Petition of a Molatto Boy called **Pardon**, of Little Compton, he being an apprentice by indenture to **Job Almy** of Little Compton, yeoman, called on evidence respecting the Burning of a Mill situate in said town and in the course of evidence, petitioner acknowledged himself guilty in Burning said Mill, at the command of his said Master, that he Burnt said Mill by the threats then offered by his said Master, all which your Petitioner saith is True--- he therefore apprehends . . . [that he] ought to be dismissed and discharged from any further service by force of said Indenture. **Job Almy** notified to appear.

This generated a case in May 1759 against **Job Almy**, papers from which are included here. The fire took place 27 July 1758. Pardon signed his mark to a statement: "Yes I did set fire to the Mill I had been to drive the Cows & when I came back I told my master I saw a Fire by **Mr cooks** Mill he told me to go back & I did & he followed me & told me to set fire to the Mill which I did on that side next our House & my Master stayd outside the Walls I went to him & he bid me go back & set fires to the other side which I did. I put the Fire between the step and the Mill the other side from our House & put some Chips to kindle the Fires."

William Willcox Junr of Tiverton, farmer, signed a deposition in court that some time in the previous November he was passing Fogland Ferry, in the same boat with **Mr. Abiel Cook** and **Mr. Job Almy** both of Little Compton, "a few rods from the Shoar Cook looks about and says to the said Almy 'who's here our Millwright; I wish you much joy?' to which the said Almy replyed 'the same to your self with your two squaws'; to which said Cook answered he intended to have (or he laid a Scheme to gett) £20,000 for his Mills, and he had Heard that the Old Colonel had a Trunkfull of Dollars which had Never been unlocked, but that he intended to shew himself such a point of law as should unlock it."

Aaron Seabury testified in court and answered questions, saying that he had "heard Mr Almy say in my Fathers House he would be avengd of Abiel Cook if it cost him a thousand pounds . . . about a fortnight or three weeks before the mill was burnt." **John Brown** testified that "that Night that Mr Cooks Mill was burnt I passd by it about half an hour after Dark before I came to the Mills I saw a small fire about as big as a Candle which seemd to be at ye south Door of the Mill & about as high as the Step after I passd by I saw an other fire some Distance from the Mill which I took to be a Lanthorn . . . the Wind that Night was about SouthWest or a little nearer the South."

Pheby Palmer of Little Compton signed her mark to a deposition written down by **Gideon Willcox,** J.P., at Tiverton 28 May 1759, saying that on 27 July last she was at the house of **Job Almy Junr** . . . "Almy was att home before ye setting of the Sun & their Remaind untill bed-time & I saw sd Almy go to bed . . . Almy then had a melater or mustee boy called or known by the name of **Pardon** which boy went about ye seting of the sun to drive a cow & mair of his masters to a lott of land called or known by the name of Wood lot & Returnd back in the Dusk of the Evening & said y^{t} there was fire by Cooks mill & said Pardon Remained at home until I went to bed & he went up chamber to bed . . . sum time in ye knight sd Almy Cald to me to come down stairs for he said he heard some body below & said as it is all of a fire . . . thought it was Abial Cooks house was on fire & when I came down we descovered that it was Abial Cooks mill was on fire & sd Almy went a few steps from the dore & came astily back & told me to git his stockkins & he would run up to the mill & when he went out of the dore again ye mill was down & at that time I heard sd Almy say although Abial Cook did not like him yet he was sory for his loss and Remembred what his boy had sd about ye fire being near ye mill & sd Almy said it was a very carles action to leave fire so near the mill."

Sarah Ned, an Indian woman, mother of the boy **Pardon,** was questioned in court and signed her testimony by mark. She said that **Job Almy** had promised to give her £50 if she went to her son and if he would say he did not burn the mill. She spoke with her son at **Mr. Church**'s, and he told her he did set fire to the mill, and she asked him what made him do it and he said "his master said if he did not do it he would beat his brains out." Asked if Mr. Almy since his prosecution had let her have a pair of shoes and on what account, she said "I did some work for Mr. Almy and askd him to get a pair of shoes for me which he did & I expected to pay for them & asked him what the Price was and [he] told me if I spoke well in Court I should pay nothing for them."

– November Term 1758 –

Inferior Court of Common Pleas

908. **Simon Pease** of Newport, merchant, administrator of **Jane Bate** late of the City of Dublin in Ireland, widow, deceased, vs. **Joseph Clarke** of Jamestown, Esq. and his wife **Rebecca**, executors of the will of **Walter Rodman**, late of said Jamestown, physician, deceased, who was executor of the will of **Charles Bate** late of the City of Dublin in the Kingdom of Ireland, mariner, deceased. **Charles Bate** by will dated 5 October 1748 bequeathed to **Jane Bate** 100 pistoles in gold and afterwards died, making aforesaid **Walter Rodman** executor and afterwards said Walter died having first undertaken to execute said will and also made his own will . . . never paid money. Judgment for plaintiffs, damages £4000. (Docket No. 5)

909. **Thomas George** of Newport, caulker, vs. **James Patterson** [who signed by mark X], now resident in Newport, mariner. On 21 December 1757 at Newport defendant had received £50 old tenor in full for a quarter share of Prizes that should be taken on board the Brigantine *Prince Frederick* whereof **James Potter** [*sic*] was commander, then bound on a cruising voyage against His Majesty's Enemies . . . proceeded and to plaintiff unknown took a valuable ship which . . . carried to Port of New York and there condemned. One full share = £480. (Docket No. 13)

910. **Sarah Shrieve** of Tiverton, widow, administratrix of **Constant Shrieve**, late of Tiverton, mariner, vs. **Daniel Willcox** of Newport, mariner, in action of trover concerning 1300 lbs. of white Muscovado Sugar which **Constant Shrieve** on 10 March 1757 did in his lifetime possess and out of his hands casually did lose, etc. (Docket No. 41)

911. **Robert Dunbar** of Newport, mariner and late master of the sloop *Success*, vs. **Joseph Wanton Jr.** of Newport, gentleman, late owner of said sloop, concerning a promise 12 May 1756 for wages on a voyage to Jamaica. (Docket No. 44)

912. **Joseph Cowley** of Newport, merchant, vs. **Thomas Webber** of Newport, huxter & shopkeeper, in an action of trespass, to recover land bounded east on Thames Street, north, west and south on land of the plaintiff, of which lot **Edward Pelham** was on 21 May 1740 seized and

by his will of that date, devised it to his daughter **Penelope** and died . . . afterwards the plaintiff intermarried with said **Penelope** and in [her] right on 4 January 1756 became likewise seized . . . . (Docket No. 45)

913. **Joseph Cowley** of Newport, merchant, vs. **John Cahoone** of Newport, joiner, to recover a lot bounded west on Thames Street, north and east on land of the plaintiff, and south on an alley or passage leading from Thames Street up to the front of the mansion house late belonging to Mr. **Edward Pelham,** deceased [*as No. 912*]. (Docket No. 46)

914. **Jonathan Manchester** of Newport, setwork cooper, vs. **Joseph Bull** of Newport, merchant, in an action of assumpsit. On 28 April 1758 at request of the defendant, the plaintiff took to board at his house **Sylvester Hart,** who was then very sick . . . defendant promised to pay. Bill of £76:6 included board for five weeks from April to June, wine and raisins, Doctor's bill. (Docket No. 49)

915. **Joseph Cowley** of Newport, merchant, vs. **Henry Gardner** of Newport, innholder, to recover a house and lot in Newport, bounded north on land of **John Freebody,** it being the house of **Edward Pelham,** deceased [*as No. 912*]. (Docket No. 50)

916. **Thomas Richardson** of Newport, distiller, vs. **Benjamin Tucker** of Newport, mariner, in an action of assumpsit. Defendant on 12 December 1757 had promised to pay or be paid to the plaintiff 200 gallons of good molasses at the return of the sloop *Victory* from sea, Capt. **John Low,** master, for value received . . . said sloop returned safe. (Docket No. 51)

917. **Richard Shearman** of Swansey, yeoman, vs. **Barnabas Hargill Jr.** of Newport, leather dresser, to recover the lower part of a dwelling and lot in Newport, of which the plaintiff was seized 14 August 1749. (Docket No. 53)

918. **Job Bennit Jr.** of Newport, gentleman, vs. **Hannah Taylor** of Newport, widow, to recover a chamber and privileges in garret and cellar and a garden with dwelling house in Newport at Easton's Point, deeded to the plaintiff 29 July 1756 by **William Bennet,** bounded south on lot no. 5, east on the street, north on lot no. 7, west on the Bay, of which he had been dispossessed by the defendant 10 October 1758. (Docket No. 58)

919. **Abner Chase** of Tiverton, merchant, vs. **John Shrieve Jr.** of Portsmouth, gentleman, in an action of assumpsit. On 20 December 1757 at Portsmouth, it had been agreed that the plaintiff would take in part of pay for a horse he had sold and delivered to the defendant for £150 Old Tenor, a certain note of hand of **Benjamin Cornell** for £132:13:6, and if he did not get it from Cornell, the defendant would pay. Depositions were made by **Charles Brownel** of Tiverton, and by **Sarah Soule**, wife of **Cornelius Soule** of Tiverton, that "sometime in the fall of the year last past [1757] came Capt. **John Shrieve** and **Abner Chase** to my house and called my self and my daughter **Susannah** to bear witness [to their agreement]." Suit withdrawn. (Docket No. 65)

920. **Freelove Boss** of Newport, spinster, vs. **William Ellery** of Newport, Esq., in an action of promise. Defendant had promised the plaintiff 23 March 1757 that if she would permit him to put a quantity of molasses into a certain storehouse in Newport that she then had the letting of, he would pay her for storage. Withdrawn. (Docket No. 78)

921. Case involving a wreck of the *King of Prussia*. On 6 December 1758 **Anthony McMillan**, now residing at Newport, mariner, late Chief Mate of the privateer brig called the *King of Prussia* commanded by Capt. **John Rolfe** in a cruize against his Majesty's Enemies, "deposed that he sail'd from Boston in sd Privateer on 9 August 1757 . . . on 14 September following they made the Island of St. Martin & Anguilla being then bound to Cruize on the south side of Hispaniola but intended to stop at the Island of St. Thomas's to Wood Water & Careen the Vessell . . . the Captain said he never had been thro' any of these Islands in his Life & enquir'd who was acquainted among his Officers . . . **Richard White** Master of sd Privateer said he was well acquainted . . . would take charge to pilot the Vessel through a Channell by Anguilla . . . Capt. Rolfe look'd at the Draught & say'd it appeard to him that there was a better Channell between Sambraro & the Dogg & Prickle Pear, but the Master said he would take Charge to carry him safe thro', he having been thro' several Times before accordingly the said Master directed the Course to be steer'd thro', was several times & frequently on the foreyard & conned the Vessell, the People that look'd out forward call'd out, Breakers, the Capt told the Master of it to which the Master replied it was nothing but the surff on the shore, & that there was no Danger, that what the People first took to be Breakers we pass'd clear of; [I] was going up the fore shrouds to look out the Vessell struck whilst [I] was up aloft, & [I] never saw the Rief till she struck on the Northermost side of the Channel . . . the Channel the Master intended to go thro' between Anguilla & the Prickle Pear is a good & safe Channel for shipps . . . [I have] seen several vessells go thro that Channel Particularly the Privateer Ship commanded by Capt **Gruchie** of Boston. . . . " He responded to questions, stating that the Master was killed on the Island of Anguilla by firing a cohorn; he didn't remember whether **Solomon Mackey** the First Lieutenant was on deck the afternoon or evening before the ship was cast away.

On 24 January 1758 **Daniel Wilcox** and **Ebenezer Washburn** of Newport testified, responding to questions, that they sailed on the ship from Rhode Island about 15 May on a cruise, took two prizes, "the ship we sent to Boston and the Snow we sent to Rhod Island"; they arrived in Boston about 17 June last, where the vessell was refitted with stores and provisions; it carried four more cannon from Boston than it had from Rhode Island; the officers and men shifted in Boston were the Master, the Chief Mate, the Capt. Quarter Master, Doctor, Gunner, and Boatswain and Carpenter and Carpenter's Mate and between 30 and 40 men and boys. They sailed from Boston some time in the beginning of last August and before reaching another port were cast away between Anguilla and the Prickley Pear sometime in September, between seven and eight of the clock in the evening under a Mainsail, foretopsail, Maintopsail for sail and forestaysail. They were steering west southerly and went six or seven knots. They made the land at Saint Martins, about 10 or 11 in the morning, Anguilla about 3 or 4 in the afternoon; the wind was East Northerly. When asked if there was any objection among the officers in going thro' that passage in the night, they answered, "Yes, **Capt. Rolfe** was for standing off, but the Master (**Richard White**) said there was no danger"; they were with three or four men upon the foreyard and one on the bowsprit. After going aground, they got their boats out but the surf was so high that they could not carry the anchors out; they stayed on the vessel and sent a boat to Anguilla for help. Part of the vessel and stores were saved: beef, pork, flour, sails and riggins, cables, one anchor, boats, twelve guns, part of the sparrs, the swivel guns, small arms, etc.; the inhabitants of Anguilla helped. The two deponents, Wilcox and

Washburn, worked to save the goods because they felt it was their duty, and were not ordered to do so, and received no satisfaction.

John Linscom, testified at Newport 1 February 1758, saying that he was Second Lieutenant and had entered on board the brigantine *King of Prussia* in Newport and sailed from Rhode Island the 15th of May last, victualed for six months; eleven days after sailing they took a ship and a snow, sent the snow to Rhode Island and the ship to Boston, proceeding with the latter. When asked why the privateer had gone to port with this prize, he said it was to see the prize safe into port, and for fear the Halifax Privateer should carry her into Halifax, and to refit and repair the damage sustained. They arrived 24 June in Boston, where the officers and men refused to do their duty, and left the privateer. **Capt. Rolfe** advertised them in the public prints to induce them to return on board. Asked whether they were deemed deserters by the captain and remaining part of the company, he replied that "then was a Committee held, and an Instrument drawn up, which . . . made them liable to lose their shares." Other officers and men were shipped at Boston in place of those who deserted, and they sailed on 9 August with greater force than when they had left Rhode Island. They first landed at Saint Martins, and soon after Anguilla, 14 September. Asked to declare all he knew about what happened from the time they landed at Anguilla to the time the vessel struck the rocks, and he replied, "**Capt. Rolfe** was for standing off that night, but the Master (**Richard White**) told him he was as well acquainted thro as he was to his own door, as he had been thro several times, and at eight of the Clock we Struck & hoisted out our Boats & sounded, in order to carry out an Anchor but found it impossible, then went on shore to Anguilla to procure the Inhabitants to assist us in saving the lives of the people & what else was possible." Their own boats were not able to save anything. A store was appointed and things brought from the wreck were put into it, marked, and an account made. More questions were posed by **Charles Wickham, Evan Malbone**, and **William Vernon**, to which Linscom replied that they had taken two more cannons on board at Boston, ten cohorns in . . . ten swivels, five or six hundred weight of bread, five or six barrels of beef and some powder, and had taken five cannons at sea out of the prize ship. Other officers carried out on the second cruise from Boston were the Master, Richard White, the Captain, Quarter Master, Doctor, Chief Mate, Gunner, Boatswain, and

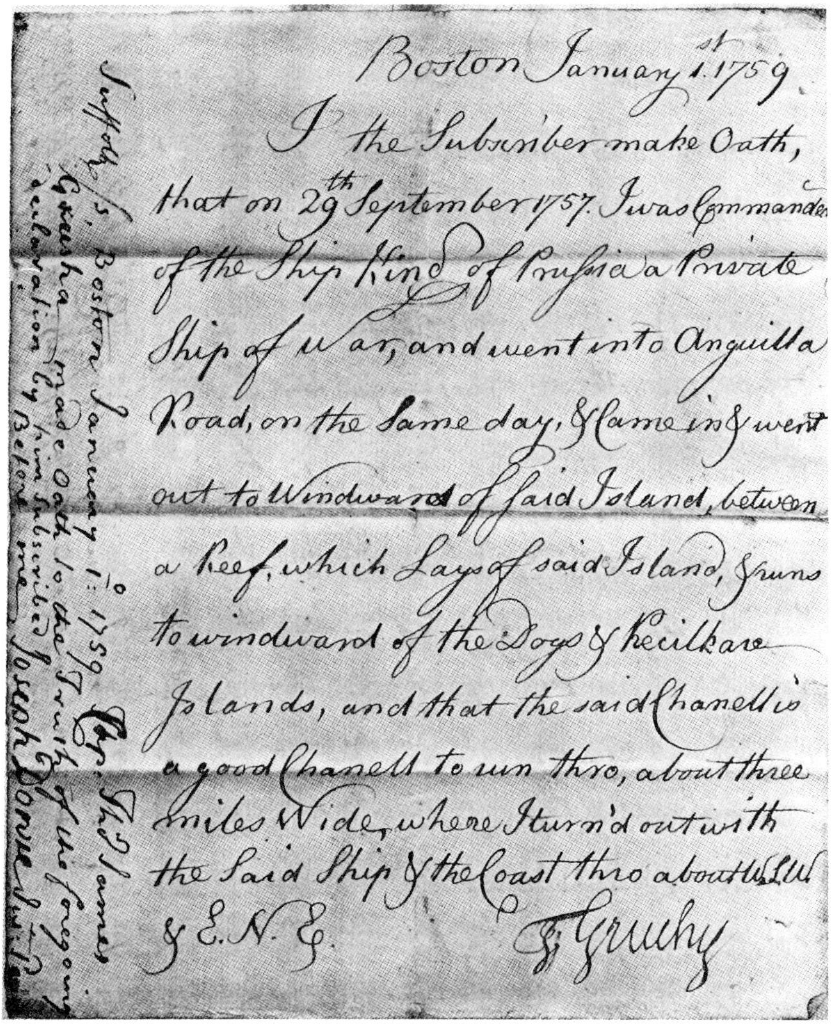

Boston January 1st 1759

I the Subscriber make Oath, that on 29th September 1757. I was Commander of the Ship King of Prussia a Private Ship of War, and went into Anguilla Road, on the Same day, & Came in & went out to Windward of Said Island, between a Reef, which Lays of said Island, & runs to windward of the Dogs & Recilkare Islands, and that the said Chanell is a good Chanell to run thro, about three miles Wide, where I turn'd out with the Said Ship & the Coast thro about W.S.W. & E.N.E.

T. Gruchy

Suffolk s/s. Boston January 1st 1759 Capt. Thos. James Gruchy made Oath to the Truth of the foregoing declaration by him subscribed Before me Joseph Dowse Just. Peace

Captain Gruchy's declaration, 1759

about thirty men. Some of the men who quit the vessel returned. It was not common for vessels to go between Prickly Pear and Anguilla in the night, and the people of Anguilla did not care to do it; Linscom knew of no necessity in their attempt. There were four or five men aloft looking out before they came upon the rocks; someone called out breakers on the starboard side which the Master said was the surf of the shore, when they were about four miles from shore. The hull was entirely lost, two cannon, the powder and shot, bread and flour, and part of almost everything except the sails. Linscom signed his testimony before **Peter Bours**, J.P., and **Job Sylvester**, J.P.

On 1 January 1759 Capt. **Thos James Grusha** testified that he had been Commander of the ship *King of Prussia* a Private Ship of War, on 29 September 1757, and "went into Anguilla Road on the same day, and came in and went out to Windward of the Island, between a Reef which Lays of sd Island, & runs to windward of the Dogs & Kecilkare Islands, and that the sd Chanell is a good Chanell to run thro, about three miles Wide, where I turn'd out with the said Ship & the Coast thro about W.S.W. & E.N.E."

John Watson of Newport, who had been on the brigantine in the capacity of Prise Master, testified 25 April 1759 that it was "fine clear weather and brisk winds in the Eastern board and being then under full sail . . . we continued our course down to the northward of sd Islands & all the after Noon and in the Evening soon after sun-setting we was about one League & a half from the Land [I] was ordered upon the Fore Yard together with **Dan^ll Wilcock** and several others in order to discover if any danger between Anguila and the Dog where we soon saw Breakers and a Reef of Head and called out . . . the answer from the Quarter Deck was Damn your Blood keep a look out you know nothing about it upon which I came down and told them I could shift for my Life as well as any of them, the People forward & in ye Top after I came down call'd out Breakers & Rocks upon our Bow the Master said it was only the shades of the Moon upon the Land & to look out for Rocks astern and in a few minutes we struck upon the Rocks. . . ."

922. **David Brayton** of Newport, mariner, and late master of the sloop *Greyhound*, vs. **John Easton** of Newport, mariner, in an action of assumpsit, that the defendant on 12 January 1757 at Boston did ship on said vessel of which the plaintiff was master, at the monthly wages of £25; (Mass. Bay currency was 45 shillings to the Dollar); from Boston to Newport where he was discharged 10 March 1757. (Docket No. 135)

923. **Samuel Sanford** of Tiverton, weaver, vs. **Millisent Sanford** of Newport, widow, aministratrix of the estate of **Peleg Sanford**, late of Tiverton, weaver, to recover money due by book and damages of £600. Bill from Samuel Sanford to Peleg Sanford of Tiverton, weaver, totaling £312:16:6, itemized: "To keeping your son **John Sanford** from April 10th 1752 to March 25th, 1753 @ 29/ pr week; To keeping your son **Isaac Sanford** from April 3d 1753 to March 3rd 1754 . . . @ 60/ pr week; To keeping [Isaac] from July 15th: 1756 to February 9th: 1757 @ 3-10 pr week; To takeing care of my Brother Peleg Sanford at my house from January 28 1757 to February 9th . . . he being sick weak & in a low condition."

Deborah Sanford, widow of Tiverton, signing by mark, testified in Tiverton 5 April 1759 before **Gideon Willcox** "Jusapse" that "sum time after my son **Peledg Sanford** lost his wife when he was a widower he brought one of his Children on my invitation but my said son Peledg was to help find for the seport of the Child & my son brought a bushel corn or half a bushel one of these i am sartain and small quantity of flower but as for the quantity I cant Remember . . . at the time of my sons desese I dont Remember as my son **Samuel** had any a count or not gainst my son Peledg . . . I dont know upon what considration my grandson **John Sanford** came to my son Samuel to live."

Isaac Manchester of Tiverton deposed 14 April 1759, that "sum time in the month of June Last past I being at ye house where **Samuel Sanford** now liveth in sd Tiverton & **Mallasent Sanford** the widow & Raleck of **Peleg Sanford** late deceased was there & the sd Samuel Sanford & Mallacent was Disscoursing about an account the sd Samuel had against the Estate of the sd Peleg Sanford . . . Mallacent demanded his account he asked her wheither she had got any money to pay him she said she did not know wheither she should have mony enough to pay him before he told her what his account was then he told her it was £500 but shew her no account as I saw And as to his keeping any of the Children which he Charges for I cannot tell anithing about that or what age they was of when they did live with him. . . ." Isaac added, "I desire that you would accept the above written as my Evidence . . . for I can tell no more about it if I were personally present and I desire you would put me nor your self to any further Trouble . . . and as I am Now much In Disposed & not Realy able to Ride so far therfore have Taken the pains to wright unto you. . . ." A list of the children of **Peleg Sanford** and **Ann** his wife is in file: "**Thomas Sanford** was Born March ye 12th: 1738/9; **John Sanford** was Born November the 21st: 1740; **Philip Sanford** was born September ye Ninth 1743; **Prissilla Sanford** was born October ye 2nd: 1745." The case went to referees: the plaintiff chose Mr. **Benjamin Pabodie**, the defendant **James Sheffield**, and the court appointed Col. **Job Bennet Jr.** Their judgment was that the plaintiff pay costs, and the defendant be discharged. (Docket No. 163)

– May Term 1759 –

924. **Abial Cook** of Little Compton, yeoman, vs. **John Horswell** of same, for money due for a plow he sold to him 10 June 1756. Deposition of **Abraham Slocum** now resident in Newport, labourer, that in the month of January 1757 he kept the Ferry at Fogland in Tivertown at which time **Horswell** and **Cook** were at the deponent's dwelling house in said Fogland when and where they made a settlement of certain monies that said **Cook** was indetted to said **Horswell**; Cook gave Horswell a note of hand for about £380; deponent was present and wrote both note and receipt; no mention made of plough. The note, dated 7 January 1757, was witnessed by **Abra'm Slocum** and **John Woodman**.

Deposition of **Stoakes Potter** of Dartmouth in County of Bristol, Province of the Massachusetts Bay, 28 May 1759, that he was "at Howse whare **Abraham Slocum** lived at a place called Fogland Ferry . . . **Horswell** asked **Cook** to pay the money he ought him and Cook said he was redy to settle. . . ." (Docket No. 15)

In a second case the same day, **Abial Cook** of Little Compton, yeoman, vs. **John Horswell** of same, for £98:10 due for keeping livestock for him 1754 to 1756. Judgment for defendant. (Docket No. 16)

925. **Joseph Boss** of Newport, Boat Builder, vs. **Francis Harrison** of Freetown, County of Bristol, Boatman, in an action of assumpsit, that on 1 August 1758 at Newport, he received one silver watch of the plaintiff to the value of £80 old tenor in consideration [for which] he agreed to deliver 10 cords of wallnut wood at £10:10 each by the last day of September.

Deposition of **Isaac Hathaway** of Freetown, mariner, that he delivered some walnut wood, above one cord, unto **Joseph Boss** in Newport some time in the fall of the year 1758 in part payment. (Docket No. 36)

926. **John Coggeshall** of Portsmouth, yeoman, vs. **William Hall Junr** of Portsmouth, yeoman alias butcher, in an action of trespass concerning 9 acres of meadow, part arable, part pasture, in Portsmouth, bounded west on the highway, north on **William Hall Jr.**, east on the sea, south on **William Hall Sr.**, of which **David Fish** of Portsmouth, blacksmith, was possessed on 10 April 1745 when he deeded it. (Docket No. 37)

927. **Christopher Turner** of Portsmouth, yeoman alias innholder, vs. **John Coggeshall** of Portsmouth, yeoman, in an action of trespass concerning a house and 16 acres in Portsmouth. Deeds entered: **Jeremiah Tallman** of Portsmouth, yeoman, to the plaintiff 4 April 17[--]; **John Dexter** of East Greenwich, yeoman, to plaintiff 9 July 1744. (Docket No. 44)

928. **Isaac Ingraham** of Newport, cooper, vs. **Hannah Goulding** of Newport, widow, in an action of trespass concerning a certain chamber, part of his dwelling house in Newport, deeded to plaintiff 7 May 1739 by **John Record** of North Kingstown, yeoman; claimed to have been dispossessed by defendant 1 May 1759. Withdrawn. (Docket No. 45)

929. **Joseph Parsley** of Newport, staymaker, vs. **David Seavers** of Newport, house carpenter alias mariner, in an action of trespass concerning one certain chamber and Bed Room adjoining, part of a dwelling in Newport on half a lot of land at Easton's Point, number 96 in First Division, bounded north and west on streets, south on Cove, east on other half of the lot; deeded to plaintiff 26 July 1757 by **Anne Maylem**. (Docket No. 47)

930. **Kathrine West** of Newport, widow, vs. **Benjamin Shearman** of Portsmouth, yeoman, in an action of assumpsit; on 5 November 1757 he

promised her that if she would go to Nursing **Joseph Shearman** then sick of the small pox at his House in Portsmouth he would pay [her] so much Money as she should reasonably deserve; she claimed she deserved £55 old tenor and gave notice 25 November and divers other times. (Docket No. 52)

931. **John Nichols** of Newport, mariner, vs. **Mary Liscom** of Newport, widow, in an action of trespass concerning 2 lower rooms and 2 chambers and part of a garret and half a cellar in a dwelling house in Newport, bounded east on the street, south on a lane, west and north on land of **Joseph Sandford**, said premises having been deeded to the plaintiff 25 March 1759 by **Henry Collins**. (Docket No. 54)

932. **Rufus Church** of Newport, house carpenter, vs. **Samuel Stanley** of Newport, Innholder, in an action of detinue, that he render to the plaintiff one Bedstead, Feather Bed and Bolster and one Coverlid to the plaintiff belonging, to the value of £70, which on 20 December 1757 he had delivered to the defendant to be by him safely kept and redelivered again when requested. (Docket No. 55)

933. **Kathrine Sargent** of Newport, widow, vs. **Bathsheba Loveland** of Newport, widow, for money due by note of 20 April 1757. (Docket No. 63)

934. **Joseph Turner** of Newport, mariner, vs. **Daniel Holloway** of Newport, mariner, in an action of assumpsit; he had promised to deliver 2 September 1758 at Newport 100 gallons of merchantable molasses immediately after ye said Holloway had made a Voyage to the West Indies, it being for Value Received; in fact, said Defendant hath made a voyage to the West Indies and arrived safe in the Harbour of Newport on 7th of May 1759 . . . on 8th of same month Plaintiff gave him notice. (Docket No. 64)

935. **Abiel Cook** of Little Compton, yeoman, vs. **Samuel Cook** of Tiverton, yeoman, in an action of promise and assumpsit: at Tiverton 18 June 1748 **John Cook** late of Tiverton made his will; he was father of plaintiff and defendant, being possessed of considerable estate both real and personal; he ordered his two sons to bring up two granddaughters, namely **Priscilla Cook** and **Thankful Cook**, daughters to his son **William Cook**, in a decent manner and to good Learning and to keep them and provide for them upon their own cost and charges if his said son **William Cook** should never come home, &c . . . said **William Cook** did never return home and he hath been at the whole charge of maintaining and educating the said **Thankful** from the 24th of May 1754 when said **John** died till he purchased this writ. **Samuel Cook** signed the writ 7 May 1759 and claimed he owed nothing; **J. Honeyman** was lawyer for the defense. (Docket No. 258)

936. **Clarke Cornel** of Portsmouth, yeoman, and his wife **Frelove**, late **Frelove Cornel** and wife of **William Cornel** late of Portsmouth, deceased, vs. **William Cornel**, (an infant of said Portmouth, labourer, son of **William Cornel**), in an action to recover her dower right in 150 acres and a dwelling in Portsmouth. It was stated that William Cornel died 10 August 1758. (Docket No. 259)

937. **Rebeccah Worden** of Portsmouth, widow, executrix of the will of **Caleb Brown**, late of Portsmouth, mariner, deceased, vs. **Thomas Remington** of Cranston, mariner, in an action of promise and assumpsit, that he on 18 December 1757 received [*blank*] from **Caleb Brown** which he promised to sell at Antigua. (Docket No. 264)

938. **Christopher Slocum**, yeoman, and **Rebeccah Slocum**, widow, both of Dartmouth, executors of the will of **Holder Slocum** of Dartmouth, yeoman, deceased, vs. **Abraham Slocum** of Portsmouth, yeoman, in an action to recover £550 old tenor due for rent to Holder Slocum.

939. **John Marsh** of Jamestown, labourer, vs. **John Remington** of Jamestown, yeoman alias husbandman, in an action of assumpsit; on 8 April 1758 at Jamestown he promised that if the plaintiff would work at Farmer's work he would pay him what he reasonably deserved; he worked 59 days and deserved 30 shillings per day; claimed £88:10.

– 1760 – Superior Court –

940. March: Petition of **William Richmond Jr.** of Little Compton, gentleman, appointed by the Tiverton Town Council as administrator of the goods of **Tobias Briggs**, a free Mustee man late of Tiverton, mariner, deceased, to sell real estate belonging to the deceased, consisting of a small dwelling house and four acres of land in Tiverton, to pay debts outstanding. (Superior Court 14,038)

941. August: Petition of **Leonard Thurber** of Warren, husbandman, for divorce from his wife **Rebecca Thurber** who had been absent for many years and committed adultery. **Mary Allen**, wife of **Joseph Allen** of Warren, on 25 April 1760 testified that in May 1758 she had been at the house of Mr. **Nathaniel Twogood** in Warren, "afternoon near night, and saw Rebecca on a bed in the chamber with a man that was not her husband and were both covered with the bed cloths."

John Thurber testified on 7 May 1760 at Warren, before John Kinnicut Justice Pleas [*sic*], that "in the year 1753 hee was impoured to make up the difficolty between lenard thurber and his wife which hee tryed to do hee want to his wife several times from under his hand with promis to take as good care of hir as hee was abele to dew and hee would fech heir in a chair or on hors back which shee plesed but shee maid som small excuse but . . . she refused to cohabit or live with him any more and whean all fair means was used to gain her to live with him and no real reson given by hir: than hee went to the to[*w*]n counsel of warin whare shee than resided and desired them to [*warn her*] out of town and hee promesed them that hee would take good care of hir as hee culd which they toock noties of but shee precured surties and still refuses to live with him and this present year in apral last past I h[*e*]ard one **John Wimbel** say that hee saw the wife of leonard thurber abead with a man that was not hair husband and more than once or twice or thrice) this Wimbel was to be sworn to the truth this [*but*] hee was wounded accidentaly and died of the wound[*in*]g before wee could have oportunity to heare his evidece." Rebecca Thurber "was notified but not present at the caption hereof." (Superior Court 14,033)

942. August: Signed petition of **Alice Brownell** of Little Compton, widow, whose "husband, **Aaron Brownell**, died between five & six years ago leaving a number of small children and some debts to pay and but a small Real Estate consisting of a Dwelling House and about ten acres of Land in Little Compton aforesaid and but a very small personal estate besides the Household Goods & a Little Stock the whole of which was by no means sufficient to pay the Debts and bring up the Children without selling the Real estate. The Account of Funeral Expenses & Debts paid & bringing up said Children already amounts to upwards of Seventeen hundred pounds — more than the Inventory of the Personal Estate. . ." The Petitioner requests permission to sell real estate to pay debts of the estate.

— 1761 — Superior Court —

943. February 10: **Mr. Shearman Clarke** of Newport, mariner, petitioning to sell real estate, rendered account of his administration on the personal estate of his father Mr. **John Clarke** late of Newport, mariner, deceased, showing debts to sundry persons totaling £7,280 and exceeding inventory. (Superior Court 14,031).

944. February 27: Petition of **Ruth Brownell** [*signed by mark*], widow of **Job Brownell**, late of Little Compton, to sell house and land there to pay debts. She stated that her children were **Susannah**, about 12, **Robert**, about 10, **Elizabeth**, about 7, **Grace**, about 4, and "one sucking Infant at my Breast." She had been left a widow with about 30½ acres in Little Compton on which was an old house, both land and house in poor repair, and the estate of her late husband was encumbered with debts totaling £1742:19:2 (Superior Court 14,029).

945. March 2: **Thomas Freebody** and **Walter Cranston**, administrators of the estate of **Nehemiah Macks** late of Newport, shopkeeper, petition to sell real estate in order to pay debts. (Superior Court 14,030)

946. May 26: **Rhodes Havens** of New Shoreham, innholder, vs. **Robert Trim** of the same place, fisherman, for money due by book; plaintiff recovered £146:10.

947. **Rebecca Slocum** of Dartmouth, widow, executrix of the will of **Holder Slocum** late of Dartmouth, deceased, vs. **Remington Greenal** of Tiverton, husbandman, otherwise called **Remington Greenal** of the Island, commonly known by the name of Nassawanna, being one of the Elizabeth Islands in Chilmark in Dukes County, for debt; recovered £18:14:06.

948. November 5: **Constant Tabor** of Newport, cordwainer, vs. **Robert Hill** of Newport, taylor, in an action of promise and assumpsit: on 10 July 1756, he at the request of the defendant, at Newport, "undertook to learn the defendant's son **Joseph Hill** the art or trade of a cordwainer and accordingly received him into his Family and instructed him in said Business for the space of two years . . . at which time the defendant promised to bind said Joseph by Indenture and he should live with him until he became 21 – 5 years from that time" and he had not done so. Depositions were made by **Joseph Howland** and **Samuel Burroughs** and it was noted that **Joseph Hill's** wages in the service of the Colony as a soldier from March to 15 December, 9 months and 12 days at 40s per month, amounted to £18:16s "in ye year 1760." Jury verdict for defendant. (Superior Court 13,988)

– 1762 – Superior Court –

949. March: **John Linscomb** of Newport, mariner, vs. **Thomas Haszard** and **John Roffe**, merchants, both of Newport, and **Henry Wall**, yeoman, of North Kingstown, in an action of promise and assumpsit: The defendants on 10 September 1760 were owners of the privateer man of war called *The Success*, commanded by **Daniel Fones**, then bound to sea. They requested the plaintiff to proceed on said cruise in the character of a Lieutenant, and he should be entitled to four shares of all prizes. Together with another privateer man of war called *Roby* commanded by **Silas Cook** they surprised and took a certain schooner called the *Friendship*, whereof **Daniel Dehariette** was master, belonging to some subject of the French king, and her cargo, back to Newport where it was condemned as a lawfull Prize. Decision by referee was for the plaintiff, £874 and costs.

950. March: Indictment of **John Shearman**, now resident in Newport, labourer alias mariner, for breaking into the mansion house of **Sarah Rumreil** of Newport, shopkeeper, widow of **Thomas Rumreil**, merchant, between the hours of 11 and 12 in the evening of 7 October 1761, and stealing a pocket book, silk purse and silver money. He was "with **Daniel Dunnevan** who came with me from New London." It was noted that Donnavan had formerly used **Mrs. Standley's** House, was middle sized, 32 years old, of fair complexion, wearing "dark brown cut wigg, blue jacket double breasted, black hair buttons, checkd long trousers, old shoes, plain smooth brass buckles." **Mary Russell**, wife of **Daniel Russell**, was summoned to testify. (Superior Court 13,986)

951. May 31: **Starr Shrieve** of Newport, mariner, vs. **Thomas King** of Newport, mariner, for trespass, to recover a half acre of land with dwelling house, bounded south on land of **John Warkman**, west and north on land of **Martha Brayton** and east on the street.

952. August: **Joseph Brownell** of Portsmouth, Esq. petitions for liberty to sell real estate to pay debts of **Moll Clarke** late of Portsmouth, a Free Negro Woman, who died intestate leaving some personal estate and real estate consisting of one acre of land with a small dwelling House; he was appointed to administer the estate 9 March 1761. (Superior Court 14,018)

953. September: **John Fry**, mariner, petitioned for divorce from wife **Ann.** It was stated that on 29 December 1759, his wife Ann, then by the name of **Ann Milward**, and being big with child and pretending that he was the father, had him arrested and induced him to marry her "to yr Pet^r's great misfortune it proved afterwards that she was with child by another man . . . [*Fry*] being beyond sea at the time said child was begot and for a long time before and afterwards." (Superior Court 13,999).

954. September: **Sarah McWilliams** of Newport petitioned for divorce from **John McWilliams**, who had violated his marriage covenant by absenting himself from her and refusing to cohabit with her for the space of 12 years past. Depositions were made by **Archibald Campbell** and **Robert Campbell** of Newport, who said he had told **John McWilliams** to take his wife home and behave as a husband ought and support her, and he refused and said he had made his estate over to his

son. **John Campbell** of Voluntown, County of Windham, Connecticut, stated that he had lived 12 years a near neighbor to **Sarah**, wife of **John McWilliams** of Newport, had seen John "often at my House and I often requested [*him*] to go and see [*her*] and talk with her"; **Mary Campbell**, wife of John also testified. (Superior Court 14,016)

955. September (on appeal from November 1761): **William Tallman** of Dartmouth, taylor, vs. **Job Cook** of Portsmouth, taylor alias labourer, in an action of trespass, charging that he "with force & arms at Portsmouth 31 August 1761 did take away from and out of the possession of the plaintiff one **Joseph Rickerson** an Indented Apprentice . . . and hath kept [*him*] from his said Masters service"; warrant for Cook's arrest dated 5 October 1761. **Joseph Martin Junr** Deputy Sheriff, on 13 October "arrested ye body of the within named Job Cook & afterwards I took **Susanna Cook** Bail for him." Case first tried in November 1761. The defendant's plea by his attorney **J. Honyman** was not guilty. Testimony given 10 November 1761 by **Shadrach Dennis** of lawful age who said that on or about 31 last August he "went to the house where Job Cook then lived, with an advertisement from William Talman to take his apprentice Joseph Ricketson which had a little while before Run away from said Talman and I found the sd Joseph near the door of said house and took him and Cook being near asked me what I was going to do with [*him*] . . . told sd Cook . . . I was going to carry him to **Butts**'s where his Master was . . . said Cook told me the boy must go into the house to get his Cloaths and I told said Cook I was affraid he would take the boy away from me if he went into the house and I did not choose he should go in but I would carry him to Butts's and send for his Cloaths, and then said Cook made Answer by God he shall go in or Else you and I will try which is Stoutest so I went into the house with the sd Cook and the boy and still kept hold of the boy and said Cook went into another Room and two women came to me and asked me what I was going to do with the Boy . . . the women took hold of the Boy and tried to get him away and seized upon my hand with which I held the Boy and tried to break my hold and one of the women said to me you damn'd son of a Bitch what! you carry the boy away you go to hell, he is my Sister's Child but I still kept hold of the boy till said Cook came out of the other Room and took up a Broom and said to me get out of doors you damn'd son of a Bitch or I will Split your Brains out so I let the boy go and went out and said I would

go and call Talman and one of the women made answer go and fetch your damn'd Talman and I will horsewhip him and then said Cook came out and pulled of his Cap & frock and Challenged me to stricke him but I did not then he told me to go into ye highway & he would give me what I wanted but I did not & thereupon came **William Talman** and **Wm Burrington** and said Talman demanded his Boy of said Cook and said Cook & the women both made answer go look [*for?*] him . . . I came away. . . ." **William Wood** testified the same day, that sometime in the year 1760 in June he had gone to the house of his son **Josiah Wood** and there he saw **William Talman, Benjamin Ricketson** & his wife and **Daniel Hat[*h*]eway** "who as I perceived had been writing Indentures binding Joseph the Son of the said Benjamin Ricketson to William Talman as an Apprentice to learn the trade of a Taylor," and if he remembered right he had been one of the subscribing witnesses to the indenture and afterwards **Susanna** the wife of **Benjamin Ricketson** delivered into his keeping one of the indentures which he kept until he heard that Joseph had run away from his master, and then Susanna Ricketson had come to demand it; he was loath to let her have it but both Benjamin and Susanna Ricketson repeatedly demanded it and "I at last delivered up said Indenture to her. . . ." **Daniel Hathaway** of Dartmouth testified that he had written the Indenture, at the house of **Josiah Wood**. **Thomas Dennis**, and **Thomas Wilcox** (who signed by mark) stated that they lived with Mr. William Talman about a month and his apprentice Joseph Ricketson lived there near the whole of that time and they saw no abuse offered to him "neither by his Master nor Mistress nor any body Else neither had we any Reason to Complain of our living and the said Joseph for the most part sat at the table with us and fared as we did." **Sarah Condall** on oath declared that on or about the month of August 1761 she was at her "Mother's house in Portsmouth in her appartment with whom she lived when came in a Man called by the Name of Dennis who had then hold of a boy named Joseph Rickerson and said that he was his Money . . . My Brother **Job Cook** being present desired said Dennis to sett down and handed him a Chair and then went into his own appartment he living in the other part of said house leaving the Man and the Boy in my Mothers appartment . . . The boy never lodged with my brother, but with my mother . . . Dennis let the boy goe."

Verdict for the plaintiff: Talman to have of Cook £300 and £26:11:0 costs; both appealed to the next Superior Court and gave bond. (Superior Court 13,951).

956. November: **Abraham Anthony** vs. Mulatto boy named **Ben**. Deposition of **Ruth Sisson** of Charlestown that she was at house of **Abraham Anthony** of Portsmouth 12 June 1760 when "came a mulotto woman known as **Amy** with her Boy named **Ben** and left him at Anthony's and in 1761 sumtime the first of May came a Negro man named **Ben Bozzard** with the molatto woman his wife to Bind said Boy as Apprintice to said Anthony but he being from home . . . Negro said he could not come again for he was going a Soldiering." Deposition of **William Sherman** that **Benjamin Bosworth** so-called, a free Negroe, etc. Deposition of **Daniel Anthony** that he being at home at the house of **Abraham Anthony** "came a Mustee or Indian woman . . . **Amy** . . . said boy to be learnt to Read . . . has been and can spell in short spellings . . . well . . . ."

Indenture: **Negro Ben**, a free Negro man of Bristol, laborer . . . bind son, mulatto boy named Ben, an apprentice unto **Nathaniel Cary** of Bristol, gentleman and **Elisabeth** his wife . . . for 13 years 9 months or till 21 years, which term will compleat 6 December 1775. Dated 5 March 1762. (Superior Court 13,913).

— 1763 —

957. May 30: **Philip Gray** of Tiverton, yeoman, vs. **Ephraim Richmond** of Tiverton, yeoman, for trespass, to recover 73 acres of land with mansion house thereon, in Tiverton, consisting of meadow, wood, and pasture, bounded west upon land of **Abiel Cook**, south on Little Compton line, east on land of **John Dennis**, and north partly on land of **John Dennis** and partly on land of **George Cook**. Plaintiff recovered possession.

958. **Peleg Thurston** of Newport, Esq. vs. **John Belithro** of Newport, distiller, for trespass, to recover a lot with dwelling house and distill house in Newport, bounded on the south side by the Point Bridge, about 85 feet, east partly on land of **George Thomas** and partly on land of the late **John Coddington**, west and north on land belonging to Friends, called Easton's Point; damages asked £15,000. Plaintiff won by default.

959. **Remembrance Corey** of Tiverton, widow, late wife of **Roger Corey** of Tiverton, deceased, vs. **Caleb Corey** of Tiverton, yeoman, in action of dower, to recover her right in one half part of the 4th Six Score Lot in the Pocasset Purchase in Tiverton, the south half of said lot with dwelling house thereon, it belonging to the "estate of **Roger Corey**, deceased, of which the plaintiff hath had nothing." Bounds listed were north on land of **John Brown**, east on fresh River, south on a highway, west on land of **Roger Corey**. Verdict for plaintiff to recover one full third part of the land in question.

960. **Anstis Coggeshall** of Newport, widow, late wife of **Thomas Coggeshall**, merchant, deceased, vs. **Benjamin Church** of Newport, mariner, and **Bathsheba** his wife, in an action of dower, to recover 106 acres of land with beach adjoining in Newport, part meadow, part pasture, part arable land. Verdict for plaintiff to recover it.

961. November 14: **Mary Flagg** of Newport, widow and administratrix of the estate of her husband **Ebenezer Flagg**, late of Newport, deceased, petitioned for permission to sell real estate to settle debts. Property was described as a lot in Newport with dwelling house and buildings fronting on Queen Street and one whole share or 27th part of Long Wharf with warehouses.

962. May. **William Shaw** vs. **Thomas Church** in action to recover four 30 shilling bills received by the hand of his Negro **Sampson**.

Nathaniel Church of Little Compton, Province of Massachusetts Bay, yeoman, on 6 January 1700, for $18, sold to **William Shaw** of the same place, yeoman, one Negro boy named **Sampson**, being 2 years of age the 27th Day of May next. Witnesses to the bill of sale were **George Brownell** and **Edw'd Richmond**.

Receipt of **Sampson Shaw** [*mark X*] [*torn*]ber 1760 at Newport, "of **Thomas Cranston**, $11 in full for my wages in the Last Campaign by order of **Jeremiah Shaw**." On 18 April 1761 a receipt was signed by **Experience** [*mark X*] **Tobey** to **Thomas Church** "for four 30 shilling Bills and one 6*d* Bill of March date 1760 and seven coppers which belongeth to me & was ordered out of my hands to be cleansed of the small pox."

Deposition of **Noah Stoddard**, dated 31 January 1763, that in December 1760 he "being at ye pest house in Little Compton he was ordered by **Thomas Church** to take the money the Negro man **Sampson** had with him . . . to air clens . . . sometime after. . .**William Shaw** came and demanded [*it*] . . . I refused . . . **Thomas Church, Esq.** one of the athority come and received it." Deposition of **Fobe Little** of Little Compton, that "some years past **William Shaw** of Little Compton came to my house and asked me to write an agreement between him and his Negro man . . . **Sampson** obliged to pay to his master 150 Old Tenor and when so fullfiled then said Shaw promised to give him his freedom and to give bonds to the town as the law directs . . . said Sampson's master obliged him to Digg his garden for him so long as he should live and make his Baskets and Brooms."

Deposition of **William Jameson** that "some time in December 1760 a Negro man called **Sampson Shaw** broke out in smallpox . . . I went with **Thomas Church Esq.** to the wigwam that said Negro lived in to carry . . . to pest house in said Town . . . said Church ordered a Squaw called **Exe** the wife of said Negro to bring all the money out and shee brought him sumthing out of the wigwam and gave to said Negro." Verdict for plaintiff, money sued for and costs. Appealed but confirmed. (Superior Court 13,940)

963. September. **Matthew Robinson** of South Kingstown, gentleman, vs. **Mary Tripp** and **Bridget Spencer** both of Newport, widows, in an action of trespass involving land and house in Newport, bounded west by highway leading to the Neck, south by land of **Robert Taylor**, east and north on land of **Abraham Redwood**, of which premises **Benjamin Tripp** of Newport, mariner, on 24 September 1757 was possessed and by deed of that date did convey to plaintiff. One half was devised to Mary for life and the whole had finally been obtained at law by **Benjamin Tripp**, son of said Mary; Mary devised her interest to him. Copy of will of Othniel Tripp [*for full transcription of will, see No. 768*]. Mary and Bridget received costs. (Superior Court 13,944)

964. March: Petition of **Stoddard Lawton** of Tiverton, mariner, for divorce: on 1 December 1760 he sailed from Newport and continued absent until January 1763; during his absence and after he had been out of the Colony upwards of 2 years his wife **Deborah** was brought to bed with a female child. Deposition of **Borden Wilcocks** of Tiverton, mariner, that on 5 December 1760 he sailed on Sloop *Two Brothers*, **Daniel Wilcocks**, Master, of this place, to Maryland; **Stoddard Lawton** was on said Sloop as a Hand; he left in Maryland; later **Borden Willcocks** was in Maryland again and saw him at James Island and they went in company up the Bay to Swan Creek until 6 June 1762. Summons were issued to --- **Irish**, wife of **John Irish** of Little Compton, midwife, and **Lillis Briggs** of Tiverton and **Anstress Willcocks.** Deposition of **Lilless Briggs** that she was at the house of **William Willcocks** in Tiverton 5 November 1762 and at that time **Deborah Lawton** who is called wife of **Stoddard Lawton** was delivered of a female bastard child.

965. May: **Benjamin Fish** of Portsmouth, yeoman, vs. **Holder Chace** of Portsmouth, yeoman. In the evening of 6 January 1763 dogs belonging to defendant killed 14 ewe sheep. Summons were issued for **David Fish Jr.** and **George Hall**, both of Portsmouth. Deposition 3 March 1764 signed by **David Fish Jr.**, who responded to questions from the plaintiff, saying that the boy who informed him of Hall's dog having the lamb was **Daniel Phillips**, 12 or 13 years old; the dog's ears were cut off but he couldn't tell about the tail; the **Widow Westgate's** dog was a "lightish coullard shagged dog." (Superior Court)

966. Will of **Joseph Tillinghast**, dated 28 December 1762; proved 5 December 1763 [*separated from case*]

In the name of God Amen I Joseph Tillinghast of Newport in ye County of Newport in the Colony of Rhode island and providence plantations in New England Shop keeper being by Divine favour of a reasonable and disposeing mind & memory and knowing it is appointed unto men once to die do make and ordain this my last will & testament that is to say principally & first of all I commit my spirit to the hand of God who gave it and my body to the earth to be buried in decent manner at the direction of my executrix hereafter to be named & appointed & as concerning such worldly estate as it has pleased God to bless me with in this life I give & dispose thereof in manner & form following.

My will is that all my just debts be paid in a reasonable time after my decease.

Item I give to my daughter **Lydia Amy** ye sum of seven hundred pounds equal to dollars at seven pounds apiece.

Item I give to my son **Joseph** ye house in which he now dwells togather with the lot of land on which the said house stands with all the improvements & appertunances thereunto belonging (except as is herein excepted) to be and remain to hm his heirs & assigns forever that is to say he pay unto my executrix (hereafter to be named) the sum of nine thousand pounds equal to dollars at seven pounds pr within the space of one year after my decease.

Item I give to my daughter **Ann Gardner** to ye value of twenty dollars a year for the space of twelve years but if my said daughter die before ye said twelve years are expired then ye money or value thereof shall be paid to my granddaughter **Freelove Easton** during the remaining part of ye said twelve years (for the use of her family) according to her direction. I also give to my said daughter Ann the use of the house she now lives in with the use of the entry between said houses also a small room in the north east corner of the seller of ye other house with the priveledge of a well as also sixteen foot square in the north east corner of the garden the improvement of said premises I give to her & her daughter Freelove Easton during their natural lives.

Item I give to my son **Samuel** ye lands in which he now lives togather with a [---] or water lott & all appertunanes thereunto belonging to him his heirs & assigns forever I also give unto him the sum of two thousand pounds equal to dolars at seven pounds pr.

Item I give to my son **Nicholas** two thousand pounds equal to dollars at 7½ pr also the warehouse and wharfe below ye house which he now lives in in Providence also one half of a store or woodhouse in Newport standing on ye wharfe I bought of **William Dyre** with a double house adjoining thereunto he keeping said wharfe in good repair so farr as adjoins ye said premises I give to him his heirs & assigns forever with ye priviledge of build^{g} further in to the water if he or they please

Item I give to my daughter **Elezebeth Cozzens** one double and one single warehouse on the wharfe I bought of **William Dyre** being to the westward of ye store or wood house so called on said wharfe she keeping in good repair said wharfe so far as adjoining ye said premises. I also give her the sum of five hundred pounds equal to dollars at seven pounds pr.

Item I give to my son **Daniel** a small lot of land near Fullers Ferry in Rehoboth as also the eastermost double house on the wharfe I bought of **William Dyre** aforesaid as also the eastermost half of ye store or wood house with ye priveledges of said wharfe and to build further out if he please he keeping in good repair said wharfe so far as may adjoin his interest said premises I give to him his heirs & assigns forever. I also give to my son Daniel the sum of two thousand pounds equal to dollars at seven pounds ppr.

Item. I give to my granddaughter **Mary Barker** two hundred pounds equal to dollars at seven pounds ppr.

Item. I give to my grandson **Nicholas Paris Tillinghast** three hundred pounds equal to dollars at seven pounds ppr.

Item. I give to my grandson **Nathaniel Tweedy** the sum of three hundred pounds equal to dollars at seven pounds ppr.

Item. I give to **Mary** my beloved wife the sum of three thousand pounds equal to dollars at seven pounds ppr as also my Indian girl to her her heirs & assigns forever as also the rents and improvements of all the remaining part of my estate during her natural life if any remains to be devided between my surviving children.

Also I appoint and ordain my Mary my said wife to be sole executrix of this my last will & testament hereby disanulling & revokeing all othr wills & bequests heretofore by me made or established ratifying & confurming this & no other to be my last will & testament. In witness herof I have hereunto set my hand & seal this twenty eighth day of December in the year of our Lord one thousand seven hundred & sixty two Sign'd sealed & published, pronounced & declared by the said Joseph Tillinghast as his last will & testament.

[*signed*] Joseph Tillinghast

In presence of **Jabez Carpenter, Archibald Campbell, William Hookey**

Newport December 5th A D 1763

In Council appeared **Archibald Champbell Wm Hookey** and on their oaths declared they saw Joseph Tillinghast sign seal & publish & declare the within written will to be his last will & testament and that he was then of a sound mind & understanding & that they with **Jabez**

Carpenter signed as witnesses to said will at the same time in the said Joseph Tillinghasts presence.

Witness Wm Coddington Council Clerk

The above & foregoing pages is a true copy of the will of Joseph Tillinghast with the several interlineations & erasements as in are in the original will & which was compared with said original will this eighth day of December 1763

Witness William Coddington Council Clerk

— May Term 1763 —
Inferior Court of Common Pleas

967. **Isaac Howland** of Newport, merchant, vs. **Myer Polock** of Newport, merchant, for trespass, charging that on 11 March 1763 he had assaulted him. Testimony of **Job Easton** that Howland was talking with others and Polock came up behind and hit him. Judgement for plaintiff. This file includes a page from the *Newport Mercury* for Monday March 21, 1763, No. 237: ships cleared [*out of Newport*] included the Sloop *Three Sallys*, **Burroughs,** master, for Gibraltar. "The house of **William Havens** of North Kingstown was consumed by fire last Monday . . . chimney fire . . . Capt. Havens was much burned in endeavoring to save his Effects." (Docket No. 40)

968. **Thomas Rogers** of Newport, housecarpenter, vs. **Gambo,** a Negro man of Newport, labourer, in action of trespass, charging that on 22 July 1762 he struck a cow belonging to the plaintiff with a boat hook. Defendant pleaded not guilty. Arbitrated by referees: **Daniel Goddard, William Robinson** and **Matthew Barker,** son of **Abraham.** (Docket No. 82)

969. **John Greene** of Boston, merchant, surviving co-partner of **Thomas Greene,** late of the same place, merchant, deceased, vs. **Giles Peckham** of Providence, shopkeeper, for debt due by book, presenting account for cloth, etc., delivered in the year 1760.

970. **Issachar Polock** of Newport, merchant, vs. **Christopher Allen** of Newport, mariner, late master of the schooner *Eagle,* for an accounting of the cargo on a voyage to Jamaica. (Docket No. 101)

971. **Joseph Cooke Jr.** of Tiverton, yeoman, vs. **George Croker** of Tiverton, blacksmith, for £45 due by note dated January 1763 at Tivertown, for "2.0.18 pds of rise at £20 per hundred [*and*] sorting of the rise." (Docket No. 328)

972. **Trustees of the Colony** vs. **Mary Updike** of Newport, widow; writ also vs. **Peter Wanton** who was not to be found, in action of trespass, for witholding a lot of land in Newport bounded east on Thames Street, south on **John Cooke**, west on the harbour, which on 16 August 1744 **Mary Updike** who was formerly **Mary Wanton** deeded to the Colony. (Docket No. 455)

– 1764 –

973. March: **Sarah Beere,** spinster of Newport vs. **Samuel Phillips,** infant, yeoman, of North Kingstown. . . . Appealed from Inferior Court of Common Pleas at Newport in November 1763, when writ stated that Sarah Beer of Newport in the County of Newport spinster an infant by her uncle and guardian **Stephen Hoockey** of said Newport shipwright complains of Samuel Phillips of North Kingstown in the County of Kings County an infant yeoman who holds the real estate of **Christopher Phillips** his grandfather as devisee in fee in North Kingstown aforesaid (which estate is improved by **William Wall, Paul Greene** and **Richard Briggs**) who was executor of the last will & testament of **Henry Beer** late of Newport in the County of Newport mariner deceased . . . **Christopher Phillips** did receive the sum of £500 on the death of the sd Henry Beer . . . on the first day of June 1747 in his capacity as executor, the same to be put to interest till the plaintiff arrived to the age of eighteen years to wit on the 16 day of April 1758 . . . Plaintiff demands £500 and interest thereon the value of £500 being equal to 500 dollars at the time the said Christopher rec^{d} the same, damage £7,000 current money of New England . . . and to recover and have of the real estate of the sd Christopher Phillips possessed and enjoyd by the sd Samuel Phillips the sum of £2,511 . . . defendant appeals to the next Superior Court. Will of Henry Beere entered in evidence:

Will of **Henry Beere**, Newport, 1746:

In the name of God Amen Henry Beere of Newport in ye County of Newport in ye Collony of Rhode Island and Providence Plantations in New England, mariner, being in good health of body and of a sound mind and understanding blessed be God for ye same and being bound on a voyage to sea and calling to mind the mortality of my body and knowing that it is appointed for all men once to die do make and ordain this to be my last will & testament. That is to say principally and first of all, I commit my soul into the hands of God who gave it me hopeing through ye merit death and passion of my blessed Lord and Saviour Jesus Christ to have full and free pardon and remission of all my sins and to inherit eternall life and as to my worldly estate, it hath pleased God to bless me with I give devise, & dispose of ye same in ye following manner and form.

Imprimus. I will that all my just debts be well and truly paid by my executors herein afternamed in some convenient time after my decease.

Item. I give and bequeath unto my loveing sister **Hannah Beere**, widdow of my brother **Charles Beere**, late of said Newport, mariner deceased, ye sum of one hundred pounds current money of New England to be paid her immediately after my decease.

Item. I give and bequeath unto my loveing nephew **Henry Beere** son of my said brother **Charles Beere** all that my lott of land which was formerly his fathers, and which I purchased of his mother **Hannah Beere** with ye house and all other the priviledges thereunto belonging to be and remain to him, his heirs & assigns forever.

Item. I give and bequeath to my two nieces, vizt: **Sarah Beere** and **Mary Beere**, daughters of my said brother **Charles Beere** the sum of five hundred pounds current money of New England to each of them ye said sum of five hundred pounds to be put out to interest immediately after my decease for their uses, and the principall & interest to be paid them when they arrive to ye age of eighteen years or day of marriages which shall first happen & ye said money to be put to interest by my executors herein afternamed.

Item. I desire that my brother **Christopher Phillips** of North Kingstown in ye County of Kings County and Collony of Rhode Island &c Esqr may take out of my personall estate, as much as will satisfie him for his time and the trouble he has been at about my affairs.

Item. I give and bequeath to each of the children of my brother Christopher Philips, namely **Christopher, Peter, Frederick & Elizabeth Philips**, and my nephew **Thomas Keeling** each ye sum of five pounds.

Item. After my debts and legacys are paid I give and bequeath all my money bonds and notes to my said nephew **Henry Beere** and all the rest of my personall estate I give & bequeath to be divided between my said nephew Henry Beere, and his sisters **Sarah Beere** and **Mary Beere** equally, and to be and remain to them their heirs & assigns forever.

And lastly I nominate, constitute, and appoint my said brother Christopher Phillips of said North Kingstown Esqr to be my whole and sole executor of this my last will & testament ratifieing allowing and confirming this and no other to be my last will & testament in witness whereof I have hereunto sett my hand and seal at Newport this twenty eighth day of April in ye nineteenth year of His Majesties Reign George ye Second King of Great Brittain &c annoque Domini one thousand seven hundred & forty six.

[*signed*] Henry Beere (seal)

in ye presence of us . . . **James Gardner, Wm Coddington Junr, Penelope Coddington** (Superior Court 13,884)

– May 1764 –

General Sessions of the Peace

974. Indictment of **Thomas Weaver Jr.** of Newport, mariner alias cooper, charged as follows: in the evening of 30th December 1763 with others unknown assembled having faces blackened and otherwise disguised . . . he broke into a chamber in Newport in possession of **Benjamin Brayton** of Newport, mariner, by breaking down the door, and seized **Hannah Brayton**, wife of Benjamin, and **Content**, daughter of Benjamin, and did drag [*them*] out and throw [*them*] in a Horse Cart and carry [*them*] to the Workhouse in Newport. **Robert Sisson Jr.** of Newport, mariner alias house carpenter, **Nathan Reed** of Newport, labourer alias mariner, son of **William Reed**, and **Goodson Langworthy** of Newport, mariner, were also indicted for the same incident.

975. **Enoch Butts** of Portsmouth, yeoman, vs. **Rebeccah Worden** of Portsmouth, widow, and **John Slocum** of Newport, yeoman, in the custody of the sheriff, in an action of the case that they perform their promise to the plaintiff made. On 1 December 1762, the plaintiff was tenant of a certain farm in Portsmouth lately belonging to one **Caleb Brown**, and on 24 May 1760 was served with an order by the Overseers of the Poor of Portsmouth to levy the rents of sd farm in order to satisfy the order, which was made up against the sd Caleb Brown for the maintenance of a Bastard Child born of the body of one **Sarah Strange** and of which sd Caleb Brown was adjudged the putative father . . . on 1 December 1762 [*Butts*] paid unto **Rebeccah Worden** and **John Slocum** the rents of sd farme and they did promise to indemnify and save him harmless.

Court order directed to the Overseers of the Poor of the Town of Portsmouth: Whereas **William Anthony, Wm Earl & Robert Dennis** all of Portsmouth, Esq^{rs}, Justices . . . made an order against the estate of Caleb Brown late of Portsmouth, mariner, deceas'd, the reputed father of a bastard child born of the body of **Sarah Strange** requiring the Overseers of the Poor of sd Portsmouth to take so much of the goods, chattles of the sd Caleb Brown and to receive so much of the rents yearly issuing out of the lands as did belong to [*him*] as would amount to the sum of £168 which charge the town had then been at & paid until 11 November 1758 & also to receive the sum of 45*s* per week yearly . . . so long as the child should be chargeable . . .

At the Court of General Sessions of ye Peace . . . at Newport on the third Tuesday of November 1758 **Rebeckah Worden** the executrix of the last will and testament of ye said **Caleb Brown** and **John Slocum** the guardian of the devisee of the real estate were cited to appear . . . **Jonathan Freeborn** and **Thomas Brownell**, Overseers of the Poor, 24 May 1760, "having made search for the within mentioned goods & chattels and cannot find any therefore we have levied the same on **Enoch Butts** by demanding the rents yearly issuing out of the real estate . . . said Butts being tenant thereon. . . .

– 1764 – May Term –

Inferior Court of Common Pleas

976. **Abner Chase** of Tiverton, yeoman, vs. **Robert Bennet Jr.** of Tiverton, mariner, in an action of the case that the defendant keep and perform his promises and assumption to the plaintiff made. On or about 10 March 1761 Bennet had contracted with Chase about 1000 cords of wood on Chase's land; 500 were to be chosen by Chase over 3 years time. **Thomas Howland** testified, "at my house in Tiverton in company with **Abner Chase** and **Robert Bennet Jr.** 18th February 1761, Chase bought of Bennet 1000 cord of wood which was standing on his

farm in Tiverton . . . 500 cord where he pleased." **Thomas Corey** gave the same testimony. **Cornelius Sowle** on 13 November 1761 testified that in the fall of 1761 he contracted to buy 6 cords of wood of **Robert Bennet Jr.** . . . "I understood **Abner Chase** was to cut the wood." **Christopher Manchester** testified that in the spring of the year last past "I contracted to cut some cordwood for **Abner Chase**, accordingly I went to cut some wood and he told me I must go up to Bennet's Farm to cut the wood . . . I went up and when I came there before I had cut any wood **Robert Bennet Senior** came to me and forewarned me cuting any wood . . . also forewarned a Negro which was cuting wood there for said **Abner Chase**." Testimony also was given by **Benjamin Palmer** of Tiverton and **Lilless Briggs**. **Stephen Taber** of Tiverton, yeoman, testified that in 1761 he purchased of **Robert Bennet** 4 cords and timber on the west end of land in Tiverton which **Robert Bennet Jr.** had purchased of **Timothy Gifford Jr.**; **Jonathan Sowle** of Tiverton made an identical deposition. **Thomas Gray Jr.** of Tiverton testified that in February he was at the house of **Thomas Howland** when Bennet said to cut at the west end of the farm . . . "Chase said "'I will cut it all if **William Manchester** will let me cart it through.' Chase and Bennet fell into discourse consearning a parcel of tops of Trees which said Chase had fell before for ship timber and Chase agreed to cut them all up into cordwood and to give said Bennet £3 a cord." In court at May term 1764, **Peleg Sawdy** deposed and said that in the month of February 1763 he indented with Abner Chase for one year to perform husbandry work "and I have cut corded & carted a Considerable quantity of Wood as Chase purchased of Bennet . . . cord wood Mill Loggs Railes Timber & Poles and Stakes & Barr Posts and Barrs of Different Lengths and was corded where it was cut to my knowledge the sd Chase soplys his own Fire, out of the Wood as was purchased of Bennet & not made no Cordage of the same, the Poles and Stakes was not corded . . . some Time in the Winter in the year 1764 I heard Robert Bennet J^{r} forwarn Abner Chase from cutting any more Wood till he had cut up all as he had cut down and corded and if said Chase had not cut his Compliment he should cut till he had for he told him that he did not want him to stand still one Minute except sd Chase will cut where sd Bennet should direct him. . . ." **Laurence Springer** and **Jonathan Hart Junr** testified that when they went to cut wood on Bennet's land for Chase, Robert Bennet came out and scared their oxen with a club . . . later they saw that "Chase's cartway was fenced up on Bennet's land near to a bad rocky gully which he had taken great pains to clear away through the which said Fence was part of the Inclosures of a small Field which was call'd Bennet's Field." **Benjamin Sawdy** of Tiverton, yeoman, deposed that on 18 January 1764 he "being agoing to the house of Abner Chase where he now liveth with my son Peleg Sawdy in order to get the said Abner Chase to release my son Peleg Sawdy from cutting one hundred cords of wood that he . . . obligd himself by a written obligation to cut . . ." Chase asked Peleg why he did not cut the wood and he said he was afraid to cut it "likewise I . . . said I woud not have him cut it for a dollar a cord by reason I thought the Danger was so great that I did not know what the Consequence might be." **Stoddard Lawton** [*signed his name* ***Stodder Lawton***] deposed at Tiverton 24 May 1764 that Chase had told his people not to pay attention to what Bennet told them, but to keep cutting and he would bear them harmless. **John Fish** of Tiverton, cooper, on oath declared [*signed by mark*] that Peleg Sawdy had asked him to assist him in cutting wood, and that Bennet had come and forewarned them, saying that they should not cut any more until Chase had cut up the wood that was already cut down and corded it; Bennet believed Chase "did not know what he had got himself, for he had fell some trees on those that was fallen down before and broke their top pieces and Bennet said that was not fair . . . he woud go and shew said Chase where he shoud cut . . ." but Chase sent them back to cut where they were. The jury found for the plaintiff £45 damage and cost of court.

977. **James Easton** and **Nicholas Easton** of Newport, yeomen, **Peter Barker** of Middletown, yeoman, **Jacob Mott Jr.** of Portsmouth, yeoman, vs. **Simeon Newton** of Newport, distiller, re land of which **Jacob Mott, Thomas Cornell**, late of Portsmouth, **William Barker** and **Samuel Thurston**, late of Newport, yeomen, were originally proprietors and which premises the defendant held of the second proprietors. (Docket No. 63)

978. **Samuel Mumford** of Middletown, yeoman, vs. **John Card** of Middletown, cordwainer, for withholding possession of a lot in Middletown with a dwelling house, bounded east on highway, north and west on land of **Clement Weaver**, south on land of **John Gould**, of which **Job Caswell** of Newport, housecarpenter, was on 4 March 1757 seized and did on that day deed to the plaintiff. (Docket No. 252)

979. **William Winpenny** of Newport, mariner, vs. **William Joy** of Newport, mariner, concerning possession of a dwelling house and gardens in Newport, bounded north on **Henry Sabin**, west on the street, south on **Joseph Jacob** and east on **Gideon Wanton Jr.**, of which premises **William Demoy** late of Newport, mariner, deceased, was in his lifetime seized, from 1 June 1763 until 10 June 1763 when he died without issue and intestate, leaving the plaintiff his next of kin and heir-at-law. File includes a deposition by **Linn Martin** of Newport "in the county of Newport and English Colony of Rhode=Island," dated 2 December 1764 before **John Davis**, J.P., that in 1755 or 1756 he sailed from Newport in the brig *Phenix*, **Benj. Hicks** master, bound to Jamaica. **William Dumoy** of Newport was a hand on board the vessel "and on our passage wee ware taken in sight of highspanaola by two French men of war and carried in to Cape Fransway and sd Dumoy and this deponant with the rest of the people ware there confind in jail and about five month after we ware taken we ware put on board of French ships to be carried to old France that is some on board one ship and some on board others and we went to old France and about a twelve month after that this deponant see one **John Yates** who belonged up to Providence . . . asked him what became of sd Dumoy and the rest of sd Hicks's people and he told [*me*] that said Dumoy dyed in France and the rest of sd crew he could not tell what became of them and sd Dumoy dyed in Denine a town so called in sd France." (Docket No. 257)

980. **Margaret Zape**, **Abigail Doodley** and **Mary Whitman**, all of Bandon in County Cork, Kingdom of Ireland, daughters of **Charles Coombs** late of Newport, clothier, deceased, complain of **Peleg Hull** of Newport, mariner, in an action of trespass, for possession of a certain lot of land in Newport, 100 feet square with dwelling house, on Easton's Point, of which premises **Charles Coombs** was in his lifetime seized on 10 May 1754 till about 10 June 1754 when he died intestate, leaving the petitioners, his only daughters. The Burgesses and Common Council of the Borough of Bandon, Cork, certified that "we know **Ann Coombs** . . . wife of Charles within mentioned to be mother of the within named Mary, Abigail, and Margaret," dated 18 March 1763 . . .

"ministers and churchwardens of the south side of the town of Bandon in the Parish of Ballymooden, Cork." (Docket No. 266)

981. **Caleb Earl** of Newport, clothier, vs. **Joshua Wilbore** of Newport, cordwainer, in action of trespass, to recover land in Newport, 20 by 80 feet, and a dwelling, of which premises **Joseph Scott** of Newport, Esq., was on 31 March 1760 seized and conveyed by deed to the plaintiff. Defendant answers that he is always called **Uzziah Wilbore**, not Joshua as in the writ. (Docket No. 270)

In November 1764, **Caleb Earl** of Newport, clothier, vs. **Usiah Wilbore** of Newport, cordwainer, re trespass. (Docket No. 244)

– November Term 1764 –

General Sessions of the Peace

982. **John Robinson** of Newport, Esq., at Portsmouth, 10 July 1764, was accused of obstructing **David Anthony** of Portsmouth, Esq., in the execution of his office, concerning laws respecting the small pox. Defendant was ill and unable to attend; case not prosecuted.

Inferior Court of Common Pleas

983. **Katherine West** of Newport, widow of **Henry West** late of Newport, butcher, dec'd, vs. **Job Almy** of Tiverton, yeoman, in action of dower, concerning a dwelling and yard in Newport of which Henry was seized 6 November 1754, bounded south 60 feet and west 77 feet on land of **William Sandford**, north 60 feet on **William Richardson**, east 88 feet on the street. Henry died 7th day [---] 1756. Defendant answered that Henry West on 27 August 1753 deeded the property in mortgage to **John Tryer**; case withdrawn.

984. **Rebecca Babboult** of Newport, widow, vs. **Mary Taggart** of Newport, widow, for money due by note. (Docket No. 19)

985. **Thomas Greene** of Newport, shopkeeper, vs. **George Cooper** of same, an infant son and heir at law to **Robert Cooper** of Newport, mariner, dec'd, for money due by book. **John Cooke** attorney. (Docket No. 20)

986. **Margaret Briggs** of Little Compton, widow and administratrix of the estate of **John Briggs** of Little Compton, yeoman, deceased, vs. **Constant Bowen** of Newport, shipwright, to recover a debt due by book. (Docket No. 22)

987. **Peter Cook** of Newport, merchant, vs. **John Collogan** of Island of Teneriffe in Dominion of King of Spain, merchant, for £29:16:2 due by note dated 3 November 1761. **John Cooke** attorney. (Docket No. 23)

988. **May Davis** of Newport, goldsmith, vs. **John Sunderlin** of Exeter, for debt due by note. (Docket No. 30)

989. **Thomas George** of Newport, gentleman, vs. **Ruth Lovel** of Newport, widow, in an action of trespass, for witholding from the plaintiff possession of one room or chamber of his dwelling in Newport. (Docket No. 34)

990. **William Gyles** of Newport, shopkeeper, vs. **Benjamin Sheffield Jr.** of Jamestown, gentleman, for non-performance of promise. Charter-Party Indenture dated 30 July 1762 signed by both, witnessed by **Joseph Vickers** and **Anthony Shaw**: plaintiff was owner of sloop *Victory*, burthen ca 30 tons, leased to the defendant for one whole voyage to be made from Newport to New Providence one of the Bahama Islands and back again. . . plaintiff promised to fit sloop at own cost . . . defendant promised to pay £250 per month and to victual and man sloop, pay Port charges, etc. Defendant did not keep and perform his covenant. (Docket No. 37)

991. **Edward Lillebridge** of Newport, cooper, vs. **John Saunders Jr.** of Westerly, mariner, for non-performance of promise, 11 October 1763, for value received from services and 3 barrels of good merchantable cider on request. **Weight Saunders** made oath concerning delivery of the writ.

992. **William Stead** of the City of London, merchant, vs. **Jacob Isaacks** of Newport, merchant, for non-performance of promise, claiming that on 28 December 1761 at Newport, one **Napthali Hart**, merchant, made a bill of exchange and directed same to **Abraham Hart** in London, for £650 Sterling.

993. **James Easton, Nicholas Easton,** of Newport, **Peter Barker** of Middletown, **Giles Slocum** and **Jacob Mott Jr.**, of Portsmouth, yeomen, vs. **James Burroughs** of Newport, mariner, for non-payment

of rent for a lot 100 by 150 feet, bounded east on New Thames Street, north on a street, south on the 16th lot, west on the harbour, of which premises **Jacob Mott** and **Thomas Cornell**, late of Portsmouth, **Wm. Barker** and **Samuel Thurston**, late of Newport, yeomen, were original proprietors. Rent was $25 New England currency annually. (Docket No. 45)

994. **Thomas Rodman** of Newport, mariner, vs. **Robert Proud** of Newport, watchmaker, in an action of trespass, charging that the defendant entered and withheld a lot and west half of a dwelling house in Newport, bounded east on land in possession of **John Dennis**, south on the street, west on land of **William Wanton**, belonging to devisees of **Samuel Rodman**, dec'd, and northerly on Queen Street, of which the plaintiff was possessed on 1 April 1764. (Docket No. 51)

995. **Ruth Thurston** of Newport, widow, **Jonathan Thurston, Joseph Thurston**, and **Elizabeth Thurston**, all of Newport, infants, children and devisees of **Jonathan Thurston**, merchant, dec'd, vs. **Constant Wilbore**, cooper, **Mary Hughs**, widow, and **Robert Pettys**, taylor, all of Newport, in an action of trespass, to recover a lot about 40 feet square with three shops or tenements, of which **Jonathan Thurston**, dec'd, was possessed on 3 August 1757 . . . In his will of that date [*he*] devised to his two sons **Jonathan** and **Joseph** half of all his estate and to his wife and daughters **Elizabeth** and **Deborah** the other half. **Deborah** died within age and without heirs, and the plaintiff was possessed of the whole until 15 April 1764. Evidence: Mortgage Deed from **William Thurston** to **Jonathan Thurston**, dated 20 August 1756; the widow of **William Thurston** appeared per her attorney **August Johnston, Esq.**, and requested her dower in the premises. (Docket No. 56)

996. **Thomas Cook** of Portsmouth, yeoman, vs. **Benjamin Hall** of Portsmouth, cordwainer alias gentleman, for £310 due by note dated 12 March 1762. (Docket No. 62)

997. **Margaret Briggs** of Little Compton, widow, vs. **Thomas Howland** of Newport, schoolmaster, for debt by book. (Docket No. 6[-])

998. **William Bull** of Newport, mariner, vs. **Jonathan Rogers** of Newport, shopkeeper alias Esq., in an action of trespass, charging that on 5 January 1764 the defendant assaulted him and hit him with a cane. Verdict for plaintiff, £24 and costs. (Docket No. 68)

999. **Jacob Rodrigues Rivera, Aaron Lopez** and **Isaachar Polock**, all of Newport, merchants, vs. **James Burroughs** of Newport, mariner, for non-performance of promise. On 3 March 1763 the defendant received of the plaintiffs goods and became their bailiff [*for*] "six firkins of butter, a barrell of indigo, sugar, sole leather, Indian corn, some good, some average, barrel staves and wax," and promised to transport it all to "a place called Orataira, a seaport in Island of Teneriffe." **John Cooke** attorney for the plaintiffs. (Docket No. 71)

1000. **Job Bennet Jr.** of Newport, Esq., vs. **Thomas Chadwick** of Newport, fisherman, in an action of trespass, to recover land and a house in Newport, bounded 32 feet on the street, of which land the defendant was possessed on 5 September 1754, when by deed of that date he sold it to the plaintiff, who enjoyed peaceable possession until 20 September 1764 when the defendant dispossessed him of it. (Docket No. 128)

1001. **Sarah Stanton** of Newport, spinster, vs. **Joseph Gould** of Newport, truckman, in an action of trespass, for withholding from her possession of a dwelling house in Newport, bounded north on land of **Benjamin Gould** and south on a lane, it being property of which **Benjamin Stanton**, late of Newport on 4 April 1760 was possessed and by will of that date devised to the plaintiff, who after his death on 10 July 1762 entered the premises and was of them possessed until 5 May 1764 when the defendant by force of arms, etc., did enter and expel her. (Docket No. 130)

1002. **Thomas Hassard** of Newport, merchant vs. **Ebenezer Slocum** of North Kingstown, boatman alias fisherman, to recover £503:8 due for sugar, corn, and salt, in 1760. (Docket No. 131)

1003. **John Baker** of Boston, merchant, administrator of the estate of **Matthew Moreau** late of Island of St. Eustatius in West Indies, merchant, dec'd, vs. **Augustus Johnson** of Newport, Esq., for an accounting of the time when the defendant was bailiff of **Matthew Moreau,** in the month of July 1758 at Newport, of the sloop *Tryal* of the burthen of about 70 tons, together with cargo ". . . 280 baggs of coffe, 64 hogsheads of sugar," etc. (Docket No. 185)

1004. **Amy Weeden** of Newport, widow, administratrix of the estate of **William Weeden** of Newport, painter, dec'd, vs. **Robert Stanton**, now resident in Newport, yeoman, for £200 Old Tenor due by note dated 9 June 1761. (Docket No. 188)

1005. **Ezekiel Burroughs**, distiller and **James Burroughs**, mariner, both of Newport, vs. **Lodowick Updike** of North Kingstown, yeoman, to recover £674:15:05 due by note dated 4 November 1763. (Docket No. 203)

1006. **Nathaniel Parent** of City and Colony of New York, mariner, vs. **Joseph Ireson** of Newport, glazier, to recover money due by note dated 10 May 1764. (Docket No. 208)

1007. **Thomas Attwood** of Newport, shopjoiner, vs. **James Bradley** of Newport, innholder, and **Elisabeth** his wife, in an action of trespass. On 11 January 1764 being specially appointed Deputy Sheriff to serve a writt at the suit of **John Batty** of Newport, inn-holder, for £54:18 due against **Thomas Thurber**, late resident of Newport, mariner, the plaintiff did serve same on the body of **Thomas Thurber** in the evening of said 11 January and had his body in custody, at which time the said **Elisabeth** did use force and arms to rescue said **Thurber** from the plaintiff and suffer him to escape. (Docket No. 296)

1008. **Abraham Anthony** of Portsmouth, yeoman, vs. **John Brown** of Warren, Esq., High Sheriff of County of Bristol. On the first Monday in March 1764, the plaintiff obtained a judgment against one **Ben** (so-called) a "Mollatta Boy lately resident in Portsmouth, labourer," for £10:19, but the defendant has kept Ben prisoner in Goal and now suffered him to escape, and the plaintiff is unable to recover judgment. Deposition of **Lydia Cockrum**, 21 November 1764, that ". . .within 7 or 8 weeks past I have seen mulatto boy **Ben** at Mr. **Hopestill Potter's** come to the well in Bristol to fetch water sundry times and on said Potter's land. . .and heard Mrs. **Hopestill Potter** tell **Simeon Munro** the Deputy Sheriff that she did not know but that she had done a damige by telling that she had seen said **Ben** out of gole." (Docket No. 298)

1009. **Joseph Bull** of Newport, mariner, vs. **May Davis** of Newport, goldsmith, for non-performance of promise 3 March 1764, when the defendant received from the plaintiff one silver tea pot of £12 value. (Docket No. 301)

1010. **William Burroughs** of Newport, house carpenter, vs. **Lodowick Updike** of North Kingstown, yeoman, to recover £143:8:3 due for boards and planks delivered. (Docket No. 210)

1011. **Gideon Cornell** of Newport, Esq., vs. **William Lake** of Newport, schoolmaster, administrator of the estate of **David Lake** late of Newport, merchant, deceased intestate. The plaintiff and **David Lake** were jointly concerned in a vessel called the snow *Windsor*, **Jer**[h] **Clark** commander, at Newport on 10 May 1760 when it was taken from Port Louis to Jamaica by an English man of war, carried into Jamaica, and then condemned. Plaintiff appealed to the Council of Appeal in Great Britain and expended about £405:12 Jamaican Currency. (Docket No. 250)

1012. **Thomas Freebody** of Newport, mariner, vs. **John Holmes** of Middletown, yeoman, in an action of trespass, charging that the defendant on 8 June 1765 "entered his close in Middletown and threw down one rod of his stone wall to the value of 10s and one rod of fence, thereby leaving open said Close and letting thereinto and drove thro said Close upwards of 200 sheep which eat up and destroyed the plaintiff's grass then growing in his Close to the value of £4." (Docket No. 251)

1013. **Thomas Richardson** of Newport and **John Lyon** of Rehoboth, merchants, vs. **John Rider** of Newport, mariner, concerning a contract of assurance in May 1760 when the plaintiffs were owners of the sloop *Sarah* whereof **Caleb Corey** was master on a trading voyage at Monte Christo and thence to Newport . . . on 30 April 1761 she was surprised and taken upon the high seas by the French Privateer Sloop *Vaillant* commanded by one **Capt. Delamorlier**.

Copy of Protest, signed by **Caleb Cory** [*sic*], 21 May 1761 before **Henry Ward** of Newport, Esq., Secretary and Public Notary. Corey, master of the sloop *Sarah*, burthen of 60 tons or thereabouts by Register and navigated by six men . . . sailed from Monte Christi on the Island of Hispaniola on 28 April last laden with molasses and some dry goods bound to Newport . . . taken 30th by a French Sloop named the *Vaillant* commanded by one Capt. **Delamorlier** . . . they took from Corey one Silver Watch being his own property. He ransomed the said vessel and cargo for the consideration of one silver watch, two silver hilted swords, some other dry goods and 1400 pieces of eight. They had plundered the sloop of some part of the rigging and the people of some of their clothes. Delamorlier took from **Lawrence Pain** who was Supercargo 526 pieces of eight which was agreed to be in part of the ransom money . . . on the next day being the first of May he was dismissed and proceeded on his voyage and arrived in Newport this day . . . by reason of the capture he desireth a Regal Protest. **Lawrance Pain**, Supercargo, and **John Sanford**, Mate of the *Sarah*, signed a statement that Corey's declaration was true.

File includes a detailed invoice of the cargo, accounting for about 65 hogsheads of molasses belonging to the owners, 11 for **Lawrence Payne**, 12 for **Caleb Corey**, master, one for **John Sanford**, five for **Ephraim Mancester**, and two for **Brayton**. Also an accounting of the items plundered, "about 5 leagues from Turks Island NNW of them" by **Monsieur De Labaton** [*sic*] in a French Privateer Sloop: including a coil of rigging, lanthorn, hammer, oar 15 feet long, cedar buckets, fish hooks, a case knife, fork, and two spoons, drawing knives, a cooper's ax, a vise, sail needles, padlocks, a pendant, and a pepper box, total value £196:5. "After which they obliged me to Ransom the said Vessel & Cargo for the following Articles": 2 silver hilted swords, 2 silver watches, 2 dozen worsted caps, several dozen stockings of various kinds including white cotton and brown thread, and a large quantity of white gloves, both men's and women's, for a total of £4195:14.

Copy of the policy of assurance [*printed form*], dated 12 May 1761, whereby **Thomas Richardson** and **John Lyon** insured for £8000 Old-Tenor "at & from Monta Christo to the Harbour of Newport in Rhode Island upon any Goods as also upon the body Tackle & apperil of & in Sloop Sarah Molasses Valued at £220 pr hogshead . . . said Vessel & goods at & from Monta Christo aforesaid and so shall continue & endure untill said Sloop shall arrive in the Harbour of Newport . . . & there be moored 24 hours in safety." At the bottom was a record of payments made to **Thomas Wickham, Moses Levy, Joshua Saunders, Joshua Amy, Stephen Wanton, John Treby, John**

Mawdsley, Daniel Fourtane, Francis Brinley Jr, George Gibbs, William Richardson, Simon Pease Jr, John Dockray, Metcalf Bowler, and **Issachar Polock**, for sums ranging from £300 to £500; three other names were crossed out (**Evan Malbone, William Vernon**, and **Charles Weeks**). (Docket No. 267)

1014. **Giles Sanford**, blacksmith, and **Elizabeth** his wife and **Israel Church**, cooper, and **Sarah** his wife, all of Middletown, vs. **Isaac Smith** of Middletown, yeoman, in an action of trespass and ejectment for possession of a certain tract of land containing about 100 acres being part meadow, part pasture, part arable, and part orchard, with a barn and cribb thereon standing and also the westermost half part of a dwelling house standing on the said premises situate in Middletown and belonging to the plaintiff. The land was part of a larger tract containing about 200 acres, bounded northwest on land lately belonging to **Peleg Smith**, dec'd, northeasterly on land of **John Holmes**, easterly on the sea or salt water, and southwesterly on land belonging to **Isaac** and **Elisha Smith**, of which larger tract of land **Edward Smith** late of Middletown, yeoman, was on 13 July 1730 seized and made his will on that day, wherein among other things he gave the larger tract in the following manner . . . [*see full transcript of will below*] and on or about 18 September 1730 he died . . . **Phillip Smith** and **Elizabeth Smith** became seized of the larger tract as tenants for life and on or about 10 March 1731 [*they*] divided the tract and premises . . . now the plaintiffs say that Phillip Smith did never come to be of a sound disposing mind and understanding as he was in at the time of the making & publishing sd will, and continued so until he died on or about 10 April 1762 . . . the plaintiffs further say that by virtue of said devises the premises descended to the plaintiffs Elizabeth and Sarah who were the only children of the sd **William Smith** who died on or about 23 November 1741, and upon the death of the sd Phillip [*they*] became seized of said premises . . . until on or about 20 October 1764 when they were dispossessed thereof by the defendant. Writ dated 29 October 1764. (Docket No. 280)

The Will of Edward Smith, Newport, 1730:

In the Name of God Amen I Edward Smith of Newport in the County of Newport in ye Colony of Rhode Island and Providence Plantations in New England yeoman being of sound and disposing mind and memory tho weak in body thanks be given unto God for ye same and knowing that it is appointed for all men once to die do therefore make and ordain this my last will and testament in manner and form following Principally I recommend my soul to God that gave it and my body to the earth to be buried in decent and Christian manner firmly believing I shall receive ye same at ye Resurrection of the just and as for such worldly estate as it hath pleased God to bestow upon me in this life I give devise and dispose of ye same in manner and form following.

Imprimus. I will that my just debts and funeral charges be well and truly paid within some reasonable time after my decease.

Item. I give and bequeath unto my son **Philip Smith** and my well beloved wife, **Elizabeth Smith** during the term of their lives the north east part of my farm whereon I now dwell with all ye houses outhouses and edifices thereon standing and being which land is bounded as followeth Viz^{t}: north west on land of my brother **Peleg Smith** north easterly on land of **Joseph Holmes**, easterly on land on ye sea or salt water, and south westerly on land by me in this will given to my sons **Isaac** and **Elisha Smith**. And further my will is that if it should please God to restore my son Philip to be of a sound and disposing mind and understanding then and in such case I give and bequeath the abovesaid land by me before given to him and his mother to him my said son in fee simple the one half thereof to be possest by my said wife during her life notwithstanding.

Item. If it should please God that my son Philip should die before he should come to be of a sound & disposing mind and understanding then and in such case I give and bequeath all ye aforesaid north east part of my farm and ye buildings thereon to my son **William Smith** and to his heirs.

If it should please God that my son William should live to enjoy the aforesaid north east part of my farm and buildings thereon as aforesaid then my will is that ye legacy of six hundred pounds by me given him in this will, to be paid him by my sons Isaac and Elisha Smith be void and if he shall have received ye same before he shall have right to enjoy or enter upon ye aforesaid north east part of my farm as aforesaid, I will and order him to repay back to my said sons Isaac and Elisha the six hundred pound legacy he recd of them, and in case he shall refuse or neglect to pay ye same by ye space of six months after his right has arrived to him in ye aforesaid north east part of my land then I will and order that my said sons Isaac and Elisha enter into ye said lands and hold them to their own use until they are paid the aforesaid sum of six hundred pounds out of the profits thereof.

Item. I give unto my son **Isaac Smith** and to his heirs all that my house and land which I purchased of **Samuel Baley** lying in Newport aforesaid, also I give to my said son Isaac and to his heirs all those lands I bought of

Margaret Wrightington and are butted and bounded as in and by ye deed thereof may fully appear. Also I give to my son Isaac my Negro man called **Primus** two oxen five cows five two year old cattle, five yearling cattle, (all neat) & one hundred sheep.

Item. I give unto my son **Elisha Smith** and to his heirs all that my land herein after mentioned and is butted and bounded as followeth viz[t]: to range from that land I purchased from **Samuel Bailey** Strait in ye line of fence that devides ye pasture from ye little meadow next to ye little swamp so called so ranging with a strait line to a place called Wood's Castle Rocks, and the same is bounded northerly on land devised in this will to my son Philip and to my wife, during their lives, easterly on ye sea and south easterly on the sea and south westerly on ye former creek according to ye former grant in the year 169[-] and westerly on land before given to my son Isaac (wherein is contained all that land purchased of **Major Henry Tew** deceased and of my brother in law **Henry Tew** as by deed will appear, the old meadow, the new meadow, the field and part of the new pasture so called to the aforementioned range. Also I give to my said son Elisha Smith my Negro boy named **Orson** one yoke of oxen five two year old cattle five yearling cattle (all neat) and one hundred sheep.

Item. I give to my sons each a drift way through each others land as they and their heirs shall from time to time have occasion for, they doing no damage willingly to one another,

Item. I give and bequeath to my son **Edward Smith** and to his heirs all that house and land I bought of my brother **Peleg Smith** lying in ye town of Newport, also I give to my said son Edward two hundred and thirty pounds to be paid him out of my personal estate also I give him one Negro boy called **Cudgh**.

Item. I give and bequeath unto my son **Henry Smith** six hundred pounds in current bills of credit to be paid him by my sons Isaac and Elisha each one half when he shall arrive to ye age of twenty one years, and further my will is that if my said sons shall not pay him the said sum of six hundred pounds (within six months after his arrivall to ye age of twenty one years of age then it shall and may be lawfull for my said son Henry to enter into all those lands given by me to my said sons Isaac and Elisha and to hold the same to their own use till he is paid ye said sum of six hundred pounds out of the profit thereof also I give him my Negro boy **Breemer**.

Item. I give and bequeath unto my son **William Smith** six hundred pounds in current bills of credit to be paid him by my sons Isaac and Elisha each one half when he shall arrive to twenty one years of age and further my will is that if my son Isaac and Elisha shall not pay him ye said sum of six hundred pounds within six months after his arrival to ye age twenty one years then it shall and may be lawfull for my said son William to enter into all ye lands given by me to my said sons Isaac and Elisha and to hold ye same to his own use till he is paid ye said sum of six hundred pounds out of ye profits thereof Also I give him my Negro boy **Cuff**.

Item. I give and bequeath unto my daughter **Mary** one hundred and fifty pounds in current bills of credit out of my personal estate also I give my said daughter Mary one feather bed and furniture,

Item, I give and bequeath unto my daughter **Elizabeth** eighty pounds in bills of credit out of my personal estate.

Item. I give and bequeath unto my daughter **Sarah** eighty pounds out of my personal estate.

Item. I give and bequeath unto my daughter **Ph[*ebe*]** one hundred and sixty pounds out of my personal estate and one feather bed and furniture.

Item. I give and bequeath unto my daughter **Hannah** one hundred and sixty pounds out of my personal estate and one feather bed and furniture.

Item. I give and bequeath unto my daughter **Dorcas** one hundred and sixty pounds out of my personal estate and one feather bed and furniture.

Item. I give and bequeath unto my daughter **Ann** one hundred & sixty pounds like money out of my personal estate and one feather bed and furniture.

Item. My will is that my son **Philip** and my wife have one third part of ye hay and grass being on that part of my land given to my sons **Isaac** and **Elisha** at my decease and my said two sons shall have ye others two thirds, and my said wife and son **Philip** shall have one third part of the grass that shall grow thereon for two years next after my decease they being at ye charge of cuting and makeing of the same with full & free liberty to carry ye same of ye said land for their wintering their stock.

Item. I give and bequeath unto my well beloved wife my Indian Woman called **Joan** and my two girls named **Jenny** and **Dinah** and two feather beds and furniture all which bequests with all those others give by me to her in this will, I give her in full satisfation of her dower.

Item. I give and bequeath unto my loving wife and to my son **Philip** all ye rest residue & remainder of my personal estate after my debts & legacies paid to be equally divided between them.

Lastly I nominate constitute and appoint my well beloved wife to be my sole executrix to this my last will and testament till my son **Philip** shall attain to be of sound and diposing mind and understanding and then my said son Philip shall be my executor to this my last will ratifieing & allowing this and no other to be my last will & testament. In witness whereof I have hereunto set my hand and seal this 1th day of July in ye fourth year of his Majestys reign, annoque Domini 1730.

Signed sealed prounounced & declared by ye said Edward Smith to be his last will and testament in presence of **Wm Barker, Nicholas Easton, Richd Ward**

Nicholas Easton and **Richard Ward** in Council this 5th October 1730 Made oath that they saw **Edward Smith** sign seal & declare the foregoing instrument to be his last will and testament and that he was of a sound mind and that they in his presence with **William Barker** at ye same time signed as witnesses. Test Wm Coddington Council Clerk

Recorded Octr 5th 1730 – pr Wm Coddington Council Clerk

Newport: The above and foregoing six pages are a true copy from ye Town Council Book of Newport No 7 Pages 183-184-185 & 186. Newport April 30th AD 1770 Witness Wm Coddington Council Clerk

1015. **Simon Newton**, distiller, of Newport vs. **Joshua Bicknell** of Warren, yeoman, and wife **Hannah**, who when sole was **Hannah Norton**, for money due for goods. (Docket No. 281)

1016. **George Pearce** of Little Compton, yeoman and executor of the will of **Elisabeth Sisson** late of Little Compton, widow, dec'd, vs. **Bathsheba Woodman** of Little Compton, widow, administratrix of the estate of **Sylvester Woodman** late of Little Compton, yeoman. Certain goods were due to Elisabeth by the will of **John Woodman**, late of Little Compton . . . **Sylvester** was executor of the will of **John Woodman**, whose wife sd **Elizabeth** then was. Case went to referees. (Docket No. 283)

1017. **Henry Knowles** of Newport, mariner, vs. **Samuel Burroughs** of Newport, shopjoyner, for £100 due by a contract of assurance. On 19 April 1760 the plaintiff had "a quantity of sugar, molasses, Indigo, and other merchandise shipt on board the sloop *Royal Thoney* whereof he was master, at a place called the Ocoyco in the West Indies . . . wanted to insure it . . . therefore caused a certain writing called a Policy of assurance used among Merchants to be made out. The Defendant did underwrite with his own name and for £22. . .. said vessel sailed from Ocoyes for Newport on or about 11 April 1760 and was seized by His Majesty's Ship *Enterprise* and all [*cargo*] carried away." (Docket No. 293)

1018. **Elnathan Hammond** and **David Moon**, shopkeepers and **Caleb Arnold**, carpenter, all of Newport, a committee appointed by members of the First Congregational Church in Newport, formerly under the pastoral care of late Mr. **Nathaniel Clapp** and **Jona. A. Helyard**, dec'd, now under pastoral care of Rev. Mr. **Wm. Vinal**, vs. **David Huntington** of Newport, to recover £22 due by bond dated 1 April 1762, originally signed by **Daniel Creulz**, baker, and **David Huntington**. (Docket No. 299)

1019. **Mary Hall** of Portsmouth, widow, and **Benjamin Hall** of Newport, Esq., executors of the will of **William Hall** late of Portsmouth, Esq., deceased, alias cordwainer, vs. **John Allin Jr.** of Portsmouth, taylor, to recover £650 due by bond dated 5 March 1748, signed by **John Allin** and **John Allin Jr.**, witnessed by **Benjamin Freeborn** and **Caleb Lawton**. (Docket No. 301)

1020. **Nathan Sheffield** of Newport, cordwainer, vs. **George Gardner** of New Shoreham, yeoman, to recover £1088:8 Old Tenor due by bond dated 1 June 1763. (Docket No. 308)

1021. **Matthew Robinson** of South Kingstown, gentleman, vs. **Temperance Grant** of Newport, widow, and **Patrick Grant**, admistrators of the estate of **Sueton Grant**, to recover £20,000 due by bond dated 10 October 1744. (Docket No. 323)

1022. **Jane Brown**, widow, **Jeremiah Brown**, merchant, both of Newport, and **Robert Brown**, yeoman, and **Matthew Robinson**, gentleman, both of South Kingstown, executors of the will of **John Brown** late of Newport, merchant, dec'd, vs. **Temperance Grant**; on 10 October 1744, the defendant was bound together with the plaintiffs to the Trustees of Colony [*probably a mortgage*]. (Docket No. 325)

1023. **Mary Ward** of Newport, widow and executrix of the will of **Richard Ward** of Newport, Esq., vs. **Phebe Havens** of Newport, widow, to recover £58:5:10 due by book, for which **Richard Ward** had, on the last Monday of May 1763, received a judgement against the defendant. (Docket No. 326)

1024. **Mary Ward** of Newport, widow and executrix of the will of **Richard Ward** of Newport, Esq., vs. **Thomas Durfey** of Middletown, innholder, to recover debt of £72:17:6, for which **Richard Ward** had, on the last Monday of May 1763, received a judgement against the defendant. (Docket No. 327)

1025. **Sarah Lawton** of Newport, widow and administratrix of the estate of **George Lawton**, late of Newport, shopkeeper, vs. **Samuel Little Billings** of Newport, taylor, for debt due by note. (Docket No. 334)

1026. **Benjamin Shearman** of Portsmouth, husbandman, vs. **John Dockray** of Newport, merchant, charging a covenant broken. On 25 March 1761, the defendant had leased to the plaintiff all his land in North Kingstown which he purchased of **Frederick Phillips, Samuel Albro,** and **Benjamin Congdon,** and also a pair of oxen. The plaintiff was to keep the fences in repair, and the defendant to pay labourers' wages, and the plaintiff to provide them with meat, drink and lodging. (Docket No. 353)

1027. **May Davis,** goldsmith, of Newport, vs. **Joseph Bull** in a case of trespass involving assault over a teapot [*cf. No. 1009*]. **John Sims** of Newport, school-master, testified in court, May term 1764, that

". . . near five of the clock in the afternoon of the ninth day of March last in this present year 1764 [*I*] went into the then shop of Mr May Davis of Newport goldsmith, where was siting Capt Joseph Bull and Mr **Isaac Touro,** and Mr Davis was standing up; [*I*] saw a peice of gold and some silver money in the hand of the sd Bull, and he speaking to Davis, sayd Then you wont take the Money? I won't take that money saith Davis. Now sayth Bull you promised my Father [**Joseph**] Nichols that if I would bring you twenty-three dollars, yould deliver me the Pot (meaning as [*I*] presumed a teapot which had ben pledged by Bull to Davis) and I believe my Father Nichols's word will be taken. I never sayed saith Davis that I would take three and twenty dollars without I was clear of the charges. You did'nt say anything about charges Faith say's Bull and my Father Nichols will swear it, And, I have a good action against you for that promise, make use of it then sayth Davis. Pray says Bull what charges have you to pay. I took the writt out of the Clerks Office I paid the Entry of the Action and the Jury. What charges have you to pay, I suppose **Jemmy Honyman** wants a few days attendance fees, and I wont pay him any. Well then, says Davis if there is no charges to pay why won't you give me from under your hand to clear me from them. Because I wont sayth Bull. I did intend to pay the charges but now I wont, for Faith you never mentioned charges to Father Nichols, and if you had'nt included the charges in your demand, what a Devil could you demand three and twenty dollars for, I had but twenty of you? Why say's Davis the note was for twenty and a half and I ask'd one dollar for interest since it became due, and there was one I gave Mr Honyman for his fee (and he was a damn'd mean fellow for takeing of it in such a damn'd iniquitous [---] says Bull) well that made twenty two and a half saith Davis & the other half dollar was for some small extra charges. Well say, saith Bull, if you'll take the money. Where is your money says Davis, I hav'nt seen it yett. I'll see your money and then I'll refuse it. Here it is Faith says Bull, and put his hand in his pocket as [*I*] thought to feel for some paper money. [*I*] then went to the other end of the shop and stood with [*my*] back to the disputants, and heard Bull say here 'tis I'll pay you Faith at dollars eight pound a piece, but instantly recalld his words, and said no I wont neither let me see fifteen and eight is twenty three, Here look here **Mr Sims** says Bull. Mr Sims hath no business with it says Davis. [*I*] still keeping [*my*] standing, heard the said Bull say, heres fifty six pounds, eight dollars, and these make twenty three will you take it. No sayeth Davis. Let it alone then says Bull. After a short pause Davis sits down, and says but, Mr Bull what part of this affier has been so iniquitous? The whole affair say'th Bull from the beginning was a contriv'd peice of damn'd villany. Then get out of my shop say's Davis, I won't say's Bull. I'll open the door for you says Davis, so you may say'th Bull. Davis stept and opened the door, and step't on one side, and say's march, march off, Bull arose in a rage and was comeing toward Davis, saying you little insignificant puppy if I had you out of doors I'd whip your gutts out. [*I*] step't between them with [*my*] face towards Bull, and sayed Pho, Pho Capt Bull what are you after, Bull then walk't along toward the door, Davis step't nimbly across the shop to the foot of the stair-case, where were two hickory sticks, [*I*] step't up to him, and sayed you shan't fight, Bull turns about & seeing the stick catch'd hold of it Davis then had it in both hands but let go one hand to take the other strik but miss'd it and catch'd a chizle rod with an iron ring at the bite end Davis pull'd the stick and Bull pull'd the same, Davis held with one hand, Bull with two, Davis with the other hand held the chizel rod, and aimed several blows at Bulls hands to make him let go, Bull being strongest had almost pull'd Davis out of doors, to prevent which Davis took advantage of being brought up by the door post, and thereby lost a peice of skin from one of his thumbs, which made him let go the stick, and Bull carryed it off in triumph." (Docket No. 392)

1028. **Elizabeth Gardner** and **Caleb Gardner** of Newport vs. **Jonathan Hazard** of South Kingstown, yeoman, to recover money due by note dated 5 July 1763. (Docket No. 394)

1029. **Penelope Stelle** of Newport, widow and administratrix of **Isaac Stelle**, late of Newport, merchant, vs. **Abiel Cook** of Little Compton, yeoman, to recover £100 Old Tenor due by note dated 29 Aug 1760, signed by **Abial Cook**. (Docket No. 407)

1030. **John Gladding** of Newport, infant, mariner, by his father and guardian **Joseph Gladding** of Newport, cordwainer, vs. **William Bull** of Newport, mariner, in an action of trespass, charging that the defendant did assault him with a rope at Cape Francois 10 March 1763. On 7 January 1764, the defendant's father **Hennery Bull** provided bail. **Jacob Mias** of Newport, mariner, deposed and said that Bull ordered Gladding to go in the boat to fetch the captain . . . Gladding was sick, not well enough to go; Bull said he was well enough . . . took a piece of rope called a ratline and beat Gladding. **John Fones** of North Kingstown, now resident in Newport, mariner, testified that he was on board the sloop *Hope* at Cape Franceway. (Docket No. 409)

1031. **Stephen Hicks** of Tiverton, gentleman and assigne of **Samuel Hicks** vs. **John Andrew**, now resident in Newport, mariner, to recover a debt of £17:15 (one dollar = 8 shillings). (Docket No. 414)

1032. **Thomas Chadwick** of Newport, fisherman, vs. **Jonathan Easton** of Newport, gentleman, to recover £42 Old Tenor due by book, for carting a load of fish to town, and carting two loads over to the pond. (Docket No. 416)

1033. **Sarah Gray** of Tiverton, widow and executrix of the will of **Philip Gray** of Tiverton, yeoman, vs. **Jonathan Grinnell** of Tiverton, yeoman, to recover debt due by note. (Docket No. 167)

1034. **Jonathan Sowle** of Tiverton, yeoman, assignee of **Joseph Sowle**, vs. **Jonathan Foster** of Westerly, yeoman, for 132 Spanish Milled Dollars, due by note dated July 1763. (Docket No. 176)

1035. **Jeremiah Clarke** of Newport, mariner, vs. **Shearman Clarke** of Newport, mariner, to recover $50 due on a contract of assurance. On 30 December 1730, the defendant did assure goods laden on board the ship *Caesar* whereof the plaintiff was master, on a voyage from Philadelphia to the Coast of Africa and from thence back to James River in Virginia . . . rate of $16 for every $100 assured . . . arrived coast of Africa 25 January 1761 and continued to trade until 22 September 1761 when departed Annamaboo on coast of Africa, bound for Guadaloupe . . . on 13 October before could get off said coast, ship and all cargo were seized by the Enemy, near to and in sight of Isle of St. John's on coast of Africa.

Depositions of **Jeremiah Clarke**, late master, and **John Bodiner**, late mariner of said *Caesar*, that on 1 April 1762 . . . ship armed with 4 carriage and 6 swivel guns and 2 cohorns and navigated by 14 men . . . [*had*] sailed from Philadelphia 10 December 1760 . . . having completed their lading they sailed . . . having onboard 116 slaves on account of the owners . . . for Guadaloupe. . .taken by French Frigate *L'Amethyst* mounting 34 guns, who carried said ship into Isle of Princes where they sold her taking the slaves on board the Frigate . . . proceeded to Port Louis on Island of Hispaniola and there disposed of slaves . . . sd Jeremiah and John took Passage from thence with Capt. **George Nichols** for this port where they arrived yesterday. Judgement by referees: defendant clear by returning half the premium; plaintiff to pay costs. (Docket No. 178)

— May Term 1765 —

1036. **John Strange** of Freetown, mariner, vs. **John Miller** of Newport, to recover money due by note. (Docket No. 257)

1037. **James Gibbs** of Newport, mariner, vs. **Ephraim Tiffany** of Warren, yeoman, who owes him £126 Old Tenor for prison fees from 5 November 1764 to 2 April 1765, or 21 weeks @ £6; the plaintiff is an insolvent debtor committed to His Majesty's Goal in Newport on an execution at the suit of the defendant; by an Act of the General Assembly passed at Newport in June 1761, he hath the right to have and recover, etc. (Docket No. 278)

1038. **Wait Easton** of Newport, widow of **James Easton**, late of Middletown, yeoman, vs. **Nicholas Easton** of Newport, Esq., in an action of dower, to recover her right in land in Newport bounded west on land lately belonging to **John Easton** and **John Bennet**, north on land lately belonging to **Benjamin Stanton** and the late **Joseph Slocum**, east on land of **Josiah Bliss**, and south on land of the defendant; her husband was possessed of said land 25 March 1740, and he died 12 April 1764. Warrants dated 31 May 1765, to summon **Wait Easton**, widow of Newport, **Job Durfey** of Middletown, husbandman and **Sarah** his wife, **Robert Lawton** of Newport, mariner, and **Mercy** his wife, said **Wait, Sarah** and **Mercy** being devisees and legatees of **James Easton** late of said Middletown, yeoman, deceased, to appear at court to warrant **Nicholas Easton** of Newport, Esq., in the possession of one third part of a certain messuage or dwelling house, barn, cheese house, and about 85 acres of land being part meadow, part pasture, and part arable land, situate in Newport, bounded westerly partly on land late belonging to **John Easton** and partly on land of **John Bennet**, northerly partly on land lately belonging to **Benjamin Stanton** and partly on land late **Joseph Slocum**'s, easterly on land lately belonging to **Josias Bliss** and southerly on land of the sd Nicholas Easton . . . against a suit pending brought by the said Wait Easton. . . . (Docket No. 388)

1039. **Jane Rogers** of Newport, widow, vs. **Jacob Jackson**, a Free Negro Man of Newport, labourer, in an action of trespass, involving the west end of a certain dwelling house in Newport to the plaintiff belonging, bounded west on land of **James Gardner**, north on land of **Samuel Holmes**, east and south on land of the plaintiff; on 20 April 1761 she was possessed thereof for life, till 19 April 1765, when deprived of it by the defendant. (Docket No. 398)

1040. **Joram Place** of Newport, mariner, vs. **Capt. Sylvester Gardner** of North Kingstown, mariner, for money due by book; for rum, barrels, shirts, etc., some on ye coast of Africa, in year 1763. (Docket No. 423)

1041. **Richard Woodman** of Newport, cooper, vs. **James Bradley** of Newport, labourer alias innholder, charging that he wilfully enticed away from the plaintiff an apprentice boy called **Paul McDaniel** knowing him to be the plaintiff's apprentice . . . by means of which he hath lost his servant. Depositions taken 3 June 1765 at Newport: **Nathaniel Emmons**, baker, said that he often fed the boy. **Thomas Jones** said that he worked in **Capt. Hill's** bake house, and the boy came in in rags, his heels out of his stockings . . . and the snow half leg deep. **Job Cook** stated that "I livd with **Mr. Woodman** going on two years . . . all the time **Paul McDaniel** had good working cloathes and a sute of good cloaths to go to meeting in . . . have seen him tear his cloaths on purpose and swear when them was gone he would have more."

1042. **John Perry** vs. **Richard Gifford**, both yeomen of Tiverton; appeal from verdict of October 1764 about an affair of June and July 1763 with 4 hogs. **Benjamin Negus** of Tiverton, labourer, testified in December 1763 that "as my brother **Job Negus** and my self was going together from Howlands ferry home & as we was agoing across the farm tht **John Perry** now lives on we fell into discourse about John Perrys loosing his hoggs & I askt my Brother if said Perry had found his hoggs & he answerd me no nor I beleive wont very Quick & further my Brother Job told me of his own free Voluntary will that his son **Thomas** told him that **Richard Gifford Thomas Negus John Brightman** & Two Black fellows that lived with sd Gifford drove sd hoggs down to ye shore & catcht them & confind them & carried them to Newport in **Peter Tallman's** boat & sold them, and as they was going by a Wharf in Newport Thomas Negus says to Gifford this won't do we shall be Catcht for here is **Joseph Cook** & **Balies** Sloop & then they Rowed down Town & sold Three of the smallest to **Mr. Workham** and one to an other man. . . . [*illegible in fold*] discourse with Thomas Negus and I told him to go and make up for he would bring more Scandal on himself than Ever he could get Clear of, and his answer to me was that if it is Ever found out I shall be Clear for I thought I was going to Carry them to the pound when we took them into the boat untill we got up with Commonfence point then Gifford says Come we will go to Newport & sell them. In [*the*] year 1764 as I was amending the wall Rich[d] Gifford says to me we will mend this wall & see if John Perrys hoggs will plague us this year as they did last year." In response to questions, Negus said he remembered that one of the smallest hogs had a black spot on his rump, and one was larger than the rest. **Pardon Cook** of Tiverton deposed that he asked Thomas Negus "which he thought would get the case John Perry or Richard Gifford & he sd he thought Perry would . . . by reason that Richard Gifford himself and John Brightman caught the hoggs & put them into the boat & carried to Newport & sold them some for five and some for five and six pence a pound . . . Gifford new they was John Perrys hoggs. . . ." (Superior Court 13,782)

1043. **Jacob Rivera** *et al* vs. **James Burroughs**, concerning the Sloop *Three Sallys*. (Superior Court 13,876)

– November 1765 –

General Sessions of the Peace

1044. **Priscilla Briggs** of Little Compton, singlewoman, lately delivered a bastard child yet living and likely to become chargeable [*to the town*] . . . said **Priscilla** accused **Stephen Woodworth** of Little Compton, labourer, as the father. **Mary Davenport**, widow, of Little Compton deposed and said that on 2 January 1764 she was carried as a midwife to **Priscilla Briggs** and delivered the child on 4 January . . . **Priscilla** was in travail the entire time. In her deposition, **Priscilla** mentioned her father **William Briggs**, deceased, and said that **Stephen Woodworth** on 2 April 1763 promised to marry her. **Mary Woodworth, Sarah Woodworth,** and **Deborah Smith** each testified that [*their brother*] **Stephen** was at home all day on 2 April; **Deborah** added that "I . . . and **Priscilla** and **Judah Head** and **Deborah Head** went from our house ye 2nd of April about 9 in ye evening . . . and **Priscilla** and I went to **Jonathan Records** and I left her there." **Priscilla** persisted in her account and **Stephen Woodworth** was ordered to post bond and pay costs, **Priscilla** to be publicly whipped 10 stripes or to pay 40 shillings Old Tenor.

1045. **Mary Pulman** wife of **John** of Exeter, labourer, "at Newport 12 September 1765 had five pieces of mettle made in the form of one Spanish Dollar and three-quarters of Spanish cobs and one half pistoreen . . . not silver . . . and did pass them to **John Dunn** of Uxbridge, wheelwright for true [*money*] . . . said **Mary Pulman** a cheat." Defendant answered that she got it of **David Codner** for cloth in his house in Exeter. Found guilty.

1046. **Mary Stoddard** of Little Compton, singlewoman, delivered a male bastard child born 19 July 1765, and accused **John Palmer Jr.** of Dartmouth as the father. John Palmer of Dartmouth and **Simeon Palmer** of Little Compton came before the justices and gave bond of £500 each.

1047. **Stoddard Lawton** of Tiverton, blacksmith alias mariner, on 21 October 1765 assaulted **Job Almy Jr.** of Tiverton, gentleman, in the house of **Job Almy, Esq.** of Tiverton.

– 1766 –
Superior Court

1048. September: **Samuel Slocum**, Town Clerk of Jamestown, *et al* vs. **Benjamin Sheffield** and **George Franklyn** of Jamestown, yeomen, and **John Barber** of North Kingstown, yeoman, concerning the estate of Capt. **Benjamin Sheffield**, claiming that they had not properly administered that estate and also the estate of the widow **Damaris Sheffield**.

Original will of **Damaris Sheffield** presented. It had been probated 23 June 1764, but **William Hazard** of Jamestown in behalf of the heirs claimed that it ought not to be probated because the testator had been judged *non compos mentis* and had a guardian who took her estate and leased it out for her support. **Samuel Slocum** and **Daniel Underwood** dissented from probate, which had been ordered by Town Council. The will was dated 15 February 1764, witessed by **John Barber, William Dyer, Samuel Youngs**, and **Jeffry Watson**. Damaris Sheffield of Jamestown, widow, in good health of body and perfet sound disposing mind and memory, appointed Benjamin Sheffield executor, and willed:

Item I Give and Bequeath unto my Three well beloved Daughters **Phebe Arnold, Abigail Carr,** and **Damaris Hull**, Five Shillings Lawfull money to Each of them, in Token of my Love, and Rememberance of them, but they have Received their Portions and part of my Estate already.

Item I Give and Bequeath unto my three Well beloved Granddaughters that is to say **Desire Fowler, Patience Nicolds**, and **Damaris Slocom**, all my Wearing apparil to be Equally Divided between them.

Item I Give and Bequeath unto my Duetifull and Well Beloved Son in Law **Benjamin Sheffield** all my Real Estate Lying and being a part of the Island Cauld and Known by the Name of Dutch Island and Lying in the Narraganset bay in the County of Newport and Colony of Rhode Island all whch I give and Bequeath unto him my said son In law Benjamin Sheffield, and unto his Heirs and assigns for Ever: I also give unto him my said son In law Benjamin Sheffield all the Rest and Residue of my Estate both Real and Personal . . . .

Jeffry Watson of South Kingstown testified at March term 1767 that he wrote **Damaris Sheffield**'s will for her in the house where she lived, upon a table by her side with no other person present "but every gift therein containd. . . . I tryed to put hir of and pirswaded hir not to make any [*will*] but she reply'd she had lived an honest woman all hir days and was desireous to dye one . . . could not be easy except she made a will, for now (said she) they will try to wrong **Benjamin Sheffield** out of the Negros his father gave him; for in the first place they insisted upon the Negros being inventoried as hir late husbands estate and Sheffield refused to have them inventoried as his fathers estate for they were gave to him years before but the Coun[*cillors*] said they should be apprized or they would give some body else letters of administration and to prevent any contention with the town council she pirswaded Sheffield to have the Negros apprized and asshured him it should make no odds with him for she would soon settel every thing with him as his father and she had agreed, and upon hir promiseing him so he had the Negros apprized and then the Councill emediately put hir under guardians and so Sheffield is like to be wronged."

Evidence in the file includes: Petition 5 January 1764 by **Phebe Arnold, Abigail Carr** and **Damaris Hull**, daughters of **Damaris Sheffield**, requesting a guardian for her; Capt. **Samuel Carr** of Newport with **Oliver Hull** of Jamestown and said **Phebe Arnold** appointed. Inventory of personal estate of Capt. **Benj[a] Sheffield** of Jamestown, shown by the widow **Damaris Sheffield**, 5 January 1764, totalling £60.12.2, including a Negro woman called **Hagar**, £30, and on 20 January were added a Negro man **Moses**, £45, Negro man **Ezekiel**, £40, Negro girl **Patience**, $10, and on 30 June, an old Indian woman **Phillis**, 4*d*.

Damaris Sheffield of Jamestown, widow, on 16 January 1764 gave power of attorney to her son-in-law **Benjamin Sheffield** of Jamestown, mariner.

Depositions of Mr. **Thomas Hazard** of Newport, merchant, **Ephraim Smith**, and Miss **Mary Frizby** of North Kingstown, who said that she had lived with **Damaris Sheffield** about two months. Depositions of Miss **Mary Cables** now residing Jamestown; of **Elizabeth Wheeler**, who said she had known **Damaris Sheffield** for 40 years and that during that time she worked at Taylor's Business for the said **Benjamin Sheffield** in his house; of **Thomas Bentley**; of **Sarah Green**, widow of **David Green** late of Jamestown, deceased, who was in her 83rd year; of Mr. **John Pain**, who was acquainted with **Damaris Sheffield** a great number of years.

Verdict 23 June 1764 for defendants with cost of suit. In September 1765, **Phebe Arnold**, widow, **James Carr**, yeoman, and his wife **Abigail**, **John Hull**, yeoman and his wife **Damaris**, all of Jamestown, appealed, but the earlier verdict was upheld. (Superior Court 13,779)

– May 1766 –

Inferior Court of Common Pleas

1049. **Benjamin Church** and **Bathsheba** his wife vs. **Benjamin Almy** concerning half the personal estate of **Thomas Coggeshall**, devised to **Bathsheba** by will. The whole estate totalled £43,632:4:3. Case begun in May 1764, finished May 1766; settled by referees **Pardon Tillinghast**, **Samuel Greene** and **Samuel Gibbs**. Summons issued to **Thomas Burges**, **James Coggeshall**, **Elisha Coggeshall**, **Benjamin Sayer**, **Nathaniel Coggeshall**, **Anstis Coggeshall**, and **Meriba Hall** of Newport. Various accountings in file, include "sundries received of **Benjamin Almy** on behalf of son **John Coggehall Almy**."

1050. **Henry Sowle** of Newport, taylor, vs. **Thomas Ninegrett** of Charlestown, gentleman, re debt of £12:17:6 due by note dated 23 December 1765. (Docket No. 2)

1051. **Elizabeth Peckham** of Middletown, spinster, daughter of **Daniel Peckham** of Middletown, vs. **John Slocum** of Middletown, husbandman, otherwise **John Slocum** of Newport, yeoman, re debt of 532 Spanish Milled Dollars due by note dated 11 November 1763. (Docket No. 10)

1052. **William Crossing** of Newport, shopkeeper, vs. **Jacob Harris** otherwise **Pearce**, a free Negro man residing in North Providence, labourer, to recover £366 due by note dated 14 December 1765 at Newport, signed by the defendant and **Deborah Pearce** and payable to the plaintiff. Defendant pleaded not guilty. (Docket No. 34)

1053. **Robert Lillibridge** of Newport, innholder, and wife **Sarah** who was one of the daughters of **Mercy Herle** [*? Haile*] late of Bristol, widow, deceased, vs. **Mary Haskel** of Bristol, widow, administratrix of sd **Mercy Herle**, for an accompt. An accounting dated May 1762 signed by **Mary Hascoll**, adm., was presented 16 May 1765 [*sic*]. Inventory dated May 1762: one Negro woman named **Luse**, £850; total was £871. Decision awarded £377:19 to the plaintiffs. (Docket No. 37)

1054. **Robert Lillibridge** of Newport, innholder, vs. **Gideon Sisson & Company** of Newport, merchant, re £1030:3:6 Old Tenor. Record of Proprietors Meeting of Long Wharff, convened at house of Mr. **Ja^s Hunt** at the *Sign of the Queen* this 24th June 1765 . . . including Mr. **Robert Lillibridge** and **Gideon Sisson**, chosen to oversee repairs of Long Wharf.

Deposition of **Job Caswell** that in the year 1765 he worked at repairing Long Wharf and **Robert Lillibridge** and **Gideon Sisson** were overseers "for carrying on of the work . . . Lillibridge worked as hard as he could carrying of logs and lifting . . . Mr. Sisson ordered we should mind nobody else but said Lillibridge." Asked whether as much work would have been done if Lillibridge had not been there, Caswell replied, "as much, but not half so well." Depositions were made also by **Edward Kenney** of Newport, carpenter, and **William Rude** of Newport, house carpenter. Decision awarded the plaintiff £387:10:10. (Docket No. 65)

1055. **Josiah Albro** of Portsmouth, weaver, vs. **Clarke Cornel** of Portsmouth, gentleman, to recover a debt due for boarding the defendant's wife 40 weeks beginning 24 April 1765 and ending 26 March 1766 at 12*s* per week. (Docket No. 67)

1056. **William Martin** of Jamestown, ferryman, counters a suit by **Griffin Barney**, ferryman, of Newport, by presenting his "account for half the freight of cattle and draft horse and sheep and hogs and lams and calfs and other things that my bot brought from your wharf [*in 1759*]." Barney had sued Martin in May 1763; paper in file: "**Jonathan Nichols** account for expences at settling Martin and Barne's accounts att june court, to sundrys of liquor £6:0:0." Referees **John Lawton, Matt^w Borden** and **Jonathan Nichols** decided for the plaintiff, £5:18:18. (Docket No. 109)

1057. **Martha Honeyman** of Newport, widow, vs. **Michael Lemy** of Newport, gentleman, to recover a debt: $12 and 1/2 and 1/8 [*sic*], for six weeks board at $2 per week for his boy, one week at 1/4 dollar . . . mending chairs . . . lb candles . . . black ball. (Docket No. 193)

1058. **Sarah Lawton** of Newport, widow and administratrix of **George Lawton** late of Newport, merchant, deceased intestate, vs. **Samuel Taylor** of Newport, fisherman, to recover debt due by a note dated 11 January 1765 to **George Lawton** in his lifetime. (Docket No. 201)

1059. **Job Bennett** of Newport, Esq., only surviving executor of the will of **Daniel Amory** late of Newport, mariner, deceased, vs. **Abraham Borden** of Westerly, to recover a debt due by note dated 25 November 1751. (Docket No. 219)

1060. **Elizabeth Gray** of Tivertown, widow, vs. **John Manchester** of same, yeoman, in an action of trespass to recover five acres lying in a triangular form in Tiverton . . . orchard, pasture, and meadow land . . . of which premises **William Gray** was possessed at his death, which occurred on or about the first day of October 1765. Deed shown, dated 29 March, acknowledged 6 June 1745, witnessed by **Philip Cory, Restcome Sanford** (recorded Bristol Co. [*Mass.*] Deeds 34:223): **Edward Gray** of Tiverton, yeoman, for £1373 to **William Gray** of Tiverton, yeoman . . . land and salt meadow in Tiverton . . . being half of land given my brother **John Gray** by his honoured father by will . . . on both sides of the great highway . . . the other half part belongeth to him, sd **William Gray** . . . whole part on the west side of the highway . . . bounded south partly on **John Manchester**, part on salt meadow of **Samuel Durfie**, west on Sapowet Creek, north partly on salt meadow of **Thomas Gray**, part on **Phillip Gray**.

Thomas Gray deposed and said that he was "well acquainted with the land in controversy between **William Gray** and **John Manchester**, both of Tiverton . . . there stood a large tree in the southwest corner of the land which my father gave to his son the sd **William Gray** . . . that being the northwest corner of sd **John Manchester's** home orchard . . . the tree so near the corner it touched the bottom stones of sd wall."

Edward Manchester of Tiverton deposed and said that he was well acquainted with the land, mentioning a large red oak tree in the southwest corner which "my father-in-law **Edward Gray** did give to his son the sd **William Gray**."

Original will of **William Gray**, as recorded (Tiverton) Book 1:341,342 and a copy of the will of **Edward Gray**, recorded Bristol County Wills 5:245-247, entered. Original deed by **George Man-**

chester [*signed by mark X*] of Tiverton, husbandman, and wife **Elizabeth**, to **Edward Gray** of same, yeoman.

Verdict was for the plaintiff, land sued for and costs. (Docket No. 324)

– November Term 1766 –

1061. **Jacob Isaacks** of Newport, merchant, vs. **Patience Burdick** of Newport, widow, executrix of the will of **Jonathan Burdick** late of Newport, mariner, who hath assets in her hands unless she has wasted same. **Jonathan Burdick** at Musqueto Cove on 25 December 1763 received of **William Pitt Esq.** £118:3:4 Jamaican currency on account for use of the plaintiff. (Docket No. 21)

1062. **Jeremiah Hazard** of North Kingstown, yeoman, vs. **George Gardner** in an action of trover, concerning a slave **Hagar. Jeremiah Hazard** had brought action in Kings County against **George Gardner** at last February Court but by reason of "extended Relationship of the Parties no trial could be had"; petition for trial in Newport Court granted in May 1766. Hazard's wife was a daughter of Gardner. The plaintiff charged that one Negro Slave named **Hagar** and a female child Slave named **Jenny,** both of the price of $80, on 11 January 1766 fell into the hands of the defendant.

Sarah Sheffield, wife of **Josiah Sheffield** of New Shoreham, deposed and said that she was in South Kingstown when **Jeremiah Hazard Jr.** was married, and referred to her father **George Gardner**. Depositions were made by **Archibald Campbell** and wife **Hannah** and by Mr. **Job Sweet** of North Kingstown. **Susannah Smith,** wife of **John Smith** of South Kingstown, deposed and said that Hagar lived with **Jeremiah Hazard Jr.** upwards of 15 or 16 years past, and she Excepted [*expected*] that Mr. Hazard's Friends gave the Negro woman to him.

Ephraim Hazard deposed and said that when he was in company with **George Gardner** and **Ruth Hazard,** wife to **Jeremiah Hazard,** about 12 February 1766, he heard that when **Hagar** was sick with that Negro boy called **Prince** that she had at his House, her sickness cost him $50 or $60. "**Jeremiah Hazard** moved the goods that came by his wife as I accepted upon the same Farm the said Hazard now lives on," but **Hagar** did not go down then. To questions, the deponent replied that it was "my home and brother Jeremiah's too"; that Mr. **George Gardner** had never given **Hagar** to Mrs. **Ruth Hazard** but had sent her down to her; and when asked if he had ever heard Mrs. **Ruth Hazard** say the Fee or Property of the Negro Woman **Hagar** was in her mother and that **George Gardner** could take her when he was a mind to or dispose of her if he would, he answered, "No, she always called her *her* Negro."

Deposition of **Capt. Benj'n Allen,** yeoman, who said that he had been leveller of Rates in North Kingstown and when he levelled the Rates he always Excepted one [*of the Hazard Negroes*]. (Docket No. 31)

1063. **Mary Pinnegar** of Newport, singlewoman, vs. **Shearman Clarke** of Newport, alias mariner, to recover a debt due by book. (Docket No. 36)

1064. **Clothier Pearce** of Newport, merchant, and wife **Mary** lately wife of **Timothy Hill** of Newport, blacksmith, deceased, vs. **John Wanton** of Newport (son of John), to recover Mary's dower rights in the 16th lot in second division of Easton's Point with dwelling, of which Timothy was possessed at his death which occurred on 1 June 1759. Deposition by **Edward Lillibridge** of Newport, cooper, who said that he bought a house of **Timothy Hill** . . . Timothy drank hard and was often incapable.

Deed dated 15 May 1759, from **Edward** and **Esther Lillibridge** to **Timothy Hill,** witnessed by **Preserved Fish** and **Abraham Dennis,** as recorded Newport Deeds 14:286.

Letters of administration to **Mary Hill,** widow of **Timothy,** dated 6 October 1760; personal inventory taken 4 May 1761 by **Thomas Weaver** and **John Davis Jr.,** £2099, recorded Newport Town Council Book 12:197 as attested 18 November 1766 by **William Coddington,** who found no accounting of the administration.

Verdict was for the plaintiff. (Docket No. 44)

1065. **Joseph Cook** of Portsmouth, husbandman, vs. **Barnet Sisson** of Richmond, yeoman, to recover £200 due by note dated 6 June 1763 at Portsmouth, witnessed by **James Sisson Jr.** (Docket No. 186)

1066. **Joseph Cook** of Portsmouth, husbandman, vs. **Peleg Thurston** of Richmond, yeoman, to recover £150 due by note dated 11 August

1763 at Richmond, witnessed by **Christopher Cadman.** (Docket No. 187)

1067. Thomas Cooke of Portsmouth, gentleman, vs. **Abraham Borden** of Westerly to recover £612 due by note dated 25 October 1768 at Newport but written at "Westly." (Docket No. 188)

1068. Sarah Lewis of Newport, widow and administratrix of **James Lewis** late of Newport, mariner, vs. **Thomas Rogers** of Newport, mariner, to recover property of her late husband. Said **James Lewis** at a place called Surriloan [*Sierra Leone*] upon the coast of Guinea, on 1 November 1764 died, possessed of one bed of the value of 50s, five pairs of stockings worth 20s, and one check shirt worth 6s; the defendant took same.

Depositions dated 3 January 1766 by **William Clark** and **Edward Stringthfield** of Newport, mariners, who said that "on board the brig *Othello* on her late voyage to the coast of Africa, **James Lewis** was Chief Mate who died at Sierraleon . . . no slave was ever marked for sd **James Lewis** or any other person until about a week after arrival at Antigua . . . about a week after arrival I discovered a boy Slave to be marked JL which I suppose the Captain had marked for sd Lewis . . . the day after arrival at Antigua the slaves were marked.

"Account of Mr. **James Lewis** with **Peleg Thurston**, [*dated*] 1763, [*includes*] cash paid in wages, to wife, and shoes for your father . . . 1764, wages brig^{t} *Elizabeth*, **Joseph Aborn** [*?master*], voyage from Newport to and from Liverpool . . . balance at £546:13:2."

Extracts from the log of the *Othello*: "Tuesday 1 October 1765 [*by* **Thomas Rogers**] slaves let go one of Anchors in Insurrection . . . 10 of men slaves killed or lost belonging to the Cargo, one to **Capt. Thos Rodman** dead, one Mr. **James Lewis,** one **Thomas Rogers**."

When first sued, **Thomas Rogers** was at sea, so lost case by default. He presented an account of **James Lewis**: "one man slave b^{t} for you £130, one boy, £102; man lost overboard and drowned. Boy sold to Mr. **John Williams** 16 November 1765 Anteg." He offered to pay **Sarah Lewis** but she would not accept. (Docket No. 262)

1069. Daniel Tillinghast of Providence and **Nicholas Paris Tillinghast** of Newport, merchants, administrators of the estate of **Paris Hendren** late of Newport, apothecary, deceased intestate, vs. **Thomas Rodman**

of Newport, physician, to recover a debt of £495 due by account on 3 September 1765. (Docket No. 280)

1070. **Samuel Vernon** and **William Vernon** of Newport, merchants in company, vs. **Thomas Rogers** as bailiff for goods on the brig *Othello*, for an accounting. [*cf. No. 1068*]

In file are: Instructions to Master: "to make voyage from Newport to Cape De Verd Islands then to the Windward Coast of Africa as high up as the Isle Delas or Sierrallon and so down to the Gold Coast Whiden and River Gaboon . . . trading at such places as you think most for our Advantage . . . proceed with your Slaves to Georgia or Charlestown in South Carolina where we shall lodge Letters for your further Proceedings . . . after stopping at Barbados for necessaries to refresh your Slaves."

Protest of **Thomas Rogers**, master of the Brig *Othello*, **William Clarke** and **George Harvey**, mariners, on board, dated 4 October 1765. "28 September last past . . . sailed from the Island of Barbadoes bound to Island of St. Christopher . . . cargo 70 slaves. On 1 October in sight of Isls Desiada and Mariegalante about three in the afternoon slaves made an Insurrection upon the ship's crew and having armed themselves with billets of wood, seized the Master and held him while others beat and wounded him in very dangerous manner. **John Hammond** the Mate coming to assistance, he was attacked and suffered a fractured scull . . . now lies in agonies of death . . . **Thomas Rogers** having recovered a little from the storm of blows, got behind the Barricade and endeavoured for near two hours by fair words and persuasion to pacify sd slaves . . . [*they*] made slight of every proposal that could be offered, shouted, laughed and made a great noise in their savage manner . . . near sunset and no hopes left of quelling them, sd master gave orders to his people to fire upon them in small arms . . . one of the slaves was killed on the spot, three wounded, thirteen jumped overboard or swam away and refused to return or be taken up, voluntarily drowning. That night, the Captain dangerously wounded, the Mate dying of his wounds, few others capable of duty, and the sheets all let fly by the sd slaves during the sd insurrection . . . [*we*] put into the first port we could reach . . . St. John in this Island, 3 October." Sworn before **William Atkinson**, Notary Public, 4 October 1765. (Docket No. 292)

1071. **Freelove Beere** of Newport, spinster, executrix of the will of **Sarah Beere** late of Newport, widow, deceased, vs. **Oliver Beere** of Newport, cooper, to recover money due by a note dated 22 May 1766 from Oliver to "my mother" **Sarah Beere,** concerning legacy he was to pay Freelove. Arbitration by **Daniel Ayrault** and **Francis Malbone;** decision 13 June 1766 was that Oliver was to pay Freelove £622, Freelove was to endorse and deliver to Oliver an order drawn on him by **Thomas Teackle Taylor** in his favour for the legacy payable to his wife **Patience Taylor** by the will of her mother **Sarah Beere.** Witnesses: **John Vial, Evan Malbone Jr.** (Docket No. 294)

1072. **Joseph Stevens** of Newport, cordwainer, vs. **Frances Gardner,** widow and **George Gardner,** merchant, both of Newport, executors of the will of **John Gardner** late of Newport, Esq., deceased, to recover £823:4 due by note dated 20 November 1755 in his lifetime. (Docket No. 304)

1073. **Thomas Forrester,** mariner, and **Joanna Dennis,** widow, of Newport, on 3 November 1765 received a judgement against **Oliver Hazard** of Jamestown, ferryman, for possession of two acres of land in Jamestown. Defendant appealed, stating that the judgement was unsatisfactory because **Joanna Dennis** had deceased before the return of the execution, and **Gardner Thurston** of Newport, clerk, was guardian to **John Dennis,** an infant under the age of 21 and heir-at-law to **John Dennis.** Writ dated 18 October 1766. (Docket No. 347)

1074. **Peter Tallman** of Tiverton, yeoman, vs. **William Durfee,** son of **Samuel Durfee,** husbandman, and **Jonathan Luther,** yeoman, of Tiverton. (Docket No. 355)

1075. **William Sawdy** of Tiverton, cooper, assignee of **Gideon Gray** of Tiverton, labourer, vs. **Lumber Hart** of Little Compton, labourer, re note dated 29 July 1765.

– 1767 –

Superior Court

1076. September: **William Durfee** vs. **Benjamin Durfee,** in action of trover concerning a Negro man slave named **Prince,** "lost" 18 March 1767, valued at $60. (Superior Court 13,780)

1077. November: **William Downing** of Newport, cordwainer, vs. **William Rhodes and William Rhodes Jr.** both of Cranston, merchants, for wages due to his apprentice **Marshall Downing** on board the Sloop *Sally and Polly* whereof **Joram Place** was late master.

Agreement between **Joram Place** and **William Rhodes** of Cranston, seaman or fisherman belonging to Sloop *Sally and Polly* "now Ryding at Anchor in Port of Newport . . . agree to go to Halifax to deliver a freight and from thence on a fishing Voyage to the gutt of Canser for three quarters of one Share of all the fish," etc. Deposition of **James Dinnes** of Rehoboth who was on board. Judgment of former court reversed; verdict for plaintiff. (Superior Court 13,698)

– 1768 –

Superior Court

1078. March. **Daniel Snell,** residing Coventry, yeoman, petitions for divorce from present wife **Abigail.** They were married some years past but then upwards of seven years ago she eloped from him leaving behind her three small children.

Depositions were taken 3 March 1768 at Plymouth from **Moses Snell** of Bridgewater, **Elisha Washburn** and **Nathaniel Jackson** of Middleborough, and Mrs. **Patiance Jackson** and **Rebeckah Peirce,** both of Middleborough, who said they had been at the house of **Daniel Snell** in Middleborough.

Deposition made by **Joseph Briggs** of Coventry who said that for two years he was very well acquainted with **Daniel Snell** in Coventry and understood he had a wife in Bridgewater.

Deposition of **Solomon Hall,** who signed by mark X, sworn to in Plymouth 2 May 1768, that **Daniel Snell** and wife parted company in January 1761. **Ezra Harlow** and **Joseph Jackson** of Middleborough testified to the same thing. (Superior Court 13,699)

1079. **Abner Durfey** of Tiverton in the county of Newport, yeoman, vs. **Bennet Bayley** of Tiverton, yeoman, in the custody of the sheriff, in an action of trespass, charging that the defendant with force of arms on 13 June 1768 an assault on his body did make and did lay violant hands on him, pull his hair & ear & ran his fist in the plaintiff's face & other enormities did do against the Peace of our Lord the King. Writ dated 18 July 1768; **R. Helme** attorney. **Perce Perry** and **Joseph Cook** both of Tiverton, yeomen, and **John Bowen** of Tiverton, Esq. summoned to attend Inferior Court in November next.

Deposition made 26 August 1768 by **Parden Cook** of Tiverton, that he was at the house of **Oliver Cook** sometime in June 1768 with **Bennet Baley** and **Abner Durfee**, "and I ask[d] Mr Baley if that he would Play a Game of Cat and y[e] sd Baley Replyd that he would not play where so Dam[d] or Cursed a Liar as Abner Durfee was . . . Abner Durfee would tell any lie to hurt a Man or his Interest . . . as y[e] sd Durfee was sitting in y[e] Cart Baley walk[d] up to him and took hold of his haire and threatend him that if it was not for the Law he would whip him . . . ." and described how Durfee kicked Baley, who then turned around and pulled him down. The defendant asked: "Did not I charge **Abner Durfee** with going to **Patience Cook** & telling her that theire was a fine Ceder Swamp on that Lot I had Purchased of **Thomas Cory** [*and*] a great many good Pines on it & his father would faine have bought it if he could [?]" Cook replied: "yes To the best of my Memory." Durfey asked and Cook answered further questions about the altercation.

David Eddy of Darthmouth [*sic*] deposed that he was at **Oliver Cook**'s house the day in question, and that Baley said "Durfee was the Damdest Liar in all Tiverton . . . a Mischief making Doog and tryd to hurt him in his tradeing . . . Durfee told him to stand of[*f*] for he wanted to have nothing to say to him." The defendant asked if he had heard Baley say that "I went down and told the Widow Cook that that Land was worth a great deal more than what **Tho[s] Cory** had sold it for [?]"; Eddy replied yes and answered other questions.

Stephen Tallman and **John Negus**, both of Tiverton, testified on 2 November 1768, describing the same event. (Superior Court 13,880)

– 1769 –

1080. **Peter Shaw** of Little Compton, labourer, vs. **Benjamin Head** (son of **William**) of Little Compton, labourer. On 23 November 1769 at the house of **William Brownill** in sd town by force of arms the defendant grabbed the plaintiff by the collar and hauled him about the flore and dragd him about the room and with his fist did strike [*him*] diver times in his face and on his nose by which blow the grestel of his nose is broke or crushd . . . very much brused . . . . [*signed*] Peter Shaw Juner." Writ dated 25 November 1769.

– April Term 1770 –

1081. April: Petition of **Amy Crowley,** administratrix of the estate of **Thomas Crowley,** late of Newport, stating that her deceased husband in his will dated 28 July 1768 and proved 21 February 1769 appointed **James Milward,** mastmaker, and **David Huntington,** shop joiner, executors thereto, and they refused; the plaintiff was appointed administratrix of the personal estate, and she requests permission to sell part of the real estate. Signed "Aameay Crowley." Permission granted. (Superior Court 13,474)

– November Term 1770 –

1082. **Giles Sanford**, yeoman, and **Elizabeth** his wife who when sole was **Elizabeth Smith** of Middletown vs. **Elizabeth Smith**, widow, **Isaac Smith**, yeoman, **William Taggert**, mariner, all of Middletown, and **Sarah Church**, wife of **Israel**, when sole **Sarah Smith** of Tiverton, for possession of part of about 200 acres of land in Middletown, bounded north on land of **Benjamin Smith,** east on the sea, south and west on land of **Isaac Smith,** formerly the estate of **Edward Smith** of Newport.

Edward Smith of Newport left a will dated 13 July 1730, bequeathing to daughter **Hannah** £160 and one feather bed and furniture. Receipt from **Hannah Seabury** of Newport to **Philip Smith,** executor, witnessed by **Isaac Smith** and **John Clarke.** Other receipts in file, all to **Philip Smith**: 30 October 1730, **Hannah Smith** to brother **Philip**

Smith for £30 legacy from will of father **Edward Smith**; 1 February 1730[/1] from **Phebe Smith** for £100 in bills in part payment of legacy of Edward Smith to daughter Phebe; 1 February 1730[/1], **Elizabeth Smith** for £20 for legacy of Edward Smith to daughter **Dorcas**; 11 June 1731, from **Hannah Smith** for £20 for legacy of Edward Smith to daughter **Hannah**; 17 July 1731, **Hannah Smith** for £50 for daughter Hannah; 20 August 1731, from **Elizabeth Smith** to son-in-law **Philip Smith** for £50 in part payment of legacy given by Edward Smith in his will to his daughter **Ann**; 13 December 1735 at Newport from **Elizabeth Smith** to son-in-law **Philip Smith,** executor, for £30 in money . . . for my part of the mustee **Tobie.**

Note to Mr. Smith from **Benjn Hall,** dated Newport, 3 December 1741: "I send this Boy to you . . . [*he is in*] poor surcumstance having neither father nor mother and his mother-in-law has not wherewith to support hir own and him. I have taken a great deal of pains to get him a good master but all in vain . . . the winter now aproaches . . . I thought [*torn*] sending him to you being an own uncle as well as my self and you having no children of your own . . .if you take care of him this winter next summer I will take all possible care to get him a master."

Deposition May 1771 by **Dorcas Peckham,** that Philip Smith was a man of sense in his youth, some time before his father's death appeared to be delirious and stupid . . . continued to be a delirious person . . . neighbours and acquaintances used to pity him for his disordered state of mind.

Summons issued for **Dorcas Smith** of Newport, spinster, and **James Mitchell** of Middletown, blacksmith, and **Jon^{n} Easton** of Newport. **Jonathan Easton,** of lawfull age, deposed and said that the knowledge he had of **Philip Smith** late of Middletown, deceased, was that the aforesd Smith appeared to be of a gloomy & melancholy disposition and unfit to transact business. **Daniel Peckham** of Middletown, yeoman, of lawful age, testified that at some time after the death of **Edward Smith** of Newport, he was well acquainted with his son **Philip Smith** and often saw him and always understood and looked upon sd Philip to be a man (though of few words) of a sound and disposing mind and understanding. **Robert Barker** of Portsmouth gave similar testimony, adding that Philip "came for shoes . . . was slow of speech . . . would hold up his foot and I asked him whether he wanted a good sole and he said yes."

Joseph Rider of Middletown testified that he worked for a summer season for **Philip Smith. John Peabody** of Middletown stated that Philip was as capable as any other man in the latter years of his life, and that he, the deponent, had worked for him and been a near neighbour in November 1764. **William Turner** of Middletown stated that he was acquainted with Philip before the death of his father and that he was a capable young man. **Peleg Rogers** of Middletown testified that he was present when the will of **Edward Smith** late of Newport, deceased, was brought to be proved . . . the widow was there . . . no objections against letters of administration being given to Philip, son of the deceased . . . deponent was acquainted with Philip from then on and thought him a man of Right Disposing mind and memory.

Mr. **Henry Tew** who was brother to **Elizabeth Smith,** widow of Edward, and **William Peckham,** brother-in-law to sd Elizabeth Smith, were members of Town Council.

John Barker of Middletown testified about **Isaac Smith,** brother of Philip, and said that Philip wrote better than Isaac, but was slow of speech and sometimes at a loss for words and was not so capable of committing his ideas.

[*This case was evidently continued; see No. 1093, below. A full transcript of the will of Edward Smith, 1730, appears in No. 1014, above. Relevant papers were found widely scattered.*]

1083. **Oliver Cook** of Tiverton, Esq., vs. **Ephraim Pearce** of Portsmouth on Prudence Island [*sic*], yeoman, for debt due by note dated 25 March 1770. (Docket No. 105)

1084. **Job Easton** of Newport, merchant, vs. **Ichabod Potter** of Newport, innholder, in action of trespass concerning land in Newport, about 7 or 8 acres bounded west on the highway from Newport to Bristol Ferry, east on land of **Nicholas Easton,** north on land of **John Slocum,** it being sold by one **Peleg Wood** to **Job Easton** 28 October 1768. (Docket No. 166)

1085. **George Helmes** of Newport, ship carpenter, vs. **John Perry** and **Samuel Bowers** both of Swansey, Co. Bristol [*Massachusetts*] and **Josiah Simmons** of North Providence, all ship carpenters, in an action of trespass. Plaintiff charged that defendants forced him from his lawful employment and work; all were then and there building a certain vessel for a sloop and defendants took possession of same. Writ dated 30 October 1770. Went to referees: **James Millward, Wm. Goddard** and **Robert Mowrey.** (Docket No. 177)

1086. **John Lawton** of Newport, innholder, vs. **George Gardner** of Newport, merchant alias gentleman, in action of trespass, to recover a messuage or dwelling house and land in Newport, bounded south 40 feet fronting Queen Street, west on land of **John Rhodes,** deceased, north on **Paul Coffin,** east on another street or lane, which the defendant sold 27 October 1767 to the plaintiff for 489 Spanish Milled Dollars. Deed in file. (Docket No. 181)

1087. **Joshua Kitson** of the City of London vs. **John Richardson** now resident in Newport, mariner, for £105:12:03 due by note dated in London 6 September 1766 to Messrs **Joseph & Garard & Sharp,** New Bern, North Carolina. Account in file: Capt. **John Richardson** to **Joshua Kitson,** 1764, for Dorchester Beer & bottles. Verdict for defendant. (Docket No. 269)

1088. **Matthew Rights** of Newport, schoolmaster, and **Susannah** his wife, sued **Benjamin Durfee** of Tivertown, yeoman, administrator of the estate of **William Durfee** late of Tivertown, merchant, deceased, to recover a bequest of 250 Spanish milled dollars made by William Durfee to the said Susannah, to be paid within twelve months after his deceased, which the defendant has promised to pay but neglected to do so. Writ filed 24 May 1768; **Henry Marchant** attorney.

The will of **William Durfee** copied into evidence:

I **William Durfee** of Tiverton in the Colony of Rhode Island and Providence Plantation in America mariner . . . this 24th day of January 1766.

Imprimis I order my Cousen **Jeames Durfee** the son of my Brother **Benjamin Durfee** of Tiverton whome I appoint sole Executor . . . to pay out of what I shall commit into his hands for that use all my Just Debts that I am in write or Justice to any men together with my funeral Charges and settlement of my Estate.

Item I give and bequeath unto **William Borden** the son of **Rebeckah Borden** the Daughter of **Thomas Borden** of Tiverton aforesd deceased which sd William Borden being about Eight or Nine years of Age now liveth with me and is under my Cear & tuition unto the said William Borden abovesaid I give that part of my homestead farm that I now live on that my honoured father bought of **Stephen Brownell** of Portsmouth in the Colony of Rhode Island aforesd w[ith] the second great lot in the first Division in pocasset purchase and is bounded as followeth Northerly by **Benjamin Brentons** Land easterly by an highway Southerly by my fathers old homesteed farm and Westerly by the River or Salt Water containing about one hundred acres of Land with the buildings thereon standing scituate lying and being in Tiverton aforesd and also I give unto the said **William Borden** aforesd one Lot of Land lying in Tivertown in the County of Bristol in the province of the Massachusetts bay [*sic*] the first great Lot in the pocasset purchase containing about twelve acres be the same more or leass haveing Respect to the Division of Mr **Benjamin Brentons** Estate for the more perfect Discription of the bounds of the premises together with the houses wharf & buildings thereon standing the above bequeths to be and remain to the said **William Borden** & to his Heirs and Assigns for ever and likewise I give unto the said William Borden abovesaid my Indores moveables or furnature of my now Dwelling house.

Item I give & bequeath unto my well beloved Cousen **Richard Durfee** son to my Brother **Richard Durfee** the one half part of the Remaining part of my homesteed farm that I have not already given unto William Borden aforesd Except his haveing any Right in the six acres that I bought out of **Capt Pearses** farm above the Lower highway beginning at the River or Salt Walter and to Extend East Southerly untill it comes to the upper highway full half ye Weidth Excepting as aforesaid the Premises above given are scituate in Tiverton aforesaid and lays adjoyned on the south side of that Land that I have given unto **William Borden** in said Will & is commonly known by my honnoured fathers home place with the buildings thereon standing and to be & Remain to him my said Cousen **Richard Durfee** his Heirs & Assigns for ever and he my Cousen **Richard Durfee** to come into the possession thereof at the Decease of his father my said Brother **Richard Durfee**.

Item I give unto my beloved Brother **Richard Durfee** the use and Improvement of the aforesd farm that I have given unto his son Richard with the housings & buildings thereon standing for ad during the Term of his Natural Life he making no strip nor wast on any of the above given Improvements by any way or means more than proper or Reasonable whereby my said Cousen may be Damnified Further my Will is that if either of these aforesaid Minors Viz: **William Borden** or **Richard Durfee** should depart this Lfe before they shall arive to Lawful age or without Lawful Issue then the Surviving Minor shall inherit the Estate of the Deceased Minor

Item I give & bequeath unto my well beloved Cousen **James Durfee** Son of my Brother **Benjamin** of Tiverton in the Colony aforesd the Remainder of my homesteed farm being the one half part that I have not given **William Borden** Minor abovesaid bounded Northerly upon that I gave unto my Cousen **Richard Durfee** southerely upon **Capt. Pearses** farm now in the Possession of **Richard Gifford** together with the six acres that is Excepted out of my Cousen Richards bequest to begin at the River or salt water & to extend East Southerly untill it comes to the Upper highway for its Length the Premises above given are Scituate in Tiverton aforesd & to be and remain to him my said Cousen **James Durfee** and to his Heirs and Assigns forever

Item Further I will and order my Cousen **James Durfee** whom I have appointed my Executor to this my last Will and Testament to make sale of my house Land and three Quarters of my Saw Mill at Asonet River together with my out Lands to Inable him to pay all my Just Debts & Legacies together with my Sloop burthened about ninety Ton and all my Whailing Craft all seafairing Eutencals of what Name & Nature soever and likewise I order my Executor abovesaid to sell all my Cattle horses all stock of any kind together with my out dores moveables or farming tackling of any kind whatsoever

Item I give unto my two Sisters Vizt: **Susannah Right** and **Martha Durfee** the Sum of five hundred Dollars to be equally divided Betwen them and to be paid unto my said Sisters within twelve months after my decease

Item Further I order my Executor to keep the within named **William Borden** the Son of **Rebeckah Borden** to School and cause him to taught [*sic*] and Instructed both in Reading Wrighting and Cyphering and in Arts and Sciances that may be thought proper for such a Child and for such an Estate as is bestowed upon him & likewise I order that after the payment of my Legacys Just Debts funeral Charges & all Charges that shall arise upon the settlement of my Estate if there be any Remainder of Money in the hand of my Executor I order the same to be put out at Intrest and Devoted towards bringing up the said **William Borden** N.B.: throug forgetfullness there is a Remainder of Real Estate that at the Decease **Mary Brenton** Wido and Releck of **Benjamin Brenton** will decend to me **William Durfee** the Testator which I give likewise unto the said **William Borden** his Heirs & assigns forever . . . .

[*signed*] William Durfey, in presents of **Stephen Borden, Daniel Cornell,** and **Ambrose Barnaby**.

On 21 April 1766 witnesses Borden and Cornell attested the will.

At May term 1768 a jury found for the plaintiffs; the defendant appealed and the case went to the September 1768 Superior Court. (No. 13,671)

1089. **Jonathan Sowle** of Dartmouth, blacksmith, assigne of **Solomon Southwick**, assigne of **Ebenezer White**, vs. **Isaac Snell** of Little Compton, cordwainer, for debt due by note. (Docket No. 290)

1090. **Charles Debbens** of Newport, cooper, vs. **John Brown** of Newport, mariner, charging defamation and claiming damages of £200. "You are a Rogue and a Thief." (Docket No. 353)

1091. **Elisha Durfy** of Newport, shopkeeper, vs. **Joseph Thurston** of Newport, merchant, in action of assumpsit. Plaintiff had evidently sold goods valued at £100 to **Abigail Stoneman** on 29 October 1769 and had not been repaid by the defendant as promised. (Docket No. 354)

1092. **Samuel Greene** of Newport, house carpenter, vs. **Nicholas Smith** now or late of Taunton [*Massachusetts*], trader alias merchant alias mariner, for debt.

– May Term 1771 –

1093. **Giles Sanford** and wife **Elizabeth** vs. **Elizabeth Smith, Isaac Smith,** and **William Taggart.**

Deed dated 24 April 1770: **Giles Sanford** of Middletown, blacksmith, and wife **Elizabeth** (one of the daughters and coheirs of **William Smith** late of Middletown, deceased), for 1000 Spanish Milled Dollars sold to **William Read** of Newport, merchant, their right in one undivided half part of the northeast part of a farm and dwelling where sd Elizabeth's grandfather, **Edward Smith,** formerly lived, in Middletown, bounded northwest on land of the late **Peleg Smith,** deceased, west on **Joseph Holmes,** east on the sea, and southwest on land which Edward gave and devised to his sons **Isaac** and **Elisha** by his will dated 13 July 1730.

Deposition 21 May 1771 of **John Taylor** of Middletown, yeoman, who said that he heard it reported at the probate of **Edward Smith's** will that three of the Town Council of Newport withdrew and would not act in granting administration to **Phillip** on account of his disorder in his understanding. The deponent would meet him and ask him what ailed him and he would put his hand upon his head and say my Head. . . .

Deposition 23 May 1771 of **Charles Gerrard** of Middletown, practitioner in Physick, who said that he "worked for **Edward Smith,** deceased, and was well acquainted with **Philip Smith** before he was delirious and after . . . after Edward's death, [*I*] worked several times for Isaac and lodged with sd Isaac where sd Phillip Smith lived . . . it was usual for [*us*] all to go upstairs together to go to bed, and after [*we*] had got into the Chamber, sd Isaac say'd he must lock the door to keep sd Philip in, for fear he should get up in the Night and go out . . . told [*me*] not to be afraid for Philip would not hurt him, and accordingly did lock the Door and took the key out . . . one night Philip got up and [*I*] asked where he was going and he said to Seconnet . . . [*I was*] obliged to go with him. . . ."

Deposition of **Sarah Dillingham,** wife of **Cornelius Dillingham** of Newport, blacksmith, that she lived with **Philip Smith** and **Isaac Smith** for four years successively before Philip died, and he was disordered in his senses . . . after a week of foul weather, he "would get his gun and fire her off to make fair weather as he say'd."

Deposition of **Dorcas Smith:**

I Dorcas Smith of Newport in the County of Newport in the Colony of Rhode Island &c Spinster on oath delares I was in ye seventeenth year of my age when my father **Edward Smith** died . . . after my fathers death I lived in part of the same house where my brother **Philip Smith** lived and until he died and several years after with my mother **Elizabeth Smith** until she died. . . . after Letters of Administration was granted to the said **Philip Smith** my brother **Isaac Smith** got in the debts that was due to my said father's estate and he paid legacies which I was an eye witness to, but refused to pay my mother the money left her without being paid for it, for he sayd it was a great deal of trouble and my mother gave him a feather bed to make him satisfaction for doing that business . . . said Philip was so distracted that my mother often sayd she was afraid of her life. . . . the said Isaac Smith would have ye land divided between my mother and said Philip and said Isaac chose two of the men that divided it and would have the upper part of said land . . . the said Isaac Smith settled all the books and accounts with my mother and I never heard said Phillip say anything about the administration or do anything about it for he seemed very much stupified and disordered in his senses and would often get up out of his bed in the night time and especially in stormy weather and would very uneasy and fire of a gun to [*torn*] fair weather as [*in crease of paper*] Mother one stormy day, it was because she had bought cattle of that colour was the cause of the storm . . . it was his common practice if he wanted to walk out on the farm or to a neighbours house to go into their part of the house and ask if he had not better go and would point with his hand and I understood more by his pointing and actions than I did by his words and as for his being capable of business I had no reason to think he was for he ordered his Negro to cut down one of his own cherry trees and said Isaac Smith was very angry with him for it . . . said Isaac demanded of said Philip his money and commanded him to go up to his said Philip's chamber and he went up with said Isaac and after some time said Isaac came down and went out and upon the whole he never appeared to me to be of a sound disposing mind and understanding after his distraction to the day of his death . . . my father the said Edward Smith departed this life ye 18th day of September anno Dom. 1730. [*signed*] Dorcas Smith

Quest: How long before the death of your father was it that your brother Philip Smith was disorderd in his senses

Ans^{r}: Between one & two year as well as I can remember

Quest: Had you and your brother Isaac Smith frequent differences

Ans^{r}: We differed once

Quest: Was it after your brother Philips death that you differed with your brother Isaac

Ans^{r}: Yes we differed about making fence with my mother

Quest: Are you acquainted with the hand writing of your brother Philip

Ans^{r}: Yes he wrote a good hand

Quest: Is the receipt which I now hand to you the handwriting of your brother Philip Smith signed by Eliz^{a} Smith & markd with the letter A

Ans^{r}: I cannot certainly tell but I believe not

Quest: Is the receipt I now deliver you the handwriting of your brother Philip Smiths signed by Hannah Smith & markd with the letter B

Ans^{r}: I cannot tell but think it is not so fair a hand as he wrote before his distraction

Quest: Which was the best writer your brother Philip or Isaac

Ans^{r}: Philip

May term 1771 Sworn to in Court Teste Josias Lyndal Clerk

[*For a full transcript of the will of Edward Smith, see Item 1014*]

1094. **Sarah Burrington** of Tivertown, widow, assignee of **David Slocum,** vs. **Mary Turner** of Portsmouth, widow, for money due by note. (Docket No. 6)

1095. **Elisha Durfey** of Newport, shopkeeper, assignee of **Benjamin Jenks** of Tivertown, yeoman, vs. **Joseph Stanton** of Charlestown, Kings County, yeoman, for 54 Spanish Milled Dollars due by note dated May 1764. (Docket No. 12)

1096. **William Trip** of Newport, infant, mariner, by father and guardian **Benjamin Trip** of Newport, mariner, vs. **John Heffernan** of Newport, for having detained from the plaintiff a chest with cloaths and bedding and money of the value of £100, which the plaintiff possessed 28 April 1771 and lost . . . later upon sd day was found in hands of the defendant.

Joshua Trip of Newport, mariner, testified that in October of the year 1770 he sailed as a Cooper of a ship belonging to **Mr. Lopez** under command of Capt. **John Heffernan,** and **William Trip,** son of **Benjamin,** was the other cooper. Before sailing the deponent heard something of sd vessel going to Europe, and asked **Mr. Lopez** if they were going to London; **Mr. Lopez** replied no, and asked what should they do with a cooper if they were going to London? They were at Jamaica sometime and sd **William Trip** understood they were bound for London and . . . had chests on shore, sd William's chest being in the Piache adjoining to a house at a distance under care of one **Mr. Battey,** a taylor. When **Capt. Heffernan** understood that the deponent and sd **William Trip** left the vessel and would not proceed to Europe he swore he would have the chests, but could not find the deponent's . . . went to the Piache and took **William Trip's** and carried it on board . . . sd William had in his chest all his wearing apparel and the deponent believed, money, as he sold 400 bushels of onions at [--] Bitt a Bushel and spent no money, and cooper's tools.

List shown of "what William Trip had in his chest at Battys the tailear in Jeameco that Capt. John Heffnand took: 7 chekd shirts, 2 frocks, 6 pair trousers, one frahand jacket, won large pr silver shubuckels, stok, 1 new pr shoes, 1 new pt pornger, 1 gal 1/2 rum, 1 velvet jacket almost new, 2 sugar boxes, 1 calabash ful of suger abote 14 or 16 pds, 1 ginney and 2 pistols . . . cupers ax, drawing knif. . ." (Docket No. 32)

1097. **Mary Borden** of Newport, widow and administratrix of **Matthew Borden** late of Newport, merchant, vs. **Bolston Coggeshall** of Portsmouth, butcher, for £116:05 Old Tenor due for rum, salt, molasses, &c, an order on **Frances Bennett.** (Docket No. 51)

1098. **John Banister** of Middletown, gentleman, only acting executor of the will of **John Banister** late of sd Middletown, Esq., together with **Thomas Banister**, gentleman, vs. **William Gardner** of Newport, hoopmaker, for debt due for hay and carting of it from 1751 to 1772 [*varying from £20 to £72 per year*]. (Docket No. 53)

1099. **Catherine Earl** of Newport, widow, administratrix of the estate of **William Earl**, tavernkeeper, deceased, vs. **John Bull** of Newport, stonecutter, for £450:14:04 due for suppers, lodging, etc. (Docket No. 61)

1100. **Samuel Greene** of Newport, house carpenter, vs. **Charles Spooner** of Newport, house carpenter, executor of the will of **Wing Spooner** late of Newport, house carpenter, deceased, for £87:07:05 Old Tenor; the defendant answered that he had no assets of **Wing Spooner** in his hands. (Docket No. 67)

1101. **Jemimah Howland** of Jamestown, widow, wife of **Job Howland** late of Jamestown, yeoman, deceased, vs. **Isaac Howland** of Jamestown, yeoman, for her dower right in land there, 32½ acres bounded west on land of Job Howland, north on land of **Benjamin Carr**, east on the sea, and south on a highway. (Docket No. 69)

1102. **Simon Hough** and **William Pratt** both of Seabrook, Co. New London, Colony of Connecticut, mariners, vs. **William Gyles** of Newport, timber merchant, in action of assumpsit. The defendant was to pay for new rigging at $10 per 100 weight. (Docket No. 68)

1103. **Henry Hunter** of Newport, distiller, vs. **James Read** of Newport, tavernkeeper, and **Mary** his wife, lately **Mary West**, for debt. (Docket No. 70)

1104. **Benjamin Kent, Esq., John Heard** and **Joseph Pearce** of Boston, merchants, executors of the will of **Jane Eustis** late of sd Boston, singlewoman, deceased, vs. **Abigail Simon** of Newport, widow, for having made illegal entry into a house and land in Newport, of which premises **Peter Simon** was seized 1 June 1769 and by deed of that date conveyed to the sd testator in her lifetime and to her heirs, and continued in peaceable possession . . . until 1 June 1770 when the defendant by force of arms. . . . (Docket No. 72)

1105. **Peter Mumford** of Newport, gentleman, vs. **Nathaniel Smith** of Newport, shipwright alias shopkeeper, for £3 due for rent. Case agreed. (Docket No. 73)

1106. **Henry Sowle** of Newport, taylor, vs. **Robert Barker** of Portsmouth, cordwainer alias yeoman, charging that in August 1767, the defendant at his own request put into the care of the plaintiff his young son called **Ezburn,** to learn the art and trade and mistery of a Taylor . . . until age 21 . . . on 24 May 1770 sd Ezburn on persuasion of the defendant, left. Verdict for plaintiff. (Docket No. 211)

1107. **Gideon Brown** of Middletown, yeoman, vs. **Thomas Weaver** (son of Thomas) of Middletown, yeoman, in action of assumpsit concerning land in Middletown which was bounded partly on land of **Thomas Weaver,** son of **Clement Weaver.** (Docket No. 225)

1108. **James Daniels** of Newport, mariner, vs. **Richard Bissell** and **Walter Harnus** of Newport, mariner, charging them with assaulting his body 9 October 1770 at Cape Nichols Mole, striking him with a club and kicking him; asked £100 damages.

John Roy of Newport, mariner, deposed and said that he was on board the sloop *Mary,* of which **Waters Hanner** [*sic*] was master, in the year 1770 at Cape Nichols Mole . . . **James Daniels** was also on board, and about a month after arriving in Port a difference arose between him and the defendants "but no blows ensued . . . **Richard Bissell** the Mate said if we wanted to fight then we must go on shore. [*He described the fight*]. . . Captain on shore haled for the Boat." **Spink Tarbox** of East Greenwich, mariner, also made a deposition about it. (Docket No. 230)

1109. **Nicholas Easton** of Newport, husbandman, vs. **Daniel Spencer** of Bedford, County Bristol, yeoman, in an action of assumpsit: defendant on 27 April 1770 had promised to deliver 160 cedar poles and rails. (Docket No. 237)

1110. **Rebecca Manchester** of Tiverton, widow, vs. **Gilbert Manchester** of Tiverton, yeoman, for trespass, charging that on 23 April 1771 the defendant illegally entered the dwelling of the plaintiff (his mother) and laid violent hands upon her and pulled, halled and jerk'd her out of the Door . . . diverse times between 1 November 1770 and 26 April 1771. Property concerned was the homestead farm of **John Manchester** devised by will to his son **William Manchester,** deceased, on both sides of the highway from Tiverton down through Little Compton.

Deposition of **Christopher Manchester sener** of Tiverton, that in the winter of 1770/1 when he went to the widow **Rebecca Manchester's** to thresh oats, **Gilbert** came and accused him "of meddling . . . sd oats was his . . . and [*threatened*] to thresh me."

Deposition of **Rhoda** and **Alice Manchester** of Tiverton that on 23 April last past "we were at home with our mother Rebecca Manchester and she at that time was taking her Negro girl to Due for some fault . . . Gilbert came . . . asked Rebecca what the Devillish Noise was . . . [*she*] asked whether it Disturbed him . . . Gilbert said there always was a Damnd Eternal Noise when she was at home and if she did not hold her tongue he would out of doors with her . . . her answer was, you put me out of doors . . . yes said he, I sware I will . . . she said, touch me if you Dare you Sorry Puppe . . . Yes, Damn you I will said he, then took her by her arm and out of Doors with her in a furious Manner." (Docket No. 248)

1111. **Elisabeth Hoockey** of Newport, widow, vs. **Malcolm Graham** of Newport, perriwigg maker, in an action of trespass, to recover a great chamber and a small room adjoining in the plaintiff's dwelling house in Newport, bounded north by land of **Elezar Trivett,** east on the street, and partly on land of **Stephen Hoockey** deceased now in occupation of **William Hoockey,** and west on Thames Street, of which the plaintiff was legally seised until 6 May 1771. **Ackurs Sisson** was attorney for the plaintiff. (Docket No. 367)

1112. **John Andrews** of Cranston, Esq., vs. **James Harding** of Newport, labourer alias trader, in action of promise and assumpsit: [*reason of case not clear*]. Document dated at New York, 27 June 1770, proof that **James Manser** was a sailor taken at Oswego and kept by the Enemy so that he could not return to Newport till the 27th of August 1757. Like proof for **David Williams. John Shepherd,** boatbuilder, was by agreement to have £80 Old Tenor per month. (Docket No. 374)

1113. **Owen Morris** of Newport, mariner, vs. **Thomas Claggett** of Newport, watchmaker. Plaintiff charged that defendant had on 10 April

1767 sold him a clock for £1200 Old Tenor, and that it was bad and deficient, and the defendant knew it to be bad and deficient and made in no workmanlike manner . . . it became of no value.

Deposition of **And^{w} Freebody** being well acquainted with **Thomas Claggett** . . . often frequented his shop . . . saw there a new chim clock going . . . asked Claggett if that was the clock that belonged to Mr. Owen Morris. He told me yes, being something curious I frequented his shop much oftener and found it always going and kept good time . . . sd Mr. Morris did not like the chiming part he then made one or two larger wheels then it was set up again for tryal in his shop some time longer and I thought it went as well as any clock soever.

Thomas Crossing of Newport testified that on or about 14 February 1771 he was in the shop of Mr. Thomas Claggett and afterwards came into sd shop Mr. **Paul Collings, Christopher Townsend, John Easton** and Mr. **Daniel Hoockey.** Claggett requested Mr. Townsend to point out the defects in the clock if any. Claggett delivered it to a Negro man by order of Mr. Paul Collings and he carried the same away.

Thomas Rogers of Newport, mariner, on 5 July 1771 deposed that he was intimately acquainted with Capt. Morris . . . oftentimes saw Mr. Thomas Claggett altering, amending and changing weights and position . . . frequently joked with Claggett in the street, telling him he had taken Morris finely in, by making a clock for him at a price much greater than he could have purchased one in England for and would never go . . . sd Claggett said it was part of his bargain that if he did not make the clock go he was to have nothing and he could and would make her go. Question: "did you ever hear Capt. Morris threaten to return her?" Answer in the affirmative.

Deposition of **Andrew Hunter** of Newport, perukemaker, dated 19 July 1771: he recommended Mr. Thomas Claggett to Capt. Owen Morris who wanted to purchase a clock and went with Morris to Claggett for that purpose . . . he made a clock which was left in the care of Mr. **Paul Collins,** brother-in-law to Morris. He stated that afterwards he spoke with Claggett who told him he was not paid for making it and that the reason Mr. Collins had not paid him was that it had not pleased him in its going. . . . The same day **James Bradley** testified that he had lived next door to Thomas Claggett's shop in the year 1768 and the clock went well.

John Morris, clockmaker of Newport, also deposed on 19 July 1771, stating that he did with the assistance of **Thomas Jackson** of the aforesd colony, clockmaker, make a weight Quarter clock for Mr. Thomas Claggett which clock was bespoke by Capt. Owen Morris . . . as good a piece of work as any clock what someever and of a right construction . . . and delivered it to sd Morris sound and in good order. When questioned about the bells, he said, "I can't say the bells are so good as I could buy in London, but they are as good as I can buy in this country in general."

Deposition of **Samuel Rockwell** of Middletown, County of Hartford, Colony of Connecticut, clockmaker, 7 August 1771, that he "hath taken a view of the clock belonging to Capt. **Owen Morris** at sd Morris' house, made at Mr. **Thomas Claggett's** shop in Newport . . . [*it*] appeared to be very good work though his view of it could not be complete . . . it being standing in the House. The deponent saith that he hath made a clock of the same kind with Morris's for Mr. **John Randall** of Providence, and that **Jackson** the maker or principal workman in Morris's clock, is a person well known to the deponent . . . worked with him . . . a good workman . . . but the deponent never employed him in a work of that construction nor doth he know that ever Jackson made such a clock before.

Gawen Browne of Boston deposed at Boston 7 September 1771 that "the clock presented me by **Josiah Collin** of Newport . . . which was by sd Collin said to be made or contracted for by Mr **Thomas Clagget** of said Newport I have view'd as she was together, & what was seen Seemeth to be good of the Inside work, but if the Quarter part runs down sooner than either the other two parts it appears wrongly calculated & ought to be altered, there Bells shou'd have been had from England set to musick they being not well cast for a Clock of this kind. The Dial wheels which turn the Moon's Age, miss each other, which ought not to be. Mr Clagget ought to send this Clock to London to be put in order, at his own Expence & get a new sett of Bells. . . ."

Christopher Townsend deposed that Jackson's "ability was not equal to a performing of the complicated nature . . . sd Jackson worked for me some time — I having purchased him of Mr. **Samuel Rockwell** of Middletown in Connecticut."

Deposition of **Benj[n] Bagnall Senior** of the persuasion called Friends, who affirmed 14 October 1771 that **Christopher Townsend** of Newport "served his apprenticeship with me . . . my opinion is that sd Christopher Townsend is a good workman and understands both the watch and clockmakers business very well." He testified also that the clock was not made agreeable to the plan which clocks of that construction generally were made and it will not perform until some alterations are made.

Thomas Jackson of Newport, clockmaker, on 26 October 1771 signed his mark to a statement that the clock was very ill used and broke twice, once by one **Ann Drake** and another time by one of sd Morris' family, who broke the [*?rae*] spring.

Deposition of **Edward Thurston Jr.** of Newport, dated 19 November 1771, that in September 1768 he was in King Street in Boston and "met by a person who goes by the name of **John Morris** (whom I had several times before seen at the shop of Mr. Christopher Townsend Jun[r] in Newport)" . . . they had a conversation about the clock, and Morris said that Claggett and Jackson could never make it perform as they did not understand that sort of work. At the house of Owen Morris in Newport, **William Henderson** looked at it and said he could put it in order for a dollar, but he refused to take it down (in pieces). . . .

In court in November 1771, **Ebenezer Rumreill** testified that he had kept a shop in the year 1768 next door to **Tho[s] Claggett** and was often in and out of his shop to know the time of day. "Claggett had a very nice chiming clock up in his shop and . . . told me it was for Capt. Owen Morris . . . always called the Regulator, and to appearance as fine a clock as ever I see." Judgement was for the plaintiff, £30 and costs.

1114. November: **Mary Channing** of Newport, widow of **John Channing** late of Newport, merchant, vs. **Ignatius Battan** of Newport, mariner, in an action of dower; defendant to set off third part of two lots in Newport and a house where he now dwells, bounded north on the street, east on lot 17 belonging to **Thomas Freebody,** south on land lately belonging to **Peter Coggeshall** but now to the defendant, west on lot 19 lately belonging to **Hezekiah Carpenter** but now to **Robert Stoddard,** another with stable adjoining; lot 4 was sold to **Robert Shearman,** west on lot formerly belonging to **Elizabeth Elliot** but now to **Isaac Howland. John Channing** died in the month of February 1771. Writ dated 22 October 1771. Suit withdrawn.

1115. **Adam Fergesson** of Newport, snuffmaker, vs. **Samuel Ross** of Richmond, Esq., for debt of 27 August 1769, £2:5 for goods, including 3 dozen bottles of snuff at £20; £60 in lawful money = £2:5. To the writ was "attached one button delivered by the defendant's wife on his estate." (Docket No. 93)

1116. **Edward Wanton** of Newport, merchant, administrator of the estate of **John Channing,** late of Newport, merchant, vs. **Stephen Saunders** of Westerly, yeoman, for debt of 21 December 1770, £21:15:4:3f, for goods: indigo, ginger, busckels, lawn apron, scissors, salt, buttons, sugar and a sieve bottom, comb, etc. It was calculated that the amount sued for was equal to £580:10:6 old tenor. (Docket No. 146)

1117. **Abigail Stoneman** of Boston, widow, vs. **Jonathan Chace** of Newport, shopjoiner and **Anne Morrison** of the same place, widow (**William Cayne** against whom also the plaintiff purchased her writ not being found to be arrested) in action of trespass. The property in convtroversy was in Newport, bounded east by land lately belonging to **Peleg Thurston,** deceased, south part on land of Peleg Thurston, part on the highway leading down to Ferry Wharf, west on a 5 ft. gangway lying between the premises and land of **Jeremiah Child** for the use of both, and north on land of **Daniel Russell,** being premises of **Jonathan Chace,** late of Newport, innkeeper, by his will of 1 June 1743 devised to his wife **Mehitable Chace** with authority to sell land in Newport lately purchased of **Peleg Carr**. The estate was not sufficient to pay the debts, and Mehitable at Newport on 2 September 1767 deeded the land to the plaintiff by **Marchant and Ellery,** attorneys. Note dated 18 November 1771 by **William Coddington,** town clerk, "examined town council records and don't find that Mehitable Chace, late widow of Jonathan Chace, ever rendered any account of her executorship on sd estate as she was sole executrix." (Docket No. 258)

1118. **William Crossing** of Newport, gentleman, vs. **Mary Borden** of Newport, widow, administratrix of the estate of **Matthew Borden** late of Newport, merchant, deceased, to recover $8 1/2 due by note dated 2 December 1767 by Matthew. (Docket No. 263)

1119. **Daniel Donham Jn^r** of Newport, gentleman, vs. **Uriel Lyon** of Newport, cooper, "for roum to the amount of £140 old tenor for Mr. **John Thurston**" due by note dated 6 February 1769. (Docket No. 274)

1120. **William Durfee** of Tivertown vs. **Richard Gifford** of the same place, yeoman, to recover money due by note. **William Cook,** sheriff, "attached a puter spoon" 29 October 1771. (Docket No. 275)

1121. **Joseph Head** of Dartmouth, yeoman, vs. **Stephen Willcox** of Dartmouth, yeoman, concerning possession of about 60 acres in Portsmouth, bounded north partly on land of **George Hall** and heirs of **Robert Burrington**, deceased, east on land lately of **Enoch Briggs**, deceased, and all other ways on highways, except for two acres purchased by **Jonathan Head** of **William Cory**. A suit was originally brought by Stephen Willcox against **Joseph Borden** of Portsmouth, yeoman, at the Court of Common Pleas at Newport in May 1769, with verdict for the plaintiff. This was overturned in an appeal in September 1770, and the premises were delivered to **Daniel Wilcox** in behalf of his father **Stephen Wilcox** on 8 April 1771 by Wm. Chaloner, Sheriff. Summons were issued for **Joseph Tripp** of Newport, **Joseph Borden,** and **Matthew Cooke** of Portsmouth [*their testimony is not in file*]. (Docket No. 124)

– 1771 –

Miscellaneous

1122. Order of the Town Council of Newport, dated 3 March 177[*1/*]2, signed by Wm. Coddington Town Council Clerk, concerning the removal of a child of **Hannah Harris** to Jamestown. Hannah upon examination by the Town Council on 3 June 1771 on oath had declared that she was born in Newport, had served her time in Jamestown with **Hazard Knowles**, her child was born in Jamestown 2 March 1770 while she was an apprentice with sd Knowles, the child's name was **Lydia** and **Benjamin Astin** was its father. The Town Council, believing that sd **Lydia Harris** was likely to become chargeable to the Town, voted that she be immediately sent by an officer to the town of Jamestown "where it was born and where said child by right belongs."

— November Term 1771 —

1123. **Amy Crawley** of Newport, widow, vs. **Henry Brightman** of Newport, labourer, in action of trespass, for witholding from her possession the northeast chamber in her dwelling house in Newport. (Docket No. 14)

1124. **James Abeel** of the City and Province of New York, merchant, vs. **Cromwell Child** of Warren, shipwright alias merchant, for £80 New York currency and £2:3 lawful money.

1125. **George Goulding Honeyman** of Newport, gentleman, vs. **Benj: Burch**, now resident in Newport, labourer alias mariner alias shoemaker, in an action of trespass, charging that the defendant assaulted him 15 October 1771 with a club. (Docket No. 48)

1126. **Thomas Vernon** of Newport, Esq. vs. **Frances Townsend** of Newport, widow, administratrix of **Solomon Townsend** late of Newport, mariner, deceased, to recover money due by note of Solomon Townsend dated 17 December 1764. (Docket No. 229)

1127. **John Melvil** of Tobago one of the British West Indian Islands, merchant, and wife **Deborah** who when sole was named **Deborah Scollay** vs. **Cullen Pollock** of Edenton, in the Province of North-Carolina, Esq. alias merchant, executor of the will of **George Pollock** late of sd Edenton, merchant. George Pollock by will in North-Carolina 11 August 1758 bequeathed unto the plaintiff's wife Deborah "Miss Deborah Scollay daughter of John Scollay of Boston, merchant," £500; the defendant was appointed executor together with **Thomas Pollock** . . . accepted the administration in 1764 and paid £250 on 10 August 1768. Plaintiffs petition for other half of legacy. Writ served on body of the defendant and on **Silas Cooke** and **Aaron Lopez** who became his Bail. (Docket No. 222)

1128. **William Green** now resident in Newport, mariner, vs. **Richard Brew** of Anamaboc on the Coast of Africa, Esq., for debt due by bill dated at "Annamabo March the 1 1768:" 2 yrs wages due on board ye *Triton* at 40/ P month; 9 mo. wages due at £3 Sterling. **Martin Benson**, mariner, deposed that the plaintiff had "sailed with him in the sloop *Triton* whereof the deponent was master . . .[*he was*] servant of Mr.

Richard Brew on Coast of Africa from the beginning of September 1769 to about the last of April . . . was a person in whom he confided and who eat and drink with the deponent on board and the defendant in his absence trusted sd Green with the voyage and cargo." Defendant claimed that the plaintiff had embezzled cargo. (Docket No. 327)

– May 1772 –

1129. **Benjamin Howland** of Tiverton, yeoman, an infant who sues by his Guardian **Gilbert Devol** of Tiverton, yeoman, vs. **Mary Richardson**, widow, **Joseph G. Wanton** Esq., **John G. Wanton, Gideon Wanton** and **Edward Wanton**, merchants, all of Newport, and **Henry Bowers** of Swansey, merchant and **Mary** his wife, **Abraham Borden** of Westerly, yeoman, **Thomas Howland** of Newport, merchant and **Sarah** his wife, **Mary Rodman** of Newport, widow, and **Abraham Borden** of Sherburn in the County of Nantucket, an infant gentleman, and **Charles Whitfield** of Newport, yeoman, and **Elizabeth** his wife, in an action of partition concerning two tracts of land in Tiverton, one of about 150 acres with a dwelling house and buildings, part meadow, part pasture, and the other part arable and wood, butted and bounded: northerly on land of the **Widow Slocum** in tenure of **Job Almy**, easterly on a Proprietors Highway, northerly and Westerly on Highwaies, being the Homestead Farm formerly belonging to **Joseph Wanton** late of Tiverton, yeoman, deceased; the other tract contains 240 acres, part meadows, part pasture, and part arable and woodland, bounded upon the River and thence running up into the woods to the Eight Rod highway that goes across the head of the Great Lots and northerly on land late in possession of **John Howland**, being two 120 acre lots. Writ dated 28 April 1772. Joseph Wanton, yeoman of Tiverton, was possessed of the land and made his will 10 August 1749, giving the aforesd lands and premises unto his son **Edward Wanton** and to the heirs male of his body and for want of such issue to his son **Gideon Wanton** and to his daughters, **Elizabeth Borden, Mary Richardson, & Sarah Spencer** to be divided among them share and share alike with provisions in case any should die; Joseph died on or about 20 March 1754 and Edward became seized of the premises, and Sarah Spencer having intermarried with **Benjamin Howland** died on or about 20 February 1756 leaving issue **Wanton Howland**, who died on or about 15 September 1756 leaving issue **Benjamin Howland** the present plaintiff, and on or about 17 October 1771 Edward Wanton died without issue.

The will of Joseph Wanton, yeoman, dated 14 August 1749, entered in evidence:

. . . unto my well beloved son **Gideon Wanton** all that my Messuage or tenement & tract or parcel of Land scituate lying & being at White wine brook in Tiverton . . . bounded on Quoquat pond & from there Extending up into the Woods untill it Comes to an Eight Rod highway at the head of the Lots . . . and also one Cow. . . . to my well beloved daughter **Elizabeth Borden** of Newport . . . Widow one Cow and the sum of £800 in currant lawfull Bills of Publick Credit old Tenor. . . . to my well beloved Daughter **Mary Richardson** Wife of **Thomas Richardson** of Newport, Esq., one feather Bead standing in the Porch Chamber in my House where I now live together with ye beding & furnature belonging to it also one Cow and the sum of £800 in currant lawfull Bills of Publick Credit old Tenor. . . . unto my well beloved Daughter **Sarah Spencer** wife of **Thomas Spencer** of Greenwich in the County of Providence . . . Practitioner in Physsick the Use & Improvement of ye house and Lot or piece of Land where she formerly lived in Tiverton . . . twelve rods wide & to extend up so far until it makes one Acre . . . for and during the term of her natural life and after her decease I give and devise the same to my well beloved Gransons **Benjamin Howland** and **Wanton Howland** sons of my said Daughter Sarah Equally to be divided. . . . [*and*] the sum of £300 in currant lawfull Bills of Publick Credit old Tenor. . . . unto my well beloved son **Edward Wanton** all that my homsteed Farm where I now live and house Lots together with all & singular the Buildings Improvements & Appurtenances to the same belonging or in any wise Appertaining Excepting out of the same the house & Lot or peace of Land herein before given to my sd Daughter Sarah. . . . Also the twelve gore Lots that extends to the Eight Rod Highway at the head of ye great Lots in Tiverton . . . also all that my Wharf and Land belonging to it in Tiverton . . . also all my Ware houses adjoyning to the sd Wharf and the land they stand on and below the highway also my one thirtyeth part of the two Lots containing about eight acres on the South Side of Howlands Ferry also my one thirtyeth part of a Ferry Right of a piece of Land of twenty Rods wide and extending up Eighty Rods to the Highway also my own [*one*] thirtyeth part of a highway of four Rods wide that Runs Eighty rods up also my one thirtyeth part of a piece of

Land left for a training Place & burying Place at the head of the Four Rod highway, also my own thirtyeth part of the Land laid out & intended for a minister which **Joseph Anthony** now hires of the Proprietors also all that my Northward farm of a [*120*] acre lot in Tiverton . . . adjoyning that part of the Lot that **John Howland** lives on also the moiety or Equal half part of a Sixty acre lot on the south side of **Joseph Wodels** Lot and Runs up to the Eight rod highway and from thence runs up to basket Swamp & also a [*50*] acre lot on ye south side of the sd [*60*] acre lot . . . to him my sd son **Edward Wanton** and to the Heirs of his body Lawfully begotten for ever and for want of such Issue then I give Devise and bequeath all & singular the Lands Tenements and Hereditaments with their & every of their Appurtenances herein given and devised to my sd son Edward, unto my sd Son **Gideon Wanton** & my sd Daughters **Elizabeth Borden, Mary Richardson** & **Sarah Spencer** Equally to be divided . . . and to their several & Respective Heirs and Assigns for ever. . . . further unto my sd son Edward one thirtyeth part of a Neck of Land called Cranbarry Neck and also my one fourth part of a Lot of Land up at the head of Freetown. . . . Edward shall have the Use and Improvement of all my Stock as Cattle Horses Sheep hogs & other Creretures & also all my Household goods for & during the Term of his Natural Life . . . my will further is that my sd son Edward shall have the Use and Improvement of all my Negroes during the term of his Natural Life except such as are not wiling to live with him and incline to be sold, Then & in that Case my sd Daughters or either of them shall have the Liberty of taking such Negro or Negroes that incline to be sold in part payment of the Legacies herein before given to them, But if my sd Daughters decline taking such Negro or Negroes that wants to be sold as aforesd, then the sd Negro or Negroes shall have the Liberty of Chosing of a Master or Mistress that will buy them provided they will give as good a prize for e'm as another will. . . . after the decease of my sd son Edward all my Stock Household Goods and Negroes aforesd not sold shall be & Remain to the Heirs of his Body . . . and for want of such Issue then I give and bequeath the same (except my silver Tankard herein after mentioned) unto my sd son Gideon and my sd Daughters Elizabeth, Mary & Sarah Equally. . . . if my son Edward dies without Issue . . . I give my Silver Tankard . . . unto my Granson **Joseph Wanton** son of my sd son Gideon but in case my sd Grandson Joseph Wanton shall happen to die before my son Edward then I give the Tankard to the sd Joseph's wife . . . if she happen to die before my son Edward then I give the same to my sd Granson Joseph Wanton's Daughter **Sarah**.

Executors were to be sons **Gideon** and **Edward Wanton**; witnesses were

Joseph Proud, Edward Tew, and **Jos. Fox**. The will was proved 1 April 1754.

The Court judged that partition be made, one fourth part to **Benjamin Howland**, one fourth to **Mary Richardson**, one fourth to **Joseph G. Wanton, John G. Wanton, Gideon Wanton**, and **Mary** wife of **Henry Bowers** (who was not attach'd) and the other fourth to **Sarah**, wife of **Thomas Howland, Mary Rodman**, and **Abraham Borden** (who was not attach'd) and **Elizabeth**, wife of **Charles Whitfield**. The defendants appealed to the next Superior Court. (Superior Court 13,372)

1130. **Susanna Womsley**, of Newport, an Infant within the age of twenty one years who sues by **Mary Womsley** of sd Newport, her mother & next Friend, vs. **Jeffrey Watson**, of South Kingstown, Esq. alias yeoman, in action of trespass, claiming £200 damages. Writ dated 25 April 1772. [*cf. Item 1144*]

"On 18 December 1771 at South Kingstown, the plaintiff being within the English Colony of Rhode Island, and being by the Laws of the Kingdom free and not subject to the Arbitrary Will and Controul of any of his Majesty's subjects . . . sd Jeffrey with Force and Arms . . . the Body of the Plaintiff (she in the Peace of the Lord the now King then and there being) without any reasonable Cause against her Will and Consent and against the Laws of the Kingdom into his Custody did take, and did falsly imprison for the space of one Day . . . eighteenth Day of December AD 1771: and . . . afterwards unto **Samuel Rose** of Richmond . . . did alien and sell as a Slave . . . to serve and obey; by means whereof the Plaintiff was further imprisoned for the Space of five Days . . . deprived of her free Will to act and do according to her own Will."

The Defendant answered that he was acting in "his Capacity as one of the Commissioners or Assignees of **James Gardner** of North Kingstown . . . yeoman, an Insolvent Debtor." Deed of Conveyance, 4 January 1771: **James Gardner** of North Kingstown, insolvent debtor, to the Committee, **Jeffrey Watson** of South Kingstown, **George Northup**, and **Peter Phillips, Esq.,** of North Kingstown; inventory included one negro wench and three children, valued at £3000.

Bill of sale dated 11 December 1771: **Jeffrey Watson** of South Kingstown as assignee of the estate of James Gardner of North Kingstown, husbandman, insolvent debtor, for £10 sold to **Col.**

Samuel Rose of Richmond, gentleman, one Negro gairl named **Susanah** of about eleven years.

Deposition of **Ebenezer Tefft** of South Kingstown, who said that on 20 December 1771, **Samuel Tifft** and **Josiah Shearman** came to his house and ordered him to "deliver up a servaunt gearl that then lived with me . . . for Jeffery Watson Esq. had given a Bill of Sale of her to one **Phelps** or Col. Rose which I cannot tell, and . . . if I refused to Deliver up sd gearl I should supject my selfe to a Lawe Sute, I told sd Samuel that I took the gearl at three years and a half of age had much rather keep hur than deliver hur to any body, his answer was I must . . . and Esq[r] Watson would make me ample satisfaction for keeping hur, for he did not want my estate to pay James Gardners debts."

Deposition of **Samuel Rodman** of South Kingstown in court, that some time in the summer of the year 1771, **Mary Wamsley** "begged his permission to tarry at his House that she mght not be taken & carried away by **Jeffry Watson Esq[r]** of South Kingstown who was in pursuit of her in order to enslave her so that she could not in peace and Security remain at her own proper dwelling place . . . the deponent suffered her so to do where she tarried about two months, under great perplexity & apprehension of Danger. . . .some time in the forepart of December AD 1771 in the Township of Richmond near sunset he saw one **Jonas Shearman** with a black child behind him and . . . stopping and conversing with the said Shearman discovered it to be **Susey,** the daughter of **Mary Wamsley,** and . . . the said Shearman then informed the deponent he was carrying her to **Col. Sam[l] Rose's,** the Deponent then moving forward left **Peter Boss, jun[r]** (who had been in the Company of the deponent on the Road) in Conversation with the said Shearman."

Deposition of **Christ[o] Gardner**: At North Kingstown, May 22[d] 1772, Christ[o] Gardner of South Kingstown of Lawfull Age and Engaged according to Law Testifieth and Saith that he well Remembers a Negro woman named **Mary** that his Honour'd Grandfather gave to his Father **Ephraim Gardner** which sd Negro liv[d] and Dyed at my fathers, and when s[d] black Mary was Living she had Several Children one Call[d] **Moll** which my father gave my Brother **James Gardner** after he was married, which Negro Moll had Several Children while she Liv[d] with my brother James Gardner, and my s[d] brother James had a Child Scaulded to Death, which I thought was don through her means as she Run out Doors when I ran to the Child with my s[d] Brother's Wife and I advised him to Prosecute s[d] Negro or sell her soon after I understood s[d] Negro Left his house, and some time after I asked my Brother James why he Did not take her up and Due something with her and he told me he never wanted to see her again for he said he would sell her the first opportunity.

Question, by **Jeffry Watson** in Behalf of **Sam[l] Rose**: Was the Child in the Pot Cittle or tub of Hot Water when you went into the Kitchen and saw her Runing out at the other Dore?

Answer: the Child was in a Kettle of Hot Water partly overset and my Brother's Wife took the Child out of s[d] Kettle and Further this Deponent saith that the said Child said Before it Died that the said Negro **Moll** Pushed him into Said Kittle of Hot Water.

Question by **Benj[a] Rodman**: Did the sd Negro Moll as you Excepted Serve her time out Before she went to Live with James Gardner?

Answer: No . . . my father gave her to my Brother James. . . .

Question by Jeffry Watson on behalf of Sam[l] Rose: Was the s[d] Negro Moll the same which you except your Brother James gave up unto the Assignees as His Proper Estate?

Answer: Yes. I Except She was.

Deposition of **Catharine Gardner,** widow of **Henry Gardner**: On 19 March 1772 at Newport, Catharine Gardner of Newport, widow and relict of Henry Gardner, late of Newport, innholder, aged sixty-nine years . . . being sworn . . . sayeth that Henry Gardner Father to her late deceased Husband Henry Gardner of Newport had in his Possession three of the **Wamsley Family,** to wit **Tom, Mary** & a little one some where in or about the year 1722. Tom served his Time out with Henry Gardner the Father and was set at Liberty. . .. Henry Gardner the Father gave unto **Ephraim** his Son and brother to the deponent's late husband **Mary** to serve out her Time or rather the Time he had in her by a Contract entered into between the said Henry the Father, and **Tom Wamsley** the Father of the Wamsley Family that the little one the said Henry Gardner gave unto Tom Wamsley and **Patience** his Wife in Lieu and free Satisfaction of a Cow & Calf, which by the Contract aforementioned . . . he . . . was to give Wamsley, the alternative being left to Wamsley & Wife whether they would take the Cow & Calf, or the Child, and they choosing the

Child. . . . **Mary Wamsley** the mother of **Bet Dyer** so called & the present Mary Wamsley served out her Time with Ephraim Gardner . . . who was Brother to the deponent's late Husband . . . after her Time was expired the said Mary Wamsley from the said Ephraim Gardner went at Liberty as a free Person and as such acted, living Some Time at the House with the deponent as a free person. . . . While there she was taken Sick and was consumptive as was apprehended whereupon, as she had Children then living with the said Ephraim Gardner, and so could be better attended and taken care of, it was thought most advisable for her to return there which she did and there died. [*Signed by* **Catharine Gardner** *with her mark*]

Deposition of **Ephraim Gardner** of North Kingstown . . . of lawful age [*who*] on oath saith that his Hon^{d} Father **Henry Gardner** gave him and to his Disposal, "a Negro girl which s^{d} Negro we called **Mary** and when [*she*] grew to the age of a woman my s^{d} father advised me to free her if She Lived to the age of Twenty fore years old, and when She arived to s^{d} age, I was Willing to free her according to the advice of my father but she was in So poor State of health not able to Earn her Living and the Town Couns^{ll} of s^{d} Town would not admit her to be free to Bring any Charge upon the Town for when She was about twenty three years old I Employed Doctors to Do for her and She Continued upon the Decline and I Sent her to **Doctor Waits** and their kept her some time for him to Docter, and after that to **Doctor Robinsons** at Newport and Their She was under his Cair, untill they both Concluded they Could not help her But said She was in a Consumption, then She was brought hom to my house a Gain and their She Continued growing weaker untill She Dyed at abought Twenty Seven years old and Never was freed, and Before s^{d} Mary was Twenty Three years old she had Several Children, and one that wee Called **Bett** — I gave my Daughter **Pinelopy Dyer,** one wee Call^{d} **Moll** I gave my son **James Gardner.** both of them was born before the s^{d} Mary arived to the age that my s^{d} father advised me to free her at and as to the Two Children of ye s^{d} Mary that is Bett and Moll, I Never Talked of freeing them but Desposed of them as I Related and the s^{d} Moll lived with my son James Gardner untill he had a Child Scaulded which the s^{d} Negro Moll was Very Much blamed about it, and then She Soon went of as I Excepted to look Somebody to buy her or to keep out of the way a While, Sundry

Times after I asked my s^{d} son James Gardner why he Did not Due Something with her, he Replied he whould sell her the first oppertunity. . . ."

Question by Mr. **Benjamin Rodman:** Was the Negro Mary that your father gave you Daughter to Patiance after she had Wamsley?

Answer: I Excepted She was, & Born before Patiance was freed.

Deposition of **Peter Boss** of South Kingstown, yeoman . . . some time in the fore part of December AD 1771 . . . in company with **Samuel Rodman** returning into South Kingston from Richmond nigh **Robert Stantons** between his House and the Bridge in the after-part of the day, met with **Jonas Shearman** on horse back who had a black Girl behind him, of whom the deponent asked what black Girl he had got there, and he not suddenly answering the deponent then asked the Girl where he brought her from and she answered from **Ebenezer Tifts** and immediately fell to crying . . . the deponent having a week or ten days before heard that **Jeffry Watson, Esq.**, was in pursuit of that Family of Wamsley to enslave them, [*he*] cautioned the said Shearman to be careful how he meddled or concerned himself in those matters as it would bring him into Trouble, and to be careful to secure himself before he delivered her to any body or carry her back again, and Shearman said he would . . . the deponent then put forward & overtook **Samuel Rodman** . . . who had passed by during the conversation had with Shearman. About the twelfth or thirteenth Day of December . . . the deponent received a Letter from **James Helm, Esq.**, requesting [*him*] to deliver a Writt . . . under the hand & Seal of the said Helm, to **Col. Samuel Rose** commanding the said Rose upon a certain Day to appear before the said Helme and bring the Girl named **Susey Wamsley** then in his Possession which is the same Girl the deponent before saw behind Shearman . . . Rose sayed the Girl was at his house but that he had sold her to **Mr Phelps** & had nothing to do with her or words to that Purpose. Upon the Deponent's return home in the Evening a precept in writing under the hand of the Hon'ble **Joseph Wanton, Esq.** Governor of this Colony, was delivered him wherewith the Deponent immediately returned to the said Colonel Samuel Rose's house, tarried there that night, and the next morning made his Business known to the said Rose and Phelps who had purchased the aforementioned Girl of Rose, he being also there . . . and by Virtue of such [*he*] took the Body of the said Susey, **Susannah Wamsley** and her had before the Governor aforesaid as by the same Precept was commanded him . . . when the deponent took the said Girl into his Custody, the said Rose forbad him so to do or to carry her away and claimed her as his property at the same time shewing to the Deponent a Bill of Sale of her from under the hand & seal of Jeffry Watson, Esq[r] as one of the Assignees of James Gardner.

Question: Did . . . Phelps at that or any other time inform you that he with . . . Rose & Jeffrey Watson, Esq[r] were jointly concerned in enslaving the Wamsley family . . . and that he was to enjoy certain proportion of the profits arising from the sale of them ? . . .

Answer: Phelps told me that Jeffry Watson Esq[r] was to give Col. Rose a Bill of Sale of them and Col. Rose to give him one, that Col. Rose was to carry them into the Colony of Connecticut & there deliver them to him the s[d] Phelps, who was then to dispose of them and they the said Watson, Rose, and Phelps to divide the purchase money among them.

Verdict: "we find that **Mary Wamsley & Susannah Wamsley** are free." (Superior Court Case 13,407)

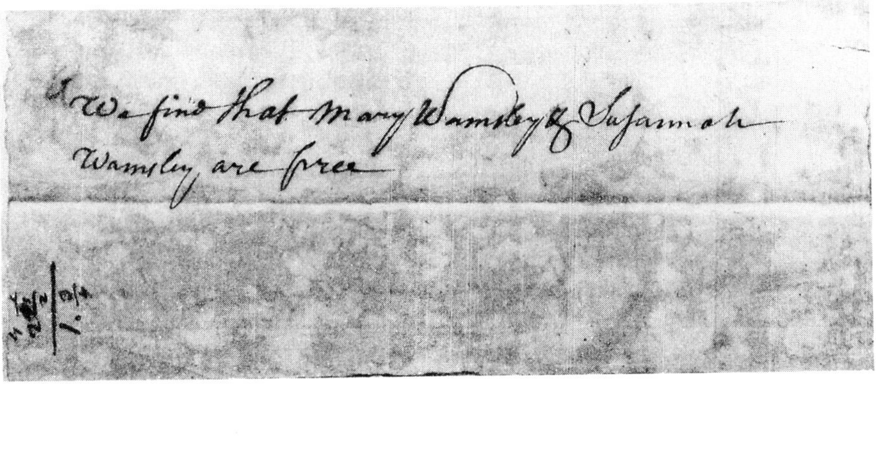
We find that Mary Wamsley & Susannah
Wamsley are free

1131. **Samuel Hull** of Newport, housewright, vs. **Joseph Peterson** of Newport, shipwright, in action of trespass to recover the easternmost half of a lot in Newport, the east half of a lot which **Joshua Morey** late of Newport purchased of **John Chapman** and was purchased by the defendant of **Hopestill Morey**, widow; bounded on the other half, belonging to **Arthur Tribut**, north on **John Chapman**, east on **David Fairbanks**. Deed shown, Joseph Peterson to Samuel Hull, 8 May 1770. (Docket No. 8)

1132. **Mary Searing** of Newport, widow, vs. **Richard Haughton Reid** of St. James in the Parish of St. James, Island of Jamaica for note due 26 December 1770 from **Cornelius Dillingham** of Newport, blacksmith. **Thomas Lillington**, one of the deputy sheriffs for the county, for want of the body of the defendant did attach a Negro man named **Primos** as estate of sd Richard Haughton Reid . . . since then has been "in my custody and bound to me as servant by certificate of indenture for a valuable consideration under hand and seal of the [*defendant*] for a term of years." (Docket No. 31)

1133. **Samuel Wilbour** of Little Compton, husbandman, and wife Phoebe who when sole was **Phoebe Gray** vs. **Philip Knight** of Warren, for debt due by note dated 22 March 1769 to Phoebe. (Docket No. 55)

1134. **Jahleel Brenton** of Newport, gentleman, vs. **Noel Allen** of Newport, blacksmith, for a house sold to him last September. (Docket No. 62)

1135. **Silas Cooke** of Newport, merchant, vs. **Henry Pinel** of Boston, mariner, for debt due 10 September 1771: 12 bottles of claret wine at 2s/3. (Docket No. 68)

1136. **John Halliburton** of Newport, physician, vs. **Catherine Brenton** of Newport, widow and devisee of **Thomas Brenton** of Newport, deceased, for debt due for medical services and drugs from 1768 to 1771, totaling £586:10. Constable Robert Lillibridge endorsed the warrant: "I attached a goldsmith shop and land it is on in possession of **Thomas Arnold**."

1137. **William Grinnell** of Newport, mariner, vs. **James Card Jr.** of Newport, mariner, to recover debt due by note given to **James Osman** 18 September 1769 at Philadelphia. Defendant promised on 14 October 1769 to pay to one **Joseph Redman** [*sheriff*] £8:06:04 in Philadelphia currency. Warrant to attach property to any value; constable Robert

Lillibridge attached "small piece of cloth on defendant's flour" [*blue cloth pinned to warrant*]. (Docket No. 92)

1138. **Thomas Gordon Stelle** of Newport, merchant, and wife **Elizabeth** when sole **Elizabeth Scott** vs. **George Scott**, merchant, **George Gibbs**, merchant, **Joseph Scott**, merchant, and **Sarah Scott**, spinster, an infant, all of Newport, in an action of partition of one farm in Portsmouth of 240 acres and a house and a farm in Little Compton of 140 acres and a house and a lot in Newport partly a tanyard, held by the parties together as undivided tenants in common: two seventh parts with one fifth of a seventh part belonging to sd George Scott in fee, one seventh with one fifth of a seventh to George Gibbs during his natural life as tenant by the curtesie; to Joseph Scott, one seventh part and one fifth of the seventh, the same amount to Sarah Scott, and the same to the plaintiff's wife Elizabeth. The farm in Portsmouth is in possession of **David Fish**; the farm in Little Compton **David Cook** now lives on and improves. Writ dated 23 April 1772. (Docket No. 144)

1139. **Samuel Slocum**, gentleman, of Jamestown vs. **Thomas Wright** of New Shoreham, mariner, for the schooner *Rhoda*, **John Wright**, master. Bill of sale 22 July 1771, Wright to Slocum, with mortgage payable 22 January 1772. Plaintiff recovered the schooner. (Docket No. 220)

1140. **Alexander Todd** and **Jacob Wincy** of City of Philadelphia, merchants, vs. **Jeremiah Brown** of Providence, mariner, for debt due by note from **Samuel Boone** of South Kingstown, yeoman, on 30 June 1769 at Newport endorsed for 70 Spanish Milled Dollars. Bill of sale for sloop *Dolphin*, with mortgage. (Docket No. 224)

1141. **Abial Cook**, yeoman, vs. **Nicholas Power**, merchant alias ropemaker, claiming £15:02:04 for debt. Bill dated at Little Compton 19 November 1771, for "my tew Negro felow work in his Rop walk named **Aaron** & **Moses** from the Date above to the twenty fifth day of March 1772 att twelve Dolors pr month." The defendant had paid "to **Sarah Green** for mending Moses & Aaron's cloaths; to **John Pytts** to pr of shoes for Aaron & Moses, 7*s* 6*d*." **William Piles** of Providence, ropemaker, deposed on 23 May 1772 that he "worked for Messrs Brown and Powers for two years as head of the Rope walk . . . sometime last fall came there two Negroes which Capt. Power hired of Mr.

Abial Cook of Little Compton and they were with us about 4 months . . . in winter . . . Moses could not work for want of cloathes and went home for some time and returned again in about a week or more . . . [*I*] never knew journeymen to be paid for the time when weather prevented them." He signed by mark; **John Shanneth** swore to the truth of the above, also signing by mark. Case went to referees, who found £12 10*s* due the plaintiff. (Docket No. 235)

1142. **Holder Chace** of Portsmouth, yeoman, vs. **Weston Hicks** of Portsouth, yeoman, in action of trespass to recover 8 acres in Portsmouth possessed by **Abigail Simon** of Newport, widow, on 6 March 1772 when she deeded it to the plaintiff. (Docket No. 264)

1143. **Bela Davenport** of Lebanon in County of Windham, Connecticut, yeoman, vs. **Eliphalet Davenport**, yeoman, and **Caleb Corey**, labourer of Little Compton, in action of trespass, to recover 90 acres and a house in Little Compton, bounded east partly on **Benjamin Head**, partly on Turnapus Pond, south on **Peter Shaw**, west on the highway, north partly on the highway, partly on **Richard Brownel**. The property had belonged to **Jonathan Davenport** who died 11 October 1751; his wife had it until her decease on 1 April 1772, then it was to go to their son **Samuel Davenport**, who had died 6 November 1762 intestate and without issue. The plaintiff is the eldest brother of Samuel and legal heir. Writ dated 8 April 1772. Verdict for plaintiff. (Docket No. 267)

1144. **Henry Wamsley** of Stonington, Connecticut, labourer, by **Elizabeth Wamsley** otherwise **Elizabeth Dyer** of Newport, singlewoman, his mother and guardian, vs. **Samuel Phelps** of Harrington [*Harwinton?*], Co. Litchfield, Connecticut, yeoman, and **Jeffrey Watson** of South Kingston, in action of trespass. On 1 January 1772 they sold him as a slave. Plaintiff produced an Indenture dated 28 November 1706 between **Thomas Wamsley**, molatto of Kingstown, husbandman, and **Henry Gardner** of Kingstown; Wamsley bound himself apprentice from 1 November for 5½ years, and in return "master shall set free from bondage his molata woman comonly called **Patience** and sd Thomas Wamsley at the end of 5½ years . . . she being his reputed wife, and in case the sd molata woman departed this life before [*the time was up,*] Thomas to be free at her death . . ."; master also to pay to **William Gardner**, cordwainer, £5. If Patience had a child during the time, it was to be free with them; their other children were to be free at four and twenty years. Witnesses were James Braman [*signed by mark*] and Theophilus Whale. Henry Gardner signed by mark, **H**. Verdict for the plaintiff, £45 and costs. (Docket No. 287) [*cf. No. 1130*]

1145. **Jonathan Easton** of Newport, yeoman, vs. **Jacob Barney** of Newport, yeoman, in action of trover: the defendant on 10 October 1771 converted to his own use 125 cedar rails of value £4 to the plaintiff belonging. **Jeremiah Greenman** deposed on 26 May 1772 at Newport that "in the month of October 1771 he was in a vessel which he was master of in Bedford in Dartmouth and did take on freight, about 100 and a quarter of Seder Rails by request of **Daniel Spencer** for **Jonathan Easton** of Newport . . . at Newport [*the rails*] were accepted by sd Easton." (Docket No. 303)

1146. **Mary Simmons** of Little Compton, widow, vs. **Isaac Manchester** of Tiverton, yeoman, in action of trespass, to recover one third part of 140 acres in Tiverton of which **William Hall** late of Little Compton, yeoman, deceased, had, by his will dated 15 December 1766, left to her the improvement during her widowhood. He died 10 February 1767 and she possessed it until 27 April 1772 when the defendant entered the premises. The land was bounded south on land of **Thomas Cook** and partly on land of **Paul Taber**, west partly on Taber, part on the highway, part on **Pardon Gray**; north partly on Gray, partly on land laid out to the widow **Mary Craw** for her thirds; east partly on land of **John Weight**, partly on **Benjamin Macomber**, partly on **Peleg Sanford**, partly on **Peleg Simmons**.

Oliver Hillard Esq. late of the Colony of Rhode Island now of Stonington, Connecticut, deposed at Stonington 1 July 1772 that he had often heard Deacon William Hall of Little Compton, now deceased, say and particularly after he had made a will and gave Mrs. Simmons and her son his estate in Little Compton, that the land he owned in Tiverton he always intended freely and clearly to give to the Church and Society in sd Tiverton to be forever for that use and benefit and that he did not intend Mrs. Simmons should have any thirds or interest in sd lands in Tiverton. **Mrs. Sarah Hillard**, wife of Oliver, deposed and said that Deacon William Hall replied that he had given Mrs. Simmons thirds of his estate in Little Compton and thought he had done pretty well by her. **Deacon Gedion Taylor** of Little Compton deposed and said that William Hall had disposed of his estate so none of his wife's relatives should have cause to complain. He had given a legacy to the church in Freetown and Little Compton and the farm in Tiverton to that church for support of the Gospel among that people . . . his wife was always free and willing to give that farm to that church for the extraordinary value that she had for **Mr. Campbel** and for the Gospel among the people . . . and this place at home for the love and good will that he had for **Isaac Simmons** and his wife's relations he had given to the widow and her son. The widow Simmons and her son **William Simmons** went to live with him. Court decided that the plaintiff had no right of action. (Docket No. 304)

1147. **Maria Kooy** of Buckfloot in the Province of Holland, widow, executrix of the will of **Pieter Cowenhoven** late of sd Buckfloot, mariner, deceased (late master of the ship *William Galley*) vs. **Edward Thurston** Esq. alias cooper and **Pardon Tillinghast**, mariner, both of Newport, executors of the will of **Benjamin Norton** late of Newport, merchant, deceased, for debt of £6,419:18 in the year 1745, due by bond dated 11 June 1745 at Newport. (Docket No. 316)

1148. **Maria Kooy** of Buckfloot in the Province of Holland, widow, executrix of the will of **Pieter Cowenhoven** late of sd Buckfloot, mariner, deceased (late master of the ship *William Galley*) vs. **William Read** of Newport, merchant, and **William Corey** of Providence, merchant, otherwise of Newport, surviving obligors to **Jonathan Nichols** late of sd Newport, merchant, deceased and **Robert Hazzard** late of South Kingstown, merchant, deceased, for debt in year 1745. (Docket No. 320)

– November 1772 –

1149. **John Thurston** of Newport, hatter, and **Hezekiah Starbuck** of Sherburn in the Island of Nantucket, mariner, and **Mary** his wife petitioned for a division of land: **John Thurston** late of Newport, taylor, on the first day of March 1771 died intestate seized of real estate in said County of Newport, to wit, one certain lot of land numberd six, and one other Half Lot of Land numberd seven both adjoining . . .

situate lying and being in Newport . . . together containing from East to West 124 feet . . . from north to south 60 feet or thereabouts . . . bounded southerly on a highway, easterly on land [*illegible in fold*] . . . **Howland**, northerly on land late of **John Banister** deceased, and Westerly on Land late of **Peter Treby** deceased as by a Map or Plat of the same under the Hand of **Samuel Easton** surveyor . . . said Premisses being Part and Parcell of a Number of Lots lately laid out by **John Chapman** together with all . . . the Messuages or Dwelling House, Out-Houses and Buildings thereon standing . . . And also a certain Lot of Land with a Dwelling House thereon standing situate in said Newport, containing 41½ feet from East to West and 59 feet in Breadth from North to South . . . bounded Easterly on Land now or late of **Anthony Shaw**, Southerly on a highway, Westerly on Land late of **Metcalf Bowler**, and Northerly on Land late of **John Banister** deceased . . . And also a certain Tract of Land . . . in Middletown . . . 54 Acres . . . bounded Southerly on Land of **Edward Thurston**, Westerly on a Highway. ..

Report of the division was made 12 June 1773 by **John Barker, James Tanner** and **Edw[*ar*]d Thurston** junr: "we have divided the whole into Six Shares, by accounting five eighth Parts: One Share drawn by **Latham Thurston**, who being the eldest son and by Law entitled to two Shares made choice of the next adjoining Share, consisting of the remaining three eight Parts of the Land, Buildings &c . . . together with 12 acres and 62 Rods of Land lying in Middletown, numbered two . . . bounded westerly upon a Highway 43 Rods, southerly upon Land of Edward Thurston, 46½ rods unto a Stone Wall, easterly upon said wall, 40 rods, northerly upon a Lot number three, 55 rods, unto the north part of the line first mentioned . . . **John Thurston** . . . a certain lot of land with the dwelling house thereon standing . . . in said Newport . . . 41½ feet from East to west, and 59 feet in breadth . . . with 10 acres and 64 rods of land in Middletown . . . bounded west upon a highway, 38½ rods, southerly upon lot number two, 55 rods, unto the stone wall aforesaid, easterly upon said stone wall, 20½ rods; northerly partly on lot number five and partly on lot number four, 73½ rods unto the northerly part of the line first mentioned. . . which share is one sixth part of the estates described in said petition. **Joseph Clarke Esq.** as Attorney to **Hezekiah Starbuck**, and **Mary Starbuck** his wife, drew by lot . . . one share . . . in Middletown . . . 18 acres, bounded southerly partly on land of **James Barker** deceased, and partly on land of **Isaac Peckham** deceased, westerly, northerly, and easterly on highways . . . with 9 acres and 120 rods . . . in said Middletown, bounded northerly upon land late belonging to **Samuel Bailey**, deceased, 41 rods; easterly upon said land, 9 rods and 11 links; northerly upon said land 7½ rods; easterly upon lot number five, 29 rods. . .. **Mary Thurston** as guardian to **Samuel Thurston** . . . 28 acres and 37 rods . . . in Middletown, numbered five . . . northerly upon land late belonging to Samuel Bailey. . . . Mary Thurston as guardian to **Paul Thurston** . . . 30 acres and 37 rods in Middletown, numbered six, easterly upon highway, northerly upon lot five, southerly upon land of Edward Thurston, westerly upon the stone wall.

– December 1772 –

1150. **Matthew Grinnell** and **John Martin**, yeomen, and **Thomas Fowler**, blacksmith, overseers of the poor of Jamestown, vs. Town Council of Newport, which on 3 March 1772 had ordered the removal of **Lydia Harris** a bastard child from sd Newport to Jamestown. The Newport Town Council did not determine that Lydia Harris was born in Jamestown and she never had legal settlement there; she was under the age of seven years and by law ought not to be removed from her mother. The Town of Newport paid Matthew Grinnel 6 shillings per week for keeping her from 23 March 1772 to 11 December 1772. (Docket No. 462)

1151. October: Summons for **John Negus** (son of **Job**), housewright, and **Ann** his wife who when sole was named **Ann Bailey,** both of Tiverton; Ann was administrator of the goods of **Bennet Bailey** late of Tiverton, yeoman, deceased; on complaint of **Daniel Hathaway** of Dartmouth, physician, for £19-2-8 due from Bennet Bailey on account from June 1760 to 29 July 1772, for boarding his Negroe **Boston** seven weeks at 8*d* per week and hiring him a Nourse and curing him of the Lues Ven; also for **Dorcas Hopes**, an Indian squaw who lived at his house, sick.

Summons issued (by **William Cook,** sheriff) to Job Negus, cordwainer, **Rebeccah Lamunnion,** singlewoman, both of Tiverton, and **Benjamin Durfee junr** and **Elizabeth Turner** of Portsmouth, singlewoman. Rebeccah Lamunyan testified that she was at the house of Bennet Bailey, and Elizabeth Turner that she was there last summer in mowing time. A letter was entered in evidence: dated Dartmouth 24 March 1766; "Dear Brother, I am endebted to **Richard Gifford** 5-14-8 which is more than your account, but if you will not Insist of that Sum from him till I come over to see you I will answer the overplus of your account to him or to you. I am your loving Brother - **Dan Hathway**." Verdict was for the plaintiff. (Superior Court Case 13,374)

1152. November 4: **Nancy Durfy**, a Negro girl slave to **William Durfy** of Tivertown, Innholder, confessed to having a male bastard child born 6 October; the child died in the night and she buried it in the orchard without telling anyone. Found not guilty. (Superior Court Case 13,475)

– May 1773 –

1153. May: Petition of **Caleb Carr** of Warwick, housewright, by **James Mitchel Varnum** and **Joseph Aplin** his attorneys, that in May 1771 he was sued by summons as surviving executor of the will of **Peleg Carr**, shopkeeper, deceased, by **John Fish** of Tiverton, cooper, and **Freelove** his wife for her legacy, and by **Cornelius Potter** of Newport in Kings County and Province of Nova Scotia, husbandman, and **Deborah** his wife. The court had returned an "erroneous judgement" in December 1772 and the petitioner, now in His Majesty's Gaol in Kent County, requests that he be released.

Copy of case: Will of **Peleg Carr** entered.

In the Name of God Amen the Twenty Eighth day of December in ye year of our Lord one thousand seven hundred & thirty six I Peleg Carr of Newport in ye County of Newport in ye Colony of Rhode Island &c Shopkeeper being of Perfect Mind and Memory thanks be given to Almighty God for ye same Calling to mind ye Mortality of my body & knowing that it is appointed for all men once to Die Do make & ordain this to be My Last Will and Testament in Manner following principally and first of all I give & Recommend my Soul into ye hands of Almighty God that Gave it me hoping through ye Merits Death & Passion of my Lord & Saviour Jesus Christ to have full and free Pardon and forgiveness of all my sins & to Inherit Everlasting Life of My Body I Commit to ye

Earth to be Decently Buried at ye Discretion of My Executor hereafter named nothing Doubting at ye General Resurrection that I shall Receive ye same again by ye Mighty Power of God and As Touching such Worldly Estate wherewith it hath Pleased ye Almighty God to Bless me I order & Dispose of ye same as followeth (vizt)

Imprimus I Will that all those Debts and Dues that in Right or Con[*tract?*] I do owe to any person or persons shall be well and truly contented & paid in a convenient time after my decease by my executor hereinafter named

Item I give and bequeath unto my beloved wife **Elizabeth Carr** the one third part of all my household goods impliments & utensils of household) after a deduction made of what I shall herein after bequeath) of whatever nature or kind soever also I give unto ye said Elizabeth Carr one Negro Woman named **Jenny** and one Negro Girl named **Chloe** all which to be & remain to said Elizabeth Carr & to her own proper use & behoof forever.

Item I give devise and bequeath unto my Beloved son **Peleg Carr** all that my now Dwelling house situate lying and being in Thames Street in Newport aforesaid being butted & bounded as followeth East upon said Thames Street south upon land belonging to Job Carr west home to ye house I purchased of **Samuel Snell** and hereinafter bequeathed to my son **William Carr** and north upon land belonging to **Daniel Russell** together with all ye land to said dwelling house belonging also I give devise and bequeath unto ye said Peleg Carr the one moiety or half part of my warehouse upon ye Ferry Wharfe to be Equally Divided between him & my sd son William Carr) butted & bounded as follwoeth East upon land belonging to **John Brown** south upon ye way leading to ye Ferry, west upon land belonging to **Samuel Carr** & north upon land of said John Brown & likewise one silver porringer all which shall be delivered to said Peleg Carr when he shall arrive to ye age of twenty one years & then to be & remain to ye said Peleg Carr his heirs and assigns and to his and their own proper use & behoof forever

Item I give devise and bequeath unto my beloved son **William Carr** all that dwelling house and land that I purchased of **Samuel Snell** situate lying and being in Newport aforesaid in ye present occupation of **Thomas Huxham** being butted & bounded as followeth east upon land herein before bequeathed by me to his brother Peleg Carr south upon a way leading down to ye Ferry, west upon land belonging to **Jeremiah Child** and north upon land belonging to **Daniel Russell** being from north to south sixty four feet or thereabout and also give devise & bequeath unto ye said William Carr two new shops situation in Newport aforesaid and in ye preset occupation of **Abraham All** taylor and [*blank*] **Hall** upholsterers & bound as followeth east upon land belonging to **Job Carr**, south upon ye way leading to ye ferry west upon said way & north upon land bequeathed to my said son Peleg Carr and further I give devise and bequeath unto my said son William Carr ye remaining moiety or half part of ye said warehouse on said Ferry Wharfe and likewise one silver porringer all which shall be delivered to ye said William Carr when he shall arrive to ye age of one & twenty years and then to be and remain to ye said William Carr his heirs and assigns and to his and their own proper use and behoof forever.

Item. I give devise and bequeath unto my beloved daughter **Ann** the wife of **Charles Bardin** of Newport aforesaid mariner the sum of three hundred pounds in good & passable publick credit of said Colony to be paid by my executors hereinafter named within twelve months after my decease and also one silver tankard marked *A C* to be deliverd her immediately after my decease and to be & remain to ye said **Ann Bardin** and to her own proper use and behoof forever

Item - I give devise and bequeath unto my well beloved sons **Robert Carr** and **Benjamin Carr** all that dwelling house and land thereunto belonging situate lying & being and adjoining to ye Point Bridge in Newport aforesaid being in length from east to west ninety feet or thereabouts and in depth fifty six feet or thereabout together with two old sheds thereon standing butted and bounded as followeth east upon a dwelling house and land thereunto belonging (which I have herein after ordered to be sold south upon a street leading o[*ver?*] said Point Bridge west upon a Cove & north upon land which I have herein after ordered likewise to be sold always reserving thereout a cart way of twelve feet for the use of persons that shall purchase ye lands ordered to be sold to be laid out to ye westward of said dwelling house and ye same to be divided equally between my said two sons Robert and Benjamin when ye youngest shall arrive to ye age of one & twenty years and then such division shall be and remain to them their heirs and assigs respectively and to each of their own proper use and behoof forever.

Item - I give and bequeath further unto my said beloved daughter **Ann Bardin** the one third part of all my household goods, impliments & utencils of household, except what I shall herein bequeath of what nature or kind soever to be and remain to her own proper use and behoof forever.

Item - I give and bequeath unto my beloved daughter **Freelove Carr** ye sum of two hundred pounds in good and passable publick bills of credit of said Colony to be put to interest by my executors in twelve months after my decease for ye use of said Freelove, and I likewise give and bequeath unto ye said Freelove Carr ye remaining third part of all my houshold goods impliments and utencils or household except what is herein otherwise bequeathed and one small silver tankard to be & remain to ye said Freelove Carr and to her own proper use & behoof forever.

Item - Whereas my said wife **Elizabeth Carr** is now with Child, if she should be delivered of a son then I give & bequeath unto him ye sum of three hudnred pounds in good and passable publick bills of credit of said Colony, and if it should happen to be a daughter then I give & bequeath unto her ye sum of two hundred pounds of like money either of which happening ye same to be put to interest by my executors in twelve months after my decease for the interest of either son or daughter which shall happen to be born.

Item - My will is and I do hereby order and appoint that my said wife **Elizabeth Carr** shall live in my now dwelling house for ye bringing up of my children until my said son Peleg Carr shall arrive to ye age of twenty one years and then I do further order and appoint that she shall live in ye dwelling house herein before devised unto my said two sons **Robert** and **Benjamin** until ye said Benjamin shall arrive to ye age of one and twenty years and after that my said four sons their Exc[r] or Adm[r] shall well and truly pay annually equally between them unto my said wife Elizabeth Carr ye sum of thirty pounds in good & passable bills of Publick Credit for and during ye term of her natural lifetime in lieu of her thirds or dower: and I do hereby [*torn*] that my executors do as soon as they can after my decease sell what shall remain of all my estate after debts and legacies are satisfied & paid shall be disposed of in manner following, one third part thereof to my sd wife Elizabeth Carr in full of her thirds, and ye remaining two thirds to be equally divided between all my children that shall be then alive.

Item - I do hereby further order and appoint that my executors shall receive ye rents and profits of all my lands & housing &c herein before bequeathed until my said sons arrive to their respective ages of one & twenty years to receive ye same and pay ye said rents and profits to my said wife Elizabeth Carr for and toward the support of and bringing up my children and in case, after my lands are sold and a dividend made as abovementioned among my children to each their part of, the interest thereof should not be sufficient for their maintenance then my executors are notwithstanding my former bequests to make up of so much of the interest of each legacy as shall be necessary for ye support of such child or children.

And lastly I do hereby constitute make ordain and appoint my beloved brothers **Daniel Carr** of said Newport cooper and **Caleb Carr** of Warwick house carpenter to be the executors of this my last will & testamant, and I do hereby utterly disallow revoke & disannull all and every other former testaments wills legacies and executors by me in any wise before this time named [*line torn*] and no other to be my last will & testament In witness whereof I have hereunto set my hand and seal ye day and year abovewritten.

The will was aigned by Peleg Carr in the presence of witnesses **Daniel Russell, Sales Carr,** and **Jas. Martin**. When it was proved 10 January 1736/7, Russell and Martin were sworn.

Receipt from **Elizabeth Carr** to **Caleb Carr,** surviving executor of the estate of Peleg Carr, deceased, for rents of dwelling house, two shops, and half a warehouse, until 6 March 1743/4, according to a legacy bequeathed to **William Carr** by my husband, Capt. Peleg Carr, deceased, dated 5 October 1741 per hand of son-in-law Peleg Carr. 6 October 1741, received of Caleb Carr . . . £5 rent due from **Peleg Thurston** for the house he lives in . . . and rent of **Lydia Yeats** shop . . . and **Abraham All's** house and shop.

10 March 1741/2, receipt from Peleg Carr to Caleb Carr . . . obliging self to pay the same towards what still remains due from my sd father's estate; witness **Charles Bardin.** (taken from TC 9:437)

Inventory included **Jenny,** Negro woman, valued at £100; **Chloe,** her daughter, £50, Negro **Jo:,** £100, and Negro **Will,** £20. (From Newport Town Council Book 10:53)

Document in file: "This may certifie that Caleb Carr surviving executor of Peleg Carr late of Newport deceased did on fifth day of October A.D. 1741 render to ye Town Council of sd Newport an acco^{tt} of his executorship by which acco^{tt} it appears that he had paid two hundred and eleven pounds one shilling and eight pence more than he had in his hands of the said Peleg Carrs estate, which acco^{tt} the Council accepted of and ordered to be recorded Newport Novr 7th 1746. attest Wm Coddington Junr Council Clerk."

Freelove Carr's discharge 2 May 1757 to "Unkle Caleb Carr of Warwick, executor of the will of Peleg Carr my deceased father, of Newport, for one small silver tankard marked **P** $^{\mathbf{C}}$ **A** given me as my legacy." Witnesses: **James** and **Deborah Tallman.**

James Talman of Warwick deposed 27 September 1771 at East Greenwich, before **Thos Aldrich**, J.P., and said that Freelove Carr had come to his house and said "she was agoing to her Uncle Caleb Carr's to see if their was anything coming to her of her father's estate given to her by will." When she came back, she said that her uncle had paid out more than the estate of her father, but there was a silver tankard and if she would take that and give him a final discharge, she should have it. James and his wife went with her and she received the tankard and signed a discharge for it. **Deborah Talman** of Warwick made similar testimony, adding that Freelove brought the silver tankard to their house, and told her that "she had got more than she ever expected for her uncle Caleb had paid out so much more than he had rec^{d} of her fathers estate . . . she was fully satisfied."

[An article based on this case was published in *The American Genealogist*, 63 (1988):223-230].

– September 1773 –

1154. **Thankful Peirce** of Jamestown, single woman, spinster, vs. **John Weeden** of Jamestown, yeoman alias housewright, in an action of promise; writ dated 19 August 1773 [*case continued from November 1772*]. Thankful claimed that on 30 August 1772 she was then unmarried and promised the defendant to marry him and she therefore refused to contract matrimony with any other man and yet continued single while he continued fraudulently and craftily to deceive her; she claimed damages of £800. The defendant said he never promised to marry her. Letters were entered as evidence; one dated 12 December 1771, to be given to her father, is bitter in tone, indicating that her father was opposed to the marriage, and his father was "whimsical," intending to cut him out of his estate; he suggests he marry her after he makes sure of his own father's estate. **Isaac Peirce** deposed and said that he feared **John Weeden** had been too familiar with his daughter, and she was pregnant. **Stephen Peirce** deposed that about 1 June 1772 he had asked John Weeden what he intended to do "in the affair between my sister and himself . . . he answered she was with child by him, he intended to marry her soon but intended to get a deed of his father's house and land first if he could." **Philip Peckham** deposed that in the first week in September 1772 **Isaac Pierce** came to him and desired him to come to his house the next morning to meet **Joseph Greene** . . . they went "and **John Weeden** came in . . . Peirce called his daughter-in-law **Ann Peirce**

and daughter **Thankful Peirce** . . . decided to put an advertisement in the News Paper, to set matter in true light that the girl might be exculpiated from been guilty of action at law and he would marry her immediately." **Ann Peirce** testified in court and mentioned her father **Gibbs** in Newport. **Samuel Slocum** testified 15 September 1773 that in May last before the sitting of the court John Weeden asked him to go to Isaac Peirce's and marry him to Thankful Peirce . . . "[*I*] told him I was agoing to town that day but when I came back . . . accordingly we went . . . Weeden said now he had come with a proper officer . . . [*Peirce*] answered there should be no marrying there that night." (Superior Court 13,349)

1155. Overseers of the poor in North Kingstown vs. Overseers of the Poor in Portsmouth, appealing a judgement of May 1773 that **Bethany Justun**'s last legal settlement was in North Kingstown. (Superior Court 13,364)

– November 1773 –

1156. **Lemuel Drew** of Liverpool in the County of Queens in Nova Scotia, mariner, vs. **Oliver Cooke** Esq. and **Mary** his wife, late when sole named **Mary Allen**, both of Tiverton, who is administratrix of the goods and chattels, etc., of **Joshua Allen** late of Portsmouth, gentleman, deceased, to recover £5 Halifacks currency which is equal to £6 lawful money, due by note signed by Allen in his lifetime at a place called Cape Gaspe on 5 August 1763. Writ dated 6 November 1773. Note witnessed by **Zebedee Grinnell**.

– March 1774 –

1157. Petition of **Elisabeth Maccollock** (signed Elizabeth M'Cullock), wife of **Kenneth,** late resident in Newport, for a divorce on grounds of desertion. She stated that they were married on or about the month of March 1771 and he was now cohabiting with another married woman. Letter dated New York 14 November 1773 from **John Dudley,** c/o Mr. **Francis Dudley,** Maiden Lane, N.Y., referred to an affidavit by **Mary Walker** re **Kenneth Mc Cullock** and **Phebe,** wife of

John Dudley, having been found at Philadelphia passing as man and wife. (Superior Court 13,361)

1158. **Rebecca Rider** of Newport, widow and administratrix of the estate of **John Rider,** late of Newport, mariner, deceased, petitoned to sell real estate, exhibiting order from Town Council dated 7 March 1774. She stated that when her husband went to sea the last time, upwards of seven years ago, he was indebted to sundry persons; there was one debt due to **William Coggeshall,** being a mortgage on part of sd John Rider's real estate for £99:13:9/3f. The file contains a note to **Nath Coggeshall** dated 12 March 1765 for 22 1/4 Dollars. (Superior Court 14,014).

– May 1774 –

1159. **Shearman Clarke** of Newport, mariner, vs. **Daniel Servat** of Newport, sailmaker alias merchant, in action of trespass, charging that the defendant at Amsterdam entered on board a certain brigantine *Betsy* whereof the plaintiff was master 12 September 1773 and against his will and consent took out from the vessel 3000 pounds weight of coffee belonging to the plaintiff, valued at £100 sterling. (Docket No. 322)

– November 1776 –

1160. **John Almy** of Tiverton, yeoman, vs. **Giles Cooke** of Portsmouth, labourer, for £211:5 due for lamb and veal, etc. (Docket No. 3)

1161. **James Center**, barber, and **Mary** his wife and **Sarah Ann Howard**, spinster, all of Newport, which said Mary and Sarah Ann are executrixes of the will of **Martin Howard**, late of Newport, Esq., vs. **George Scott** of Newport, yeoman, for debt due by note. (Docket No. 11)

1162. **Thomas Claggett** of Newport, watchmaker, vs. **Lemuel Allen** of the Island of Prudence in township of Portsmouth, yeoman, but now resident in Freetown, Co. Bristol [*Massachusetts*], yeoman, and **George Allen** of said Prudence, mariner, to whom all the real estate of **Caleb Allen** late of Portsmouth, yeoman, deceased, in and by the last will and testament of said Caleb devised, for £13:7:9 due by Caleb's note dated 26 June 1773, and also for one eight-day clock, £10:6:3, cleaning the clock, and mending a jewel for his daughter **Rebecca**, 1/6. (£13:7:9 = 44 5/8 Dollars) (Docket No. 13)

1163. **Joseph Tomkins** of Little Compton, labourer, vs. **Mary Rogers**, widow, and **Aaron Wilbur Esq.** of Little Compton, labourer, for debt. (Docket No. 32)

1164. **Caleb Bentley** of North Kingstown, mariner, vs. **Mary Franklin** of Jamestown, widow, in an action of trespass, charging that on 15 July 1775 with others she did enter a certain lot of marshland, about 4 acres, in Jamestown, belonging to the plaintiff, and "mow the grass thereon growing and . . . did carry away 4 tons of grass, to the value of £30." (Docket No. 40)

– May Term 1782 –

1165. **Robert Crooke** of the City and County of Newport, merchant, administrator of the estate of **Juby Grinnell** late of Newport, widow, vs. **John Langworthy** of Dartmouth, sailmaker. Juby Grinnell of Newport died on or before 30 January 1781 possessed of [*list of goods*], and sd John Langworthy then and there possessed himself of the same. **Will of Juby Grinnel** shown, dated 1 September 1780:

. . . to **Tony Taylor** one gold ring; to **Peggy Thurston** one gold ring; to my granddaughter **Abigail Orquar** one ear ring; to **Nancy Coggeshall** three paper dollars; to **Thomas Freebody** two gold rings; to **Cubit Brown** two beds, a table, chairs, pewter, other household goods and all my sons wearing apparel and money my son left for my maintenance . . . one gold necklass and locket which I am to have a deason hansom buring out of that. Witnesses: **John Pabodie, Benjamin Church**.

1166. **Jeremiah Clark** of Newport, mariner, and wife **Sarah**, daughter and heir at law of **Joseph Wanton**, late of Providence, Esq., deceased, vs. **Gideon Wanton** of Newport, gentleman, **Stephen Ayrault Wanton, Sarah Wanton, Frances Wanton**, all of Newport, infants under 21 who by their grandfather **Stephen Ayrault** of Newport, merchant, and **Edward Wanton**, late of said Newport, merchant, deceased, which said Joseph, Gideon and Edward were children of **Gideon Wanton**, deceased.

Reference to board for mother **Mary** and for **Quam**; rents received from estate of Joseph Wanton, deceased, of Tiverton.

Bill dated at Newport 5 September 1780: to Estate of **Mary Wanton**, widdow, deceased, to **John Townsend**, for a Mahogany Coffin, 15½ Dollars = £4:13.

Receipted bill from **Polly Bull**, signed **Mary Bull**, 1780, "to my attending to take care of Mrs. Wanton from September 3, 1776 to 3rd September 1780 is 223 weeks at 3/ per week, received of John G. Wanton." "Polly Bull's account of afares of Mary Wanton: an inventory of what I found Left in ye House when I moved in to take care of it: 2 large tables, one old desk, one old dressing table, one tin kitchen [*illegible*], one parrot cage, one stand, one candlestick; one skillet and one pair handirons mother lent me; six or seven books of no great consequence."

— November Term 1782 —

1167. **Jeremiah Clarke** of Newport, gentleman, and **Sarah** his wife [*who*] is Daughter and Heir at Law of **Joseph Wanton** of Providence, Esq. deceased, **Gideon Wanton** of Newport, Gentleman and **Henry Bowers** of Swansey in the County of Bristol and Commonwealth of Massachusetts, Merchant and **Mary** his wife and **Stephen Ayrault Wanton, Sarah Wanton, Francis Wanton** all of Newport, infants within the age of twenty one years, children and devisees of the Real estate of **Edward Wanton** late of Newport, merchant, deceased, who sue by their Grandfather and Guardian **Stephen Ayrault** of Newport, merchant, which sd Joseph, Gideon, Mary & Edward were the children of Gideon Wanton late of Newport, Esq., deceased, vs. **John G. Wanton** of Newport, gentleman, in an action of partition. Continued from May 1782.

1168. **Benjamin Howland**, gentleman, **Thomas Howland**, Esq. and **Sarah** his wife who late when sole was named **Sarah Borden**, and **John Howland**, yeoman, all of Tiverton, **Mary Rodman**, widow of Leister, County of Worcester, Mass., who when sole was named **Mary Borden, Elizabeth Whitfield**, widow, late **Elizabeth Borden, Nancy Borden**, spinster, **Abraham Borden**, mariner, **Mary Borden**, spinster, **Mathew Borden**, infant mariner, **Walter Borden**, infant mariner, all of Newport, children and heirs of **Mathew Borden** late of Newport, yeoman, deceased, vs. **Almy Thurston**, widow, who when sole was named **Almy Richardson, Thomas Robinson**, merchant and **Sarah** his wife who when sole was **Sarah Richardson, Thomas Richardson**, gentleman, **William Robinson**, yeoman, and **Elizabeth** his wife who when sole was **Elizabeth Richardson** and **Gideon Wanton** Esq., all of Newport, and **Henry Bowers** or Swanzey, gentleman, and **Mary** his wife who when sole was **Mary Wanton** and **Stephen Ayrault Wanton**, guardian of **Sarah Wanton**, spinster, and **Francis Wanton**, spinster, Sarah and Frances under 21 years and children and heirs of **Edward Wanton** late of Newport, gentleman, deceased, in an action of Partition of three farms in Tiverton with buildings thereon, of which plaintiff and defendants are tenants in common. One farm was called the Homestead Farm, about 50 acres, bounded west on the Four Rod Highway, north on land belonging to heirs of **Holder Slocum**, east on Eight Rod Highway, south on land of **John Almy**; the second farm was about 120 acres, bounded west on the River or Salt Water, north on land of **Nathaniel Briggs**, east on the Eight Rod Highway, and south on land of **Susannah Barker**; the third farm was about 200 acres, bounded west on Eight Rod Highway, north on land of **Joseph Barker**, east on a highway, and south on land of **Western Hicks**.

1169. **Joseph** and **John Rogers** of Providence, merchants, vs. **Solomon Southwick** of Newport, Esq., in an action of trespass involving 11 acres in Newport bounded by **John Collins** and **Peleg Anthony**, referring to deed of 20 April 1777 by said Solomon and wife **Ann**.

1170. **Joseph Sherman** of Tiverton, Esq. vs. **Philip Sisson** of Dartmouth, yeoman, devisee of the real estate of **Thomas Sisson** late of Tiverton, yeoman, deceased. Plaintiff stated that he had from 20 April 1778 to 15 April 1781 found and provided meat, drink, washing and lodging for a certain Negro man **Jack** belonging to Thomas Sisson late of Tiverton, deceased, for which Thomas Sisson had promised to pay. Bill: figured at 12 shillings a week = $93.

Bill dated 6 February 1779 for clothing, coffin, funeral charges and digging grave, "looking after him in last sickness, fetching Doctor several times . . . **Dr. Cob's** Bill.

Deposition of **John Sears** at North Providence 14 November 1782, that the affair was settled by Mr. **Isaac Vencent** of Rochester. **Isaac Vincent**, **Philip Taylor** and **Walter Cook** chosen referees; verdict for plaintiff £52:1:5 and costs.

1171. **Ebenezer Shearman** of Newport, mariner, vs. **John Harris**, cordwainer, and wife **Deborah** of Newport in an action of trespass involving 7 acres in Newport bounded west on land late of **John Thurston** now of **Charles Handy**; defendant sold same 8 April 1774 to **Anthony Shaw** of Newport, carpenter, who sold it 30 September 1782 to plaintiff.

1172. **Ebenezer Shearman** of Newport, mariner, vs. **John Shearman** and **Peleg Shearman**, both of Newport, gentlemen, in an action of trespass involving land and dwelling in Newport of which **Elisha Shearman** late of Newport, deceased, was in his lifetime seised and on 8 May 1772 by deed conveyed to plaintiff; defendant entered premises 1 October 1782. Mortgage deed shown, witnessed by **Samuel** and **John Green**.

1173. **John Wanton** of Newport, gentleman, vs. **John Bull** of Newport, stone cutter, in an action of trespass involving lot and house in Newport, about 6 acres, bounded northwest on Broad Street, northeast on **Elisha Smith** and partly on **Nathaniel Mumford** and partly on **George Scott**, southeast on George Scott, southwest partly on **John Bull** and partly on highway to be laid out, which **Henry Bull** of Newport, Esq., deceased, on 23 September 1768 deeded to **William Bull** of Newport, mariner, who continued seised of it until 13

November 1781. **William Davis**, Esq. of Newport, Sheriff of County, by virtue of an Act of the General Assembly for regulating the method of assigning real estate sold by execution, etc., and for satisfaction of an execution, levied on the premises . . . deeded all estate of said William Bull to the plaintiff, who was on 1 October 1782 dispossessed by defendant. Plea of defense claimed Henry Bull was incapable when he made the deed and was then under guardianship; that the deed was obtained by William in fraud and deceit. Suit withdrawn.

1174. **Job Wilbur** of Little Compton, currier, vs. **John Cook** of Tiverton, Esq., for money due 28 May 1782, 102 1/2 silver dollars, for value received.

– November Term 1783 –

1175. **Gideon Almy** of Tiverton, yeoman, vs. **Sarah Gray** of Tiverton, widow and administratrix of **Edward Gray** late of Tiverton, deceased, in action of debt due 1 October 1780. (Docket No. 21)

1176. **Joseph Borden** of Tiverton, yeoman, vs. **John** and **Parker Earle** of Portsmouth, yeomen, and **Oliver Earle** of Newport, mariner, devisees of real estate of **Ruth Earle** late of Portsmouth, widow, deceased, for debt she incurred 21 May 1777: bill included "18 months house rent for your daughter-in-law Ruth Earle, cheese, wood, corn," etc. (Docket No. 23)

1177. **Samuel** and **Ebenezer Slocum** of the Island of Patience in the township of Portsmouth, yeomen, and **Edward Slocum** of East Greenwich, blacksmith, executors of the will of **Ebenezer Slocum** of Patience Island, yeoman, deceased, vs. **Samuel Dyer** of Newport, to recover a debt due 1775 at Newport. (Docket No. 41)

1178. **Gideon Almy**, yeoman, and **John Almy**, yeoman, both of Tiverton, vs. **Abiel Cook** in an action of trespass. The plaintiff on 20 December 1782 was owner of half the schooner *Lark* of burthen of 15 tons, when the defendant took her into his possession. (Docket No. 45)

Deposition of **Abraham Gifford** of Dartmouth that in 1782 late in the fall or the beginning of winter, he saw **Abiel Cook** of Tiverton, yeoman, with his son come on Davis Wharf in Dartmouth at a place called Paquacheck Point and "...take off the sales... Running of and from a schooner... put them on two horses and carry them home to his House." [*There follows a list of sails taken by the defendant.*]

Deposition of **Christopher Gifford**, at Dartmouth 12 November 1784: "**Isaac Cory** brought said schooner into the Acokset River in July 1782 . . . very leakey . . . **Abiel Cook** came with an officer and attached said schooner and put her in my care . . . got me to put her in order fit for service . . . boards out and eat to pieces, not fit for any sarvis. . . ."

Deposition of **John Head**, 12 November 1784, that he helped **Christopher Gifford**, etc.

1179. **Margery Northrup** of North Kingstown, widow and **Katherine Kilborn** and **Lydia Heath** of Newport, widow and heirs-at-law of estate of **Clement Stanton**, deceased, vs. **James Taylor** of Newport, cordwainer, in an action of trespass involving dwelling house on Broad Street. Clement Stanton died 6 October 1783. (Docket No. 157)

1180. **Henry Oman** of Newport vs. **Catherine Kilburn** of Newport, widow and administratrix of the estate of **John Kilburn** late of Newport, merchant. Deposition of **George Olney**, Agent, of Town of Providence, that sometime before 11 February 1777 **Ezekiel Burr**, Esq. late of Providence, deceased, showed him a letter signed by **Henry Oman** in which he obligated himself to pay or account for what **William Porteous** and **William Duncan** had purchased at sales of prize ships *Th[etis?]* and *Union*. (Docket No. 178)

1181. **Gideon Worden** of Portsmouth, husbandman, vs. **William Cook** of Tiverton, trader, for $10, 8 shillings due for services, 2 days time and expenses in March 1782. Judgment for plaintiff. (Docket No. 192)

1182. **Jeremiah Tallman Rogers** of Tiverton, an infant under 21, yeoman, by **Patience Rogers** of Tiverton, spinster, his mother and guardian, vs. **Stephen Tallman** of Tiverton, yeoman, in an action of trespass for the possession of one farm of about 50 acres and dwelling house belonging to **Stephen Tallman [Sr.]** of Tiverton, deceased, who died 11 May 1783 and left it to plaintiff by his will. (Docket No. 103)

Glossary

(See List 4 [pages 587-588] for types of cases abstracted in this book, which includes many of the grounds for controversy. Specific goods and and services in controversy will be found throughout the index and in List 5 [pages 589-592].)

The following definitions are drawn from Henry Campbell Black *et al.*, *Black's Law Dictionary*, abridged sixth ed. (St. Paul, Minn.: West Publishing Co., 1991) and the *Oxford English Dictionary* (CD-ROM version), selected for 17th and 18th century usage.

Bailiff: Person acting in administerial capacity who has the custody and administration of lands or goods for the benefit of the owner, and is liable to render an account thereof.

Defendant: The party against whom relief or recovery is sought ... the person defending or denying.

Deponent: One who deposes, gives under oath testimony that is reduced to writing.

Deposition: The testimony of a witness taken upon oral question or written interrogation, *outside* of court, and put in writing, to be used as evidence in a court case.

Detinue: A form of action for recovery of personal chattels from one who acquired possession of them lawfully, but retained it without right, together with damages for the detention.

Execution: The carrying out of something, such as a judgment of the court. This often involved seizing and selling property of a defendant in order to satisfy a judgment against him.

Fee in tail: to be held by exclusive heirs (*entailed*), as directed by a will (as in primogeniture, when property passes to the eldest son).

Fee simple: to hold to a person or his heirs forever, absolutely, and simply.

Mandamus: "We command." A judicial writ directed to an inferior court, an officer, etc., commanding some specified thing to be done.

Nihil dicit: "He says nothing." Name of a judgment which may be taken as of course against a defendent who omits to plead or answer plaintiff's declaration or complaints within time limits . . . judgment for want of a plea.

Non suit: A term broadly applied to a variety of terminations of an action which do not adjudicate issues on the merits of the case. In early use, the cessation of a suit resulting from the voluntary withdrawal of the plaintiff.

Plaintiff: A person who brings an action ... seeks remedial relief for an injury to rights; a complainant.

Protest: In maritime law, a written and notarized statement by the master of a vessel, declaring that damage suffered by the ship on a voyage was caused by storms or other perils of sea, without negligence on his part.

Seized or **seised** [of property]: from *seisin*, possession of real property, in *fee simple, q.v.* (thus *seised in fee simple* means to hold legal title to the land in question).

Trespass: Unlawful interference with one's person, property, or rights.

Trover: Action for the recovery of damages against a person who had found another's goods and wrongfully converted them to his own use.

Writ: A written judicial order for instituting an action. (The writ is usually the first document found in a case, giving the reason for the suit and sometimes ordering the arrest of the defendant.) There are many kinds of writs, such as **writ of execution,** which directs the sheriff to enforce the judgment of the court.

INDEX

Please note:

The following index is by **item number**. (Pagination for the abstracts has been intentionally omitted in order to minimize confusion.) The index includes the names of all individuals and ships found in the abstracts, and names of places *other than Newport*, which is mentioned so frequently that indexing it would be of questionable value. Although an attempt has been made to include subjects, we do not claim that this aspect of the index is exhaustive.

Lists arranged in specific categories will be found on pages 579 - 609, following this index. Cross-references to the lists will be found throughout the index. Categories are:

List 1. **Persons of Color**, by name, broken down into types (Indian, mulatto, mustee, negro). Individuals listed are also included in the alphabetical index. *page 579*

List 2. **Places**, grouped by country and/or state. These names will also be found as they occur alphabetically in the index. *page 580*

List 3. **Documents and Records**, by type (e.g., wills copied). *page 584*

List 4. **Grounds for Cases**, by type (e.g., trespass), excluding cases of debt. The list is probably not complete, but is included for the sake of general interest and easy reference. *page 587*

List 5. **Items**, goods and services mentioned in cases. This list may well be incomplete, but it is included to indicate the wide variety of things that were of concern to the people named in these records, and to enable the reader to pick out items of interest. Many, but not necessarily all, of the items appear also in the index. *page 589*

List 6. **Public Houses and Ships**. These names will also be found as they occur alphabetically in the index. *page 593*

List 7. **Occupations**, by trade or social status, of persons who are named in the abstracts. Use the index to look up item numbers. The same person may appear in more than one category. *page 594*

– A –

— B —

— C —

– H –

– J –

– N –

– Q –

– R –

– T –

LISTS

The lists are arranged alphabetically within the following categories:

LIST 1. PERSONS OF COLOR

Please note that the same individual may be listed in more than one category.

INDIAN
Abraham, 21
Ahannah, James, 80
Amy, 956
Audrey, 35A
Boston, 198
Briggs, Robin, 875
Cubit, 50
Daniel, Betty, 385
Dick, 198
Exe, 963
Faraoh, Sarah, 428
George, 241
Grate Plain James, 105
Greenwell, Joseph, 576
Grinel, John, 797
Hannah, 12, 428
Hoopes, Dorcas, 1151
James, 102
Jane, 24
Jeffery, 658
Jenny, 1098
Joan, 1014, 1098
Joash, 102
Joseph, 102
Myantonomy, 232
Nebe, Isaac, 116
Ned, Sarah, 907
Paris, Sampson, 884

INDIAN, *cont'd*
Pasco, Joseph, 105
Perrey, John, 72
Peter, Betty, 566
Peter, 658
Phillis, 658, 1048
Pierce, Joseph, 664
Poheag, Peter, 883
Pum Homm, 232
Queakin, Jacob, 65
Sambo, Mary, 428
Sarah, 35A
Scooner, Robin, 391
Sotanoman, 232
Thompson, Betty, 566
Tillinghast [girl], 966
Tom, 12
Will/Wills, Peter, 613
Wilson, Toby, 72
Worwick, 198

MULATTO
Anthony, Isaac, 540
Cranston, Thomas, 202
Dunbar, James, 744
Godfrey, Jesper, 202
Isaac, 540
Pardon, 907

MULATTO, *cont'd*
Wamsley, Patience, 1144
Wamsley, Tom, 1144

MUSTEE
Amy, 956
Briggs, Tobias, 940
Tobie, 1082

NEGRO
--- girl (of Manchester), 1110
--- man (of John Brown), 707
--- man (of Sarah Peters), 724
--- servant (of Freeborn), 684
Aaron, 1141
Andrew, 21
Bartholomew, Cesar 900
Ben, 956
Bess, 35A, 172
Boston, 1151
Breemer, 1014
Bristow, 752
Brownel, Samuel, 811
Butman, John, 198
Cadman, James, 198

LIST 2. PLACES

The general index may contain further references to any particular place named.

LIST 3. DOCUMENTS AND RECORDS

The following lists are intended for general reference only. There is great variation in the way such records appear in the cases, from a casual mention in a deposition to an actual transcription. The following have been noted, but the listing in any particular category is almost certainly not complete.

LIST 4. GROUNDS FOR CASES

debts due by book or on notes are not included; coverage of other categories may not be complete

BASTARDY
Arnold, Sarah, 786
Astin, Benjamin, 1122
Bowin, Kathrine, 290
Bradford, Thomas, 122
Briggs, Priscilla, 1044
Cratty, Ann, 672
Davenport, Elizabeth, 798
Fish, Alice, 802
Green/Card, Catharine, 333
Greenman, Eunice, 133
Harris, Hannah, 1122
Lawton, Deborah, 964
Lowrea, Abigail, 723
Palmer, John, 1046
Stoddard, Mary, 1046
Strange, Sarah, 975
Woodman, Thomas, 1044

DETAINURE, re:
bed and bedding, 932
gold necklace, 69
gun, 148
sea chest & contents, 1096

DIVORCE
Fry, 953
Lawton, 964
Maccollock, 1157
McWilliams, 954
Snell, 1078
Thurber, 941

INDENTURES
of Ann Humery, 699
of Ben Bosworth, 957,
of James Dunbar, 744
of Caleb Kinion, 264
of Tom Wamsley, 1144

INDICTMENTS
Aspin, Samuel, 494
Basson, Isaac, 103
Chadwick, Mercy, 496
Chapman, Johannah, 170
Child, Jeremiah, 171
Coomes, Solomon, 149
Ellis, Elizabeth, 169
Faraoh, Sarah, 428
Havens, Samuel, 779
Hopkins, Elizabeth, 426
Hulines, James, 80
Indian apprentices Joseph and James, 102
Indian Dick, 198
Morrow, Peter, 378
Scipio, Negro, 497
Shearman, John, 950
Taber, John, 671
Weaver, Thomas, 974
Wilcox, Jeremiah, 329

PARTITIONS
Boss land, S. Kingstown, 237;
Dutch Island, 513;
Jamestown, 722;
Newport, tanyard, 1138;
Portsmouth - Little Compton, 1138;
Scott land, 1138;
Three Farms, Tiverton, 1168;
Thurston land, 1149
Tiverton land & house, 1129

PROMISE, re:
cargo, 999
charter party indenture, 990

PROMISE, *cont'd*:
child support, 975
debt, 621
delivery of rum, 856
house painting, 598
lost money, 567
lottery, 548, 562, 571
making desk, 382
marriage, 133, 793, 828, 1154
misuse of property, 118
molasses delivery, 267
molasses storage, 920
New Shoreham, 480
silver tea pot, 1009
storage of molasses, 920
third party, 785
tupentine delivery, 835
wages on voyage, 911
wine on voyage, 766

TRESPASS, re:
abuse of servant, 512
affray, 681
assault, 45, 140, 539, 555, 871, 967, 998, 1027, 1030, 1079, 1125
assault on maids, 515
beating with cane, 739
black oak trees, 773
bodily harm, 709
Boston Neck, 139
cabbages, 421
cattle, 160, 182
character, 45
Charlestown property, 813
church land, 706
coffee from ship, 1159
cow, 642
cutting off ear, 555

LIST 5. ITEMS

LIST 6. PUBLIC HOUSES AND SHIPS

LIST 7. OCCUPATIONS AND SOCIAL STATUS

Apothecaries,
Creese, Thomas
Tweedy, John
Apprentices,
Barker, Ezburn
Collins, William
Corey, John
Dennis, John
Downing, Marshall
Easton, John
Gibbs, James
Harris, Hannah
House Carp
Humery, Ruth
Maddin, Mary
Manchester, Benjamin
McDaniel, Paul
Pardon [Indian]
Peckham, Benjamin
Smith, Isaac
Townsend, Christopher
Wamsley, Thomas
Woodman, Thomas
Bakers,
Child, Jeremiah
Claggett, Caleb
Creulz, Daniel
Davis, John
Emmons, Nathaniel
Fitch, George
Rogers, Samuel
Barbers,
Alison, John
Brown, William
Center, James
Elsworth, Clement
Forth, James
Lassells, William
Northam, Robert
Wilburne, Richard
Blacksmiths,
Allen, Noel
Arnold, Eleazer
Bazin, John
Bissell, Job
Blacksmiths, *cont'd,*
Brayton, Stephen
Briant, Abraham
Brooks, John
Collins, Samuel
Croker, George
Dillingham, Cornelius
England, James
Fish, David
Fish, Robert
Fowler, Thomas
Haydon, Samuel
Hill, Timothy
Howland, Jabez
Inman, Benjamin
Lawton, Stoddard
Manchester, Stephen
Mitchell, James
Morse, Joshua
Mott, Adam
Newton, David
Odlin, Robert
Olney, William
Reynhart, Tobias
Sanford, Giles
Slocum, Edward
Snow, Joseph
Sowle, Jonathan
Stephens, John
Walker, Nathaniel
White, Oliver
Wilcox, Daniel
Wilcox, Hezekiah
Blockmaker,
Carr, Caleb
Bloomers (iron workers),
Boarman, John
Church, Caleb
Pitts, Joseph
Boatbuilders,
Boss, Joseph
Ross, William
Shepherd, John
Vial, John
Boatmen,
Baker, Jonathan
Bennet, John
Briggs, Daniel
Burroughs Thomas
Butler, Henry
Clark, John
Collins, Thankful
Cooper, Samuel
Dublin, John
Elderton, Roger
Harrison, Francis
Hicks, John
Mitchell, -- Mr.
Pendleton, Edmund
Slocum, Ebenezer
Smith, Benjamin
Spencer, Thomas
Talbutt, Samuel
Underwood, Phillip
Bookbinders,
Franklin, James
Lipscombe, James
Todd, Daniel
Book Keepers,
Banister, Samuel
Venable, James
Braziers,
Langworthy, Southcott
Morrow, Peter
Brewers,
Headley, Henry
Headley, John
Lance, John
Sabeere, Daniel
Bricklayers,
Card, Richard
Plats, Thomas
Sawdey, Benjamin
Smith, Charles
Staples, Thomas
Wright, Henry
Butchers,
Allen, James
Bennet, William

Butchers, *cont'd*,
Brownel, Samuel
Butts, John
Coggeshall, Baulston
Cornell, Thomas
Easton, Peter
Fairchild, Major
Hall, William
Huxham, Thomas
Ireson, Richard
Jones, Thomas
Kerby, Edward
Mott, Samuel
Palmer, George
Perks, Christopher
Phillips, Mial
Plats, John
Plats, Thomas
Pougher, Daniel
Roe, Peter
Sanford, John
Sheran, Richard
Topham, John
Tripp, Peleg
West, Henry
Carpenters,
Arnold, Caleb
Bennet, Job
Clark, Richard
Coggeshall, Peter
Hopkins, Thomas
Johnson, Joseph
Kenney, Edward
Reynolds, John
Shaw, Anthony
Sheffield, William
Starr, Thomas
Thomas, George
Ward, Nehemiah
Carters,
Bell, James
Caswell, Jared
Cook, Constant
Crandal, Samuel
Gibbs, John
Jerson, Richard
Partelow, John

Carters, *cont'd*,
Potter, Hopestill
Scipio
Tiffany, Joseph
Caulkers,
Cook, George
George, Thomas
Northam, Robert
Chairmakers,
Proud, Joseph
Taber, John
Chaise Maker,
Dunam, Daniel
Charcoal [Dealer],
Fish, Robert
Chirurgeons,
Clarke, John
Crossing, Thomas
Harriss/Harrys, John
Clerks (*see also ministers*),
Coddington, William
Cotton, Nathaniel
Eliot, Jared
Honeyman, James
Thurston, Gardner
Clockmakers,
Jackson, Thomas
Morris, John
Clothiers,
Coombs, Charles
Cundall, Joseph
Earl, Caleb
Howard, Martin
Jeffers, George
Linscom, James
Taylor, John
Taylor, William
Coachmaker,
Aspin, Samuel
Coaster,
Strowbridge, John
Comber,
Lynscomb, James
Confectioner,
Barden, Charles
Coopers,
Alcock, Nathaniel

Coopers, *cont'd*,
Arnold, Sion
Atwood, Joseph
Atwood, Thomas
Beere, Oliver
Bundey, James
Carr, Job
Chander[s], Benjamin
Child, Jeremiah
Church, Israel
Corey, Samuel
Cranston, John
Davis, Samuel
Debbens, Charles
Downing, William
Easton, John
Fish, John
Gardner, John
Hall, Benjamin
Hoag, John
Holden, Charles
Rouse, Emanuel
Ingraham, Isaac
Ingraham, John
Lillebridge, Edward
Lyon, Uriel
Macomber, Ephraim
Maylem, Mark
Osband, John
Osbon, John, Jr.
Sawdy, William
Shapley, Daniel
Sisson, Caleb
Snell, Isaac
Staples, Daniel
Stevens, Joseph
Strange, Lott
Taylor, Samuel
Thurston, Edward
Trip, Joshua
Trip, William
Weaver, Thomas
Weston, John
Wilbore, Constant
Wilbore, Joshua
Wilbore, Usiah
Woodman, Richard

Cordwainers,
Alcock, Nathaniel
Allen, Samuel
Baggs, John
Barker, Robert
Basson, Isaac
Baxter, Thomas
Belcher, Joseph
Benson, John
Bently, William
Berry, Richard
Blades, William
Card, John
Carr, Job
Cary, James
Chaffee, Joel
Clinton, Joseph
Coggeshall, Josiah
Cook, John
Corey, Samuel
Darling, Samuel
Dennis, Ezekiel
Downing, William
Dunn, Nathaniel
Easton, Joshua
Fish, Daniel
Fowler, Nicholas
Gardner, John
Gardner, William
Gladding, Joseph
Grantland, John
Gubbins, William
Hall, Benjamin
Hall, Parker
Hall, William
Harris, John
Holmes, John
Humery, Return/Turn
Jeffers, John
Jeffries, Thomas
Johnson, Ezekiel
Kelton, Samuel
King, William
Manchester, Baze
Marreno, Charles
Negus, Job
Peckham, Benjamin

Cordwainers, *cont'd*
Potter, Stephen
Potter, Thomas
Rhodes, John
Rogers, Peleg
Roy, John
Sabin, Joseph
Sheffield, Nathaniel
Shrieve, Daniel
Sisson, Caleb
Smith, Ephraim
Snell, Isaac
Stevens, Joseph
Tayer, John
Taylor, James
Tunly, John
Weaver, Thomas
Webster, John
Weeden, Jeremiah, Jr.
Whitehead, Samuel
Wilbore, Joshua
Wilbore, Usiah
Winslow, James
Yeats, Jeremiah

Curriers,
Bently, Benjamin
Bently, William
Jackson, James
Maddin, Thomas
Risbey, William
Townsend, Nathan
Vaughan, Lovelace
Wilbur, Job

Cutter,
Parry, William

Distillers,
Belithro, John
Brown, John
Burroughs, Ezekiel
Coffin, William
Cutlove, William
Eccles, Brice
Gidley, John
Hunter, Henry
Malem, John
Newton, Simeon
Richardson, Thomas

Distillers, *cont'd,*
Whitehorn, John

Ditcher,
Jones, Morgan

Doctors,
-- German,
Rodman, John,
Terry, Ebenezer

Engraver,
Brown, John

Esquires,
Andrews, John
Anthony, David
Banister, John
Bennett, Job
Borland, Francis
Brown, John
Brownell, Joseph
Bull, Henry
Burr, Ezekiel
Byfield, Nathaniel
Carr, Caleb
Carr, Nicholas
Champlin, Christopher
Church, Thomas
Clarke, Joseph
Coddington, John
Coggeshall, Thomas
Cole, Elisha
Cook, John
Cook, Oliver
Cornell, Gideon
Cranston, Samuel
Davis, William
Dexter, John
Easton, Nicholas
Ellery, Benjamin
Ellery, William
Freeborne, Gideon
Gardner, John
Green, Job
Hall, Benjamin
Hall, William
Helm, James
Hilliard, Oliver
Howard, Martin
Howland, Daniel

Esquires, *cont'd,*
Howland, John
Howland, Thomas
Johnson, Augustus
Johnston, August
Kay, Nathaniel
Kelly, Denis
Kent, Benjamin
Lawton, George
Nicholls, Jonathan
Nichols, Benjamin
Perry, James
Phillips, Peter
Pierce, Ezekiel
Pitt, William
Richardson, Thomas
Robinson, John
Rogers, Jonathan
Ross, Samuel
Scott, Joseph
Sherman, Joseph
Southwick, Solomon
Spencer, William
Thurston, Edward
Thurston, Peleg
Tripp, Peleg
Updike, Daniel
Wanton, Gideon
Wanton, Joseph
Watson, Jeffrey
Farmer,
Arnold, John
Farriers,
Tuck, Adam
Willson, Joseph
Fellmongers,
Baley, Thomas
Bennett, John
Brown, Thomas
Hawkins, James
Staniford, Jeremiah
Feltmakers,
James, William
Pinigar, William
Whitehorn, Richard
Ferrymen,
Barney, Griffin

Ferrymen, *cont'd*
Bill, Joshua
Durfey, Thomas
Eldred, Thomas
Hazard, Oliver
Johnson, Ezekiel
Martin, William
Nickols, Jonathan
Northup, Thomas
Shepley, Daniel
Thomas, Benjamin
Underwood, William
Warner, William
Fishermen,
Chadwick, Thomas
Rhodes, William
Slocum, Ebenezer
Taylor, Samuel
Gardener,
Tennant, John
Gentlemen,
Abbott, Daniel
Almy, Christopher
Almy, Job
Arnold, Josiah
Banister, John
Banister, Thomas
Bennit, Job
Borden, Abraham
Bowers, Henry
Brenton, Jahleel
Brown, Peleg
Bull, Benjamin
Bull, Henry
Campbell, Charles
Carpenter, Hezekiah
Carr, Nicholas
Cary, Nathaniel
Caswell, Job
Champlin, Christopher
Church, Benjamin
Clarke, Jeremiah
Clarke, Lawrence
Cole, John
Cooke, Thomas
Cornel, Clarke
Cornell, Benjamin

Gentlemen, *cont'd,*
Cornell, Thomas
Crossing, William
Donham, Daniel
Durfee, Richard
Dyre, William
Easton, Jonathan
Fell, Christopher
Gardner, George
George, Thomas
Greene, James
Greene, Jeremiah Fones
Hall, Benjamin
Hicks, Stephen
Hill, John, Jr.
Holmes, John
Holmes, Joseph
Honeyman, George
Goulding
Howard, Martin
Howland, Benjamin
Hull, Samuel
Johnson, George
Lake, David
Langford, John
Lawton, George
Lemy, Michael
Little, Oatis
Little, Samuel
Mason, John
Mumford, Peter
Newdigate, Nathaniel
Ninegret, Charles
Ninegret, Thomas
Pelham, Edward
Pelham, Thomas
Potter, Ichabod
Richardson, Thomas
Richmond, William
Robinson, Matthew
Rose, Samuel
Sanford, William
Shearman, John
Shearman, Peleg
Sheffield, Benjamin
Shrieve, John
Slocum, Samuel

Gentlemen, *cont'd*,
Staniford, John
Thomas, George
Updike, Daniel
Walton, John
Wanton, Edward
Wanton, Gideon
Wanton, John
Wanton, John G.
Wanton, Joseph
Ward, Richard

Gentlewomen,
Carr, Elizabeth
Harwood, Mary

Glaziers,
Anthony, Jacob
Currie, Robert
Easton, John, Jr.
Easton, Peter
Forrester, John
Green, Thomas
Gulley, William
Ireson, Joseph
Wood, William

Glovers,
Mathews, David
Swan, Samuel

Goldsmiths,
Brenton, Benjamin
Davis, May
Dixwell, Basil
Hutton, John
Pollard, William
Russell, Daniel
Townsend, Thomas
Whiting, John

Gunsmiths,
Carr, Samuel
Sabin, Henry
Tisdale, Henry

Hatters,
Clark, Samuel
Devotion, Constant
Julian, John
Mitchel, Benjamin
Pinnigar, William
Sanford, Samuel

Hatters, *cont'd*,
Thurston, John
Underwood, Daniel
Whitehorn, Richard
Willson, Benjamin
Wrightington, Thomas

Hoopmaker,
Gardner, William

Horse Jockey,
David Ingersole

House Carpenters,
Bennet, Job, Jr.
Bennet, Joseph
Burroughs, Ezekiel
Burroughs, William
Cadey, William
Caswell, Job
Chapman, Israel
Church, Rufus
Coggeshall, Caleb
Collins, Thomas
Conner, Francis
Dunham, Daniel
Dunham, Thomas
Godfrey, Wm
Greene, Samuel
Hedges, John
Hedges, Joseph
Jenkins, Jedediah
Knowlton, Joseph
Lawton, William
Peckham, James
Peckham, Jeremiah
Peckham, Thomas
Phillips, Peter
Rogers, John
Rogers, Joseph
Rogers, Thomas
Rude, William
Seaver[s], David
Sisson, Robert
Spooner, Charles
Spooner, Wing
Starr, Thomas
Tew, James
Thomas, Richard, Jr.
Tilley, Simeon

House Carpenters, *cont'd*,
Wightman, Daniel
Wilbour, Peleg
Wilcox, John
Wyatt, Benjamin

Housewrights,
Carr, Caleb
Hull, Samuel
Negus, John
Ward, Nehemiah
Weeden, John

Husbandmen,
Allen, David
Allin, John
Anthony, Samuel
Ashby, Edward
Austin, James
Babcock, Joseph, Jr.
Ballard, Isaac
Barber, Samuel
Bates, Francis
Bly, William
Brand, William
Brownell, Thomas
Burgess, Edward
Caswel, Timothy
Clark, Emmanuel
Coggeshall, Newby
Collins, Thankful
Collins, Thomas
Cook, John
Cook, Joseph
Cornell, George, Jr.
Dunn, Nathaniel
Durfee, Samuel
Durfee, William
Durfey, Job
Easton, Nicholas
Elderton, Roger
Gardner, James
Greenal, Remington
Hall, James
Hazleton, William
Holway, Samuel
Jennings, Gabriel
King, William
Kinyon, Ebenezer

Husbandmen, *cont'd*,
Lawton, William
Lewis, George
Lillibridge, John
Manchester, Job
Marsh, John
Maxon, Joseph, Jr.
Metchelf, George
Mitchell, Edward
Moot, Edward
Moot, John
Morss, Joseph
Mott, Edward
Nichols, James
Niles, Ebenezer
Northup, Henry, Jr.
Northup, Nicholas
Palmer, John
Phelps, John
Philips, Richard
Phillips, John
Phillips, William
Place, Joseph, Jr..
Place, Nathan
Popplestone, Edward
Potter, Cornelius
Potter, Ichabod
Reed, John
Remington, John
Reynolds, John
Robbins, Richard
Rogers, Robert
Rogers, Thomas
Shearman, Benjamin
Shelden, John, Jr.
Sherman, Thomas
Slocum, John
Tippets, William
Vaughan, Daniel
Weaver, William, Jr.
Webb, George
Webster, John
Wilbour, Samuel
Wilcox, Joseph
Wilson, James
Wing, John
Wood, William

Husbandmen, *cont'd*,
Worden, Gideon
Young, Nicholas

Huxter,
Webber, Thomas

Innholders,
Akin, James
Barker, Peleg
Batty, John
Bayley, Thomas
Billings, Richard
Bradley, James
Briggs, John
Bull, Ezekiel
Butts, John
Coffin, William
Duin, Thomas
Durfee, Thomas
Durfy, William
Gage, Thomas
Gardner, Henry
Gillet, Thomas
Goslin, Thomas
Lawton, John
Lillibridge, Robert
Lyndy, Jandifor
May, James
Nichols, Jonathan
Owins, George
Palmer, Christopher
Potter, Benjamin
Potter, Ichabod
Rees, Thomas
Shippy, John
Sisson, James
Stanley, Samuel
Sweet, Samuel
Sweet, Sylvester
Sweeting, Henry
Tifft, Joseph
Turner, Christopher

Innkeepers,
Bull, Ezekiel
Card, Elisha
Chace, Jonathan

Jailkeeper,
Stevens, Thomas

Jeweler,
Winnock, Joshua

Joiners,
Attwood, Thomas
Baley, Constant
Bennet, Job, Jr..
Bennitt, Robert
Bingham, Thomas
Bull, Henry
Cahoone, John
Chaplin, Joseph
Clark, Richard
Dee, William
Fairwater, Daniel
Greene, Samuel
Hedges, John
Hodges, Joseph
Langworthy, James
Peckham, Reuben
Phillips, Jonathan
Robinson, William
Smith, Edward
Townsend, Christopher

Journeyman,
Creese, Thomas

Laborers,
Allen, Oliver
Austin, David
Austin, James
Barzee, Henry
Ben (mulatto)
Benchley, William
Bradley, James
Briggs, Job
Briggs, Philip
Brightman, Henry
Burch, Benjamin
Carter, Robert
Cooke, Constant
Cooke, Giles
Coomes, Solomon
Corey, Caleb
Cornel, William
Fuller, Margaret
Gambo (negro)
Gray, Gideon
Greenall, Daniel, Jr.

Laborers, *cont'd,*
Grinel, John (Indian)
Hamilton, William
Hammond, Thomas
Harding, James
Hart, Lumber
Havens, Samuel
Head, Benjamin
Hicks, Thomas
Ingraham, Benjamin
Isaac (mulatto)
Jackson, Jacob
Jackson, John
Jerson, Richard
Kettle, Ephraim
King, William
Lake, David
Marsh, John
Morse, Benjamin
Morse, John
Mott, Jonathan
Nebe, Isaac (Indian)
Negro, Anthony
Nichols, James
Perkins, William
Phillips, John
Pierce, Joseph
Reed, Nathan
Richmond, Edward, Jr.
Riggers, William
Rogers, Isaac
Shaw, Peter
Shearman, Stephen
Sisson, Gilbert
Slocum, Abraham
Springer, Benjamin
Tomkins, Joseph
Toms, John
Wamsley, Henry
West, Clement
Wilbur, Aaron
Wilcox, Jeremiah
Will, Peter
Withers, John
Wood, Newport
Wright, Benjamin

Linguister,
Belon, Daniel

Mariners,
Allen, Christopher
Allen, George
Amory, Daniel
Andrew, John
Anthony, David
Babcock, Richard
Baker, Benjamin
Barbour, John
Barker, Edward
Barney, Jonathan
Bartholomew, Cesar
Bate, Charles
Battan, Ignatius
Beard, Jno
Beauchamp, Isaac
Beauchamp, John
Beere, Charles
Beere, Henry
Bell, William
Bennet, Robert
Bentley, Caleb
Bissell, Richard
Blyth, William
Bodiner, John
Borden, Abraham
Borden, Matthew
Borden, Walter
Boss, Edward
Bradford, Theophilus
Brayton, Benjamin
Brayton, David
Brenton, Benjamin
Briggs, Robin
Briggs, Tobias
Bristow, John
Brock, Peter
Brooks, Thomas
Brown, Caleb
Brown, James, Jr.
Brown, Jeremiah
Brown, John
Brown, Joseph
Brown, William, Jr.
Bryant, Joseph

Mariners, *cont'd,*
Bull, Joseph
Bull, Nathan
Bull, William
Burdick, Jonathan
Burroughs, James
Cahoone, John
Cain, Edward
Cain/Cane, John
Card, James
Carr, John
Chace, Abraham
Chace, Ezekiah
Chapman, John
Chapman, Richard
Church, Benjamin
Clark, Jeremiah
Clark, John
Clark, William
Clarke, Jeremiah
Clarke, Shearman
Cochran, John
Codden/Coden, James
Coddington, Edward
Coggeshall, Baulston
Coggeshall, Freegift, Jr.
Coggeshall, Peter
Coldwell, John
Collins, James
Collins, William
Cook, Ebenezer
Cook, Silas
Cooper, Robert
Cornish, Peter
Cowenhoven, Pieter
Cranston, John
Cranston, William, Jr..
Cupid, John
Daniels, James
Davis, John
Davis, Thomas
Day, Joseph
Degrove, Adolph
Degrove, Deric Adolph
Demoy, William
Dennis, John
Dunbar, Robert

Mariners, *cont'd,*
Dunbar, William
Duncan, James
Dunwell, John
Durfee, Job
Durfey, Richard
Earle, Oliver
Easton, John
Edmondson, James
Eldred, John
Erwin, John
Fanning, William
Finney, Jeremiah
Fling, John
Fones, John
Fones, Joseph
Forrester, Thomas
Freebody, Thomas
Fry, John
Gardner, Benoni
Gardner, Robert
Gardner, Sylvester
Gavett, William Anthony
Gibbs, James
Gibbs, John
Gladding, John
Goddard, William
Graham, Joseph
Green, Elisha
Grinnell, William
Harnus, Walter
Harper, David
Harvey, George
Harvey, Seth
Hastings, James
Hathaway, Abiah
Hockeday, Joseph
Holland, James
Holloway, Daniel
Holmes, Samuel
Hough, Simon
Hulines, James
Ingraham, Benjamin
Jackson, John
James, William
Jennings, Josias
Johnson, John Arthur

Mariners, *cont'd,*
Jones, Henry
Jones, Richard
Joy, William
Keeling, Thomas
Kempton, Manassah
Kilbee, John
King, Thomas
Kinnion, Caleb
Kinsman, Thomas
Knowles, Henry
L'homedieu, Benjamin
Langworthy, Goodson
Lawton, Robert
Lawton, Stoddard
Lewis, James
Little, Robert
Long, Jacob
Lusk, John
Lynscomb, John
Mac Daniel, John
Marrow, Nathan
Marshall, Peter
Mawdsley, John
Mc Lester, Alexander
Mc Millan, Anthony
Mias, Jacob
Mitchel, George
Mitchell, James
Mitchell, John
Moore, Josa Tho.
Moore, Thomas
Morris, Owen
Morse, Edward
Nichols, John
Nichols, Jonathan
Nickerson, David
Osborn, James
Parent, Nathaniel
Patterson, James
Penny, Christopher
Phillips, Michael
Pierce, Joseph
Pinel, Henry
Pitman, Benjamin
Place, Joram
Porter, Peter

Mariners, *cont'd,*
Potter, William
Power, Joseph
Pratt, William
Reed, Nathan
Remington, Stephen
Remington, Thomas
Rennols, Richard
Richardson, John
Rider, John
Robins, Samuel
Robinson, Richard
Rodman, Thomas
Rogers, Thomas
Rous, John
Roy, John
Russel, Joseph
Sabins, Elizer
Sanford, John
Saunders, John
Scott, Joseph
Seavers, David
Sharp, Lewis
Sharp, Lewis
Shearman, Ebenezer
Shearman, John
Sheffield, Benjamin
Sheffield, Samuel
Shepherd, Henry
Shrieve, Constant
Shrieve, Starr
Sisson, Caleb
Sisson, Robert
Slocum, Thomas
Smith, Benjamin
Smith, John
Smith, Nicholas
Smiton, William
Spink, Nicholas
Spinney, Zebulon
Stafford, Joseph
Stanbrough, Hubbart
Starbuck, Hezekiah
Stirtevant, William
Stoddard, Thomas
Strange, John
Strange, Melatiah

Mariners, *cont'd*
- Strange, Sylvanus
- Stringthfield, Edward
- Strowbridge, John
- Sutton, Aaron
- Sweeting, Henry, Jr.
- Sweeting, Nathaniel
- Taggert, William
- Tallman, Jeremiah
- Tarbox, Spink
- Tennant, John
- Thurber, Thomas
- Thurston, Joseph
- Tillinghast, Benjamin
- Tillinghast, Pardon
- Tillinghast, Philip
- Toman, Thomas
- Trip, Joshua
- Trip, William
- Tripp, Benjamin
- Trobridge, John
- Tucker, Benjamin
- Turner, Joseph
- Updike, Daniel
- Updike, James
- Von Heinem, Solomon
- Wallen, John
- Washburn, Ebenezer
- Waterman, Resolved
- Watson, Thomas
- Weaver, Thomas
- Webb, George
- Wells, Hugh
- White, Nicholas
- Whitfield, Charles
- Wilcocks, Daniel
- Wilcox, Daniel
- Wills, Peter
- Willson, Joseph
- Wilson, James
- Wilson, Jeremiah
- Wilson, Joseph
- Wilson, William
- Wing, John
- Winpenny, William
- Wright, Thomas

Masons
- Braman, James
- Chadwick, John
- Clark, John
- Green, Elisha
- Havens, Thomas
- Plats, Thomas
- Robert
- Rounds, George
- Sawdey, Joseph
- Smith, Charles
- Staples, Thomas
- Swan, William
- Wilcox, Robert

Mastmaker,
- Milward, James

Merchants
- Abbott, Daniel
- Abeel, James
- Abrahams, Israel
- Almy, Christopher
- Almy, Job
- Almy, William
- Apthorp, Charles
- Armitage, Jonathan
- Arnold, Benedict
- Austell, Moses
- Ayrault, Daniel
- Ayrault, Stephen
- Baker, John
- Bannister, John
- Barker, Robert
- Blackstock, James
- Boon, Samuel
- Borden, Matthew
- Borland, Francis
- Boss, Edward
- Bowdoin, James
- Bowers, Henry
- Brown, James
- Brown, Jeremiah
- Brown, John
- Bull, Joseph
- Byvanck, Evert
- Campbell, Cuthbert
- Carr, Peleg
- Carr, Robert

Merchants, *cont'd*
- Chaloner, Walter
- Channing, John
- Chase, Abner
- Cheesebrough, David
- Child, Cromwell
- Church, Benjamin
- Clarke, Weston, Jr.
- Coddington, John
- Codwise, Christopher
- Coggeshall, Daniel
- Coggeshall, Thomas
- Coles, Barak
- Collins, Arnold
- Collins, Henry
- Collins, Paul
- Collogan, John
- Cook, Peter
- Cooke, Silas
- Corey, William
- Cowley, Joseph
- Cranston, John
- Cranston, Walter
- Crawford, Gideon
- Crawford, William
- Crooke, Robert
- Devotion, John
- Dickinson, John
- Dockray, John
- Dunbar, George
- Dyre, William
- Easton, James
- Easton, Job
- Easton, John
- Ellery, Benjamin
- Ellery, William
- Ferrari, Francis
- Fitch, Samuel
- Fletcher, Thomas
- Fogg, Edward
- Foye, William
- Freebody, John
- French, William
- Gardner, George
- Gardner, William
- Gibbs, George
- Gibbs, Robert

Merchants, *cont'd*
Gidley, John
Gill, Richard
Grant, Sueton
Greene, John
Greene, Thomas
Hart, Napthali
Hassard, Thomas
Haszard, Benjamin
Hazzard, Robert
Heard, John
Hewlett, John
Holmes, Samuel
Howland, Daniel
Howland, Isaac
Howland, Thomas
Isaacks, Jacob
Jones, John
Jones, Joseph
Jones, William
Kent, Benjamin
King, Matthew
Lake, David
Langford, John
Lawton, George
Lippett, Moses
Livingston, Henry
Lopez, Aaron
Lucas, Augustus
Lyon, John
Lyte, George
Mallbone, Godfrey
Metcalf, Jonathan
Mew, Richard
Moreau, Matthew
Mumford, William
Newbury, Benjamin
Nichols, Clement
Nichols, Jonathan
Nichols, William
Norton, Benjamin
Pearce, Clothier
Pearce, Joseph
Pease, Simon
Philips, Caleb
Polock, Issachar
Langworthy, Southcott

Merchants, *cont'd*,
Polock, Myer
Powel, Adam
Powel, John
Power, Nicholas
Read, William
Redwood, Abraham
Rhodes, Samuel
Rhodes, William
Richards, William
Richardson, Thomas
Rivera, Jacob Rodrigues
Robinson, Thomas
Rogeral, John
Rogers, John
Rogers, Joseph
Sabeer, John
Scott, Christopher
Scott, Edward
Scott, George
Scott, John
Scott, Joseph
Servat, Daniel
Shelton, Robert
Sisson, Gideon
Smith, Daniel
Smith, Nicholas
Stead, William
Stelle, Isaac
Stelle, Thomas Gordon
Taylor, Robert
Thom/Thorn, Stephen
Thompson, Isaac
Thurston, Jonathan
Tilinghast, Joseph
Tillinghast, Charles
Tillinghast, Daniel
Tillinghast, Jonathan
Tillinghast, Nicholas Paris
Tillinghast, Pardon
Tillinghast, Philip
Tillinghast, Samuel
Todd, Alexander
Vale, John Baptist
Van Rans'l, Cornelius
Vernon, Samuel
Vernon, William

Merchants, *cont'd*,
Wanton, Edward
Wanton, George
Wanton, Gideon
Wanton, John
Wanton, John G.
Warner, Oliver Ring
Whipple, Joseph
Whitfield, Charles
Wickham, Samuel
Wincy, Jacob
Woodbridge, Dudley

Midwives
Corey, Elizabeth
Fry, Mary
Irish, [Mrs. John]

Millers
Butts, John
Cross, Samuel
Davis, Jeffery

Millwright,
Green, James

Ministers (*see also* clerks),
Clapp, Nathaniel,
Helyard, Jona. A.
Vinal, William,

Painters,
Fletcher, John
Gibbs, William
Hunt, Edward
Weeden, William

Paver [Pavier, Payver]
May, William

Pedler,
Jackes, Tho

Periwig makers,
Caswell, William
Graham, Malcolm
Mortimer, Richard

Perukemakers,
Cummings, David
Hedges, Bethiah (___)
Hunter, Andrew
Melvil, David

Pewterers,
Clarke, Samuel
Langworthy, Lawrence

Physicians,
Brett, John
Halliburton, John
Harris, John
Hathaway, Daniel
Hooper, Henry
Jackson, George
Mortan, Frankland
Peters, John
Robinson, James
Rodman, John
Rodman, Thomas
Rodman, Walter
Rowan, Andrew
Stewart, George
Tallman ---
Tallman, Stephen
Talman, John
Vigneron, Norbert
Plasterer
Hawkins, William
Post Rider
Hill, Thomas
Practitioners of Physick,
Arnold, Oliver
Crossing, Thomas
Gerrard, Charles
Greene, Daniel
Hooper, Henry
Overbeck, John
Rodman, Walter
Spencer, Thomas
Ropemakers,
Ayres, Thomas
Gosler, John Leopold
Piles, William
Power, Nicholas
Tilley, James
Tilley, William
Rugweaver,
George, John
Sadlers,
Case, Robert
Coggeshall, Joshua
Haydon, Adam
Rossam, Edward
Salter, Thomas
Sadlers, *cont'd,*
Wood, Peleg
Sailmakers,
Hatch, Nathaniel
Langworthy, John
Servat, Daniel
Treby/Tribee, Peter
Sailors,
--deson, Uriah
Day, Joseph
Frank, Samuel
Manser, James
Pearce, James
Persey, James
Robbin, Samuel
Sheld, James
Schoolmasters,
Campbell, Archibald
Chapman, John
Davison, Henry
Egland, John
Gould, James
Hammatt, John
Howland, Thomas
Kaies/Keas, William
Lake, William
Rights, Matthew
Rutter, Nathaniel
Sims, John
Schoolmistress,
Mitchell, Sarah
Scrivener,
Fox, Joseph
Seafaring Man,
Anderson, Laurence
Servants,
Cratty, Ann
Dunbar, James
Hambleton, Elisha
Jackson, David
Jacobs, Mary
Osborn, James
Osborne, Henry
Smith, John (Indian)
Witherill, Sarah
Manchester, Jonathan
Setwork Coopers,
Mosher, Philip
Ship Captains,
Grusha, Thomas James
Heffernan, John
Nichols, George
Richards, William
Richardson, John
Rolfe, John
Ship Carpenters,
Bowers, Samuel
Helmes, George
Hicks, John
Lambart, Daniel
Migood, Nicholas
Perry, John
Perry, Samuel
Simmons, Josiah
Tompkins, Samuel
Ship Commanders,
Clark, Jeremiah
Delamorlier, Capt
Shipmasters,
Aborn, Joseph
Allen, Christopher
Brayton, David
Burroughs ---
Cowenhoven, Pieter
Dunbar, Robert
Fones, Joseph
Hanner, Waters
Herbert, William
Lemote, Geo
Low, John
Place, Joram
Sears, Isaac
Stoddard, Robert
White, Richard
Wilcocks, Daniel
Wright, John
Shipwrights
Arnold, James
Beere, John
Belcher, Benjamin
Bowen, Constant
Brown, Nathanel
Bull, James

Shipwrights, *cont'd*,
Child, Cromwell
Cook, George
Easton, James
Goddard, Ebenezer
Hoockey, Samuel
Jeffrey, John
Jones, David
Lambert, Daniel
Luther, Benjamin
Marsh, Jonathan
Martindale, John
Peterson, Joseph
Place, John
Sheffield, James
Smith, Nathaniel
Taylor, Robert
Shoemaker,
Burch, Benjamin
Shopjoiners,
Attwood, Thomas
Baley, Joseph
Burroughs, Samuel
Shopkeepers,
Chace, Jonathan
Huntington, David
Ayrault, Daniel
Barker, Robert
Boucher, Thomas
Carr, Job
Carr, Peleg Capt.
Claggett, Thomas
Cook, John
Crossing, William
Dexter, James
Dixwell, Basil
Dunbar, George
Durfey, Elisha
Dyre, William
Freebody, John
French, William
Fryers, John
Gardner, Caleb
Gardner, James
Gardner, Thomas
Gidney, Bartholomew
Grant, Temperance

Shopkeepers, *cont'd*
Greene, Daniel
Greene, Thomas
Gyles, William
Hadwen, John
Hammond, Elnathan
Hawden, James
Larrance, John
Lawton, George
Levy, Moses
Moon, David
Pane, Solomon
Peckham, Giles
Pembrooke, Elkanah
Phillips, Thomas
Potter, Hopestill
Rhodes, John
Rogers, James
Rogers, Jonathan
Rumreill, Ebenezer
Russell, Daniel
Smith, Nathaniel
Smith, Thomas
Thurston, Edward, Jr..
Tillinghast, Joseph
Toppan, William
Von Heinem, Solomon
Wanton, John
Wanton, Philip
Webber, Thomas
Weeden, Jonathan
White, Daniel
Wood, Michael
Snuffmaker,
Fergesson, Adam
Spinsters,
Arnold, Sarah
Baggs, Content
Beere, Freelove
Beere, Sarah
Bennet, Mary
Borden, Mary
Borden, Nancy
Boss, Freelove
Clarke, Sarah
Collins, Sarah
Dyre, Mary

Spinsters, *cont'd*,
Greenman, Eunice
Harvey, Hannah
Hewit, Elizabeth
Hicks, Leah
Howard, Sarah Ann
Langford, Elizabeth
Little, Elizabeth
Mitchell, Sarah
Moon, Hope
Palmer, Mary
Palmer, Phebe
Peckham, Elizabeth
Peirce, Thankful
Pinniger, Mary
Rogers, Patience
Scott, Sarah
Shearman, Mary
Smith, Dorcas
Thompson, Betty
Wanton, Frances
Wanton, Sarah
Westcott, Freelove
Wing, Amy
Wing, Deborah
Wing, Phoebe
Staymaker,
Parsley, Joseph
Stonecutters,
Bull, John
Stephens, John
Stevens, William
Stonemason,
Green, Elisha
Storekeeper,
Terry, Ebenezer
Surgeons,
Hooper, Henry
Huckle, William
Keith, Robert
Nixon, Samuel
Surveyors,
Easton, Samuel
Green, William
Mumford, John
Tailors,
Arnold, Caleb

Tailors, *cont'd*
Battey, Mr.
Brown, James
Cleveland, Palmer
Cotton, John
Cozzens, Leonard
Dunbar, Mordecai
Duncan, Robert
Fletcher, Francis
Greene, Benjamin
Hill, James
Hunt, John
Jameson, William
Jennings, Gershom
Marshall, Peter
Milliman, Aaron
Newton, Matthew
Otis, Nicholas
Pettys, Robert
Pike, Samuel
Read, Daniel
Rogers, John
Russell, John
Shepherd/Sheppard, Ebenezer
Smith, William
Sowle, Henry
Tallman, Dictus Darias
Tallman, Jeremiah
Tedder, William
Thurston, John
White, John
Wilson, Joseph, Jr.

Tallow Chandler,
Dyer, Nathaniel

Tanners,
Bayley, Thomas
Bennett, John
Borden, Samuel
Brown, James
Brown, Joseph
Cleveland, Palmer
Collins, William
Dunbar, Mordecai
Easton, Peter
Freeborn, Joseph
Hagger, Benjamin

Tanners, *cont'd,*
Markie, Thomas
Newton, Matthew
Olney, William
Phillips, Christopher
Phillips, Samuel
Phillips, Thomas
Pike, Samuel
Pitcher, John
Snell, Samuel
Tedder, William
Trip, Robert
Vallence, William
Vaughan, Daniel
Wight, Joseph
Young, Alexander

Tavernkeepers,
Earl, William
Purdy, Sarah (___)
Read, James
Tift, Joseph

Timber Merchant,
Gyles, William

Tinman,
Newell, Timothy

Traders,
Belton, Jonas
Belton, Joseph
Cook, William
Courtney, John
Goodfellow, Thomas
Harding, James
Inman, Benjamin
Kilbee, John
Olds, Robert
Renshon, Christiana
Smith, Nicholas
Strange, Melatiah
Wolford, Julian

Upholsterer,
Moore, John

Victuallers,
Bull, Ezekiel
Mott, Samuel
Stevens, Thomas

Vintners,
Barden, Charles

Vintners, *cont'd,*
Beatty, Hugh
Bright, William
Channing, John
Coles, Barak
Gilburt, Francis
Heffernan, William
Hicks, Deborah (____)
Jackson, Stephen
Mason, Alexander
Nichols, Mayes
Rogers, Samuel
Snell, Samuel
Swan, William
Sweet, Samuel
Sweet, Silvester
Webb, Samuel
Whiting, Timothy
Wilson, Jeremiah

Watchmakers/menders,
Claggett, Thomas
Proud, John
Proud, Robert

Weavers,
Albro, Josiah
Allen, Ralph
Bayley, John, Jr.
Bennet, Caleb
Berry, Elisha
Butts, John
Cook, William
Cooper, Samuel
Cornell, Clark
Davis, John
Folkner, John
Fowler, James
Gereardy, John
Haley, John
Healy, Joseph
George Jeffers
May, James
Moon, John
Morris, Richard
Phillips, Joseph
Potter, Ichabod
Sanford, Peleg
Sanford, Samuel

Weavers, *cont'd,*
Shearman, Benjamin
Shearman, Philip
Shearman, Samson
Shearman, William
Thomas, George
Toppin, William
Tripp, Othniel
Whaley, Lawrence
Whitford, Ezekiel

Wheelmaker,
Axton, Young

Wheelwrights,
Jarrat, Charles
Tilley, Simeon

Whitesmith,
Clark, Noah

Wine cooper,
Henry Whitton

Yeomen,
Allen, Benjamin
Allen, Caleb
Allen, Lemuel
Allen, Zechariah
Almy, Gideon
Almy, Job
Almy, John
Anderson, John
Anthony, Abraham
Arnold, Benedict
Arnold, Thomas
Babcock, Joseph, Jr.
Babcocke, Robert
Bailey, Bennet
Baley, Samuel
Barker, Peter
Barker, Robert
Barker, William
Barney, Jacob
Bicknell, Joshua
Blye, William
Boone, Samuel
Borden, Abraham
Borden, Joseph
Borden, Matthew
Borden, Thomas
Boss, Edward

Yeomen, *cont'd,*
Boss, Peter
Bradford, Thomas
Briggs, John
Brightman, William
Brown, Abraham
Brown, Charles
Brown, Eseck
Brown, Gideon
Brown, Robert
Brown, Thomas
Brownell, George
Bull, Ephraim
Butts, Enoch
Carpenter, Solomon
Carr, Caleb
Carr, James
Carr, John
Carr, Robert
Cary, Benjamin
Case, John
Case, Joseph
Case, Joseph 2d
Chace, Holder
Champlin, Joshua
Chase, Abner
Church, Nathaniel
Clarke, John
Clarke, Lawrence
Coggeshall, Abraham
Coggeshall, Benjamin
Coggeshall, Freegift
Coggeshall, James
Coggeshall, John
Coggeshall, Joshua
Coggeshall, Peter
Coggeshall, Thomas
Coggeshall, William
Coleman, John
Collins, Thomas
Congdon, Benjamin
Cook, Abial
Cook, John
Cook, Joseph
Cook, Samuel
Cook, Stephen
Cook, Thomas

Yeomen, *cont'd,*
Corey, Caleb
Corey, Samuel
Cornel, Clarke
Cornell, Thomas
Cory, William
Cranston, John
Davenport, Bela
Davenport, Eliphalet
Dawley, Michael
Dennis, John
Dennis, Joseph
Dennis, Robert
Devol, Gilbert
Dexter, John
Dickinson, Charles
Dunn, Richard
Durfee, Benjamin
Durfey, Thomas
Dyre, Edward
Dyre, Samuel
Dyre, William, Jr.
Earl, Oliver
Earle, John
Earle, Parker
Easton, James
Easton, Jonathan
Easton, Nicholas
Easton, Stephen
Edey, Zechariah
Elderton, Roger
Eldred, John
Eldred, William
Fanning, James
Fish, Benjamin
Fish, Daniel
Fish, Jeremiah
Fish, William
Fones, John
Foster, Jonathan
Franklin, Abel
Franklyn, George
Freeborn, Gideon, Jr.
Freeborn, John
Gardner, Ephraim
Gardner, George
Gardner, James

Yeomen, *cont'd,*
Gardner, Joseph
Gardner, Samuel
Gardner, William
Gifford, Richard
Goreham, Shubael
Gorton, Hezekiah
Gould, John
Gould, Thomas
Graham, Joseph
Gray, Edward
Gray, Philip
Gray, William
Green, Daniel, Jr.
Green, David
Green, Job
Green, John
Green, Peter
Green, William
Greene, Daniel
Grinnel, Daniel, Jr.
Grinnell, Jonathan
Grinnell, Matthew
Hack, William
Hall, Benjamin
Hall, Nathaniel
Hall, William
Hambleton, David
Hammond, Thomas
Hannah, Robert
Harris, Toleration
Hazard, Jeffery
Hazard, Jeremiah
Hazard, Jonathan
Hazard, Thomas
Head, Joseph
Herrindeen, William
Herington, William
Hicks, Thomas
Hicks, Weston
Hill, John
Hill, Jonathan
Hix, Thomas
Holland, Henry
Holloway, Timothy
Holway, Benjamin
Hollyman, Ezekiel

Yeomen, *cont'd,*
Holmes, John
Howland, Benjamin
Howland, Isaac
Howland, Job
Howland, John
Hull, John
Hull, Teddeman
Ingersole, Thos
Irish, Joseph
Jackways, Nathan
Jackwise, Thomas
Jenkins, Job
Jenkins, Zechariah
Jenks, Benjamin
Jennings, Joseph
King, William
Kinnion, John
Knight, Joseph
Knowles, Henry
Larkin, Edward
Lawton, George
Lawton, Isaac, Jr.
Lawton, John
Lawton, Robert
Lewis, Samuel
Lillibridge, Thomas
Little, Nathaniel
Long, Ezekiel
Luther, Jonathan
Mackoon, Daniel
Macomber, Benjamin
Manchester, Gilbert
Manchester, Isaac
Manchester, John
Manton, John
Martin, John
Minor, Rufus
Morey, Roger
Morgan, James
Morse, John
Mory, Benjamin
Mott, Edward
Mott, Jacob
Mumford, John
Mumford, Joseph
Mumford, Samuel

Yeomen, *cont'd,*
Mumford, Thomas
Nichols, David
Nichols, William
Nickolls, James
Northup, Benjamin
Northup, Stephen
Northup, Thomas
Paine, John
Palmer, Ichabod
Pearce, Ephraim
Pearce, George
Pearce, Jonathan
Peck, Daniel
Peckham, Daniel
Peckham, Phillip
Pelham, Edward
Pendleton, Edmund
Perry, Benjamin
Perry, John
Perry, Samuel
Phelps, Samuel
Phillips, Samuel
Pigot, George
Pitkin, Ozias
Potter, Edward
Potter, Ichabod
Potter, John
Potter, Thomas
Quithel, Benjamin
Randel, Matthew
Rathbone, Thomas
Raynolds, John
Record, John
Remington, Gershom
Remington, John
Reynolds, Elisha Capt.
Reynolds, James
Reynolds, John, Jr.
Richmond, Ephraim
Ripley, David
Robins, Richard
Robinson, William
Rogers, Isaac
Rogers, Jeremiah Tallman
Rogers, John
Rogers, Samuel

Yeomen, *cont'd*
Rogers, Thomas
Rowse, George
Sanders, Edward
Sanford, Giles
Saunders, Stephen
Scott, George
Scott, Sylvanus Capt
Shaw, Peter
Shaw, William
Shearman, Benjamin
Shearman, Joseph
Shearman, Richard
Shearman, Thomas
Sheffield, Benjamin
Sheffield, Isaac
Sheffield, Jeremiah
Sheffield, Joseph
Shelden, John
Sisson, Barnet
Sisson, John
Sisson, Philip
Sisson, Thomas
Slocum, Abraham
Slocum, Christopher
Slocum, Ebenezer
Slocum, Giles
Slocum, Holder
Slocum, John
Slocum, Samuel
Smith, Benjamin
Smith, Daniel
Smith, David
Smith, Edward
Smith, Isaac
Smith, John
Smith, Prince
Smith, William
Snell, Daniel
Sowle, Jonathan
Spencer, Daniel
Spencer, Michael
Spencer, Robert
Spink, Nicholas
Squire, Daniel
Stafford, Thomas
Stanton, Benjamin

Yeomen, *cont'd,*
Stanton, Joseph
Stanton, Robert
Sweet, Jeremiah
Sweet, John
Taber, Stephen
Tallman, Darias
Tallman, Peter
Tallman, Stephen
Taylor, John
Tew, Henry
Tew, Richard
Thomas, Samuel
Thurston, Peleg
Thurston, Samuel
Tibbitts, George
Tiffany, Ephraim
Tillinghast, John
Towsley, Abner
Tripp, Job
Tripp, Joseph
Tripp, Peleg
Tucker, Morrice
Turner, Christopher
Updike, Lodowick
Updike, Richard
Vaughan, John
Wanton, Joseph
Warner, John
Wastcote, Zerobabell
Watson, Jeffrey
Watson, John, Jr.
Weaver, Thomas
Weeden, John
Weight, John
Weight, Thomas
Wells, Benjamin
Wells, John
West, Clement
Whipple, Noah
Whitfield, Charles
Whitford, Pasko
Wickes, William
Wightman, George
Wilbore, John
Wilcock, Daniel
Wilcocks, Edward

Yeomen, *cont'd,*
Wilcocks, Edward
Wilcox, Daniel
Wilcox, Jeremiah
Wilcox, John
Wilcox, Robert
Wilcox, Stephen
Wilkenson, William
Willcox, Josiah
Willcox, Stephen
Wilson, James
Wilson, Jeremiah
Wilson, Samuel
Wing, Benjamin
Wing, John
Woodman, Edward
Woodman, Robert
Woodman, Sylvester
Worden, Gideon

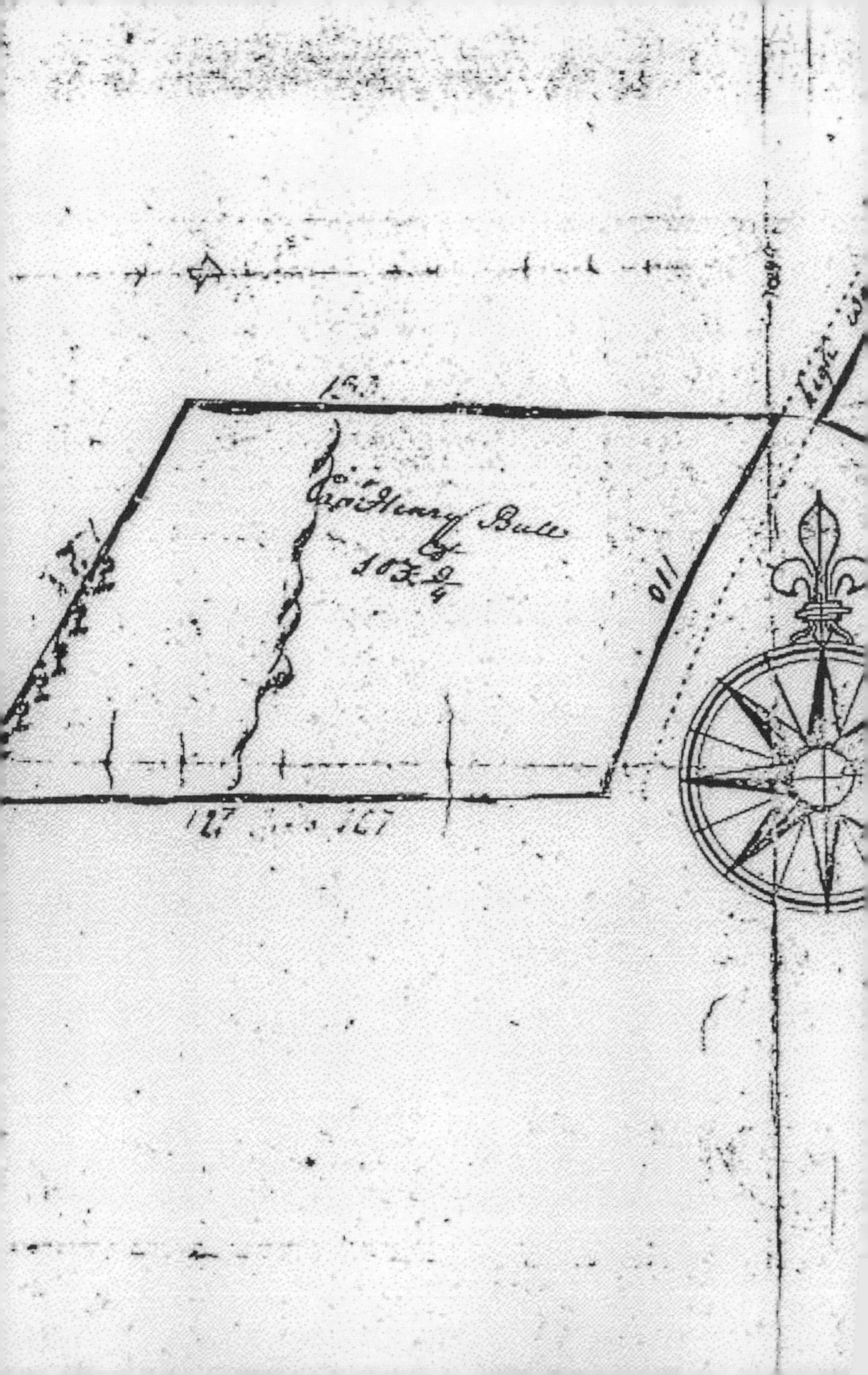
Henry Bull